THE JOSSEY-BASS HANDBOOK OF

NONPROFIT LEADERSHIP AND MANAGEMENT

FOURTH EDITION

DAVID O. RENZ
ROBERT D. HERMAN, EDITOR EMERITUS

JB JOSSEY-BASS™
A Wiley Brand

Published by John Wiley & Sons, Inc., Hoboken, New Jersey
Published simultaneously in Canada

For general information about our other products and services, please contact our Customer Care Department within the United States at (800) 762-2974, outside the United States at (317) 572-3993 or fax (317) 572-4002.

Wiley publishes in a variety of print and electronic formats and by print-on-demand. Some material included with standard print versions of this book may not be included in e-books or in print-on-demand. If this book refers to media such as a CD or DVD that is not included in the version you purchased, you may download this material at http://booksupport.wiley.com. For more information about Wiley products, visit www.wiley.com.

Library of Congress Cataloging-in-Publication Data is available:

ISBN 9781118852965 (Hardcover)
ISBN 9781118852866 (ePDF)
ISBN 9781118852941 (ePub)

Cover Design: Wiley
Cover Image: © iStock.com/konradlew

Printed in the United States of America

10 9 8 7 6 5 4 3 2 1

CONTENTS

PART ONE: THE CONTEXT AND INSTITUTIONAL SETTING OF THE NONPROFIT SECTOR   1

v

FIGURES, TABLES, AND EXHIBITS

Figures

Tables

Exhibits

THE CONTRIBUTORS

Rikki Abzug is a professor and convener of management at the Anisfield School of Business, Ramapo College of New Jersey. A researcher of organizational governance, sector theory, social purpose organizations, and neo-institutionalism in organizations, Dr. Abzug is co-author (with Jeffrey Simonoff) of *Nonprofit Trusteeship in Different Contexts* and (with Mary Watson) *Human Resources in Social Purpose Organizations,* as well as the author or co-author of a myriad of scholarly peer-reviewed articles in journals, including *Organization Science, The Academy of Management Journal, Nonprofit and Voluntary Sector Quarterly, Nonprofit Management & Leadership,* and *Voluntas: International Journal of Voluntary and Non-Profit Organizations.* Dr. Abzug has been a management and market research consultant and has also provided consulting services in nonprofit and board development to management groups in the United States, Poland, and the Ukraine. She served on the Board of the Association for Research on Nonprofit Organizations and Voluntary Action (ARNOVA), was a founding leadership council member of the Alliance for Nonprofit Governance (now, Governance Matters), and has been active in a variety of other professional and trade associations. Before joining the faculty of Ramapo, Dr. Abzug was the chair of the Nonprofit Management Program at The New School for Social Research in New York City. Prior to her work at the New School, Dr. Abzug was the associate director of Yale University's Program on Nonprofit Organizations and a faculty member at New York University's Stern School of Business.

James E. Austin is the Eliot I. Snider and Family Professor of Business Administration, Emeritus, and co-founder of the Social Enterprise Initiative at the Harvard Business School. He is one of the pioneering researchers and authors in the field of nonprofit-business alliances and the author of the award-winning books *The Collaboration Challenge* and, with M. May Seitanidi, *Creating Value in Nonprofit-Business Collaborations*. Austin has provided advisory services to private companies, governments, international development agencies, educational institutions, and nongovernmental organizations, and has served as a special advisor to the White House.

Marcia A. Avner teaches in the Masters in Advocacy and Political Leadership Program (MAPL) at Metropolitan State University. Avner is a consultant whose practice, Avner Advocacy, includes strategy design, training, curriculum development, and facilitation. She works with nonprofits, foundations, and academic centers on initiatives to advance public policies and civic engagement. Avner also serves as a senior fellow at the Minnesota Council of Nonprofits, where she was public policy director from 1996 to 2010. Her career includes service as the deputy mayor of St Paul, Minnesota, the assistant commissioner for Energy in Minnesota, and communications director for a U.S. Senator. The unifying thread in Avner's work is the commitment to advancing advocacy in the nonprofit sector and the broader community. Avner has authored *The Lobbying and Advocacy Handbook for Nonprofit Organizations: Shaping Public Policy at the State and Local Level* (2nd ed., 2013) and *The Board Member's Guide to Lobbying and Advocacy* (2004).

Jeanne Bell, MNA, is executive director at CompassPoint (www.compasspoint .org)—a national nonprofit leadership and strategy practice based in Oakland, California. She is the co-author of *The Sustainability Mindset: Using the Matrix Map to Make Strategic Decisions* (Jossey-Bass). In addition to frequent speaking and consulting on nonprofit strategy and finance, Bell has conducted a number of research projects on nonprofit leadership over the past ten years including, most recently, *UnderDeveloped: A National Study of the Challenges Facing Nonprofit Fundraising*. She serves on the boards of *The Nonprofit Quarterly* and Intersection for the Arts.

Woods Bowman was professor emeritus in the School of Public Service at DePaul University, Chicago, Illinois until his death in July, 2015, in an auto accident. He was also senior fellow of the Midwest Center for Nonprofit Leadership of the Henry W. Bloch School of Management at the University of Missouri at Kansas City. He taught undergraduate and graduate courses at DePaul and received its Excellence in Public Service Award. His research was in the areas of financial management of nonprofit and governmental organizations, the economic value of volunteers in nonprofit organizations, taxation and fiscal policy of nonprofits, and a theory of membership association finance. His book, *Finance Fundamentals for Nonprofits: Building Capacity and Sustainability,* was chosen for a research award from the Association for Research on Nonprofit Organizations and Voluntary Action (ARNOVA). Other publications include numerous journal articles and contributions to edited volumes. He also wrote and taught about ethics in various settings for practitioners and students, including a regularly appearing column in *The Nonprofit Quarterly.* Prior to joining DePaul he served for fourteen years as a member of the Illinois General Assembly and later as the chief executive officer of Cook County, Illinois. Earlier in his career he was a member of the faculty of the Department of Economics at the University of Illinois at Chicago, where his research focused on urban economics and land use policy. Before that he was a research economist at the Federal Reserve Bank of Chicago. Bowman earned a bachelor's degree in economics and a bachelor's degree in physics from the Massachusetts Institute of Technology, a master's degree in public administration, and a Ph.D. degree in dconomics, both from the Maxwell School of Syracuse University.

William A. Brown is a professor in the Bush School of Government and Public Service at Texas A&M University and holds the Mary Julia and George Jordan Professorship. He serves as the program director for the Certificate in Nonprofit Management. He teaches the Nonprofit Management, Social Innovation, and Entrepreneurship, Human Resource Management, and Capstone courses. He received a bachelor of science degree in education from Northeastern University with a concentration in human services. He earned his master's degree and doctorate in organizational psychology from Claremont Graduate University. Prior to joining Texas A&M University, he was an assistant professor at Arizona State University, where he worked as the program coordinator of their Certificate in Nonprofit Management and Leadership and was an affiliated faculty member with the Center for Nonprofit Leadership and Management. He has worked with numerous organizations in the direct provision of services, consulting, and board governance. He served on the board of the Association for Research on Nonprofit Organizations and Voluntary Action (ARNOVA) from 2007 to 2012 and chaired the Education Committee from 2009 to 2011. His research focuses on nonprofit governance, strategy, and organizational effectiveness. He has authored numerous research articles, technical reports, and several practice-oriented publications. Examples of his work include exploring the association between board and organizational performance and developing the concept of mission attachment. Publication outlets include *Nonprofit and Voluntary Sector Quarterly, Nonprofit Management & Leadership, International Journal of Volunteer Administration,* and *Public Performance and Management Review.* He has completed an edited volume entitled *Nonprofit Governance: Innovative Perspectives and Approaches* (Routledge, July 2013) with Chris Cornforth. A textbook entitled *Strategic Management in Nonprofit Organizations* was published in March 2014 (Jones & Bartlett).

Jeffrey L. Brudney, Ph.D., is the Betty and Dan Cameron Family Distinguished Professor of Innovation in the Nonprofit Sector at the University of North Carolina Wilmington. The Urban Institute calls him "the foremost research expert on volunteer management programs and community volunteer centers in the United States." Dr. Brudney has received numerous honors and awards for his professional activities. In 2015 he received the Award for Distinguished Achievement and Leadership in Nonprofit and Voluntary Action Research (formerly called the Award for Distinguished Lifetime Achievement) from the Association for Research on Nonprofit Organizations and Voluntary Action (ARNOVA). His book, *Fostering Volunteer Programs in the Public Sector: Planning, Initiating, and Managing Voluntary Activities,* earned the John Grenzebach Award for Outstanding Research in Philanthropy for Education. In addition to receiving other awards for research, Dr. Brudney has been honored with the Mentor's Award of the American Political Science Association for providing "exceptional guidance to graduate students or to junior faculty members." Dr. Brudney serves on the United Nations Volunteers Programme Technical Advisory Board on the *State of the World's Volunteerism Report.* He recently concluded his term as editor-in-chief of *Nonprofit and Voluntary Sector Quarterly,* the leading academic journal in nonprofit and voluntary studies worldwide.

John M. Bryson is McKnight Presidential Professor of Planning and Public Affairs at the Hubert H. Humphrey School of Public Affairs at the University of Minnesota. He works in the areas of leadership, strategic management, collaboration, and the design of engagement processes. He wrote *Strategic Planning for Public and Nonprofit Organizations* (4th ed., Jossey-Bass, 2011), and co-wrote with Barbara C. Crosby *Leadership for the Common Good* (2nd ed., Jossey-Bass, 2005). Dr. Bryson is a fellow of the National Academy of Public Administration and received the 2011 Dwight Waldo Award from the American Society for Public Administration for "outstanding contributions to the professional literature of public administration over an extended scholarly career."

Nancy E. Day is an associate professor of human resources and organization behavior at the Henry W. Bloch School of Management at the University of

Missouri–Kansas City (UMKC). She also serves as UMKC's faculty ombudsperson. She teaches graduate and undergraduate courses and has served as executive MBA director, department chair, and interim associate dean. Her research has been published in such journals as the *Academy of Management Learning & Education, Human Resource Management, Personnel Psychology, Personnel Review, Employee Relations,* and the *Journal of Leadership and Organizational Studies.* Before joining the faculty, Dr. Day was a consultant in the practice areas of compensation and performance management as well as an HR practitioner. She has served on the board of World and Work (and the American Compensation Association), as president of the Midwest Academy of Management, and as a long-time member of the Academy of Management. She currently serves the Academy as chair of the Ethics Ombudsperson Committee.

Alnoor Ebrahim is an associate professor at the Harvard Business School. His research and teaching focus on the challenges of performance management, accountability, and governance facing organizations with a social purpose. He is author of the award-winning book, *NGOs and Organizational Change: Discourse, Reporting, and Learning* and is co-editor of *Global Accountabilities: Participation, Pluralism, and Public Ethics* (both with Cambridge University Press). Professor Ebrahim's research is closely integrated with practice. He recently served on a working group established by the G8 to create global guidelines on impact measurement for investors, and on an advisory board of the Global Impact Investing Network. He has authored commissioned reports on civil society relations with the World Bank and the Inter-American Development Bank, and he consults to international NGOs on their challenges of global governance and accountability. Dr. Ebrahim holds a BSc degree from MIT and a Ph.D. from Stanford University, where he studied environmental planning and management.

Shannon Ellis, MNA, is a project director at CompassPoint. She supports nonprofit leaders as they hone and develop their organizational strategy, build their financial literacy, and increase their organizations' sustainability. She also teaches public and customized workshops for nonprofits, as well as in CompassPoint's cohort leadership programs. Ellis has a deep personal commitment to social equity and believes that nonprofits have an important role to play as we move toward a more just society. She has worked in nonprofits throughout her career and is a Certified Nonprofit Accounting Professional.

Brenda Gainer is director of the Social Sector Management Program and holds the Royal Bank Professorship in Nonprofit Management at York University in Toronto, Canada. She teaches marketing, resource development, and philanthropy; alternative approaches to social value creation (social enterprise, fair trade and co-operatives); and leadership in the nonprofit sector. Her published work appears in a wide variety of journals and conference proceedings, and she is on the editorial board of a number of academic and practitioner journals. Before embarking on an academic career, Gainer worked in the areas of aboriginal rights, women's issues, and arts and culture. She has also developed capacity-building leadership programs for immigrant and refugee-serving NGOs, child welfare organizations, and the social housing sector. She has served on the board of Canada Helps, a web-based organization dedicated to increasing philanthropy in Canada, as well as a number of other Toronto organizations. Her professional service includes advisory boards for Statistics Canada and other government agencies and two terms as vice president of the Nonprofit Academic Centers Council. Most recently she served two terms as a board member of the International Society for Third Sector Research, and she is a past president of the association.

Virginia C. Gross is a shareholder with Polsinelli PC, concentrating her practice on providing advice and counsel to tax-exempt organizations. She counsels exempt organizations on all aspects of tax-exempt and nonprofit organizations law. Clients include charitable and educational organizations, private foundations, health care entities, associations, supporting organizations, social welfare organizations, and social clubs. Gross has worked with numerous nonprofit boards of directors and trustees regarding their nonprofit governance and best practices. She is a frequent writer and speaker on nonprofit law topics. Her publications include *Nonprofit Governance: Law, Practices & Trends* (Wiley) and *Nonprofit Law for Colleges and Universities* (Wiley), as well as *Private Foundations–Distributions (Sec 4942)*, a Tax Management Portfolio (BNA). Gross earned her J.D. from the University of Texas and her B.S. degree from Texas A&M University and is listed in Best Lawyers in America for Nonprofit Organizations/Charities Law for 2008–2016. She is currently serving as a member of the Exempt Organizations subcommittee of the IRS Advisory Committee on Tax Exempt and Governmental Entities. Gross has served on numerous governing boards and provides extensive pro bono legal services to many charities and other nonprofit organizations.

Peter Dobkin Hall was Hauser Lecturer on Nonprofit Organizations at the John F. Kennedy School of Government, Harvard University. Associated with Yale's Program on Non-Profit Organizations from 1978 to 1999, he also held teaching appointments in Yale's Department of History, Divinity School, Ethics, Politics, and Economics Program, and School of Management. Hall's publications include *Sacred Companies: Organizational Aspects of Religion and Religious Aspects of*

Organizations (1998), *Inventing the Nonprofit Sector and Other Essays on Philanthropy, Voluntarism, and Nonprofit Organizations* (1992), *Lives in Trust: The Fortunes of Dynastic Families in Late Twentieth Century America* (1992), and *The Organization of American Culture, 1700–1900: Organizations, Elites, and the Origins of American Nationality* (1982). (It is with great sadness that we note the passing of Peter in the spring of 2015.)

Scott T. Helm is the associate director of the Midwest Center for Nonprofit Leadership at the University of Missouri–Kansas City, as well as a teaching faculty member at the Henry W. Bloch School of Management at the University of Missouri–Kansas City. Using his background in economics and nonprofit management, Helm has spent the last decade working with nonprofit organizations, assisting them with program evaluation, market research, commercialization, business planning, strategic planning, and board training. Helm's primary research focus is social entrepreneurship. His work in this area has led to publication, presentations at international and national academic conferences, as well as projects with local nonprofit organizations on how to innovate. His writing has garnered awards, including the *Nonprofit Management and Leadership* 2011 Editors' Prize for Volume 20 for the article, "Beyond Taxonomy: An Empirical Validation of Social Entrepreneurship in the Nonprofit Sector," written with Fredrik Andersson.

Robert D. Herman is professor emeritus of the Department of Public Affairs and senior fellow with the Midwest Center for Nonprofit Leadership, both of the Henry W. Bloch School of Business and Public Administration at the University of Missouri–Kansas City (UMKC). He is a founder of UMKC's Master of Public Administration nonprofit management program, one of the first to be created in the United States. Herman's research has concentrated on the effective leadership of nonprofit charitable organizations, including chief-executive-board relations, and his most recent research has focused on nonprofit organizational effectiveness. He has published extensively, including scholarly and practitioner publications such as *Public Administration Review, Nonprofit Management and Leadership, Nonprofit and Voluntary Sector Quarterly,* and he is co-author of *Executive Leadership in Nonprofit Organizations* (with Dick Heimovics, 1991) and co-editor of *Nonprofit Boards of Directors* (with Jon Van Til, 1989). Herman is the founding editor of the *Jossey-Bass Handbook of Nonprofit Leadership and Management* (1994; 2nd ed., 2005). Herman has served in numerous leadership roles in the field of nonprofit studies, including past president of the Association of Voluntary Action Scholars (now know as the Association for Research on Nonprofit Organizations and Voluntary Action, or

ARNOVA). Herman received his B.A. degree in economics from Kansas State University and his M.S. and Ph.D. degrees, both in organizational behavior, from Cornell University.

Bruce R. Hopkins concentrates on the representation of tax-exempt organizations, practicing with the Bruce R. Hopkins Law Firm, LLC, Kansas City, Missouri. He is the Professor from Practice at the University of Kansas School of Law. He has authored or co-authored more than thirty books on nonprofit law subjects, including *The Law of Tax-Exempt Organizations* (11th ed.); *The Tax Law of Charitable Giving* (5th ed.); *The Law of Fundraising* (5th ed.); *Private Foundations: Tax Law and Compliance* (4th ed.); *Bruce R. Hopkins' Nonprofit Law Dictionary; Nonprofit Governance: Law, Practices, and Trends;* and *Tax-Exempt Organizations and Constitutional Law: Nonprofit Law as Shaped by the U.S. Supreme Court.* He writes a monthly newsletter, the *Bruce R. Hopkins" Nonprofit Counsel.* He is listed in the Best Lawyers in America for Nonprofit Organizations/Charities Law, 2007–2016. He earned his JD and LLM degrees at the George Washington University, his SJD degree at the University of Kansas, and his B.A. degree at the University of Michigan. He is a member of the bars of the District of Columbia and the State of Missouri.

Thomas H. Jeavons currently serves as an adjunct professor of philanthropic studies at Indiana University–Purdue University Indianapolis, and he has served for many years as a trustee of the Jessie Ball duPont Fund. Previously he was the executive director of ARNOVA; and before that was the general secretary of Philadelphia Yearly Meeting, the largest Quaker judicatory in the United States. His academic career included serving as the founding director of the Johnson Center for Philanthropy and Nonprofit Leadership at Grand Valley State University. He holds a Ph.D. in management from the Union Institute, an M.A. in theology from the Earlham School of Religion, and a B.A. in philosophy from the University of Colorado.

Matthew T. A. Nash is managing director for social entrepreneurship at Duke University's Innovation & Entrepreneurship Initiative and is a fellow and past executive director of the Center for the Advancement of Social Entrepreneurship (CASE) at Duke's Fuqua School of Business. A visiting lecturer at Duke's Sanford School of Public Policy, where he teaches courses in social innovation, Nash was the founding center director of the Social Entrepreneurship Accelerator at Duke, a development lab for scaling innovations in global health, funded by the U.S. Agency for International Development. Prior to joining the CASE team, he was a senior consultant in strategy and change management with the public-sector practice at IBM Business Consulting Services (formerly PricewaterhouseCoopers

Consulting). Previously, he led the Leadership Institute at Yale's Center for Public Service and volunteered with the U.S. Peace Corps as a nongovernmental organization development consultant in Romania. He is a graduate of the Yale School of Management (MBA) and Yale College (B.A.). A recipient of Vice President Al Gore's "Hammer Award" for reinventing government, Nash has been honored by Ashoka and the Cordes Foundation for innovation in social entrepreneurship education.

Sarah K. Nathan, Ph.D., is associate director of the Fund Raising School, the nationally known professional training program for fundraising practitioners. In this role, she supports faculty and curriculum development. Recently, she managed the publication of the fourth edition of *Achieving Excellence in Fundraising*, and she is currently directing a national study of the fundraising profession. Previously, she was assistant professor of nonprofit management and philanthropy at Bay Path University, where she taught and advised online graduate students in the Master's of Nonprofit Management and Strategic Fundraising degree programs. Dr. Nathan holds a master's degree and doctorate in philanthropic studies from the Indiana University Lilly Family School of Philanthropy.

Brent Never is an associate professor of nonprofit leadership, Henry W. Bloch School of Management, University of Missouri–Kansas City. His research considers the spatial and geographic implications of a decentralized human service system. Using geographic information systems (GIS) and spatial regression methods, he has worked to identify communities underserved by human services. In addition, he has co-edited a special issue of *Nonprofit and Voluntary Sector Quarterly* considering the impact of Elinor and Vincent Ostrom on nonprofit studies. Dr. Never's research has been funded by national and regional foundations. He was a Fulbright Scholar (2003–2004 to Benin and 2007 to Northern Ireland), and in 2011–2013 was awarded a Young Scholar Research Grant from the Kresge Foundation. He has published in *Nonprofit and Voluntary Sector Quarterly, Nonprofit Management & Leadership, Voluntas,* and *Nonprofit Policy Forum.* In addition, Dr. Never regularly writes for the practitioner audience in the *Nonprofit Quarterly.* He holds a Ph.D. in public policy from Indiana University-Bloomington.

M. May Seitanidi (FRSA) is an associate professor of strategy at Kent Business School, University of Kent. She is a visiting fellow at the International Centre for Corporate Social Responsibility (ICCSR) at Nottingham University Business School, University of Nottingham, and a visiting professor in CSR at LUISS Business School, Rome, Italy. Her work for over twenty years, as a practitioner and academic, focused on all types of cross-sector social interactions, previously on philanthropy and socio-sponsorship, and currently on social partnerships. She was the founder of the Hellenic Sponsorship Centre (1994), the magazine *Sponsors and Sponsorships* (1995) and the *Annual Review of Social Partnerships* (2006), promoting cross-sector collaboration for the social good. In 2007 she founded the International Symposia Series on "Cross Sector Social Interactions" (CSSI) organized by academics at leading universities around the world. She has served as a consultant and trainer for many private, public, and nongovernmental organizations. Books include *The Politics of Partnerships* (2010, short-listed for the SIM 2013 Best Book Award), *Social Partnerships and Responsible Business. A Research Handbook* (2014, co-authored with Andrew Crane), and *Creating Value in Nonprofit-Business Collaborations: New Thinking & Practice* (2014, co-authored with James E. Austin and received the 2014 Finalist Terry McAdam Best Book Award Book of the Alliance for Nonprofit Management).

Jung-In Soh is a doctoral student in the Andrew Young School of Policy Studies' Department of Public Management and Policy at Georgia State University. With a background in direct social service provision in local government and nonprofit agencies, her research interests include nonprofit finance and effectiveness.

Steven Rathgeb Smith is the executive director of the American Political Science Association. Previously, he was the Louis A. Bantle Chair in Public Administration at the Maxwell School of Citizenship and Public Affairs at Syracuse University. He also taught for many years at the University of Washington, where he was the Nancy Bell Evans Professor at the Evans School of Public Affairs and director of the Nancy Bell Evans Center for Nonprofits & Philanthropy. In addition, he has taught at Georgetown, American, and Duke universities, and Washington University in St. Louis. From 1997 to 2004, he was editor of *Nonprofit and Voluntary Sector Quarterly* and, from 2006 to 2008, president of the Association for Research on Nonprofit Organizations and Voluntary Action. Dr. Smith has authored and edited several books, including, most recently, *Nonprofits and Advocacy: Engaging Community and Government in an Era of Retrenchment* (The Johns Hopkins University Press, 2014; co-edited with Robert Pekkanen and Yutaka Tsujinaka).

Eugene R. Tempel, Ed.D., is president emeritus of the Indiana University Foundation, founding dean emeritus of the Indiana University Lilly Family School of Philanthropy, and a professor of philanthropic studies. He led the world's first school devoted to research and teaching about philanthropy, is an internationally recognized expert on the philanthropic sector, and has four decades of leadership and fundraising experience. A member of several nonprofit boards, Professor Tempel is a past chair of the national Association of Fundraising Professionals'

Ethics Committee. The author of several works in the field, he has won numerous awards and has been named among the fifty most influential nonprofit sector leaders thirteen times by *The NonProfit Times*, which also named him the sector's first "Influencer of the Year" in 2013.

John Clayton Thomas is a professor in the Department of Public Management and Policy in the Andrew Young School of Policy Studies at Georgia State University in Atlanta, Georgia. Dr. Thomas teaches master's- and doctoral-level courses on program evaluation and performance measurement and has written four books and more than sixty articles in the areas of program evaluation, performance measurement, citizen-government relationships, and other aspects of public management. Dr. Thomas has also consulted and conducted training for state and local governments and nonprofit agencies in Colorado, Georgia, New York, South Carolina, Pennsylvania, Texas, and Missouri. He holds a Ph.D. in political science from Northwestern University and a B.A. (magna cum laude) and M.A. in journalism and mass communications from the University of Minnesota.

Mary R. Watson is executive dean at The New School in New York City. In this role she leads a portfolio of graduate schools in the fields of management, public policy, environment, international affairs, media studies, and writing, as well as an adult undergraduate program in liberal arts. Watson's research and creative practice explore shifting labor market inequalities, including sustainable global supply chains, executive career paths, ethics in multinational operations, design inspired leadership, and the future of work and learning. She plays a leadership role in networks advancing social and environmental innovation, including the Ashoka Changemaker campuses and Management Education for the World, and she is on the advisory board of Social Accountability International. Watson has taught in the United States, South Korea, India, Austria, and Australia, and she is recipient of The New School's Distinguished University Teaching Award. She earned her Ph.D. in organization studies from Vanderbilt University.

Dennis R. Young is executive in residence in the Maxine Goodman Levin College of Urban Affairs at Cleveland State University and professor emeritus at Georgia State University. Previously he was a professor of public management and policy in the Andrew Young School of Policy Studies where he directed GSU's Nonprofit Studies Program and held the Bernard B. and Eugenia A. Ramsey Chair in Private Enterprise. From 1988 to 1996 he was director of the Mandel Center for Nonprofit Organizations and Mandel Professor of Nonprofit Management at Case Western Reserve University. He is the founding editor of the journal *Nonprofit Management and Leadership* and founding and current editor of *Nonprofit Policy Forum*, and a past president of the Association for Research on Nonprofit Organizations and Voluntary Action (ARNOVA). His books include *A Casebook of Management for Nonprofit Organizations*, *Economics for Nonprofit Managers* (with Richard Steinberg), *Corporate Philanthropy at the Crossroads* (with Dwight Burlingame), *Effective Economic Decision Making for Nonprofit Organizations*, *Wise Decision-Making in Uncertain Times*, *Financing Nonprofits*, *Handbook of Research on Nonprofit Economics and Management* (with Bruce A. Seaman), *Civil Society, the Third Sector and Social Enterprise: Governance and Democracy* (with Philippe Eynaud and Jean-Louis Laville), and *The Social Enterprise Zoo* (with Elizabeth A. M. Searing and Cassady V. Brewer). In 2013, his 1983 book *If Not for Profit for What? A Behavioral Theory of the Nonprofit Sector Based on Entrepreneurship* was digitally reissued with new commentaries from contemporary scholars by the Georgia State University Library. Young received ARNOVA's 2004 Award for Distinguished Achievement and Leadership in Nonprofit and Voluntary Action Research and the Award for Innovation in Nonprofit Research from the Israeli Center for Third Sector Research at Ben Gurion University in 2005. In 2010 he was awarded an honorary doctorate from the University of Liege in Belgium for his work on social enterprise and entrepreneurship. He served on the governing board of the National Council of Nonprofits from 2008 to 2014 and the Advisory Board of the Foundation Center/Atlanta from 2005 to 2015.

THE EDITOR

David O. Renz is the Beth K. Smith/Missouri Chair in Nonprofit Leadership and the director of the Midwest Center for Nonprofit Leadership, the nonprofit leadership research and development center of the Henry W. Bloch School of Management at the University of Missouri–Kansas City. Renz earned a master of arts degree in industrial relations in 1978 and a Ph.D. with a concentration in organization theory and administration in 1981, both from the University of Minnesota.

Renz teaches and conducts research on nonprofit and public service governance and leadership, especially, on strategies for improving nonprofit organization and board effectiveness. He writes extensively for both the scholarly and practice communities and has published reports, chapters, and articles in a wide variety of journals, including *Nonprofit Management and Leadership, The Nonprofit Quarterly, Strategic Governance, Public Productivity and Management Review, Public Administration Review*, and *Nonprofit and Voluntary Sector Quarterly*.

Renz has served public service organizations in many capacities, including consulting and service on many councils, task forces, and governing boards. He is past president of the Nonprofit Academic Centers Council, a network of university-based nonprofit centers that he helped found, and has served as an officer and on the governing boards of many nonprofit field-building organizations, including the Association for Nonprofit Research and Voluntary Action

(ARNOVA), the Fieldstone Alliance, and the Forum of Regional Associations of Grantmakers. In 2015, he served as the founding president of the Governance Section of ARNOVA. He also is active in several networks of nonprofit capacity building consultants and organizations, including the Alliance for Nonprofit Management and the statewide nonprofit association, Nonprofit Missouri. For eight years, Renz also served as executive director of Kansas City's Clearinghouse for Midcontinent Foundations. Prior to joining the University of Missouri system, he was a Minneapolis-based consultant and taught at the University of St. Thomas. His career includes several senior executive positions in government, including executive director of the Metropolitan Council of the Twin Cities and assistant commissioner of administration for the State of Minnesota Department of Labor and Industry.

INTRODUCTION TO THE FOURTH EDITION

David O. Renz

It is a pleasure to have the opportunity, on behalf of founding editor Robert Herman and all of us associated with *The Jossey-Bass Handbook of Nonprofit Leadership and Management*, to present this fourth edition. With Robert's retirement, it became my privilege to assume the role of editor for the 2010 edition of the *Handbook*, and now we have the opportunity to share the fourth edition with nonprofit leaders, managers, and students throughout the United States and the world. Needless to say, my aspiration is to sustain the legacy and value of the first three editions while increasing the relevance and impact with the latest and most substantive of insights into the changing and expanding world of nonprofit leadership and management. All chapters of this fourth edition of the *Handbook* present the most current of research, theory, and practice in the field of nonprofit leadership and management, written in a manner that is practical and relevant. To ensure that the *Handbook* continues to meet the needs of this fast-changing field, we have further developed our changes in emphasis in three important areas. First, we continue to focus our attention on the challenges that confront essentially all nonprofit leaders and managers with regard to heightened demands for accountability, transparency, and the need to demonstrate outcomes and results. Alnoor Ebrahim's seminal chapter on how to understand and address the complexities and implications of the "many faces of nonprofit accountability" sets the stage for this, and the issues and themes he highlights are addressed from the perspective of specific fields in subsequent chapters on ethics, finance, advocacy, marketing, and more.

Second, we continue to focus our attention on the increasingly popular phenomenon of social entrepreneurship, and all of the ways it is defined and understood, with additional focus on its implications for nonprofit leadership and management. The foundation for this discussion is Matthew Nash's revised chapter on social entrepreneurship and social innovation, and the majority of the chapters in the book reflect the need to consider the implications of this phenomenon with regard to each of their topics. Integral to this is the third area of emphasis, the increasingly complex and dynamic world of nonprofit financial management. The financial environment and character of the sector has been changing quite dramatically over the past fifty years, as Brent Never illustrates and explains in his chapter on the changing context of nonprofit management, and all chapters in the financial section of this edition have been revised to address this. Two chapters that were new to the third edition have been substantially revised to reflect the additional complexity of this new environment and the resulting financial leadership and management challenges that confront nonprofits and their leaders. First is the framing chapter on financial leadership by Jeanne Bell and Shannon Ellis, and second is the foundational chapter on nonprofit finance and resource development by Dennis Young and Jung-In Soh.

For this fourth edition, we also have substantially enhanced the chapter-by-chapter resources and tools that we make available to readers and educators via the *Handbook*'s Internet resource site. All who purchase the *Handbook* are invited to visit the Wiley Premium Content Internet resource site (www.wiley.com/go/JBHandbook) where they will find an extensive array of supplemental resources designed to help readers make the most of the information presented in each chapter. Among the resource materials on the site are supplemental readings lists, annotated website reference lists with hot links to useful chapter-relevant Internet resources, plus application resources such as worksheets and checklists that can be used to begin to apply the knowledge and information relevant to each chapter. In addition, for educators, a special password-protected website has been created. Among the resources on this unique access-controlled site are the *Handbook* instructor's manual and chapter-specific teaching materials, including PowerPoint presentations, discussion guides and questions, sample assignments, and related teaching tools. Educators who wish to gain access to these teaching resources should go to www.wiley.com/college/JBHandbook and register to secure access.

This edition of the *Handbook* arrives at a very interesting time in the development of the nonprofit sector (throughout this volume, we will use the label "nonprofit sector" to refer to the sector that others sometimes label "the third sector," "civil society," "the independent sector," or "the social sector"; and we generally will use the label "nonprofit organization" to refer to both nonprofits and organizations that typically are referred to as "nongovernmental organizations" or "NGOs" in many parts of the world). The pace at which the sector and its organizations change continues to accelerate, driven by a complex mix of internal and external dynamics. This edition goes to press as the nonprofit sector finds itself recovering from the effects of one of the most challenging and troubling of economic times. The results and implications of this difficult era are yet to be fully understood, although early signs suggest that the nonprofit world has been changing (and continues to change) in fundamental ways. As Brent Never discusses in this volume, the nonprofit sector as a whole is quite resilient. Some segments have recovered relatively well, yet many other segments—especially small and community-based organizations—have not been able to recover very well from the effects of the recession. "Lifeline" or "safety net" nonprofits continue to struggle from the "triple whammy"—continued higher demand for services, coupled with significant declines in governmental financial support and only recent rebound in philanthropic support (in the United States, but not everywhere), combined with a very slow recovery in nonprofits' own internal resources (to the extent they ever existed). Five years after the recession seemed to end, it remains true in the United States and in many other nations that the safety nets are fraying, the level of stress throughout the sector remains significant, and there is no potential to return to the conditions of the past. It is indeed a new era for nonprofit leaders and managers!

Challenges and threats notwithstanding, the dynamics of the current times also offer opportunity and hope. The enthusiasm that many have for the fast-growing interest in social entrepreneurship (no matter how you define it) is bringing new and sometimes different kinds of energy to the field. Some reflect the tensions of competition from new organizational forms (for example, hybrids that blur the lines between nonprofit and for-profit enterprise and for-profits that are created with the explicit goal of social impact rather than financial gain for their founders). Many of today's changes are the result of the very innovation and creativity that the nonprofit sector can be so good at fueling—the adoption of new ways of understanding charity and social good and the development of entrepreneurial new ways of meeting the needs of people and communities. In addition, fundamental shifts are under way throughout the United States and many other nations as a direct result of key demographic changes, as new cultures, perspectives, and generations become more fully integrated into the leadership of the sector. The pace and depth of technological change and the increased presence of various social media certainly fuel additional forces for change in the sector. And a new generation of enthusiasm for volunteering and community service seems to be emerging as well. From a leadership and management perspective, the challenges confronting the sector are exceptional. Yet so, too, are the opportunities—for those prepared to step in and make the difference!

The *Jossey-Bass Handbook of Nonprofit Leadership and Management* emerged in response to the need for a single volume that would offer a comprehensive and thorough treatment of the functions, processes, and strategies integral to nonprofit organization leadership and management. Writing in the preface\nobreak to the second edition of this *Handbook*, editor emeritus Herman observed that all too often advice on financial management, human resource management (for both paid and volunteer personnel), and organizational strategies and leadership has been available only in fragmentary pieces published in far-flung periodicals that are not readily available (p. xvii). In recent years, the volume of literature of the field has grown and developed in impressive ways. And yet, the need for a single comprehensive volume on nonprofit leadership and management remains. We are proud that this fourth edition of the *Handbook* (with its supplemental Internet resources) will extend the legacy as we meet this need with timely, substantive, and readable knowledge and information that is uniquely suited to the challenges of Twenty-First Century nonprofit leaders and managers.

Intended Audience

This volume is designed to provide comprehensive and in-depth explanations of effective leadership and management practices, relevant to and applicable throughout any nonprofit organization. We intend the *Handbook* to be of value to all who practice nonprofit leadership or management, as well as those who aspire to do so. It will be especially useful to anyone who has come to a management or leadership position from a program service background, to anyone who has moved from a relatively specialized management niche into a position with extensive general responsibilities, and to all who seek a solid core of support for the wide range of knowledge and skills that nonprofit leadership requires. In addition to those in paid staff positions, this volume will benefit board members and other volunteer leaders who are interested in enlarging their understanding of the nature of nonprofit organizations and their management. This *Handbook* also will be useful to those, both in formal education programs and in self-directed learning, who want to prepare for careers in nonprofit management. Finally, we want this book to continue to be an important resource to those who work with nonprofit organizations as consultants, technical assistance providers, regulators, and funders, and to inform their efforts to build the capacity, sustainability, and impact of the nonprofit sector across the globe.

Overview of the Contents

This volume is organized into five parts, and each part addresses the challenges of a significant part of the puzzle that is nonprofit management and leadership. Part One provides an overall perspective on the context and institutional setting within which nonprofit organizations and the sector as a whole have developed and currently operate, with observations about the ways this context is likely to change for the future. Nonprofit organizations have been shaped and will continue to be shaped by the historical times and forces, by social institutions, laws and regulations, and political and economic trends and events. The chapters in Part One consider how these large-scale phenomena have affected and are affecting nonprofit organizations and their leadership and management. In Chapter One, Peter Dobkin Hall succinctly describes the complex history of philanthropy and nonprofit organizations in the United States, exploring how and why the nonprofit sector has developed as it has. In Chapter Two, Bruce Hopkins and Virginia Gross offer a timely and current explanation of the national-level legal and regulatory environment in which U.S. nonprofit organizations operate. This chapter provides insight into recent legislative changes and discusses how the U.S. Internal Revenue Service is likely to proceed with implementation and enforcement. In Chapter Three, Brent Never provides an assessment of the impact of large-scale economic, political, and demographic forces on various segments of the nonprofit sector in the United States and discusses their implications for nonprofit management. Alnoor Ebrahim, in Chapter Four, describes the increasingly strong press for accountability in the nonprofit sector, discusses alternative ways that accountability can be understood, and offers key insights for ways nonprofit leaders might address them.

Part Two examines the ways that leadership is provided in nonprofit organizations, including the work of governance and strategic management. Boards of directors of nonprofit organizations govern their organizations and, therefore, are central to the process of nonprofit leadership. Many also engage in some forms of management work. There is clear evidence that there is an important relationship between board effectiveness and the effectiveness of nonprofit organizations, and nonprofits need effective boards. In Chapter Five, I describe the leadership and management functions of governing boards (including the legal and fiduciary responsibilities of boards and their members), discuss some of the major challenges that confront boards, and offer a board development framework that explains how nonprofit leaders can help build board capacity. In Chapter Six, Robert Herman examines the crucial role of chief executives in leading and managing nonprofit organizations and describes the board-centered, external, and political leadership skills of especially effective chief executives. Nonprofit executives and other leaders have the challenge of creating and sustaining organizational cultures and practices that uphold the highest of ethical standards. Thomas Jeavons offers important insight into the ethical challenges that leaders must address and provides important advice about how this can be achieved in Chapter Seven.

Leading and managing strategically is essential to nonprofit success, and one of the key leadership tasks facing boards and top executives is that of organizing and managing the work of the organization to ensure it achieves its mission. In Chapter Eight, William A. Brown presents a broad and strategic overview of the work of strategic management and the key elements that compose it. John Bryson, in Chapter Nine, builds on the these key concepts with a very complete and thoughtful explanation of the work of executives and boards in developing organizational strategy, including a comprehensive model of the strategic planning processes by which this might best be accomplished. Finally, for this part of the book, Robert Herman and I, in Chapter Ten, offer a general perspective and set of insights that we have developed from the research on the elusive concept of nonprofit organizational effectiveness, how it is related to leadership and management, and discuss its implications for organization and management practice. Each of these chapters offers important insights into the processes, dynamics, and practices that have an impact on the degree to which nonprofit organizations are effectively governed and led.

The contributions in Part Three begin to get at the heart of nonprofit organizational management operations. Effective nonprofit leaders and managers understand that their organizations develop, grow, and thrive because they have developed an important mutually beneficial relationship with the world they exist to serve. Similar to all organizations, nonprofits succeed because they offer value and make a valuable difference in the communities and societies they emerge to serve. The chapters of Part Three of this *Handbook* build on Part Two to explain how nonprofit organizations start, develop, grow, and (sometimes) disappear. In Chapter Eleven, Matthew T. A. Nash helps us understand various ways that nonprofits and other social ventures get their start, and how those with socially innovative ideas hone and develop them to become functioning organizations that make a difference—that achieve a social impact. This is the realm of the increasingly popular but oft-misunderstood topic of "social entrepreneurship." Scott T. Helm, in Chapter Twelve, builds on the concepts presented in Nash's chapter with practical information about the development of a social venture, including, in particular, the processes by which nonprofit leaders can use the concepts and practices of business planning to effectively operationalize their visions for community service and impact.

In Chapter Thirteen, Brenda Gainer explains nonprofit marketing, the discipline that enables us to understand how to effectively develop and manage relationships and engage in the exchanges that every enterprise must develop with its key constituents, clients, and stakeholders to survive. And in Chapter Fourteen, Marcia A. Avner explains the process of advocacy by nonprofits, including a discussion of the most effective approaches that nonprofits can employ to engage constituents and exercise influence in governmental policy processes to have an impact on legislation and policy that will affect their work and their clients' lives. James E. Austin and M. May Seitanidi offer a new perspective on collaboration in Chapter Fifteen, and explain how nonprofits can understand and develop valuable collaborative relationships and alliances—alliances that have the greatest potential for generating additional benefit and impact for all partners. Of course, the press for nonprofits to show that the work they and their programs do makes a difference requires that nonprofit leaders and managers understand how to assess and communicate about the performance and impact of these programs. The final chapter of Part Three, Chapter Sixteen by John Clayton Thomas, addresses the core principles of program evaluation and offers guidance for how nonprofits can most pragmatically assess program effectiveness and results.

The chapters of Part Four collectively address the multiple facets of the process of securing, allocating, using, and accounting for financial resources, all with the orientation of maximizing the potential for mission impact and results. Jeanne Bell and Shannon Ellis set the tone in Chapter Seventeen with their discussion of strategic financial leadership; they discuss how the strategic orientation of effective financial leadership has the potential to open the door to new possibilities for nonprofit development and sustainability. Of course, raising money through philanthropic channels is a time-honored approach to securing funds for nonprofits. In Chapter Eighteen, Sarah K. Nathan and Eugene R. Tempel outline the key elements of an effective fundraising program for a typical nonprofit and explain key options that exist for nonprofits that seek gifts and donations. Dennis R. Young and Jung-In Soh approach the financial resource question from a broader and more strategic perspective in Chapter Nineteen, where they discuss the range of options for securing financial resources and present a framework to inform decisions about the critical question of revenue mix. In Chapter Twenty, Steven Rathgeb Smith examines the nature and implications of nonprofit-government contracting and how this has evolved in the

United States, discusses the key benefits, challenges, and dynamics associated with it, and offers advice for ways that nonprofits might maintain an appropriate level of engagement and autonomy when engaged in this common yet potentially problematic nonprofit revenue relationship. Part Four closes with the most operational chapter on financial management. Woods Bowman's explanation in Chapter Twenty-One of the fundamental tools and techniques of nonprofit financial management addresses the challenges of financial sustainability, the need for mission-based decision making, and how to ensure that financial managers are good stewards who are using the financial resources of the organization to achieve the greatest benefit and impact. Readers are especially encouraged to supplement their review of this chapter with the extensive set of resources and tools that Bowman provides on the *Handbook*'s Internet resource site.

Regardless of the mission, size, history, or geographic location of the organization, every nonprofit must be able to attract, retain, reward, and motivate its people. There is a valuable body of knowledge about human resource management and how it can be handled effectively, and the chapters of Part Five apply the insights of this field to the work of nonprofit managers. Mary R. Watson and Rikki Abzug lead into the topic in Chapter Twenty-Two, with an overview of human resource management and an explanation of the human resource systems, processes, and practices that are important to any well-functioning nonprofit organization. Nancy E. Day explains in Chapter Twenty-Three how to approach one of the most challenging yet important of human resource management issues, the challenge of compensating work and rewarding performance. Finally, in Chapter Twenty-Four, Jeffrey L. Brudney discusses the segment of the human resource world that is most unique to the nonprofit sector—the volunteer. Brudney presents a comprehensive explanation of the effective volunteer management program and how it should be developed and operated, and explains how a nonprofit can systematically and strategically implement a program that will enable it to attract, organize, lead, and manage the volunteers it needs and wants.

Finally, in the Conclusion, I discuss the ways that the sector may be developing and changing and offer a few observations about the future of nonprofit leadership and management. I am optimistic about the future of the sector and the capacity of the talented people who lead and manage it, and I share thoughts about various ways that nonprofit leaders and managers can address the myriad of conflicting and complicating forces that buffet the sector and their organizations.

Like the three editions that precede it, this fourth edition of the *Handbook* is designed to present the latest and most relevant leadership and management information currently available on this extensive range of topics. The authors and I have taken care to integrate the best of what we know about current practice with the guidance and insight that derives from the latest in research and theory. It is our goal that this fourth edition, like its predecessors, will become a valued and widely used reference and resource, informing leaders, aspiring leaders, managers, and aspiring managers for many years to come.

Acknowledgments

It is both a privilege and daunting responsibility to serve as the editor for a new edition of a resource as widely known, respected, and valued as *The Jossey-Bass Handbook of Nonprofit Leadership and Management*, and I want to express my great personal thanks to all who have helped bring this new edition to life. This must, of course, begin with thanks to editor emeritus Robert Herman. Bob is an exceptional colleague and friend, and he has been very supportive of our efforts to bring this fourth edition to press. Bob, thank you for entrusting yet another generation of the *Handbook*'s legacy to my care; I hope you find it a fitting extension of the work you began more than twenty years ago when you launched the first edition of the *Handbook*!

My acknowledgements also must begin, of course, with a deep thank you to each and every chapter author. For most, this was their second or third round of service, and I greatly appreciate their willingness to tackle yet another round and to do so with such enthusiasm and energy. For some, this was their first opportunity to become a part of the project and they, too, showed great enthusiasm and energy for the work. All confronted tight deadlines and endured regular editorial harassment, yet every one invested an exceptional amount of effort and delivered their best. This is truly an outstanding group of colleagues, and it has been a pleasure to work with each and every one of them!

Sadly, it is a bittersweet challenge to acknowledge the exceptional contributions of two of our team of authors, in particular, because both have died in tragic automobile accidents during the past year. Both were sage analysts and exceptional leaders who invested decades of their lives in the development of nonprofit studies as a field, and we mourn their loss. Peter Dobkin Hall, preeminent nonprofit historian and one of the most thoughtful and significant leaders of the field, has been the author of the history of the sector chapter since the first edition of the *Handbook* was published. We lost Peter in April of 2015 and this loss is still being felt throughout our community.

Another of the giants in our field, Woods Bowman, is a man whom I was privileged to call a valued colleague and friend in the profession. A preeminent scholar and writer on nonprofit finance, public policy, and ethical leadership and management, Woods began work two years ago on his chapter on nonprofit financial management for this volume, and he completed the chapter in the spring of 2015. We had expected to work together to develop additional resources and conduct programs and workshops on the material he developed, but we lost Woods in the summer of 2015. He was a dedicated public servant as well as a prominent leader in the field of nonprofit management research, and he wrote extensively for both academic and practice audiences (including a widely followed column on nonprofit ethics and frequent articles on nonprofit financial management for the *Nonprofit Quarterly* magazine). Words cannot express the sense of loss so many of us feel as we reflect on the exceptional times we had working with Woods, a loss that never will be forgotten.

I am very appreciative of the essential support that I have received from Matthew Davis and Caroline Maria Vincent, our editors at Jossey-Bass, and senior editorial assistant, Heather Brosius. They have provided essential support throughout the various transitions of this project, and they responded with good humor and care as I lurched my way along this path. Thank you for all of your help!

Similarly, a great vote of thanks is due to each of my colleagues at the Midwest Center for Nonprofit Leadership—Mark Culver, Cindy Laufer, Scott Helm, Fredrik Andersson, and Nimisha Poudyal; and to my colleagues in the Department of Public Affairs at the University of Missouri–Kansas City: Arif Ahmed, Hye-Sung Han, Anne Williamson, Scott Helm, Sarah Martin-Anderson, Brent Never, Nick Peroff, and especially Barbara Domke. All tolerated my cycles of inattention and distraction with grace and encouragement, and they all stepped up to the plate to provide help whenever it was needed. I especially appreciate the assistance that Nimisha provided with specific elements of this project as we worked to bring it to closure. To all of you: it is a true pleasure to work with such exceptional professionals!

Finally, there are no words to adequately express my thanks to Sandy, my wife and partner in life, for her exceptional support and encouragement during this challenging project and always, and to our daughter, Sarah, our son Christian, and his family—our daughter-in-law, Margaret, and our very special granddaughter, Mia. Their care, support, and encouragement have meant everything to me, especially since this project has taken too much from our time together! Thanks for everything, guys!!

David O. Renz

PART ONE

THE CONTEXT AND INSTITUTIONAL SETTING OF THE NONPROFIT SECTOR

It is important to recognize that the nonprofit sector has developed within a larger institutional and social context, and that nonprofit organizations of today have been and will continue to be shaped by historical forces, social institutions, laws and regulations, and significant political and economic trends and events of the nations and cultures in which they develop and operate. All of these have had an important influence on the modern practice of nonprofit leadership and management, and all have important implications for the future of the sector. The chapters of Part One provide the background and information that help us understand this context, and they examine the ways these large-scale phenomena are affecting nonprofit leadership and management.

This part of the book contains four chapters. In Chapter One, Peter Dobkin Hall describes and analyzes the implications of the historical evolution of the U.S. nonprofit sector and how nonprofit organizations are affected by and affect many our society's major institutions. Bruce R. Hopkins and Virginia C. Gross explain in Chapter Two the federal-level legal and regulatory environment within which U.S. nonprofit organizations, particularly charities, operate, and share observations on the implications of this evolving framework for the practice of nonprofit management. In Chapter Three, Brent Never describes some of the most significant of large-scale changes of the economic, political, and demographic environments of the sector and discusses, in particular, how nonprofit organizations in the United States are affected by changes in their evolving relationship with government over the past fifty years. Finally, in Chapter Four, Alnoor Ebrahim examines the increasingly strong push for nonprofit accountability and provides a useful framework by which to consider how nonprofit leaders can understand and respond. This press for greater accountability is a critical element that is shaping most aspects of modern nonprofit management, in the United States, Europe, and across the globe, and cannot be ignored. Ebrahim's chapter offers an invaluable perspective for making sense of the multiple and often conflicting demands on the nonprofit sector.

It is clear that three of the four chapters in Part One have a very explicit focus on the context of nonprofit organizations in the United States. In some respects, this may appear to make them less relevant to the nonprofit and nongovernmental organization world beyond the borders of the United States. Alternatively, these chapters can be viewed as case examples from one nation, cases that exemplify the principles and dynamics that have their counterpart in every nation and continent of the world. History, legal framework, and socio-political and economic dynamics of the recent past are fundamental elements of pivotal significance to the nonprofit and nongovernmental organization context of every nation. The specifics of such contexts will be different for every nation, but the reader from outside the United States is encouraged to consider what may be the comparable trends and dynamics that are relevant to the nonprofit sector and civil society in their own nation. In some nations, the context will be relatively similar; in others, the context will be significantly different. Nonetheless, since context fundamentally affects why and how nonprofits and nongovernmental organizations emerge, operate, thrive, and die, the important question for the nonprofit leader is how such contextual conditions have been and will continue to shape the unique character of their sector and their work as leaders and managers for their own specific circumstances. In contrast to the first three chapters, Ebrahim's treatise on accountability in Chapter Four is broadly generalizable across all nations and cultures; it is the specific forms and vehicles of accountability that will vary from nation to nation.

CHAPTER ONE

HISTORICAL PERSPECTIVES ON NONPROFIT ORGANIZATIONS IN THE UNITED STATES

Peter Dobkin Hall

Although charitable, educational, and religious organizations are thousands of years old (for example, the Roman Catholic church) and some in the United States (for example, Harvard College) were founded in colonial times, the concept of "nonprofit organizations" as a unified and coherent "sector" dates back only to the 1970s.

In fact, over 90 percent of nonprofit organizations currently in existence were created since 1950. Worldwide, most nongovernmental organizations (or NGOs, as they are called outside the United States) have come into being in the past thirty years. Nonprofits and NGOs are the most rapidly growing organizational domain in the world.

It is difficult to define what nonprofit organizations are, what they do, and how they do it. They vary enormously in scope and scale, ranging from informal grassroots organizations with no assets and no employees to multi-billion-dollar foundations, universities, religious bodies, and health care complexes with thousands of employees or members. Although some provide traditional charitable, educational, and religious services, the laws in many countries, including the United States, permit them to provide almost any kind of good or service on a not-for-profit basis. Sources of revenue vary: some are supported by donations, others depend on income from sales of goods and services, many receive most or all of their revenues from government. Modes of governance range from the autocracy of sole trustees selected from among the descendants of charitable donors to broadly representative boards composed of ex officio elected officials or directors elected by members of organizations.

Because of the complexity and diversity of nonprofit organizations, the term itself has a variety of meanings. It can refer to entities classified by the Internal Revenue Code as 501(c)3 charitable tax-exempts—or to a more inclusive universe of 501(c)4 civic organizations, which are themselves exempt from taxation but do not allow deductibility of donations. Good arguments can be made for including other noncharitable nonprofits such as cemeteries, veterans and fraternal/sororal organizations (such as the Masons and the Elks), political parties, and other organizations covered by Section 501(c). However inclusive, restricting the term to organizations accorded nonprofit status by the tax code remains problematic, since it does not include churches and other religious organizations that enjoy the privileges of 501(c)3s but are not legally required to incorporate or seek exempt status. There is also a vast realm of unincorporated associations (such as Alcoholics Anonymous and other self-help groups) that perform many of the functions of incorporated nonprofits as providers of charitable, educational, and religious services but whose assets do not merit—or ideology does not permit—formal institutionalization.

Because their numbers have grown so rapidly, because they are so diverse, and because their impact is so far-reaching—touching on every aspect of our lives and every level of institutions—nonprofits have been the focus of intense controversy as legislators, the courts, and the public have struggled to come to terms with this organizational revolution. At the same time, because the nonprofit universe has been in a process of emergence, those within it have had to struggle to define and legitimate it.

For all of these reasons—diversity, complexity, and disagreement about how to define them—nonprofits pose particular difficulties for scholars trying to explain their history. Although elements of the "nonprofit sector" date back to Biblical and Classical times (for example, religious bodies), other important aspects of it are entirely new (for example, hospitals and universities). At best, in trying to understand the history of nonprofits, we can identify the various ideas and institutions that constitute today's nonprofit domain and show how they have evolved over time.

Associations in Early America

The basic legal vehicles of today's nonprofits—the corporation and the trust—were known to colonial Americans. Philanthropy and volunteer service—giving money and time—were also features of early American life. But because the colonists understood the role of government and the rights and responsibilities of citizenship so differently, these vehicles and practices little resembled the forms they take in modern America.

To begin with, there was no clear demarcation between public and private realms. All corporations, to the extent that they were permitted to exist, were considered to be public agencies (Davis, 1918; Dodd, 1960; Hurst, 1970; Seavoy, 1982). Most common were municipal corporations: townships (Hartog, 1983). In most colonies, religious congregations were public corporations supported by taxation and enjoying monopoly powers. The early colleges, Harvard (1638), William & Mary (1689), and Yale (1701), were sustained by government grants and governed by clergymen who, as officials of the government-supported ("established") churches, were public actors (Whitehead, 1976). No private corporation as we understand the term today existed in America before the 1780s. Many of these institutions—churches, townships, and colleges—accepted gifts and bequests from donors and held them in trust as endowments, although it would be decades before American courts would have the power to enforce or adjudicate trusts.

Citizens often pitched in to maintain roads, build meeting houses, fight with militias, and assist with other public tasks (McKinney, 1995). Although superficially resembling modern volunteers, these citizens were usually compelled by law to labor on behalf of the public. Service of this kind was a common way of paying taxes in a primitive colonial economy in which barter usually took the place of money. Militia duty and service in public office was often required by law—and those who failed to "volunteer" to serve were often punished by fines.

Despite obvious differences, these colonial institutions resembled modern nonprofits in important ways (Zollmann, 1924). They were self-governing, with decisions made by members who often delegated power to governing boards. More important, they had no owners or stockholders. As public bodies they were exempt from taxation. And, like modern nonprofits, they could accept donations and bequests for charitable purposes, such as supporting education and relief for the poor.

During the 18th Century, population growth, economic development, and closer contact with England and other European countries changed American institutions. More people and the founding of new towns made it harder to maintain social and political unity. Artisans, merchants, and laborers living in seaports, who depended on trade and were exposed to new ideas from Europe, developed ways of thinking and living that were different from those of subsistence farmers in isolated landlocked villages. Even in the back country, conflict developed between farmers who began to grow crops for sale to urban merchants—thus tying themselves to the emerging market economy—and those who continued to produce largely to satisfy their own needs. To complicate matters, England's efforts to integrate the colonies into its growing commercial empire brought political changes. In many colonies, elected officials were replaced by royal appointees and the Congregationalist religious monopoly was broken by the establishment of Anglican churches.

New ideas accompanied these social, economic, and political changes. Out of a century of religious warfare and political strife in Europe came philosophies that asserted the "natural rights" of citizens, including freedom of speech, assembly, and worship, and questioned the authority of arbitrary and oppressive government (Bailyn, 1992). New ideas also included more sophisticated understandings of law, particularly as it affected economic rights (Horowitz, 1977; Katz, 1971; Katz, Sullivan, and Beach, 1985; Nelson, 1975).

Closer ties to Europe brought not only new ideas, but also new institutions. After an apprenticeship as a printer in London, young Benjamin Franklin returned with firsthand knowledge of the various kinds of voluntary associations being formed by English tradesmen (Morgan, 2003). Freemasonry, a fraternal order whose members were committed to a variety of radical political and religious ideas, spread rapidly through the colonies in the mid-1700s. Masonry provided a model for other forms of private voluntary associations, most notably Franklin's "Junto," a club of young Philadelphia tradesmen who pooled their books, trained one another in debating and writing, and supported one another's political and economic ambitions.

Closer ties with Europe also transformed American religious life as evangelists associated with dissenting sects crossed the ocean to spread their doctrines (Ahlstrom, 1972; Butler, 1990; Finke and Stark, 1992; Hatch, 1989). Soon American cities and towns were filled with competing churches, with Methodists, Baptists, and other religious enthusiasts crowding out the older Congregationalists and Methodists. Although Pennsylvanians and Rhode Islanders had long enjoyed religious toleration, the notion that people could freely choose how to worship and were free to form and support their own congregations, free of government interference, was a novel idea to most Americans. In many places, religious dissenters demanded and succeeded in obtaining many of the same rights as members of established churches, including exemption of their congregations from taxation. This set an important precedent for the secular associations that would proliferate in the 19th Century.

The American Revolution drew on all these intellectual and organizational developments: religious revivals and political theories that affirmed the importance of individual rights, experience in organizing voluntary associations, and the use of associations in politics. Groups such as the Sons of Liberty and the Committees of Correspondence helped mobilize citizens to fight for American independence.

Voluntary Associations in the New Republic, 1780–1830

Despite their importance during the Revolution, many Americans distrusted voluntary associations and feared the power of wealthy private institutions. These feelings were fueled by popular uprisings such as Shay's Rebellion, in which Revolutionary veterans led armed resistance to tax collectors, and the establishment of the Society of the Cincinnati, an association of army officers that, critics believed, desired the creation of a titled aristocracy. This distrust fueled resistance to efforts to charter corporations and to enact legal reforms that would make it easier to create and enforce charitable trusts.

Led by Virginia, many states actively discouraged private charity (Miller, 1961; Wyllie, 1959). In 1792, the Commonwealth annulled the British laws that authorized the establishment of charitable trusts and confiscated endowments administered by the Anglican church. Favoring public over private institutions, Virginia established the first state university in 1818 (Dabney, 1981). This would become a common pattern in many southern and western states.

The South was not alone in its suspicion of private charitable enterprise. In 1784, New York established the Regents of the University of the State of New York, a regulatory body that oversaw all charitable, education, religious, and professional organizations. In the 1820s the state enacted laws limiting the size of institutional endowments and the size of bequests that testators could leave to charity.

In contrast, the New England states actively encouraged private initiatives of all sorts. By 1800, Massachusetts and Connecticut had chartered more corporations than all the other states combined. Voluntary associations—formal and informal; religious and secular—flourished. By the 1820s, legal reforms gave further encouragement to private charities by protecting trustees from liability and liberalizing the kinds of investments they could make. As a result, New England states became national centers for education, culture, and science, as the wealth from their industrializing economy poured into the coffers of their colleges, hospitals, libraries, and museums (Hall, 1982).

These growing differences in the treatment of private associations, charity, and philanthropy inevitably had political consequences. With the rise of popular politics and the intensification of efforts to disestablish churches in states where some religious groups still enjoyed monopoly privileges and tax support, conservative elites went on the defensive, using colleges and other private institutions to protect their power. These struggles came to a head in the Dartmouth College Case (Tobias, 1982; *Trustees*, 1819). In 1819, the U.S. Supreme Court was asked to decide whether the state of New Hampshire had exceeded its powers in taking over a privately endowed educational institution and turning it into a public institution. The court, in ruling that a corporation was a private contract and hence protected by the contracts clause of the United States Constitution, gave assurance to donors that the institutions they founded and supported would be safe from government interference. Later, in the Girard Will Case, the Court would affirm the legal basis for private philanthropy, even in states such as Pennsylvania, which had annulled British charities statutes.

Because the Constitution granted significant power to the states, these federal court decisions had limited impact. Every state had its own laws governing corporations, associations, and charities. Some, like those of New England, encouraged private philanthropy and protected charitable corporations. Most, however, restricted private initiatives and, as a matter of public policy, favored public ones. This preference did not, it should be noted, preclude private giving to public institutions. State colleges and universities, public libraries, and other government-run agencies benefited from this growing practice of public philanthropy.

During the first half of the 19th Century, voluntary associations played increasingly important roles in the nation's public life. Political parties, which were embryonic in 1800, had become powerful national institutions. As Americans became concerned about slavery, drunkenness, violations of the Sabbath, treatment of the insane, and other causes, voluntary associations, organized on a national basis with state and local chapters, became the preferred vehicles for social movements promoting reform. Churches began organizing themselves into national denominations that supported a wide variety of educational and charitable initiatives, domestic and foreign missions, and substantial publishing enterprises (Foster, 1965; Mathews, 1969). Fraternal organizations, the Masons and Odd Fellows, commanded the loyalties of hundreds of thousands of Americans (Skocpol, Ganz, Munson, Camp, Swers, and Oser, 1999).

Beginning in the 1830s, emigrants, displaced by war, revolution, and economic distress, began to flock to our shores. Some, like the Germans, brought with them their own rich traditions of voluntary action. Others, like the Irish, brought forms of charitable engagement. The Roman Catholic church, to which many Germans and Irish belonged, began creating a benevolent empire of schools, orphanages, temperance societies, and social welfare organizations to serve its members. Although its hierarchical structure excluded laity from involvement in church governance, the church became an increasingly important factor in the nation's associational life (Dolan, 1992; Oates, 1995).

In addition to these national associations, there were thousands of free-standing local charitable corporations and voluntary associations devoted to practically every imaginable purpose (Ryan, 1981). As the French visitor Alexis de Tocqueville noted while visiting America in the 1830s:

> Americans of all ages, all conditions, and all dispositions constantly form associations. They have not only commercial and manufacturing companies, in which all take part, but associations of a thousand other kinds, religious, moral, serious, futile, general or restricted, enormous or diminutive. The Americans make associations to give entertainments, to found seminaries, to build inns, to construct churches, to diffuse books, to send missionaries to the antipodes; in this manner they found hospitals, prisons, and schools. If it is proposed to inculcate some truth or foster some feeling by the encouragement of a great example, they form a society. Wherever at the head of some new undertaking you see the government in France, or a man of rank in England, in the United States you will be sure to find an association. (de Tocqueville, [1835] 1945, II, p. 106)

In his enthusiasm, de Tocqueville somewhat exaggerated the universality of voluntary associations. Although they were used for many purposes and by people at all levels of society, including women and African Americans, who were excluded from the political process, there remained significant geographical variations in citizens' willingness to use them, depending on whether state laws restricted their activities and authorities were willing to subsidize them directly, through government grants and contracts, or indirectly through tax-exemption.

In states where private initiative was discouraged, tasks of education, healing, and care for the dependent and disabled were often carried out by public agencies. Public provision did not preclude private support, however. State universities accepted private donations. Fire fighting in most towns and cities was provided by volunteer companies. Along with newer forms of voluntary action, older traditions of public philanthropy and voluntarism continued to flourish.

Nation Building, 1860–1920

Associations, private charities, and giving and volunteering all played prominent roles in the Civil War, which provided opportunities for further advancing the claims of private eleemosynary enterprise. Among the first units to rally to the defense of the Union were private military companies, groups of civilians for whom soldierly training was a form of recreational and social activity. Once the fighting began in earnest, private groups rushed to care for the injured and provide comfort for soldiers still in the field. The United States Sanitary Commission, the United States Christian Commission, and other groups organized fundraising events, made clothing and bandages, and mobilized volunteers in towns and cities throughout the country to meet the medical, public health, and other needs of armed forces (Brockett, 1864; Cross, 1865; Frederickson, 1965; Moss, 1968).

At the war's end, the victorious Union faced the immense task of "reconstructing" states devastated by fierce fighting and preparing millions of free slaves for freedom (Butchart, 1980; Fleming, 1906; McFeely, 1968; Richardson, 1986). To do this, the government turned to voluntary organizations to build and staff schools, teach civic and vocational skills to newly freed men and women, and reform southern industry and agriculture (Swint, 1967). Reconstruction also showed some of the darker possibilities of voluntary associations, as embittered southerners organized groups such as the Ku Klux Klan to terrorize blacks and the northern volunteers who were helping them.

The Civil War transformed America, not only establishing the preeminent authority of the federal government in important areas such as civil rights, but also unifying the country economically and culturally. Military needs had forced standardization of railroad equipment, consolidation of the telegraph industry, and the creation of a national financial market, centered in New York. Government spending and growing demand from an increasingly urbanized population fueled the increases in the scope and scale of manufacturing and commercial enterprises that sought national and international markets. The government-funded Transcontinental Railroad, completed in 1869, opened vast areas of the West for agricultural and industrial development. Growing industries and advancing technology required managers and experts for efficient and profitable operation.

Educational institutions found opportunities in this prospect of unbounded growth. "The American people are fighting the wilderness, physical and moral, on the one hand, and on the other are struggling to work out the awful problem of self-government," declared Harvard's new president, Charles W. Eliot, in 1869. "For this fight they must be trained and armed" (Eliot, 1869). Having spent the war years in Europe studying the relationships between higher education and economic development, Eliot himself was well prepared to lead the transformation of Harvard, a sleepy local college before the war, into a modern research university.

Eliot's clarion call was met with enthusiasm. Gifts and bequests to the university increased from $1.6 million for the period 1841–1865 to $5.9 million for the years 1866–1890 (Sears, 1922). Business leaders largely replaced clergymen and lawyers on its governing boards (Veblen, 1918). Curricular reforms encouraged specialization, while new graduate departments and professional schools provided facilities for advanced training and research (Hawkins, 1972; Rudolph, 1968; Veysey, 1965). Harvard's transformation into a research university set the pace for American higher education—and the generosity and imagination of its donors set a standard for philanthropists throughout the country (Curti and Nash, 1965).

Universities became hubs for a universe of new associational and philanthropic institutions and activities (Bledstein, 1976; Geiger, 1986, 1993; Hawkins, 1992). Hospitals, museums, and other arts organizations became research centers, closely tied to university medical schools, scientific disciplines, and new programs in the fine arts and music (DiMaggio, 1986; Fox, 1963; Starr, 1982). New academic disciplines and professions gave rise to professional and scholarly societies (Buck, 1965; Haskell, 1977). University-trained managers and experts became increasingly important not only to industry, but also to governments, which were beginning to grapple with the social welfare, public health, transportation, and policing problems of growing cities (Brint, 1994; Wiebe, 1967).

Beginning in the 1870s, the American economy was shaken by a series of crises. The collapse of the stock market in 1873 was the beginning of a depression that lasted for years and impoverished hundreds of thousands of workers. Economic distress encouraged the growth of labor unions and radical political organizations whose conflicts with employers and government authorities became increasingly violent. In 1877, a national railroad strike provoked large-scale rioting and looting in major cities. In 1886, labor's campaign for a ten hour workday culminated in the Haymarket bombing in Chicago, which killed a dozen policemen and led to the round-up and execution of radical politicians and journalists.

Among the few calm voices in the period was that of a Pittsburgh steel executive, Andrew Carnegie (Wall, 1970). An immigrant from Scotland, Carnegie had worked his way up from being a child laborer in a textile mill to serving as the right-hand man of the president of the Pennsylvania Railroad. From there, he became a pioneering and fabulously successful steel manufacturer. By the 1880s, he was well on his way to becoming one of America's wealthiest men.

In 1886, Carnegie began writing a series of articles on the labor crisis that argued that shorter hours, better working conditions, and employer recognition of workers' right to organize were in the interests of both capital and labor. At the same time, he suggested that the enlarged scope and scale of modern industry had fundamentally changed not only economic relationships, but also the nature of political life (Carnegie, 1886a, 1886b). He summed up his thinking in an 1889 essay, "Wealth," which urged the "men of affairs" who had most profited from advanced industrial development to use their "genius for affairs" to reinvest their fortunes in society. Inherited wealth, he believed, was bad both for heirs and for society—and he went so far as to recommend confiscatory estate taxation to prevent the passing on of large fortunes (Carnegie, 1889). More important, he argued that intelligent philanthropy could not only eliminate the root causes of social problems, but sustain the competitive processes essential to continuing progress.

Carnegie was harshly critical of traditional charity, which, he believed, only responded to suffering rather than addressing the causes of poverty. "It were better for mankind that the millions of the rich were thrown into the sea," he wrote, "than so spent as to encourage the slothful, the drunken, the unworthy. Of every thousand dollars spent in so-called charity today, it is probable that nine hundred and fifty dollars is unwisely spent—so spent, indeed, as to produce the very evils which it hopes to mitigate or cure" (Carnegie, 1889). "The best means of benefiting the community," Carnegie urged his fellow millionaires, "is to place within its reach the ladders upon which the aspiring can rise"—"institutions of various kinds, which will improve the general condition of the people; in this manner returning their surplus wealth to the mass of their fellows in the forms best calculated to do them lasting good" (Carnegie, 1889). This included libraries, parks, museums, public meeting halls (like New York's famous Carnegie Hall), and educational institutions.

In popularizing the idea that businessmen could use the same "genius for affairs" that had made them rich to reform society, Carnegie set an example for his fellow tycoons. Before Carnegie, most philanthropy had been small-scale and conventional. After Carnegie, philanthropy, organized and focused through foundations, would assume an unprecedented scale and scope, becoming an important source of innovation in addressing problems of education, health, and social welfare.

The consolidation of American political, economic, and social institutions between the Civil War and the First World War was as much the result of the actions of elite institutions such as universities and powerful leaders such as Andrew Carnegie as it was the outcome of associational activity at all levels in society (Sklar, 1988). In the second half of the 19th Century, America became, in Arthur Schlesinger Sr.'s phrase, "a nation of joiners" (Schlesinger, 1944, p. 24). Immigrants, who flooded the nation in ever growing numbers, organized mutual benefit associations that gave them solidarity and provided help in times of sickness and distress (Li, 1999; Soyer, 1997). Physicians, lawyers, engineers, and other professionals organized associations to set standards, exchange information, and pressure government (Abbott, 1988; Auerbach, 1976; Calhoun, 1965; Calvert, 1967; Kimball, 1995). Businesses organized trade associations to advocate for legislation favoring their interests (Naylor, 1921). Wage earners organized trade unions to press employers to improve pay and working conditions. War veterans organized the Grand Army of the Republic to promote sociability and advocate for pensions and other benefits. Advocacy groups, which drew members from across the social spectrum, agitated for prohibition, women's suffrage, civil service and charities reform, and other causes (Clemens, 1997). Most important of all were the fraternal and sororal organizations—the Freemasons, Odd Fellows, Knights of Columbus, Rebekahs, and dozens of others—whose chapters became centers of sociability and civic activity, as well as sources of social insurance, for men and women throughout the country (Beito, 2000; Dumenil, 1984; Kaufman, 2002; Skocpol, 2003).

Widespread participation in these broad-based associations was probably the most powerful and effective school of democracy. By participating in associations, citizens learned how to be self-governing, argue and persuade, raise funds and manage finances, and form alliances and coalitions. The fact that most of these associations were national entities whose architecture mirrored that of government itself—with nation, state, and local organizations—helped bind the nation together by accustoming Americans to engaging with one another beyond the locality. If, as de Tocqueville suggested, Americans in the first half of the 19th Century had learned the principle of association in their schoolyards, in the second half of the century associations became the great school of democracy, teaching adults and children alike the values and skills needed for a vibrant and inclusive public culture.

New Charitable Vehicles, 1890–1930

The kind of large-scale targeted giving Carnegie recommended faced a number of obstacles. The most important of them were legal barriers to private charity in states such as New York. At the time that Carnegie wrote, New York state courts had already invalidated a million dollar bequest to Cornell on grounds that the donation, if accepted, would render the university's endowment larger than the amount that the legislature had authorized it to hold. They had also invalidated former presidential candidate and corporation lawyer Samuel Tilden's multimillion-dollar charitable bequest to establish the New York Public Library (Ames, 1913). Without major legal reform, the wealthy, who were increasingly gravitating to New York—the nation's financial center—could not be philanthropically generous even if they wanted to be.

Another obstacle was the lack of organizational vehicles for large-scale philanthropy. Wealthy men like the devoutly religious John D. Rockefeller, who controlled America's petroleum industry by the 1890s, tried to be conscientious givers, personally considering and carefully weighing the thousands of begging letters that poured into their offices (Chernow, 1998; Harr and Johnson, 1988). Rockefeller's situation was summed up by his chief assistant, John W. Gates, who exclaimed to his employer, "Your fortune is rolling up, rolling up like an avalanche!...You must keep up with it! You must distribute it faster than it grows! If you do not, it will crush you and your children and your children's children" (Harr and Johnson, 1988, p. 82). The solution was the creation of corporate entities, staffed by experts, to scientifically distribute this surplus wealth. The problem was that American charities law had traditionally required that charitable trusts be specific in designating classes of beneficiaries.

The failure of the Tilden Trust, combined with anxieties about the increasing anger of average Americans toward the rich and big business, fueled a coordinated effort to reform charities laws in the leading industrial states ("American Millionaires," 1893). By 1893, New York, Pennsylvania, Ohio, and Illinois had altered their charities statutes, permitting the kind of wholesale philanthropy that Carnegie had advocated. Philanthropists proceeded cautiously onto this new legal ground. The first recognizably modern foundations included Rockefeller's General Education Board (established in 1901) to benefit black schools in the South but later broadened to include higher education nationally, Andrew Carnegie's Carnegie Endowment for the Advancement of Teaching (established in 1905), and Margaret Olivia Slocum Sage's Russell Sage Foundation (established in 1907) to systematically address social welfare issues on a national basis (Fosdick, 1962; Glenn, Brandt, and Andrews, 1947; Hammack and Wheeler, 1994; Lagemann, 1999). In 1911, Carnegie took the bold step of establishing the largest foundation of all, the Carnegie Corporation of New York, for the general purpose of "the advancement and diffusion of knowledge and understanding" (Lagemann, 1992).

John D. Rockefeller, not to be outdone and smarting from the court-ordered breakup of the Standard Oil monopoly, applied to Congress for a charter for a $100 million foundation dedicated to "the betterment of mankind" (Fosdick, 1952). The request set off a furor among politicians and journalists who worried about the influence foundations of this size could have on public policy and about their economic power. Rockefeller eventually obtained a charter from the New York State legislature in 1913.

Concerns about the power of foundations and the continuing concentration of wealth continued to grow. In 1915, the Congress empanelled a special Commission on Industrial Relations that held well-publicized hearings over a period of two years (U.S. Congress, 1916). The charges aired during these hearings led foundations to be cautious and secretive about their involvement in public affairs—a stance that would fuel public suspicions of philanthropy's motives and methods that would erupt periodically for the rest of the century (Katz, 1981).

Grantmaking foundations were not the only new charitable vehicles created in the decades before the First World War. In 1910, Cleveland, Ohio's Chamber of Commerce convened a committee to consider problems of charitable fraud, abuse, and inefficiency. Appeals for charity were multiplying, but donors had no way of knowing whether they came from reputable organizations. The number of charitable organizations seeking aid was increasing, producing duplicated efforts and wasted resources. The donor base was shrinking, with an increasing proportion of donations coming from a smaller number of donors. The committee eventually brought forth a new kind of charity—the Community Chest (Cutlip, 1965; Seeley et al., 1957). Led by businessmen, the Chest proposed to conduct a single annual fund drive for all of Cleveland's charities. The Chest's distribution committee would assess the city's charities and allocate funds to the most worthy. The Chest proposed to broaden the donor base by soliciting employees of the city's business firms. Aggressively publicized, the Chest idea spread rapidly. By 1930, hundreds of towns and cities had adopted this form of federated fundraising. The Community Chest is the ancestor of today's United Way.

Cleveland also fostered cooperation among the city's social agencies through its Charities Federation. Establishing lines of communication between agencies allowed them to coordinate their activities, improve their management, and use their resources more efficiently. It also enabled private agencies to work more closely with government to address social problems.

The Community Chest and the Charities Federation addressed problems of current giving and spending. In 1925, Cleveland banker Frederick Goff sought to make the establishment and management of charitable endowments more efficient. He proposed the idea of the community foundation, an institution empowered to receive charitable trusts of various sizes and for various purposes

(Hall, 1989a; Hammack, 1989; Magat, 1989). These would be placed under common management under the authority of a board made up of leading bankers. A distribution committee, often made up of public officials and others serving ex officio, would allocate undesignated or discretionary funds to worthy organizations. Like the Community Chest, the community foundation was intended to democratize charitable giving while giving civic leaders control of a community's charitable resources.

None of these innovations would have been possible without the enthusiastic backing of business leaders. Not only did their ideas and money sustain charitable, educational, and religious institutions, but their companies became important to the effort to improve society (Hall, 1989b; Heald, 1970). Under the banner of "welfare capitalism," corporations not only contributed generously to community institutions, they also established pension plans, initiated educational programs, and supported social and athletic activities for their employees and their families (Brandes, 1976; Brody, 1980). Many firms sold products intended to improve Americans' health and quality of life.

These charitable innovations were only a small part of a far broader associational revolution in the first third of the 20th Century. In the first quarter of the 20th Century, membership in fraternal and sororal organizations peaked in numbers of organizations and membership (Skocpol, 2003). Businessmen's service organizations—Rotary, Kiwanis, Lions, and others—appeared in every town and city (Charles, 1993). Businesses organized trade associations to advocate, lobby, and educate the public and government about their interests. Herbert Hoover, writing in 1922, envisioned these trade associations working closely with other kinds of "voluntary organizations for altruistic purposes" to advance public welfare, morals, and charity, to elevate public opinion, to improve public health, and to solve social problems combining the pursuit of self-interest with higher values of cooperation and public service (Galambos, 1966; Hawley, 1974, 1977; Hoover, 1922; Karl, 1969, 1976). A nation based on public interest voluntarism, he believed, would not need the radical remedies of socialism and communism to address problems of inequality and injustice.

Accompanying this associational revolution was a related transformation of fundraising (Cutlip, 1965). As the needs of hospitals, universities, and other organized charities grew, fundraising became professionalized. Firms such as John Price Jones & Company combined sophisticated business methods with aggressive marketing techniques in raising funds for the World War I loan drives and, later, for Harvard and other universities.

Reform-oriented social movements and other kinds of organized advocacy continued to grow during this period (Sealander, 1997). Efforts to eliminate child labor, enfranchise women, restrict immigration, and protect the rights of minorities influenced public policy through demonstrations, advertising campaigns, lobbying, and litigation. Particularly notable were the efforts of the NAACP (National Association for the Advancement of Colored People) and other groups in the vanguard of the effort to halt the epidemic of lynchings and race riots in which thousands of black citizens perished between 1890 and 1930. Sadly, perhaps the most influential social movement of the period was the revived Ku Klux Klan, which, during the 1920s, commanded the loyalty of hundreds of thousands of followers throughout the country, directing its energies against African Americans, Jews, Catholics, labor organizers, and others.

Big Government, the Nonprofit Sector, and the Transformation of Public Life, 1930–1980

Between 1930 and 1980, American public life was transformed by huge growth in the scope and scale of government, which in turn stimulated commensurate expansion of private institutions. The two were closely connected, since government, as it took on increasing responsibilities for managing economic, political, and social domains, was able to use its awesome power to stimulate growth and activity in the private sectors. Just as public sector activities such as construction of the interstate highway system and petroleum industry subsidies stimulated the growth of the privately owned automobile industry, so public sector subsidies of charitable giving (tax breaks for donors, exemptions for charities, voucher programs such as the G.I. Bill, and increasingly generous grants and contracts) stimulated the growth of nonprofit enterprises of every kind.

This was an incremental process. In the 1930s, no one envisioned that the emergency powers assumed by the federal government to deal with the Depression would become permanent and central features of public life. Nor could anyone imagine the extent to which the increasing activism of government would stimulate the growth of the private sector.

The nation was ill-prepared to deal with the catastrophic economic collapse that began with the stock market crash of October 1929. Even if the discipline of economics had been better developed, its retrospective insights could not have offered much understanding of this unprecedented event. In any event, government lacked the necessary tools of economic management to engage problems of mass unemployment and business failure on this scale.

President Hoover, a millionaire mining engineer who had entered politics with an international reputation as a humanitarian, was philosophically opposed to the idea of big government. His attempts to deal with the Depression through the system of voluntary associations whose growth he had fostered as secretary of commerce and later as president, proved ineffective. His successor, Franklin D. Roosevelt, entered office with similarly conservative views. The centerpiece of his recovery program, the National Recovery Administration (NRA)—with its motto, "we do our part"—was similarly based on voluntaristic principles, promoting economic revival through cooperation between business and government (Himmelberg, 1976).

When the NRA was declared unconstitutional in 1935, Roosevelt turned to more activist remedies, with attempts to restore consumer buying power through massive public works projects like the WPA (Works Projects Administration) and the CCC (Civilian Conservation Corps), agricultural subsidies, and through a national system of social insurance (Social Security). He also proposed major tax reforms, which introduced steeply progressive income and estate taxes with the intent of using the tax system to redistribute the wealth owned by the richest Americans. These tax reforms had little impact on average Americans, few of whom earned enough money to owe income tax. But they proved to be a powerful incentive for the wealthy to avoid taxation through large-scale charitable giving.

Roosevelt's New Deal established the paradigm for the later growth of government. Although the federal government increased the scope of its responsibilities and assumed leadership for making policy in important areas, most federal programs were carried out by state and municipal agencies and by nongovernmental organizations funded by government contracts, user fees, and private contributions indirectly subsidized through tax exemptions and deductions.

During the Second World War and afterward, as the United States assumed leadership of the free world, federal government policies played a key role in stimulating growth in the number and importance of nonprofit organizations. The most important of these involved taxation (Webber and Wildavsky, 1986; Witte, 1985). The income tax, which few Americans had had to pay before the 1940s, was universalized: not only were most wage and salary earners subject to it, but also the government began withholding estimated tax liabilities from employees' paychecks. At the same time, tax rates were sharply increased on estates and business corporations. New tax policies were not only intended to gather revenue for government. Through "loopholes"—exemptions, deductions, and tax credits—tax policy was used to encourage charitable giving to private institutions classified as tax exempt by the Internal Revenue Service (IRS) (Howard, 1997). The growth of nonprofit organizations was also stimulated by increased spending in the form of government grants, contracts, and vouchers (like the GI bill, which subsidized higher education for returning soldiers).

These policies had dramatic effects (Weisbrod, 1988). By 1940, there were only 12,500 charitable tax-exempt organizations registered by the IRS—along with 179,742 religious congregations (which did not have to apply for exemption) and 60,000 noncharitable nonprofits (such as labor unions and fraternal associations) that enjoyed various tax privileges.[1] By 1980, there were 320,000 charitable tax exempt nonprofits—as well as 336,000 religious bodies and 526,000 noncharitable nonprofits. By 2006, there would be more than 600,000 charitables, 400,000 religious congregations, and 600,000 noncharitables—a total of more than a million and a half nonprofits of various types (Hall and Burke, 2006). Government policies played a crucial role in fueling the growing scope and number of nonprofit organizations, not only indirectly through creating incentives to individuals and firms for contributing to private organizations serving governmental ends, but also directly, through grants and contracts. By the 1970s, between 12 percent and 55 percent of total nonprofit revenues were direct payments from the federal government (Salamon, 1987).

Although the scope and scale of its responsibilities vastly increased in the second half of the 20th Century, the size of the federal government—at least as measured in the size of its civilian workforce—did not. The number of federal civilian employees remained unchanged between 1950 and 2000, while the number of state and local employees doubled and tripled and the number of nonprofit organizations grew from the thousands to over a million. Quite clearly, "big government" as it developed after the second World War took a very different form than conventionally supposed. Doing its work through states and localities and through policies that encouraged flows of resources to private actors, the American welfare state was a remarkable example of what Lester Salamon has called "third-party government." (See Chapter Three for more about the relation between governments and nonprofit organizations.)

Of the proliferating organizations of the nonprofit sector, none attracted more attention in the decades following the war than foundations (Andrews, 1950). As taxes on incomes and estates increased, the founders of the huge fortunes built in the boom years of the 20th Century were increasingly likely to use foundations as mechanisms for avoiding taxation. When Henry Ford died in 1947, stock in his closely held company was divided into two classes (Greenleaf, 1964; MacDonald, 1956; Nielsen, 1971; Sutton, 1987). The voting stock was retained by the family, while the nonvoting securities were given to the Ford Foundation, which sold them at an immense profit. The Ford Motor

Company passed to the next generation without paying a penny in taxes—and the largest foundation in the world was created in the process.

Stratagems like this helped fuel an enormous increase in the number and importance of foundations. Numbering only 203 in 1929, the number of foundations with assets exceeding a million dollars grew to 2,058 by 1959—with the vast majority of these established within the decade (Andrews, 1956; *Foundation Directory,* 1960, pp. ix–lv). In 1929, their assets represented only 10.7 percent of the total property controlled by charitable tax-exempt organizations; by 1973, their share was 21.7 percent. Thanks to liberalized laws regarding corporate philanthropy, the growing universe of private and community foundations was further enlarged by corporate foundations and organized corporate contributions programs (Andrews, 1952; Hall, 1989b; Himmelstein, 1997; Useem, 1987).

Although Ford and other foundations established by wealthy families at this time undoubtedly performed valuable services, some politicians and journalists wondered whether average citizens, who were becoming increasingly sensitive to their own tax burdens, either approved of the loopholes that permitted multi-millionaires to evade taxes or sympathized with the sometimes controversial uses of foundation grants (Andrews, 1969; Lundberg, 1968; Nielsen, 1971). Between 1952 and 1969, congressional committees' investigations of foundations and "other tax-exempt entities" cast an increasingly skeptical eye on their activities. With the federal government assuming primary responsibility for education, health, and social welfare, many wondered whether private philanthropy, subsidized by tax breaks, had outlived its usefulness.

Despite these periodic outbursts of regulatory enthusiasm, funds from foundations, corporations, and new government programs (such as the National Institutes of Health, National Science Foundation, National Endowment for the Arts, and National Endowment for the Humanities, among others) continued to fuel the growth and transformation of nonprofit enterprise. On the one hand, industries such as the performing arts and health care, which had been almost entirely for-profit in ownership before 1950, became dominated by nonprofit firms in the course of the next half-century. On the other hand, industries like elder care, which had been largely nonprofit, became for-profit in ownership as government social and medical insurance programs made nursing homes an increasingly profitable enterprise.

The increasing centrality of government also encouraged the growth of special interest advocacy organizations, as stakeholders affected by or benefiting from government programs sought to influence legislators in their favor (Berry, 1977, 1997; Jenkins, 1987; Jenkins and Eckert, 1986; Jenkins and Halcli, 1999). Policy research ("think tanks") and policy advocacy groups such as the Business

Advisory Council, the Conference Board, the Committee for Economic Development, and the Business Roundtable formed a privatized policy establishment (Critchlow, 1985; Rich, 2004; Smith, 1991a, 1991b).

Increasing government activism and foundation funding also stimulated grassroots social movement activity intended to influence public policy. The Civil Rights movement of the 1950s and 1960s gave rise to a host of movements promoting the rights of women, children, the unborn, and the disabled, the health of the environment, and a variety of international causes (Berkeley Art Center Association, 2001; Fleischer and Zames, 2001; Minkoff, 1995; Minton, 2002; Proietto, 1999; Stroman, 2003). On the whole, these social change organizations differed in significant ways from their 19th-Century predecessors. Earlier organizations had been broadly based membership organizations in which volunteers and local chapters played central roles. Late 20th-Century social change organizations were increasingly likely to be based in the national capital and to be run by professional managers, policy experts, communications specialists, and lobbyists (Skocpol, 2003).

Changing political culture, combined with a more educated, affluent, and mobile citizenry, helped kill off traditional kinds of voluntary associations. Membership in fraternal and sororal organizations began to drop sharply after the Second World War as Americans moved to the suburbs and substituted television and other privatized forms of entertainment and recreation for more collective forms of social engagement (Skocpol, 1999). Even such venerable organizations as the Parent-Teacher Association (PTA) began to decline, as suburban parents preferred to devote their energies to parent-teacher organizations focusing more narrowly on the schools their own children attended rather than broader educational issues (Crawford and Levitt, 1999). According to political scientist Robert Putnam, all forms of civic engagement—voting, attending public meetings, church attendance, and participation in athletic associations such as bowling leagues—declined sharply after the 1960s (Putnam, 2000).

Taking the place of traditional voluntary and membership-based engagement was a growing domain of narrowly focused, professionally managed nonprofit organizations that drew their revenues from a mix of earned revenues, government and foundation grants and contracts, and corporate contributions (Hall, 2003). These organizations were more likely to provide specific kinds of services (child day care, elder care, education, health services) and to engage in advocacy, lobbying, and public education than to promote generalized sociability and civic engagement. Regarding public culture in the later 20th Century, management guru Peter Drucker would write that "the nonprofit organizations of the so-called third sector . . . create a sphere of effective citizenship . . . , sphere of personal achievement" in which the individual "exercises influence, discharges responsibility, and makes decisions." Drucker concludes:

> In the political culture of mainstream society, individuals, no matter how well-educated, how successful, how achieving, or how wealthy, can only vote and pay taxes. They can only react, can only be passive. In the counterculture of the third sector, they are active citizens. This may be the most important contribution of the third sector. (Drucker, 1989, p. 204)

In his enthusiasm for the possibilities of the sector, Drucker overlooked the fact that organizations that did not depend on volunteers or donations, that did not seek to recruit members, and that were narrowly focused on service provision and advocacy were likely to primarily engage the energies and interest of "knowledge workers" empowered by the high-tech economy rather than the mass of citizens.[2] It appeared that the "nation of joiners" celebrated by Schlesinger in 1940 was left without opportunities for joining.

The major exception to this trend was religion. Although rising more slowly than the general population, membership in religious bodies and attendance at worship services increased steadily through the second half of the 20th Century (Finke and Stark, 1992; Fogel, 2000). More impressive were increases in the number of congregations and new religious organizations (Roof, 1999). While the mainstream denominations (Catholic, Protestant, Jewish) declined, their place was being taken by free-standing congregations, often evangelical in persuasion, and by groups that stood outside of Western religious traditions (Eck, 2001; Wuthnow, 1998). In addition, ecumenical and parachurch organizations such as Habitat for Humanity, which drew on members' religious commitment but were nonsectarian, grew steadily (Baggett, 2001; Bender, 2003; Wuthnow, 1994). New religious organizations were more likely to be politically active: the conservative revolution of the 1980s and 1990s owed much to its ability to mobilize voters and bring pressure to bear on legislators (Reed, 1996). More important, the new religious organizations were likely to be broadly based in ways that crossed lines of class, occupation, education, and ethnicity in ways that made them especially potent in imparting civic values and skills (Verba, Schlozman, and Brady, 1995).

As religious organizations have assumed a new visibility in public life generally, they have also gained recognition as centrally important parts of the nonprofit sector (Cherry and Sherill, 1992; Demerath, Hall, Williams, and Schmitt, 1998; Wuthnow, 1988; Wuthnow, Hodgkinson, and Associates, 1990).

This is the case not only because they constitute some 40 percent of the nonprofit universe and command two-thirds of all volunteers and donations, but also because they serve as paths of recruitment into secular activities and as platforms for secular or faith-based service provision in a variety of areas. The debate over charitable choice stemming from the welfare reforms of the mid-1990s was not so much an argument about church-state separation as it was an effort to codify government support for faith-based social services that had been a feature of America's human services regime for decades (Carlson-Theis and Skillen, 1996; Chaves, 2001; Cnaan, 1999, 2002; Hall, 2001).

Originally associated with the conservatives' political agenda, particularly with the programs pushed by the second President Bush, by the end of the first decade of the 21st-Century charitable choice had been embraced by both parties. The Democrat's abandonment of efforts to maintain a "wall of separation" between church and state was doubtless due to the fact that among the chief beneficiaries of federal funding were the inner city African American congregations crucial to President Obama's 2008 victory.

The Conservative Revolution and the Nonprofit Sector, 1980–2000

For much of the 20th Century, foundations and secular nonprofit organizations had been generally associated with liberal political causes. Conservatives, regarding nonprofits as liberal—if not subversive—organizations had not only sought to curtail their privileges, but also had generally avoided using nonprofits to advance their own purposes. This began to change after the defeat of Barry Goldwater in 1964, when conservative leaders realized that criticizing liberalism was insufficient as a basis for political success: victory required alternative policies and relentless efforts to sway the public in their favor (Hodgson, 1996). To achieve their ends, conservatives would have to overcome their aversion to nonprofits in order to create their own "establishment" of think tanks, advocacy organizations, and foundations (Berry, 1997; Blumenthal, 1986; Rich, 2004).

A number of factors fueled this resolve. One was the emergence of a new cadre of monied conservatives, mostly from fast-developing areas of the South and West, whose wealth was based on defense production and extractive industries (Sale, 1975). They had a vital economic interest in being able to sway government policies in their favor. Another factor was the political mobilization of conservative Christians, particularly in the South, due to civil rights legislation and court decisions—on school prayer, abortion, and tax exemption for segregated private schools—that they believed threatened their way of life. The convergence of big new money and a mass-based religious movement with a social agenda created new opportunities for conservative Republicans to begin organizing around "wedge issues" such as reproductive rights that broke up long-standing liberal political coalitions. The mobilization of conservative voters, in turn, created the conditions for articulating a positive set of conservative policies that could credibly challenge liberal orthodoxies.

Although moderate Republicans regained control of the party after the Gold-water defeat, the conservatives worked doggedly to seize control of the local and state party organizations—helped along by the Watergate scandal, which discredited the moderate leadership of Richard Nixon. By the eve of the 1980 election, conservatives were ready to take power with Ronald Reagan as their standard-bearer.

Reagan assumed office with strong opinions on the role of nonprofit organizations in public life. He believed that big government had stifled private initiative and he intended to undo the damage through a combination of "jawboning" higher levels of corporate giving (through the President's Task Force on Private Initiatives) and by cutting government spending. What he, like most Americans, failed to understand was the extent to which the nonprofit sector had become dependent on government spending. By the time he took office, nearly a third of the annual revenues of private research universities came from government grants and contracts, and direct federal support for nonprofits in industries such as human services ranged as high as 90 percent. All in all, as an influential Urban Institute report pointed out in 1982, the federal government had become the largest single source of revenue for secular nonprofit organizations and, for this reason, massive cuts in government social spending would be likely to devastate the nonprofit sector (Salamon and Abramson, 1982).

Through the 1980s and into the 1990s, the emphasis in conservative social policy was on devolution (shifting responsibilities to states and localities) and privatization (shifting responsibilities for service provision to private sector actors). The rationales for these policies included the belief that more local and private service provision would not only be more flexible and responsive to the needs of beneficiaries, but also that competition for contracts among private providers would produce greater efficiency and effectiveness in service provision (Olasky, 1992).

While it remains to be seen whether privatized social services have fulfilled any of these promises, it is clear that among the most important impacts of these policies was to increase the need for professionally trained nonprofit managers and entrepreneurs—people who could master an increasingly complex and turbulent policy and funding environment. Although Republican leaders like George H. W. Bush might enthuse about the "thousand points of light" comprising America's community-serving nonprofit organizations, the reality was that these organizations were being driven by circumstances into being less and less responsive to client and community needs, while becoming more businesslike in their attitudes and operations. At the same time, as traditional manufacturing and commercial businesses either disappeared or were driven from urban centers to the suburbs, for-profit enterprises were being rapidly replaced by nonprofit service providers, making the nonprofit sector an increasingly important part of the national economy.

Despite the election of centrist Democrat Bill Clinton in 1992, the conservative revolution entered a new and more radical phase in 1994, when Republicans took control of the House of Representatives and increased their plurality in the Senate. Under the banner of a "Contract with America," conservative leaders set out to dismantle the government social programs created during the previous century (Gillespie and Schellhas, 1994). This agenda went well beyond the desire to devolve and privatize without altering the basic tasks of social programs. Rather, it was based on a fundamental challenge to a variety of liberal articles of faith: that the tax system should be used to redistribute wealth, that alleviating poverty required changing social conditions, and that church and state should be strictly separated. Asserting that liberal social programs had succeeded in creating a "permanent underclass" by rewarding welfare recipients for deviant behavior, the conservatives proposed to eliminate most entitlement programs and to strictly limit eligibility. The key to dealing with poverty and dependency, conservatives believed, was changing the values and behavior of the poor. The dependent, the disabled, and the unemployed would have to rejoin the workforce and, in doing so, regain their self-respect and self-sufficiency. Not surprising, given their heavily sectarian constituency, conservatives looked to religious bodies and faith-based organizations to play central roles in transforming the values and behavior of the poor. Section 104 of the Personal Responsibility and Work Opportunity Reconciliation Act of 1996 set forth the terms of government's new relationship to religious nonprofits.

Although the conservative revolution in many ways favored nonprofit enterprise, especially with the huge expansion of contracted programs, it also fueled intensified competition between organizations, not only because for-profit businesses were invited to bid against nonprofits for government grants and contracts, but also because of a shift from producer-side subsidies, which went directly to service providers, to consumer-side subsidies, which enabled clients to choose among providers (Salamon, 2005, pp. 84–85). Whereas conservative school reforms encouraged nonprofits through voucher programs and charter schools, they also put nonprofit schools in competition with for-profit enterprises such as the Edison Schools, which, with its access to equity financing, had the capacity to operate entire urban school systems. In such an environment, skilled management, entrepreneurial attitudes, and political acumen became crucial to the survival of nonprofits.

Health care, which until the 1970s had been dominated by nonprofits, underwent major changes as legislators sought to control the rising cost of entitlement programs such as Medicare and Medicaid (Gray, 1983, 1986, 1991). As government became more vigilant about health care costs, hospitals were forced to become more businesslike in their operations. Many converted to for-profit ownership. Others, while remaining nonprofit, turned their operations over to for-profit firms. Seeking economies of scale, hospitals consolidated into national and regional chains, as did formerly nonprofit health insurance plans such as Blue Cross Blue Shield.

In putting nonprofits in competition with for-profits offering similar services and in demanding higher levels of accountability for decreasing government funding, conservative policies helped erode many of the boundaries between nonprofit and for-profit enterprise (Weisbrod, 1997; Hall, 2003). Nonprofits had to become more commercial and more entrepreneurial to survive. Whether nonprofits' commitments to missions of public service could survive such relentless attention to the bottom line remained in doubt as the 21st Century dawned (Weisbrod, 1998).

The New Century and the Transformation of Philanthropy

The model of "modern" philanthropy as it had come to be by the middle of the 20th Century was intended to accommodate the essentially undemocratic character of large charitable endowments established by the wealthy with the mores of democratic politics and society. To this end, tax and regulatory regimes strove to reduce donor control, limit opportunities for private benefit, make governance more representative and accountable, and support activities in harmony with established public policies. An important component of this involved promoting the professionalization of management in foundations and their nonprofit beneficiaries on the assumption that trained expertise would be better qualified to discern public priorities than either donors or the general public.

Establishing and maintaining consensus over the way philanthropy should be managed and the purposes it was to serve was fairly easy before the 1980s because most large foundations were concentrated in urban centers in the Northeast and upper Midwest and were run by men who shared similar privileged backgrounds. With very few exceptions, foundations were pillars of the "Liberal Establishment," which ran the nation's major universities, cultural institutions, and federal government agencies. Henry Ford II alluded to this liberal bias in his 1977 letter of resignation from the board of the Ford Foundation. The fact that "the Foundation is a creature of capitalism," he wrote, is

> a statement that, I'm sure, would be shocking to many professional staff people in the field of philanthropy. It is hard to discern recognition of this fact in anything the Foundation does. It is even more difficult to find an understanding of this in many of the institutions, particularly the universities, that are the beneficiaries of the Foundation's grant programs.[3]

Although the conservative revolution of the 1980s helped broaden the range of viewpoints represented by philanthropic leaders, it did little to change how philanthropy was done, since the new conservative institutional infrastructure followed the pattern of its liberal counterpart, domestically focused, professionally managed, and based on foundation support of conventional nonprofit recipients, such as universities, cultural institutions, and policy think tanks.

What fundamentally changed philanthropy was not political pluralism, but a tidal wave of new wealth accumulation, originating in the revolution in information technology, globalization, and the financialization of the economic system. The new billionaires, largely younger men who were still in their prime as active business leaders, embraced far more activist views of how to manage their surplus wealth. Results-oriented, they expected their philanthropy to express their values and to yield measurable impacts. Because the sources of their wealth were global, they took particular interest in global problems of hunger, disease, environment, and economic development.

The $35 billion Bill & Melinda Gates Foundation, which described itself as "the largest transparently operated private foundation in the world," epitomized many of the features of the contemporary philanthropic revolution. Based in Seattle, Washington, it was established in 1994 by Microsoft founder and chairman Bill Gates to pursue "the interests and passions of the Gates family"

(Bill & Melinda Gates Foundation, 2009). The foundation's major foci included a Global Health Program, whose significant grantees have been The Global Alliance for Vaccines and Immunization, The Institute for OneWorld Health, Children's Vaccine Program, University of Washington Department of Global Health, HIV Research, and the Aeras Global TB Vaccine Foundation. Its Global Development Program has funded financial services for the poor (through such social enterprises as the Grameen Bank), agricultural development (focusing on rice research and promoting a green revolution in Africa), Global Libraries, a United States Program (funding schools, libraries, and scholarships). The Gates Foundation's resources were vastly increased in 2006 by financier Warren Buffett's pledge to donate most of his own private fortune—estimated at $30 billion.

Although hardly comparable in size, the philanthropic activities of financier George Soros have been no less globally influential—though in a very different way. A refugee from Nazism, Soros's primary interest has been politics and the development of democratic societies in Central and Eastern Europe. He has also generously funded progressive social movement activity in the United States. Like Gates, he has also given substantial support to poverty eradication efforts in Africa and to social enterprises such as the Grameen Bank.

The philanthropy of Google founders Sergey Brin and Lawrence Page has moved in very different directions from that of Gates, Buffett, and Soros. Founded in 1998 as an online search engine, Google was, as of 2009, valued at more than $23 billion and employed more than 19,000 people worldwide. Although they created a company foundation, their major interest has been the company and its products, which they have viewed—much as Henry Ford viewed the Model T—as primary instruments of social transformation. Their most innovative philanthropic initiative was their establishment in 2006 of Google.org, a for-profit foundation intended to carry out a wide range of activities including product development, political activism, and medical research (Hafner, 2006; Hansell, 2005; Rubin, 2008). Google's philanthropic activities represent an important example of "social enterprise" which, in combining commitments to business and social change, represent a significant departure from traditional conceptions of charity.

Kiva Microfunds, founded in 2005 by California entrepreneurs Matt and Jessica Flannery, offers yet another approach of philanthropy. Drawing its inspiration from the Grameen Bank and other Third World–based microfinance programs, Kiva works globally to match Western microlenders with "field partners" in the developing world (Walker, 2008). Within two years of its establishment Kiva had made nearly $20 million in loans to nearly a quarter million individuals.

Not all big philanthropy has involved the wealthy in the developed world helping the poor in the developing world. A notable feature of economic and cultural globalization has been the growth of diaspora groups who, while living in parts of the world to which they have emigrated, have succeeded in their adopted homelands while retaining significant ties to their countries of origin—and who, although often possessing dual citizenship, make their native lands primary recipients of their philanthropic largesse. These philanthropically active transnational populations now include Indians, Pakistanis, Chinese, Latin Americans, and, of course, Jews, who set the pattern for this kind of transnational philanthropic orientation (see Geithner, Johnson, and Chen, 2004; Merz, 2005; Merz, Chen, and Geithner, 2007; Najam, 2006).

Within a quarter of a century, philanthropy has gone from being centered in North America and Western Europe and focused on aid by advanced industrial nations to developing countries to a genuinely transnational collection of enterprises and initiatives sustaining complex multidirectional flows of aid and influence.

The Nonprofit Sector and the Global Challenge

Nonstate actors—nonprofit organizations, NGOs (nongovernmental organizations), network organizations—are assuming extraordinary importance with the globalization of the world's economy (Anheier and Salamon, 1998; Salamon and Anheier, 1996, 1997).[4] Despite growing global flows of goods, information, and labor, the nation state remains the primary unit of governmental organization, and international governmental bodies remain weak. For this reason, nongovernmental organizations operating transnationally have become the major mechanisms of world governance (Lindenberg, 1999).

These organizations have a variety of forms (Khagram, Riker, and Sikkink, 2002). Some mediate relationships between states (Brown and Fox, 1998; Brown, Khagram, and Moore, 2000; Brown and Moore, 2001). Some, like the U.S. Agency for International Development, are governmental bodies operated to serve the interests of the United States by promoting economic development. Others, like the World Bank, the International Monetary Fund, the World

Health Organization, and UNESCO, are international quasigovernmental bodies connected to the United Nations and governed by boards representing the U.N.'s member states.

Many NGOs, such as CARE, the International Red Cross, and a variety of religious charities, are based in the United States or Europe but carry on their operations elsewhere (Biberson and Jean, 1999; Foreman, 1999; Gnaerig and MacCormack, 1999; Henry, 1999; Offenheiser, Holcombe, and Hopkins, 1999). Others are genuinely transnational, based on coalitions of indigenous and transnational NGOs. Often operating in opposition to nation states, these promote human rights, sustainable development, and environmental objectives (Edwards, 1999; Fisher, 1993, 1998). Unlike the quasigovernmental bodies, which deal primarily with governments, these transnational NGOs work directly with indigenous peoples, communities, and organizations. Among the most important of these are groups such as CIVICUS, which promotes the development of nonprofit sectors throughout the world. Some of the largest grantmaking foundations, notably Ford, Rockefeller, and the Bill &Melinda Gates foundations, have global programs that fund health, education, research, and economic development activities in developing countries.

The tragic events of 9/11 called attention to the significance of NGOs and network organizations connected to religious movements. Along with terrorist networks such as Al Qaeda, there are Islamic charities and foundations that operate worldwide to support religious education, provide relief, and support economic and political development in Muslim communities.

In some respects, transnational organizations are nothing new. The scientific community has long been transnational and anchored in nongovernmental professional and disciplinary bodies. Transnational human rights advocacy dates back at least as early as the anti-slave trade movement of the late 18th Century. Most major religious bodies are transnational organizations. International relief organizations have been operating since the 19th Century. Grantmaking foundations have had international programs since the 1920s (Curti, 1965).

Contemporary global and transnational NGOs differ from their predecessors in important respects. Most important, many are genuinely transnational, located either in many countries or, as in the case of Al Qaeda, not anchored in any nation state. Beyond the reach of national authorities, these entities are difficult to police and control (Brown and Moore, 2001; Goodin, 2003). Of equal importance is the extent to which transnational NGOs are linked to indigenous organizations outside the advanced nations of Europe and North America. Their capacity to give voice to victims of authoritarian regimes, protest economic exploitation, and resist the power of Western corporations and governments has dramatically transformed global public policymaking. Advances in information technology have vastly increased the influence of transnational NGOs by making information available that corporations and governments may attempt to suppress and making it possible for transnational and indigenous groups to form coalitions and alliances. Recent worldwide protests against economic globalization and the U.S. invasion of Iraq may signal the emergence of new kinds of political forces.

The nature of globalization and the role of transnational nonstate actors is far from clear. To some, they represent a kind of neocolonialism, the means by which an integrated global economy, anchored in the advanced nations of the West, is being created. To others, they represent a new empowering force for democracy and social and economic justice. One thing is clear, however: nonprofit organizations, so highly developed in the United States in the course of the 20th Century, offer important possibilities to nations engaged in creating their own civil societies.

Conclusion

This chapter has traced a long and complex strand of institutional development. Beginning in the 17th Century, when the nation state was still emergent, legal systems primitive, and boundaries between government and private initiative ill-defined, it has traced the ways in which voluntary associations, eleemosynary corporations, and philanthropy became indispensable components of the national state and the industrializing economy in the United States in the 19th Century. It has suggested that neither business nor government could stand alone: both required broadly based participation by citizens, producers, and consumers in organizations and activities that created the shared values and skills that enabled formal institutions of government and business to function effectively.

In the years between 1830 and 1950, the private, donative, and voluntary character of much of nonprofit enterprise seemed self-evident, as did the boundaries between public and private initiative. In the second half of the 20th Century, these defining characteristics became less well-defined as nonprofits became more dependent on government subsidy and increasingly entrusted with responsibilities formerly borne by government agencies, on the one hand, and more commercial and entrepreneurial, on the other hand.

Globalization, which has enabled nonprofits to operate beyond national borders, has further eroded traditional boundaries between public and private domains and commercial and charitable activities. Because privatization is a global movement, NGOs outside the United States are increasingly taking the place of nation states in service provision, relief, and development assistance. Many development activities, such as microloan programs, more resemble commercial activities than charitable ones. And, overall, important aspects of the emergent global institutional order depend on the governance functions of NGOs rather than governmental entities.

In significant ways, today's centrally important but poorly demarcated roles and responsibilities of nonprofits and NGOs more resemble those of three centuries ago, when the nation state was aborning, than the associations and eleemosynary corporations of a century ago whose character and functions were relatively well defined and clearly bounded.

History shows, if nothing else, that ownerless collectivities of the nonprofit type are remarkably flexible instruments that can be put to a multitude of uses, whether empowering the masses in democracies, shaping public opinion for the benefit of elites, carrying out the tasks of government in authoritarian regimes, promoting peace and prosperity, or spreading terror. What the future holds in store for nonprofits is anybody's guess.

Notes

1. There are few tasks more difficult than accurately counting the number of nonprofit organizations in the United States. The fundamental difficulty involves how to define the nonprofit universe. In corporation law, a nonprofit is any nonstock corporation that does not distribute its surplus, if any, in the form of dividends. Under the federal tax code, a nonprofit is any organization or association classified in Section 501(c) of the IRS Code—a universe that includes not only charitable entities—501(c)3s—but also many other kinds of organizations, including political parties, labor unions, cooperatives, cemetery companies, and black lung trusts. Because some of these noncharitable nonprofits, like those classified as 501(c)4s (social welfare organizations, civic organizations, and associations of employees), engage in many of the same educational and service provision activities as do charitables, though without donors' deductibility of donations, excluding them from a definition of the nonprofit sector posits an unreasonably narrow definition. To complicate matters, religious bodies, which enjoy tax exemption and deductibility of donations by right (and hence are not required to apply for these privileges) are not included in IRS statistics of registered nonprofits—despite the fact that they are the largest single category of nonprofit organization in the United States and account for more than half the donated funds received by American nonprofits. To further complicate matters, many groups engaged in charitable, educational, religious, and other activities associated with nonprofits are unincorporated and do not seek exempt status (Smith, 2000).

2. It is impossible to provide exact figures on the number of donative and voluntary nonprofits versus those supported by dues, fees, commercial income, and grants and contracts from government, corporations, and foundations. Studies of local organizational populations (Hall, 1999) and national membership associations (Skocpol, 1999, 2003) suggest a vast die-off of traditional donative, voluntary, and membership associations and their replacement by professionally managed nonprofit organizations. Despite these trends, such organizations as religious congregations—one of the most vigorously expansive nonprofit domains—remain heavily dependent on volunteers and almost entirely dependent on donations. Counterbalancing this, however, is the huge growth of nonprofit service providers incident to the court-ordered deinstitutionalization of the mentally disabled. These use no volunteers and depend entirely on government subsidies.

3. As quoted in www.discoverthenetworks.org/funderProfile.asp?fndid=5176, retrieved December 28, 2009.

4. Walter W. Powell's seminal article on network organizations defines them as "reciprocal patterns of communication and exchange" characterized by "lateral or horizontal patterns of exchange, interdependent flows of resources, and reciprocal lines of communication" (Powell, 1990, pp. 295–296). An example of a network organization is the open source network of computer programmers cooperating to develop the LINUX operating system. These entities lack the hierarchical structures and financial incentives that are typical of conventional firms.

References

Abbott, A. D. *The System of Professions: An Essay on the Division of Expert Labor*. Chicago: University of Chicago Press, 1988.

Ahlstrom, S. E. *A Religious History of the American People*. New Haven, CT: Yale University Press, 1972.

American Millionaires and the Public Gifts. *Review of Reviews*, 1893, 37(7), 48–60.

Ames, J. B. The Failure of the Tilden Trust. In J. B. Ames, *Essays in Legal History and Miscellaneous Legal Essays*. Cambridge, MA: Harvard University Press, 285–297, 1913.

Andrews, F. E. *Philanthropic Giving*. New York: Russell Sage Foundation, 1950.

Andrews, F. E. *Corporation Giving*. New York: Russell Sage Foundation, 1952.

Andrews, F. E. *Philanthropic Foundations*. New York: Russell Sage Foundation, 1956.

Andrews, F. E. *Patman and the Foundations: Review and Assessment*. Occasional Paper Number Three. New York: The Foundation Center, 1969.

Anheier, H. K., and Salamon, L. M. *The Nonprofit Sector in the Developing World: A Comparative Analysis*. New York: St. Martin's Press, 1998.

Auerbach, J. S. *Unequal Justice: Lawyers and Social Change in Modern America*. New York: Oxford University Press, 1976.

Bailyn, B. *The Ideological Origins of the American Revolution*. Cambridge, MA: Belknap Press of Harvard University Press, 1992.

Baggett, J. P. *Habitat for Humanity: Building Private Homes, Building Public Religion*. Philadelphia, PA: Temple University Press, 2001.

Beito, D. T. *From Mutual Aid to the Welfare State: Fraternal Societies and Social Services, 1890–1967*. Chapel Hill, NC: University of North Carolina University Press, 2000.

Bender, C. *Heaven's Kitchen: Living Religion at God's Love We Deliver*. Chicago: University of Chicago Press, 2003.

Berkeley Art Center Association. *The Whole World's Watching: Peace and Social Justice Movements of the 1960s and 1970s*. Berkeley, CA: Author, 2001.

Berry, J. M. *Lobbying for the People: The Political Behavior of Public Interest Groups*. Princeton, NJ: Princeton University Press, 1977.

Berry, J. M. *The Interest Group Society*, 3rd ed. New York: Longman, 1997.

Biberson, P., and Jean, F. The Challenges of Globalization of International Relief and Development: Medecins Sans Frontieres. *Nonprofit and Voluntary Sector Quarterly*, 1999, 28 (Supplemental), 104–108.

Bill & Melinda Gates Foundation, "Guiding Principles" at http://www.gatesfoundation .org/about/Pages/guiding-principles.aspx, retrieved December 28, 2009.

Bledstein, B. *The Culture of Professionalism: The Middle Class and the Development of Higher Education in America*. New York: Norton, 1976.

Blumenthal, S. *The Rise of the Counter-Establishment: From Conservative Ideology to Political Power*. New York: Harper & Row, 1986.

Brandes, S. *American Welfare Capitalism*. Chicago: University of Chicago Press, 1976.

Brint, S. *In an Age of Reform: The Changing Role of Professionals in Politics and Public Life*. Princeton, N.J.: Princeton University Press, 1994.

Brockett, L. P. *The Philanthropic Results of the War in America. Collected from Official and Other Authentic Sources, by an American Citizen*. Dedicated by permission to the United States Sanitary Commission. New York: Sheldon & Co., 1864.

Brody, D. The Rise and Decline of American Welfare Capitalism. In D. Brody (ed.), *Workers in Industrial America*. New York: Oxford University Press, 1980, 48–81.

Brown, L. D., and Fox, J. (eds.). *The Struggle for Accountability: The World Bank, NGOs, and Grassroots Movements*. Cambridge, MA: MIT Press, 1998.

Brown, L. D., and Fox, J. *Transnational Civil Society Coalitions and the World Bank: Lessons from Project and Policy Influence Campaigns*. Working Paper #3. Cambridge, MA: Hauser Center for Nonprofit Organizations, Harvard University, 1999.

Brown, L. D., Khagram, S., and Moore, M. H. *Globalization, NGOs and Multi-Sectoral Relations*. Working Paper #1. Cambridge, MA: Hauser Center for Nonprofit Organizations, Harvard University, 2000.

Brown, L. D., and Moore, M. H. *Accountability, Strategy and International Non-Governmental Organizations*. Working Paper #7. Cambridge, MA.: Hauser Center for Nonprofit Organizations, Harvard University, 2001.

Bryer, D., and Magrath, J. New Dimensions of Global Advocacy. *Nonprofit and Voluntary Sector Quarterly*, 1999, 28 (Supplemental), 168–177.

Buck, P. H. (ed.). *Social Sciences at Harvard, 1860–1920: From Inculcation to the Open Mind*. Cambridge, MA: Harvard University Press, 1965.

Butchart, R. E., *Northern Schools, Southern Blacks, and Reconstruction, 1862–1875*. Westport, CT: Greenwood Press, 1980.

Butler, J. *Awash in a Sea of Faith: Christianizing the American People*. Cambridge, MA: Harvard University Press, 1990.

Calhoun, D. H. *Professional Lives in America: Structure and Aspiration, 1750–1850*. Cambridge, MA: Harvard University Press, 1965.

Calvert, M. A. *The Mechanical Engineer in America: Professional Cultures in Conflict*. Baltimore, MD.: Johns Hopkins University Press, 1967.

Carlson-Thies, S. W., and Skillen, J. W. (eds.). *Welfare in America: Christian Perspectives on a Policy in Crisis*. Grand Rapids, MI: Eerdmans, 1996.

Carnegie, A. An Employer's View of the Labor Question. *Forum*, 1886a, 1, 114–125.

Carnegie, A. Results of the Labor Struggle. *Forum*, 1886b, 1, 538–551.

Carnegie, A. Wealth. *North American Review*, 1889, 148, 653–664; 149, 682–698.

Charles, J. A. *Service Clubs in American Society: Rotary, Kiwanis, and Lions.* Urbana: University of Illinois Press, 1993.

Chaves, M. Religious Congregations and Welfare Reform: Assessing the Potential. In M. Silk and A. Walsh (eds.), *Can Charitable Choice Work? Covering Religion's Impact on Urban Affairs and Social Services.* Hartford, CT: Pew Program on Religion and the News Media, Leonard E. Greenberg Center for the Study of Religion in Public Life, Trinity College, 2001.

Chernow, R. *Titan: The Life of John D. Rockefeller, Sr.* New York: Random House, 1998.

Cherry, C., and Sherrill, R. (eds.). *Religion, the Independent Sector, and American Culture.* Atlanta, GA: Scholars Press, 1992.

Clemens, E. S. *The People's Lobby: Organizational Innovation and the Rise of Interest Group Politics in the United States, 1890–1925.* Chicago: University of Chicago Press, 1997.

Cnaan, R. A. *The Newer Deal: Social Work and Religion in Partnership.* New York: Columbia University Press, 1999.

Cnaan, R. A. *The Invisible Caring Hand: American Congregations and the Provision of Welfare.* New York: New York University Press, 2002.

Crawford, S., and Levitt, P. Social Change and Civic Engagement: The Case of the P.T.A. In T. Skocpol and M. Fiorina (eds.), *Civic Engagement in American Democracy.* Washington, DC: Brookings Institution Press, 1999.

Critchlow, D. T. *The Brookings Institution, 1916–1952 : Expertise and the Public Interest in a Democratic Society.* DeKalb: Northern Illinois University Press, 1985.

Cross, A. B. The War and the Christian Commission. Baltimore, MD, 1865.

Curti, M. *American Philanthropy Abroad.* New Brunswick, NJ: Rutgers University Press, 1965.

Curti, M., and Nash, R. *Philanthropy and the Shaping of American Higher Education.* New Brunswick, NJ: Rutgers University Press, 1965.

Cutlip, S. M. *Fund Raising in the United States: Its Role in America's Philanthropy.* New Brunswick, NJ: Rutgers University Press, 1965.

Dabney, V. *Mr. Jefferson's University: A History.* Charlottesville, VA: University Press of Virginia, 1981.

Davis, J. S. *Essays on the Earlier History of American Corporations.* Cambridge, MA: Harvard University Press, 1918.

Demerath, N. J. III, Hall, P. D., Williams, R. H., and Schmitt, T. (eds.) *Sacred Companies: Organizational Aspects of Religion and Religious Aspects of Organizations.* New York: Oxford University Press, 1998.

DiMaggio, P. J. Cultural Entrepreneurship in Nineteenth Century Boston. In P. J. DiMaggio (ed.), *Nonprofit Enterprise in the Arts.* New York: Oxford University Press, 1986.

Dodd, E. M. *American Business Corporations until 1860, with Special References to Massachusetts.* Cambridge, MA: Harvard University Press, 1960.

Dolan, J. P. *The American Catholic Experience: A History from Colonial Times to the Present.* South Bend, IN: University of Notre Dame Press, 1992.

Drucker, P. F. *The New Realities: In Government and Politics, in Economics and Business, in Society and World View.* New York: HarperCollins, 1989.

Dumenil, L. *Freemasonry and American Culture, 1880–1939.* Princeton, NJ: Princeton University Press, 1984.

Eck, D. L. *A New Religious America: How a "Christian Country" Has Become the World's Most Religiously Diverse Nation.* New York: HarperCollins, 2001.

Edwards, M. International Development NGOs: Agents of Foreign Aid or Vehicles for International Cooperation? *Nonprofit and Voluntary Sector Quarterly*, 1999, 28 (Supplemental), 25–37.

Eliot, C. W. The New Education. *Atlantic Monthly*, 1869, 23, 203–220, 358–367.

Finke, R., and Stark, R. *The Churching of America, 1776–1990: Winners and Losers in Our Religious Economy.* New Brunswick, NJ: Rutgers University Press, 1992.

Fisher, J. *The Road from Rio: Sustainable Development and the Nongovernmental Movement in the Third World.* Westport, CT: Praeger, 1993.

Fisher, J. *Nongovernments: NGOs and the Political Development of the Third World.* West Hartford, CT: Kumarian Press, 1998.

Fleischer, D. Z, & Zames, F. *The Disability Rights Movement: From Charity to Confrontation.* Philadelphia: Temple University Press, 2001.

Fleming, W. L. (ed.). *Documentary History of Reconstruction: Political, Military, Social, Religious, Educational & Industrial 1865 to the Present Time.* Cleveland, OH: Arthur H. Clark Company, 1906.

Fogel, R. W. *The Fourth Great Awakening and the Future of Egalitarianism.* Chicago: University of Chicago Press, 2000.

Foreman, K. Evolving Global Structures and the Challenges Facing International Relief and Developing Organizations. *Nonprofit and Voluntary Sector Quarterly*, 1999, 28 (Supplemental), 178–197.

Fosdick, R. B. *The Story of the Rockefeller Foundation.* New York: Harper & Row, 1952.

Fosdick, R. B. *Adventure in Giving: The Story of the General Education Board, a Foundation Established by John D. Rockefeller.* New York: Harper & Row, 1962.

Foster, C. I. *An Errand of Mercy: The Evangelical United Front, 1790–1837.* Chapel Hill, NC: University of North Carolina Press, 1965.

Foundation Directory—Edition I. New York: Russell Sage Foundation, 1960.

Fox, D. M. *Engines of Culture: Philanthropy and Art Museums.* Madison, WI: State Historical Society of Wisconsin, 1963.

Frederickson, G. M. *The Inner Civil War: Northern Intellectuals and the Crisis of the Union.* New York: HarperCollins, 1965.

Galambos, L. *Competition and Cooperation: The Rise of a National Trade Association.* Baltimore, MD: Johns Hopkins University Press, 1966.

Geiger, R. L. *To Advance Knowledge: The Growth of American Research Universities, 1900–1940.* New York: Oxford University Press, 1986.

Geiger, R. L. *Research and Relevant Knowledge: American Research Universities Since World War II.* New York: Oxford University Press, 1993.

Geithner, P. F., Johnson, P. D., and Chen, L. C. (eds.). *Diaspora Philanthropy and Equitable Development in China and India.* Cambridge, MA: Harvard University Press, 2004.

Gillespie, E., and Schellhas, B. (eds.). *Contract with America: The Bold Plan by Rep. Newt Gingrich, Rep. Dick Armey and the House Republicans to Change the Nation.* New York: Times Books, 1994.

Glenn, J. M., Brandt, L., and Andrews, F. E. *The Russell Sage Foundation, 1907–1947.* New York: Russell Sage Foundation, 1947.

Gnaerig, B., and MacCormack, C. F. The Challenges of Globalizations: Save the Children International. *Nonprofit and Voluntary Sector Quarterly*, 1999, 28 (Supplemental), 140, 146.

Goodin, R. E. *Democratic Accountability: The Third Sector and All.* Working Paper #19. Cambridge, MA: Hauser Center for Nonprofit Organizations, Harvard University, 2003.

Gray, B. H. (ed.). *The New Health Care For Profit: Doctors and Hospitals in a Competitive Environment*. Washington, DC: National Academy Press, 1983.

Gray, B. H. (ed.). *For-Profit Enterprise in Health Care*. Washington, DC: National Academy Press, 1986.

Gray, B. H. *The Profit Motive and Patient Care: The Changing Accountability of Doctors and Hospitals*. Cambridge, MA: Harvard University Press, 1991.

Greenleaf, W. *From These Beginnings: The Early Philanthropies of Henry and Edsel Ford, 1911–1936*. Detroit, MI: Wayne State University Press, 1964.

Hafner, K. Philanthropy Google's Way: Not the Usual. *New York Times*, September 14, 2006.

Hall, P. D. *The Organization of American Culture, 1700–1900: Institutions, Elites, and the Origins of American Nationality*. New York: New York University Press, 1982.

Hall, P. D. The Community Foundation in America. In R. Magat (ed.), *Philanthropic Giving: Studies in Varieties and Goals*. New York: Oxford University Press, 1989a.

Hall, P. D. Business Giving and Social Investment in the United States. In R. Magat (ed.), *Philanthropic Giving: Studies in Varieties and Goals*. New York: Oxford University Press, 1989b.

Hall, P. D. Vital Signs: Organizational Population Trends and Civic Engagement in New Haven, Connecticut, 1850–1998. In T. Skocpol and M. P. Fiorina (eds.), *Civic Engagement in American Democracy*. Washington, DC: Brookings Institution, 1999.

Hall, P. D. Historical Perspectives on Religion, Government, and Social Welfare in America. In M. Silk and A. Walsh (eds.), *Can Charitable Choice Work? Covering Religion's Impact on Urban Affairs and Social Services*. Hartford, CT: Pew Program on Religion and the News Media, Leonard E. Greenberg Center for the Study of Religion in Public Life, Trinity College, 2001.

Hall, P. D. The Welfare State and the Careers of Public and Private Institutions since 1945. In L. J. Friedman and M. D. McGarvie (eds.), *Charity, Philanthropy, and Civility in American History*. New York: Cambridge University Press, 2003.

Hall, P. D., and Burke, C. B. Voluntary, Nonprofit, and Religious Entities and Activities. In S. Carter, et al. (eds.), *Historical Statistics of the United States—Millennial Edition*. New York: Cambridge University Press, 2006.

Hammack, D. C. Community Foundations: The Delicate Question of Purpose. In R. Magat (ed.), *An Agile Servant*. New York: The Foundation Center, 1989, 23–50.

Hammack, D. C., and Wheeler, S. 1994. *Social Science in the Making: Essays on the Russell Sage Foundation, 1907–1972*. New York: Russell Sage Foundation, 1994.

Hansell, S. Google Earmarks $265 Million for Charity and Social Causes. *New York Times*, October 12, 2005.

Harr, J. E., and Johnson, P. J. *The Rockefeller Century*. New York: Scribner, 1988.

Hartog, H. *Public Property and Private Power: The Corporation of the City of New York in American Law, 1730–1870*. Ithaca, NY: Cornell University Press, 1983.

Haskell, T. L. *The Emergence of Professional Social Science: The American Social Science Association and the Nineteenth-Century Crisis of Authority*. Urbana: University of Illinois Press, 1977.

Hatch, N. O. *The Democratization of American Christianity*. New Haven, CT: Yale University Press, 1989.

Hawkins, H. *Between Harvard and America: The Educational Leadership of Charles W. Eliot*. New York: Oxford University Press, 1972.

Hawkins, H. *Banding Together: The Rise of National Associations in American Higher Education, 1887–1950*. Baltimore, MD: Johns Hopkins University Press, 1992.

Hawley, E. W. (ed.). *Herbert Hoover as Secretary of Commerce: Studies in New Era Thought and Practice.* Iowa City: University of Iowa Press, 1974.

Hawley, E. W. Herbert Hoover, the Commerce Secretariat, and the Vision of an "Associative State." In E. J. Perkins (ed.), *Men and Organizations.* New York: Putnam, 1977.

Heald, M. *The Social Responsibilities of Business: Corporation and Community, 1900–1960.* Cleveland, OH: Case Western University Press, 1970.

Henry, K. M. CARE International: Evolving to Meet the Challenges of the 21st Century. *Nonprofit and Voluntary Sector Quarterly,* 1999, 28 (Supplement), 109–120.

Himmelberg, R. F. *The Origins of the National Recovery Administration: Business, Government, and the Trade Association Issue.* New York: Fordham University Press, 1976.

Himmelstein, J. L. *Looking Good and Doing Good: Corporate Philanthropy and Corporate Power.* Bloomington, IN: Indiana University Press, 1997.

Hodgson, G. *The World Turned Right Side Up: A History of the Conservative Ascendancy in America.* Boston, MA: Houghton-Mifflin, 1996.

Hoover, H. *American Individualism.* Garden City, NY: Doubleday, 1922.

Horowitz, M. J. *The Transformation of American Law, 1780–1860.* Cambridge, MA: Harvard University Press, 1977.

Howard, C. *The Hidden Welfare State: Tax Expenditures and Social Policy in the United States.* Princeton, NJ: Princeton University Press, 1997.

Hurst, J. W. *The Legitimacy of the Business Corporation in the Law of the United States, 1780–1970.* Charlottesville: University Press of Virginia, 1970.

Jenkins, J. C. Nonprofit Organizations and Policy Advocacy. In W.W. Powell (ed.), *The Nonprofit Sector: A Research Handbook.* New Haven, CT: Yale University Press, 1987.

Jenkins, J. C., and Eckert, C. M. Channeling Black Insurgency: Elite Patronage and the Development of the Civil Rights Movement. *American Sociological Review,* 51, 1986, 812–830.

Jenkins, J. C., and Halcli, A. L. Grassrooting the System? The Development and Impact of Social Movement Philanthropy, 1953–1990. In E.C. Lagemann (ed.), *Philanthropic Foundations: New Scholarship, New Possibilities.* Bloomington, IN: Indiana University Press, 229–256, 1999.

Karl, B. D. Presidential Planning and Social Science Research: Mr. Hoover's Experts. *Perspectives in American History,* 1969, 347–409.

Karl, B. D. Philanthropy, Policy Planning, and the Bureaucratization of the Democratic Ideal. *Daedalus,* Fall 1976, 129–149.

Katz, S. N. The Politics of Law in Colonial America: Controversies over Chancery Courts and Equity Law in the Eighteenth Century. In D. Fleming and B. Bailyn (eds.), *Law in American History.* Boston: Little, Brown, 1971, 257–288.

Katz, S. N. The American Private Foundation and the Public Sphere, 1890–1930. *Minerva,* 1981, 19, 236–270.

Katz, S. N., Sullivan, B., and Beach, C. P. Legal Change and Legal Autonomy: Charitable Trusts in New York, 1777–1893, *Law and History Review* 1985, 3, 51–89.

Kaufman, J. For the Common Good? *American Civic Life and the Golden Age of Fraternity.* New York: Oxford University Press, 2002.

Khagram, S., Riker, J. V., and Sikkink, K. (eds.). *Restructuring World Politics: Transnational Social Movements, Networks, and Norms.* Minneapolis, MN: University of Minnesota Press, 2002.

Kimball, B. A. *The "True Professional Ideal" in America: A History*. Lanham, MD: Rowman & Littlefield, 1995.

Lagemann, E. C. 1992. *The Politics of Knowledge: The Carnegie Corporation, Philanthropy, and Public Policy*. Chicago: University of Chicago Press, 1992.

Lagemann, E. C. *Private Power for the Public Good: A History of the Carnegie Foundation for the Advancement of Teaching*. New York: College Entrance Examination Board, 1999.

Li, Ming-huan. *We Need Two Worlds: Chinese Immigrant Associations in a Western Society*. Amsterdam, NL: Amsterdam University Press, 1999.

Lindenberg, M. Declining State Capacity, Voluntarism, and the Globalization of the Not-For-Profit Sector. *Nonprofit and Voluntary Sector Quarterly*, 1999, 28 (Supplemental), 147–167.

Lundberg, F. *The Rich and the Super-Rich; A Study in the Power of Money Today*. New York: Lyle Stuart, 1968.

MacDonald, D. *The Ford Foundation: The Men and the Millions*. New York: Reynal, 1956.

Magat, R. (ed.). *An Agile Servant: Community Leadership by Community Foundations*. New York: The Foundation Center, 1989.

Mathews, D. The Second Great Awakening as an Organizing Process. *American Quarterly*, 1969, 21, 23–43.

McFeely, W. S. *Yankee Stepfather: General O.O. Howard and the Freedmen*. New Haven, CT: Yale University Press, 1968.

McKinney, H. J. *The Development of Local Public Services, 1650–1860: Lessons from Middletown, Connecticut*. Westport, CT: Greenwood Press, 1995.

Merz, B. J. (ed.). *New Patterns for Mexico: Observations on Remittances, Philanthropic Giving, and Equitable Development*. Cambridge, MA: Harvard University Press, 2005.

Merz, B. J., Chen, L. C., and Geithner, P. F. (eds.). *Diasporas and Development*. Cambridge, MA: Harvard University Press, 2007.

Miller, H. S. *The Legal Foundations of American Philanthropy*. Madison, WI: Wisconsin State Historical Society, 1961.

Minkoff, D.C. *Organizing for Equality: The Evolution of Women's and Racial-Ethnic Organizations in America*. New Brunswick, NJ: Rutgers University Press, 1995.

Minton, H. L. *Departing from Deviance: A History of Homosexual Rights and Emanicipatory Science in America*. Chicago: University of Chicago Press, 2002.

Morgan, E. S. *Benjamin Franklin*. New Haven, CT: Yale University Press, 2003.

Moss, L. *Annals of the United States Christian Commission*. Philadelphia: Lippincott, 1968.

Najam, A. *Portrait of a Giving Community: Philanthropy in the Pakistani-American Diaspora*. Cambridge, MA: Harvard University Press, 2006.

Naylor, E. H. *Trade Associations: Their Organization and Management*. New York: The Ronald Press Company, 1921.

Nelson, W. E. *Americanization of the Common Law: The Impact of Legal Change on Massachusetts Society, 1760–1830*. Cambridge, MA: Harvard University Press, 1975.

Nielsen, W. *The Big Foundations*. New York: Columbia University Press, 1971.

Oates, M. J. *The Catholic Philanthropic Tradition in America*. Bloomington: Indiana University Press, 1995.

Offenheiser, R., Holcombe, S., and Hopkins, N. Grappling with Globalization, Partnership, and Learning: A Look Inside Oxfam America. *Nonprofit and Voluntary Sector Quarterly*, 1999, 28 (Supplemental), 121–139.

Olasky, M. N. *The Tragedy of American Compassion*. Washington, DC: Regnery Gateway, 1992.

Powell, W. W. Neither Network nor Hierarchy: Network Forms of Organization. *Research in Organizational Behavior 12*. Greenwich, CT.: JAI Press, 1990.

Proietto, R. The Ford Foundation and Women's Studies in American Higher Education: Seeds of Change? In E. C. Lagemann (ed.), *Philanthropic Foundations: New Scholarship, New Possibilities*. Bloomington: Indiana University Press, 229–256, 1999.

Putnam, R. D. *Bowling Alone: The Collapse and Renewal of American Community*. New York: Simon and Schuster, 2000.

Reed, R. *Active Faith: How Christians Are Changing the Soul of American Politics*. New York: The Free Press, 1996.

Rich, A. *Think Tanks, Public Policy, and the Politics of Expertise*. New York: Cambridge University Press, 2004.

Richardson, J. M. *Christian Reconstruction: The American Missionary Society and Southern Blacks, 1861–1890*. Athens: University of Georgia Press, 1986.

Roof, W. C. *Spiritual Marketplace: Baby Boomers and the Remaking of American Religion*. Princeton, NJ: Princeton University Press, 1999.

Rubin, H. Google Offers a Map for Its Philanthropy. *New York Times, January* 18, 2008.

Rudolph, F. *The American College and University: A History*. New York: Knopf, 1968.

Ryan, M. P. *Cradle of the Middle Class: The Family in Oneida County, New York, 1790–1865*. New York: Cambridge University Press, 1981.

Salamon, L. M. Partners in Public Service: The Scope and Theory of Government-Nonprofit Relations. In W. W. Powell (ed.), *The Nonprofit Sector: A Research Handbook*. New Haven, CT: Yale University Press, 1987.

Salamon, L. M. The Rise of the Nonprofit Sector. *Foreign Affairs*, 73(4), July/August 1994, 110–122.

Salamon, L. M. The Changing Context of American Nonprofit Management. In R. Herman and Associates (eds.), *The Jossey-Bass Handbook of Nonprofit Leadership and Management* (2nd ed.). San Francisco: Jossey-Bass, 2005.

Salamon, L. M., & Abramson, A. J. *The Federal Budget and the Nonprofit Sector*. Washington, DC: Urban Institute, 1982.

Salamon, L. M., and Anheier, H. K. *The Emerging Nonprofit Sector: An Overview*. New York: St. Martin's Press, 1996.

Salamon, L. M., and Anheier, H. K. *Defining the Nonprofit Sector: A Cross-National Analysis*. New York: St. Martin's Press, 1997.

Sale, K. *Power Shift: The Rise of the Southern Rim and Its Challenge to the Eastern Establishment*. New York: Random House, 1975.

Schlesinger, A. M. Biography of a Nation of Joiners, *American Historical Review*, 1944, 50(1), 1–25.

Sealander, J. *Private Wealth and Public life: Foundation Philanthropy and the Reshaping of American Social Policy from the Progressive Era to the New Deal*. Baltimore, MD: Johns Hopkins University Press, 1997.

Sears, J. B. *Philanthropy in the Shaping of American Higher Education*. Washington, DC: Bureau of Education, Department of the Interior, 1922.

Seavoy, R. E. *The Origins of the American Business Corporation, 1784–1855*. Westport, CT: Greenwood Press, 1982.

Seeley, J. R., Junker, B. H., Jones, R. W., Jr., Jenkins, N. C., Haugh, M. T, and Miller, I. *Community Chest: A Case Study in Philanthropy*. Toronto: University of Toronto Press, 1957.

Sklar, M. J. *The Corporate Reconstruction of American Capitalism, 1890–1916 : The Market, the Law, and Politics*. New York: Cambridge University Press, 1988.

Skocpol, T. Advocates without Members: The Recent Transformation of American Civic Life. In T. Skocpol and M. Fiorina (eds.), *Civic Engagement in American Democracy.* Washington, DC: Brookings Institution Press, 1999, 461–510.

Skocpol, T. *Diminished Democracy: From Membership to Management in American Civic Life.* Norman: University of Oklahoma Press, 2003.

Skocpol, T., and Fiorina, M. P. (eds.). *Civic Engagement in American Democracy.* Washington, DC: Brookings Institution, 1999.

Skocpol, T., Ganz, M., Munson, Z., Camp, B., Swers, M, and Oser, J. How Americans Became Civic. In T. Skocpol and M. P. Fiorina (eds.), *Civic Engagement in American Democracy.* Washington, DC: Brookings Institution, 1999.

Smith, D. H. *Grassroots Associations.* Thousand Oaks, CA: Sage, 2000.

Smith, J. A. *The Idea Brokers: Think Tanks and the Rise of the New Policy Elite.* New York: The Free Press, 1991a.

Smith, J. A. *Brookings at Seventy-five.* Washington, DC: Brookings Institution, 1991b.

Soyer, D. *Jewish Immigrant Associations and American Identity in New York, 1880–1939.* Cambridge, MA: Harvard University Press, 1997.

Starr, P. *The Social Transformation of American Medicine.* New York: Basic Books, 1982.

Stroman, D. F. *The Disability Rights Movement: From Deinstitutionalization to Self-Determination.* Lanham, MD: University Press of America, 2003.

Sutton, F. X. The Ford Foundation: The Early Years. *Daedalus,* 1987, 116, 42–91.

Swint, H. L. *The Northern Teacher in the South, 1862–1870.* New York: Octagon Books, 1967.

Tobias, M. *Old Dartmouth on Trial.* New York: New York University Press, 1982.

Tocqueville, A. de. *Democracy in America.* (vol. 2) (Henry Reeve, trans.). New York: Random House, 1945 [orig. publ. 1835].

Trustees of Dartmouth College v. *Woodward,* 4 Wheaton 625 (1819).

U.S. Congress. *Industrial Relations: Final Report and Testimony Submitted to Congress by the Commission on Industrial Relations.* 64th Congress, 1st Session, S. Doc. 154. Washington, DC U.S. Government Printing Office, 1916.

Useem, M. Corporate Philanthropy. In W. W. Powell (ed.), *The Nonprofit Sector: A Research Handbook.* New Haven, CT: Yale University Press, 1987.

Veblen, T. *The Higher Learning in America; A Memorandum on the Conduct of Universities by Business Men.* New York: B. W. Huebsch, 1918.

Verba, S., Schlozman, K. L., & Brady, H. *Voice and Equality: Civic Voluntarism in American Politics.* Cambridge, MA: Harvard University Press, 1995.

Veysey, L. R. *The Emergence of the American University.* Chicago: University of Chicago Press, 1965.

Walker, R. Extra Helping: Kiva.org. *New York Times,* January 27, 2008.

Wall, J. F. *Andrew Carnegie.* New York: Oxford University Press, 1970.

Webber, C., and Wildavsky, A. *A History of Taxation and Expenditure in the Western World.* New York: Simon & Schuster, 1986.

Weisbrod, B. A. *The Nonprofit Economy.* Cambridge, MA: Harvard University Press, 1988.

Weisbrod, B. A. The Future of the Nonprofit Sector. *Journal of Policy Analysis and Management,* 1997, 16(4), 541–555.

Weisbrod, B. A. (ed.). *To Profit or Not to Profit: The Commercial Transformation of the Nonprofit Sector.* New York: Cambridge University Press, 1998.

Whitehead, J. S. *The Separation of College and State: Columbia, Dartmouth, Harvard, and Yale, 1776–1876.* New Haven, CT: Yale University Press, 1976.

Wiebe, R. M. *The Search for Order.* New York: Hill & Wang, 1967.

Witte, J. F. *The Politics and Development of the Federal Income Tax.* Madison: University of Wisconsin Press, 1985.

Wuthnow, R. *The Restructuring of American Religion: Society and Faith Since World War II.* Princeton, NJ: Princeton University Press, 1988.

Wuthnow, R. *After Heaven: Spirituality in America since the 1950s.* Berkeley: University of California Press, 1998.

Wuthnow, R. (ed.). *I come away stronger: How Small Groups are Shaping American Religion.* Grand Rapids, MI: Eerdmans, 1994.

Wuthnow, R., Hodgkinson, V. A., and Associates. *Faith and Philanthropy in America: Exploring the Role of Religion in America's Voluntary Sector.* San Francisco: Jossey-Bass, 1990.

Wyllie, I. G. The Search for an American Law of Charity. *Mississippi Valley Historical Review,* 1959, 46, 203–221.

Zollmann, C. *American Law of Charities.* Milwaukee, WI: Bruce, 1924.

CHAPTER TWO

THE LEGAL FRAMEWORK OF THE NONPROFIT SECTOR IN THE UNITED STATES

Bruce R. Hopkins and Virginia C. Gross

Nonprofit law is derived from many sources, principally the federal tax law and state corporation and fundraising law. At the federal level, additional bodies of nonprofit law are in the antitrust, consumer protection, health, labor, postal, securities, and other fields. Various forms of law, basically statutes enacted by the U.S. Congress and state legislatures, the promulgation by agencies of regulations and rules, and the issuance of federal and state court opinions constitute nonprofit law. Thus, the few pages of this chapter are inherently insufficient to summarize the federal and state law applicable to nonprofit organizations. Nonetheless, the following synopsis of this body of law is provided as an overview to understand the basics of nonprofit law and the governance responsibilities of nonprofit organizations, and to assist the leadership and management of these organizations to be in an informed position to ask questions of legal counsel.

Nonprofit Organizations

A fundamental precept in nonprofit law is the concept of the *nonprofit organization*. This term does not mean an organization that is prohibited by law from earning a profit (that is, an excess of gross earnings over expenses). In fact, it is quite common for nonprofit (and tax-exempt) organizations to generate profits.

Rather, the definition of nonprofit organization essentially relates to requirements as to what must be done with the profit earned or otherwise received. This fundamental element of the law is subsumed in the doctrine of private inurement (discussed below).

This concept in law of a nonprofit organization is best understood through a comparison with the concept of a *for-profit* organization. A fundamental distinction between the two types of entities is that the for-profit organization has owners that hold the equity in the enterprise, such as stockholders of a corporation. The for-profit organization is operated for the economic benefit of its owners; the profits of the business undertaking are passed through to them, such as by the payment of dividends on shares of stock. That is what is meant by the term *for-profit organization*: It is an entity that is designed to generate a profit for its owners. The transfer of the profits from the organization to its owners is private inurement—the inurement of net earnings to them in their private (personal) capacity. For-profit organizations are supposed to engage in private inurement.

By contrast, a nonprofit organization is not permitted to distribute its profits (net earnings) to those who control it, such as directors and officers. To do so would be to violate the prohibition against private inurement to which nearly all tax-exempt organizations are subject. That is why the private inurement doctrine is the substantive defining characteristic that distinguishes nonprofit organizations from for-profit organizations for purposes of the law. There are thus two categories of profit: one is at the *entity* level and one is at the *ownership* level. Both nonprofit and for-profit organizations can yield entity-level profit; the distinction in law between the two types of entities pivots on the latter category of profit.

A nonprofit organization can take many forms, most prominently a corporation, but can also be an unincorporated association or a trust. Most states have a statutory regime governing nonprofit corporations and trusts. These regimes address the formation, governance, purposes, operations, and dissolution of the entities.

Tax-Exempt Organizations

A nonprofit organization is not necessarily a tax-exempt organization, although most nonprofit entities qualify for some classification as an exempt entity under the tax rules. Whether a nonprofit organization is entitled to tax exemption, initially or on a continuing basis, is a matter of law. If a nonprofit organization qualifies for a tax exemption, at the federal or state law levels, or both, then it is entitled to the exemption. (There is, however, no constitutional law right to a tax exemption, except perhaps for religious organizations.)

The law requires some categories of nonprofit organizations that are eligible for tax-exempt status at the federal law level to apply to the IRS for *recognition* of that exemption. This is generally accomplished by the filing of an application for recognition of exemption (usually Form 1023, 1023-EZ, or 1024). Most charitable organizations, certain employee benefit organizations, prepaid tuition plans operated by private educational institutions, health insurance insurers, and credit counseling organizations that desire exemption as social welfare organizations are required to timely application for recognition of exemption. Political organizations must, to be exempt, file a notice with the IRS (Form 8871). Organizations seeking classification as a social welfare organization and programs that offer Achieving a Better Life Experience (ABLE) accounts for disabled persons must also file a notice with the IRS. For other categories of organizations desiring tax-exempt status, application for recognition of exemption with the IRS is optional, but provides some assurance as to the claimed exempt status.

Additional rules apply with respect to *group exemptions*. This is a regime by which organizations that are affiliated with a central tax-exempt organization can be exempt without applying to the IRS for recognition of exemption, provided the central organization successfully files for recognition of tax-exempt status on behalf of the group. This regime can be effective for national or regional organizations with local chapters or affiliates.

The IRS can revoke a recognition of tax exemption for good cause, such as a change in the law, but an organization that has been recognized by the IRS as being exempt generally can rely on that determination as long as there are no substantial changes in its character, purposes, or methods of operation. If material changes occur, the organization should notify the IRS; it may have to undergo a reevaluation of its exempt status.

In a law sense, there really is no such thing as a completely tax-exempt organization. Nearly all exempt organizations are subject to tax on their unrelated business income. Many types of exempt organizations can have some or all of their investment income taxed if they engage in political activities. Public charities can incur taxes if they undertake legislative or political campaign activities. Private foundations are potentially liable for a variety of excise taxes, including a tax on their investment income. Social clubs, political organizations, and certain other nonprofit entities are also required to pay tax on their net investment income. Even with complete exemption from federal taxation, a nonprofit organization may have exposure to state or local income, sales, use, or property taxation; each state has its own set of laws regarding qualification for these exemptions.

Categories of Tax-Exempt Organizations

There are over seventy categories of tax-exempt nonprofit organizations in the federal tax law. Not all of them have comparable exemption at the state law level.

Charitable and Like Organizations

Tax exemption is provided for a variety of charitable organizations, which are described in Section 501(c)(3) of the Internal Revenue Code ("Code"). Charitable organizations include those that provide relief for the poor or distressed; promote health; lessen the burdens of government; advance education, science, or religion; promote social welfare; and promote youth sports and protection of the environment. Exemption also is available for cruelty prevention organizations, amateur sports organizations, public safety testing organizations, cooperative hospital service organizations, cooperative educational service organizations, and charitable risk pools. Limitations apply as to private inurement, private benefit, and impermissible advocacy (namely, substantial legislative activities and any political campaign activity).

Religious Organizations

Tax exemption is provided for churches and similar institutions, conventions or associations of churches, integrated auxiliaries of churches, religious orders, apostolic organizations, and other religious organizations, including certain communal groups and retreat facilities. These organizations are also tax-exempt by reason of Code § 501(c)(3).

Educational Organizations

Tax exemption is provided for private schools, including colleges and universities, albeit with a variety of requirements, including the necessity of a disseminated policy as to nondiscrimination on the basis of race. A *school* is an educational institution that has a regular faculty, a regularly enrolled student body, a curriculum, and a place where the educational activities are regularly carried on. Tax exemption is provided as well as for other organizations that instruct individuals or the public, including those that promote sports for the benefit of youth. The term *educational* is not well-defined; the federal tax law distinguishes it from *propagandizing*. Nonprofit schools and other educational organizations generally are also tax-exempt by reason of Code § 501(c)(3).

Scientific Organizations

Tax exemption is provided to organizations that engage in scientific research in the public interest. Scientific organizations are typically also tax-exempt by reason of Code § 501(c)(3). There can be controversy as to whether an activity involves *research* as opposed to *commercial testing*.

Social Welfare Organizations

Tax exemption is provided to organizations that operate for the promotion of social welfare (such as civic leagues), in the sense of benefiting those in a community. This category of organizations may include advocacy organizations, that is, those entities that attempt to influence legislation and/or engage in political campaign activity. Generally, these organizations are described in Code § 501(c)(4).

Labor, Agricultural, and Horticultural Organizations

Tax exemption is provided for organizations that engage in collective action to better the working conditions of individuals engaged in a common pursuit. The principal type of this category of tax-exempt organization is the union. Likewise, exemption is provided for organizations that engage in activities to improve the grade of agricultural or horticultural products, and develop a higher degree of efficiency in the activity. Generally, these organizations are described in Code § 501(c)(5).

Business Leagues

Tax exemption is provided for business leagues, namely, associations of people united by common interests, as well as chambers of commerce, boards of trade, real estate boards, and professional football leagues. The principal categories of tax-exempt organizations in this context are trade and business associations, and professional societies. The purpose of these associations is to promote conditions within the line of business they represent. Business leagues typically serve a membership, but are not engaging in exempt activities by providing services to individual members. Generally, these organizations are described in Code § 501(c)(6).

Social Clubs

Tax exemption is provided for organizations that provide pleasure and recreation for the benefit of their members. These tax-exempt organizations, which include country clubs and hobby clubs, are required to pay tax on their net investment income and nonmember income. Generally, these organizations are described in Code § 501(c)(7).

Fraternal Societies

Tax exemption is provided for fraternal beneficiary organizations operating under the lodge system and providing certain benefit to their members, and for domestic fraternal societies operating under the lodge system that devote their net earnings to charitable purposes. Generally, these organizations are described in Code § 501(c)(8) or (10).

Veterans' Organizations

Tax exemption is provided for organizations of past or present members of the U.S. armed forces, or related auxiliaries or foundations, where at least 75 percent of the members are past or present members of the U.S. armed forces and substantially all of the other members are spouses or otherwise related to the members. Generally, these organizations are described in Code § 501(c)(19).

Political Organizations

Tax exemption is provided for parties, committees, associations, funds, and other organizations operated primarily for the purpose of accepting contributions or making expenditures, usually for the purpose of assisting one or more individuals in getting elected to public office or preventing a candidate from becoming elected to a public office. Generally, these organizations are described in Code § 527.

Other Tax-Exempt Organizations

Other types of nonprofit organizations that are eligible for tax exemption under the federal tax law are title-holding organizations, credit unions, small insurance companies, various mutual and cooperative organizations, crop financing entities, health maintenance organizations, homeowners' associations, and a variety of employee benefit funds.

Tax-Exempt Organizations Law Basics

Eight principles of law at the federal level compose the basics of the law of tax-exempt organizations, particularly for charitable entities.

Primary Purpose Test

The primary purpose of an organization determines (in part) whether it can qualify as a tax-exempt organization and, if so, which category of exemption is applicable. The focus in this context is on purposes, not activities. These purposes are usually stated in the organizational documents of a tax-exempt entity, such as its articles of incorporation, constitution, or trust document.

Organizational Test

A formal organizational test is applicable to charitable organizations, which focuses on the content of an organization's statement of purposes and the necessity of a dissolution clause in its organizational documents. This statement describes the mission of the entity, although there may also be a mission statement. A dissolution clause preserves the assets and net income of an organization for charitable purposes, should it dissolve or liquidate. Although there rarely is a formal organizational test for any of the noncharitable tax-exempt organizations, these tests are inherent in each category of exemption.

Operational Test

An operational test is applicable to charitable organizations, which focuses on how an organization functions in relation to the applicable requirements for tax-exempt status. These fundamental requirements are advancement of one or more exempt purposes, and avoidance of private inurement, private benefit, substantial legislative activity, and political campaign activity. Although there rarely is a formal operational test for noncharitable tax-exempt organizations, these tests are inherent in each category of exemption.

Private Inurement Doctrine

The doctrine of private inurement is one of the most important sets of rules constituting the federal law of tax-exempt organizations. This doctrine is a statutory criterion for federal income tax exemption for several categories of exempt organizations, including charitable entities.

The private inurement doctrine requires that a tax-exempt organization subject to it be organized and operated so that, in antiquated language, "no part of... [its] net earnings... inures to the benefit of any private shareholder or individual." What this doctrine means is that none of the income or assets of a tax-exempt organization subject to the private inurement doctrine may be permitted to directly or indirectly unduly benefit an individual or other person who has a close relationship with the organization, when that person is in a position to exercise a significant degree of control over the entity.

The purpose of the private inurement rule is to ensure that the tax-exempt organization involved is serving exempt rather than private interests. It is thus necessary for an organization subject to the doctrine to be in a position to establish that it is not organized and operated for the benefit of persons in their private capacity, informally referred to as *insiders*, such as the organization's founders, trustees, directors, officers, members of their families, entities controlled by these individuals, or any other persons having a significant personal and private interest in the activities of the organization.

The doctrine of private inurement does not prohibit transactions between a tax-exempt organization subject to the doctrine and those who have a close relationship with it. Rather, the private inurement doctrine requires that these transactions or arrangements be tested against a standard of *reasonableness.* The standard calls for a roughly equal exchange of benefits between the parties; the law is designed to discourage a disproportionate share of the benefits of the exchange flowing to an insider.

The private inurement doctrine does not prohibit the payment of compensation to employees of a charitable organization, provided the compensation is reasonable and not excessive. The reasonableness standard focuses essentially on comparability of data, that is, on how similar organizations, acting prudently, transact their affairs in comparable instances. Thus, the rule addressing the matter of the reasonableness of compensation is that it is generally appropriate to assume that reasonable and true compensation is only such amount as would ordinarily be paid for like services by like enterprises under like circumstances.

The sanction for violation of the private inurement doctrine is revocation (or denial) of the tax-exempt status of the organization involved.

Private Benefit Doctrine

A tax-exempt organization's charitable status can be revoked if there is a finding that the organization is serving a private, rather than a public, benefit. To be exempt, a charitable organization must establish that it is not organized or operated for the benefit of private interests such as designated individuals, the organization's creator or the creator's family members, shareholders of the organization, or persons controlled, directly or indirectly, by such private interests.

The prohibition against private benefit is not limited to situations in which benefits accrue to an organization's insiders. An organization's conferral of benefits on "disinterested persons" (persons who are not insiders) may cause it to serve a private interest. Unlike the private inurement doctrine, the private benefit doctrine permits incidental private benefit. This is an important distinction, inasmuch as, technically, any amount of private inurement may jeopardize a charitable organization's tax-exempt status, while an incidental amount of private benefit is allowable. Unlike private inurement, private benefit can exist even where an arrangement is otherwise reasonable. For example, the IRS has found that a charity was conferring impermissible private benefit on a for-profit management company managing a school, where the management company controlled nearly all the operations of the school.

The sanction for violation of the private benefit doctrine is revocation (or denial) of the tax-exempt status of the organization involved.

Intermediate Sanctions

The intermediate sanctions rules (Code § 4958) emphasize the taxation of persons who engaged in impermissible private transactions with certain types of tax-exempt organizations, rather than revocation of the tax-exempt status of these entities. With this approach, tax law sanctions—structured as penalty excise taxes—may be imposed on those persons who improperly benefited from the transaction and on certain managers of the organization who participated in the transaction knowing that it was improper. These taxes are applied to the amount of the excess benefit derived from the transaction. The taxes consist of an *initial* tax and an *additional* tax. The law as to excess benefit transactions applies with respect to tax-exempt public charities and exempt social welfare organizations. These entities are collectively termed, for this purpose, *applicable tax-exempt organizations.*

A person who has a close relationship with an applicable tax-exempt organization is a *disqualified person.* A disqualified person generally is a person who has, or is in a position to have, some type or degree of control over the operations of the applicable tax-exempt organization involved. The term *disqualified person* is defined in this context as (1) any person who was, at any time during the five-year period ending on the date of the transaction involved, in a position to exercise substantial influence over the affairs of the organization (whether by virtue of being an organization manager or otherwise), (2) a member of the family of an individual described in the preceding category, and (3) an entity in which individuals described in the preceding two categories own more than a 35 percent interest.

At the heart of the intermediate sanctions regime is the *excess benefit transaction.* In general, an excess benefit transaction is a transaction in which an economic benefit is provided by an applicable tax-exempt organization, directly or indirectly, to or for the use of a disqualified person, and the value of the economic benefit provided by the organization exceeds the value of the consideration (including the performance of services) received for providing the benefit. Any difference, other than an insubstantial one, between the value provided by the exempt organization and the consideration it received from the disqualified person is an *excess benefit.*

An excess benefit transaction includes a payment of unreasonable (excessive) compensation by an applicable tax-exempt organization to a disqualified person with respect to it. The value of services, in the intermediate sanctions setting, is the amount that ordinarily would be paid for like services by like organizations under like circumstances. Compensation in this context includes all economic benefits (other than certain disregarded benefits) provided by an applicable tax-exempt organization, to or for the use of a person, in exchange for the performance of services, including all forms of cash and noncash compensation.

A key component of the intermediate sanctions rules is the *rebuttable presumption of reasonableness.* When activated, this presumption shifts the burden of proof to the IRS to prove that an element of a transaction or arrangement was unreasonable. (The IRS can rebut this presumption with relevant facts of its own.) This presumption comes into play where the decision to engage in the transaction was made by an independent board or board committee, the board considered appropriate data as to comparability, and the decision was properly and timely documented (including in minutes).

The intermediate sanctions rules entail an initial tax, which is 25 percent of the excess benefit, payable by the disqualified person or persons involved. The transaction must be undone, by placing the parties in the same economic position they were in before the transaction was entered into; this is "correction" of the transaction. If the initial tax is not timely paid and the transaction is not timely and properly corrected, an additional tax may have to be paid; this tax is 200 percent of the excess benefit. Board members are subject to a tax of 10 percent of the amount involved if they knowingly participated in the excess benefit transaction, unless the participation was not willful and was due to reasonable cause. The board members subject to the 10 percent excise tax are jointly and severally liable for this tax, which is capped at $20,000 per transaction.

Commensurate Test

Pursuant to an infrequently used standard, termed the *commensurate test*, the IRS may assess whether a charitable organization is maintaining program activities that are commensurate in scope with its financial resources. The IRS has used the commensurate to revoke the tax exemption of charities with high fundraising costs relative to its other expenditures. The IRS has announced that it is going to make greater use of this test.

Public Policy Doctrine

Tax exemption as a charitable organization is available only when the organization is operating in conformance with federal public policy. For example, pursuant to this body of law, a private school cannot be exempt if it has a racially discriminatory policy as to the admission of students, an entity cannot be exempt if it promotes child pornography and exploitation, and an organization cannot qualify for exemption if it impedes IRS inquiries.

Legislative Activities Law

Considerable law restricts the ability of nonprofit organizations to engage in lobbying; these rules are principally directed at charitable organizations. Lobbying involves engaging in activities designed to influence the adoption of legislation, and are distinct from political activities, which involve activities in support of or in opposition to a candidate for political office.

Charitable Organizations. Tax-exempt public charities may engage in legislative activities to the extent that lobbying is not a *substantial* part of their overall functions. This rule is known as the *substantial part test.* Thus, an insubstantial portion of a public charity's activities may constitute lobbying; the term *insubstantial* in this context is not well-defined. These rules apply with respect to attempts to influence a legislative branch, usually in connection with the development of legislation. In contrast to public charities, private foundations may not engage in any lobbying without incurring an excise tax.

A mechanical test for measuring allowable lobbying, the *expenditure test,* may be elected by a charity. Pursuant to this rule, generally 20 percent of an organization's expenditures may be for lobbying (subject to a $1 million upper limit); several exceptions from the concept of lobbying are available under these rules. Excessive lobbying may lead to the imposition of excise taxes or revocation of exemption or both. More stringent rules are applicable to private foundations.

Social Welfare Organizations. There are no federal tax law limitations on attempts to influence legislation by tax-exempt social welfare organizations, other than the general requirement that the organization primarily engage in efforts to promote social welfare.

Associations (Business Leagues). There are no federal tax law limitations on attempts to influence legislation by tax-exempt business leagues, other than the general requirement that the organization primarily engage in activities appropriate for these organizations. The federal tax law, however, includes rules restricting the tax deductibility of dues paid to these organizations to the extent a portion of the dues is used for lobbying.

Other Exempt Organizations. Generally, the limitations on lobbying applicable to charitable organizations are also application to health insurance insurers. There are no federal tax law limitations on attempts to influence legislation by any other types of tax-exempt organizations, other than the general requirement that the organization primarily engage in efforts to advance its exempt purpose.

Political Activities Law

The federal tax law generally discourages political campaign activity by nonprofit, tax-exempt organizations. There is an absolute prohibition on political campaign activity by charitable organizations—a rule that is frequently violated.

Charitable Organizations. A charitable organization, to be tax-exempt, may not participate or intervene in a political campaign on behalf of or in opposition to a candidate for public office. This absolute prohibition encompasses political campaign contributions, endorsements, use of facilities, and signage on organization property. Leaders of charitable organizations may, however, engage in political activity in their personal capacity. Political activity may lead to the imposition of excise taxes (Code § 4955) and/or revocation of exemption. More stringent rules are applicable to private foundations.

Social Welfare Organizations. A tax-exempt social welfare organization can engage in political campaign activity, without jeopardizing its exemption, but this type of activity cannot be its primary function.

Associations (Business Leagues). There are no federal tax law limitations on political campaign activity by tax-exempt business leagues, other than the general requirement that the organization primarily engage in activities appropriate for these organizations. The federal tax law, however, includes rules restricting the tax deductibility of dues paid to these organizations to the extent a portion of the dues is used for political activity.

Political Organizations. Most political organizations have as their primary exempt function the involvement in political campaign activity, either in support of or in opposition to one or more candidates for public office.

Other Exempt Organizations. Generally, the limitations on political campaign activity applicable to charitable organizations are also application to health insurance insurers. The federal tax law is silent as to the extent to which other types of tax-exempt organizations can engage in political campaign activity, in relation to their eligibility for exempt status.

Public Charities and Private Foundations

The realm of Code§ 501 (c) (3) charitable organizations is divided into two classes: public charities and private foundations. Every tax-exempt charitable organization is presumed to be a *private foundation* (Code § 508). A showing that the entity is a public charity may rebut this presumption. Because of this presumption, a charitable organization that loses its public charity status becomes, by operation of law, a private foundation.

Definition of Private Foundation

Generically, a private foundation is a charitable entity that is funded from one or just a few sources, has ongoing funding in the form of investment income, and typically makes grants, usually to public charities, for charitable purposes. More technically, a private foundation is a tax-exempt charitable organization that is not a public charity. There are three basic types of charitable organizations that are not private foundations: the institutions, publicly supported charities, and supporting organizations. A fourth form of public charity is the public safety testing organization.

Institutions

Certain tax-exempt *institutions* are classified as public charities regardless of the source of their financial support (Code § 509(a)(1)). The principal types of institutions are churches, certain other religious organizations, formal educational institutions, hospitals, medical research organizations, agricultural research organizations, and governmental units.

Publicly Supported Organizations

Publicly supported charitable organizations are forms of public charities. The *donative* type of publicly supported charity (Code §§ 170(b)(1)(A)(vi), 509(a)(1)) normally receives a substantial part of its support (other than exempt function revenue) in the forms of contributions or grants from the public or one or more governmental units. The term *substantial* in this context generally means at least one-third, although a charity's public support can be as low as 10 percent if the charity can meet other criteria for public charity status. Generally, support from a member of the public cannot, to be public support, exceed 2 percent of the total amount of support the organization received during the measuring period, which is the entity's most recent five years (including its current year).

The *service provider* type of publicly supported charity (Code § 509(a)(2)) normally receives more than one-third of its support in the form of contributions, grants, membership fees, and fee-for-service revenue from *permitted sources*, and normally does not receive more than one-third of its support in the form of gross investment income and net unrelated business income. Permitted sources do not include disqualified persons with respect to the organization. Public support for these organizations is determined for a measuring period, which is the entity's most recent five years (including its current year).

Supporting Organizations

Supporting organizations are forms of public charities (Code § 509(a)(3)). Essentially, a *supporting organization* must be organized and operated exclusively for the benefit of, to perform the functions of, or to carry out the purposes of one or more qualified supported organizations. Typical functions of a supporting organization are fundraising, operation of separate programs, and maintenance of an endowment fund. There are four basic types of supporting organizations: Type I, II, III functionally integrated or Type III nonfunctionally integrated. Stringent law provisions are directed at Type III supporting organizations (both functionally integrated and nonfunctionally integrated), particularly those that are not functionally integrated with a supported organization. All supporting organizations are subject to an organizational test, operational test, control test, and relationship test. To meet the relationship test, Type III supporting organizations must satisfy a notification requirement, a responsiveness test, and an integral part test.

A private foundation may not treat as a qualifying distribution (a permissible grant) an amount paid to a Type III supporting organization that is not a functionally integrated Type III supporting organization or to any other type of supporting organization if a disqualified person with respect to the foundation directly or indirectly controls the supporting organization or a supported organization of the supporting organization. An amount that does not count as a qualifying distribution under this rule is regarded as a taxable expenditure.

A Type III supporting organization must notify each organization that it supports of information regarding the supporting organization in order to help ensure the responsiveness by the supporting organization to the needs or demands of the supported organization(s). In addition, a Type III supporting organization must be responsive to the needs or demands of one or more supported organizations. This is typically accomplished by having at least one overlapping officer or director of each of the organizations. Type III supporting organizations that are nonfunctionally integrated are subject to a payout requirement, which requires that they distribute a certain amount annually to one or more of their supported organizations and the distributed amount must be sufficiently important to the supported organization to ensure that it has sufficient reason to pay attention to the supporting organization's role in its operations.

A supporting organization must annually demonstrate that one or more of its disqualified persons (other than its managers and supported organization(s)) do not, directly or indirectly, control it. This is done by means of a certification on its annual information return.

Generally, a supported organization of a supporting organization is a public charity that is classified as one of the institutions or is a publicly supported charity. Under certain circumstances, however, a tax-exempt social welfare organization, labor organization, or business league (association) can qualify as a supported organization.

Private Foundation Rules

Private foundations are subject to a battery of rules prohibiting self-dealing with disqualified persons, excess business holdings, jeopardizing investments, and taxable expenditures (Code §§ 4940-4948). An income payout in the form of qualifying distributions is mandated. They must pay an excise tax on their net investment income. They are prohibited from holding certain investments and making certain grants and expenditures. The sanctions for violating these rules include a series of excise taxes.

Donor-Advised Funds

A donor-advised fund, although not a separate legal entity, is often seen as an alternative to a private foundation. A *donor-advised fund* is a fund or account (1) that is identified by reference to one or more donors, (2) that is owned and controlled by a sponsoring organization, and (3) as to which a donor or a donor advisor has advisory privileges with respect to the distribution or investment of amounts held in the fund or account. A *sponsoring organization* is a public charity that maintains one or more donor-advised funds. Various impermissible distributions from a donor-advised fund can give rise to a tax (Code §§ 4966, 4967).

Governance

Nonprofit governance is a matter of a great deal of attention in recent years. *Governance* refers to how an organization is governed, meaning how is it controlled and managed. Generally, the body of law applicable to the governance of a tax-exempt organization is state, not federal, law. The nature of the governance of a nonprofit, exempt organization depends mainly on the form of the entity. The state act governing the creation and operation of a nonprofit entity will address matters relating to the organization's governance.

Tax-exempt organizations that are corporations are typically governed by either a board of directors or a board of trustees. If the exempt organization is a trust, it may have a board of trustees or be governed by a single, sometimes corporate, trustee. How the nonprofit organization is organized determines how its directors are selected. Some nonprofit organizations are established with a self-perpetuating board of directors, meaning that the directors elect their successors. In the case of a nonprofit organization formed as a membership entity, the members of the nonprofit organization typically elect the directors.

In the rare instance of a nonprofit corporation organized as a stock corporation, which is allowable only in a few states, the stockholders elect the directors. With trusts, the trust document often appoints the trustees. Certain director positions may be ex officio, with the individual serving as a director because of a position held in another entity. However selected, the governing board of a nonprofit organization is responsible for overseeing its affairs. A nonprofit organization's officers are usually elected by the governing body or by the organization's members, with the election process typically governed by the organization's bylaws.

State law usually mandates at least three individuals serve as the governing body, although some states require only one. Some nonprofit corporations have very large boards of directors; state law does not set a maximum on the number of directors of nonprofit organizations. Some agencies and organizations suggest a minimum of three or five directors in their good governance guidelines. The prevailing view is that nonprofit entities should have enough board members to allow for full deliberation and diversity of thinking on governance and other organization matters.

The composition of a nonprofit organization's governing board is generally a matter of state law, but currently there are four exceptions to this general rule: (1) tax-exempt health care organizations are required to satisfy a community benefit test, which includes having a community board; (2) organizations qualifying as a publicly supported charity by reason of the facts-and-circumstances test may need to have a governing board that is representative of the community, as a community board is one of the factors considered in meeting the test; (3) organizations that qualify as supporting organizations are subject to certain requirements as to their board composition and selection; and (4) entities qualifying as exempt credit counseling organizations are subject to board composition requirements regarding financial independence from the organization. In addition, publicly supported organizations wishing to exclude a large grant as an "unusual grant" will find that having a large, representative governing body is favorable for purposes of treating the grant in this manner.

There is no general requirement that a nonprofit organization have a certain number of independent board members. The inclusion of independent directors on the board of a nonprofit entity is, however, considered a good governance practice. An independent board member is generally one with no financial or family connections with the organization, other than serving as a board member. IRS agents, when reviewing initial applications of exempt organizations, often try to impose their own views on board compositions, such as requiring the addition of independent directors; such views are not correct assertions of the law.

As a practical matter, the IRS does not favor small, related boards of directors other than with private foundations. New organizations applying for recognition of tax-exempt status may encounter resistance from the IRS if their governing board is comprised of only a few, related individuals. One IRS representative stated publicly that "outside of the very smallest organizations, or possibly family foundations," an active, independent, and engaged board of directors is the "gold standard" of board composition.

Duties of Directors

The board of a tax-exempt organization is collectively responsible for developing and advancing the organization's mission; maintaining the organization's tax-exempt status, and (if applicable) its ability to attract charitable contributions; protecting the organization's resources; formulating the organization's budget; hiring and evaluating the chief executive; generally overseeing the organization's management; and supporting fundraising that the organization undertakes. Embodied in state law are fiduciary duties for members of the governing body of a nonprofit organization. Fiduciary duties arose out of the charitable law of trusts and impose on directors and trustees standards of conduct and management. One of the principal responsibilities of board members is to maintain financial accountability and effective oversight of the organization they serve. Board members are guardians of the organization's assets, and they are expected to exercise due diligence to see that the organization is well-managed and has a financial position that is as strong as is reasonable under the circumstances. Fiduciary duty requires board members of nonprofit organizations to be objective, unselfish, responsible, honest, trustworthy, and efficient. Board members, as stewards of the organization, should always act for the organization's good and betterment, rather than for their personal benefit. They should exercise reasonable care in their decision making and not place the organization under unnecessary risk.

The distinction as to legal liability between the board as a group and the board members as individuals relates to the responsibility of the board for the organization's affairs and the responsibility of individual board members for their actions personally. The board collectively is responsible and may be liable for what transpires within and what happens to the organization. As the ultimate authority, the board should ensure that the organization is operating in compliance with the law and its governing instruments. If legal action ensues, it is often traceable to an inattentive, passive, or captive board. Legislators and government regulators are becoming more aggressive in demanding higher levels of involvement by and accountability of board members of tax-exempt organizations; this is causing a dramatic shift in thinking about board functions, away from the concept of mere oversight and toward the precept that board members should be far more involved in policy-setting and review, employee supervision, and overall management of the organization. Consequently, many boards of exempt organizations are becoming more vigilant and active in implementing and maintaining sound policies and procedures.

In turn, the board's shared legal responsibilities depend on the actions of individuals. Each board member is liable for his or her acts (commissions and omissions), including those that may be civil law or even criminal law offenses. In practice, this requires board members to hold each other accountable for deeds that prove harmful to the organization.

The duties of the board of directors of a tax-exempt organization essentially are the duty of care, the duty of loyalty, and the duty of obedience. Defined by case law, these are the legal standards against which all actions taken or not taken by directors are measured. They are collective duties adhering to the entire board; the mandate is active participation by all of the board members. Accountability can be demonstrated by showing the effective discharge of these three duties.

The duty of care requires that directors of a tax-exempt organization be reasonably informed about the organization's activities, participate in decision making, and act in good faith and with the care of an ordinarily prudent person in comparable circumstances. In short, the duty of care requires the board—and its members individually—to pay attention to the organization's activities and operations.

The duty of care is satisfied by attendance at meetings of the board and appropriate committees; advance preparation for board meetings, such as reviewing reports and the agenda prior to meetings of the board; obtaining information, before voting, to make appropriate decisions; use of independent judgment; periodic examination of the credentials and performance of those who serve the organization; frequent review of the organization's finances and financial policies; and compliance with filing requirements, particularly annual information returns.

The duty of loyalty requires board members to exercise their power in the interest of the tax-exempt organization and not in their personal interest or the interest of another entity, particularly one with which they have a formal relationship. When acting on behalf of the exempt organization, board members are expected to place the interests of the organization before their personal and professional interests.

The duty of loyalty is satisfied when board members disclose any conflicts of interest; otherwise adhere to the organization's conflict-of-interest policy; avoid the use of corporate opportunities for the individual's personal gain or other benefit; and do not disclose confidential information concerning the organization.

The duty of obedience requires that directors of a tax-exempt organization comply with applicable federal, state, and local laws, adhere to the organization's governing documents, and remain guardians of the organization's mission. The duty of obedience is complied with when the board endeavors to be certain that the organization is in compliance with applicable regulatory requirements, complies with and periodically reviews all documents governing the operations of the organization, and makes decisions in advancement of the organization's mission and within the scope of the entity's governing documents.

Developments in Nonprofit Governance

Congress, the IRS, and other groups have been attempting to exercise more influence and control over the governance of tax-exempt organizations, especially charities. At this time, however, there is little federal law applicable to the governance of tax-exempt organizations. While a few provisions of the Sarbanes-Oxley Act passed in 2002 apply to nonprofit organizations, Congress has not yet enacted laws that affect the governance, oversight, and management of nonprofit organizations to any significant degree. The IRS, with its redesign of the Form 990, which is the annual information return filed by most nonprofit organizations, has done more to conform the governance practices of tax-exempt organizations than any other agency. Many in the nonprofit community questioned the IRS's authority to regulate the manner in which nonprofit organizations are governed. Most believe the IRS is effectively trying to make law by virtue of the questions it asks on the redesigned Form 990 and through the exempt organization application process. The IRS, however, stated that it has no intentions of backing away from the issue of nonprofit governance and will continue to "educate, engage, and indeed irritate" in the area of nonprofit governance.

Certain states have enacted laws regarding the accountability of nonprofit organizations, with the states of California and New York having the most extensive sets of rules concerning governance and accountability of nonprofit organizations, mainly due to California's enactment of the Nonprofit Integrity Act in 2004 and New York's adoption of the Nonprofit Revitalization Act of 2013. Most state provisions, to the extent they exist, require audited financial statements for nonprofit organizations with revenues in excess of a certain threshold.

Corporate Policies

With a few noted exceptions, a nonprofit entity is not legally required to have corporate policies. The prevailing view by the IRS and watchdog organizations in the nonprofit community, however, is that a well-governed nonprofit organization is more effective and more compliant, and that policies and procedures are an indication of a well-governed entity. As a result, tax-exempt organizations should consider implementing policies that are applicable and relevant to their organization, both as a matter of good governance and to demonstrate that they are effectively governed in the event of an audit or investigation. These policies include a conflicts-of-interest policy, whistle-blower policy, document retention and destruction policy, code of ethics, investment policy, travel and reimbursement policy, and fundraising policy, just to name a few.

One of the nonprofit buzzwords of the day is "transparency." Most good governance guidelines have, as one of their tenets, a principle that a nonprofit organization should make information regarding the entity widely known and available to the public, including information about its mission, activities, finances, board, and staff. Some of these matters are already part of the law applicable to tax-exempt organizations. Others represent opinions on good governance, but are not legal requirements.

As more situations involving apparent lack of governance at the board level over tax-exempt organizations surface, exempt organizations and those that advise them need to pay increasing attention to the entities' governance practices and procedures. Members of the public and nonprofit watchdog organizations likely will be unsympathetic to an organization bled dry by a wayward executive director or a nonprofit steered away from its original mission by self-interested directors when adherence to good governance principles could have avoided the matter. Exempt organizations should take care to see that its governance affairs are in order, whether or not subject to a legal requirement to do so.

Reporting Rules

Nonprofit, tax-exempt organizations are subject to many reporting rules.

Annual Information Returns. Nearly every organization that is exempt from federal income taxation is required to annually file an information return with the IRS (Code § 6033). For many tax-exempt organizations, this return is Form 990. Small (that is, entities with less than $200,000 in gross receipts or $500,000 in total assets) exempt organizations can file Form 990-EZ. Private foundations (of any size) file Form 990-PF. Political and other exempt organizations may file Form 990 or 1120-POL or both. Homeowners' associations file Form 1120-H. Black lung benefit trusts file Form 990-BL. Very small organizations (that is, those with less than $50,000 in gross receipts) are required to electronically file a Form 990-N (the e-postcard). Exceptions to this filing requirement are available for a variety of organizations, including churches, their integrated auxiliaries, governmental entities and their affiliates, and organizations that are part of a group exemption and included on a group return filed by the central or parent organization.

Unrelated Business Income Tax Returns. A tax-exempt organization with unrelated business income is generally required to file an income tax return, reporting the income, expenses, and any tax due (Form 990-T).

Split-Interest Trust Returns. A split-interest trust is required to annually file a return (generally Form 1041A, perhaps Form 5227) with the IRS.

Nonexempt Charitable Trust Returns. A nonexempt charitable trust is required to annually file a return (Form 1041A, perhaps 5577) with the IRS.

Apostolic Organizations' Returns. Apostolic organizations are required to annually file a partnership return with the IRS (Form 1065).

State Annual Reports. Nonprofit organizations, particularly nonprofit corporations, are generally required to file annual reports with the states in which they are formed, headquartered, and do business.

Charitable Solicitation Act Reports. Charitable and other types of nonprofit organizations that engage in fundraising are generally required to file annual reports with each state in which they solicit funds.

Disposition of Gift Property Rules. A charitable organization that disposes of charitable gift property within three years of the date of the gift is generally required to report the transaction (on Form 8282) to the IRS.

Disclosure Rules

Generally, a tax-exempt organization must make its IRS application for recognition of exemption (including documents submitted in support of the application and any letter or other document issued by the IRS regarding the application) and its three most recent annual information returns available for public inspection. Exempt organizations other than private foundations and political entities are not required to disclose the names and addresses of their donors and may redact this information prior to providing copies or otherwise making information returns available. Public charities are required to make their Forms 990-T available for public inspection. The IRS has also established a procedure for requesting copies of these documents and returns from the IRS using IRS Form 4506-A, Request for Public Inspection or Copy of Exempt or Political Organization IRS Form.

Documents required to be disclosed must be made available for inspection at the organization's principal office and certain regional and/or district offices during regular business hours, and organizations are required to provide copies of these documents to those who request them, either in person or in writing. Copies must be provided without charge, other than a reasonable fee for reproduction and mailing costs.

A tax-exempt organization is not required to comply with the requests for copies of its application for recognition of exemption or annual information returns if the organization has made the document widely available. For this purpose, making the documents widely available is satisfied if an organization posts the documents on a web page that the organization establishes and maintains, or if the documents are posted as part of a database of similar documents by other exempt organizations on a web page established or maintained by another entity, provided certain other criteria are met. The rules for public inspection of the documents will continue to apply, even if the organization makes the documents widely available to satisfy the requirements regarding copies.

If the IRS determines that a tax-exempt organization is the subject of a harassment campaign and that compliance with the requests would not be in the public interest, the tax-exempt organization does not have to fulfill a request for a copy that it reasonably believes is part of the campaign. The document disclosure rules apply to the notice that must be filed by political organizations to establish their tax-exempt status and to the reports they must file.

Unrelated Business Rules

One of the principal aspects of the law of tax-exempt organizations is the body of law concerning the conduct of unrelated business (Code §§ 511-514). For an exempt organization to conduct an unrelated business, it must be engaged in a trade or business that is regularly carried on and that is not related to the organization's exempt purposes.

Requirement of Business

A *business* of a tax-exempt organization is an activity that is carried on for the production of income from the sale of goods or the performance of services. Nearly every undertaking of an exempt organization, including its programs, is a business. Businesses of exempt organizations are, for this purpose, either related or unrelated.

Regularly Carried On Rule

A business of a tax-exempt organization, to be considered an unrelated business, must be regularly carried on. Generally, this element of regularity is measured annually; if a season is involved, that is the measuring period.

Substantially Related Standard

A business of a tax-exempt organization, to be considered a related business, where the conduct of the business activity has a causal relationship to the achievement of an exempt purpose (other than through the production of income) and the causal relationship is substantial.

Exceptions as to Activities

Various exceptions from treatment as unrelated business are available for activities of tax-exempt organizations, including volunteer-conducted businesses, convenience businesses, sales of donated items, certain entertainment activities, the conduct of trade shows, certain hospital services, the dissemination of low-cost articles, and the exchanging or rental of mailing lists.

Exceptions as to Income

Various exceptions (in the form of *modifications* of the general rule) from treatment as unrelated business income are available for income received by tax-exempt organizations, including dividends, interest, annuities, royalties, rent, capital gains, and research income.

Social Clubs and Like Organizations' Rules

Special unrelated business rules are applicable to social clubs, veterans' organizations, voluntary employees' beneficiary associations, and supplemental unemployment benefit trusts.

Unrelated Debt-Financed Income Rules

In computing a tax-exempt organization's unrelated business taxable income, there must be included with respect to each debt-financed property that is unrelated to the organization's exempt function—as an item of gross income derived from an unrelated trade or business—an amount of income from the property subject to tax in the proportion to which the property is financed by the debt.

Tax Computation

The unrelated income tax rates payable by most tax-exempt organizations are the corporate rates, although exempt organizations formed as trusts are subject to the trust income tax rates. In computing unrelated business taxable income, exempt organizations may deduct expenses that are directly connected with the carrying on of the trade or business. A specific deduction of $1,000 is available, as is a charitable deduction. Taxable unrelated business income is reported on Form 990-T.

Subsidiaries

It is common for nonprofit, tax-exempt organizations to have one or more subsidiaries. Generically, this type of arrangement is known as *bifurcation*: a splitting of functions that might otherwise be conducted by one organization so that some of the functions are conducted by one entity and the balance of the functions are conducted by the other entity. Common reasons for formation of a subsidiary by a tax-exempt entity are to insulate the exempt entity from the liability risks of the subsidiary's activity or because the subsidiary's activity is not related to the nonprofit entity's exempt purpose. If one or more subsidiaries exist, the board members should know why; if there are no subsidiaries, the board members should, from time to time, deliberate and seek advice as to whether a subsidiary might be of advantage to the nonprofit organization.

A subsidiary may be a tax-exempt organization or it may be a for-profit organization. Before addressing those distinctions, however, there are six law aspects of the parent-subsidiary relationship that the should be considered, irrespective of the type of subsidiary: the form of the subsidiary, the nature of control of the subsidiary, funding of the subsidiary (initially and on an ongoing basis), day-to-day management of the subsidiary, revenue flow from the subsidiary to the parent, and, perhaps, liquidation of the subsidiary.

- *Form.* If the subsidiary is a nonprofit organization, the legal forms are: nonprofit corporation, unincorporated association, trust, or limited liability company. If the subsidiary is a for-profit organization, the typical choices are for-profit corporation or a limited liability company. Matters can become more complicated where the nonprofit parent is not the sole owner of the for-profit subsidiary.

- *Control.* If the subsidiary is a nonprofit organization, the parent can control it by overlapping governing boards, membership (where the parent is the sole member of the subsidiary), appointments, ex officio positions, or some combination of the foregoing. If the subsidiary is a for-profit organization, the control feature will be manifested by ownership, either by stock in the corporation or membership interest in the limited liability company.

- *Funding.* The parent must decide how much money or property, if any, to transfer to the subsidiary and should understand the federal tax consequences of the transfer. If the subsidiary is a for-profit entity, the transfer may be in the nature of a capitalization, such as in exchange for stock or membership interest. The parent may make loans to the subsidiary.

- *Management.* If the parent organization is unduly involved in the day-to-day management of the subsidiary, the activities of the subsidiary may be attributed to the parent. This type of attribution usually causes federal tax problems, either in the form of endangering tax exemption or unrelated business income taxation.

- *Revenue flow.* Revenue can flow from a subsidiary to a nonprofit parent in two basic ways: payment of net earnings (such a dividends, in the case of a for-profit subsidiary) or payment for services or assistance (such as rent or interest). The second category of these payments may be taxable to the parent as unrelated business income. A special rule exempts certain types of revenue from a subsidiary from unrelated business income taxation (Code § 512(b)(13)).

- *Liquidation.* If the subsidiary is terminated or dissolved, and liquidated into the parent, the subsidiary may have to pay income tax on the capital gain resulting from the transfer of assets to the parent, that have appreciated in value.

If the subsidiary is a tax-exempt charitable organization, it may be a supporting organization. Typical parents of charitable subsidiaries are social welfare organizations, associations (business leagues), and labor organizations. A charitable organization may be the parent of a charitable subsidiary, such as may be the case with a "foundation" related to a domestic public charity or a fundraising entity affiliated with a foreign charitable organization.

A charitable organization may be the parent entity and have a subsidiary that is a tax-exempt, noncharitable entity. Two common illustrations of this form of bifurcation are lobbying arms (social welfare organizations) of public charities and certification organizations (business leagues) associated with public charities. Other arrangements involving nonprofit, tax-exempt parents and nonprofit, exempt subsidiaries are those using title-holding companies, political action committees and other political organizations (but not by charitable organizations), and various types of employee benefit funds.

Some of these subsidiaries may be for-profit, taxable entities, usually utilized to conduct a business activity that is both substantial and unrelated to the tax-exempt activities of the parent entity. Particular consideration needs to be given to choice of entity in this context; a standard corporation (C corporation) is likely to be the answer, in that flow-through entities (such as S corporations and limited liability companies) can give rise to tax dilemmas for the tax-exempt parent. In some instances, revenue received by an exempt organization parent from its subsidiary is taxable as unrelated business income.

Joint Ventures

Nonprofit, tax-exempt organizations may participate in partnerships and other forms of joint ventures, such as those utilizing limited liability companies. Most of the law in this area concerns public charities as general partners or members in these ventures. Ventures may be whole-entity or ancillary. The IRS is particularly sensitive to the potential for private inurement or private benefit in these circumstances.

The term *partnership* generally has a technical meaning; partnerships are recognized forms of business entities, either as general partnerships or limited partnerships. The term *joint venture*, however, is much broader; a nonprofit organization can be involved in a joint venture with one or more other nonprofit entities or one or more for-profit entities. On occasion, the joint venture form can be imposed on an arrangement between a nonprofit organization and one or more other organizations by operation of law.

A public charity (or perhaps another form of tax-exempt organization) can be a (or the) general partner in a general partnership and not endanger its exempt status where (1) the participation of the exempt organization in the partnership is in furtherance of an exempt purpose, (2) the exempt organization is insulated from the day-to-day responsibilities of being the general partner, and

(3) the limited partners are not receiving an unwarranted economic benefit from the partnership.

The federal tax law recognizes the concept of the *whole-entity joint venture.* This type of vehicle was started by tax-exempt health care institutions, which placed the entirety of the institution in a venture (unlike most joint ventures, where only a portion of nonprofit resources are involved). The other venturer(s) may be nonprofit or for-profit. Where it is the latter, the IRS and the courts will look to see whether the exempt venturer has "ceded control" over its operations to the for-profit venturer. If it has, the nonprofit organization will likely lose its tax-exempt status, on the basis of violation of the private benefit doctrine.

The federal tax law developed in the context of whole-entity joint ventures is being applied to other ventures involving nonprofit organizations, where less than the entire entity is placed in the venture. These are termed *ancillary joint ventures.* It may be that an ancillary joint venture is wholly in furtherance of charitable or other exempt purposes, in which case tax exemption is not at issue. Or the involvement of an exempt organization in an ancillary joint venture may be, from the organization's standpoint, incidental, thus eliminating any private benefit doctrine problems. This open question remains: What happens when a tax-exempt, charitable organization is involved in an ancillary joint venture, to more than an insubstantial extent, and loses control of its resources in the venture to a for-profit co-venturer? The logical, albeit perhaps harsh, answer is that the organization would lose its exempt status.

The joint venture vehicle of choice, when only tax-exempt organizations are involved, is the limited liability company. These companies, which can have one or more members, are generally treated, for federal tax law purposes, as partnerships, which means that they are not themselves taxed, but instead are flow-through entities causing their members to be taxable on the venture's income. Issues may arise, however, with trying to obtain property and sales tax exemptions for these flow-through entities.

Limited liability companies may also be used in situations with for-profit partners. While the for-profit venturers tend to favor this approach, which avoid double taxation, tax-exempt organizations may want to avoid a flow-through entity, so as not to have taxable unrelated business income and possibly jeopardize their tax-exempt status if the venture does not further exempt purposes. For this reason, some tax-exempt organizations form a for-profit subsidiary to be a member of the joint venture, to serve as a "blocker" entity to escape the unrelated business income tax and perhaps to avoid jeopardizing the nonprofit organization's exempt status.

The single-member limited liability company is usually disregarded for tax purposes. This feature allows a tax-exempt organization to place activities in a limited liability company to protect against legal liability, yet still treat them for federal tax purposes as activities directly conducted by the exempt organization.

Other Aspects of Law of Exempt Organizations

Seven other aspects of the law of tax-exempt organizations warrant mention for the benefit of the leadership and management of nonprofit organizations.

Gaming

In general, the conduct of gaming (or gambling) activity by a tax-exempt organization constitutes an unrelated business or a nonexempt function that may jeopardize the organization's exempt status. An exception in the unrelated business context is available for the conduct of bingo games, where they are lawful under state law.

Withholding of Taxes

As is the case with for-profit employers, nonprofit organization employers are required to withhold income and other taxes and remit them to the appropriate government. Members of the board of nonprofit organizations can be personally liable for these taxes owed (and not paid by the organization).

Unemployment Tax

Tax-exempt organizations generally are required to pay federal and state unemployment taxes with respect to their employees.

Nonexempt Membership Organizations

Special rules apply that can limit the deductibility of expenses in computing taxable income, in situations where a nonprofit organization is a nonexempt membership entity.

Maintenance of Books and Records

Tax-exempt organizations are required to keep records sufficiently showing gross income, expenses, and disbursements, and providing substantiation for their annual information returns. The IRS frequently revokes the exempt status of organizations that do not maintain adequate records.

Personal Benefit Contracts

The federal tax law denies a charitable contribution deduction in connection with, and imposes penalties on tax-exempt organizations that engage in transactions involving, certain personal benefit contracts (Code § 170(f)(10)).

Commerciality Doctrine

Tax-exempt organizations, particularly public charities, which operate in a commercial manner (that is, in the same manner as for-profit entities) may have their exemption revoked by the IRS. Commercial activity may alternatively be considered an unrelated business. Factors as to commerciality include the extent of the sale of goods and services to the public, pricing policies, and competition with for-profit businesses.

Charitable Giving Rules

The federal tax law is replete with detailed rules concerning the charitable contribution deduction, for income, gift, and estate tax purposes.

Charitable Deduction. The federal tax law provides for an income tax charitable contribution deduction for gifts to charitable, governmental, and certain other types of tax-exempt organizations (Code § 170). These deductible contributions may be made in the form of money or property. Various percentage limitations may restrict the amount of a charitable contribution deduction in a year. Many special rules apply in this context for particular types of charitable gifts, such as those of inventory, scientific research property, vehicles, and intellectual property. These rules can limit the amount of the charitable deduction, sometimes confining it to the amount of the donor's basis in the property. Generally, gifts to a public charity will receive more favorable treatment under these rules than gifts to a private foundation.

Property Valuation. In connection with charitable contributions of property, rather than cash, often the major issue affecting the deductibility of the gift is the matter of the fair market value of the property at the time of its contribution. Various "accuracy-related" penalties can apply with respect to an overvaluation of property in this context.

Gift Restrictions. A gift may be made to charity that involves the imposition of conditions or restrictions. In many instances, such a restriction is lawful (such as for scholarships, a form of research, or for an endowment). A restriction or condition may, however, be unlawful, may result in unwarranted private benefit, or may reduce or eliminate the amount of the allowable charitable deduction.

Split-Interest Trusts. Contributions may be made to charity by means of a split-interest trust. The resulting charitable contribution deduction (if any) is based on the value of the partial interest contributed to the charity by means of the trust. For a charitable deduction to be available in this context, various requirements must be satisfied, such as those for charitable remainder trusts, pooled income funds, and other types of gifts of remainder interests. These vehicles are used in the realm of the type of charitable fundraising known as *planned giving*. If a charitable organization does not have a planned giving program, the board member may wish to inquire as to why that is the case.

Charitable Remainder Trusts. The *charitable remainder trust* (Code § 664) is the mainstay of a typical planned giving program. This term is nearly self-explanatory: the entity is a trust, in which has been created a remainder interest that is destined for one or more charitable organizations. One or more income interests are also created by means of this type of trust. These trusts, if they qualify under the federal tax law, are tax-exempt entities.

A qualified charitable remainder trust must provide for a specified distribution of income, at least annually, to one or more beneficiaries (at least one of which is not a charitable organization) for life or for a term of no more than twenty years, with an irrevocable remainder interest to be held for the benefit of, or paid over to, the charitable organization. The manner in which the income interests in a charitable remainder trust are ascertained depends on whether the trust is a charitable remainder annuity trust or a charitable remainder unitrust.

In the case of the *charitable remainder annuity trust*, the income payments are a fixed amount (hence the term *annuity*). With a *charitable remainder unitrust*, the income payments are in an amount equal to a fixed percentage of the fair market value of the assets in the trust. Conventionally, once the income interest expires, the assets in a charitable remainder trust are distributed to the charitable organization that is the remainder beneficiary. The assets (or a portion of them) may, however, be retained in the trust; if this type of a retention occurs, the trust will likely be classified as a private foundation. With these charitable giving instruments, the person establishing the trust receives a charitable deduction for the value of the charitable remainder interest at the time the trust is established.

Charitable Gift Annuities. A charitable gift annuity is based on an agreement between the donor and the charitable donee. The donor agrees to make a gift and the donee agrees to provide the donor (or someone else, or both) with an annuity for a period of time. Charitable gift annuities may be subject to state law registration requirements.

Federal Law as to Fundraising

The federal tax law includes five bodies of law that pertain to fundraising.

Special Events. *Special events* are social occasions (such as annual balls, games of chance, and sports events) for the benefit of charities that use ticket sales and underwriting to generate revenue. These events, however, may raise federal tax law issues, such as unrelated business and inappropriate gaming. Special event fundraising is the subject of specific reporting rules as part of the annual information return.

Gift Substantiation Rules. The income tax charitable contribution deduction is not allowed for a contribution of a monetary gift unless the donor maintains a suitable record of the contribution. For a charitable contribution of $250 or more to be deductible, certain substantiation requirements must be met. This principally entails a written communication from the charitable donee to the donor, containing specified information. More detailed substantiation requirements apply in connection with larger noncash contributions. Other charitable gift substantiation rules may arise in other contexts, such as with respect to contributions of vehicles or intellectual property.

Quid Pro Quo Contribution Rules. The federal tax law imposes certain disclosure requirements on charitable organizations that receive *quid pro quo contributions*, which are payments made partially as a contribution and partially in consideration for goods or services provided by the one organization. Fundraising events, such as luncheons and galas, often result in quid pro quo contributions. Penalties apply for violation of these rules.

Noncharitable Organizations Gifts Disclosure. The federal tax law imposes certain disclosure requirements in connection with contributions to tax-exempt organizations other than charitable entities. These rules, targeted principally at exempt social welfare organizations, are designed to prevent circumstances when donors are led to believe that the gifts are deductible when they are not. Penalties apply for violation of these rules.

Appraisal Requirements. A contribution deduction is not available, in an instance of a gift of property with a value in excess of $5,000, unless certain appraisal requirements are satisfied, including an obtaining by the donor of a qualified appraisal and use of the services of a qualified appraiser. A *qualified appraisal* is an appraisal document prepared by a qualified appraiser in accordance with generally accepted appraisal standards. A *qualified appraiser* is an individual with verifiable education and experience in valuing the type of property for which the appraisal is performed.

State Law as to Fundraising

Many states have elaborate laws—charitable solicitation acts—that apply to charitable and other nonprofit organizations that engage in fundraising in their jurisdictions. These laws require charitable organizations soliciting gifts to register with and annually report to the state. Fundraising consultants and paid solicitors may also have registration and reporting requirements; bonds may also be necessitated. These laws can impose several other requirements, such as dictation of the contents of a contract between a charity and a professional fundraiser.

Organization of IRS

The leadership of nonprofit organizations, and those who represent these entities, should understand the organization of the IRS. Among the many reasons for this is to gain a perspective on the IRS audit function. Generally, an IRS audit is less traumatic if the overall process is understood.

The IRS is an agency (bureau) of the Department of the Treasury. One of the functions of the Treasury Department is assessment and collection of federal income and other taxes. Congress has authorized the Secretary of the Treasury to, in the language of the Internal Revenue Code, undertake what is necessary for "detecting and bringing to trial and punishment persons guilty of violating the internal revenue laws or conniving at the same." This tax assessment and collection function has largely been assigned to the IRS.

The IRS website proclaims that the agency's mission is to "provide America's taxpayers with top quality service by helping them understand and meet their tax responsibilities and by applying the tax law with integrity and fairness to all." The function of the IRS, according to its site, is to "help the large majority of compliant taxpayers with the tax law, while ensuring that the minority who are unwilling to comply pay their fair share."

The IRS is headquartered in Washington, D.C.; its operations there are housed principally in its National Office. An Internal Revenue Service Oversight Board is responsible for overseeing the agency in its administration and supervision of the execution of the nation's internal revenue laws. The chief executive of the IRS is the Commissioner of Internal Revenue. The National Office is organized into four operating divisions; the pertinent one is the Tax Exempt and Government Entities (TE/GE) Division, headed by the Commissioner (TE/GE). Within the TE/GE Division is the Exempt Organizations Division, which develops policy concerning and administers the law of tax-exempt organizations. The components of this Division are Rulings and Agreements, Customer Education and Outreach, Exempt Organizations Electronic Initiatives, and Examinations.

The Examinations Office, based in Dallas, Texas, focuses on tax-exempt organizations' examination programs and review projects. This office develops the overall exempt organizations enforcement strategy and goals to enhance compliance consistent with overall TE/GE strategy, and implements and evaluates exempt organizations examination policies and procedures. Two important elements of the Examinations function are the Exempt Organizations Compliance Unit and the Data Analysis Unit.

Applications for recognition of exemption are filed with the IRS office in Covington, Kentucky. Tax-exempt organizations file their annual information returns with the IRS office in Ogden, Utah.

IRS Audits

The IRS, of course, has the authority to examine—audit—nonprofit, tax-exempt organizations. Due to funding cuts since 2010, the IRS can devote only limited resources to audits and, statistically, exempt organizations have been subject to a lower audit risk than for-profit organizations. Nevertheless, the examinations function of the Exempt Organizations subdivision has become focused on data-driven decision making using the Form 990 and its related schedules to determine potential noncompliance with the tax laws. Thus, the IRS is focused on more objective case collection for examinations and employing more sophisticated methods for selecting returns (and thus the organizations) to audit.

Reasons for IRS Audits. The reasons for an IRS examination of a nonprofit, tax-exempt organization are manifold. Traditionally, the agency has focused on particular categories of major exempt entities, such as health care institutions, colleges and universities, political organizations, community foundations, and private foundations. Recent years have brought more targeted examinations, such as those involving credit counseling entities and down payment assistance organizations.

An examination of a tax-exempt organization may be initiated on the basis of the size of the organization or the length of time that has elapsed since a prior audit. An examination may be undertaken following the filing of an annual information return or a tax return, inasmuch as one of the functions of the IRS is to ascertain the correctness of returns. An examination may be based on a discrete issue, such as compensation practices or political campaign activity. Other reasons for the development of an examination include media reports, a state attorney general's inquiry, or other third party reports of alleged wrongdoing.

IRS Audit Issues. The audit of a nonprofit, tax-exempt organization is likely to entail one or more of the following issues:

- The organization's ongoing eligibility for exempt status
- Public charity/private foundation classification
- Unrelated business activity
- Extensive advocacy undertakings
- One or more excise tax issues
- Whether the organization filed required returns and reports
- Payment of employment taxes
- Involvement in a form of joint venture

Types of IRS Examinations. There are four basic types of IRS examinations of nonprofit, tax-exempt organizations. A compliance check is not technically an audit. Also, there are special procedures for inquiries and examinations of churches.

Common among the types of IRS examinations of tax-exempt organizations are *field examinations*, in which one or more revenue agents (typically, however, only one) review the books, records, and other documents and information of the exempt organization under examination, on the premises of the organization or at the office of its representative. IRS procedures require the examiner to establish the scope of the examination, state the documentation requirements, and summarize the examination techniques (including interviews and tours of facilities).

The IRS's office/correspondence examination program entails examinations of tax-exempt organizations by means of office interviews or correspondence or both. An *office interview* case is one where the examiner requests an exempt organization's records and reviews them in an IRS office; this may include a conference with a representative of the organization. This type of examination is likely to be of a smaller exempt organization, where the records are not extensive and the issues not particularly complex. A *correspondence examination* involves an IRS request for information from an exempt organization by letter, fax, or e-mail communication.

Office or correspondence examinations generally are limited in scope, usually focusing on no more than three issues, conducted by lower-grade examiners. The import of these examinations should not be minimized, however. A correspondence examination can be converted to an office examination. Worse, an office examination can be upgraded to a field examination.

For larger, more complex organizations, the IRS may conduct a *team examination program* (TEP) audit. TEP initiatives have a fundamental objective, which is to avoid fragmenting of the exempt organization examination process by using multiple agents. The essential characteristics of the TEP approach are that the team examinations are being used in connection with a wider array of exempt organizations, the number of revenue agents involved in an examination is somewhat smaller, and the revenue agents are less likely to semi-permanently carve out office space in which to live at the exempt organization undergoing the examination. The TEP agents, however, are still likely to want an office, for occasional visits and storage of computers and documents.

A TEP case generally is one for which the annual information return of the tax-exempt organization involved reflects either total revenue or assets greater than $100 million (or, in the case of a private foundation, $500 million). Nonetheless, the IRS may initiate a team examination where the case would benefit (from the government's perspective) from the TEP approach or where there is no annual information return filing requirement. IRS examination procedures include a presumption that the team examination approach will be utilized in all cases satisfying the TEP criteria.

In a TEP case, the examination will proceed under the direction of a case manager. One or more tax-exempt organizations revenue agents will be accompanied by others, such as employee plans specialists, actuarial examiners, engineers, excise tax agents, international examiners, computer audit specialists, income tax revenue agents, and/or economists. These examinations may last about two years; a post-examination critique may lead to a cycling of the examination into subsequent years. The IRS examination procedures stipulate the planning that case managers, assisted by team coordinators, should engage in when launching a team examination; these procedures also provide for the exempt organization's involvement in this planning process.

The foregoing types of IRS audits are those normally used to examine nonprofit, tax-exempt organizations. The IRS has within it a Criminal Investigation Division, however; the agents of which occasionally are involved in exempt organization examinations.

Compliance Checks. An overlay to the IRS program of examinations of tax-exempt organizations is the agency's *compliance check projects*, which focus on specific compliance issues. These projects, orchestrated by the Exempt Organizations Compliance Unit, are a recent invention of the IRS; they are designed to maximize the agency's return (gaining data and assessing compliance) on its investigation efforts. The IRS stated that its exempt organizations examination and compliance-check processes are among the "variety of tools at [the agency's] disposal to make certain that tax-exempt organizations comply with federal tax law designed to ensure they are entitled to any tax exemption they may claim."

Usually, in the commencement of these projects, the IRS contacts exempt organizations only by mail to obtain information pertaining to the particular issue. An exempt organization has a greater chance of being a compliance check target than the subject of a conventional audit. A compliance check, however, can blossom into an examination.

Recent compliance check projects have focused on executive compensation, political campaign activities by public charities, hospitals' compliance with criteria for their exemption, intermediate sanctions reporting, tax-exempt bond financing, community foundations' law compliance, various aspects of the operations of colleges and university, public charities with large fundraising costs, and exempt organizations with considerable unrelated business income.

Reference Resources

An extensive set of nonprofit law and IRS readings, references, and resource materials, including updates that become available subsequent to the publication of this book, is available at the Internet resource website that offers supplementary premium content for this *Handbook*.

CHAPTER THREE

THE CHANGING CONTEXT OF NONPROFIT MANAGEMENT IN THE UNITED STATES

Brent Never

The nonprofit sector in the United States is not well understood by the average nonprofit leader or employee, much less by the average citizen. My task in this chapter is to provide a foundation for understanding the nature of the sector in America today, explain the context within which the sector operates, and offer some observations about how the sector may continue to evolve and change in the coming five to ten years. It is within this context that nonprofit organizations continue to grow and develop, and it is within this context that the leaders and managers of the nonprofit sector will engage in their work of leading, managing, and operating their organizations.

Introduction

Metaphors are often used in organization theory to describe how sectors evolve over time. Sometimes, organization populations are like animals on the Serengeti, flexing in size as the local water pool increases or decreases. Other times, organizations are like amoeba, moving gradually across the landscape, largely immune to the hustle and bustle of the environment. Since the 1980s, many scholars have become enamored with the metaphor of an "iron cage" that tightly bounds organizations by the institutional constraints of society at large. Metaphors are wonderful tools to focus our attention on important dynamics when the world seems too complex to comprehend. At the same time, they can go too far and steer us away from understanding nuance and the details that inform why human beings make the choices they do. This chapter discusses the dynamics of today's nonprofit sector while pointing out the nuance in how the American nonprofit sector has reacted to very real constraints. The sector is neither an antelope nor an amoeba, but perhaps a willow tree that bends in seemingly unbearable headwinds yet does not break. It is resilient in the face of many challenges (Salamon, 2012), yet is so rooted in the fabric of American society that it continues to grow.

My job in this chapter is to provide context for the current state of the American nonprofit sector—a significant sector that constitutes about 10 percent of the American labor force (Salamon, 2012, p. 8)—and discuss how it might evolve in the near future. First, I present a broad overview of what we know about the sector and, perhaps more important, what we do not know. Like an iceberg, what we can see above the water line is a mere sliver of the entire sector (Smith, 1997). Second, I consider the relationship of the nonprofit sector to the constraints it faces. In particular, I look at how public and private funding sources can shape the choices of nonprofit managers. I use three central questions to organize this discussion: How? Why? and Where? Over time we have changed in how we focus on nonprofit organizations, with a new question dominating each era of study. Next, I look at the challenges and opportunities for the sector. Last, I conclude with thoughts about how this resilient sector will look in the future. The central idea that undergirds the nonprofit sector is that formal rules and informal norms channel behavior such that the look of the sector today is the result of how these channels have developed, and that the future scope will be largely shaped by the constraints that are being instituted today. Nonprofit organizations work within a dense matrix of expectations and, while innovation and entrepreneurship are prized, the rules of the game continue to shape what nonprofits are able to accomplish.

I encourage you to consider this information in the context of your own knowledge of nonprofit organizations. Does this information ring true for you? Do you come to similar conclusions as to the pressures that your organizations face? One of the most exciting aspects of studying nonprofit management today is that experts are still trying to grapple with what it is, how it acts, and what it will be. So your interpretation is valuable.

The Nonprofit Sector in America

Many Americans have difficulty giving an example of a nonprofit organization but, if pushed, might offer an example such as the American Red Cross or the YMCA. Most would be staggered by the idea that there are 1.18 million registered nonprofit public charities in the United States, with an additional 95,992 private foundations (National Center for Charitable Statistics [NCCS], 2015). Add in 83,827 501(c)(4) social welfare organizations, that are becoming increasingly important in political campaigns, plus 45,783 fraternal beneficiary societies, 1,844 state-chartered credit unions, and even 8,958 cemetery companies, and pretty soon they are amazed at the scope and breadth of the sector. Nonprofits are instrumental in an American's life from cradle to grave. One can be born in a nonprofit hospital, attend a nonprofit preschool, participate in a nonprofit basketball league, be educated at a nonprofit university, join a nonprofit parent-teacher organization, move on to being a member of the American Association of Retired People, be housed at a nonprofit nursing home, and maybe even be given hospice care by a nonprofit palliative-care organization. Using the lens of what is called the three-sector theory, nonprofits in America exist because they either address a market failure (such as youth development for disadvantaged youth) or they provide supplementary services for which the voting public does not wish to pay (such as a symphony) (Steinberg, 2006). While market failures exist throughout the world, Americans have a long tradition of turning away from government for providing services; the large, dynamic nonprofit sector provides that crucial bridge that may be provided by the state in other societies.

One of the most important insights about the American nonprofit sector is that there has always been a dynamic relationship between the top-down structures put in place by society (today these are formal laws but, as Hall explains in Chapter One of this *Handbook*, America has always had strong informal societal norms influenced by religious teachings) and the bottom-up desire of Americans to fulfill their expressive, advocacy, and service needs through organizations that are non-government and also non-market. Observers have marveled for centuries about how Americans self-organize themselves at every turn, ranging from the abolitionist societies of the early nineteenth century to the Tea Party organizations of the early 21st Century. Alexis de Tocqueville (2003 [1835])) observed that Americans have a fundamental belief in the democratic ideal whereby all ideas have potential merit, with organizational forms following to fulfill these ideas. Americans for centuries have believed in the ethic popularized by the movie *Field of Dreams* (1989): "If you build it, they will come." We continue to see this today, with the tremendous growth in nonprofit organizations. From 1995 to 2015, the number of nonprofit organizations (inclusive of public charities and other 501(c) organizations) has grown by 45 percent; in that same period, public charities have increased in number from 576,133 organizations to 1,182,187, or a 105 percent increase (National Center for Charitable Statistics, 2015).

The inductive nature of creating nonprofit organizations also has a seemingly dark side: nonprofit death. While Americans have a proclivity to create nonprofit organizations, they also let them die with tremendous frequency. When using the IRS Exempt Organization Master File, we find that from 2005 to 2014 we created 503,212 nonprofit organizations, yet 578,835 died or were dropped from the database (McLean, 2014). This results in undeniable disruption for those employed by these organizations (although the majority of the organizations are small and have few or no paid employees), and the millions of Americans who rely on their services (Never, 2013). But it is this continual churn of organizational birth and death that leads to a dynamic sector that continually reinvents itself as needs evolve.

This democratic stance toward organizational creation is commendable, but it does not entirely explain the nature of the American nonprofit sector today. The type of organizations that we have is also determined by the legal framework that incentivizes the creation of new nonprofit organizations (see Chapter Two by Hopkins and Gross for an explanation of the U.S. nonprofit legal framework). In the United States, the costs of creating a nonprofit organization are very low (for example, a nominal fee for incorporation with a state and a small amount of paperwork to be filed with and processed by the Internal Revenue Service). The benefits to creating a nonprofit can be large, particularly the benefits of tax exemption for all nonprofits and tax deductions for many donors to 501(c)(3) public charities. This basic framework provides an impetus for Americans to be great organizational creators (Hammack, 2002). So, in the end, the nonprofit sector is a legal creation that gives form and support for a great American democratic impulse.

What Is the Nonprofit Sector?

What is the nonprofit sector? The answer is at least as complex as the answer to the question What is the business sector? As Hopkins and Gross indicate, nonprofit organizations are legal creations, but for the purposes of this chapter I will explore how the legal framework defining different types of nonprofit organization affects what we know about the American nonprofit sector, which comes from two sources: from states, where we find nonprofit incorporation filings, and from the U.S. Internal Revenue Service, where we find tax returns. Most nonprofits (but notably not congregations, such as churches and synagogues) incorporate within their home states. The information that we can garner from state incorporations is highly variable based on the state. Perhaps the most important information that we see is the "birth" of an organization, as incorporation is usually the first step in creating a nonprofit. Many organizations will incorporate but will not apply for nonprofit tax-exempt status for a long time; sometimes organization members do not seek donations, so there is no need for nonprofit tax-deductions, while other times the seeming hassle of applying for exempt status precludes this action. Given that scholars would have to seek incorporation records from every state in order to have a full national picture of nonprofit birth, we see less scholarship using incorporation.

One of the most influential datasets that we have about American nonprofits is the IRS tax records, which are based on the organizations' filings of Forms 990. Because our most systematic information about registered nonprofits comes from a tax agency, it is unsurprising that what we know about nonprofits is largely limited to financial matters. The data was digitized in the early 1990s, meaning that scholars could begin to work directly with the data from the returns. It is surprising to think that the nonprofit sector is incredibly important in our lives (our faith institutions, schools, hospitals, and arts organizations are often nonprofits), yet in many ways we only have a hazy vision of the scope of the sector. For example, Kirsten Grønbjerg and her Indiana Nonprofit Project team spent over fifteen years mapping the sector in one state, yet there continue to be holes in our knowledge. It is important to consider how our picture of the sector, drawn from IRS 990 tax returns, is fuzzy and potentially inaccurate. First, full financial data is only available for 501(c)(3) public charities and public foundations included in the publicly available database. Second, a somewhat limited set of organizations is required to file an annual Form 990 (or the Form 990-EZ). Public charities with gross receipts over $200,000 must file the regular Form 990, and those with revenues from $50,000 to $199,999 are required to file the shorter Form 990-EZ.[1] What this means is that the very smallest organizations, with revenues below $50,000, only file the Form 990-N (or e-postcard). This form only indicates that the organization indeed does exist but gathers no other data. Congregations—churches, synagogues, mosques, and others—are not required to file with the IRS. Last, organizations that simply do not want to qualify for the charitable tax deduction also need not file. This is becoming an increasingly actively used strategy as some social enterprises seek other legal forms (see Chapter Twelve for more discussion of this aspect of nonprofit development). Smith (1997) estimates that upwards of 90 percent of nonprofit associations are not accounted for in the NCCS database.

Public Charities. Public charities are organizations that address one of approximately a dozen exempt purposes and exist to provide a public benefit. In exchange for this public benefit, the organizations receive tax-exempt and tax-deductible status (see Chapter Two for more explanation of this status). Using the Form 990 tax returns, we see that human service organizations comprise about one-third of all public charities (see Table 3.1). Human services is a diverse category including youth services, vocational training, recreation and sports, housing, legal services, and a category for general human services where one finds organizations that provide a range of services, such as the YMCA. Education (preschool, education services, and higher education) is the next largest category (17.3 percent), followed by health (11.8 percent). Public and societal benefit organizations (11.3 percent) are civil rights, community improvement, philanthropy and voluntarism, science and technology, and general public benefit organizations. The variation within the categories is large, not to speak of the great diversity of organizations across categories, making comparisons very difficult.

It is important to understand that, for every organization type listed in the table, there will be many sub-types with quite different characteristics. For example, among the 45,155 health organizations there are 4,220 hospitals. There is exceptional diversity even among these hospitals. For example, these

TABLE 3.1. Types of Nonprofit Organization (2013)

Organization Type	Number	Percentage
Arts, Culture, and Humanities	40,940	10.7
Education	66,059	17.3
Environment	18,306	4.8
Health	45,155	11.8
Human Services	129,611	33.9
International	8,897	2.3
Mutual Benefit	1,017	0.3
Public and Societal Benefit	43,347	11.3
Religion	28,525	7.5
Unknown	537	0.1
Total	382,934	

Source: National Center for Charitable Statistics, 2015.

hospitals range in annual revenue from $4.68 billion at the Cleveland Clinic to $27,565 at the Community Health Center of Western Illinois (National Center for Charitable Statistics, 2015). Interestingly, residential mental health facilities and reproductive health facilities are not in the health category. Likewise, education organizations range from exceptionally large universities (Harvard University, with annual revenues of $5.8 billion) to very small community preschools (such as the Rainbow Corners Nursery School, with annual revenues of $0). It becomes very hard to talk about education nonprofit organizations without being very specific about niche, whether it be a subfield (such as school auxiliaries like parent-teacher organizations) or location (such as nursery schools in Cleveland).

There is a particular challenge in identifying and knowing much about religious congregations in the United States, even though they constitute the largest category of recipients of individual philanthropy in America. Congregations have been essential to American nonprofit organizational development from the very first settlements in the British colonies. With that said, the Free Exercise clause of the First Amendment of the U.S. Bill of Rights has in effect caused a distinct separation between the conduct of the government and the conduct of congregations. The IRS has made only very limited attempts to regulate congregational affairs and has erred on the side of not requiring documentation of congregational activities, revenues, and expenses and, hence, we have limited sector-wide governmental data on congregations. Data sources do exist, such as the Association of Religion Data Archives (www.thearda.com) and the Association of Statisticians for American Religious Bodies (www.asarb.org). Since 1952 there has been a decennial census of American congregations, with the 2010 iteration showing 344,894 congregations and 150.7 million adherents representing 48.8 percent of the U.S. population (Grammich, Hadaway, Houseal, Jones, Krindatch, Stanley, and Taylor, 2012). Many scholars have chronicled the linkage between congregations and voluntary action (Cnaan, Kasternakis, and Wineburg, 1993; Grønbjerg and Never, 2004), although a comprehensive assessment of the impact of congregations on American life has been a particular challenge.

Private Foundations. Private foundations hold a large and perhaps outsized image in the minds of Americans. The category of foundations can be divided into different types of private grant-making foundations (for example, corporate foundations, private independent foundations, private operating foundations) as well as public foundations (such as community foundations). Overall, there were just under 96,000 foundations in the United States in 2013, giving an estimated $54.7 billion to charitable causes that year (Foundation Center, 2014).

The largest private independent foundation in the United States is the Bill & Melinda Gates Foundation, which had total assets valued at $41.3 billion in 2013 and gave more than $3.2 billion in 2012 (NCCS, 2015). While the amount of foundation giving is important, context is necessary to understand the relative size or magnitude of the resources that come from foundations. For example, the total of all U.S. foundation giving in 2013 ($54.7 billion) is dramatically less than the 2016 budget request for the U.S. federal government, which was $3.99 trillion (Office of Management and Budget, 2015). Thus, while the foundation segment of the U.S. nonprofit sector is a significant part of the revenue puzzle for many public charities, it is not a sufficient piece to fund most or all service delivery for the vast majority. Salamon (1987) has articulated well the problem of philanthropic insufficiency: no matter how generous we are as a society, we simply do not give enough to scale nonprofit services large enough to achieve impact. Foundations often will leverage their limited resources to create outsized effects, yet it also is true that foundations cannot provide the funding necessary to take up the slack when the public sector withdraws from funding service delivery.

Big Questions for Nonprofit Leaders

Funding has shifted significantly for nonprofit organizations in the US since the mid-1980s. As Salamon and Lund (1984) report, the "Reagan Revolution" of that era championed the cutting of federal funding for social services. In the 1990s, there was a further movement toward contracting out services, with governments at all levels opting to move the production of human services to private providers, nonprofit and otherwise. Government funding remains an essential revenue source for human service organizations (see Chapter Twenty of this *Handbook* for an extensive discussion of the nature and dynamics of government contracting with nonprofits for delivery of services), yet there are tough questions from public-sector leaders about the role of government in supporting these services. Here I summarize the evolution in the nature of the questions that have been asked about the role of government in funding of nonprofit service delivery in the United States.

The Johnson Administration (1963–1969) championed the War on Poverty, and through the Social Security Amendments (1965), sought the help of the nonprofit sector in extending services to disadvantaged populations. The precipitous growth of the human service segment of the nonprofit sector tracked with an increased support among Americans for the position that public monies should go to supporting those most at risk, and the nonprofit sector was well positioned to grow with this support (Smith and Lipsky, 1993). Funders' chief question at the time was "how": How are nonprofits going to provide the necessary services? The Nixon Administration highlighted that government was unable to handle the complexity of poverty, which enhanced the impetus toward other providers using government money to address need. *How* is the question that is most appropriate when the funding is sufficient. Government officials seek to understand how providers will be better able to address social problems than government would itself.

The "Reagan Revolution" in the United States in the 1980s was predicated on a fundamental reordering of priorities about the role of government and, in particular, the federal government, in the lives of all Americans. President Reagan, in his First Inaugural Address in 1981, communicated the view that the national government was outsized in its influence on Americans and ultimately impeded ordinary citizens from achieving whatever they would like to achieve. The result of this "revolution" was a movement of funding away from nondefense nondiscretionary purposes. The block grants that were the cornerstone of federal funding for human services in the 1970s were seen as excessive federal largesse and the philosophy was that states and local communities should take charge of how their own public monies were spent. The key question of this time was "*why*": Why should government support a particular program? The "how" question that was important in the previous generation became less prominent because sufficient funds for programs were not there. To be successful in this environment, nonprofit leaders needed to articulate that their work remained important to the common weal before they explained how they could perform these services.

The 1990s brought a twist to the Reagan Revolution, this time with the Democratic Clinton Administration leading the charge. The federal government had downsized and, it was said, needed to become both efficient and nimble. The reinvention movement, popularly conceptualized by David Osborne and Ted Gaebler (1992) and championed by Vice President Al Gore, also emerged at this time, in response to the perceived need for government to be responsive to the people. Three large changes resulted. First was a focus on continuing the movement toward third-party service provision. Second was a movement toward accountability for both government and its contractors. And third, there was increased pressure for the enhancement of consumer (citizen) choice of services.

Third-party service provision, from the standpoint of the nonprofit sector, continued to open avenues for great government support for nonprofits. While the Reagan Administration wanted to see less government production of services, which came from an ideological belief that smaller government unleashes the potential for private-sector development, the reinvention movement focused on the power of competition to lower costs and increase responsiveness to citizen needs. With the focus on competition came an agnostic view as to the type of provider; it was equally acceptable for the provider to be in either the nonprofit or for-profit sector. The health, vocational training, and daycare fields were opened to for-profit as well as nonprofit service providers, pushing nonprofit organizations to consider not only how they serve their clients but also whether their services were competitive with what other organizations (other nonprofits as well as for-profits) could produce. Contracts, by which payments flow when services are rendered within the agreed-to scope, became more prevalent; as opposed to grants that typically supported the general functioning of an organization. Service contractors would have less latitude as to how they produced services.

Pushes for accountability fell on the shoulders of both the government contracting agencies and the private contractors under these conditions. A signature piece of legislation, the Government Performance and Results Act (GPRA) of 1993, required government agencies to determine long-term strategic goals and create performance systems to reach those goals. Using this approach, government would be required to prove that it accomplished its goals efficiently and, ultimately, effectively. In an era of third-party service provision, this meant a strong focus on the accountability of contractors. Performance-based contracting filtered down to nonprofit contractors that typically worked in complex and difficult mission fields, where the results of the work often are much more difficult to assess or prove. For example, areas as complicated as vocational training and career services for welfare recipients, where preparing unskilled workers for the workforce can require interventions beyond simple training (perhaps ranging from childcare to substance abuse treatment), were now subject to rigorous accountability measures that would determine whether the contractor would receive future contracts. For nonprofits, the technical aspects of contract development and administration as well as program evaluation were barriers for those organizations that could not hire employees with the right skills, contract evaluation out, or provide the funding to develop employees from within. As Salamon (2012) reports, at this period training in nonprofit management became more prevalent due to a need for technically competent personnel able to navigate the increasingly complex funding environment.

Further, reinvention was predicated on the idea that citizens are consumers of services and need to be treated as clients. This means that service recipients should have choice. With competition at the ideological core of reinvention, consumers will be able to choose those services that fulfill their needs. For some, this would mean that services are located closer or are provided by employees who look like them, while for others this could mean access to a broader array of offerings. Two approaches have been used to encourage consumer choice (Salamon, 2002). One is the use of vouchers, such as in child daycare services, where parents can choose a provider accepting vouchers that best maximizes whatever values that they see fit: convenience, quality, comprehensiveness, and so forth. The second is government-supported fees-for-service. The most common example is Medicaid insurance for poor individuals. Medicaid recipients can choose a medical provider (that must be willing to accept Medicaid payment), and the reimbursement for services flows directly from the Medicaid administrator to the provider organization. This type of system required a paradigm shift for nonprofit service providers, moving from simply receiving clients who came through the door to actively competing to attract those clients. The funding only flows to an organization if an individual chooses it, and competitors often are in the private sector where marketing has been practiced for decades. Nonprofits needed to focus on identifying potential clients, determine the modality of communication that would best resonate, and then actually attract those clients to the service.

The Great Recession (2007–2009) has had a profound effect on how Americans feel about government, and the question of "why" has become prevalent. Throughout the recession itself, the federal government used spending as a means to both support economic activity (such as transportation construction) and deliver services for those most impacted. The American Recovery and Reinvestment Act (ARRA) of 2009, commonly known as the stimulus bill, was one of the very first responses from the Obama Administration. While derided by some as an unorganized mish-mash of government largesse, ARRA did provide funding for human services that eventually were provided by nonprofit service producers: vocational rehabilitation for disabled individuals ($540 million), job training to those who lost jobs to outsourcing ($1.6 billion), commodities for food banks ($150 million), meals for adult and child daycare ($100 million), extension of welfare (Temporary Assistance to Needy Families or TANF) payments to states ($2.4 billion), and temporary support for increased Medicaid spending ($90 billion) (*The Wall Street Journal*, 2009). There was a sense that nonprofit organizations had a special and important role in aiding the truly disadvantaged, partly because they were the most able to move resources and services out to communities.

State governments had a different initial experience with the recession. Because the federal government is able to run a deficit, it is uniquely positioned to stimulate economic activity in the near term and then consider the consequences of that deficit spending in the longer term. States, which must balance their budgets every year, largely rely on property, income, and sales taxes. Revenues from all three types of taxes were hard hit by the recession, with areas where real estate values plummeted being particularly affected. Although some ARRA money did flow to and through states, the impact of the shortfall of tax revenues was almost immediate. What this meant for the states' contractors, both nonprofit and for-profit, was slow payment for services rendered, slow enactment of contracts and, ultimately, decreased resources for future contracts. The Urban Institute, in its national survey of nonprofit human service organizations in 2009, found that 50 percent of nonprofits froze or reduced salaries, 39 percent were forced to draw on reserves, and 38 percent laid off employees (Boris, de Leon, Roeger, and Nikolova, 2010a, p. 19). The impacts were not even across states. For example, 72 percent of Illinois nonprofits experienced late payments, as compared to 24 percent of Texas nonprofits (Boris, de Leon, Roeger, and Nikolova, 2010b, p. 116). In particular, states that had fewer economic difficulties (such as those benefiting from the fracking revolution in oil drilling) were able to better support their contractors. Unfortunately, this broadly mirrored the strength of the economies in these states, with those having the worst problems also having the most difficulty in fulfilling their contract obligations.

The difficulties throughout the funding environment served to highlight the impact of the reinvention movement on the human services sector in particular. Boris, de Leon, Roeger, and Nikolova (2010a, p. 9) found that 53 percent of human service nonprofits have cost-reimbursable government contracts, the most common type of contract. Cost-reimbursable contracts in practice mean that nonprofits bear the initial cost of providing a service (human, physical, and financial capital) and then apply for reimbursement. As states extended the timeline for reimbursement, nonprofit contractors were forced to bear those medium-term costs. Sixty-eight percent of respondents found that government payments not fully covering the costs of contracted services was a problem (Boris, de Leon, Roeger, and Nikolova, 2010a, p. 13). Typically, nonprofit organizations are able to cross-subsidize the provision of services, with those services not fully covered by contracts being subsidized by other revenue streams such as individual donations. As the recession lengthened, contracts became even harder to support with those other revenues. The complexity of contracting also was a drain on nonprofit contractors: 76 percent of respondents felt that the complexity and time required to report on government contracts was a problem; 76 percent also felt the same about the application process (Boris, de Leon, Roeger, and Nikolova, 2010a, p. 13).

Even though the recession officially ended in 2009, its impacts on government funding were more long-lasting. For states, this has been particularly pronounced and is acutely felt by many, even in 2016. Given the dependence on property and income taxes, states with sluggish real estate or labor markets continue to face the need to cut. Many states have determined that, given many competing demands, human services are of less importance than education or criminal justice, and they have decreased their funding for human services. One type of funding has increased significantly, and that is Medicaid spending in the thirty-two states that opted to expand their coverage under the Affordable Care Act. The resulting pass-through money serves to support nonprofit community health centers and hospitals (and for-profit competitors, too), while in states without expansion these nonprofit health providers often must face the additional cost of serving those without insurance coverage.

The protracted nature of the economic slump across the country has helped to bring forward the question of '*why*': why does government need to be supporting particular services? Dennis Young (2006) developed a three-part way of categorizing how nonprofits interact with governments: complementary, supplementary, and adversary. Nonprofits act as complements to governments when they provide those services that government wants provided but either does not have the means or desire to produce. Governments use contracts and grants to move service production off of their books in these cases. Medical services for the poor, mental health care, substance-abuse treatment, and vocational training are all provided by nonprofits in a complementary manner. Supplementary services are those that government has decided not to support but communities might find valuable. In many cases, fine arts, reproductive services for the poor, and higher education are supplemental and provided by nonprofits. Last is the category of adversary organizations, those that are expressive in that they exist to communicate the feelings of citizens to their government. Social-movement organizations such as Greenpeace are in the adversary mode.

A great debate has occurred over the past five years as to what services currently provided in a complementary mode should be considered supplemental. One of the most visible debates has been around Medicaid expansion, with many states struggling with the question of why they must greatly expand medical coverage to poor individuals. The eighteen states that have decided to forego the expansion in effect are saying this care is supplemental and should be supported by other revenue sources. When a service such as this is declared supplemental, it almost always means that any service production will be done by a nonprofit because of the inherent market failure of trying to provide medical services to those unable to pay. Likewise, there is a vigorous debate about the place of higher education in the government-nonprofit relationship. Some states have decided to reinvigorate their investment in public (nonprofit) universities, while others have moved toward a supplementary stance, pushing those universities to either raise fees-for-service (tuition) or find additional private philanthropic support. Last, support for nonprofit arts organizations has firmly moved away from a complementary mode, with the National Endowment for the Arts funding in 1995 being $15 million more than in 2015 (even before taking inflation into account) (National Endowment for the Arts, n.d.).

Proponents of moving services traditionally produced by nonprofits to the supplementary mode have historically sought to draw on a great strength of the nonprofit sector: the ability to draw on the generosity of private philanthropy to support services that ultimately benefit communities. President H. W. Bush (1989–1993) articulated that there are a "thousand points of light," voluntary- and community-based efforts to improve the lives of our own communities. For almost four-hundred years, we have drawn on a strong American ethic of using private financial and human capital to build stronger communities. Americans are undeniably a generous society, but the key question is how generous. Key nonprofit fields rely extensively on government grants and contracts, and there is little doubt that private philanthropy would not be able to provide sufficient financial capital to serve community needs.

The "how" and "why" questions remain important, but I argue that the important question of the future is "where." The services that nonprofits produce, and the labor that volunteers give, are almost entirely place-based. It is hard to consider outsourcing mental-health counseling or child daycare from the United States to India (the commute would be atrocious!). While American for-profit corporations have experimented with outsourcing, the nonprofit sector is largely connected to communities. For decades, nonprofits have been selected for government support for the very reason that they are more connected to the communities that they serve and are able to move resources to the people who need them. The reinvention movement viewed contractors in general, and nonprofit contractors more specifically, as those local laboratories that exude a democratic ideal of being close to and of the neighborhoods they serve. With the advent of welfare reform in 1996, President Clinton affirmed that faith-based organizations are uniquely situated to use deep community connections in addressing some of society's most intractable problems, and the commitment of the federal government to support faith-based organizations has become deeper during the Bush and Obama Administrations. In a different vein, President Obama has drawn on the excitement for social enterprise by creating the Office of Social Innovation and Civic Participation, with the idea that new, innovative enterprises would be able to quickly scale to address some of the challenging problems that have dogged communities for decades. Social enterprise can span from nonprofit to for-profit solutions, yet many are place-based.

The "where" question is a difficult one. Being fundamentally place-based, nonprofits are well-positioned to understand their clients. Often, the program staff also live in the community, with localized knowledge being a treasured commodity. At the same time, many community-based nonprofits rely on gut instinct to think about the "where" question, rather than using data to understand client needs and location. While the software tools needed to analyze geography are becoming more intuitive and cheaper (with several open-source options), nonprofit leaders have not had to traditionally focus on "where." The previous generation of stakeholder demands focused on efficiency and effectiveness, meaning that the limited funding available for capacity development has gone toward performance measurement. Major corporations enlist entire teams of geographic information systems (GIS) analysts to determine the best location for a pharmacy, grocery store, or fast-food outlet because place-based services, such as selling hamburgers, means that success can be determined by careful analyses of place. Most nonprofits do not have this capacity; perhaps only the largest hospital systems and universities have in-house GIS expertise. The federal and state governments have less funding to support human services and are beginning to ask where they should be putting these limited dollars. Likewise, foundations and individual philanthropists are beginning to be savvier about wanting to know where their money is going.

Place-based initiatives are as old as Jane Addams' Hull House of the 19th Century, yet they have reached a new level of importance for public policy and foundation leaders (Hopkins and Ferris, 2015). At the heart of initiatives such as the Harlem Children Zone is the confluence of answers to the "how," "why," and "where" questions. How? By creating a small, geographically designed focus area, they are able to concentrate resources on multifaceted challenges. Why? Because up to this point, public solutions have failed and there is a market failure such that private providers will not enter into the market. Where? A section of Harlem, New York, with an even smaller subset of school-aged children and their families. Nonprofits can capitalize on bringing together answers to all three of these questions.

There is a negative side to the "where" question. The American system of human service and health service delivery for the disadvantaged is largely a patchwork of nonprofit producers that follow the spatial contours of public policy and private philanthropy. States that expanded Medicaid stand to have stronger systems of nonprofit and for-profit health providers, compared with those that did not. Communities with wealth are more likely to generate private philanthropy for human services. For example, many would be surprised to know that the largest community foundation in the country is located in Tulsa, Oklahoma, home to a large petroleum industry. Thus, the spatial patterning of nonprofits is not equal, even taking population density into account (Never, 2014). When we examine the expenditures of human service nonprofits on a county-by-county basis across the United States (data drawn from the NCCS Core Files) and consider how each county's expenditures compare with the national average it becomes quite apparent that there is a pronounced state-level effect that largely separates those states in the north-eastern United States from the rest of the country. This mirrors the history of the development of the sector, with support for human services being prevalent in the industrialized north for a century. States in this region tend to be supportive of Democratic presidential candidates and policies that comparatively support investment in human services.

In many ways, the American system of human, health, and higher-education service delivery is privately produced (both nonprofit and for-profit producers) and to a certain extent publicly financed. It capitalizes on competition to create more choice for the most disadvantaged. One could also look at the system as fragmented and unequal. With publicly produced services—such as street sweeping, education, parks—the question of location can have a fundamental place in the political discussion about service provision. If one street is plowed and the next one is not, a city councilperson can count on a complaint. Likewise, discussions about closing publicly produced services such as schools or health clinics can be met with loud protest. With third-party delivery, in particular when working with disadvantaged populations, there is an additional level between the end-users and the funding body. The result is a chance for clients to lose their voice in evaluating service producers.

Not all nonprofits are created equally, and not all are equally strong. As the experience of the Great Recession shows, some nonprofit contractors are better able to weather the difficult times than others are. Financial health is a significant issue. Many scholars have used accounting ratios developed in the private banking industry to assess the financial health of nonprofits. When using these assessments, we find there is a strong likelihood for financially sick nonprofits to be less able to deliver the same quality of services as those that are financially strong. I have documented an important aspect of this problem in a 2014 study. I mapped the locations of financially distressed human service nonprofits

(2007–2009) and found a significant relationship between the percent of minority population in a Census tract and the number of distressed nonprofits (Never, 2013). This leads to several questions: Are we funding those nonprofits located in minority communities at a level that would be commensurate with a majority community locality? Does a decentralized system lend itself to an unequal provision of quality services to minority populations? Should funders be building the capacity of organizations serving minority communities? These questions have yet to be addressed by public leaders.

Challenges and Opportunities for the Future

Nonprofit organizations have become deeply and inextricably woven into the fabric of our society. While not always recognized by the general public, nonprofit organizations represent a cradle-to-grave response to societal problems, moving from daycare and preschool to youth soccer leagues, colleges and universities, hospitals and community health centers, substance-abuse treatment, legal aid, and hospice care. Many visitors to the United States, especially since the travels and writings of Alexis de Tocqueville, are befuddled by how much we Americans rely on the nonprofit sector to perform functions that are performed by the state elsewhere in the world. To add another level of complexity, we see that, even though many nonprofits that provide public services are private-sector organizations, a primary mechanism for supporting their service delivery is public funding. This hybrid system allows for great variation and innovation, yet many challenges and opportunities lie ahead for nonprofit organizations in America.

Challenges

A challenge that also is an opportunity is the ongoing debate about the "why" question: Why should government be involved in education, health, or human services? Americans have always had a strong commitment to libertarian ideals, yet the Tea Party Movement (and yes, nonprofit organizations affiliated with the movement) has captured the attention of millions of Americans. The movement is predicated on the idea that government should not directly produce most services and that it should greatly scale back its funding for services produced by contractors. Nonprofit organizations may stand to lose access to government funding as this debate progresses to policy decisions, yet societal problems will not go away and will require the use of experts grounded in the community to continue to address them. A continued challenge of this type for the sector is to illustrate that it offers a means to provide quality services efficiently and directly to those most in need. The opportunity is that, in many mission categories, the private sector does not have the expertise or the inclination to compete against nonprofit organizations.

A second challenge is the fact that public funding increasingly comes with strings attached. During the recent recession, nonprofits faced the reality that government contracts often did not fully cover the cost of providing the service. While this has always been a reality, with nonprofits able to turn to private philanthropy (individual and foundation-based), a focus on accountability has increased the costs not directly tied to service provision—costs such as credentialing and licensure, program evaluation and reporting, and the continual need to search for new revenue streams. These costs are important. At the same time, there is a pressure from the public-at-large and channeled through charity watchdogs such as Charity Navigator to decrease the share of resources going to administrative overhead and increase the share going to programming (Lecy and Searing, 2015). Government grants and contracts have signaled stability and credibility, but nonprofit leaders will have to determine whether seeking them is worth these increasing costs.

A final challenge is the increased competition that the sector faces from for-profit and hybrid social enterprises. In arenas where market failure is prevalent, nonprofits were the go-to solution. Increasingly, private-sector organizations have become key players in domains in which government funding can be used to make providing services profitable. For example, hospice care is increasingly provided by for-profit franchises as Medicare covers the service costs at an attractive rate. But the new challenge comes from social enterprises that may or may not be nonprofits. For-profit enterprises such as B Corporations, L3Cs, and other LLC forms have captured the imaginations of many social entrepreneurs and consumers alike. Organizations of these other forms are able to access certain forms of financial capital in ways that allows them to be more flexible and nimble, as compared with nonprofits, which are traditionally limited to public contracts and private philanthropy. It remains to be seen the extent to which these forms will become prevalent in providing solutions to societal problems, but they will be part of the discussion for which nonprofits will need an answer.

Opportunities

There are, no doubt, many challenges but, as Salamon (2012) articulates, the nonprofit sector is a resilient sector. The opportunities spring from the unique position of nonprofit organizations in our communities and the minds of our public leaders. The first opportunity comes from the fact that the American population is rapidly aging. Over 10,000 "Baby Boomers" in the United States are turning sixty-five every day. As the demographic bubble that the Boomers represent gets older, they will require more medical services that many times will be provided by nonprofits. More money will be spent by Medicare and Medicaid, leading to stable funding for the health and affiliated service organizations. Many older adults want to continue to live in their homes as long as possible, leading to greater needs for home health, Meals on Wheels, recreational programs, faith activities, and coordination services, all very likely to be provided by the nonprofit sector. Further, Baby Boomers include a large pool of skilled retirees who could be valuable volunteers, helping to expand the capacity of the sector they serve.

The next opportunity is due to the rising Millennial generation that increasingly feels the need to have social impact as a necessary part of any work activity. Nonprofits and other social enterprises present attractive employment opportunities for Millennials, as well as host sites for substantive volunteer engagement. This upcoming generation will also begin to rewrite the social contract with government, which may include a greater place for policies that support the most disadvantaged in society.

The final opportunity is borne out of the shift underway in many states as the nature of the nonprofit service relationship moves from the complementary to the supplementary mode. While government may not have the funding or the will to support services previously considered public, nonprofits remain uniquely positioned to allow citizens to maximize their preferences. For example, while federal arts funding has decreased, many metropolitan areas are seeing a boom in the visual and fine arts. Arts incubators, regional festivals, and small theaters that draw on private philanthropy not only generate support for arts development but ultimately can be key components for creating livable cities. In addition, nonprofits are able to receive tax-advantaged philanthropy, which is a particular benefit not available to the other forms of social enterprise.

Conclusion

There is no doubt that the nonprofit sector in the United States is multifaceted and resilient. It represents the democratic nature of America. If you have an idea, there are few barriers to you giving it a try. At the same time, one would be remiss to say that managing a nonprofit organization is simple. While there may be a low bar to entry, in order to thrive, organizational leaders need to be savvy as to the opportunities and constraints that are so essential to the development of the sector.

Government continues to be the cornerstone for how the sector develops. Government dictates how the nonprofit legal form exists and, increasingly importantly, how competing forms of social enterprise are allowed to function. The continued availability of tax exemption and tax deductibility means that nonprofit organizations continue to hold important advantages over rival forms but, at the same time, those tax benefits come at the cost of being beholden to governmental oversight. Nonprofits also remain in the public's eye, with continued criticism for excessive executive salaries and other perceived signs of excess. Government also continues to be a cornerstone of nonprofit funding, although this funding has moved toward government-reimbursed fee-for-service. Last, nonprofit leaders must increasingly question whether working with government merits the significant costs associated with accountability. Demands for accountability must be met with a technically proficient workforce able to systematically measure and report how organizations are impacting their communities.

The state of the nonprofit sector is in flux, but the place of nonprofit organizations in American life remains strongly fixed. Nonprofits fit well with the can-do attitude of the American narrative. America can be considered a generous society not only because Americans give a lot, but because of the strength of the sector to which Americans give. Without a vibrant nonprofit sector, giving would be for naught.

Note

1. All financial statistics reported in this chapter are presented in terms of U.S. dollars, unless otherwise noted.

References

Boris, E. T., de Leon, E., Roeger, K., and Nikolova, M. *Human Service Nonprofits and Government Collaboration: Findings from the 2010 National Survey of Nonprofit Government Contracting and Grants.* Washington, DC: The Urban Institute, 2010a.

Boris, E. T., de Leon, E., Roeger, K., and Nikolova, M. *National Study of Nonprofit-Government Contracting: State Profiles.* Washington, DC: The Urban Institute, 2010b.

Cnaan, R. A., Kasternakis, A., and Wineburg, R. J. Religious People, Religious Organizations, and Volunteerism in Human Services: Is There a Link? *Nonprofit and Voluntary Sector Quarterly,* 1993, 22, 33–51.

Foundation Center. Key Facts on U.S. Foundations, retrieved at http://foundationcenter
.org/gainknowledge/research/keyfacts2014/pdfs/Key_Facts_on_US_Foundations_
2014.pdf, 2014.

Grammich, C., Hadaway, K., Houseal, R., Jones, D. E., Krindatch, A., Stanley, R., and
Taylor, R. H. *2010 U.S. Religion Census: Religious Congregations & Membership Study*.
Kansas City, MO: Nazarene Publishing House, 2012.

Grønberg, K. A., and Never, B. The Role of Religious Networks and Other Factors in Types
of Volunteer Work. *Nonprofit Management & Leadership*, 2004, 14, 263–289.

Hammack, D. C. Nonprofit Organizations in American History: Research Opportunities
and Sources. *American Behavioral Scientist*, 2002, 45, 1638–1674.

Hopkins, E. M., and Ferris, J. M. (eds.). *Place-Based Initiatives in the Context of Public Policy
and Markets: Moving to Higher Ground*. Los Angeles: The Center on Philanthropy and
Public Policy, Sol Price Center for Social Innovation, University of Southern California,
2015.

Lecy, J. D., and Searing, E. "Anatomy of the Nonprofit Starvation Cycle: An Analysis of
Falling Overhead Ratios in the Nonprofit Sector." *Nonprofit and Voluntary Sector Quarterly*, 2015, 44, 539–563.

McLean, C. Vital Records: Births and Deaths in the Nonprofit Sector. *Nonprofit Quarterly*,
2014, 21, 4–8.

National Center for Charitable Statistics. NCCS Data Files. Washington, DC: Urban Institute, 2015.

National Endowment for the Arts. National Endowment for the Arts Appropriations
History. Retrieved at https://www.arts.gov/open-government/national-endowment-
arts-appropriations-history, n.d.

Never, B. Divergent Patterns of Nonprofit Financial Distress. *Nonprofit Policy Forum*, 2013,
5, 67–84.

Office of Management and Budget. *Fiscal Year 2016 Budget of the U.S. Government*.
Washington, DC: U.S. Government Printing Office, 2015.

Osborne, D., and Gaebler, T. *Reinventing Government: How the Entrepreneurial Spirit is Transforming the Public Sector*. New York: Plume, 1992.

Salamon, L. M. Partners in Public Service: The Scope and Theory of Government-
Nonprofit Relations. In W. W. Powell (ed.), *The Nonprofit Sector: A Research Handbook*.
New Haven, CT: Yale University Press, 1987.

Salamon, L. M. The New Governance and the Tools of Public Action: An Introduction. In
L. M. Salamon (ed.), *The Tools of Government: A Guide to the New Governance*. New York:
Oxford University Press, 2002.

Salamon, L. M. *The Resilient Sector: The State of Nonprofit America*. Washington, DC: Brookings Institution Press, 2003.

Salamon, L. M. The Resilient Sector: The Future of Nonprofit America. In L. Salamon
(ed.), *The State of Nonprofit America*. Washington, DC: Brookings Institution Press, 2012.

Salamon, L. M., and Lund, M. S. Governance in the Reagan Era: An Overview. In L. M.
Salamon and M. S. Lund (eds.), *The Reagan Presidency and the Governing of America*. Washington, DC: The Urban Institute, 1984.

Smith, D. H. The Rest of the Nonprofit Sector: Grassroots Associations as the Dark Matter
Ignored in Prevailing "Flat Earth" Maps of the Sector. *Nonprofit and Voluntary Sector
Quarterly*, 1997, 26, 114–131.

Smith, S. R., and Lipsky, M. *Nonprofits for Hire: The Welfare State in the Age of Contracting*. Cambridge, MA: Harvard University Press, 1993.

Steinberg, R. "Economic Theories of Nonprofit Organizations." In W. W. Powell and R. Steinberg (eds.), *The Nonprofit Sector: A Research Handbook*. (2nd ed.). New Haven, CT: Yale University Press. 2006.

Tocqueville, A. de. *Democracy in America*. London, UK: Penguin Classics, 2003 [1835]).

The Wall Street Journal. Getting to $787 Billion. Retrieved from http://online.wsj.com/public/resources/documents/STIMULUS_FINAL_0217.html, 2009.

Young, D. R. Complementary, Supplementary, or Adversarial? Nonprofit-Government Relations. In E. T. Boris and C. E. Steuerle (eds.), *Nonprofits and Government: Collaboration and Conflict*. (2nd ed.) Washington, DC: The Urban Institute Press, 2006.

CHAPTER FOUR

THE MANY FACES OF NONPROFIT ACCOUNTABILITY*

Alnoor Ebrahim

Calls for greater accountability are not new. Leaders of organizations, be they nonprofit, business, or government, face a constant stream of demands from various constituents for accountable behavior. But what does it mean to be accountable?

At its core, accountability is about trust. By and large, nonprofit leaders tend to pay attention to accountability once a problem of trust arises—a scandal in the sector or in their own organization, questions from citizens or donors who want to know whether their money is being well spent, or pressure from regulators to demonstrate that they are serving a public purpose and thus merit tax-exempt status. Amid this clamor for accountability, it is tempting to accept the popular normative view that more accountability is better. But is it feasible, or even desirable, for nonprofit organizations to be accountable to everyone for everything? The challenge for leadership and management is to prioritize among competing accountability demands. This involves deciding both *to whom* and *for what* they owe accountability. The purpose of this chapter is to provide an overview of the current debates on nonprofit accountability while also examining the trade-offs inherent in a range of accountability mechanisms.

---

*This chapter is a much expanded and revised version of an entry that was first published in the *International Encyclopedia of Civil Society* (Ebrahim, 2010).

Numerous definitions of accountability have been offered by scholars and practitioners in the nonprofit and nongovernmental sector. Many describe accountability in terms of a "process of holding actors responsible for actions" (Fox and Brown, 1998, p. 12) or as "the means by which individuals and organizations report to a recognized authority (or authorities) and are held responsible for their actions" (Edwards and Hulme, 1996b, p. 967). The literature further identifies four core components of accountability (Ebrahim and Weisband, 2007):

1. *Transparency,* which involves collecting information and making it available and accessible for public scrutiny
2. *Answerability or justification,* which requires providing clear reasoning for actions and decisions, including those not adopted, so that they may reasonably be questioned
3. *Compliance,* through the monitoring and evaluation of procedures and outcomes, combined with transparency in reporting those findings
4. *Enforcement or sanctions* for shortfalls in compliance, justification, or transparency

For many observers, it is enforceability that ultimately gives any accountability mechanism power or "teeth." Other observers, however, find such an approach to be too narrow in its dependence on punitive forms of compliance. They broaden this perspective by suggesting that accountability is not just about responding to others but also about "taking responsibility" for oneself (Cornwall, Lucas, and Pasteur, 2001, p. 3). As such, accountability has both an *external* dimension in terms of "an obligation to meet prescribed standards of behavior" (Chisolm, 1995, p. 141) and an *internal* one motivated by "felt responsibility" as expressed through individual action and organizational mission (Fry, 1995). For example, the One World Trust in the United Kingdom, which assesses the accountability of large global organizations—multinational corporations, international NGOs, and intergovernmental agencies—defines accountability as "the processes through which an organization makes a commitment to respond to and balance the needs of stakeholders in its decision making processes and activities, and delivers against this commitment" (Lloyd, Oatham, and Hammer, 2007, p. 11).

At the very least, what the preceding definitions share is an understanding that accountability centers on the relationships among various actors, with some giving accounts of their behavior and others receiving and judging those accounts. Most discussions about the concept thus also pose two further questions: Accountability to whom? And accountability for what?

Accountability to Whom?

Accountability relationships are complicated by the fact that nonprofits are expected to be accountable to multiple actors: upward to their funders or patrons, downward to clients, and internally to themselves and their missions (Edwards and Hulme, 1996a; Kearns, 1996; Lindenberg and Bryant, 2001; Najam, 1996). "Upward" accountability usually refers to relationships with donors, foundations, and governments and is often focused on the use of funds. Accountability to clients refers primarily to "downward" relationships with groups receiving services, although it may also include communities or regions indirectly impacted by nonprofit programs. The third category of accountability concerns nonprofits themselves. This internal (or horizontal) accountability centers on an organization's responsibility to its mission and staff, which includes decision makers as well as field-level implementers. Some scholars have even suggested that there are as many types of accountability as there are distinct relationships among people and organizations; some characterize this condition as "multiple accountabilities disorder" (Koppell, 2005; Lerner and Tetlock, 1999).

At a minimum, to whom one is accountable varies with organization type, be it a membership organization, a service-delivery nonprofit, or a network engaged in policy advocacy. Although these three "types" of nonprofits do not capture the diversity in the sector, they illustrate critical differences:

- *Membership organizations* are largely oriented toward serving the interests of their members, and are often run by and for their members (e.g., the American Association of Retired Persons, cooperatives and unions, and clubs and societies). The mechanisms of accountability available to members include the exercise of "voice" by voting for the organization's leaders, "exit" by revoking membership and dues or joining another organization, and "loyalty" by attempting to reform the organization either by influencing leaders or by running for a leadership position.[1] Because the members or clients are internal to the organization, membership organizations combine internal accountability (to members of the organizations) with downward accountability (to clients, who are members). In short, there is a structural equality between principals and agents, and thus a significant potential for the use of exit, voice, and loyalty options.
- *Service organizations* typically provide a range of services to their clients or beneficiaries, ranging from health and education to housing and rural

development. Their clients are usually not involved in creating the nonprofit in the way that members are; they are external actors to the organization and therefore have less voice in shaping its activities and direction. For many, the demands of funders or patrons (that is, upward accountability) tend to be the most formalized, for example, through grant contracts, reporting requirements, and formal evaluations. This imbalance is reproduced in their relations with clients, who are often in a "take it or leave it" relationship with respect to services offered (Uphoff, 1996, p. 25), except in highly competitive contexts in which clients have multiple service providers from which to choose. A key accountability challenge lies in increasing "downward" accountability from funders to the nonprofit, and from the nonprofit to clients.

- *Policy advocacy networks* display characteristics that are common to membership as well as service organizations, and also characteristics that are unique. For example, organizations such as the Sierra Club and Amnesty International both have individual members who pay dues and thus have the option of taking their dues elsewhere should the organization fail to satisfy their interests. But they are not self-help organizations in the way that cooperatives are, and most members do not have direct access to organizational decision making or even to other members (nor do they necessarily desire such access), despite the fact that they elect board members. They are more like clients of service organizations. In other words, although their options for exit (revoking membership dues) are potentially powerful, their actions are likely to be remote and isolated. On the other hand, some network organizations attract members by virtue of their policy advocacy work—thereby seeking to hold policymakers and public officials accountable to the views and values of their members. The mechanisms of accountability available to them are advocacy-oriented (voice), including lobbying, litigation, protest, negotiation, fact-finding, and demanding transparency in the reporting of information and events. Networks in which the members are organizations, rather than individuals, involve an additional layer of accountability that depends on negotiation and coordination among member organizations. Accountability is collective in the sense that it depends on reliable coordination and pooling of resources among key players.[2]

In short, the demands of accountability "to whom" are multifold and can seldom be reduced to simple terms. Accountability is a relational concept; it varies according to the relationships among actors, and it also varies across different types of organizations (for example, membership, service, and advocacy networks). Furthermore, asymmetric relationships among stakeholders are likely to result in a skewing toward accountability mechanisms that satisfy the interests of the most powerful actors. In other words, accountability is also about power, in that asymmetries in resources become important in influencing who is able to hold whom to account.

Accountability for What?

Given that nonprofit organizations face demands for accountability from multiple actors, it follows that they are expected to be accountable for different things by different people. These expectations may be broken down into four broad, but far from comprehensive, categories: accountability for finances, governance, performance, and mission (Behn, 2001; Ebrahim, 2009).

Questions about *finances* have received considerable attention in the wake of various accounting scandals and crises not only in the nonprofit world but also in the private sector (for example, the fall of firms such as Enron and WorldCom in 2001 and 2002, as well as industry-wide failures in mortgage-backed securities and financial derivatives markets in 2008). Public policy responses, particularly to firm-level failures, typically call for greater disclosure of financial transactions, transparency in the use and oversight of funds by executives and trustees, and protections for whistle-blowers who reveal information about mismanagement. Accountability in this context is constituted as coercive or punitive, with an emphasis on disclosure and a reliance on legislative or regulatory oversight, backed up by threats of sanctions for noncompliance, such as fines, imprisonment, or loss of tax-exempt status.

The second type of expectation focuses on organizational *governance,* which, especially in the United States and United Kingdom, has often centered on the role of the board of directors. The board is the nexus of standards of care, loyalty, and obedience: board members are responsible for seeking and considering adequate information on which to base decisions (care), for disclosing conflicts of interest and placing the organization's interests over personal ones (loyalty), and for acting within the organization's mission while also adhering to internal organizational protocols for decision making (obedience). The board's fiduciary responsibilities typically focus on its financial oversight role, about how the organization raises and spends money, follows donor intent, and whether it is in compliance with the law. The basic premise is that boards are responsible for oversight of internal controls and legal compliance, such that failures within an organization are reflective of failures of guidance and oversight at the board level.

But boards are increasingly also expected to be accountable for the broader purposes of the organization: for its performance in achieving results, for identifying
an effective strategy, and for focusing on a mission that creates the greatest social
value.[3] These functions require much more than fiduciary oversight, demanding
that boards play a more "generative" role (Chait, Ryan, and Taylor, 2005), particularly in the development and maintenance of mission (McFarlan and Epstein,
2009). Chapter Five of this volume focuses more broadly on the design and work
of nonprofit organizations' governing boards, and Chapter Two includes important information about their legal characteristics.

Thus, the third broad stream of accountability demands centers on *performance*, built on the premise that organizations should be held to account for
what they deliver. The purpose of such accountability is to demonstrate "results."
Performance-based accountability often uses tools such as logic models (called
logical framework analysis in the international development world), in which a
project's objectives and expected results are identified in a matrix with a list of
indicators used in measuring and verifying progress. This kind of accountability relies on a range of technical and professional skills related to performance
measurement, indicator development, evaluation and impact assessment, all of
which converge toward metrics that link goals to outcomes. This type of accountability is encouraged by funder reporting requirements that reward clear outputs
and outcomes. Some critical observers have cautioned, however, that an overem-
phasis on measurable outcomes can lead to a push for quick fixes, potentially
conflicting with or even undermining the work of nonprofits engaged in relationship building and empowerment-related work, and whose efforts may take
time to bear fruit (Benjamin, 2008; Lindenberg and Bryant, 2001, p. 214). They
stress a need to examine long-term effectiveness and less easily measurable goals
related to political and social change.

This leads to a fourth and more emergent type of accountability that focuses
on the very core of nonprofit activity: organizational *mission*. If nonprofits exist
for purposes of public good, why not ask them to demonstrate progress toward
achieving that mission? One might describe this as a mission-centered variant
of performance-based accountability, which it extends in two respects. First, it
embraces a long-term view of performance measurement by emphasizing iteration and learning—on the basis that nonprofit managers are unlikely to know
how best to achieve their goals and what to measure along the way, but repeated
trials and critical scrutiny can lead to new insights and convergence. This suggests there are no panaceas to social problems, but instead that social problem
solving requires an ability to cope with uncertainty and changing circumstances.
It also indicates a critical role for nonprofit boards in internalizing the mission,

regularly monitoring performance against it, and periodically reviewing it in light of changing external conditions (McFarlan and Epstein, 2009). And second, organizational goals and strategies are themselves subject to adaptation, as managers learn more about the social problems that they are trying to understand and solve. A central managerial challenge becomes putting in place processes that can engender systematic critical reflection and adaptation while remaining focused on solving social problems (Ebrahim, 2005).

These four "whats" of accountability—for finances, governance, performance, and mission—are not mutually exclusive but are instead integrative. For example, boards have not only fiduciary responsibility but also serve the mission and oversee performance. Donors consider mission in selecting which organizations to fund, and many provide considerable flexibility with respect to performance assessment. And chief executives are expected to work with boards and staff to align mission, strategy, and performance.

Accountability How?

If nonprofits are expected to be accountable to multiple actors (accountability to whom) and for multiple purposes (accountability for what), what then are the mechanisms of accountability actually available to them (accountability how)? And how can we compare these mechanisms?

The following discussion explores five broad (but far from comprehensive) types of accountability mechanisms used by nonprofits in practice: reports and disclosure statements, evaluations and performance assessments, industry self-regulation, participation, and adaptive learning (Ebrahim, 2003). The comparative strengths and weaknesses of each of these mechanisms are also further analyzed. This discussion does not examine challenges of democratic accountability, in which nonprofits may claim to represent the views of a specific community; this would require a separate discussion on representation.

In beginning, it may be helpful to differentiate between those mechanisms that are "tools" and those that are "processes." In basic terms, accountability tools refer to discrete devices or techniques used to achieve accountability. They are often applied over a limited period of time, can be tangibly documented, and can be repeated. For example, financial reports and disclosures are tools that are applied and repeated quarterly or annually and are documented as financial statements, ledgers, or reports. Performance evaluations are also often carried out at specific points in time, usually at the end of a specific project, and result in an evaluation report. However, process mechanisms such as participation and adaptive learning are generally more broad and multifaceted than tools, while also being less tangible and time-bound, although each may use a set of tools for achieving accountability. Process mechanisms thus emphasize a course of action rather than a distinct end product, in which the means are important in and of themselves. These distinctions are discussed in greater detail below.

Disclosure Statements and Reports

Disclosure statements and reports are among the most widely used tools of accountability and are frequently required by federal or state laws in many countries. These include, for example, application requirements for tax exemption under section 501(c)(3) of the Internal Revenue Code, and annual filings of the Form 990 which requests disclosures on finances, organizational structure, and programs. Furthermore, state law provisions also often include registration and reporting statutes that involve annual financial reporting (Fremont-Smith, 2004).

On the one hand, such legal disclosures enable some degree of accountability to donors, clients, and members who wish to access these reports, and also serve as means for nonprofit boards to fulfill their fiduciary responsibilities. On the other hand, donors and clients of a nonprofit organization in the United States generally have very limited legal standing to challenge an organization for falling short of legal requirements, with primary responsibility falling on the attorney general as the representative of society at large or on the Internal Revenue Service for matters of tax exemption. At the same time, legal requirements can also be abused by governments to keep tabs on organizations that challenge them, as has been documented in many parts of the world (International Center for Not-for-Profit Law (ICNL), 2006). These problems have become more pronounced in a post 9/11 context, where nonprofit activities are subject to greater scrutiny by their governments, funders are being asked to prove that their moneys are not being channeled to activities of concern to state security, and some subsectors, such as Muslim charities, suffer "from a loss of the presumption of innocence" (Jordan and Van Tuijl, 2006, p. 8). Apart from legally mandated reports, donors require regular reports from organizations that they fund. The nature of these reports varies considerably among funders and projects, and it is not uncommon for nonprofit staff to complain about multiple reporting requirements.

Such reports and legal disclosures are significant tools of accountability in that they make available (either to the public or to oversight bodies) basic data on nonprofit operations. Their distinct and tangible nature makes them easily accessible. Yet the bulk of this reporting emphasizes upward reporting of financial data, with only limited indication of the quality of nonprofit work and almost no attention to downward accountability to stakeholders. These are external approaches to accountability, enforced through punitive threats such as the loss of nonprofit status or revocation of funds. Although no doubt important as deterrents, these external approaches have limited potential for encouraging organizations and individuals to take internal responsibility for shaping their organizational mission, values, and performance or for promoting ethical behavior.

Evaluation and Performance Assessment

Another widely used set of tools for facilitating accountability includes various kinds of evaluation, including performance and impact assessments. Funders commonly conduct external evaluations of nonprofit work near the end of a grant or program phase, and are increasingly employing mid-term assessments as well. Such evaluations typically aim to assess whether and to what extent program goals and objectives have been achieved, and they can be pivotal to future funding. These appraisals may focus on short-term results (activities or outputs, such as training programs offered or jobs secured) or medium- and long-term results (outcomes and impacts, such as sustained improvements in client income, health, natural resource base, and so forth). Internal evaluations are also common, in which nonprofit staff gauge their own progress, either toward the objectives of externally funded programs or toward internal goals and missions.

As a means of accountability, evaluations often run into conflicts among nonprofits and funders over whether they should be assessing activities, processes, outputs, or outcomes and impacts (accountability for what). As donors increasingly demand information about long-term outcomes and impacts, many nonprofit leaders have expressed concern about the difficulty, reliability, and expense of such measurement, particularly in accounting for causal factors well beyond their control. Randomized control trials, regarded by some as a gold standard for evaluation, are costly to conduct and are feasible only when cause-effect relationships are sufficiently linear and testable (Center for Global Development, 2006; Jones, Jones, Steer, and Datta, 2009; Rogers, 2009; White, 2009). Moreover, the question of what should be evaluated may vary according to different stakeholders (accountability to whom). When an organization's work is fairly straightforward to measure (for example, a nonprofit that aims to serve meals to the poor), and performance criteria are likely to be shared across different stakeholder groups, a simple logic model can be helpful in clarifying results. However, when performance criteria vary among stakeholders, such as in empowerment and rights-based work or policy advocacy, nonprofit leaders face the challenge of prioritizing and coordinating among multiple interests and constituents.

Control over evaluations thus remains a central tension between nonprofits and their stakeholders, and particularly with funders who must make decisions on allocating or cutting funding. Some scholars have shown that funders can come to somewhat different conclusions about the same set of nonprofits as a result of how they frame their evaluations (Tassie, Murray, and Cutt, 1998, p. 63). A related concern raised by small nonprofits is that their limited staff and resources are stretched too thin by evaluation and reporting requests of funders, and that nonprofit size and capacity should be key factors in determining the scale of an appraisal. These concerns notwithstanding, the strength of evaluation as a mechanism of accountability lies in its explicit attention to results (whether those be outputs or outcomes) and the impetus it provides to nonprofits for collecting some form of performance data.

Self-Regulation

Nonprofits have also increasingly turned to industry-wide accountability standards. The term *self-regulation,* as used here, refers specifically to efforts by nonprofit networks to develop standards or codes of behavior and performance. These standards have emerged partly as an effort to redeem the image of the sector (as a result of public scandals or exaggerated claims of performance) while establishing norms around quality, and in some instances to forestall potentially restrictive government regulation.

Standards and their certification are most ubiquitous and longstanding in the education and health care sectors, where there is a mix of government oversight and industry self-regulation, and a combination of public, private, and nonprofit players. In education, for example, certification of teachers and educational facilities is common but not always required. Moreover, the entire higher education industry is organized around programs that must be accredited in order to grant degrees (in business, law, medicine, education, public administration, public health, accounting, city planning, and social work, to name just a handful). Similarly, the health care field relies on certification and licensing of its professionals (doctors, nurses, administrators, technicians, and others) and also offers certification of facilities and services.

More broadly, the past two decades have seen the emergence of an array of voluntary codes of conduct and third-party certification standards across nonprofit industries—intended to send signals of good housekeeping to the outside world. Hundreds of national and international codes have been documented globally. For example, the Independent Sector in the United States, and Bond in the United Kingdom (formerly British Overseas NGOs for Development), together list over a hundred standards and codes promoted by charity watchdogs, nonprofit and NGO associations, foundations, individual organizations, and governments.[4] Some standards systems are inclusive in nature, seeking to improve governance across a spectrum of nonprofits, and are typically sponsored by umbrella associations. Others are exclusive in nature, seeking to screen organizations and professions through a certification process (Gugerty and Prakash, 2010).

In the United States, a widely cited set of standards was developed in 1993 by InterAction, a membership association of U.S. private voluntary organizations active in international development. The 1990s also saw the rise of state-level nonprofit associations adopting and promoting codes and certification standards; the most heavily promoted was the "Standards of Excellence" developed by the Maryland Association of Nonprofit Organizations (MANO). Most of these standards lay out, in considerable detail, requirements concerning governance, organizational integrity, finances, public communication and disclosure, management and hiring practices, and public policy involvement. For instance, governance standards typically require organizations to have an independent board of directors and even specify some of the tasks of the board and minimum frequency of meetings. Integrity standards emphasize truthfulness in conduct and require that each organization develop a written standard of conduct (including conflict of interest) for its directors, employees, and volunteers. InterAction's code further provides guidelines and requirements for promoting gender equity, diversity, and people with disabilities. These standards have had impacts beyond the United States. For example, a code of ethics used by the Canadian Council for International Co-operation contains content very similar to InterAction's code. Although implementation of these standards is often based on self-certification (as for InterAction), some organizations require external or third-party certification (as for MANO).

Whether and how the adoption of such self-regulation actually improves nonprofit accountability remains to be empirically tested. At the very least, their value is symbolic, sending signals about sector identity and values to an increasingly skeptical public. Even then, self-regulatory efforts face at least two challenges. First, as the number of such standards has grown, it has become difficult for donors and citizens to compare them. Their power as seals of good housekeeping may thus rely on two, distinct pathways—either more clear differentiation among codes or a consolidation among them. Second, although most self-regulatory efforts have focused internally on the governance and operations of their members (accountability for what), few have been explicit about accountability to key constituents (accountability to whom). A notable exception is the Humanitarian Accountability Partnership, established in 2003, which specifically prioritizes accountability to its intended beneficiaries (disaster survivors), and which requires all participating organizations to articulate an explicit "accountability framework."[5]

Participation

As an accountability mechanism, participation is quite distinct from disclosure reports and evaluations because it is a process rather than a tool, and it is thus part of ongoing routines in an organization. In examining participation, it is helpful to distinguish between four levels or kinds of participation common to nonprofit and public activities (Arnstein, 1969; Gardner and Lewis, 1996). At one level, participation refers to information about a planned intervention being made available to the public, and it can include public meetings or hearings, surveys, or a formal dialogue on project options. In this form, participation involves consultation with community leaders and members, but decision-making power remains with the project planners. A second level of participation includes public involvement in actual project-related activities, and it may be in the form of community contribution toward labor and funds for project implementation, and possibly in the maintenance of services or facilities. At a third level, citizens are able to negotiate and bargain over decisions with nonprofits or state agencies, or even hold veto power over decisions. At this level, citizens are able to exercise greater control over local resources and development activities. And finally, at a fourth tier of participation, are people's own initiatives that occur independently of nonprofit- and state-sponsored projects. Examples of this kind of participation include social movements such as the environmental and women's movements.

The first two forms of participation are commonly espoused by state agencies, donors, and nonprofits and are based on an assumption that social problems such as poverty can be eliminated by increasing local access to resources and services. At both of these levels, little decision-making authority is vested in communities or clients, and actual project objectives are determined by nonprofits and funders long before any participation occurs. This sort of participation has been criticized by some observers as being a feel-good exercise in which "the sham of participation translates into the sham of accountability" because "[u]nlike donors, [communities] cannot withdraw their funding; unlike governments, they cannot impose conditionalities" (Najam, 1996, pp. 346–347). The act of participation or the exercise of "voice" and "exit" is largely symbolic in such settings. The primary argument is that without some mechanism for addressing unequal power relations, participation appears unlikely to lead to downward accountability (Cooke and Kothari, 2001).

There have been a number of innovations in this area since the year 2000, especially in combining participation with evaluation to involve communities in evaluating nonprofits, or nonprofits in evaluating funders. For example, the Grantee Perception Reports, developed by the Center for Effective Philanthropy in the United States, seek anonymous feedback from nonprofit grantees about their relationships with funders (Center for Effective Philanthropy, 2004). Similarly, a Comparative Constituency Feedback tool developed by Keystone Accountability in the United Kingdom aims to give nonprofits or funders data on how their constituents view and evaluate their relationships and interventions (Bonbright, Campbell, and Nguyen, 2009). There have also been innovations in participatory budgeting, pioneered by citizens in municipalities in Brazil, and social audits and public hearings in which citizens assess the work of NGOs and governments (Malena, Forster, and Singh, 2004). Each of these approaches combine tools of evaluation and performance assessment with processes of participation to enhance downward accountability.

Adaptive Learning

Another process mechanism is adaptive learning, in which nonprofits create regular opportunities for critical reflection and analysis in order to make progress toward achieving their missions. Building such learning into an organization requires at least three sets of building blocks: *a supportive learning environment*, where staff are given time for reflection and the psychological safety to discuss mistakes or express disagreement; *concrete learning processes* and practices that enable experimentation, analysis, capacity building, and forums for sharing information; and *supportive leadership* that reinforces learning by encouraging dialogue and debate and by providing resources for reflection (Garvin, Edmondson, and Gino, 2008). Learning, as such, seeks to "improv[e] actions through better knowledge and understanding" (Fiol and Lyles, 1985, p. 803) or, in more technical terms, to "encod[e] inferences from history into routines that guide behavior" (Levitt and March, 1988, p. 320).

As an accountability mechanism, adaptive learning focuses internally on organizational mission rather than externally on accountability to funders, although it may also enhance the latter. It also offers a way for nonprofit leaders to address a common myopia—the focus on immediate short-term demands at the expense of longer-term and more sustained results. The central managerial challenge becomes putting in place processes that can engender systematic critical reflection and remain focused on achieving the mission.

This is easier said than done. Evaluations or performance assessments that reward success while punishing failure (for example, through revocation of funds or additional conditions on funding) seem unlikely to engender learning since they encourage nonprofits to exaggerate successes while discouraging them from revealing and closely scrutinizing their mistakes. At the same time, onerous data requirements can lead nonprofits to develop monitoring and evaluation systems that, although satisfying donor needs for information, are of limited value for internal learning and decision making.

Despite these impediments, a number of global nonprofit organizations have been experimenting over the past decade with building learning into their work. This has been especially true of multisite organizations seeking to share knowledge across teams in dozens of countries. For example, ActionAid International revamped its entire planning and reporting processes in 2000, launching a new Accountability, Learning, and Planning System (ALPS). Its aim was to reduce unnecessary internal bureaucracy, while reshaping the expert-driven task of measurement and reporting into a more critical and reflective process (ActionAid International, 2006, p. 4; David and Mancini, 2004). Many other international nonprofits, such as CARE and Oxfam, have undertaken their own experiments to find practical and useful approaches to measurement, reporting, and learning. At the same time, there has been a burst in the development of participatory tools for evaluation and learning such as outcome mapping, constituency feedback, and most significant change techniques (Bonbright, Campbell, and Nguyen, 2009; Davies and Dart, 2005; Earl, Carden, and Smutylo, 2001; Khagram, Thomas, Lucero, and Mathes, 2009).

Discussion and Implications

Key characteristics of the accountability mechanisms discussed in this chapter are summarized in Table 4.1. The first column lists each of the five mechanisms and distinguishes among those that are tools and those that are processes.

TABLE 4.1. Characteristics of Accountability Mechanisms

Accountability How? (tool or process)	Accountability to Whom? (upward, downward, internal)	Accountability for What? (finances, governance, performance, mission)	Inducement (internal or external)	Organizational Response (compliance or strategic)
Disclosures/ Reports (tool)	Upward to funders and oversight agencies Downward (to a lesser degree) to clients or members who read the reports	Finances and performance, depending on what is being reported	Legal requirement Tax status Funding requirement (external threat of loss of funding or tax status)	Primarily compliance, with a focus on letter of law and short-term results
Evaluation and Performance Assessment (tool)	Upward to funders Significant potential for downward from nonprofits to communities and from funders to nonprofits	Performance, often short-term outputs but with increasing emphasis on impacts	Funding requirement (external) Potential to become a learning tool (internal)	Primarily compliance at present, with possibilities for longer-term strategic assessments
Self-Regulation (tool and process	To nonprofits themselves, as a sector To donors as a seal of good housekeeping	Finances and governance, depending on what the codes of standards emphasize	Erosion of public confidence due to scandals and exaggeration of accomplishments (external loss of funds; internal loss of reputation)	Strategic if it raises industry standards and enables policy voice Compliance if standards are weak and adopted pro-forma
Participation (process)	Downward from nonprofits to clients and communities Internally to nonprofits themselves Significant potential downwards from funders to nonprofits.	Depends on the purpose of participation, e.g., whether to seek input on implementation (performance) or to influence agendas (governance)	Organizational values (internal) Funding requirement (external)	Primarily compliance if participation is limited to consultation and implementation Strategic if it increases power of clients in influencing nonprofit agendas, or increases power of nonprofits in influencing funders
Adaptive Learning (process)	To nonprofits themselves Downward and upward to stakeholders	Mission and performance	Improve performance in order to achieve mission (internal)	Strategic if it focuses attention and resources on how to solve social problems

The second and third columns respond to the questions of "accountability to whom" and "accountability for what"? For example, disclosure statements and reports are currently used primarily for upward accountability from nonprofits to donors, and tend to focus on reporting about annual or quarterly performance and finances. Similarly, tools of evaluation and performance assessment are also mostly targeted toward satisfying funder demands for assessing performance, although they have a tremendous, underutilized potential for downward accountability—by making nonprofits more accountable to communities and by making funders more accountable to nonprofits. Although funders frequently require nonprofits to seek community input in evaluating projects, they rarely seek nonprofit input in evaluating themselves. Similarly, participation, which is primarily conceived by nonprofits as a tool of downward accountability to communities, has received only scant attention as a tool for increasing the responsiveness of funders to nonprofits. Self-regulation, often driven by a crisis of confidence in the sector, is seen as enabling accountability within the sector and also to donors who seek a seal of good housekeeping. And it is only adaptive learning processes that tend to focus on accountability to organizational mission, although related mechanisms such as performance assessment also have the potential to do so.

There are several broad implications to these observations. First, although traditional approaches to improving accountability, such as increased oversight through reporting and disclosure requirements, enable a degree of upward accountability, they are of limited use for enhancing downward accountability. A more balanced approach thus requires a greater role for nonprofits in evaluating funders and for clients in evaluating nonprofits. The emergence of feedback tools such as grantee perception reports and constituency voice suggest that it is possible to find low-risk ways for nonprofits to express their views on funders. These efforts notwithstanding, the key point is that downward accountability mechanisms remain comparatively underdeveloped.

A second implication is that improving accountability within nonprofits themselves also needs attention to a range of mechanisms. The fourth column in Table 4.1 focuses on the inducements or drivers behind each accountability mechanism. In many cases the inducements are external, such as legal requirements for annual reports (for example, for retaining nonprofit tax status) or requests by donors for quarterly progress data, backed up by sanctions for noncompliance (such as loss of funding). External inducements can also be more subtle, such as the erosion of public confidence in nonprofits as a result of scandals or exaggerated claims of achievement.

The key point here is that although externally driven mechanisms matter, the legitimacy and reputation of the social sector needs to be buttressed by internally driven mechanisms. To be sure, internal inducements exist and are often driven by core values, for example, about participation and democratic practice. But for a sector that views itself as largely mission-driven, there is an urgent need for nonprofit leaders to take performance assessment seriously in order to justify activities with substantiated evidence rather than with anecdote or rhetoric. Funders and regulators also bear responsibility in this regard. Funders that want nonprofits to measure impacts, but at the same time are unwilling to fund management capacity building and overhead costs for performance measurement, end up undermining both the nonprofits and themselves.

The third implication concerns the primary type of organizational response that a mechanism generates—whether it is *compliance-driven* or *strategy-driven* (see last column in Table 4.1). Compliance-driven accountability is a reactive response to concerns about public trust. It is about doing what one has to do, such as complying with the law, disclosing whatever information is necessary in order to account for resource use, and taking fiduciary responsibility seriously in order to prevent fraud or malfeasance. Under this approach, nonprofit leaders share information about their performance or operations largely because funders or regulators demand it. Strategy-driven accountability, on the other hand, is a proactive approach to addressing concerns about public trust (Brown, Moore, and Honan, 2004; Jordan, 2007). It is focused on improving performance and achieving mission. Under this approach, nonprofit leaders seek and share information that can help them achieve their long-term goals.

The most common mechanisms of accountability, such as disclosure statements, reports, and project evaluations, mainly serve a compliance purpose because they tend to focus on accounting for funds and reporting their short-term results (often within specified budget cycles). The complex nature of nonprofit work suggests, however, that attention to more strategic processes of accountability are necessary for lasting social and political change. While reporting requirements that are biased in favor of easily measurable assessments of progress might be sufficient for funding and regulatory purposes, they undervalue adaptive assessments that are essential for understanding how a nonprofit might improve its work. A strategy-driven accountability requires building internal capacity in nonprofits for adaptive learning.

Self-regulation may also be seen as a strategic response in the sense that it is targeted toward change at a sector-wide level, not only by raising the standards for an industry, but also by forming umbrella organizations that can engage in national-level policy debates. But self-regulation also runs the risk of becoming a compliance response if the adopted standards are weak, pro forma, and do not actually improve behavior.

Conclusions

In the end, accountability is both about being held to account by external actors and standards and about taking internal responsibility for actions. An integrated perspective suggests that nonprofit leaders face multiple, and sometimes competing, accountability demands: from numerous actors (upward, downward, internal), for varying purposes (finances, governance, performance, mission), and requiring various levels of organizational response (compliance and strategic).

The current emphasis among nonprofits and funders on the upward and compliance dimensions of accountability is problematic, as it skews organizational attention toward the interests of those who control critical resources. In such cases, patrons hold powers of punishment and can revoke funds, impose conditionalities, or even tarnish nonprofit reputations. The predominant emphasis on compliance-driven accountability tends to reward nonprofits for short-term responses with quick and tangible impacts, while neglecting longer-term strategic responses or riskier innovations that can address more systemic issues of social and political change.

Yet it is inescapable that nonprofits will continue to face multiple and competing accountability demands. After all, funders have a right to demand accountability for their resources, and many are increasingly attentive to the concerns and interests of nonprofits they support. The critical challenge for nonprofit leaders lies in finding a balance between upward accountability to their patrons while remaining true to their missions. At the same time, few nonprofits have paid serious attention to how they might be more accountable to the communities they seek to serve. The above review of accountability offers four key insights for practice:

- Nonprofit leaders must be deliberate in prioritizing among accountabilities. They cannot be accountable to everyone for everything. But it is a fact of life in the social sector that they will continue to be pulled in all directions. Rather than aiming simply to comply with the demands of the most powerful actors, nonprofit leaders need to focus their attention on accountabilities that really matter.

- Nonprofits are expected to be accountable for multiple purposes: finances, governance, performance, and mission. These expectations cannot be handled separately, but require integration and alignment throughout the organization.

- There are many mechanisms of accountability available to nonprofits—including, for example, better information disclosure, evaluation and performance assessment, industry codes and standards, participation, and adaptive learning (to name just a few). Nonprofit leaders must adapt any such mechanisms to suit their organization—whether it is a membership-based organization, a service-delivery nonprofit, or an advocacy network (among others).

- The broader conclusion is that accountability is not simply about compliance with laws or industry standards but is, more deeply, connected to organizational purpose and public trust. Nonprofit leaders might thus pay greater attention to strategy-driven forms of accountability that can help them achieve their missions. New innovations are unlikely to lie in oversight and punishment, but in creative forms of adaptation and learning in order to solve pressing societal problems.

Notes

1. These options of exit, voice, or loyalty draw from Hirschman (1970).
2. Nonprofit organizations engaged in policy advocacy face an additional accountability challenge increasingly leveled by their critics: "Whom do you represent? Who elected you?" This challenge is less of a problem for organizations that are membership based, and who can thus claim to be accountable to their members for their lobbying and advocacy activities. Nonmembership organizations, however, tend to claim authorization on the grounds of what, rather than whom, they represent—such as a set of values, a social purpose or mission, expertise and experience in an issue area such as health or education, or a particular set of interests such as those of marginalized or unorganized groups (Peruzzotti, 2006, pp. 52–53).
3. The author is grateful to Herman "Dutch" Leonard for this insight, which underpins a "Governing for Nonprofit Excellence" executive education program at Harvard Business School chaired by Professor Leonard.
4. See www.independentsector.org/issues/accountability/standards2.html and www.bond.org.uk/pages/quality-standards-codes-and-inititatives-2.html (both accessed November 11, 2009).
5. For examples of codes, see InterAction (www.gdrc.org/ngo/pvo-stand.html), Maryland Association for Nonprofits (www.marylandnonprofits.org/html/standards/index.asp), the Philippine Council for NGO Certification (www.pcnc.com.ph), the

International NGO Accountability Charter (www.ingoaccountabilitycharter.org), and the Humanitarian Accountability Partnership (www.hapinternational.org/standards.aspx); accessed November 24, 2009.

References

ActionAid International. ALPS: Accountability, Learning and Planning System. Johannesburg: ActionAid International, 2006.

Arnstein, S. R. A Ladder of Citizen Participation. *American Institute of Planning Journal,* 1969, 35(4), 216–224.

Behn, R. D. *Rethinking Democratic Accountability.* Washington, DC: Brookings Institution Press, 2001.

Benjamin, L. M. Account Space: How Accountability Requirements Shape Nonprofit Practice. *Nonprofit and Voluntary Sector Quarterly,* 2008, 37(2), 201–223.

Bonbright, D., Campbell, D., and Nguyen, L. The 21st Century Potential of Constituency Voice: Opportunities for Reform in the United States Human Services Sector. Alliance for Children & Families, United Neighborhood Centers of America, and Keystone Accountability, 2009.

Brown, L. D., Moore, M. H., and Honan, J. Building Strategic Accountability Systems for International NGOs. *Accountability Forum,* 2004, 31–43.

Center for Effective Philanthropy. *Listening to Grantees: What Nonprofits Value in Their Foundation Funders.* Cambridge, MA: The Center for Effective Philanthropy (CEP), 2004.

Center for Global Development. *When Will We Ever Learn? Improving Lives Through Impact Evaluation.* Washington, DC: Evaluation Gap Working Group, Center for Global Development, 2006.

Chait, R. P., Ryan, W. P., and Taylor, B. E. *Governance as Leadership: Reframing the Work of Nonprofit Boards.* Hoboken, NJ: John Wiley & Sons, 2005.

Chisolm, L. B. Accountability of Nonprofit Organizations and Those Who Control Them: The Legal Framework. *Nonprofit Management and Leadership,* 1995, 6(2), 141–156.

Cooke, B., and Kothari, U. (eds.). *Participation: The New Tyranny?* London and New York: Zed Books, 2001.

Cornwall, A., Lucas, H., and Pasteur, K. Introduction: Accountability Through Participation: Developing Workable Partnership Models in the Health Sector. *IDS Bulletin.* 2001, 31(1), 1–13.

David, R., and Mancini, A. Going Against the Flow: Making Organisational Systems Part of the Solution Rather than Part of the Problem. *Lessons for Change in Policy & Organisations* (No. 8), 2004.

Davies, R., and Dart, J. The "Most Significant Change" (MSC) Technique: A Guide to Its Use. 2005. Available at http://www.mande.co.uk/docs/MSCGuide.htm

Earl, S., Carden, F., and Smutylo, T. *Outcome Mapping: Building Learning and Reflection into Development.* Ottawa: International Development Research Centre, 2001.

Ebrahim, A. Accountability in Practice: Mechanisms for NGOs. *World Development,* 2003, 31(5), 813–829.

Ebrahim, A. Accountability Myopia: Losing Sight of Organizational Learning. *Nonprofit and Voluntary Sector Quarterly,* 2005, 34(1), 56–87.

Ebrahim, A. Placing the Normative Logics of Accountability in "Thick" Perspective. *American Behavioral Scientist,* 2009, 52(6), 885–904.

Ebrahim, A. Accountability. In H. Anheier and S. Toepler (eds.), *International Encyclopedia of Civil Society*. New York: Springer, 2010.

Ebrahim, A., and E. Weisband (eds.). *Global Accountabilities: Participation, Pluralism, and Public Ethics*. Cambridge: Cambridge University Press, 2007.

Edwards, M., and Hulme, D. (eds.). *Beyond the Magic Bullet: NGO Performance and Accountability in the Post-Cold War World*. West Hartford, CT: Kumarian Press, 1996a.

Edwards, M., and Hulme, D. Too Close for Comfort? The Impact of Official Aid on Nongovernmental Organizations. *World Development,* 1996b, 24(6), 961–973.

Fiol, C. M., and Lyles, M. A. Organizational Learning. *Academy of Management Review,* 1985, 10(4), 803–813.

Fox, J. A., and Brown, L. D. (eds.). *The Struggle for Accountability: The World Bank, NGOs, and Grassroots Movements*. Cambridge, MA: The MIT Press, 1998.

Fremont-Smith, M. R. *Governing Nonprofit Organizations: Federal and State Law and Regulation*. Cambridge, MA: Belknap Press of Harvard University Press, 2004.

Fry, R. E. Accountability in Organizational Life: Problem or Opportunity for Nonprofits? *Nonprofit Management and Leadership,* 1995, 6(2), 181–195.

Gardner, K., and Lewis, D. *Anthropology, Development and the Post-Modern Challenge*, London: Pluto Press, 1996.

Garvin, D. A., Edmondson, A.C., and Gino, F. Is Yours a Learning Organization? *Harvard Business Review,* 2008, 109–116.

Gugerty, M. K., and Prakash, A. (eds.). *Voluntary Regulation of NGOs and Nonprofits: An Accountability Club Framework*. Cambridge, UK: Cambridge University Press. 2010.

Hirschman, A. O. *Exit, Voice, and Loyalty: Responses to Decline in Firms, Organizations, and States*. Cambridge, MA: Harvard University Press, 1970.

International Center for Not-for-Profit Law (ICNL). Recent Laws and Legislative Proposals to Restrict Civil Society and Civil Society Organizations. *International Journal of Not-for-Profit Law,* 2006, 8(4), 76–85.

Jones, N., Jones, H., Steer, L., and Datta, A. *Improving Impact Evaluation Production and Use*. London: Overseas Development Institute, 2009.

Jordan, L. A Rights-Based Approach to Accountability. In A. Ebrahim and E. Weisband (eds.), *Global Accountabilities: Participation, Pluralism, and Public Ethics*. Cambridge, UK: Cambridge University Press, 2007, 151–167.

Jordan, L., and P. Van Tuijl (eds.). *NGO Accountability: Politics, Principles, and Innovations*. London and Sterling, VA: Earthscan, 2006.

Kearns, K. P. *Managing for Accountability: Preserving the Public Trust in Nonprofit Organizations*. San Francisco: Jossey-Bass, 1996.

Khagram, S., Thomas, C., Lucero, C., and Mathes, S. Evidence for Development Effectiveness. *Journal of Development Effectiveness,* 2009, 1(3), 247–270.

Koppell, J. G. S. Pathologies of Accountability: ICANN and the Challenge of Multiple Accountabilities Disorder. *Public Administration Review,* 2005, 65(1), 94–108.

Lerner, J. S., and Tetlock, P. E. Accounting for the Effects of Accountability. *Psychological Bulletin,* 1999, 125(2), 255–275.

Levitt, B., and March, J. G. Organizational Learning" *Annual Review of Sociology,* 1988, 14, 319–40.

Lindenberg, M., and Bryant, C. *Going Global: Transforming Relief and Development NGOs*. Bloomfield, CT: Kumarian Press, 2001.

Lloyd, R., Oatham, J., and Hammer, M. *2007 Global Accountability Report*. London: One World Trust, 2007.

Malena, C., Forster, R., and Singh, J. *Social Accountability: An Introduction to the Concept and Emerging Practice*. Washington, DC: The World Bank, 2004.

McFarlan, F. W., and Epstein, M. W. Non-Profit Boards: It's Different: A Businessman's Perspective. Draft book manuscript (cited with permission), 2009.

Najam, A. NGO Accountability: A Conceptual Framework. *Development Policy Review,* 1996, 14, 339–353.

Peruzzotti, E. Civil Society, Representation and Accountability" In L. Jordan and P. Van Tuijl (eds.), *NGO Accountability: Politics, Principles and Innovations.* London and Sterling, VA: Earthscan, 2006, 43–58.

Rogers, P. Matching Impact Evaluation Design to the Nature of the Intervention and the Purpose of the Evaluation. In R. Chambers, D. Karlan, M. Ravallion, and P. Rogers (eds.), *Designing Impact Evaluations: Different Perspectives,* Working Paper 4. New Delhi: International Initiative for Impact Evaluation, 2009. Available at 3ieimpact.org

Tassie, B., Murray, V., and Cutt, J. Evaluating Social Service Agencies: Fuzzy Pictures of Organizational Effectiveness. *Voluntas: International Journal of Voluntary and Nonprofit Organizations,* 1998, 9(1), 59–79.

Uphoff, N. Why NGOs Are Not a Third Sector: A Sectoral Analysis with Some Thoughts on Accountability, Sustainability, and Evaluation. In M. Edwards and D. Hulme (eds.), *Beyond the Magic Bullet: NGO Performance and Accountability in the Post-Cold War.* West Hartford, CT: Kumarian, 1996, 23–39.

White, H. We All Agree We Need Better Evidence. But What Is It and Will It Be Used? In M. W. Lipsey and E. Noonan (eds.), *Better Evidence for a Better World.* Working Paper 2. New Delhi: International Initiative for Impact Evaluation (3ie), 2009. Available at 3ieimpact.org

PART TWO

LEADING AND GOVERNING NONPROFIT ORGANIZATIONS

Governance and leadership are two of the most important areas in which nonprofit organizations differ significantly from businesses and government agencies, and this part of the *Handbook* examines the various ways that leadership and strategic direction are provided to nonprofit organizations. In most nations of the world, governing boards (boards of directors or boards of trustees) of nonprofit organizations are legally accountable for leadership, governance, and oversight of the affairs of the nonprofit organization, and they are expected to provide effective leadership in establishing and developing their organizations' missions, visions, values, and strategic directions. No less central in providing organizational leadership are those who serve as chief executives of nonprofit organizations. They work with their governing boards to provide leadership, develop strategic direction, and manage the operations of their organizations.

The six chapters in Part Two of this volume collectively examine the leadership roles that boards, their members, and chief executives are expected to serve in nonprofit organizations, explore the challenges that sometimes hinder boards or executives from implementing their prescribed and expected roles, and discuss various strategies and techniques that have proved useful in enhancing the effectiveness of both boards and executives. The first chapter in this part,

Chapter Five, explains the work of governing boards and draws on the growing body of knowledge that we have developed from research and practice to explain how boards and their members can execute their roles effectively. In Chapter Six, Robert D. Herman examines the many dimensions of the work of chief executives and discusses what it takes for executives to succeed, including their pivotal role in helping their governing boards perform effectively. In Chapter Seven, Thomas H. Jeavons discusses the work of executives and managers, with particular attention to creating and sustaining organizational cultures and practices that articulate and uphold high ethical standards.

Leading and managing strategically is essential to nonprofit success, and one of the key leadership tasks facing boards and top executives is that of organizing and managing the work of the organization to ensure it achieves its mission. In Chapter Eight, William A. Brown presents a broad and strategic overview of the work of strategic management and the key elements that compose it. Chapter Nine by John M. Bryson builds on these concepts with a very complete and thoughtful explanation of the work of executives and boards in developing organizational strategy, including a comprehensive model of the processes by which this might best be accomplished. Robert D. Herman and I, in Chapter Ten, offer a general perspective and set of insights that we have developed from the research on the elusive concept of nonprofit organizational effectiveness, how it is related to leadership and management, and discuss its implications for organization and management practice. Each of these chapters offers important insights into the processes, dynamics, and practices that have an impact on the degree to which nonprofit organizations are effectively governed and led.

CHAPTER FIVE

LEADERSHIP, GOVERNANCE, AND THE WORK OF THE BOARD

David O. Renz

Every incorporated nonprofit organization, in the United States and in most other nations of the world, is legally required to have a governing body. Typically labeled a "board of directors" or "board of trustees," this governing board is the group of people entrusted with and accountable for the leadership and governance of the nonprofit corporation. It is the board that has the ultimate authority and responsibility for the performance of a nonprofit organization and, even when the organization employs people in executive and staff roles, it is the board that ultimately is accountable to the community, to the state, and to clients and beneficiaries.

Since the mid-1990s, governing boards increasingly have become a focus of attention and interest as a growing body of evidence affirms that effective board performance is integral to nonprofit organization performance and success. Boards are charged with leading as well as overseeing the work of nonprofits in the increasingly dynamic and complex environment of nonprofit and civil society work, and the challenge of doing this well under such conditions has led to greater interest in the work of boards, how they are organized, and how they can and should contribute to the success and effectiveness of the organizations they govern, lead, and serve.

When we consider most of what nonprofit leaders know about boards and nonprofit governance, we find they rely to a surprising degree on conventional wisdom, anecdotes, horror stories, and the ad hoc impressions and prescriptions of various board consultants and authors. However, as the research on nonprofit governance and boards has grown since the mid-1990s, important and useful insights for leaders have emerged as scholars and practitioners from a growing range of disciplines and fields have examined boards and the ways that they are organized, the practices they employ, and the impact they have on nonprofit performance (Renz and Andersson, 2013). Nonetheless, as Ostrower and Stone observe in their 2006 report on the research literature on nonprofit boards and governance, "major gaps in our theoretical and empirical knowledge about boards continue to exist" (p. 612). They explain this is partly because "boards are complex entities that defy sweeping generalizations," and partly due to the fact that there is an incredible degree of heterogeneity in the range of settings in which boards work. In particular, it is important to acknowledge that we have much less research experience with boards and the work of governance in smaller, community-based nonprofits (Ostrower and Stone, 2006). It can be very difficult to know just what guidance should apply to any one particular board, given this exceptional diversity. Nonetheless, there is an important and growing body of knowledge and information that informs the design and practice of nonprofit governance and the work of boards. That is the focus of this chapter.

I discuss nonprofit boards and governance from three perspectives in this chapter. First, and as a foundation, I introduce governance and discuss the legal duties and fiduciary responsibilities that are the distinct province of a nonprofit board.[1] Second, I discuss the typical duties and responsibilities of governing boards and those who serve as members of boards, and describe some of the recent changes in expectations for board service. Finally, I discuss some of the key concerns that have been voiced regarding board performance and offer a general framework for thinking about how to build board capacity. In the context of this framework, I highlight some of the important findings of recent research on board performance and discuss strategies for enhancing board effectiveness.

The Legal Dimensions of Board Work

The board of directors is the primary group of people entrusted with and accountable for the leadership and governance of the nonprofit corporation. Nonprofit corporations are entities authorized by a state to be formed for the purpose of engaging in some form of public service, or for providing benefits or services to a group of members, and state laws generally require that each such corporation has a governing body that oversees the work and ultimately is legally accountable. Acting as a collective, this governing body has both the authority and the accountability for the work of the organization (that is, corporation). It is common for many boards to hire staff to do the actual work of the organization, often with support from volunteers. Nonetheless, it is the governing board that ultimately is accountable for all acts undertaken in the name of the nonprofit corporation (including by staff and volunteers), whether or not those acts are formally approved by or implemented by the board itself. This accountability exists regardless of the size or nature of the nonprofit organization (and regardless of whether the organization employs staff.)

From a legal perspective,[2] a nonprofit board and its members have three fundamental duties:

- *Duty of Care,* which requires that the board take the care and exercise the judgment that any reasonable and prudent person would exhibit under similar circumstances in the process of making informed decisions. This includes acting in good faith consistent with what you as a member of the board truly believe is in the best interest of the organization. The law recognizes and accepts that board members may not always be correct or make the best decisions, but it holds them accountable for being attentive, diligent, and thoughtful and prudent in considering and acting on a policy, course of action, or other decision. Active preparation for and participation in board meetings where important decisions are to be made is an integral element of the duty of care.
- *Duty of Loyalty,* which calls upon the board and its members to consider and act in good faith to advance the best interests of the organization. In other words, board members will not authorize or engage in transactions except those by which the best possible outcomes or terms for the organization can be achieved. This standard constrains a board member from participating in board discussions and decisions when they as an individual have a conflict of interest (that is, their personal interests conflict with organizational interests, or they serve multiple organizations whose interests conflict).
- *Duty of Obedience,* which requires obedience to the organization's mission, bylaws, and policies, as well as honoring the terms and conditions of other standards of appropriate behavior such as laws, rules, and regulations.

Boards and their members are obligated to honor these standards with regard to all decisions and actions of the board, and those who do not may be subject to civil and even criminal sanctions (including, in the

United States, sanctions imposed by the federal Internal Revenue Service in cases of inappropriate personal benefit).

There has been a significant increase in the attention paid to clarifying and enforcing the legal responsibilities of nonprofit boards and their members since the mid-1990s. National, state and provincial authorities all have placed increased emphasis on the need for nonprofit boards to be actively accountable for the quality of their governance and oversight of their organizations, and a number of governments have adopted legislation intended to increase nonprofit board performance and accountability (for example, the State of California's 2009 revisions to its nonprofit laws; the New York Nonprofit Revitalization Act of 2013; the 2011 Canada Not-for-Profit Corporations Act). Many also have provided formal policy "guidance" and direction intended to spur increased self-regulation (for example, U.S. Internal Revenue Service, n.d.; The Panel on the Nonprofit Sector, 2005). The increasingly competitive and demanding environment of nonprofits, including increased competition between nonprofits and for-profit businesses, is likely to lead to calls for even more legal accountability in the future.

It is worth noting that there are many others who want boards to improve their practice as well, and some of them are more troubled by many boards' lack of connectedness and accountability to their constituent communities. Nonprofits exist to serve these communities, these advocates assert, so it is time for boards to develop new and more effective ways to engage more fully and effectively with their clients and beneficiaries (Freiwirth, 2013; Freiwirth and Letona, 2006). In spite of the fact that there often is less direct legal accountability for this aspect of board work, some communities and stakeholder groups are beginning to explore ways to enhance this type of accountability. It is unclear whether this is a growing trend, but greater nonprofit stakeholder activism in several parts of the United States in 2015 and 2016 resulted in changes to the governance and board practices of several nonprofit and public service organizations (for example, Sweet Briar College; see McCambridge, 2015).

The Fiduciary Responsibility of Boards

Boards and board members often are reminded that they have a "fiduciary responsibility" to the organization and, ultimately, to the larger community they serve. At its core, "fiduciary responsibility" is the responsibility to treat the resources of the organization as a trust, and the responsible board will ensure that these resources are utilized in a reasonable, appropriate and legally accountable manner. Although the phrase often is used to refer specifically to financial resources, it actually applies to the stewardship of all of the assets and resources of the organization.

In general, the appropriate exercise of fiduciary responsibility includes:

- Adoption of a set of policies to govern the acquisition and use of financial and other resources
- Establishment, on a regular basis (usually annual), of a budget that allocates financial resources to the programs and activities that will accomplish the organization's mission, vision and goals and outcomes (preferably, in alignment with a strategic plan)
- Development and implementation of an ongoing system for monitoring and holding staff and volunteers accountable for their performance with regard to these policies and budgets
- Development and implementation of an ongoing system to monitor, assess, and report on the overall fiscal condition and financial performance of the organization
- Implementation of an independent external review process (such as an independent audit) on a regular basis (usually annual), to assess the organization's fiscal condition and health, including the effectiveness of its systems and policies for the protection and appropriate use of financial resources

The Legal Responsibilities of the Individual Board Member

The legal responsibilities of a board member flow directly from the responsibilities of the board as a whole. Each board member, individually, is accountable for honoring the same three fiduciary duties as is the entire board: to exhibit due care, loyalty, and obedience on behalf of the organization on whose board the member serves. This standard of personal conduct requires active and informed preparation and participation in the conduct of board business, including raising questions and issues that would reasonably be raised by any prudent person. Of course, a board member who does not attend meetings or who attends but does not participate or know what is under consideration does not meet these standards. At best, such members are not helping the organization; at worst they are endangering the organization and the interests of the people it serves. Such members also are at risk of personal liability and "intermediate sanctions" should certain kinds of inappropriate organizational or board behavior occur. (See the Internet resource website for this *Handbook* for more information on risk management and the liability of board members and other volunteers, as well as Chapter Two for general information about nonprofit law.)

All board members are responsible for doing their best to help ensure that the board as a whole is performing its legal responsibilities, and individual board members can be held liable as individuals for inappropriate organizational acts. Among the circumstances under which board members have been held personally liable (for more information, see Herman, 2006) are the following:

- When the organization has not paid certain taxes, especially payroll taxes
- The board enters into inappropriate arrangements or contracts with a board member, particularly including conflicts of interest
- The board has violated employment laws or contracts (a common example: the handling of the termination of an executive director)
- The board has failed to take reasonable steps to protect others from harm in a situation they knew or should have known was potentially dangerous (for example, in addressing dangerous facilities conditions, or in failing to address inappropriate individual behaviors of staff such as harassment or sexual misconduct)

Governance, Strategy, and the Work of the Board

As common as nonprofit boards are, they and their work tend to be rather misunderstood—even by those who work with and serve on them! Central to the confusion is the blurring of two key concepts: governance and board. The two are fundamentally different: *governance* is an organizational function, whereas a *board* is a structure of the organization that exists (at least theoretically) to govern—to perform the work of governance. When we treat them as the same thing, we plant the seeds of much of the confusion that bedevils our understanding of boards and board effectiveness.

Governing boards, by definition, exist to govern. They often do more, as discussed later in this section but, at the least, they are to govern. For a nonprofit organization, what does this mean? Governance is the process of providing strategic leadership to the organization, a process that begins with making informed organizational choices: choices about why we're here, what we want to accomplish, how best to achieve those results, the resources we'll need to do these things and how we will secure them, and how we will know whether we are making a difference. It comprises the functions of setting direction, making decisions about policy and strategy, overseeing and monitoring organizational performance, and ensuring overall accountability. Nonprofit governance is a political and organizational process involving multiple functions and engaging multiple stakeholders. There is significant evidence that effective governance is closely related to the success of the nonprofit organization (summarized in Herman and Renz, 2008). Governance is primarily the province of an organization's governing board, yet often it is not theirs alone. This is especially true in larger organizations that employ staff, where it is not unusual for the chief executive officer (often known as the executive director) and sometimes others to play a part in the governance process, as well.

Decisions about strategy and policy are central to the process of governance, based on the assumption that organizations can cause desired results to occur by choosing appropriate courses of action. In principle, strategy is the process of selecting among alternative courses of action—using the organization's mission, vision, and desired outcomes as the basis for the selection—with the expectation that implementing the chosen courses of action will enable the organization to achieve the desired outcomes to achieve the social impact the organization aspires to achieve.

Effective governance and strategy are integral to the sustainability and long-term effectiveness of a nonprofit operating in today's complex and competitive world. To succeed, nonprofits (like all organizations) must continuously renew the link between what they do and the needs and interests of the community they serve. As noted above, strategy involves gathering information and using it to inform the key decisions to be made by the leaders of the organization, with the expectation that good strategic choices will result in organizational success. Unlike the for-profit world, where these choices are largely grounded in options for making money for someone, nonprofits essentially always begin (as they should) with a focus on mission accomplishment. Their choices are about how best to have an impact. They must ensure they are providing the services needed and valued by their clients and constituents, and in ways that are consistent with the organization's core values and principles. As the organization serves its clients and the community, governance involves making assessments about how well or poorly the organization is doing and then making choices about how to refine its work to be more effective. The deeper process and practices by which this is accomplished is often referred to as strategic management, which is further explained in Chapter Eight. The strategy development and change process is explained in Chapter Nine.

The Work of the Nonprofit Board

In general, there are four fundamental categories of work that boards typically perform for any organization: governance and strategic direction, resource development and acquisition (financial and other resources), coaching and supporting, and monitoring and oversight (including its legal responsibilities). But how a board does each of these four is going to be quite different from organization to organization, and even within any one organization from time to time. That's because, apart from the standard legal duties, the work of a board must change over time as it ensures that it effectively addresses the organization's needs given its strategic direction and state of development.

Leadership Is Key. Every board exists to provide leadership to its organization, to its staff, and to its volunteers. Usually, this involves strategy and planning—defining or clarifying the organization's mission, vision, strategic direction, and goals. It includes clarifying why the organization exists, how the community will benefit from the work the organization will do, and what the organization is to accomplish. For the agency with paid staff, the work of setting direction and goals should be done together with the executive staff but, in the end, it is the board that makes the final decision.

Decisions about strategic direction also include deciding which programs will be implemented to accomplish the mission and goals. Programs are the sets of activities that involve the actual operations or work of the organization and, similar to the work of setting goals, decisions about programs are best made in collaboration with the executive staff (especially in cases of professional operations and practices). The imperative is to determine which programs are likely to be of greatest benefit in enabling the organization to accomplish its goals.

One of the most important acts of leadership for any board is the selection of the top staff person, the person who will lead the accomplishment of the work. In larger organizations with staff, this is the executive director or the chief executive officer (CEO); they will be recruited, selected, and supervised by the board or its key leaders. But even small agencies with no paid staff need to be clear about who will lead the work. Typically, this will be the board president or board chair but, to avoid confusion and conflict about who does what, it is important for the board to be clear in making and articulating this decision.

The board's work doesn't end with the selection of an executive director or CEO though. The board and its members have a responsibility to provide encouragement and support for their executive. This may involve serving as a "sounding board" or coach, and offering advice to the executive when he or she seeks it. It also involves setting specific goals with the executive—preestablished standards by which the board will judge the executive's job performance. If the executive is having significant performance problems, it is the board's job to support the executive with the additional training, direction, coaching, or other support that will help him or her be successful.

One of the most common expectations of governing boards for nonprofits is that of raising money and attracting other essential resources (such as donations of equipment, supplies, and talent). Not all boards handle the actual solicitation of funds, but every board is responsible for ensuring that its organization has adequate resources to implement the plans it has adopted. If the resources are inadequate, the board needs to implement activities to secure additional resources, decide to eliminate or cut back on certain programs, or how to implement some mix of both. When the agency has a professional fundraising team (usually including the chief executive), the board's fundraising work is handled in collaboration with them. Board members almost always can help in unique ways ("opening doors," helping nurture contacts with prospective donors) and it is important to capitalize on this help. In small organizations with no staff, it is entirely the board's job to solicit and secure such support.

Leadership and direction for the organization also include setting policies to guide the decisions of managers and the work of the staff and volunteers. Useful policies offer direction that guides the decisions and actions of all who work in the organization (including the board itself). Further, it is the board's job to have systems in place to ensure accountability and enable the board to monitor whether the organization and its people are following its policies.

What About Accountability? Of course, it is also the board's responsibility to ensure that the resources of the organization, once they are acquired, are used efficiently and effectively in the accomplishment of the work. In the United States, regulatory agencies expect the board to be the chief steward of the nonprofit's resources, and they demand that the board ensure that the organization make the most of its financial and other resources. To do this well, the board needs to have a financial management system in place that will enable it to guide and regularly monitor how agency resources are used. A useful system will enable the board to evaluate compliance with financial goals, plans, policies, and procedures, and a board should regularly review financial reports and assessments (including, for larger agencies, the results of annual audits) that will enable it to assess how well the organization is performing when it comes to its finances.

The board's responsibilities with regard to accountability, however, go beyond the issue of financial performance. It is the board's responsibility to ensure that the organization has systems in place to enable it to evaluate how well agency programs and activities perform. Similar to the issue of financial performance, the focus here is on how well the organization is achieving the results that it has promised in response to what its clients and community want and need. As with finances, it is important that the board have a system in place that gathers and reports on the results of the work. The goal is to enable the board to "close the loop" with information that enables it to evaluate whether the results are worth the resources that have been invested in their accomplishment.

Building Bridges and Staying in Touch. Effective boards also take care to nurture and strengthen their organization's relationships with constituents throughout the community, both those who receive benefits or services and those who are in important leadership positions in the political and donor communities. Nonprofits exist to meet community needs, and it is important for the board to be well connected to both sets of clients so it can make legitimate and useful judgments about whether the organization's programs and activities are valued by those they are designed to serve. This includes evaluating whether community conditions have changed to the degree that changes are needed in the agency's programs. It also involves making sure that the organization has the political support it needs to do its work. Organizations that are out of touch with their constituents, sooner or later, become irrelevant and disappear. Boards are a critical resource to help the organization (especially the chief executive and other organizational leaders) monitor and understand how the agency is perceived and whether changes are needed to sustain or increase its credibility and success.

Numerous nonprofit board consultants and authors have created lists of core functions and responsibilities to help boards understand their work. There is some variation among lists, and no one list is applicable to all organizations and boards, yet there are key responsibilities that appear in one form or another on almost all lists. Typically, it is a governing board's responsibility to:

1. *Lead the Organization:* provide overall leadership and strategic direction (including mission, vision and key goals) for the organization.
2. *Establish Policy:* be proactive in establishing policies that will guide the organization.
3. *Secure Essential Resources:* make sure the organization secures the resources that it needs to accomplish its mission, vision, and goals.
4. *Ensure Effective Resource Use:* ensure that the organization makes effective use of its resources to accomplish its mission, vision, and goals.
5. *Lead and Manage Chief Executive Performance:* provide strategic direction, support and advice, and performance feedback to the organization's chief executive (executive director). (*Note:* Even in organizations that do not employ staff, the board still is responsible for providing direction and oversight to the person or persons who manage and direct the work of the organization.)
6. *Engage Constituents:* actively help the organization develop and sustain effective ongoing relationships with its key constituents.

7. *Ensure and Enable Accountability:* make certain that the organization has established standards and implemented systems by which to ensure that it is accountable, ethical and effective in serving the community it exists to serve.

8. *Ensure Board Effectiveness:* see that the board itself operates at a high level of performance and effectiveness.

Exhibit 5.1 discusses the key activities that are associated with each of these core functions.

EXHIBIT 5.1. THE CORE FUNCTIONS OF THE PUBLIC SERVICE GOVERNING BOARD

A. LEAD

Lead the Organization

1. Articulate the mission and an inspiring vision for the organization
2. Determine the organization's strategic direction and focus, and how the organization fits into the "bigger picture" for the future
3. Instill and maintain a strategic perspective and focus for the work of the organization (this is governance versus management)
4. Specify the organization's long-term (multi-year) goals and outcomes
5. Provide advice and counsel to executive leadership
6. Seek and nurture opportunities for service and innovation

B. ESTABLISH POLICY

Establish Proactive Policy to Guide Organizational Action

1. Establish policies to guide executive decision making and action, and the implementation of organizational programs and operations
2. Determine the core programs and services of the organization
3. Establish key intermediate-term organizational goals (1–3 years)
4. Approve overall organizational design (structure and core processes)
5. Ensure that strategic plans and policies guide resource allocation

C. SECURE ESSENTIAL RESOURCES

Ensure That The Organization Secures the Resources Needed to Accomplish Its Mission, Vision, and Goals

1. Enable the organization to secure the resources necessary to implement the programs and services that are central to the achievement of the mission, vision, and goals
2. Make sure the resource mix is appropriate to the mission, vision, and long-term goals

D. ENSURE EFFECTIVE RESOURCE USE

Ensure That The Organization Makes Effective Use of Its Resources to Accomplish Its Mission, Vision, and Goals

1. Allocate resources to implement the organization's strategic plans (i.e., budget)
2. Ensure that effective systems are in place to enable the board and executive leadership to monitor and document that financial and other resources are managed and used effectively to accomplish the organization's purposes and plans
3. Make sure the organization's systems and policies are adequate to safeguard and guide the use of resources and assets (including appropriate management of risk)

E. LEAD AND MANAGE CHIEF EXECUTIVE PERFORMANCE

Ensure Effective CEO Performance

1. Recruit, select, hire, and set appropriate compensation for the chief executive
2. Provide regular performance direction and feedback to the chief executive
3. Serve as a confidential sounding board and resource advisor
4. Articulate board and executive roles and role distinctions (avoid micromanagement)
5. Ensure that there is a clear performance management structure in place that enables appropriate levels of accountability throughout the organization

F. ENGAGE CONSTITUENTS

Ensure an Effective Ongoing Relationship Between Organization and Key Constituents

1. Maintain strong relationships with key stakeholders
2. Facilitate and enhance effective two-way ongoing communication with key stakeholders
3. Enhance the external image and credibility of the organization
4. Make sure that organizational accountability information is regularly and accurately reported to relevant stakeholders
5. Encourage and support the processes for enhancing interorganizational and interagency communication and coordination
6. Discern and evaluate external trends and dynamics to assess their implications for the organization, and share this information with organization
7. Help constituents link with appropriate parts of the organization (as they have needs and problems to address)
8. Keep private the information that legally or ethically must remain private

G. ENSURE AND ENABLE ACCOUNTABILITY

Ensure Organizational Accountability and Stewardship

1. Ensure that appropriate systems exist and function well to monitor, assess, and document organizational performance and outcomes
2. Ensure that appropriate systems exist and function well to assess, document, and report on organizational compliance with policies, regulations, bylaws, and other mandates and guides for organizational action (including sunshine laws, etc.)
3. Ensure that organizational performance and outcomes information are reported in a timely, accurate, and useful manner to all relevant stakeholders
4. Monitor use of financial and other resources to ensure that they are managed and used efficiently and effectively to accomplish the organizations purposes and plans
5. Determine the performance information to be reported to the board, in what forms and manner, and how often (per previous, items 1, 2, and 4)
6. Make sure that the organization is responsive to constituent requests for information
7. Clarify to whom the organization is to be accountable and ensure that systematic accountability is maintained with them

H. ENSURE BOARD EFFECTIVENESS

Ensure a High Level of Board Performance and Effectiveness

1. Attract and retain well-qualified, committed members to serve on the board
2. Establish and monitor compliance with policies to guide board operations
3. Clarify board roles and responsibilities in helping the organization accomplish its mission, vision, and long term goals (including maintenance of distinctions between governance and management roles in the organization)
4. Prepare and educate members to work and serve effectively (including orientation, member education, ongoing information and education sessions)
5. Establish and regularly refine a functional, effective board design (structure and process for board and all subsidiary entities)
6. Engage in regular self-assessment and development planning (including individual member performance feedback)

A Special Note on Boards and Fundraising

One of the most common and, for many organizations, important roles associated with nonprofit board service is that of fundraising, of developing the financial resources needed to support the operations and programs of the organization. Fundraising is not a legal responsibility for a governing board, yet it is a governing board's responsibility to ensure that its organization has the resources it needs to finance its operations and effectively deliver its programs. How boards choose to handle this responsibility varies from organization to organization and field to field. Some hire executives and staff with the explicit understanding that they will take the lead in raising funds, some engage fundraising consultants to do most of the work, and some rely largely or entirely on board members themselves to raise funds. Many boards employ a combination of these approaches. (Chapter Eighteen addresses more fully the entire topic of philanthropic fundraising; we address only the board-related aspects of it here.) But when all is said and done, the board has ultimate responsibility for ensuring that the necessary resources are secured. This is a pivotal aspect of board leadership.

Of course, even though it's a common board responsibility, many board members dislike or are even afraid of the work of fundraising. "I hate to pester my friends for money," some say. "I'm just not cut out to beg," others say. They really do hate the idea! And if these perspectives were accurate characterizations of fundraising, almost everyone would! But they're not!

Successful fundraisers operate from a different perspective. They appreciate that fundraising is not about begging, conning, or "guilting" people into giving money—it's about creating opportunities for others in our community to join us in making a difference in the lives of those who are served by our agency or organization. It's about inviting people to become part of a cause that they appreciate. Giving is a natural human phenomenon, and charity and giving are a part of every culture. And most people do like the idea of giving when they have confidence that their gifts will make a difference in their community and improve lives. Of course, they want it to be about results—so our work starts with having effective organizations that do make a difference, and then being prepared to share the story of how that is happening and what it will take to sustain and grow the work.

So what does it take to be successful in raising money? You probably already know most of this!

- People give to the causes they care about, so we need to network and find the people who care about the work of our organization. Don't pester the people who don't care about the cause—keep reaching out and networking to find and share the story with the ones who do. They're the ones who will thank you for asking!

- People want to invest in making a difference, and they need to have confidence that their money will achieve results they care about. Therefore, when we ask people to give, we need to understand and be prepared to share the following information:
  - Who will my money benefit, and why would I care?
  - What difference will my money make, and how? If I invest in your organization, how will you use the money and what results can I expect?
  - Why should I trust you with my hard-earned money? How do you make sure my money will be used efficiently and well to achieve results I value?
- People give to people whom they trust. Therefore, fundraising involves developing and affirming relationships between those who give and those who will use the money to make the difference. No gift of any significance is going to be given before the donor gains trust and confidence that the people of the organization will be good stewards of their money. And they really want to know who is leading and overseeing the work—that is another reason why prospective donors often look critically at the governing board and top executives when they consider a gift. (By the way, that's also why many major donors ask how many members of the board themselves have made gifts to the organization. Why, they often ask, should I give to an organization that can't even attract gifts from its own board? It's a fair question!)
- People often have specific ideas about how or for whom the money they give will be used. They may have a favorite program, for example, or there may be a particular type of client they want to benefit from their gift. For example, some donors have a special interest in helping only children or people with certain health challenges or needs. Some major donors will like the idea of having their names on a building or linked to a particular program. And some prefer to remain anonymous and keep their giving confidential. We are well advised to take care to understand what the prospective donors care about and do all we can to ensure that our options meet their needs. And always remember: any restrictions that a donor places on the use of a gift is legally binding. If someone gives money for a particular program, it is illegal as well as unethical to use the money for any other purpose.
- There are many ways that people want to give, and we are much more likely to be successful if we offer options that match their interests. For example, some may wish to give via frequent small gifts (such as regular payroll deductions), some may wish to give only once or twice per year, and some may wish to give as part of some kind of fun group experience (such as a charity golf tournament, a charity casino night, a happy hour auction). Some may have very little money

today but they would like to leave a legacy, and they may be willing to include your cause in their will or name your organization the beneficiary of their IRA or life insurance policy.

Board members and other fundraisers are wise when they plan to capitalize on all of the previous points as they prepare to raise money. In fact, planning and preparation are central to fundraising success. Before going to anyone to ask for funds, get organized. Too many boards and organizations "shoot themselves in the foot" because they jump into fundraising without planning, organizing, or preparing their people for the process. It is very worthwhile to take time to work together to make plans, prepare information and resource materials, identify your best prospects and determine who and how they best could be approached, and what it is that you want to ask of them. And when we ask board members to participate in the fundraising process, we have an obligation to provide them with the information and training that will help them understand and implement this work successfully. Few of us are "naturals" at raising money. Yet, too often, we just tell our board members and volunteers to go raise money without helping them get ready to do this important work. Of course, that's often the source of board members' and volunteers' complaints and fears about fundraising. People don't like to be asked to do things they don't have confidence they can perform reasonably well. In fundraising, as in all other work, it's unfair to complain about performance if we have not provided people with the knowledge, training, and resources they need to be successful.

Fundraising is about creating opportunities for people to invest in work that they consider worthwhile and important and, when it is done ethically and effectively, it can be exceptionally rewarding for both the donor and the board members who help with fundraising. Effective fundraisers are successful because they connect with people who care as much as they do about the cause and mission, tell the story of the work in a way that appeals to those who are motivated to give, and offer these prospective donors the opportunity to make gifts in ways that will appeal to and work well for them. It's pointless to fool or harass people who don't care in an effort to get them to give. But engaging people who care to leave a legacy, people who care about the cause and want to make a difference—that's a win-win!

The Work of Individual Board Members

Interest in nonprofit boards and how they work has grown substantially in recent years, and more and more people are embracing the opportunity to serve on a board. This is good news. But the trend has a challenging side to it, as well.

The average person working with a governing board, executive and board member alike, has limited understanding of the work to be done by a board or what is expected of him or her. In spite of all the talk about the importance of effective boards and good governance, we find that the majority of people in the nonprofit sector (including even a significant share of those who have prior board experience) actually have only vague and general notions about the roles and responsibilities of a board member.

The uncertainty and confusion are understandable. Research indicates that most boards do not do a very good job of preparing people for their work on and with boards. This may be partly because every board seems to be a little (or a lot) different from any standard model, and partly because we are so busy that we don't feel that we can afford to take the time to be sure that we're all on the same page. We become so busy doing the work that we don't take the time to make sure that we understand the work! The lack of shared understanding is amplified by our discomfort with our uncertainty. A good share of the time, an executive or board member with confusion or questions assumes he or she is the only one who is uncertain and will be unwilling to ask for clarification—and yet that person usually is not alone in his or her uncertainty.

Obviously, it is important for every board member to honor his or her legal responsibilities, but the roles and responsibilities of the individual board member of a typical nonprofit board are more extensive than mere legal compliance. Every board should develop and communicate its own set of member expectations, focused on the needs and interests of that specific organization and what it needs from its board. The following are among the most common of responsibilities or expectations that a typical nonprofit is likely to have of its board members:

- Participate actively (attend all meetings of the board, serve on committees or task forces, prepare in advance for meetings and other key board activities, engage in independent and critical thought in all areas of board work, and attend special events and other key organizational activities as requested).
- Be knowledgeable and ensure that they understand and act consistently with the mission, vision, and overall work and strategic direction of the organization; the bylaws and policies that guide the work of the board; and the board's expectations of them as a member of the board.
- Do their homework to ensure that they are appropriately informed about issues and matters that will be the subjects of board deliberation, decision making or monitoring, and important issues that are likely to have an impact on the success of the board and organization.
- Provide active support for the fundraising and other resource development activities of the organization, including making a regular personal financial

contribution to the organization (at a significant level, according to the member's capacity) and assisting the organization in connecting with those people and organizations that may be able to assist in funding and supporting the organization.

- Serve as an ambassador and advocate on behalf of the organization, helping support networking and the development of connections with community and other leaders.
- Provide encouragement and active support for the work of the staff and volunteers, taking care that board activities do not undermine staff roles, functions or performance.
- Serve with honor and integrity, including:
  - Help enhance the image and credibility of the organization through their work, taking care that their personal behavior reflects well on the work and reputation of the organization.
  - Address sensitive matters in confidence and with discretion, exhibiting the best of ethical sensitivity and performance.
  - Honor and actively support all board decisions, once they have been made, and treat the content of board deliberations with confidence and discretion.
  - Avoid actual and perceived conflicts of interest, to the greatest degree possible, and exhibit the highest of ethical standards in all personal conduct.
- Support and actively contribute to the board's efforts to work effectively as a team, including taking an active and constructive role in helping the board do its work, embracing the challenges and opportunities of board work with a positive attitude and energy, bringing a sense of perspective and humor to the work of the board, and providing encouragement and support to fellow board members (including taking time to celebrate the successes and accomplishments of the organization, the board and its members).

Characteristics of Typical Nonprofit Boards

As noted earlier in this chapter, nonprofit boards are an exceptionally diverse and heterogeneous lot, so a discussion of "typical" characteristics must be broad and general. Nonprofit boards typically have specific positions (offices) and work units (committees and task forces) that help the board organize and accomplish its work. The typical nonprofit board in the United States is composed of from nine to twenty-four members and, according to some of the most recent surveys of U.S. nonprofits (BoardSource, 2015; Larcker, Donatiello, Meehan, and Tayan,

2015, p. 25; Ostrower, 2007), the average for nonprofit board size in America is from ten to thirteen members (median size is nine to eleven). BoardSource, which conducts annual surveys, reports that average board size has been decreasing slightly over the past twenty years, from an average size of twenty members in 1994 to fifteen in 2014 (BoardSource, 2015, p. 9). BoardSource also reports that boards of national and international nonprofits tend to have slightly smaller boards. Most boards in the United States have specified terms of office for their members, and 71 percent have limits on the numbers of terms a member may serve on a board. Three-year terms are most common, and about two-thirds of all U.S. nonprofits limit consecutive reelection to a maximum of three terms (40 percent impose a limit of two consecutive terms) (BoardSource, 2015).

Board composition, diversity, and inclusion are regular topics of interest and a source of significant concern for many. We know more about board membership of larger and more affluent institutions than we do about boards of smaller and community-based organizations (Ostrower and Stone, 2006), and what we know indicates that the diversity of nonprofit board membership in the United States does not reflect the diversity of the communities these organizations exist to serve. In fact, board composition in the United States (including racial and ethnic membership) has remained relatively unchanged since the late 1990s (BoardSource, 2015). In 2014, U.S. nonprofit boards were composed largely of white, non-Hispanic members; more than 80 percent were Caucasian and slightly fewer than half of members were women (p. 53). In an earlier study, Ostrower and Stone (2006) report that only about 3 percent of board members were Hispanic; and fewer than 7 percent of board members were under the age of 35. Nearly 70 percent of nonprofit executives reported in 2014 that they were dissatisfied with the diversity of their boards and that this is an organizational issue, even though 80 percent of these organizations reported that they have been making active efforts to improve board diversity (BoardSource, 2015, pp. 11–12).

Officers

Most nonprofit organizations have multiple officers, and the laws of most states in the United States require certain offices—most commonly, chair (sometimes called president), secretary, and treasurer (sometimes the roles of secretary and treasurer are combined).

Chair. The board chair is the chief voluntary officer of the organization, responsible for organizing and conducting the meetings of the board. Further, it is the chair's responsibility to facilitate the board's work as a team, and to ensure that meetings and other board activities are organized and conducted in an effective manner. It is common for the board chair to oversee the performance of the organization's chief executive on behalf of the board, although some organizations elaborate the process by assigning the chair to lead a process in conjunction with a committee of the board (often the executive committee) or even the full board. There is a small but growing body of research that affirms what many would expect: the performance and effectiveness of the board chair has significant impact on the effectiveness of the board and the satisfaction of its members (Harrison, Murray, and Cornforth, 2013).

Secretary. The work of a corporate secretary involves ensuring that accurate records are retained for the nonprofit, including copies of all official documents, communications and correspondence of the organization (including articles of incorporation, bylaws, and legal notices and filings), as well as notices and minutes of all official meetings of the board. The secretary may not personally prepare the minutes but is accountable for ensuring that accurate and complete minutes of all official meetings are kept.

Treasurer. The treasurer oversees the processes of financial management and accountability for the organization, helping make sure that all resources are used appropriately and their use is documented. This includes ensuring the preparation and retention of complete and accurate financial reports and records. In small organizations, the treasurer often is involved in the actual financial operations of the organization; in larger organizations he or she maintains general oversight of financial affairs and sees that regular reports are provided to the board, regulators, and other key stakeholders. The treasurer may not personally keep financial records and maintain accounts, but he or she is accountable for ensuring that these records are maintained and available to authorities.

Committees and Task Forces

Boards engage in much of their work as a full group and, ideally, all members work as a team to accomplish the work of the board. Nonetheless, more than 90 percent of U.S. nonprofit boards also have created committees and task forces to help the board do its work (Ostrower, 2007), and these entities are part of the governance system of the organization. For most boards, some of these units are permanent or "standing" structures, whereas others accomplish a specific task and then disappear. It is increasingly common for boards to refer to the permanent structures as "committees" and the limited-term entities as "task forces" or "ad hoc committees," although some organizations do use the labels interchangeably. It is common for board committees to be composed entirely of board members, yet a growing number of nonprofits also invite non-board members with unique expertise, knowledge, or interests to serve. (However, it must be noted that some states such as California recently have changed their laws to disallow non-board members to serve as members of committees when the committees have the authority to act in place of the full board.) Key standing committees typically are specified in the organization's bylaws, which also should explain their purpose and role(s).

The following are among the most common types of standing committees:

1. *Executive Committee.* This committee is typically composed of the officers, and sometimes also will include committee chairs or selected other board members. It usually has the authority to act on behalf of the board between meetings and to address organizational emergencies. Some executive committees have the authority to act independently, but many are required to have their actions subsequently ratified by the full board.

2. *Nominating Committee.* This committee has the responsibility for recruiting candidates for board and committee membership and preparing a "slate" of candidates or nominees for consideration and action by the full board; many also nominate officers. It is increasingly common to define this committee's responsibilities to include a year-round cycle of board development activities, including new member orientation, member self-assessment, board self-assessment and development, and the development of board training programs and retreats. When operating with this enlarged portfolio, such committees often are called Board Development or Governance Committees.

3. *Fundraising* or *Development Committee.* This committee usually is responsible for working with staff and board to organize and implement the organization's fundraising events and activities, including the solicitation of major gifts and grants.

4. *Finance Committee.* This committee is responsible for planning, monitoring, and overseeing the organization's use of its financial resources, including developing a budget to allocate the organization's funds. This committee will develop for board action the financial policies the organization requires. Unless the organization has a separate Audit Committee, the Finance Committee also will oversee and review the organization's independent audit or financial review.

5. *Personnel Committee.* This committee usually is responsible for planning, monitoring, and overseeing the organization's use of its human resources (paid and

volunteer). This committee will develop needed personnel policies, including policies guiding performance management and supervision, employee compensation and benefits, and handling of grievances.

6. *Program Committee.* It is not unusual for nonprofits to have one or more committees to oversee the organization's system(s) for delivering quality services to clients, and to engage in some form of monitoring and oversight to ensure that these services are provided in a timely and responsible manner. Such committees may handle certain relations with community leaders and interest groups that have key interests in the programs of the organization, as well as planning for program development or refinement to meet future needs.

It is important that committees and task forces only do work that legitimately is the responsibility or prerogative of the board, and care must be taken to ensure that these structures complement rather than interfere with the staff operations of the organization and the general oversight that should be provided by the full board. Many boards in older organizations have concluded that they have too many committees; since the mid-1990s it has become something of a trend among U.S. nonprofit boards to decrease the number of standing committees and use task forces more frequently to address specific issues of strategic importance as they arise (BoardSource, 2015; Taylor, Chait, and Holland, 1996).

Building Board Capacity to Serve

Nonprofit boards are today feeling more pressure than ever to perform well, and these demands to perform more effectively are coming from nearly all quarters. Although each is demanding something a little different, federal and state regulatory officials, various taxation authorities (the Internal Revenue Service and state departments of revenue), foundation officials, donors, and even clients and other key beneficiaries are calling for boards to be better, stronger, and more effective. Even board members themselves, for the most part, say their boards could be more effective (BoardSource, 2015; Larcker, Donatiello, Meehan, and Tayan, 2015).

Characteristics of the Strong Nonprofit Board

What are the characteristics of the well-developed board—the board that is able to recruit, retain, and mobilize its members to do the essential work of a board of directors? A review of the literature suggests the following key characteristics:

- The effective board organizes its work in ways that make effective (and often creative) use of the limited amount of time that members can commit to the organization.
- The effective board is good at matching the skills, abilities, and interests of its members with the work it needs to do, and it invests in preparing its members to do this work.
- The effective board understands that, at core, success is grounded in building effective relationships—relationships among the members of the board, relationships between members and the board as a whole, relationships between the members and the overall organization, and relationships with external constituencies. These boards take care to nurture and sustain these relationships.
- The effective board recognizes that one of the most valuable assets it brings to the nonprofit is its members—their time, talent, and service. It understands that the highest and best use of member time is to provide leadership, strategic direction, and oversight to the agency, and it recognizes the opportunity cost inherent in dribbling away member time by involving them in irrelevant activities that divert their attention from the most important work they could do.
- The effective board creates an infrastructure of support that helps members accomplish their work efficiently and effectively. Member time and talent are effectively leveraged because the support, systems, and technology exist to enable their work. Two kinds of infrastructure are provided:
  - Infrastructure that supports members' work together, such as communications technologies and information systems, and
  - Systems to provide the information that the board needs to accomplish its work.
- The effective board is thoughtful about and takes the time to reflect on what its does well and what could be improved—and it uses this information to improve both board performance and the quality of each member's experience as a board member. The effective board understands that board effectiveness is a journey and a process, not a specific state of being. It is thoughtful about growing its capacity to perform, and focuses on the high-leverage targets of opportunity for growing board capacity.

Competencies of Effective Boards

What are the key elements of nonprofit board effectiveness? Why do some boards perform well when many others do not? One of the foundational research initiatives to examine these questions was implemented by Thomas Holland and colleagues in the mid-1990s. They examined the differences between boards that were reported to be more versus less effective and identified six core competencies that were associated with the best-performing of these boards. Even the most effective of these boards varied in the degree to which they had mastered each of the six, but there were clear relationships between the degree to which each board exhibited each of the competencies and their overall performance as a board. The six key dimensions of board competence are the following (Holland and Jackson, 1998, pp. 122–123):

- *Contextual competence:* the board understands and takes into account the culture, values, mission, and norms of the organization it governs.
- *Educational competence:* the board takes the necessary steps to ensure that members are well informed about the organization, the professions working there, and the board's own roles, responsibilities, and performance.
- *Interpersonal competence:* the board nurtures the development of its members *as a group*, attends to the board's collective welfare, and fosters a sense of cohesiveness and teamwork.
- *Analytical competence:* the board recognizes complexities and subtleties in the issues its faces, and it draws upon multiple perspectives to dissect complex problems and to synthesize appropriate responses.
- *Political competence:* the board accepts that one of its primary responsibilities is to develop and maintain healthy two-way communications and positive relationships with key constituencies.
- *Strategic competence:* the board helps envision and shape institutional direction and ensure a strategic approach to the organization's future.

Helping Boards Meet the Challenge

Nonprofit governing boards often are criticized for poor performance, and there seem to be an increasing number of egregious examples of board dysfunction. However, it is time to recognize that we're really not doing enough to help governing boards and their members to be successful as they serve in these special roles of public trust. About half of all mid-sized and larger U.S. nonprofits' boards report that they have engaged in some regular board development process (BoardSource, 2015). There is clear and growing evidence that nonprofit boards that engage in a regular systematic approach to board development are more effective and their members are happier and more productive on behalf of the organization (BoardSource, 2015; Renz and Andersson, 2013). Appropriate board development activities can have a positive impact on board member performance as well as overall board effectiveness. Brown (2007, 2013) reports that effective member recruitment, selection, and orientation practices enhance board member engagement and performance; other research suggests that a well-designed program of board development can make a difference in the performance of a nonprofit board and, ultimately, in the financial performance of the organization (Holland and Jackson, 1998). Similarly, Cornforth (2001) reports a direct relationship between the effectiveness of nonprofit boards and (a) the knowledge and skills of board members, (b) the clarity of their board member roles and responsibilities, and (c) board members and executives coming together on a periodic basis to assess how well they are working together. It is a reasonable to conclude that activities that improve board members' knowledge and skills and clarify their roles and responsibilities will therefore enhance board effectiveness as well.

One of the major impediments that keeps the typical board from engaging in ongoing board development is the sense (or worry) that it will involve too much effort and time, and that it will be a distraction from "our real work." However, an effective board development approach will not divert attention from important matters. To the contrary, it will focus attention in a more efficient way on one of the core responsibilities of every nonprofit board—the responsibility to be a good steward of its members' time and talent and to ensure its own effectiveness. In other words, effective boards engage in a systematic ongoing process of development because they understand that this will make a difference in the value they deliver for the organization, and because it makes a difference to those who serve on the board. It's no fun to serve on a dysfunctional board!

Being systematic does not require a board to be exceptionally elaborate about its approach, nor to consume hundreds of hours of member time each year. Indeed, one of the greatest challenges confronting most boards today is that they barely can find the time to get enough members together to handle the regular required business, much less to take time for what some might consider "add on" activities. Thus, efficiency in the development process is important. However, the irony is that those boards that take a minimalist approach to development generally undercut their ability to bring members together for the small amount of business they do try to accomplish because service on their board is so boring and unrewarding! Members attend meetings (if they do at all) only out of a sense of duty or obligation rather than because they feel their time and talents are being used well to make a difference. Efforts to minimize development time actually can backfire when it comes to member commitment as well as board performance!

Eight Core Principles for Growing a Board

There are eight principles that board leaders will do well to recognize as they consider the range of options they might employ to build their boards' capacity.

- *Principle 1.* Nonprofit organizations cannot be successful for the long term unless they have governing boards that are effective. There is a high correlation between nonprofit organizational effectiveness and board effectiveness (Brown, 2007; Herman and Renz, 2008; Renz and Andersson, 2013). A board's effectiveness is important to the organization's performance and quality of service to the community.

- *Principle 2.* Board design is about the future, and all board development needs to be done with the future in mind—both the conditions that the organization will face in the future and the organization's needs for the future to address those conditions. Hockey star Wayne Gretzky is reputed to have said that his success as a hockey player was due to the fact that he always made it a point to "skate to *where the puck was going to be*!" Boards should take this point to heart! Some of the most important of board work involves bridging from the realities of today to the vision for tomorrow.

- *Principle 3.* There is no one single design or model for board development that automatically will be best for all organizations. The board is part of two larger systems—the organization and the larger community environment—and so its design and development need to be aligned with the needs and characteristics of these environs. Boards serve different functions and roles at different points in the life and development of their organizations, and these differences must be taken into account when determining the most useful board development process. Further, the research to date on board development initiatives suggests no one model seems to be better than another. In fact, there is evidence that what makes a difference in board development is the organized use of any thoughtful and well-developed systematic approach to development (Gill, 2005; Nobbie and Brudney, 2003).

- *Principle 4.* Focus on principles, not "best practices." The notion that there are practices that are universally best is flawed—at best, there are "promising practices" that are worthy of consideration, but one can never claim that a given practice will be "best" until the organization's issues, needs, and circumstances are taken into account (Herman and Renz, 2004, 2008). There are many good resources that offer examples of useful practices (for example, checklists, training programs, board development tools; consult the Internet resource website for this *Handbook* for further information). But until an organization knows what it needs, these are merely resources.

- *Principle 5.* Leadership is critical and pivotal to board success and, therefore, to board development. Every change process, including every development process, needs to have at least one champion who will make it his or her goal to advance the development process (Kotter, 1996). However, serving as "champion" is not the only leadership role in any board; responsibility for leadership must be shared among all members of a team, as they provide both mutual support and encourage mutual accountability for the board's work.

- *Principle 6.* Structures never guarantee performance in organizations (or communities), although they can get in the way and screw things up. Performance derives from the behavior of people, and it is not possible to guarantee performance through the creation of structures. Therefore, we need to develop and keep only as many board structures (such as offices, committees, terms, reporting relationships) as are useful for the next stage of board work. It is important to take care to nurture the "soft" or process aspects of the board's work, because the processes are the dynamic vehicles for bringing structures to life (see the next principle).

- *Principle 7.* Effective boards, by definition, are teams. Teams are groups of people who are working together in a mutually-accountable way to accomplish a shared goal or outcome (Katzenbach and Smith, 2003). If this definition does not describe a governing board, then that board is not living up to its legal and ethical obligations as a board! The shared outcome always is defined as the success of the organization. Thus, team building is always an important dimension of any legitimate approach to board development.

- *Principle 8.* Every effective development process must "meet" the people of the organization or board "where they are," and each organization and board must build from the level of development and capacity that exists at the time they begin the development process. Regardless of what you wish, the board is currently at some level of development that must be recognized for what it is—the starting point for growing the board. So the process starts at this point. Further, it must be recognized that there are going to be limits to how much can be done or what a board can accomplish in a given time period. It makes no sense to assume or wish that a board is better positioned than it is (nor worse than its situation is). Nowhere is this going to be more true than in working with an all-volunteer group of people from the community, people who always will need to balance their board work with the other demands of life, family, and work. To this end, do not wait until or look for the "perfect time" to start a development process—conditions never will be close to perfect for any typical board. Start now and begin with whatever is feasible to begin to help your board develop.

The Board Builder's Challenge: Taking the Long-Term Developmental Perspective

Strong and effective boards do not develop overnight, they don't happen by accident, and they do not remain effective indefinitely. Strong and effective boards grow to be effective because their leaders have invested in their capacity. Thus, a growing number of thoughtful nonprofit board and executive leaders are taking care to invest the time and resources needed to build the capacity for sustained long-term board performance and impact. They recognize that this makes a difference in the value and impact for the organization. They also recognize that it contributes in another very important way: it makes a difference in the quality of the governance and leadership experience for those who serve on the board and those who work with the board. This may well make the difference in retaining the board members who contribute the most to the board's success. The ability to achieve a long-term difference in board performance will be substantially enhanced if the leader recognizes that there exists this interconnected set of elements that collectively affect board capacity.

In this section I introduce a board development framework, discuss the process by which boards develop and grow, and suggest the ways that the concepts of the framework might be used to inform and guide board development activity. I discuss how the cycle begins for new organizations with new boards, although my emphasis is on the ways that existing boards can use this development cycle perspective to enrich their capacity and build their impact.

The Board Development Cycle

Effective boards grow and develop (intentionally or not, knowingly or not) through a relatively predictable process that progresses through eight specific phases, each of which contributes importantly to development. These phases of development are unlikely to occur in a distinct linear sequence, yet we do observe that there is a general progression through them that is common to most boards. This progression in development builds to become a renewing cycle that boards use to their advantage. In reality, this developmental process tends to be implemented rather intuitively, since few boards give much overt thought to their overall development and growth. However, when understood and used in a systematic manner, this approach makes it possible for a board to develop in more efficient and effective ways.

The effective board grows and develops in capacity to serve as it:

- *Organizes* itself to efficiently and effectively accomplish the work it must do for the organization
- *Attracts* to the board table a group of people who will enable it to do this work well
- *Prepares* these people to effectively serve in their roles as members
- *Helps* these members work together as a team to accomplish their work
- *Focuses* members' attention on the right issues and questions
- *Engages and motivates* its members to retain their involvement and service
- *Employs* members' time well, in meetings and other activities
- *Evaluates and develops* its own performance, as a group, and uses this information to refine its design and practices to improve its effectiveness for the future

The eight phases in the process of governing board growth and development undoubtedly take different forms for each board, yet every effective board addresses each in some active way as it develops.

Of course, in real organizational life, these elements tend to blur, overlap and interact in ways that cause them to influence each other. And in young and relatively undeveloped boards, led by inexperienced leaders, many of these elements are likely to be implement informally and even unknowingly—yet each of these elements is addressed in some way, in better or worse ways, by every board that actually grows to operate as a board. Figure 5.1 illustrates the general sequence and flow of the eight elements of the board development cycle.

Each of the eight elements of the board development cycle illustrated in Figure 5.1 contributes uniquely to the capacity and performance of a board. Some of these elements are most usefully implemented in a sequence (for example, recruiting and selecting members logically precedes building those members' capacity). However, it also is likely that many of these elements will overlap in their implementation (for example, "ensuring strategic focus" relates to essentially all of the other elements). Therefore, it is useful to recognize that the eight elements of the board development cycle are neither mutually exclusive nor do they occur in a purely sequential, lockstep way. In fact, for boards just beginning to address development, working on any one of these, individually and separately, can have utility for building board capacity if that element is a key source of dysfunction or difficulty. However, the extended value of the board development cycle framework lies in the recognition that the

FIGURE 5.1. The Board Development Cycle

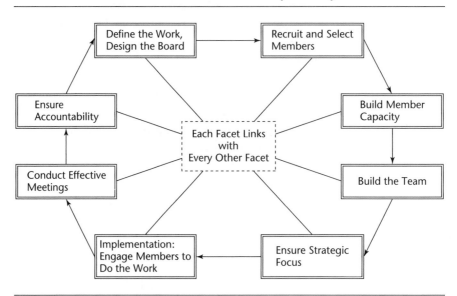

value of each element is substantially enhanced by linking it to and growing it with other elements in the cycle.

The following presents the sequence of the board development cycle from the perspective of a new organization that is just starting out with the development of its board. Each section offers a basic explanation of that element of the cycle and provides a few insights into its importance to overall board function. (Additional information about each of the eight is available at the Internet resource website for the *Handbook*. Included on the site are ideas and suggestions for various development options and activities that might be considered useful by a board working to address each element.)

Element A: Define the Work, Design the Board

The board of directors of a nonprofit organization should design itself based on the needs of the organization and the work that the board will need to do to support the organization's next generation of work. And until the board knows what is needed from it, it cannot usefully determine what it should do or how to organize to do it. The wise board organizes itself from the perspective of clarity about the needs of the organization and what it can do to uniquely add value to mission accomplishment, and then designs itself to do that work. The contributions that must be made by the board of a small start-up organization are going to be quite different from the contributions of the board of a mature organization. The work is going to be different. And some board designs match some stages of organization development better than do others. (For a very useful perspective on how boards and organizations must align as they progress through their various "life stages," see the 2008 work of Susan Kenny Stevens.)

So the process needs to begin with gaining clarity about the work and results that the board will need to deliver to advance the work of the organization in its next generation of service. Board design includes multiple elements, including structures (such as committees, task forces, offices) and processes (leading, meeting, making decisions, monitoring, communicating). And it is based on a clear delineation of the roles that the board will play in the leadership, governance and management of the organization. For the organization with staff (paid or volunteer), this definition will include explicit distinctions in the roles to be served by the board and its members as compared to that of the chief executive and other staff. Research indicates that much board member dissatisfaction is rooted in members' lack of clarity about their roles and the work they are to do. In fact, lack of role clarity is one key reason that people leave the organization. Role clarity is especially critical when aligning the work of the board and the chief executive; lack of clarity is a recipe for unproductive conflict waiting to happen. (The complex and sensitive topic of how to sustain a productive board-executive relationship is addressed extensively in Chapter Six of this volume.)

Element B: Recruit and Select Members

Recruitment and selection of the right group of members is one of the most fundamental elements of board development. To echo the advice of management author Jim Collins (2005), an essential element of organizational success is to ensure that you have "the right people on the bus." Every board must find people to serve, and every board engages in activities that will make this happen. The key concern is whether the board is thoughtful, systematic, and disciplined about member recruitment. Far too many boards haphazardly pursue the wrong candidates for the wrong reasons, place them on the board, and then become terribly frustrated when things go poorly. A large proportion of board performance problems can be traced directly back to an ineffective or counterproductive member recruitment and selection process. Ignore this element at your peril!

Recent research documents that effective recruitment and selection practice is very significant to board effectiveness (for example, Brown, 2007;

Cornforth, 2001). The effective nonprofit board will engage in a recruitment and selection process that builds on the insights it gained during its work on Element A (Define the Work, Design the Board). From its understanding of the work it needs to do for the organization in the future, it will then identify what it needs from its next generation of members (knowledge, skills, abilities, connections, and other characteristics), assess its current capacity from the perspective of these needs, and then engage in a systematic process of seeking, locating, and recruiting additional members who will be right for the next-generation work of the board. It will take care to find the right matches between the organization's needs and the needs and interests of prospective members, including taking care to ensure that its membership is appropriately diverse and reflective of the community the organization exists to serve. None of this is to suggest that this element must be implemented in a drawn-out and bureaucratic way: it is possible to be proactive and systematic without getting bogged down in an excessive process.

Element C: Prepare Members to Serve

Effective boards recruit people to serve as members because they bring knowledge, skill, and an array of talents and assets that the board envisions will be important to its future success. But it is not enough to simply bring talented people to the board; the effective board will help its members to put these talents to work in ways that are particularly useful for both the organization and the member. This type of preparation often begins with helping the new member understand the nature and scope of his or her role as he or she becomes an active member of the board, and an increasing number of boards offer some form of useful member orientation process for their new members. In fact, this member preparation usually begins at the recruitment and selection stage with an explicit description of the roles and expectations that the board has for its members (for example, requirements for meeting attendance, or whether members work on fundraising).

This is a good start, but the effective board will provide much more in the way of preparation and support for its members. Recent research also confirms that member development activities for members are positively related to effective board performance (for example, Brown, 2007; Holland and Jackson, 1998). Such development helps members better understand their work, the work of the organization, the challenges that the organization and board believe will be most important to address as they proceed with their work, what they envision will be the board's role in helping to address these issues, and how the board works together as a group or team. Further, a strong board will provide regular ongoing support to all of its members, not only those who are new, to help them serve effectively. Every member's knowledge and understanding will need to grow and develop as the organization's circumstances evolve. This dimension of support for members is not only important from a board perspective; many board members value their time on a board because they gain new knowledge, skills, and perspectives through their board service that they can use in other venues of their lives. As such, member development can become a motivator as well as a support for improved board member performance.

Element D: Build the Board as a Team

Much of the power of the effective board derives from the synergy that results from individuals coming together to do things that they could not do as well by themselves. When individual board members first meet, they are a group. Yet board work is inherently *team work*. The board's authority and responsibility, legally and ethically, derives from its work as a *collective* body. The thoughts and decisions of specific individuals, no matter how bright or relevant, cannot be represented as the work of the board unless and until the board *collectively* adopts them as its own. In other words, a board must develop to the level of working as a team in order to serve effectively.

Taylor, Chait, and Holland (1996) report that high-performing boards actively work to build their capacity to work as a team. In their words, these boards "focus on the constellation, not the stars!" While some board leaders may debate whether a board is or needs to be a team, it is entirely clear (as a matter of definition) that a board cannot truly function as a board unless its members come together to serve as a team. If there is no shared purpose the board members are working together to accomplish, then they cannot possibly be serving effectively as a board. If nothing else, the duty of loyalty compels it! Of course the typical board member joins a board for just this purpose—to work with others to help see that the organization progresses in its efforts to accomplish its mission and vision.

Of course, it is one thing to assert that a board is or should be working as a team, it is another to actually achieve this. A critical yet often overlooked element of board effectiveness is investing time and attention in helping the board's members work *together* effectively. This is central to this element of the board development cycle. Ironically, many board members and leaders know a fair amount about teams and how to grow them because they've had team development training at work, provided by their employers! And yet it is rather uncommon to find a board whose leaders are capitalizing on widely available information and resources that exist to support team building and development to enhance their board's effectiveness.

Element E: Create and Sustain a Strategic Focus

Boards are "all over the map" when it comes to their work. Some operate exclusively at the policy governance and leadership level of work, some serve in both governing and management roles, and still others serve all roles in the organization—as governor, manager, and as operations staff. But the one level at which all boards must work is the strategic level, doing the work of governance and leadership. One of the greatest challenges many boards face is that of sustaining their focus at the strategic level. For understandable but problematic reasons, boards often become so involved in the details that they lose all sense of their unique responsibility to make strategic choices. Indeed, in organizations with staff, this can become a critical source of tension between the board and the organization's top levels of executive management; board members become heavily involved in management or operations and become resented for their duplication of or interference with the work of the rest of the organization (the so-called problem of board micro-management).

This board development element is especially linked to all other elements of the board development cycle. Several aspects of creating and sustaining a strategic focus must be integrated with each of the other elements. For example, the issue of strategic focus and the board's role is central to board design issues, such as committee and role descriptions. But the challenge of strategic focus is equally relevant when we recruit members to serve on the board. If a board does not ensure that the members it recruits are able to work with an appropriately strategic focus, then it is doomed to fighting an uphill battle for its entire tenure.

There are multiple ways that boards and their leaders can help to ensure that the board works with and provides the strategic focus that the organization needs. Useful resources are available at the *Handbook*'s Internet resource site.

Element F: Implementation: Engage Members to Do the Work

Certain aspects of board development are likely to be most effectively accomplished as the board and its members actually engage in the process of implementation; that is, doing the work planned and organized during the earlier stages of board development. Key among them is the set of issues associated with engaging and motivating members to play their roles—the entire process of handling board members as a special type of volunteer. We know quite a lot about volunteer management and what it takes to engage and motivate volunteers, yet, similar to our tendency to ignore the extensive team development literature, we find that most boards are not adequately attentive to matters of engaging the board member as volunteer. (The guidance on volunteer management provided in Chapter Twenty-Four is especially relevant to this point.)

Element G: Conduct Effective Meetings

The crucible within which boards do much of their most critical and essential work is the meeting—the time during which board members come together to organize and implement their work on behalf of the organization. Too long, too short, too disorganized, too narrow, too unfocused—the complaints and concerns are multiple and frequent. Meetings are among the most disliked elements of board service for many members, yet the typical board chair or meeting leader spends surprisingly little time organizing and conducting meetings to ensure that they are efficient and effective venues for board work. There are boards that have developed strategies to use meetings to full advantage and to do so in ways that are motivating and energizing for all who participate. These meetings capitalize on the diverse and unique talents at the table, and they create a productive and engaging environment that results in board accomplishment. These meetings are used as tools to advance board performance, and they are effectively organized and conducted by chairs who have mastered the art of the effective meeting.

As with the topics of team development and volunteer management, there is a practical body of literature that exists to help board leaders understand how to organize and conduct meetings effectively. And as with team development, board leaders as a group have tended to ignore the practical advice that this literature offers for using the board meeting effectively. A few useful resources on the topic of board meeting management are included in the *Handbook*'s Internet resource website.

Element H: Assess and Enhance Board and Member Accountability

Accountability is an increasingly critical issue in all corners of the nonprofit world, and it is an issue that boards must address at multiple levels. As noted earlier in this chapter, new guidelines and expectations are being recommended and sometimes even mandated by a myriad of actors, including state and federal regulators, watchdog agencies, funders, and even constituent advocacy groups. Growing pressures are developing across the sector for enhanced "self-regulation." But the effective board is not reacting to these external calls for accountability, it is taking the lead. A growing number of nonprofit boards today are engaged in at least basic forms of self-assessment and development (BoardSource, 2015), usually via some form of self-assessment and subsequent development activity. Effective boards recognize both the imperative and potential benefits of doing so.

Effective boards set goals for their own performance, both long and short term, and they implement processes by which to assess their accomplishments and evaluate how they could be more successful. Some boards have linked self-assessment processes to gather information to assess whether board members meet the expectations that they set (for example, attendance, personal giving). Some board members are uncomfortable with such activities, but a growing number support board self-assessment and consider such efforts appropriate and beneficial. These boards are proactively developing their own systems and practices for gathering performance information at multiple levels—about organization performance, about board performance, and even about the performance of individual board members. It is essential to point out, however, that the focus of these systems is not merely on gathering and presenting performance information with a "report card" mentality—it is about using this information as the basis for refining and redesigning operations to continuously improve effectiveness. A growing number of useful tools exist to help boards engage in self-assessment initiatives. They include the Holland and Jackson's (1998) Board Self-Assessment Questionnaire that focuses on the six competencies discussed earlier in this chapter; a BoardSource self-assessment system that is based on Ingram's ten core responsibilities of nonprofit boards (Ingram, 2008) that now is available online; and the relatively new online Board Check-Up system developed by board researchers Yvonne Harrison and Vic Murray. (Details and links to all of these resources are available on the chapter's Internet resource site.)

Regardless of the specific tools and approach, effective boards take time on a regular basis to reflect on what is working well and what might be improved, and they use this information to help inform how they might refine their design and practices to be of most value to the organization and to the board's own members. And this discussion is not couched in terms of "What's bad?" or (even worse) "Who's to blame?" It is framed from a developmental perspective with a focus on two key themes: (1) What does our organization need of us, in our next generation of work as a board, to uniquely add value to the accomplishment of the organization's mission? and (2) How might we refine the way we are organized and do our work to make the most effective use of the resources that we, as a board, have at our disposal? As the board considers its findings from the assessment process, the next step is to use these findings to refine the board's design for its next generation of work—which is the linkage to the focus of Element A of the Board Development Cycle: Define the Work, Design the Board.

Where to Start?

A nonprofit organization might begin the development cycle with any of the elements, although there are two most likely phases at which a board will enter the cycle. In the case of the new organization that is just beginning to organize its board, leaders usually will begin (knowingly or not) with the work of Element A: Define the Work, Design the Board. Those engaged in creating the board are going to engage in some form of design, and their design will be based on some sense of what the board's work needs to be. They may be analytical and thoughtful about the work to be done and choose the design that best advances it, or they may simply imitate some other board design (too many boards simply copy their bylaws from those of another organization without giving any thought to whether those bylaws will be suited to the work their board needs to do). However it occurs, the fact is that some kind of design is adopted when an organization officially starts its existence.

For the board of the nonprofit that has been in operation for some time, it would be typical for the organization to enter the cycle at Element H: Assess and Enhance Board and Member Accountability. This is the phase during which the organization takes stock of its situation, assesses how well its design and actual performance meet the needs and expectations of the organization, and considers what this means for its next generation of service. It is during this phase that the organization determines whether changes are likely to be needed and, if so, generates information that will inform the next phase of work.

Effective nonprofit agencies invest time, energy, and money in building and sustaining their effectiveness. This section of the chapter has explained how boards may be developed and sustained through the use of a board development cycle comprising eight relatively sequential yet overlapping elements. Each element adds unique value to the success of the board, each poses its own design and development challenges, and each contributes in its own way to board success.

Conclusion

Governance is a central and essential component of the leadership of nonprofit organizations, and the boards of directors that engage in the work of governance are central to the success of the organizations they serve. In this chapter I have provided a basic overview of the nature and scope of a typical nonprofit organization's governance processes, including the basic ways that boards of directors typically provide leadership and direction to their organizations, and explained the ways that these roles can have an important impact on the success of the organization. I also have discussed a systematic approach to building and sustaining the performance of a nonprofit board. There is no question that when knowledgeable and motivated volunteers take the time to serve on nonprofit boards, we all benefit. Likewise, serving as a member of a nonprofit organization's board of directors can be one of the most influential and enjoyable roles that any volunteer can play, and the rewards of effective service accrue to both the volunteer and their community. Such service, performed well, is essential to the future of our organizations, our communities, and civil society.

Notes

1. The beginning of this chapter is adapted from the author's chapter on "Governance of Nonprofits" (Renz, 2004), and has been adapted with permission.
2. As with any general discussion of legal matters, we must present an important warning and disclaimer. This chapter is intended only to offer general information, and its contents do not constitute legal advice. Boards and members with specific legal questions and concerns should consult legal counsel and the relevant regulatory authorities for definitive information and answers. Please also recognize that this chapter focuses largely on nonprofit organizations in the United States. Laws and legal expectations vary from state to state, even though a large number of states in the United States have adopted nonprofit corporation laws that are based on the same model statute, and nonprofit laws vary even more substantially from nation to nation. It makes a significant difference where the organization was founded and incorporated, and where it operates its programs and services. For further information, please consult the reference and resource materials and Internet links that are listed at the end of this chapter.

References

BoardSource. Leading with Intent. A National Index of Nonprofit Board Practices. Washington DC: BoardSource, June 2015.

Brown, W. Board Development Practices and Competent Board Members: Implications for Performance. *Nonprofit Management and Leadership*, 2007, 17(3), 301–317.

Brown, W. Antecedents to Board Member Engagement in Deliberation and Decision-Making. In C. Cornforth and W. Brown (eds.), *Nonprofit Governance: Innovative Perspectives and Approaches*. Abingdon, Oxon, UK: Routledge, 2013.

Brudney, J. L., and Murray, V. Do Intentional Efforts to Improve Boards Really Work? The Views of Nonprofit CEOs. *Nonprofit Management and Leadership*, 1998, 8(4), 333–348.

Collins, J. *Good to Great and the Social Sector*. San Francisco: HarperCollins, 2005.

Cornforth, C. *What Do Boards Do? The Governance of Public and Nonprofit Organizations*. London: Routledge, 2001.

Freiwirth, J. Community Engagement Governance: Engaging Stakeholders for Community Impact. In C. Cornforth and W. Brown (eds.), *Nonprofit Governance: Innovative Perspectives and Approaches*. Abingdon, Oxon, UK: Routledge, 2013.

Freiwirth, J., and Letona, M. E. System-Wide Governance for Community Empowerment. *Nonprofit Quarterly*, 2006, 13(4), 24–27.

Gill, M. D. *Governing for results: A director's guide to good governance*. Victoria, British Columbia, Canada: Trafford. 2005.

Harrison, Y., Murray, V., and Cornforth, C. The Role and Impact of Chairs of Nonprofit Organization Boards of Directors. In C. Cornforth and W. Brown (eds.), *Nonprofit Governance: Innovative Perspectives and Approaches*. Abingdon, Oxon, UK: Routledge, 2013.

Herman, M. L. *Pillars of Accountability: A Risk Management Guide for Nonprofit Board*. (2nd ed.). Washington, DC: Nonprofit Risk Management Center, 2006.

Herman, R. D., and Renz, D. O. Doing Things Right and Effectiveness in Local Nonprofit Organizations: A Panel Study. *Public Administration Review*, 2004, 64, 694–704.

Herman, R. D., and Renz, D. O. Advancing Nonprofit Organizational Effectiveness Research and Theory: Nine Theses. *Nonprofit Management and Leadership*, 2008, 18, 399–415.

Holland, T., and Jackson, D. Strengthening Board Performance: Findings and Lessons from Demonstration Projects. *Nonprofit Management and Leadership*, 1998, 9 (2), 121–134.

Ingram, R. T. *Ten Basic Responsibilities of Nonprofit Boards* (3rd ed.). Washington, DC: BoardSource, 2008.

Katzenbach, J., and Smith, D. K. *The Wisdom of Teams: Creating the High-Performance Organization*. New York: HarperBusiness, 2003.

Kotter, J. P. *Leading Change*. Boston: Harvard Business School Press, 1996.

Larcker, D., Donatiello, N., Meehan W., III, and Tayan, B. *2015 Survey on Board of Directors of Nonprofit Organizations*. Palo Alto; CA: Stanford Graduate School of Business and the Rock Center for Corporate Governance, June 2015.

McCambridge, R. Sweet Briar College: One More Stakeholder Revolt Against an Out of Touch Board? Nonprofit Quarterly Newswire. March 13, 2015. https://nonprofit quarterly.org/2015/03/13/sweet-briar-college-one-more-stakeholder-revolt-against-an-out-of-touch-board/ (downloaded March 15, 2015).

McCambridge, R. Making the Most of Stakeholder Revolt: Recapturing of the San Diego Opera and Sweet Briar College. *Nonprofit Quarterly*, Winter 2015.

Nobbie, P. D., and Brudney, J. L. Testing the Testing the Implementation, Board Performance, and Organizational Effectiveness of the Policy Governance Model in Nonprofit Boards of Directors. *Nonprofit and Voluntary Sector Quarterly*, 2003, 32(4), 571–595.

Ostrower, F. *National Survey of Nonprofit Governance*. Washington, DC: Urban Institute, 2007.

Ostrower, F., and Stone, M. Governance Research: Trends, Gaps and Prospects for the Future. Paper presented at Association for Research on Nonprofit Organizations and Voluntary Action Conference, Miami, Florida, Nov. 27–Dec. 1, 2001.

Ostrower, F., and Stone, M. Boards of Nonprofit Organizations: Research Trends, Findings, and Prospects for the Future. In W. W. Powell and R. Steinberg (eds.), *The Nonprofit Sector: A Research Handbook* (2nd ed.). New Haven, CT: Yale University Press, 2006.

The Panel on the Nonprofit Sector. Strengthening Transparency, Governance, Accountability of Charitable Organizations: A Final Report to Congress and the Nonprofit Sector. Washington, DC: Independent Sector, June 2005.

Renz, D. O. Governance of Nonprofits. In D. Burlingame (ed.) *Philanthropy in the U.S.: An Encyclopedia*. Santa Barbara, CA: ABC-CLIO, 2004, pp. 191–199.

Renz, D., and Andersson, F. Nonprofit Governance: A Review of the Field. In C. Cornforth and W. Brown (eds.), *Nonprofit Governance: Innovative Perspectives and Approaches*. Abingdon, Oxon, UK: Routledge, 2013.

Stevens, S. K. *Nonprofit Lifecycles: Stage-Based Wisdom for Nonprofit Capacity* (2nd ed.). Long Lake, MN: Stagewise Enterprises, 2008.

Taylor, B. E., Chait, R. P., and Holland, T. P. The New Work of Nonprofit Boards. *Harvard Business Review*, 1996.

U.S. Internal Revenue Service. Governance and Related Topics. 501c3 Organizations. www.irs.gov/pub/irs-tege/governance_practices.pdf (downloaded January 31, 2016).

CHAPTER SIX

EXECUTIVE LEADERSHIP

Robert D. Herman

Nonprofit organizations are distinctive forms of organization, differing in fundamental ways from business and government. Like businesses, nonprofit organizations engage in voluntary exchanges to obtain revenues and other resources, and like governments, they often provide service with public goods characteristics. Unlike businesses, nonprofit charitable organizations have no conceptually clear maximization criterion. Unlike governments, they cannot levy taxes. Robert Payton (1988) described philanthropy as voluntary (private) action for the public purposes. Nonprofit organizations—particularly those classed as 501(c)(3) publicly supported charities under the U.S. Internal Revenue Code—are the chief instruments for actualizing philanthropy.

The distinctive character of nonprofit organizations presents special challenges for the executive (top staff) leadership of such organizations. A chief executive, in conjunction with the board, must integrate the realms of mission, resource acquisition, and strategy. To oversimplify but phrase the issue more memorably, *mission, money, and management* are interdependent. Making progress on mission achievement depends, in part, on the potential for resource acquisition. Any mission, no matter how worthy, is likely to fail if the organization lacks necessary and sufficient resources to pursue it. Conversely, the acquisition of some kinds of resources can influence the mission. Moreover, decisions about strategies for acquiring resources must be consistent with the mission and ethical values of the organizations. Actions in one realm affect the other realms. The leadership challenge is to see that decisions and actions in one realm are not only consistent with those in other realms but also mutually reinforcing.

Obviously, leadership does not and cannot occur only at the top of an organization; however, leadership is fundamentally the responsibility of the chief executive and the board. In fact, the chief executive–board relationship is crucial to effective organizational leadership. The chief executive position in nonprofit organizations is usually demanding and difficult. Those demands and difficulties can be more effectively met if CEOs both understand and develop the skills to focus on the essential relationships and tasks it entails. In these pages, I first describe the psychological centrality of CEOs. In spite of the formal hierarchical structure that makes the CEO subordinate to the board, the day-to-day reality as it is experienced by most CEOs, board members, and staff is that CEOs are expected to accept the central leadership role in nonprofit organizations. This often requires that CEOs take responsibility for enabling their boards to carry out the boards' duties.

Leadership issues are among the most studied and written about in management and the social sciences generally. This chapter will not review the general leadership literature, though it will rely on some findings that are especially germane to the position of nonprofit CEOs. By and large I will rely on research that has specifically focused on CEOs of nonprofit organizations. I begin with a description of the central role that CEOs perform in nonprofit organizations and then consider the skills that differentiate effective chief executives from those who are not as effective; those skills focus on the executives' relation with their boards. Next, I address the importance of executive leadership in the external environment—specifying strategies for leadership across boundaries. I continue by describing research on the "political" skills of effective CEOs and provide guidelines for thinking and acting in politically effective ways. The importance of this criterion of leadership is also examined in light of the hesitancy of chief executives to espouse or advocate political action as an important aspect of their leadership. The closing summary emphasizes that the essence of effective executive leadership is a responsive external orientation in which the strategies pursued are directed at the tasks of mission accomplishment and resource acquisition.

Executive Centrality

Similar to other formal organizations, a nonprofit organization is typically understood as necessarily hierarchical, with the board of directors in the superior position. The board is expected to define mission, establish policies, oversee programs, and use performance standards to assess financial and program achievements. The chief executive is hired to assist the board and works at the board's pleasure. This conception is the application of what organizational theorists have labeled the "purposive-rational" model (Pfeffer, 1982) or the "managed systems" model (Elmore, 1978) to nonprofit organizations. This model, generally derived from Max Weber's description of bureaucracy (1946), as well as the nature of many organizations over the last century or two, conceives of organizations as goal-directed instruments under the control of rational decision makers where responsibility and authority are hierarchically arranged. This rational, managed systems model is also the commonplace or conventional "theory" of many organizational participants. It is how, many people believe, organizations do and should work.

Much of the substantial normative literature on nonprofit boards accepts this conventional model (for example, Houle, 1997, and Carver, 1997), putting the board at the top of the hierarchy and at the center of leadership responsibility. Based on a legal requirement and a moral assumption, the normative literature has advanced a heroic ideal (Herman, 1989) for nonprofit boards. As Hopkins and Gross explain in greater depth in Chapter Two of this volume, United States law holds that a nonprofit board is ultimately responsible for the affairs and conduct of the organization. The moral assumption is that the board conducts the organization's affairs as a steward of the public interest, in a manner consistent with the wishes and needs of the larger community. Notwithstanding the wide dissemination of this normative model, a substantial body of research over the past three decades (for example, BoardSource, 2015) shows the actual performance of boards often falls short of the ideal and is a source of concern and difficulty for chief executives. Much of this literature has been reviewed and summarized by Ostrower and Stone (2006) and Renz and Andersson (2013). Further, as they state in a report on a 2011 survey of more than three thousand U.S. nonprofit chief executives, Cornelius, Moyers, and Bell found that 67 percent planned to leave their jobs within five years and an additional 7 percent already had given notice to their boards and were in the process of leaving their organizations. In both this survey and an earlier (2006) iteration, they found executive dissatisfaction with board performance to be strongly correlated with chief executive turnover (Bell, Moyers, and Wolfred, 2006). Clearly the relationship between chief executives and their boards can be a difficult one.

The notion that chief executives are simply agents of the board cannot be supported. Recognizing that the relationship between boards and chief executives is more complex than the normative model envisions, many people have invoked a "partnership" or "team" metaphor to describe (and prescribe) the executive-board relationship. Such terms are more appropriate than the conventional model's depiction of the relation as superior-subordinate. However, the partnership and team conceptions remain misleading.

Middleton (1987, p. 149) used the phrase "strange loops and tangled hierarchies" to describe more accurately the complex executive-board relationship. Boards retain their legal and hierarchical superiority (and sometimes must exercise it), whereas executives typically have greater information, more expertise, and a greater stake in and identification with the organization. Thus each party is dependent on the other, but they are not exactly equals. This complex, interdependent relation is not fundamentally changed even when nonprofit organizations adopt the corporate model of designating the chief executive "president" and letting the executive vote on board decisions. Ostrower's study (2007) of U.S. nonprofit organizations based on a stratified sample drawn from the IRS form 990 database found that having CEOs as voting board members is negatively associated with the accountability practices of having an audit, a conflict of interest policy, and a whistle-blower policy, indicating some shortcomings of that practice.

The complex executive-board relationship can be better understood, and more effective standards and practices relating to the executive-board working relationship can be developed, if other organizational models are used. Herman and Renz (2004, 2008) have found that a "social constructionist model" of organizations provides important insights into the chief executive's organizational role and the dynamics of effective executive-board relations. In contrast to the managed systems model, the social constructionist perspective abandons assumptions of hierarchically imposed order and rationality, emphasizing that what an organization is and does emerges from the interaction of participants as they attempt to arrange organizational practices and routines to fit their perceptions, needs, and interests. The social constructionist model recognizes that official or intended goals, structures, and procedures may exist only on paper. Actual goals, structures, and procedures emerge and change as participants interact and socially construct the meaning of ongoing events.

In research on critical events in nonprofit organizations Heimovics and Herman (1990) studied the "self-serving" hypothesis, which holds that individuals see themselves as causes of successful outcomes and others or luck as responsible for failure. In studying local nonprofit charitable organizations, they found that in successful events board presidents, chief executives, and senior staff credited chief executives with contributing the most to that outcome, although presidents and staff also attributed high responsibility to themselves. In unsuccessful events, board presidents and staff, consistent with this hypothesis, saw the chief executive as most responsible, assigning less responsibility to themselves or to luck. However, in the unsuccessful events, chief executives assigned more blame to themselves than to others. Accepting responsibility for things not going well is very unusual (and may contribute to burnout and turnover). In short, all (including chief executives themselves) see the executive as centrally responsible for what happens in nonprofit organizations. What does the reality of executive centrality imply for more effective action?

I believe that two possibilities are indicated. One, since chief executives are going to be held responsible, they should take full control, running things as they think best. The board then becomes either the proverbial rubber stamp or a combination rubber stamp and cash cow. Obviously, there are many instances of this manipulative pattern. Alternatively, since chief executives are going to be held responsible and since they accept responsibility for mission accomplishment and public stewardship, they should work to see that boards fulfill their legal, organizational, and public roles. I believe that this second implication is the much wiser choice. Not only is it consistent with legal and ethical duties, but it is also more likely to enhance organizational effectiveness. I am not advocating that chief executives dominate or "demote" their boards. Boards, in addition to their legal and moral duties, can contribute a great deal to achieving their organizations' missions. What the research results and experience demonstrate is that chief executives can seldom expect boards to do their best unless chief executives, recognizing their centrality, accept the responsibility to develop, promote, and enable their boards' effective functioning.

Board-Centered Leadership Skills of Chief Executives

The view that chief executives must often enable and develop their boards' abilities to carry out their duties and responsibilities is based on research on the leadership skills of effective nonprofit chief executives. Herman and Heimovics (1990) wanted to determine what behaviors or skills distinguished especially effective nonprofit chief executives from others. A sample of especially effective chief executives was created by asking several knowledgeable participants in a metropolitan nonprofit sector to identify executives they judged to be highly effective. The nominators held positions—such as heads of foundations, federated funding agencies, technical assistance providers, and coalitional organizations—that required them to make and act on judgments of executive effectiveness. Chief executives who received at least two independent nominations as highly effective were included in the effective sample.

A comparison sample was selected from among executives who received no nominations and who had held their position for at least eighteen months. Executives from both the effective and comparison samples were interviewed, via the critical event approach. The transcribed interviews were coded by trained raters to note the presence of various leadership behaviors by using an inventory developed by Quinn (1983). Recognizing that a CEO's relationships with the board and staff would probably differ, the raters coded executive leadership in relation to each.

The results confirmed the importance of distinguishing between executive leadership in relation to the board and the staff. Analysis showed that executive leadership in relation to staff and in relation to the board are independent and distinct factors. Effective and comparison executives differed little in leadership with their staffs. The most important finding was that the effective executives provided significantly more leadership to their boards. This does not mean that the effective executives ordered their boards around. Rather, as the descriptions of their behavior in the critical events showed, the effective executives accepted responsibility for supporting and facilitating their board's work. The effective executives valued and respected their boards. As a result, they see their boards as at the center of their work. Their leadership is board-centered.

The comparison executives' relations to their boards often fit the pattern described by Murray, Bradshaw, and Wolpin (1992) as that of CEO dominance. In an Israeli study of nonprofit chief executives, Iecovich and Bar-Mor (2007) found CEO dominance to be the most common pattern and that although a number of variables were related to CEO dominance in bivariate analyses, in a regression analysis only the number of hours spent by the board chair in his or her duties predicted (negatively) CEO dominance. In a few cases the boards seemed to dominate the CEO.

The following six behaviors specifically characterize the board-centered leadership of the especially effective executives:

- *Facilitating interaction in board relationships.* The effective chief executive is aware of, and works to see that board members engage in satisfying and productive interaction with each other and with the executive. The executive is skilled at listening (that is, at hearing the concerns behind the words) and at helping the board resolve differences.
- *Showing consideration and respect toward board members.* The effective executive knows that board service is an exchange and seeks to be aware of the needs of individual board members. The executive also works with the board president to find assignments that meet those needs.

- *Envisioning change and innovation for the organization with the board.* Given their psychological centrality and their centrality in information flows, chief executives are in the best position to monitor and understand the organization's position in a changing environment. However, appropriate response to this external flux requires that board members be apprised of the trends, forces, and unexpected occurrences that could call for adaptation or innovation. The executive encourages the board to examine new opportunities and to look for better ways of doing things and better things to do. In short, the executive challenges the board consistently to think and rethink the connections among mission, money (and other resources), and management strategy.
- *Providing useful and helpful information to the board.* In addition to the usual routine information, such as financial statements, budget reports, and program service data, boards need relevant and timely information that can aid in decision making. Since the executive will have access to a great deal of information of all kinds and quality, he or she must find ways of separating the important from the trivial and of communicating the important to the board. One key rule followed by effective executives is "no surprises." The temptation to hide or delay bad news is understandable, but it must be resisted. Effective executives realize that problems are inevitable and know that by sharing the bad news, solutions are more likely to be found.
- *Initiating and maintaining structure for the board.* Like other work groups, boards require the materials, schedules, and work plans necessary to achieve their tasks. Effective executives take responsibility to work with the board president and other members to develop and maintain consistent procedures. In many effective organizations, the board has annual objectives. It is important that the chief executive support the work of the board in reaching those objectives.
- *Promoting board accomplishments and productivity.* The effective executive helps set and maintain high standards (about attendance, effort, and giving). Through the board president and committee chairpersons, the executive encourages board members to complete tasks and meet deadlines.

These findings, based on research on nonprofit charitable CEOs, are reinforced by the results of research in general leadership. Based on his review and integration of the literature Yukl (2012) has concluded that several skills are the most important leadership functions of effective managerial leaders. Among those are (1) creating alignment on objectives and strategies, (2) building task commitment and optimism, (3) building mutual trust and cooperation, (4) strengthening collective identity, (5) organizing and coordinating activities, (6) encouraging and facilitating collective learning, and (7) developing and empowering people. The similarities of these behaviors to those discussed earlier are obvious.

Executives who have (somehow) learned how to use these leadership skills in relation to their boards, as well as their staffs (including volunteers), have hard-working, effective boards. It is not clear how some chief executives learned these board-centered leadership skills. Perhaps they had coaching in such skills by a mentor who has those skills. Perhaps they are people who have always been attentive and responsive to others. Perhaps they have developed such skills based on tacit knowledge (or intuition). Ritchie, Kolodinsky, and Eastwood (2007) found that nonprofit chief executive intuition was positively related to three of four organizational effectiveness measures. Clearly, work on understanding how board-centered leadership skills are developed is needed.

Leadership Across the Boundaries: Impact in the External World

As noted above, the board-centered executive is likely to be effective, in large part, because he or she has grasped that the work of the board is critical in adapting to and affecting the constraints and opportunities in the environment. In short, the effective executive knows that leadership is not solely an internal activity. Research specifically on nonprofit charitable CEOs (see Herman and Heimovics, 1990, 1991), as well as other research, suggests a number of specific strategies for enhancing external impact.

Spend Time on External Relations

Spending time on external relations may seem too obvious to deserve mention. However, both systematic evidence and experience show that routine activities and the inevitable day-to-day office problems can easily absorb nearly all an executive's time. Executives must learn to delegate much of the management of internal affairs and focus on the external. Dollinger (1984) found that small business owners and managers who spent more time on boundary-spanning or external activities were more successful.

Develop an Informal Information Network

Information about what happened in the past (such as is found in financial statements and program evaluations) is important, but information about what might happen in the future (whether that future is next week or next year) is even more important. Information on possible futures is much more likely to be widely scattered, partial, and ambiguous. To acquire, evaluate, and integrate this "soft" information, executives (and others) need to communicate with government agencies, foundations, accrediting bodies, professional associations, similar nonprofit organizations, and so forth. They must attend meetings and lunches, breakfasts, and legislative sessions.

Important, useful information is more likely to flow when the parties are more than acquaintances. Face-to-face communication helps build reciprocal credibility and trust.

A successful network is built and sustained when people are willing and able to understand and accept the interests of others, and it requires exchanging reliable information without violating confidentiality. It means not only investing time but also helping others with their concerns in exchange for help with your own. As Huff (1985) observes, a network is important for more than sharing information. Networks are also deeply involved in making sense of an often rapidly changing field. Different kinds of information are available from different parts of an organization's environment. Information gleaned from a professional associate will be different from that available from a corporate giving officer. Both are likely to be important to a particular policy or program delivery issue. The whole network has an important role in defining emerging issues and in pointing the way to new program practices.

Know Your Agenda

Strategic planning provides organizations with a rational process for deriving specific goals and objectives from their missions. Thus the strategic plan structures the executive's work. Both Kotter (1982) and Huff (1985) found that executives supplement the strategic plan with agendas that are both more immediate and more long-range. The executive's agenda, whether taken directly from the plan or consistently supplemental to it, provides a short list of goals or outcomes that the executive sees as crucial. Knowing and using the agenda to focus work offers a basis for effectively allocating time and effort. A limited, focused agenda also helps bring order and direction in a complex and rapidly changing environment. Concentrating on the agenda also allows the executive to use external interactions to advance those goals. Huff (1985) has described three strategies effective executives often employ in advancing their agenda as (1) dramatizing events, (2) "laying a bread crumb trail," and (3) simplifying.

Dramatizing events entails calling attention to the relationship between networking events and the executive's agenda. For example, an executive who wants to add staff fluent in Spanish to expand services to Spanish-speaking communities might send information about growth in the city's Latino population and its service needs to board members. The executive might also feature a digest of such stories in the organization's newsletter and see that the newsletter goes to regular funders. The key is to dramatically or memorably connect public issues to the organization's agenda.

Another good example of how to dramatize events comes from the chief executive of an agency serving the developmentally disabled. She encouraged a friend who taught creative writing at a local university to engage a class in developing a story about a day in the life of her agency. The story was included in the materials made available to those attending an annual banquet and awards dinner for the organization. The story was presented to many stakeholders and others to give them a "real feel for the work of the agency." Clearly, the executive director had additional uses for the story. The description skillfully catalogued the creative work of a staff constrained by limited resources. Copies of the story became part of the publicity program of the agency and were included in reports to funders and in grant applications.

Just as dramatizing external events is a way of focusing attention, so is the "*laying of a bread crumb trail.*" Over time, through various communications, a chief executive points the way to an important decision. As Huff (1985, p. 175) puts it, organizational action requires that an executive edit his or her concerns "into a smaller number of items that can be comprehended by others. Repetition of these concerns is almost always necessary to gain the attention of others and convince them of serious intent." Such a strategy is probably widely applicable, but we find it especially germane in executive-board relations.

Consider, for instance, the strategy of the chief executive of an organization that operates group homes for the mentally ill. The organization's original facility, called Tracy House, was an old building in great need of repair. Operations at the house did not quite break even. Surpluses from the operation of other facilities covered the shortfall. The executive, based on what he was hearing from the network of licensing, funding, and accrediting bodies, believed that new standards would require modifications that, combined with no growth in state daily rates, would mean operating the facility at a larger deficit. So he began laying a bread crumb trail for board members, both formally in board meetings and informally in conversations in other settings. Part of his problem was that a few board members had a strong emotional attachment to Tracy House; they had personally painted it and made repairs to meet licensing standards. Instead of pointing out again that Tracy House was decrepit, he provided an update on the state funding prospects, noting the financial implications for each facility, which made the burden of carrying the home's deficit obvious. Some time later, he mentioned the possibility of federal housing funds becoming available for group home construction, observing that this would permit the organization to "get out from under" Tracy House. In this way, when the decision was finally made to sell Tracy House, it was a foregone conclusion. The trail of markers not only defined and focused the issue but also brought everyone to the same conclusion, making what could have been a painful decision easy.

The last strategy identified by Huff is to *keep things as simple as possible*. A complex and interdependent world enhances the tendency for inaction and drift. Before we can make a decision about X, we have to see what happens with Y, and Y depends on what A and B do. To make decisions and take action, individuals must risk simplifying the situation. As Huff (1985) observes, behaving as though the situation is simpler than you know it to be can help bring about more simplicity. Acting in relation to the agenda is an important way of simplifying, or creating order in a disorderly world.

Improvise and Accept Multiple Partial Solutions

The point of leadership across the boundary is to position the organization in the larger environment and match its capabilities with the demands for its services and the resources available. Of course, the inevitable fact is that neither organizational capabilities nor environmental demands and resources are static. A short, clear agenda and the strategies to carry it out provide a compass pointing the way to where the executive, who has integrated to the greatest extent possible the preferences of the stakeholders, wants to go.

The metaphor of the compass, however, is not complete because the executive (reflecting the stakeholders' varying preferences) wants to go to several places. For example, the agenda might include increasing total revenues, diversifying revenue sources, acquiring a new facility, and expanding a particular program. Not only are these different goals, but there are likely to be different paths to each. Furthermore, the most direct path to one may make paths to the others longer or more difficult to find. Finding the combination of paths that most efficiently leads to goals may often be beyond calculation, particularly when the environment keeps changing. The upshot is that executives must sometimes be willing and able to improvise, to take an unexpected path when it presents itself. Sometimes chief executives find they cannot, at least within a crucial period, reach a goal in exactly the form imagined. As Huff (1985, p. 167) observes, an "administrator's ability to perceive issues is almost always bigger than the ability to act on issues. As a result, the administrator often must be content to work on a small part of the larger whole." That is, sometimes the organization may have to go someplace a little different from what was at one time imagined because that is where the only available path leads. Huff suggests that a "specific action should rarely be taken unless it is compatible with several different issues" (p. 168). Or in the terms of our metaphor, an action that leads to movement on paths to two or three places at once is particularly useful.

For an especially compelling illustration of this sort of creative leadership, consider the case of a nonprofit organization that required a facility with large spaces. For several years, the organization used an old warehouse that a business corporation provided for free. However, the corporation made it clear that it was interested in selling the warehouse and that the organization might have to relocate. As a few years passed and the corporation lacked success in selling the warehouse and had little apparent necessity for doing so, the issue of obtaining a suitable, more permanent facility was increasingly put on the back burner. One day, the chief executive received a call from a corporate officer saying that a tentative agreement to sell the warehouse had been reached and that the organization would have to vacate in six months. The first thing the chief executive did was to call the board. Staff members were also quickly informed to avoid the spread of rumors. The chief executive found that many board members and staff assumed that the organization should try to find another old warehouse. However, the executive knew that old warehouses had disadvantages: high energy costs, lack of parking, inaccessibility, and so forth. The executive thought this was an excellent opportunity to rethink what sort of facility would be most appropriate.

After conferring with the board chairman and other key board members, a facility planning committee was formed. The executive was interested in connecting the facility issue to other agenda issues, especially those of enhancing collaboration with other community organizations and adding a demonstration day-care program for children. As the facility planning committee identified alternative ways of securing a replacement facility and the costs associated with each, a board member suggested that the executive meet with an official from a local community college. Although the college was not in the same service field as the organization, the college had enough money available through a bond issue to construct a new building but not enough money to finish and equip the building. Following quick negotiations, the organization agreed to provide funds to finish and equip the facility in exchange for a ten-year lease of two floors at a very low rental rate. This solution, although not perfect, moved the organization along on several agenda issues simultaneously. This progress was achieved because the executive worked with and through the board and linked action on one issue with progress on others.

Promote Responsiveness to Stakeholders

In studying the effectiveness of nonprofit charitable organizations, Herman and Renz (2004) adapted an instrument developed by Tsui (1984). In an important study of managerial effectiveness Tsui, Ashford, St. Clair, and Xin (1995) used her instrument to measure how those who work with a ("focal") manager assess the effectiveness of that manager. The items Tsui, Ashford, St. Clair, and Xin used asked respondents (in their study, respondents were subordinates, peers, and superiors of the focal managers) to assess the extent to which the manager was performing the way the respondent would like, was meeting the respondent's expectations, and extent to which the respondent would change how the manager behaved.

The study identified several strategies managers might use when facing discrepant or conflicting expectations from stakeholders, including making an extra effort to meet expectations, trying to influence expectations, explaining actions, distorting feedback from stakeholders, revising their own expectations downward, and avoiding dissatisfied stakeholders. They collected data from and about mid-level managers in both business (94 managers, 713 respondents) and government (316 focal managers, 1,906 respondents). Their results showed that extra effort was very strongly related and explained action strongly related to effectiveness ratings, whereas avoidance and trying to influence stakeholder expectations were negatively related to effectiveness (because distorting feedback and revising expectations are not observable by stakeholders these strategies were not studied).

Their results also showed that managers who were rated as frequently using extra effort and explanation seldom used avoidance or attempted influence, and vice versa. Managers were also found to behave consistently with all types of stakeholders. These results, demonstrating that individuals judge managerial effectiveness of the basis of the responsiveness to their expectations, seemed to Herman and Renz (2004) likely to apply throughout an organization. Nonprofit leaders, chief executives, and boards who practice responsiveness are likely to encourage and promote such practices throughout the organization.

Herman and Renz (2004) found that an adapted instrument measuring stakeholder judgments of *organizational responsiveness* was highly correlated to a different measure of organizational effectiveness, including for institutional funders as well as board members and senior staff. Although they collected no direct evidence on whether organizational members exhibited extra effort, explained actions, or engaged in other ways of being responsive to stakeholders, this set of results (from Herman and Renz and Tsui, Ashford, St. Clair, and Xin) seems strong enough to warrant including promoting responsiveness to stakeholders, as well as external stakeholders, as a skill for chief executives (and others) to develop and practice.

These five admonitions are also reinforced by Yukl's integration of the general leadership literature (2012). Among the skills he concludes were most important for effective managerial leadership are helping interpret the meaning of events and obtaining necessary resources and support. These skills seem, in the case of nonprofit CEOs, especially relevant with regard to relations with external stakeholders, although they could also be included in the list presented pages 172–173, as some of the skills listed there could be listed here as well.

In emphasizing the importance of externally oriented leadership, I do not wish to suggest that internal operations can be ignored by chief executives. However, I believe that nearly all executives and boards are well aware of the importance of managing internal operations well. What seems to be less well comprehended is the importance of understanding and influencing, when possible, people and systems beyond the organization's boundaries. Effective executive leadership beyond the boundaries is based, in part, on a "political" orientation and on political skills. In the next section, I define what I mean by a political orientation, describe research that finds effective executives are more politically skillful than others, and suggest how executives can enhance their political acumen.

Using the Political Frame

Research has shown that not only do successful executives provide significantly more leadership for their boards than those not deemed especially effective, but they also work with and through their boards to position their organization in its environment. Special effort is extended externally across the boundaries of the organization to manage the organization's dependence on the factors that determine the availability of the resources to carry out the mission and to establish the legitimacy of the organization. In short, effective executives cross boundaries to seek and act on opportunities in the environment to help shape the future health and direction of the organization.

Effective executives have been found to be more likely than other executives to "frame" their orientations toward external events in political ways. This political orientation helps explain how effective executives work "entrepreneurially" to find resources and revitalize missions for their organizations.

Effective chief executives use a political frame to understand and deal with the challenges of resource dependency their organizations face (Heimovics, Herman, and Coughlin, 1993; Heimovics, Herman, and Jurkiewicz, 1995). A multiple-frame analysis for understanding organizations and leadership, developed by Bolman and Deal (2013), forms the basis for understanding the political orientation of the effective executive. Bolman and Deal identify four distinct organizational perspectives, or "frames," that leaders may adopt to think about the many realities of organizational life: (1) structural, (2) human resource, (3) political, and (4) symbolic. Knowledge of these frames, their various strengths, and their appropriate use can help leaders understand and intervene in their organizations more effectively. The following brief discussion summarizes these frames.

In the *structural frame,* clarity in goal setting and role expectations provides order and continuity in organizations. Clear procedures and policies and the view of the organization as a rational and hierarchical system are characteristic of this frame. Adherence to accepted standards, conformity to rules, and the creation of administrative systems confer on the organization its form and logic. Following procedures (for example, personnel systems and board performance standards) to define individual and organizational effectiveness is also characteristic of this frame, as is the emphasis on certainty in mission and clarity of direction. Leaders who rely strongly on the structural frame regard effectiveness as largely determined by clear procedures and clear goals.

According to the *human resource frame,* people are the most valuable resource of any organization. The effective leader, as defined by this frame, searches for an important balance between the goals of the organization and the hopes and aspirations of its members by attending to individual hopes, feelings, and preferences, valuing relationships and feelings, and advocating effective delegation. Nonprofit leaders who use this frame believe in delegation because it not only "empowers" others to take initiative but also provides opportunities for personal growth and development. This frame defines problems and issues in interpersonal terms and encourages open communication, team building, and collaboration.

The *political frame* assumes ongoing conflict or tension over the allocation of scarce resources or the resolution of differences—most often triggered by the need to bargain or negotiate to acquire or allocate resources. As viewed within the political frame, conflict resolution skills are necessary to build alliances and networks with prominent actors or stakeholders to influence decisions about the allocation of resources. The informal realities of organizational life include the influence of coalitions and interest groups. Politically oriented leaders not only understand how interest groups and coalitions evolve but can also influence the impact these groups have on the organization. Those who use the political frame exercise their personal and organizational power and are sensitive to external factors that may influence internal decisions and policies.

According to the *symbolic frame*, realities of organizational life are socially constructed. Organizations are cultural and historical systems of shared meaning wherein group membership determines individual interpretations of organizational phenomena. Organizational structure, politics, and human relations are inventions of the cultural and historical system. Leaders evoke ceremonies, rituals, or artifacts to create a unifying system of beliefs. This frame calls for charismatic leaders to arouse "visions of a preferred organizational future" and evoke emotional responses to enhance an organization's identity, transforming it to a higher plane of performance and value (Bass, 1985).

Heimovics, Herman, and Coughlin (1993) began research on the use of frames by revisiting the critical-incident interviews that served as the source of data for Herman and Heimovics's (1990) work on board-centered behaviors and the psychological centrality of the chief executive. Analysis revealed that the structural frame was the dominant frame for both the effective and comparison executives. The substantial reliance on the structural frame may be a reflection of the attention paid by both groups of executives to aspects of events that may be relatively close at hand, immediately demanding, and perhaps amenable to action.

The use of the political frame differed significantly, however, between effective and comparison executives. The comparison executives were almost twice as likely to employ the structural frame and 70 percent more likely to use the human resource frame than the political frame. By contrast, the political frame was the second most common frame for the effective executives, who were almost as likely to use it as the structural frame. Most significant, effective executives were twice as likely as the comparison executives to engage in actions defined by the political frame.

The findings on the substantial use of the political frame by effective executives are reinforced by additional data. Most of the critical events described by both groups of executives occurred in the environment external to their organizations. Both effective and comparison executives were more likely to choose an external event than an internal event to describe as critical. Examples of environmental events were usually incidents that dealt with the challenges of resource dependency, such as mergers, alliances, fundraising strategies, legislative lobbying, collaboration with other agencies, relations with government officials, new program developments, or program decline. These kinds of events were distinguished from internal critical events, such as a personnel action or problems with implementing an administrative system or procedure. Analysis of the data by location of events (internal or external) was undertaken to determine whether this variable explained differences in frame use. Again, significant differences between in the use of the political frame were found in the two groups of executives. Comparison executives were substantially less likely to rely on the political frame than the effective executives were when dealing with events in the external environment of the organization, where the political frame is often likely to be most important.

Effective executives not only relied more on the political frame but also dealt with events in more cognitively complex ways than those not deemed to be especially effective. That is, effective executives integrate and employ multiple frames and do not rely on single perspectives, as the comparison executives do. It seems very likely that the use of multiple frames by effective executives contributes to a deeper understanding of the complexities and volatility of the leadership challenges faced in the fast-changing and complicated environment of nonprofit organizations. The ability of nonprofit executives to understand and act politically, as well as through other frames, in relation to complex sets of interrelated actors helps explain why some executives are more effective than others.

Heimovics, Herman, and Jurkiewicz (1995) provide an interesting extension to the findings about the political orientation of effective chief executives. They conducted a second, independent four-frame analysis of the interviews using Argyris's distinctions between espoused theories and theories-in-use. For Argyris (1982), espoused theories are values and actions about which individuals are conscious and aware and which they often use to describe (their) effective leadership as distinct from what they might actually do, their theory-in-use. An espoused theory could be considered a personal philosophy or a statement of a leadership belief, but it is not necessarily a description of a particular action taken. Argyris has shown that commonly there are incongruities between what people espouse as their leadership action and how they actually behave. This was the case in this research.

Recall that effective executives were twice as likely as the comparison executives to engage in actions defined in the political frame. However, both sets of executives were much more inclined to present (espouse) their leadership from the structural and human resource frame than the political. Furthermore, both the effective executives and those not deemed especially effective enacted more political behavior than they espoused. In summary, whereas the use of the political frame was the most strongly distinguishing criterion of executive effectiveness, executives without respect to effectiveness acted in political ways and advocated a less politicized philosophy. Why might this be the case?

The espoused structural frame argues for the importance of rationality and the values of structures that best fit organizational purposes and environmental demands. Apparently, nonprofit executives prefer to present themselves as structured and orderly and embracing of the human resource frame. Perhaps it is important to appear as if one is ordered and rational and concerned about others regardless of whether one predominantly behaves that way. Pfeffer (1981, 2010) argues that power is most effectively exercised unobtrusively and that overt political pronouncements are divisive and likely to be met with challenges. Wrong (1988) distinguished between political operatives who say and those who do. He concludes that the doers are more effective. In short, it may be important and effective to act in accordance with the political frame; it may not be acceptable to espouse this frame as part of a leadership philosophy. Nonetheless, the research clearly suggests that nonprofit executive leadership effectiveness must encompass the ability to operate within a political framework, regardless of the proclivity to espouse a political agenda.

Summary

Nonprofit leaders continually face the challenge of integrating mission, money, and management strategy. Both boards and chief executives play crucial and interdependent roles in meeting this continuing challenge. Both must ask, "How well are we collectively meeting our responsibilities—to define and refine the organization's mission, to secure the resources necessary to achieve our mission, and to select and implement strategies appropriate to and effective in mission accomplishment and resource acquisition?" Chief executives must ask this question not only of themselves but also in relation to their boards. Are their boards meeting these responsibilities? If the answer is yes, a chief executive will surely want to understand how this happy state of affairs has been achieved and take pains to see that it is maintained. If the answer is no, a chief executive will want to consider the following four fundamental executive leadership strategies. The research described here suggests that executives who use these strategies are more likely to lead organizations that effectively meet their responsibilities.

- *Effective executives accept and act on their psychological centrality.* The research shows that chief executives, board members, and others often regard the chief executive as primarily responsible for the conduct of organizational affairs. This is, I'm sure, a frequent fact of life in nonprofit organizations, no matter how strongly any of us might want it to be otherwise. This fact suggests that chief executives must often accept the responsibility for enabling their boards to carry out their leadership roles.

- *Effective executives provide facilitative leadership for their boards.* Boards can make a difference in how nonprofit organizations meet the challenge of integrating mission, money, and management. Boards are much more likely to be active, effective bodies when they are supported by a chief executive who, recognizing his or her psychological centrality, is willing and able to serve the board as enabler and facilitator.

- *Effective executives emphasize leadership beyond their organizations' boundaries.* Given the extensive dependence of nonprofit organizations on their external environment, executives generally recognize the importance of "networking" and other external activities for understanding the changes in that environment. Beyond the information-gathering value of external relations, some executives recognize the importance and value of affecting events in the environment. Exercising external leadership is difficult and demanding, since executives often can bring little, if any, financial or political power to bear. The leadership resources they are likely to have in greater abundance are expertise, trustworthiness, the moral stature of their organizations, skills in coalition building and conflict resolution, and their organizations' responsiveness to external stakeholders.

- *Effective executives think and act in political ways.* Effective executives are realists. They recognize and accept that their organizations and the larger world are composed of groups with differing interests. Thus an important part of the leadership role consists of building coalitions, bargaining, and resolving conflicts. Politically astute executives are not immoral or manipulative. However, they are comfortable with the fact that interests differ and sometimes conflict. They are also comfortable with and skilled at negotiating, compromising, and forming alliances, although they are unlikely to proclaim these political skills as an aspect of their leadership strategies.

These four executive leadership strategies are highly interrelated. An executive who enhances his or her board-centered leadership skills is also likely to become more attentive to externally oriented leadership. An executive who becomes more active in and skilled at leadership in the external environment will be likely to develop more politically oriented ways of thinking and behaving. Obviously, these skills are increments to a solid base of other knowledge and skills, such as those of program services, financial management, human resource management, fundraising, planning, evaluation, and the like. These board-centered, external, and political leadership skills are what distinguish especially effective nonprofit chief executives.

References

Argyris, C. *Reasoning, Learning, and Action: Individual and Organizational*. San Francisco: Jossey-Bass, 1982.

Bass, B. M. *Leadership and Performance Beyond Expectations*. New York: The Free Press, 1985.

Bell, J., Moyers, R., and Wolfred, T. *Daring to Lead 2006: A National Study of Nonprofit Executive Leadership*. San Francisco: CompassPoint Nonprofit Services and Meyer Foundation, 2006.

BoardSource, *Leading with Intent: A National Index of Nonprofit Board Practices*. Washington, D.C.: BoardSource, 2015.

Bolman, L. G., and Deal, T. E. *Reframing Organizations: Artistry, Choice, and Organizations* (5th ed.). San Francisco: Jossey-Bass, 2013.

Carver, J. *Boards That Make a Difference* (2nd ed.). San Francisco: Jossey-Bass, 1997.

Cornelius, M, Moyers, R., and Bell, J. *Daring to Lead 2011: A National Study of Nonprofit Executive Leadership*. San Francisco: CompassPoint Nonprofit Services and the Meyer Foundation, 2011.

Dollinger, M. J. Environmental Boundary Spanning and Information Processing Effects on Organizational Performance. *Academy of Management Journal*, 1984, 27, 351–368.

Elmore, R. F. Organizational Models of Social Program Implementation. *Public Policy*, 1978, 26, 185–228.

Heimovics, R. D., and Herman, R. D. Responsibility for Critical Events in Nonprofit Organizations. *Nonprofit and Voluntary Sector Quarterly*, 1990, 19, 59–72.

Heimovics, R. D., Herman, R. D., and Coughlin, C.L.J. Executive Leadership and Resource Dependence in Nonprofit Organizations: A Frame Analysis. *Public Administration Review*, 1993, 53, 419–427.

Heimovics, R. D., Herman, R. D., and Jurkiewicz, C. L. The Political Dimension of Effective Nonprofit Executive Leadership. *Nonprofit Management and Leadership*, 1995, 5, 233–248.

Herman, R. D. Concluding Thoughts on Closing the Board Gap. In R. D. Herman and J. Van Til (eds.), *Nonprofit Boards of Directors: Analyses and Applications*. New Brunswick, NJ: Transaction, 1989.

Herman, R. D., and Heimovics, R. D. An Investigation of Leadership Skill Differences in Chief Executives of Nonprofit Organizations. *American Review of Public Administration*, 1990, 20, 107–124.

Herman, R. D., and Heimovics, R. D. *Executive Leadership in Nonprofit Organizations: New Strategies for Shaping Executive-Board Dynamics*. San Francisco: Jossey-Bass, 1991.

Herman, R. D., and Renz, D. O. Multiple Constituencies and the Social Construction of Nonprofit Organization Effectiveness. *Nonprofit and Voluntary Sector Quarterly*, 1997, 26, 185–206.

Herman, R. D., and Renz, D. O. Doing Things Right and Effectiveness in Local Nonprofit Organizations: A Panel Study. *Public Administration Review*, 2004, 64, 694–704.

Herman, R. D., and Renz, D. O. Advancing Nonprofit Organizational Effectiveness Research and Theory: Nine Theses. *Nonprofit Management and Leadership*, 2008, 18, 399–415.

Houle, C. O. *Governing Boards*. San Francisco: Jossey-Bass, 1997.

Huff, A. S. Managerial Implications of the Emerging Paradigm. In Y. S. Lincoln (ed.), *Organizational Theory and Inquiry: The Paradigm Revolution*. Thousand Oaks, CA: Sage, 1985.

Iecovich, E., and Bar-Mor, H. Relationships Between Chairpersons and CEOs in Nonprofit Organizations. *Administration in Social Work*, 2007, 31, 21–40.

Kotter, J. P. *The General Managers*. New York: The Free Press, 1982.

Middleton, M. Nonprofit Boards of Directors: Beyond the Governance Function. In W. W. Powell (ed.), *The Nonprofit Sector: A Research Handbook*. New Haven, CT: Yale University Press, 1987.

Murray, V. V., Bradshaw, P., and Wolpin, J. Power in and Around Nonprofit Boards: A Neglected Dimension of Governance. *Nonprofit Management and Leadership*, 1992, 3, 165–182.

Ostrower, F. *Nonprofit Governance in the United States: Findings on Performance and Accountability from the First Representative National Study*. Washington, DC: Urban Institute Center on Nonprofits and Philanthropy [http://www.urban.org/publications/411479.html], 2007.

Ostrower, F., and Stone, M. Boards of Nonprofit Organizations: Research Trends, Findings, and Prospects for the Future. In W. W. Powell and R. Steinberg (eds.), *The Nonprofit Sector: A Research Handbook* (2nd ed.). New Haven, CT: Yale University Press, 2006.

Payton, R. *Philanthropy: Voluntary Action for the Public Good*. Old Tappan, NJ: Macmillan, 1988.

Pfeffer, J. *Power in Organizations*. New York: Ballinger, 1981.

Pfeffer, J. *Organizations and Organization Theory*. Boston: Pitman, 1982.

Pfeffer, J. Power: *Why Some People Have It and Some Don't*. New York: HarperCollins. 2010.

Quinn, R. E. Applying the Competing Values Approach to Leadership: Toward an Integrative Framework. In J. G. Hunt and others (eds.), *Managerial Work and Leadership: International Perspectives*. New York: Pergamon Press, 1983.

Renz, D.O., and Andersson, F.O. Nonprofit Governance: A Review of the Field. In C. Cornforth and W. Brown (eds.) *Nonprofit Governance: Innovative Perspectives and Approaches*. Abingdon, Oxon, United Kingdom: Routledge, 2013.

Ritchie, W. J., Kolodinsky, R. W., and Eastwood, K. Does Executive Intuition Matter? An Empirical Analysis of Its Relationship with Nonprofit Organization Financial Performance. *Nonprofit and Voluntary Sector Quarterly*, 2007, 36, 140–155.

Tsui, A. S. A Role Set Analysis of Managerial Reputation. *Organizational Behavior and Human Performance*, 1984, 34, 64–96.

Tsui, A. S., Ashford, S., St. Clair, L., and Xin, K. Dealing with Discrepant Expectations: Response Strategies and Managerial Effectiveness. *Academy of Management Journal*, 1995, 38, 1515–1543.

Weber, M. *From Max Weber: Essays in Sociology* (H. H. Gerth and C. W. Mills, trans. and eds.). New York: Oxford University Press, 1946.

Wrong, D. *Power: Its Forms, Bases, and Uses*. Chicago: University of Chicago Press, 1988.

Yukl, G. A. *Leadership in Organizations* (8th ed.). Upper Saddle River, NJ: Prentice Hall, 2012.

CHAPTER SEVEN

ETHICAL NONPROFIT MANAGEMENT

Core Values and Key Practices
Thomas H. Jeavons

Since the mid-1980s, scandals in the nonprofit sector and the corporate world have given rise to heightened concerns about ethics, accountability, and public trust for all types of organizations. Charitable organizations and those who run them have behaved badly on occasion before, but they have probably never received such intense public scrutiny as over the last quarter-century. Now, in an era of twenty-four-hour news networks, Internet news feeds, and social media, even small missteps can become major public relations nightmares. Moreover, the public's readiness to believe the worst about most institutions has been reinforced by the pervasive evidence of the greed and moral myopia of major corporations that contributed to the "great recession" and to the widespread economic chaos and human suffering it created.

High-profile ethical scandals involving nonprofits, and the damage they can cause, have been seen before. During the 1990s, following the United Way of America scandal, the public's faith in nonprofit institutions generally fell. Then, in the aftermath of efforts to make nonprofits more accountable, there was some rebound in public trust (Independent Sector, 2002). But since the beginning of the new century the frauds, abuses of power, failures of governance, and evasions of accountability that were so evident in cases like those of the American Red Cross, the Smithsonian, and the Catholic Church (to name just a few prominent examples) have generated reasons for public faith in nonprofits to erode again.

Since 1973 a significant decline in public confidence in many major institutions has been widespread (O'Neill, 2009, pp. 251–252). This represents a real problem for government and business, but even more so for nonprofits. Why more so for nonprofits? Because nonprofit organizations—at least public charities (the 501(c)(3)s)—are especially dependent on the public's trust and goodwill to gain the support they need for the work they do. These organizations are sometimes described as "values-expressive," as being instrumental and critical to building "social capital" (a concept that centers on trust), and as being instruments of collective action for serving the public good (Lohmann, 1992; Payton & Moody, 2008; Putnam, 2000). If they are not organizations of integrity, organizations that are trustworthy, then they generally will not be able to function effectively. The logic of this is obvious. Why would people want to give their money or time to an organization if they have reason to doubt that organization is representing itself and the work it does honestly and is using the contributions it receives well for the purpose of fulfilling its stated mission?

The responsibility for assuring the ethical behavior of a nonprofit organization resides with both its managers and its board members (or trustees). The roles and responsibilities of governing boards are spoken to in Chapter Five of this volume. I would just remind us here—with emphasis—that boards are the ultimate fiduciary agents for nonprofits, so their attention to issues of integrity must be as consistent as those of any executive. That said, this chapter will focus primarily on the responsibilities of professional staff, the managers. The discussion here is about "professional ethics."

Attention to professional ethics has followed an interesting trajectory over the last four decades. There was a notable surge of interest in these matters following the Watergate scandal in the mid-1970s, after it was observed that the majority of those involved were educated at some of the nation's most prestigious law schools. A similar surge of interest in ethics has risen in the aftermath of high-profile corporate scandals over the last several decades. The professional association of business colleges and schools even required more attention be paid to ethics in the curricula of their member institutions. Yet, the responses of commentators and institutional leaders and the changes in professional school curricula over the last thirty years have been inadequate to end the cycle of recurring scandals; and these responses often reflect two troubling assumptions about ethics and the professions.

The first assumption is that careful, skilled thinking about ethical matters is more the business of philosophers and academics than of practitioners. While persons "training for the professions" may be required to take courses in or complete assignments relating to ethical issues of their profession, many involved—especially the students—assume that these courses and assignments are of secondary importance. Why would they assume that? Because both practitioners and students can see (from observing their fields) that the skills one must master to build a "successful career" are the technical and practical skills of their profession; and that often an inability to think clearly about and act appropriately on the ethical issues has not created a major stumbling block to professional advancement.

The second problematic assumption is found among many who, even while they admit the importance of ethical questions and issues, believe these questions and issues may be dealt with as discrete concerns in professional practice, isolated from others. This perspective is evident in the tendency to have one course on ethics in a professional program or to have one or two sessions in courses on other subjects take up ethical issues, rather than trying to have the ethical implications of every aspect of professional practice dealt with wherever they might arise in a professional education.

I lift up these assumptions here because they are both, I believe, patently false. Moreover, both undermine the maintenance of appropriate ethical standards in the behavior, management, and operation of nonprofit organizations. (Indeed, this is true for organizations of any kind.)

The analysis that follows builds on two contrary assumptions. The first is that reflecting critically and actively on ethical issues is an obligation of every professional, including nonprofit managers. The capacity for and inclination to socially responsive, historically grounded, critical, ethical judgment should be one outcome of any sound professional education program, and one of the capacities of a "professional" as "reflective practitioner" (Schön, 1983, 1987). The second is that a concern for the ethical implications of one's decisions and actions is salient in every aspect of professional practice and—for the considerations of this volume—in relation to every facet of the life of nonprofit organizations.

Indeed, I will argue here, as the chapter title implies, that *we are most likely to see consistently ethical behavior among nonprofit managers and organizations only where an emphasis on ethical values and behavior is deeply embedded in the cultures of these organizations.* So building and reinforcing that kind of organizational culture becomes a primary responsibility for those desiring that ethical practice be a hallmark of all the functions, including management, of their organizations.

Chapter Overview

The argument I will make here is that ethical behavior in and by nonprofit organizations cannot be effectively assured simply by employing encouraging rhetoric about ethics, nor just by establishing specific rules for ethical behavior. This point can be readily demonstrated by examining the historical record and the common experience of most managers and organizational analysts. Anyone with significant experience in organizational life knows there is often a marked disparity between rhetoric and practice, between "espoused values" and "operative values," in organizational behavior (Argyris & Schön, 1978). They also know that rules about ethics (and other matters) can be, and frequently are, followed "in the letter" while being totally ignored or violated "in the spirit."

Thus, the claim argued here is that truly ethical behavior will be assured only by creating an organizational culture in which key ethical ideals and expectations are incorporated in the "core values" (Schein, 1985) of an organization and thus permeate its operations. Achieving this will almost certainly involve the use of appropriate rhetoric about values, and it may involve promulgating codes of ethics within the organization. More important, though, it must involve modeling of the core values in the behavior of key individuals in an organization and reinforcement of those values through the organization's structures and reward systems.

Additionally, I will argue that because of the unique historical, societal dimensions of their character and function, the expectations about what constitutes ethical behavior in and by nonprofit, public benefit charities differ from those placed on other organizations. Specifically, questions of trust and integrity go to the essence of the reason for the existence of these organizations and their ability to satisfy public expectations. The existence of most charitable nonprofit organizations, their capacity to garner resources—and so to survive and carry out their missions—depends on their moral standing and consistency (see Douglas, 1987; Hansmann, 1987; Jeavons, 1992; Ostrander and Schervish, 1990; Payton & Moody, 2008).

There is an implicit social contract supporting the presence and function of private, public benefit nonprofits in our society. Simply summarized, these organizations are given special standing and specific legal advantages over other private organizations with the understanding they will serve the public good. The public expects these organizations to be motivated by and adhere to such a commitment in their performance. The public also expects these organizations will honor a set of widely accepted moral and humanitarian values—deriving from the organizations' historical and philosophical roots—and that they will not act in a self-serving manner.

Accordingly, if the managers of public benefit nonprofits wish to ensure the ethical behavior of their organizations, staffs, and themselves, then they need to create and maintain organizational cultures that honor in practice (as fundamental) a set of "core values" that are in keeping with the historic, philosophical, moral, and religious roots of the voluntary sector, and that meet current public expectations. In this context, trust is the essential lifeblood of the nonprofit sector—trust that nonprofits will fulfill this implicit social contract. To ensure that this trust is sustained, I will argue, five core values must permeate these organizations, shaping their ethics. These values are integrity, openness, accountability, service, and charity (in the original sense of that term).

We begin by considering what ethics are and are not. We will look at a number of definitions of ethics, with a particular eye toward the origins, character, and purposes of ethical norms or standards. Then we need to examine more closely the kinds of ethical norms that are usually applied to nonprofit, public-benefit organizations in American culture, the factors that have shaped these norms, and the purposes they serve.

Having formed a well-grounded perspective on the norms or standards for ethical behavior in and by nonprofit organizations, we next need to ask how such behavior can be assured. What is the relationship between values and behavior? Assuming an organization does ascribe to or articulate the "right" values, how can one help ensure that those values are captured and reflected in all aspects of its operations, by all its members?

In essence, this is to ask about the integrity of an organization, about how to make certain that it is—and will continue to be—what it claims to be. Specifically, how can one make certain that there will be conformity between the values an organization claims to represent and the purposes it says it intends to serve on the one hand, and its actual operations on the other? Finally, this chapter concludes with some specific suggestions about how a "culture of integrity" can be created and sustained in nonprofit organizations. Assuming nonprofit organizations wish to act ethically, it is only by creating and sustaining such an organizational culture that this intention is likely to be fulfilled consistently. Let us begin, then, by examining the nature of "ethics" and "ethical behavior."

What Are "Ethics"?

As a field of study, "ethics" refers to "the study of moral topics, including moral issues, moral responsibilities, and moral ideals of character."* In a normative sense, "ethics" may be seen as referring to "justified moral standards," which is to say, not just what people do believe about how they should act, but also what they *should* believe. As this chapter is directed more to practitioners of management

---

* I am indebted for this definition, and for much of the formulation of the material that follows on ethical theory, to Mike W. Martin, professor of philosophy at Chapman University.

and other "lay people" than to scholars, however, we need to think also about more common uses of the term ethics.

Webster's *New World Dictionary of the American Language* (2nd college ed. 1970) defines ethics as a "system or code of morals of a particular person, religion, group, profession; etc." The *Oxford English Dictionary* (compact ed., 1971) notes that the word "ethics" comes from the Greek term "ethos," meaning "custom, usage, manner or habit," and goes on to offer the following definitions (for ethics): "the moral principles by which a person is guided" and "the rules of conduct recognized in certain associations or departments of human life." The derivations of the term, as well as the differences we see in these common definitions, highlight two facets of the origins and purposes of ethics that are useful to examine.

One set of issues involves the derivations of and justifications for specific ethical systems and values. Exploring various types of ethical theories—duty ethics, utilitarianism, virtue ethics—can be a valuable exercise. However, given limitations of space, it is not helpful here, as it would divert us from our focus on applied ethics in nonprofit management. (Please see the *Handbook*'s Internet resource website for useful resources and references on this topic.)

On the other hand, the definitions of ethics just examined also remind us that much of what we typically think about as ethical principles or judgments, especially when our concern is application and practice, do not derive from philosophical absolutes, but rather from reference points of social or community standards. To play with the words, one's ethics (as we typically use the term) may be as much a matter of "ethos"—what is expected or socially acceptable, what is customary—as a matter of indisputable moral vision. Of course, these two aspects of ethics are often intertwined. What a particular community views as ethically acceptable will often be determined by what its members believe some source of absolute moral authority (God, perhaps) requires.

Understanding these things about the origins and meaning of ethics helps us see that when we raise and examine questions about ethics—ethics generally, professional ethics, the ethics of nonprofit managers, or the ethics of the behavior of nonprofit organizations—there are two reference points we need always to bear in mind. One is a point of moral absolutes, and the other is community standards and expectations. For our purposes, when we think about the ethics of nonprofit organizations and their management, we must ask two kinds of questions: (1) What are we morally obligated to do and not do? (2) What does society require or expect of us? Moreover, ethical questions should be considered in that order, giving preference to moral obligations over customary ones.

Professional Ethics

One volume claims that ethics are "a set of rules that apply to human beings over the totality of their interrelationships with one another, and that take precedence over all other rules" (Gellerman, Frankel, and Ladenson, 1990, p. 41). If we accept this, then we need to ask, "How are such rules more specifically defined by and applied to particular spheres of professional activity, in contrast to the broader reach of our lives?" (For a wonderfully insightful exploration of the interplay between professional and personal ethics, see Martin, 2000.)

Some scholars claim that one of the elements that define a "profession" (as opposed to other kinds of work) is that every specific profession involves a commitment to publicly articulated goals and social and societal purposes for that profession's practice and to standards for and approaches to that practice that should be shared by all its practitioners. It is because they meet societal needs with special expertise, it is argued, that professions are given certain privileges—like self-regulation, control over standards for training and entry into practice, and (thus) control over their own markets and competition. These prerogatives are provided in exchange for the profession's commitment (implicit, at least) to meet public needs and serve the public good (see Bellah and Madsen, 2007; Flores, 1988; Larson, 1977; Hatch, 1988; and Martin, 2000). Interestingly, here we have another implicit social contract. A classic paradigm for this is the medical profession and physicians with their Hippocratic Oath and the other specific expectations about their obligations to society in the provision of medical care.

Following this line of reasoning, one commentator on "professional values" argues that in our culture "professionals are viewed as morally committed to pursuing the dominant value that defines the goals of their professional practice.... They are expected to pursue such goals on a social as well as individual level.... And they are expected to do so even when self-interest may have to be sacrificed in that pursuit" (Alan Goldman, 1986, cited in Gellerman, Frankel, Ladenson, 1990, p. 5).

It may not be immediately clear what "the dominant value" that defines the goals of the practice of management generally is or should be. Still, it can be argued that the dominant value that should define the practice of management of public benefit nonprofits is "a commitment to serve the greater good." Such organizations are (or were) often created specifically to advance the common good, usually by providing services, and (as I will show) often in situations where the establishment of trust in the integrity and commitment to service of the agency is a paramount concern.

In sum, the claim here is that the ethical operation of nonprofit agencies and ethical nonprofit management require the articulation and internalization of standards for behavior and ways of being for those agencies and their managers that adequately reflect the sector's origins in the moral spheres of our culture and that meet the current, morally justifiable expectations of our society. Before moving on to look closely at those origins and expectations and the standards for behavior they necessitate, however, I want to comment briefly on how this perspective contrasts with some current views of the purposes of professional ethics, because those views are especially dangerous if they are adopted in the nonprofit world.

Misunderstanding Professional Ethics

One commonly articulated rationale for ethical behavior in professional practice is that it is simply "good for business." This may be the case. It may well be possible to demonstrate that it is (generally) true that "honesty [and other ethical behavior] is the best policy." Looking at some of the business practices that led to the economic crisis of 2008/2009, it is certainly clear that unethical behavior can have disastrous consequences for the common good. What is also clear, however, is that this utilitarian perspective does not provide an adequate underpinning for behaving ethically. Still, this is often the only, or at least the most prominent rationale or motivation given, for the development and practice of "sound business ethics."

Consider, for example, a long-running advertisement for a prestigious business school's seminars on ethics that said the reasons for learning and, presumably, practicing "good business ethics" is to "build stable, profitable relationships, strengthen employee loyalty...and avoid litigation." One would hope that all these results would ensue for the ethical organization. Still, we need to ask, "How well does a focus on these goals hold up as the rationale or motivation for behaving ethically?" What if lying about something that has recently occurred is more likely to help a firm avoid litigation than telling the truth? Is lying acceptable then? What if misusing funds to provide extra perquisites for employees is more effective in gaining their loyalty than using funds properly? What if there are cases in which "more stable, profitable relationships" can be better secured through bribery or deceit than through honest competition? The point here is that when commitments to or judgments about ethical behavior are based primarily on utilitarian cost/benefit calculations, they may be weak indeed.

It is easy to argue for the practical benefits of ethical behavior as the primary justification for adhering to ethical standards. But, as the examples just cited highlight, such a justification is easily undermined. Ironically, it is most easily undermined in just those situations when sound ethical choices may be most difficult to discern and most important to make.

One potential advantage of nonprofit, public-benefit organizations in this sphere is that they can—and should—root their judgments about commitments to ethical behavior in the moral traditions from which the nonprofit sector sprang. As one scholar reminds us: "Institutions that enunciate, transmit, and defend ethical values fall within the boundaries of nonprofit sector. Educational, religious, and advocacy organizations constitute a majority of [the] membership and have shaped the sector itself" (Mason, 1992a). Put more plainly, as a monograph on "Ethics and the Nation's Voluntary and Philanthropic Community" noted, "Those who presume to serve the public good assume a public trust" (Independent Sector, 1991, p. 1).

Understanding that ethical judgments must be based on firmer moral and social considerations lets us look more closely at the particular ethical values—and the character of the public trust—that can and should shape the ethical perspectives of nonprofit managers, whatever the practical advantages (or disadvantages) of ethical behavior may be.

Core Values for the Voluntary Sector

Many explanations have been offered for the origins and use of the nonprofit organizational form. Scholars differ as to which explanations are most valid. (For useful discussions of this question, see Columbo and Hall, 1995; Douglas, 1987; Hansmann, 1987; Hopkins, 1998; O'Neill, 2003; Salamon, 1999; Van Til, 1988.) One explanation that holds substantial explanatory power revolves around two issues or dynamics that economists and organizational theorists call "market failure" and "contract failure" (or an "agency problem").

Too simply put, the market failure theory suggests that private nonprofits tend to arise to provide services where agencies of governments cannot or will not provide the service for some reason, and the nature of the service needed is such that for-profit businesses cannot make a sufficient return on their investment to be induced to offer it. Contract failure and agency theory suggest nonprofits are needed to provide services when those who want a service offered are not in a position to provide it themselves and it is also the case that those paying for the service are unable to judge the quality of that service because of the nature, location, or setting of the service to be provided. In such circumstances, it is argued, people create or use private nonprofit (rather than for-profit) organizations because they feel nonprofits will have less incentive to cheat either consumers or supporters. That is, they think this type of organization—acting as their agent—is less likely to skimp on the amounts or quality of services offered because its board and managers have less opportunity to enrich themselves by that behavior in this organizational structure.

Note it is assumed that in these cases the people paying for the services are often not the consumers of the services. Often they are donors. This being so, they prefer to work through an organization that, as an agent, can be expected to provide that service in the manner that they (the donors) would provide it themselves if they could. Consequently, they seek an agent they believe to be highly committed for moral reasons to providing that service for others. Crassly put, they want an agent who is involved "for the cause," not "for the money."

A quick analysis of both these situations tells us what is likely to be one of the most important and desirable ethical qualities of nonprofit organizations in the public's eyes. In these circumstances trust is a key consideration. That being so, we can project what operational and ethical values will need to be evident in organizations to earn and retain the public's trust. Among the most significant, as already noted, are integrity, openness, accountability, and service.

Also on that earlier list, though, is "charity" in the original sense of the term—from the Latin *caritas*. Obviously, there are some nonprofit organizations that would not be expected to be "charitable" as that word is often used—that is, "generous" or "eleemosynary." Most people do not expect these to be characteristics of trade associations, for example. Still, the majority of the organizations that populate the nonprofit or voluntary sector are service providers dependent in some way on the philanthropic traditions and practices of our society. Indeed, the majority are religious or have religious roots (Jeavons, 2003). And all these are expected in that context to be basically "caring" organizations, willing to put the public good and the welfare of others above their own private interests.

It is important to understand how this last expectation presumes a moral quality ascribed to such organizations deriving from their historical and sociological functions in our society. The fact is that nonprofit philanthropic and service organizations occupy a distinctive place in American society because of their origins—largely in religious or other idealistic voluntary associations—and because they have traditionally been vehicles for preserving, transmitting, or promoting social values. Because of their historical development and their contemporary roles, these institutions carry much of the burden of mediating civic, moral, and spiritual values in the public realm and from one generation to the next (Curti, 1958; Parsons, 1960). Thus, they are objects of special public expectations that they will behave in morally honorable ways.

So there are ethical qualities that are essential in the character and behavior of public benefit nonprofits. These organizations are expected to—and should—demonstrate integrity, openness, accountability, service, and a caring demeanor. What is required of managers in this context is that they give continuing attention to assure that these ethical values are reflected in every aspect of these organizations. This requires that the managers model ethical qualities in their own behavior as well as articulate and foster them as ideals for others. Considering carefully the meaning of these values in organizational behavior should allow us to see better how managers can undertake these responsibilities and work toward creating a culture of integrity.

Ethical Management in Ethical Organizations

It will be useful now to consider the key ethical attributes of nonprofit managers and their organizations more fully. In this process we should undertake an analysis at two levels—the individual and the organizational—asking, for example: "What does it mean for a manager to do his or her work with integrity and for an organization to operate with integrity?"

I cannot, in this one section, make an exhaustive analysis nor offer numerous illustrations of how these ethical qualities would be evident in each of the many aspects of the operations of nonprofit organizations. Authors of other chapters in this volume who address other aspects of nonprofit management discuss questions, and may offer considerations, of how ethical issues may arise in different facets of the work of nonprofit organizations. Other literature on nonprofits offers other useful insights. We know, for instance, that nonprofits are not immune to financial fraud in various forms; but researchers have done some good work in determining the nature and scope of such fraud, and in suggesting strategies to reduce fraud (see Archambeault, Webber, and Greenlee, 2015; Greenlee, Fischer, Gordon, and Keating, 2007).

That noted, my intention is to offer a broader context within which to think further in ethical terms about the material presented in the other chapters of this *Handbook* (and in real life). Ideally, the relationship between this chapter, focused specifically on ethics, and those others, addressing other facets of nonprofit leadership, management, and accountability should set the ground for a dialogue about a wide range of ethical issues nonprofit managers face.

Integrity

It may be most useful to describe integrity as "honesty writ large." That is, integrity has to do with conformity between appearance and reality, between intention and action, between promise and performance, in every aspect of a person's or organization's existence. If trust is essential to support the operation of charitable nonprofit organizations, and if being trustworthy is one of the most basic qualities the public looks for in them, then integrity in this sense becomes a fundamental ethical characteristic they must possess.

At the organizational level, integrity is most obviously demonstrated to be present or absent by comparing an organization's own literature—fundraising materials, reports, mission statements, and such—with its actual program priorities and performance. For instance, an organization that claims to exist to serve the poor, but regularly spends extensive resources on enlarging itself, enhancing its own image before the public, or attending to the comfort of its staff must be suspect. So, too, one wonders about educational institutions that say they are devoted to providing the best education possible to students, but spend more of their resources on things intended to improve their own status—image-enhancing athletics, high-profile research projects, or "star" faculty members—than on facilities and activities for teaching and learning.

This is not to say that staff in such organizations should not have reasonable salaries and benefits; that being in the public eye for fundraising purposes may not be valuable to support the work to be done; or that an organization might not be able to improve its service delivery by growing or its teaching by employing active researchers. However, careful examinations of budgets, allocations of staff time, and the application of other resources sometimes reveal that nonprofit organizations that were created to serve the public good are giving more attention to caring for and improving themselves than others. Moreover, the public is highly sensitive to these issues. If we need proof of this, we would do well to recall the huge controversies involving United Way of America in the early 1990s or recall the many uproars that have occurred over recent years regarding excessive compensation levels for CEOs of large universities, hospitals, and foundations—all 501(c)(3)s.

It is instructive, in fact, to briefly review some details the story of the United Way of America, because its scandal caused long-term and profound damage to almost all local United Ways and injured the credibility of charities more generally. In the spring of 1992 it was revealed that the head of the United Way of America was receiving a salary of almost $500,000, traveling about the world first-class, and setting up subsidiary organizations run by his friends and relatives.

When millions of small donors to local United Ways found out that a portion of their gifts was going to support a lavish lifestyle for an executive of a charitable organization, many were outraged. Despite the massive efforts of local United Ways to explain that only a tiny portion of income went to the national organization, which was a legally separate entity, the giving to local United Ways (and to many community service agencies) fell significantly the next year, and in many cases took years to recover. Some would argue the declining influence of United Ways in many places, while having multiple causes, began its downward trend here.

This case illustrates with exceptional clarity how disparities between the ethical promise (implicit or explicit) and the real performance of one charitable organization may precipitate dramatic difficulties for the entire nonprofit sector. As one of the first economists to study the nonprofit sector observed: "Whenever any nonprofit is found to have abused its trusted position, the reputation of trustworthy nonprofits also suffers" (Weisbrod, 1988, p. 13). This observation of thirty years ago seems only to grow truer as media scrutiny of nonprofits intensifies.

Indeed, we have seen this anew in the last decade. From 2002 to 2008 the charitable sector and the public were treated to a long-running spectacle staged by the Senate Finance Committee chaired by Senator Charles Grassley. Under Grassley's leadership, the Committee launched one investigation after another—and broadcast one charge after another—about the alleged misuse and waste of funds by nonprofits. Targets of these charges included organizations as venerable as the American Red Cross. Seizing on a relatively small number of cases, some of which were admittedly egregious, the senator and Finance Committee staff were able to generate an extraordinary amount of bad publicity for charitable institutions as a whole. These investigations raised significant questions about nonprofits' operations that in many cases needed attention. But in a broader context, all the noise made by the Senate Finance Committee mostly served to make all nonprofits ethically suspect because of the bad behavior of a very small minority.

One example of the kind of behavior that raises such issues about integrity can be drawn from a smaller study of relief and development agencies (Jeavons, 1994). One of the agencies studied engaged in practices that were not illegal, but would certainly have caused questions in the minds of donors (and others), if they had become aware of them. At least two practices were ethically questionable.

First, this agency sometimes used what are called "representational" images in their fundraising materials. That is, brochures told stories about a family or person in need, often desperate need, and included pictures of their plight that were quite striking. However, sometimes these stories were actually composites of stories of a number of people in the impoverished area, put together for maximum effect, or the pictures were not of the persons or family mentioned at all, but rather were pictures the agency calculated most likely to "pull on donors' heart strings." The needs were real, and the stories and pictures conveyed the needs quite effectively; but this approach lacked integrity because the stories and pictures were not factually true.

Some persons would argue that this is morally wrong because, simply enough, it is dishonest, regardless of the fact that it raises money for a good purpose. Others argued the ends justified the means, because the stories were essentially true. Yet, even persons within this organization admitted that if donors had become aware of this practice they might have been upset. The donors' expectations of high moral standards—in this case, higher standards of truthfulness—for such an organization would have been violated.

Second, this same agency often made general appeals with brochures featuring projects for which it could most easily raise money, with the brochures giving a strong impression (although not a specific promise) that the money raised would go to those particular projects. But in fact, those projects were fully funded from other sources, and the donations were used for other purposes. Again, this was done in a way that ensured there was no illegality, but neither was there clear integrity.

One is left to wonder, in such an organizational climate: What other ethical standards were allowed to slide? and How well were the funds that were raised being used? If one is inclined to think that these kinds of decisions are purely matters of strategic choice, one needs to see the contrast between this organization and other relief and development agencies.

Many other agencies studied had specific rules against using "representational images" and policies that require donors to be consulted before their gifts are used for projects other than the ones for which they were solicited. The managers in those agencies described their standards and policies as points of pride, as conscious choices made to uphold the ethical character of their organizations and their work. Those managers pointed out that it was vital to maintain the highest moral standards in all facets of their operations, lest the willingness to compromise at one point become the beginning of a lowering of standards more generally—the first step on the proverbial "slippery slope."

This small example from long ago presaged similar more recent problems for a much more visible charity. Charges like these, but on a far larger scale, were raised about the Red Cross's fundraising in the aftermath on the terrorist attacks on the United States on September 11, 2001. While there may have been good, even compelling reasons that some of the millions of dollars of funds not needed in New York City should have been set aside for emergencies elsewhere, doing so without prior permission from—or at least explanations to—donors was not acceptable to the public. The fallout caused that organization great embarrassment.

These examples ask us to examine again the meaning of integrity at the individual level for managers and management. "Integrity" may have different meanings for different individuals, but in the context of professional ethics it must mean doing one's job as honestly and as fully in adherence to one's professed principles as possible. Careful observers of organizational behavior have noted that managers and leaders in organizations, or particular parts of organizations, can have a significant effect in setting behavioral standards, either as a matter of personal influence or because of their control of reward systems, or for both reasons.

The manager who wants her or his employees to deal honestly with others had better deal honestly with them, and, further, had better reward honesty and discourage any dishonesty. If the manager is willing to cut corners, tell "little" lies, or act in self-serving ways, it becomes more likely employees will see this as acceptable, at least in the work setting. A manager who wants the organization she or he oversees to be known for its integrity and to be trustworthy must begin by being completely trustworthy in her or his dealings with all those who are part of the organization and make it clear that similar behavior is expected of all those people.

Put more simply, integrity must be one of the hallmarks of nonprofit management. It is an ethical obligation, both as a matter of morality, because it is right, and as a matter of societal necessity, because the public expects nonprofit organizations to show integrity. Recent history shows that failing to uphold the highest standards for personal and organizational integrity can have enormous consequences for nonprofit managers and their agencies or institutions.

Openness

It would not be accurate to call the quality of openness a "moral" value, at least within the context of the most common value systems of American culture. So the claim here about openness as an ethical value is not based so much on moral absolutes—as may be the case for integrity—as on social values and expectations. In this context, we might think of openness as a "derivative virtue." We might also note, however, that in businesses as well as nonprofits, efforts to make organizations more transparent to stakeholders are gaining ground as leaders recognize that being trustworthy is often critical to success in both spheres.

In any case, in the history of philanthropy in America, whenever an organization or individual tries to hide philanthropic endeavors from public view, the result—if they are discovered—has almost always been to raise profound skepticism about the motivation for and character of those endeavors. The public's attitude here has been: "If they are really doing good, why would they be reluctant (or embarrassed) to have us see what they are doing?"

This is especially true for organizations. It is possible to put forth a reasonable argument, even one based on religious grounds (see Matthew 6:2-4 of the Bible or the Mishneh Torah), for individuals "doing good works" anonymously or in secret. However, organizations operating in the public sphere, especially in areas of service or advocacy that can have an impact on public policy or community life, find it hard to argue convincingly that there is any value to secrecy about how they make their choices and do their work. Indeed, it may be crucial for these organizations to conduct their business in a way that is open to public scrutiny.

One compelling reason for this is that openness undergirds other ethical behavior. The organization that operates openly cannot afford to cut other ethical corners. Being "transparent"—something of a buzzword in governance discussions now—makes integrity mandatory, unless one wants to suffer serious criticism. For example, in the case of the relief and development agencies (earlier), it seems clear that the one that engaged in questionable tactics would not have been able to operate transparently and retain its donor base.

Another reason for openness is historical. There have long been critical questions raised about the roles philanthropic and service organizations play in shaping people's and communities' lives. (See, for instance, Griffin, 1957, or Nielsen, 1985.) One cause for this concern is that some organizations appear to have had ulterior motives, for example, intentions of "social control" or protection of the interests of the privileged, embedded in their work. It is clear that some of the impetus for legislation regulating the operation of foundations (in 1969) came from supposedly philanthropic entities being formed and using their tax-exempt status as a way to protect family fortunes from taxation while still controlling family businesses (Bremner, 1988). Here again, recent scandals in the conduct of some nonprofit organizations reinforce the case to be made for their being subject to public scrutiny.

In addition, those who are concerned about the continuing vitality of nonprofit organizations and who recognize that maintaining a climate of trust is essential to that vitality, argue that operating openly is one of the best ways to build trust. Organizations that wish to engage people's support and good faith can find no better way to do so than to do good works well, and then welcome inquiries and inspection by anyone interested in their methods.

A similar logic applies to those who lead these organizations, in terms of their leadership and management. In the effort to build the support and commitment of staff, volunteers, and donors, a manager's willingness to talk openly and honestly about rationales for programs, the reasons for and ways in which decisions are made, and approaches to problem solving can be invaluable. Additionally, many nonprofits (as voluntary associations) come out of a populist democratic tradition in American culture. So it can be argued that they really ought to be operated in such a democratic manner to represent and further that tradition—that this may be another significant part of their role and social obligation in this society, (For very helpful discussions of these issues, see Lohmann, 1992; O'Neill, 2003; or Van Til, 1988.)

Finally, this means that openness should be seen as a core ethical value for nonprofit organizations and their managers in the business of decision making, in matters of raising and allocating resources, and generally in the manner of their operation. Moreover, openness is a necessary prerequisite to accountability, which is the next core value we examine.

Accountability

Not only is it important for nonprofit public-benefit organizations to be open about the things they do, and how and why they do them, but it is important that they be ready to explain and generally be accountable for their choices. This is an extension of the implicit social contract of privilege and trust these organizations enjoy in our society. By accepting the privilege of tax-exemption and the right to solicit tax-deductible contributions, public-benefit nonprofits also accept an obligation to be ready to answer for their behavior and performance—not only to their membership, but also to the communities they serve and to the broader public as well, for they are using financial resources that would otherwise have gone into the public treasury.

Looked at in contractual terms, we see these organizations are granted the right to solicit tax-deductible contributions, or at least are granted tax-exempt status, on the assumption that they are serving the public good and will put their resources to work as effectively as possible on behalf of the causes or people they claim to serve. Indeed, the character and language of the legal discourse about these issues, employing terms like "public benefit" or "mutual benefit" organizations, confirms these assumptions (see Simon, 1987). From this implicit social contract derives a clear ethical obligation to perform according to promise, to be subject to evaluation, and be answerable for a failure to perform.

In fact, issues of nonprofits' accountability are very complicated, much more so than public discussions of these issues typically suggest. To really understand these issues for different nonprofits, one must ask multiple questions. "To whom is a nonprofit accountable?" is only the first; and the answer is likely to be "to multiple constituencies." In addition, one should also ask, "For what aspects of their operations should they be accountable, by whom will they be held accountable, and in what manner?" Some would argue that, while all nonprofits should have some public accountability, these specifics of "to whom and how" are matters that should be thought about strategically and that need to be determined according to the stakeholders involved (Kearns, 1996).

In other words, all nonprofit organizations have an ethical responsibility to be accountable to their supporters, their members, and their donors; and the public-benefit organizations have a larger responsibility to be accountable to the broader public for the ways in which they undertake to fulfill their philanthropic purposes. Evidence of increasing public expectations in this regard can be found in the growth in recent years of "watchdog" groups like the Better Business Bureau's Wise Giving Alliance and Guidestar. Nonprofits themselves have manifested their willingness to be more accountable by forming mutual accountability networks in particular fields, like the Evangelical Council for Financial Accountability. In 2007 Independent Sector issued a report on *Principles of Good Governance and Ethical Practice*, which they encouraged all their members (and others) to see as an outline of the ideals and behaviors all nonprofits should pursue and for which they should be accountable. In addition, more states have enacted laws to mandate financial disclosure and regulate fundraising practices of nonprofits.

How does this obligation of accountability extend to nonprofit managers? In much the same way as the obligations of integrity and openness do. First, if this is a quality managers and leaders want to see others demonstrate in their organizations, then it is one the managers had better model in their own behavior. Then it becomes an expectation that they can articulate credibly to other staff, trustees, and volunteers.

Second, managers can establish this commitment most firmly by holding themselves accountable to their organization's board and working to build a board that will hold them properly accountable for their performance. Executives who view themselves as free agents and try to isolate their boards from full information about and active involvement in the work of the organization and boards that hire an executive, then fall into a passive, "rubber stamp" role in evaluation and governance have been key contributing factors to poor performance and ethical problems in a number of nonprofits. The most useful literature on the board and executive relationships has pointed out that a full and vital partnership between executives and managers is essential (Drucker, 1990; Herman and Heimovics, 1991; Middleton, 1987).

Ironically, the situation may require an executive to encourage (or even educate) a board to play a more active role in evaluating the executive's—and the organization's—performance. In this way, if the board is representative of, or at least in touch with, the needs and feelings of the larger community, then the executive is soliciting oversight and potentially helpful feedback from those the organization should serve. The executive is also modeling a quality she or he should hope to encourage in all staff—general accountability for performance and receptivity to constructive criticism.

Service

The grounds for the ethical obligation here are virtually identical with those for accountability. Nonprofit organizations, especially public-benefit organizations, exist and are granted specific privileges (as noted earlier) with the explicit understanding that they are committed in some way to serve the public good. Those that are classified as "mutual benefit" organizations, which include trade associations, fraternal organizations, and such, are not beholden in the same way to serve "the public" in the broadest sense, but they are still certainly expected to serve their membership. The point being that *service*, service to people or service to a cause, is the reason for being of all these organizations. (*Note:* Sometimes that "service" includes advocacy, speaking out about community needs and assets to others, as well as trying to meet those needs themselves.)

The social contract extended to these organizations assumes that they will devote themselves primarily to service. In accepting the privileges they have been granted, charitable organizations incur the ethical obligation to be service-oriented. Moreover, in accepting the support (membership dues, donations, volunteers' time) of people who sustain them, these organizations reinforce their ethical obligations.

The ethical obligation to service should be manifest in the conduct of managers in a number of ways, in those managers making practical and strategic choices that give precedence to fulfilling the mission of their organization over possibilities for advancing their own status and careers. One hopes that these two goals can go hand-in-hand. But there are situations in which executives can make a choice that yields a short-term gain for the organization and makes the executive look good—improving his or her chances for a better next job—even though that choice harms the organization in the long run.

Many people now make a career of work in the nonprofit sector, especially in the field of fundraising. We could not have a meaningful discussion, as we do in this book, of nonprofit management as a "profession" if people did not commit themselves to and build careers in this area. This creates the basis for our discussion of professional ethics. However, it also creates a context in which managers can easily work with more concern for their own advancement than for the people or cause their organization is supposed to serve—and that can be problematic.

This is not to say that managers are required to sacrifice themselves—their health, their basic financial security, or their personal well-being—for the benefit of their organization. Nonprofit organizations, especially cause-oriented ones, are notorious for exploiting their staff in the name of noble ideals (see Greene, 1991). But the undergirding values of the nonprofit sector are altruistic, or at least service-centered; while it is fine to be concerned for one's own career, it is never acceptable for managers to advance themselves at the expense of the people and causes they have promised to serve.

In addition, observation suggests that the willingness of managers and leaders to see themselves as "servants" of others may be crucial to focusing others in an organization on that organization's commitment to service. Here the notion of "servant leadership" (Greenleaf, 1977) takes on both profound significance and immediate salience.

Charity

The last, but certainly not least important ethical obligation of nonprofit, public-benefit organizations is to charity, in the original sense of the term. The word "charity" comes from the Latin *caritas*. This means more than giving to those in need. It originally was translated as "love"—the love of neighbor and committed concern for the welfare of others illustrated in the parable of the Good Samaritan. It meant caring, putting the welfare of others on a par with one's own. It meant being generous with one's own resources, not out of a sense of pity, but out of a sense of a relationship with and concern for others.

It can surely be argued that for nonprofit organizations an ethical obligation to "charity" in this sense derives from reciprocity. Many of these organizations depend on the generosity of their supporters for their existence and ought to display such generosity themselves. Furthermore, at least in the case of many public-benefit nonprofits, the motivation of most of their supporters rests in no small way on a belief that these organizations are committed to caring for others. As noted earlier, the basis of many of these organizations' support is the expectation that they will be vehicles for building a better world or a more caring and just society.

This expectation is manifest in an interesting range of phenomena. For instance, the preference of many clients and supporters of social service agencies for private nonprofit groups appears to be based on an assumption that they will provide services in a more personal, more caring way than a government agency would. In industries where potential employees—for example, teachers, nurses, or social workers—might work for either government or private organizations, the preference of some for private nonprofits is often explained in terms of their expectation (or experience) of these organizations as more caring work environments. This expectation is certainly confirmed by the public indignation that is often evident when an organization that is itself the beneficiary of charity turns around and acts in uncaring ways.

The way in which this expectation applies to the ethics of management seems obvious. An uncaring or mean-spirited manager can undermine the caring quality of an organization as fast as any negative influence imaginable. If one wants the participants in an organization to treat its clients (and one another) with love and respect, it is hardly likely that treating the participants coldly or unfairly will help that occur. Managers and leaders help set the tone of an organization's life—whether they intend to or not—and that tone is almost certainly going to be reflected in the way that organization and all of its staff interact at every level with various constituencies.

Finally, organizations of the nonprofit sector have been seen as having a special role in transmitting civic, social, and ethical values in our society from one generation to the next. If that is true, then we have yet another reason to be concerned that these organizations reflect the highest ideals for a caring society. It is clear that some managers do see their responsibilities in this light. Discussing the kind of "witness" his organization wants to make to all those who deal with it, the president of a Christian relief and development agency said, "We have a major challenge in living up to our commitment [to care for people]; not just for children eight thousand miles away, but also for the people at our elbow" (Jeavons, 1994, p. 265).

From Ideals to Operative Values

If we can agree, then, that these five concepts or ideals—integrity, openness, accountability, service, and charity—describe key ethical qualities and obligations of nonprofit organizations and their managers, we may ask how these ideals are translated into behavior.

At the individual level, this may be easy. If one assumes that people can choose what to value and choose to embody those values in their actions, then ethical behavior is primarily a matter of choice and will. If this is the case, then the managers of nonprofit organizations simply need to choose to act with integrity, to be open and accountable in their work, to make commitment to service and charity a cornerstone for their decision making and interactions with others. They need to do these things because they are the right things to do. They need to do these things because that is what the public that supports (and can withdraw its support) wants and because the failure to uphold these obligations can have very significant negative consequences. However, this still leaves the question of how ethical ideals become the operational values of an organization as a whole.

At this point, we need to turn to the work that has been done on "organizational culture." In particular, I want to draw on the careful research and analysis reported by Edgar Schein in *Organizational Culture and Leadership* (1985).

Some early thinking about organizational culture tended to focus, sometimes shallowly, on "rites and rituals" of organizational life (see Deal and Kennedy, 1982; Peters and Waterman, 1982). Schein takes a different tack, arguing that an excessive focus on what he calls "the manifestations of culture" will obscure the fact that very similar rituals, conventions, or regular practices in various companies are undertaken for very different reasons. Thus, to understand organizational culture one must focus on the essential values these visible practices are meant to express. These values are "the substance of culture," in Schein's view.

Indeed, Schein argues that some values represent the basic assumptions of a group of people, like the membership of an organization, about the way the world is and how they, as a group, can function most successfully in it. These "core values" will shape the organization's behavior, not only by dictating what are right or acceptable responses to different kinds of situations, but even more fundamentally by shaping the way those situations are perceived, by influencing what people see as important or unimportant.

Schein's views are reinforced by other scholars who contend that the most effective (and "unobtrusive") controls on the behavior of individuals in organizations may be achieved by either selecting people who will come to the organization with certain (shared) basic understandings about organizational or professional goals and practices or by orienting them toward those understandings, goals, and practices once they arrive (Perrow, 1986).

Schein argues that leaders or managers can shape the direction, character, and operations of an organization most fundamentally and effectively by shaping the core values of the participants within it or by selecting new participants who share those values. Indeed, he claims "there is a possibility—underemphasized in leadership research—that the only things of real importance that leaders do is to create and manage culture" (1985, p. 2). The implications of this for people who are concerned about creating and maintaining organizations that behave ethically are obvious.

Managers' capacities to create a culture of integrity take root in the connection between the ethical behavior of those managers and the maintenance of the highest ethical standards of behavior of their nonprofit organizations. This is where ethical ideals come to be accepted as "givens" and where the expectation that these ideals will be honored permeates every employee's thinking. This can only occur when these ethical values are both articulated and modeled by those in positions of responsibility and leadership. In this way, leaders and managers can shape the core values of an organization as a whole and the individuals within it around ethical ideals.

One place where such a dynamic can most readily be observed is in some religious service organizations that maintain a strong commitment to honor very clear and sometimes constricting ethical ideals in their operations, while still competing successfully for donor support in a highly competitive market. (For a detailed description of such groups, see Jeavons, 1994.)

Creating and Maintaining a Culture of Integrity

Finally, we must see that clear, strong commitments to ethical ideals and behavior on the part of managers is a prerequisite to creating organizational cultures of integrity in nonprofits that will enable the organizations themselves to behave ethically. The importance of the example of leadership in this process cannot be overemphasized. As one commentator has observed, "CEOs . . . are ultimately accountable for [their] organization's ethical posture. . . . No organization can rise above the ethical level of its manager" (Mason, 1992b, p. 30).

Clearly, a manager who tells others about the importance of behaving ethically while behaving otherwise him- or herself is likely to have little positive influence on the organization. In fact, such a manager is likely to have a destructive influence, generating cynicism about and indifference to ethical concerns throughout the organization. Ultimately a manager whose own behavior models the best values but who does not talk about their significance for the organization's life may still have a less positive influence than is needed.

Even when the management of an organization is consistent in both preaching and practicing desired values, more will probably be needed to create and sustain a culture of integrity. Organizational structures and reward systems must also support and encourage ethical behavior among all employees and volunteers. People's best intentions can be undermined or confused by organizational structures and processes that lead them to make choices that have negative ethical consequences.

One wonders, for instance, how often in nonprofit service agencies (of various types) reports of problems with programs or relationships to their clients are stifled or mistakes that could reveal ways to improve their service are never mentioned, because their staffs (and volunteers) are rewarded only for successes. As is true in many organizations that are hierarchically ordered, some nonprofits have a tendency to punish the bearers of bad news—and even reward the bearers of false news when it is good. Encouraging employees to be less than honest about policies and programs that are failing leaves an organization less able to perform its mission. The leadership and management of a nonprofit organization must put in place systems that reward participants for honesty in every form, even forms that lead to the revelation of difficulties and deficiencies.

Similarly, one has to wonder about organizations that continually emphasize short-term goals and focus solely on raw numbers (dollars raised) in evaluating development efforts, rather than asking questions about the quality of relationships with donors and other potentially positive effects of fundraising, such as its educational impact on constituencies they are trying to reach. Where narrower emphases and reward systems dominate, what is the impact on fundraisers' approaches to donors? Are they as honest and caring as they should be? What is the effect on individual and organizational reporting? Is the information about fundraising costs and results as complete and fully revealing as it should be? (For a fuller examination of these issues, see Jeavons and Basinger, 2000.)

Questions about the relationship between reward systems and structures and ethical behavior become even more complex when the behaviors at issue are not so simple or when more subtle matters are involved. For instance, what about a situation in which questions are being asked about whether a "progressive nonprofit organization" is exploiting its employees or whether it is being true to the values it claims to represent in the ways it treats them.

For example, I once worked with an organization that claimed that one of the principles to which it was committed was that it "values people . . . [and] does not permit the accomplishment of goals at the expense of people." However, the organization had a structure for and approach to fundraising that emphasized continually increasing the number of dollars raised and reducing administrative costs without consideration for the effects of such goals and policies on the relationships among staff or between donors and staff. Furthermore, rewards in the organization—both raises and promotions—were distributed in a highly competitive system according to an assessment of performance based almost solely on quantitative measures. The outcome was that managers tended to push staff to achieve "more impressive" results (that is, raise more money) without regard to the impact that pressure might have on either the donors they worked with or the staff themselves. These seemed a direct contradiction to articulated values, and led to high staff turnover.

One could look as well at the famous United Way of America scandal, mentioned earlier. How did an organization that was formed specifically to serve and support local United Ways and to promote a philosophy of service, volunteering, and giving come to be an example of self-serving, empire-building management practices? In part, at least, this seems to have been a result of organizational structures that insulated the top management from the constituencies they were supposed to be serving, making them less aware of and accountable to the people the organization most needed to hear, local United Ways' donors and clients.

In addition, the staff leadership seemed to spend most of its time with, and came to pattern itself after, business leaders—in the effort to gain support and resources from them. However, in the process, the United Way of America's executive leadership came to think like for-profit corporate executives, and appear to have come to believe that organizational growth was an end worth pursuing in itself. The fact that particular strategies for attaining this end were undermining United Way's stated mission was overlooked. The result was a misuse of donated funds, a clear abuse of public trust, and some erosion of the very spirit of giving and volunteering the organization was created to promote.

The point is that organizational structures and processes and systems of rewards and disincentives must be put in place and consciously maintained to reinforce whatever rhetoric about ethical values an organization puts forth. Moreover, all this must be supported by the managers and leaders of the organization, demonstrating personal commitment to those ethical values by their own behavior. The creation and maintenance of an organizational culture of integrity—one where integrity, openness, accountability, service, and charity consistently predominate; one that will lead to consistently ethical behavior on the part of nonprofit organizations—cannot be achieved absent these elements in an organization's life.

Summary

In this chapter I have shown that ethical questions and issues must be primary concerns of all nonprofit managers and that these issues and questions are salient in all aspects of the operation of nonprofit organizations. It has been argued that the ethical values most important for nonprofit managers and organizations to honor center on the qualities of integrity, openness, accountability, service, and charity. We have seen how these particular ethical ideals are prescribed for nonprofit organizations by virtue of the distinctive history of the voluntary and nonprofit sector and the roles that these organizations play in American society. It is crucial that nonprofit organizations embody these ethical ideals in practice, both because ethical conduct and character is what moral duty requires and because the public expects this of nonprofit organizations that say they are serving the public good. Only in this way can nonprofits fulfill the implicit social contract that supports their existence in our society.

It is important to note the educational implications of this. The last three decades have seen the emergence of a number of programs around the country to educate people specifically for the work of managing nonprofit organizations. How much attention do these programs give to helping those people understand the special history and unique roles and expectations that should shape the way these organizations function and are managed? (Some would say not enough.) Those being educated to take on the responsibilities of management and leadership in nonprofit organizations must be taught sound approaches to, as well as the profound importance of, reflection on the ethical issues embedded in the various facets of the life of these organizations.

Managing an organization so that core ethical values are embodied in the organization's life requires more than rhetoric. It requires managers to demonstrate these values in their own conduct in their professional lives and service. It also requires that they create and maintain organizational structures and dynamics by which ethical conduct is rewarded and unethical conduct, in any manifestation, is discouraged. This has to involve an examination of all organizational systems and structures, from fundraising strategies to human resources policies to accounting systems, to ensure that those structures and systems do not generate pressures on personnel to ignore or violate the standards and assumptions for ethical behavior espoused in broader contexts. Other chapters in this *Handbook* offer more illustrations of how ethical questions might arise in specific facets of the work of nonprofit organizations and their managers.

The significance of these matters cannot be overemphasized. The lifeblood of the nonprofit sector is trust. Without trust on the part of donors, clients, and the larger public, nonprofit organizations will not be able to do the important work, to fulfill the crucial roles, which are theirs in our society. Nothing will erode this foundation of trust as quickly as new (or continuing) scandals involving unethical behavior by nonprofit organizations and their managers.

When faced with the temptation to cut an ethical corner, tell a little lie, not bother with full disclosure, or let the ends justify the means, it is essential the leadership and management of nonprofit organizations understand the implications of such actions and refuse to compromise on rigorous ethical standards. We have to remember that noble ends are never served by ignoble means. We have to understand that inevitably our "ethical chickens will come home to roost."

Nonprofit, public-benefit organizations have special responsibilities to serve the public good in our society, to do the right thing for those in need and for important causes and those who care about them—because it is right. This represents the ethical and essential foundation of the nonprofit sector. Without this foundation intact, it is quite likely the whole structure of the sector, including its moral and social capital and the special privileges that support its operations, could slowly dissolve. Attention to sustaining the highest levels of ethical conduct must be a primary concern of every nonprofit manager.

References

Archambeault, D. S., Webber, S., and Greenlee, J. Fraud and Corruption in U.S. Nonprofit Entities: A Summary of Press Reports 2008–2011. *Nonprofit & Voluntary Sector Quarterly*, 2015, 44(6), 1194–1224.

Argyris, C, and Schön, D. A. *Organizational Learning*. Reading, MA; Addison-Wesley, 1978.

Bellah, R. N., and Madsen, R. *Habits of the Heart: Individualism and Commitment in American Life* (2nd ed.). Berkeley, CA: University of California Press, 2007.

Bremner, R. H. *American Philanthropy* (2nd ed.). Chicago: University of Chicago Press, 1988.

Columbo, J. D., and Hall, M. H. *The Charitable Tax Exemption*. Boulder, CO: Westview Press, 1995.

Curti, M. American Philanthropy and the National Character. *American Quarterly*, 1958, 10, 420–437.

Deal, T. E., and Kennedy, A. A. *Corporate Cultures: The Rites and Rituals of Corporate Life.* Reading, MA: Addison-Wesley, 1982.

Douglas, J. Political Theories of Nonprofit Organization. In W. Powell (ed.), *The Nonprofit Sector: A Research Handbook.* New Haven, CT: Yale University Press, 1987.

Drucker, P. F. *Managing the Nonprofit Organization.* New York: HarperCollins, 1990.

Flores, A. (ed.) *Professional Ideals.* Belmont, CA: Wadsworth Publishing, 1988.

Gellerman, W., Frankel, M. S., and Ladenson, R. (eds.). *Values and Ethics in Organization and Human Systems Development.* San Francisco: Jossey-Bass, 1990.

Goldman, A. H. Professional Values and the Problem of Regulation. *Business and Professional Ethics Journal,* 1986, 5(2), 47–59.

Greene, S. G. Poor Pay Threatens Leadership. *Chronicle of Philanthropy.* 1991, 28–31.

Greenleaf, R. K. *Servant Leadership.* Ramsey, NJ: Paulist Press, 1977.

Greenlee, J., Fischer, M., Gordon, T. P., and Keating, E. K. An Investigation of Fraud in Nonprofit Organizations: Occurrences and Deterrents. *Nonprofit & Voluntary Sector Quarterly,* 2007, 6(4), 676–694.

Griffin, C. S. Religious Benevolence as Social Control, 1815–1860. *Mississippi Historical Review,* 1957, 44(3), 423–444.

Hansmann, H. Economic Theories of the Nonprofit Sector. In W. Powell (ed.), *The Nonprofit Sector: A Research Handbook.* New Haven, CT: Yale University Press, 1987.

Hatch, N.O. *The Professions in American History.* Notre Dame, IN.:University of Notre Dame Press. 1988.

Herman, R. D., and Heimovics, R. D. *Executive Leadership in Nonprofit Organizations: New Strategies for Shaping Executive-Board Dynamics.* San Francisco: Jossey-Bass, 1991.

Hopkins, B. R. *The Law of Tax-Exempt Organizations* (7th ed.). Somerset, NJ.: John Wiley & Sons, 1998.

Independent Sector. *Ethics and the Nation's Voluntary and Philanthropic Community.* Washington, DC: Independent Sector, 1991.

Independent Sector. Keeping the Trust: Confidence in Charitable Organizations in an Age of Scrutiny. Washington, DC: Independent Sector, 2002.

Independent Sector. *Principles for Good Governance and Ethical Practice: A Guide for Charities and Foundations.* Washington, DC: Independent Sector, 2007.

Jeavons, T. H. When Management Is the Message: Relating Values to Management Practice in Nonprofit Organizations. *Nonprofit Management & Leadership,* 1992, 2(4), 403–421.

Jeavons, T. H. *When the Bottom Line Is Faithfulness: The Management of Christian Service Organizations.* Bloomington, IN: Indiana University Press, 1994.

Jeavons, T. H., and Basinger, R. B. *Growing Givers Hearts: Treating Fundraising as Ministry.* San Francisco: Jossey-Bass, 2000.

Jeavons, T. H. The Vitality and Independence of Religious Organizations. *Society,* 2003, 40(4), 27–36.

Kearns, K. P. *Managing for Accountability.* San Francisco: Jossey-Bass, 1996.

Larson, M. S. *The Rise of Professionalism: A Sociological Analysis.* Berkeley, CA: University of California Press, 1977.

Lohmann, R. *The Commons: New Perspectives on Nonprofit Organizations and Voluntary Action.* San Francisco: Jossey-Bass, 1992.

Martin, M. W. *Meaningful Work: Rethinking Professional Ethics.* New York: Oxford University Press, 2000.

Mason, D. E. Keepers of the Springs: Why Ethics Make Good Sense for Nonprofit Leaders. *Nonprofit World,* 1992a, 10(2), 25–27.

Mason, D. E. Ethics and the Nonprofit Leader. *Nonprofit World,* 1992b, 10(4), 30–32.

Middleton, M. Nonprofit Boards of Directors: Beyond the Governance Function. In W. Powell (ed.), *The Nonprofit Sector: A Research Handbook*. New Haven, CT: Yale University Press, 1987.

Nielsen, W. *The Golden Donors: A New Anatomy of the Great Foundations*. New York: Dutton, 1985.

O'Neill, M. *Nonprofit Nation: A New Look at the Third America*. San Francisco: Jossey-Bass, 2003.

O'Neill, M. Public Confidence in Nonprofit Organizations. *Nonprofit and Voluntary Sector Quarterly*, 2009, 38(2), 237–269.

Ostrander, S. A., and Schervish, P. G. Giving and Getting: Philanthropy as a Social Relation. In Van Til and Associates, *Critical Issues in American Philanthropy: Strengthening Theory and Practice*. San Francisco: Jossey-Bass, 1990.

Parsons, T. *Structures and Process in Modern Societies*. Glencoe, IL: The Free Press, 1960.

Payton, R. L., and Moody, M. M. *Understanding Philanthropy*. Bloomington, IN: Indiana University Press, 2008.

Perrow, C. *Complex Organizations: A Critical Essay* (3rd ed.). New York: Random House, 1986.

Peters, T. J., and Waterman, R. *In Search of Excellence*. New York: HarperCollins. 1982.

Putnam, R. *Bowling Alone: The Collapse and Revival of American Community*. New York: Simon & Schuster, 2000.

Salamon, L.M. *America's Nonprofit Sector: A Primer*. New York: The Foundation Center. 1999.

Schein, E. *Organizational Culture and Leadership* (2nd ed.). San Francisco: Jossey-Bass, 1985.

Schön, D. A. *The Reflective Practitioner*. San Francisco: Jossey-Bass, 1983.

Schön, D. A. *Educating the Reflective Practitioner: Toward a New Design for Teaching and Learning in the Professions*. San Francisco: Jossey-Bass, 1987.

Simon, J. G. The Tax Treatment of Nonprofit Organizations: A Review of Federal and State Policies. In W. Powell (ed.), *The Nonprofit Sector: A Research Handbook*. New Haven, CT: Yale University Press, 1987.

Van Til, J. *Mapping the Third Sector*. New Brunswick, NJ: Transaction Press, 1988.

Weisbrod, B. *The Nonprofit Economy*. Cambridge, MA: Harvard University Press, 1988.

CHAPTER EIGHT

STRATEGIC MANAGEMENT

William A. Brown

This chapter explores decision areas that nonprofit managers consider as they work to achieve public benefit outcomes and sustain organizational operations. The strategic management processes seek alignment among management practices and environmental opportunities while identifying priorities for organizational success. The chapter introduces a framework to guide strategic decision making in three areas. Strategic management is a process that comprises strategy formation (What are we going to do?) and strategy implementation (How are we going to do it?) (Hitt, Ireland, and Hoskisson, 2007). Planning relates to strategy formation and is primarily a process that guides conversations about an organization's purpose, helps integrate perspectives from multiple stakeholders, and provides the steps to develop goals and objectives that will move the organization forward. As John Bryson explains in Chapter Nine of this *Handbook*, effective planning is linked to "strategic thinking and acting." This chapter identifies critical areas managers should consider while planning and implementing activities.

Miles and Snow (1978) explain that strategy encompasses interpreting environmental conditions and designing the organization's systems to foster success:

> the effectiveness of organizational adaptation hinges on the dominant coalition's perceptions of environmental conditions and the decisions it makes concerning how well the organization will cope with these conditions. (p. 21)

Successful strategy is contingent on appropriate interpretation of environmental conditions and the formulation of an organizational response to address those conditions (Mintzberg, 1979). Strategy in any organization is developed by its "dominant coalition"—the set of key decision makers who guide priorities and control resources. No organization can drive out all of the paradoxes and contradictions, but strategic management is the process by which to facilitate alignment among the various functions and activities to achieve organizational objectives. Strategic management encompasses most of the topics discussed in this *Handbook* (such as managing programs, developing financial resources, and managing people); effective strategic managers develop coherent approaches that integrate the work of these different areas.

Before discussing nonprofit strategic management, it is necessary to explain a couple of concepts from strategy literature. First, leaders co-create the priorities and overall approach that guides how the organization operates, who it serves, and which funders to work with. Typically, changes to strategic orientations are *incremental* in nature and happen through modest adjustments to practices (Quinn, 1989). Managers need to ensure that their strategic perspective is articulated and shared. Rarely is it fully captured in a binder on a shelf, but key decision makers should understand and agree on the general perspective that will guide the organization's operations. The idea of agreement and consistency among organizational participants and structures is called *alignment*, and empirical literature documents that alignment among organizational functions is better (Schiemann, 2009).

To understand alignment, Miles and Snow (1978) developed a typology to guide strategic thinking. They identified four basic strategic orientations of organizations: Prospectors, Defenders, Analyzers, and Reactors. *Prospectors* are innovators seeking to expand and create new products and services, while *Defenders* seek efficiency and consistency in a select number of services. *Analyzers* are not the first to develop services but are quick to integrate service innovations once identified. *Reactors* lack a coherent method. They are inconsistent and unable to implement tactics reliably. Research across organizational forms (nonprofit, for-profit, international, small, and large firms) suggests that these organizational "types" are identifiable and, given varying operational contexts, any of these types might be a reasonable strategic model by which to frame management decisions (Andrews, Boyne, Law, and Walker, 2009; Ketchen, Combs, Russell, Shook, Dean, Runge, et al., 1997; Miles, Snow, Mathews, Miles, and Coleman, 1997). Reactors, on the other hand, are non-optimal performers. These "types" are not necessarily pure throughout an organization (Andrews, Boyne, Law, and Walker, 2009). Some departments and divisions might be more entrepreneurial

(Prospector-like), while other departments or divisions might be working to improve efficiencies (Defender-like). These typological boundaries are not concrete, yet they provide a useful tool to consider how organizational systems work together to improve performance.

Fundamental to strategic management is the idea of *differentiation;* in order to be successful an organization should understand how it is distinctive from others. In a for-profit context, the other entities are typically competitors trying to attract *customers.* For nonprofits that might be less true, but the concept of *comparative advantage* is useful because, even in cooperative relationships, organizational entities look for distinctive or unique capabilities in a potential partner. Furthermore in a competitive funding environment, nonprofits need to consider how they are unique in the services they provide and the values they embody. As nonprofit managers address the various contingencies of their organization, they should consider how they are *positioned* to differentiate their own organization from other entities.

One more element that informs this chapter is the recognition that many nonprofits are small- to moderate-sized organizations, and this limits choices. Nonprofit managers confront needs far bigger than their organizations can address, and resource constraints frustrate even the best organizations. So the chapter keeps strategic management concepts simple and identifies priorities for nonprofit managers. This chapter is designed to relate to, yet not duplicate, the guidance offered by other chapters throughout this *Handbook.* For example, I will acknowledge and note the importance of collaboration and alliances and effective human resource practices with the expectation that the reader will then review the content of each related chapter for additional information on each of these topics.

Nonprofit Strategic Management Cycle

Nonprofit strategy is becoming more sophisticated to better reflect the unique character of nonprofits (Backman, Grossman, and Rangan, 2000; Brown, 2014; Chew and Osborne, 2009; Courtney, 2002; Kong, 2007); this includes the need to consider multiple stakeholders, the potential for collaborations, and the mixed influences of complex market forces. This chapter draws on a modified version of the "adaptive cycle" model proposed by Miles and Snow (1978) in their cutting-edge study exploring *Organizational Strategy, Structure, and Process,* to offer guidance on decision making that is relevant to the unique conditions nonprofit managers confront. The model identifies the three main topics (see Figure 8.1).

FIGURE 8.1. The Nonprofit Strategic Management Cycle

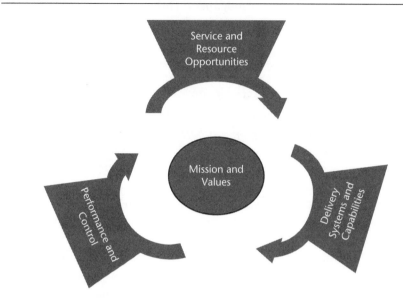

1. The need for *services and resource opportunities* (that is, market opportunities);
2. The mechanisms that will be used to offer services and secure resources (that is, *delivery systems and capabilities*); and
3. The practices used to monitor *performance and control* operations.

  This chapter is organized to address each of these decision areas or "problems." The first area (service and resource opportunities) considers the nature of the external environment. It is particularly important to describe the need for services and the make-up of the resource environment. The second section reviews the challenges of developing a service delivery system that relies on paid and unpaid organizational participants. In addition, that section examines how nonprofits often form alliances and work cooperatively. Finally, the chapter identifies the processes a nonprofit can put in place to monitor and address performance. This is particularly important for nonprofit strategy because of the difficulty in determining success. All of these "problems" are interconnected and, although the chapter addresses them one by one, organizational practices are inter related and decisions in one area are associated with decisions and activities in all the others. All parts of the nonprofit strategic management cycle work together to frame choices and facilitate performance.

Mission, vision, and values are in the center of the strategic management cycle. These define the purposes of the organization, distill key principles regarding social value objectives, and explain the philosophical perspective of the organization. This worldview is a critically important aspect of the organization's strategic position (Checkland, 2000). Vision statements articulate what the organization hopes to accomplish—What is the future state of the community, issue, or field that will result from the nonprofit's work? Values statements explain the key principles that guide operations and can be quite powerful, but often lack sufficient credibility to be fully functional (Lencioni, 2002). Yet as valued-based organizations, values statements and related management concepts are among the most important and distinctive elements in nonprofits (for more on this, read Jeavons' Chapter Seven in this book). Mission and vision statements are central for several reasons, but fundamentally they are an abbreviated rationale for the nonprofit's existence and provide a cornerstone for subsequent decision making. Clarifying and establishing the purpose and reason for being is preeminent in strategic decision making for a nonprofit. The mission helps frame how an organization approaches everything it does. It is the core or heart of a nonprofit.

Service and Resource Opportunities

Nonprofits consider both the need for services and resource opportunities available in the external environment. For-profit entities typically have an easier time identifying their customer because there is usually a direct connection between the product or service, the customer, and resource generation. This is not necessarily the case for nonprofits. It is unusual for nonprofits to operate in an exchange relationship comparable to selling a product that can fully sustain organizational operations (Moore, 2000). So nonprofits must look at "needs" in the community and the potential resource opportunities. So, although a "pure" nonprofit operates to fulfill its tax-exempt purposes, a realistic nonprofit meets those needs by considering the resource environment. Nonprofits must consider resources as part of their operating domain because funders have a significant impact on the types of services provided and nonprofits may also facilitate philanthropic needs (Jeavons, 1994). This idea is not without controversy (Eikenberry, 2009). Some contend that resources are the "means" to achieve the "ends" articulated in the mission statement and hence are not the real market nonprofits exist to serve. However, the resource dependent nature of nonprofits and the lack of exchange with beneficiaries (customers) imply that "the reason for being" is also driven by the practicalities of resources. This is a fundamental, if uncomfortable, reality for many nonprofits.

Multiple "Markets"

A nonprofit can benefit by considering primary markets (the tax-exempt purposes) and secondary markets (resource opportunities). The operating domain includes the need for services, the funding opportunities, workforce potential (labor pool of volunteers and paid employees), the nature of other service providers, and the socio-political interests of the community (see Figure 8.2). The operating domain is at a minimum "two-headed," and the existence of multiple target audiences makes it much harder to satisfy everyone (Andreasen and Kotler, 2008). Extensive literature is dedicated to analyzing market opportunities and evaluating the strengths and weaknesses of other providers (Chew and Osborne, 2009; Porter, 1998), and different chapters in this *Handbook* discuss alternative ways that nonprofits can examine their options.

"Where does my organization 'fit' in relation to other providers?" This is a basic question in strategic management. There is some concern that the

FIGURE 8.2. Multiple Nonprofit Markets and Strategic Inputs

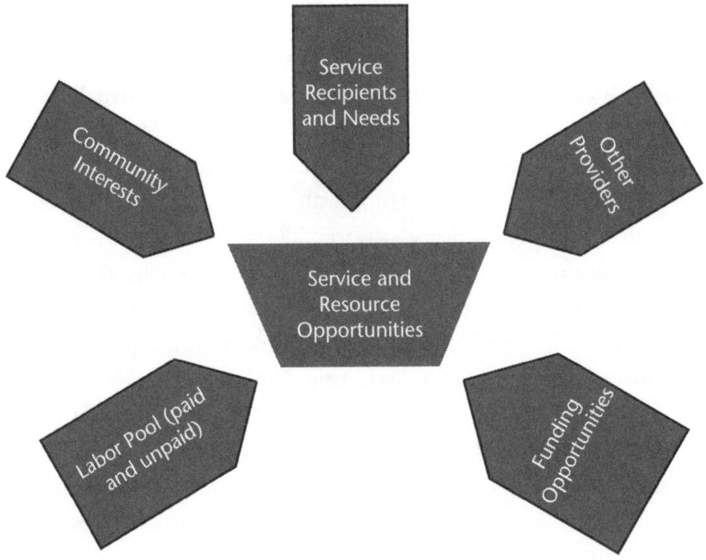

nonprofit sector is cluttered, that there are too many nonprofits doing more or less the same thing. Nonprofit managers should be cognizant of other organizations and stakeholders operating in a similar service arena. It is vital to consider how one nonprofit differentiates itself from another. Nonprofits may appear similar but there should be several ways that each is unique (including core values) (Frumkin and Andre-Clark, 2000). This differentiation is important for meeting community needs but also to attract resources.

An example of a start-up volunteer center illustrates how external forces influence strategic choices. The center was trying to determine where and how to move forward with the idea of "promoting volunteerism" in a particular regional area. The existence of the volunteer center was instigated by a funder. Community leaders had recognized for quite some time that there was a need for more coordinated services and infrastructure to serve the nonprofit community, but it wasn't until a key funder helped the center be established that the "need" was addressed. Based on the interests of the funder, certain market choices are already determined, such as the geographic service area. The funder becomes part of the "dominant coalition" of decision makers helping to articulate and define the strategic purposes (as illustrated in Lake, Reis, and Spann, 2000). There are numerous other choices to be made. For example, there are various types of volunteers (corporate, students, faith-based, individual community members, and required community service), and the center needed to decide which to prioritize. The center also considered who else was providing similar services. For instance, this center was in a university town and needed to understand how the university did or did not meet the needs of student volunteers. Inevitably, resources influenced the focus of activities. Who was willing to help pay for services? So resource questions guided how the center developed in addition to the needs and demands of the beneficiaries.

A related concept is the existence of multiple "bottom lines" (Jeavons, 1994). Take for example, Teach for America, which seeks to "eliminate educational inequity." Their strategy provides teachers to some of the most disadvantaged student populations in America. Concurrently, Teach for America seeks to recruit and influence some of the best and brightest college-educated students (that is, future leaders) in America. They hope to influence and change the volunteers, while meeting needs. They are educating not only school-aged students, but they are also educating college graduates about the American education system. Only some "corps members" will remain as teachers, but the corps members will forever understand the challenges in American education. Part of Teach for America's success is related to understanding the multiple markets. There was indeed a need for teachers in low-income communities, but there was also a desire among well-educated socially conscious individuals to make a difference, and Teach for America was able to serve both of these objectives simultaneously. This recognition of multiple markets (resources and needs) is fundamental to nonprofit strategy. These examples illustrate the complex and multifaceted "markets" that nonprofits understand when defining their operating domain. (Chapter Thirteen of this *Handbook* addresses in depth the topic of nonprofit marketing.) The next section explores in more detail needs, service recipients, and resource markets.

Service Recipients and Needs: Understanding the Need for Services

By defining a social need and/or unacceptable social condition nonprofits make a rationale for operations. "A need is a measurable gap between two conditions 'what is' (the current status or state) and 'what should be' (the desired status or state)" (Altschuld and Kumar, 2010, p. 3). Nonprofits address a whole range of "gaps," including spiritual gaps, knowledge gaps, and social/cultural gaps. Definition and articulation of the social condition is fundamentally the public benefit justification that managers utilize to defend their tax-exempt status. How that condition is defined is based on interpretation and worldview (Checkland, 2000). Various actors within the organization engage in defining and describing community needs. At the organizational level, board members and executive leaders define broad categories of social priorities. These are often articulated in the organization's mission. Program managers further define social conditions to guide particular program initiatives, within the broad scope of the mission.

There are many factors to consider regarding needs and demand for services. Needs can shift and change and thereby make the current level of services unnecessary. Nonprofits do not necessarily respond to such changes in the same way that a for-profit business might (Lynk, 1995; Zaleski and Esposto, 2007). Some studies document that nonprofits don't take advantage of the market dominance in a "typical" way. When there is limited competition it appears nonprofits may try to expand services or take on more difficult cases. Confusion with market forces is not all that surprising because nonprofits do not operate exclusively on the exchange basis (that is, services = revenue). Other factors also drive those decisions, including resources, governance models, and executive leadership.

This lack of market sensitivity might be a good thing because it means nonprofits remain focused on their charitable purposes. However, given the potential for power differentials between service recipients and the nonprofit, there is some recognition that some nonprofits may not attend to the needs of beneficiaries in the way they should (Bruce, 1995; Pavicic, Alfirevic, and Mihanovic, 2009). Some explanations include the recognition that in many instances the nonprofit is the only service provider. Beneficiaries often don't have a choice of providers and have to accept what is given. Even if there are other providers, the need or demand for services often outstrips the capabilities of all providers, so providers do what they can but are cognizant of the excessive demand. There is also the potential for providers to assume a professional or even moral justification to control services because they "know what is best." In an effort to get something done, nonprofits may inadvertently overlook beneficiary preferences. Nonprofits are morally accountable to beneficiaries but not financially accountable, and the ambiguity and power differential can be difficult to negotiate. (Chapter Four of this volume discusses in depth the multiple dynamics of nonprofit accountabilities.)

Funding Opportunities

Even more pressing for most nonprofits than demand for service is the nature of the resource environment. There is tremendous complexity in the funding environment given the range of revenue sources, such as government, corporations, individuals, foundations, and the various mechanisms through which donors can participate (grants, major gifts, annual contributions) (Delfin and Tang, 2008; Grønbjerg, 1993). Nonprofits must ensure consistent and reliable funding to sustain operations, but funders can lose interest or shift priorities and stop funding these operations.

An example is an organization dedicated to prevention services, primarily by providing programming on public school campuses. They were quite good at providing clinical and educational services related to drug abuse prevention and addiction within the school system. Most, if not all, of their services were offered on campus. Funding came through contracts with the local school district. As the educational priorities changed, demand increased for time on academics and resources were limited, so the program was losing contracts with the school district. Eventually, significant contracts were not renewed. The organization needed to consider how to respond: "our primary market is going away." Some on the board thought: "This is it, we were good at what we did and now the sponsor no longer wants our services. Our program is over." Others on the board, in particular, the new executive director, felt the organization was about *prevention* and, although they had operated in one way in the past, they needed to consider other ways to provide services to the community at large. The need for prevention services and drug abuse treatment wasn't going away—if anything, drug use and abuse was going up. The sponsor, however, was not interested in paying for those services in the same way as they had.

The executive pushed forward and developed a new program model that allowed them to expand their "market" (community-based prevention services) while staying true to their mission. They might never have become involved in what became an award-winning community program without this push from the funder. The organization continued to expand their funding base to limit the influence of just one sponsor. For most nonprofits it is inevitable that a major funder is going to have a significant impact on their services. Funding can be a "push" as, in this instance; a lack of resources pushed the organization out of a service niche. Funding can also be a "pull" whereby organizations are drawn toward particular funding opportunities. If the organization is not careful, this can become a source of "mission creep"—the problematic condition in which a nonprofit loses track of its purpose and spends too much energy following the resource market, slowly and modestly shifting to accommodate resource opportunities at the expense of attention to mission. It is important to remember that funding considerations need to be addressed in alignment with mission and service priorities (Jennings, 2004). One without the others is not optimal.

Leadership in Strategic Management

The story of prevention services also illustrates the role of the executive and board (Goodstein and Boeker, 1991; Ritchie, Kolodinsky, and Eastwood, 2007). Changes in leadership allow an opportunity to implement new models, identify new opportunities, and implement new approaches. Strategic perspectives are often held in the mind of the key decision makers, sometimes articulated but rarely captured in their entirety or in a plan sitting on a shelf. As an example, when discussing the role of the mission statement in decision making, one executive explained that the mission was used to constrain ideas for services and could be used to block new ideas. "We could do that if you want to change the mission statement," he would say to board members who suggested ideas he felt were outside the organization's purview. Other executives might frame the mission more like a planter from which program ideas "grow" (Brown and Iverson, 2004). For them, the mission statement is used to build new ideas and strategies. This is how the executive at prevention services described what was happening to their organization. Neither one of these frames is necessarily "right" or "wrong" in a generic sense. Strategic approaches should be grounded in the context, but these examples illustrate that executives have a strong influence over how the nonprofit operates. Therefore, changes at the top can, by design or at times inadvertently, shift the way a nonprofit operates.

The influence of executives is often quite pronounced when long-time founders leave the organization. Successful founders often have excellent intuition about strategic direction and how to operate the organization (Ritchie, Kolodinsky, and Eastwood, 2007). However, if that strategy was not shared with board members, or board members deferred to the executive in ways that were not healthy, then it is possible that there might be significant differences of strategic opinion between them and a new executive. A new executive may bring a different approach, one that may be needed given the development state of the organization, yet this can lead to conflict because "that's not the way we do things around here." If those perspectives are not well articulated, then there might be trouble. This is what happened in the earlier example of the organization providing prevention services. The shift to expand the market did not come without conflict on the board. Many board members were dedicated to the older model, and it took time to educate them about the new opportunity and the shifting resource environment.

Riding Against the Wind

One more illustration about recognizing the power of external environment opportunities might be helpful. I ride road bikes with a group of friends, and every Saturday we go for 40- to 50-mile bike rides. Imagine our group is a non-profit organization. We have several purposes: we want to get some exercise and we want to have fun. One of things we consider when we head out is which way the wind is blowing. Imagine if you will that the resource environment is like the wind. When the wind is at our back we go faster, feel stronger, and generally have more fun, all the while we don't have to work as hard. We travel more miles with less effort. If the wind is blowing at us, we have to work a lot harder to go the same distance. We also have to coordinate our effort a lot more. By working together and taking turns at the front, we can get through the wind. We don't mind doing that sometimes because it does make us stronger. The wind isn't always at our back but, at the same time, we are not always "riding against the wind."

The dynamics of the resource and service market are similar in that nonprof-its position themselves to take advantage of the prevailing winds. If we fight the wind in every ride, we will be exhausted and potentially give up in frustration. Of course, following every breeze isn't viable either because we would never get home. So we consider how much we can benefit from the prevailing wind to make the best use of our energy while making sure we can get home. Nonprofits that ignore the resource and market opportunities are like bike riders always head-ing into the wind or, worse, riders who don't even know which way the wind is blowing. Some days they sail along without any effort—getting further and further from home, having a grand time. Other days the wind works against them. They are not ready and maybe even somewhat clueless about why it is so hard. External forces are quite powerful and to ignore them or to operate as if they don't matter is to operate in peril.

Delivery Systems and Capabilities

The high-level strategic conversations related to markets and opportunities often engage board members. There is, however, a whole other level of management activity that is more operational. It has to do with implementation. Once questions about market opportunities are resolved, the next issue is considering how the organization is going to get things done. Opportunities are only viable if the organization has the ability to capitalize on them. Part of the grief experienced in strategic planning results when ideas and opportunities are discussed apart from the practicalities of organizational systems. Miles and Snow called this the "engineering" problem. Nonprofit managers need to address issues such as ensuring that beneficiaries have access to services, building diversified revenue streams, engaging the political system, collaborating with key service partners, and building values into organizational decision making (see Figure 8.3). One of the most fundamental aspects of the "engineering problem" is the nature of human resources (Brown, Andersson, and Jo, 2015). Who can carry out the services we have chosen? Strategic human resource management is an extensive field, encompassing a large number of elements including job design, recruitment, selection, evaluation and performance (Pynes, 2004). Watson and Abzug provide a more complete explanation of the practice of nonprofit human resource management in Chapter Twenty-Two of this book, but it is essential to this discussion of strategic management to affirm that nonprofits also must address the dynamics of human resource management from the perspective of organizational strategy and management.

Committed Human Resources

With upwards of 70 to 80 percent of expenditures allocated to staffing in the typical nonprofit, human resource capabilities are the most significant lever to achieve organizational objectives. Furthermore, for many nonprofits, volunteer labor exponentially expands the workforce. Kong (2007) makes the case that "intellectual capital" makes nonprofits unique and strategic objectives

FIGURE 8.3. Factors That Influence Service Delivery

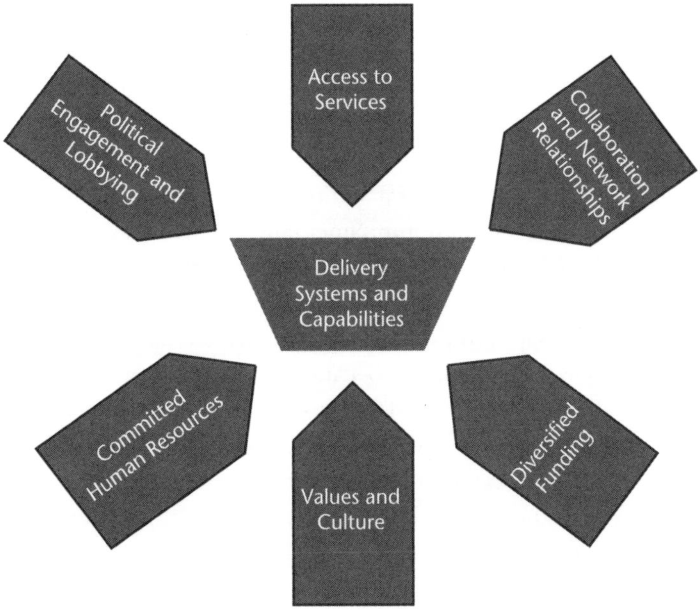

- Access to Services
- Political Engagement and Lobbying
- Collaboration and Network Relationships
- Delivery Systems and Capabilities
- Committed Human Resources
- Values and Culture
- Diversified Funding

should be framed to consider how a nonprofit can better utilize their people and relationships. The human resource school of strategic management also recognizes that working with people makes everything possible (Courtney, 2002). Traditional human resource dimensions include motivation factors, person-organizational fit, job design, and the like. Given the strategic management focus of this chapter, I will only introduce these topics; Part Five of this *Handbook* is devoted entirely to the work of leading and managing the human resource domain.

The strategic human resource management field recognizes that human resource practices make a difference in organizational performance. However, nonprofits often have some unique constraints in how such practices are utilized (Akingbola 2006; Rodwell and Teo, 2008). Part of this is explained by the small size of most nonprofits, yet some argue that nonprofits' challenges are due to a lack of discipline to implement more rigorous practices. The implementation of effective practice is further complicated by the engagement of unpaid staff members, that is, volunteers. Leading and managing volunteers poses its own unique challenges, as Jeffrey Brudney discusses in Chapter Twenty-Four. Volunteers can be difficult to control, and the ease with which they enter and exit from various roles in the organization (leadership, fundraising, program delivery) further complicates how volunteers are managed (Pearce, 1993).

Further, as discussed in depth in Chapters Twenty-Two and Twenty-Three, organizational commitment is an important issue that has significant strategic implications across the entire nonprofit "workforce." A committed workforce, whether paid or unpaid, is motivated to work harder and achieve better results for the organization. Several studies suggest that commitment to the organization and the mission are fundamentally important and a unique advantage for nonprofits (see, for example, Brown and Yoshioka, 2003; Preston and Brown, 2005). As values-based organizations, nonprofits attract and retain workers partly because they tap into the expressive needs of employees (Mason, 1995). People join and stay with nonprofits because they want to make a difference; they believe in the values and purposes. The extent to which nonprofits emphasize the expressive benefits of and help workers "see" a connection between their work and the purposes of the organization affects the degree to which people are going to be satisfied with their role in the organization, and this increases the likelihood they will put forth the effort necessary to achieve organizational priorities.

How do we encourage commitment? It is not simple but, from a strategic perspective, nonprofit executives need to ensure a high level of alignment and consistency in values and ethical practices. This *Handbook*'s chapter on ethical management (Chapter Seven) makes the case that nonprofits need to be able to rely on trust and cooperation because of the inherent difficulty in determining performance measures; stakeholders inside (paid and unpaid employees) and outside the organization need to be able to trust nonprofit leaders to operate ethically. Nonprofits are held to that higher standard because of the very nature of who they are. Employee commitment is partially driven by the ethical practices of leadership and supervisors. Since most nonprofits are not going to be able to pay as much as their for-profit counterparts, and most nonprofits are not able to offer the employment stability of the public sector, organizational participants expect a positive work environment that reflects the principles and values espoused by the organization. Their values propositions are potentially the most distinctive aspect of nonprofit organizations and can make them very appealing to donors, volunteers, and paid employees (Frumkin and Andre-Clark, 2000).

Collaboration and Network Relationships

Another important consideration in the development of service delivery is the potential of collaborative relationships. If an organization doesn't have adequate internal capacity, a good option may be to work with other organizations to achieve organizational objectives. This is particularly true for nonprofits in complex operating environments with multifaceted social issues and the challenges of resource limitations (Sowa, 2009). Collaborative strategies can be difficult, yet they are necessary and sometimes may even be the only approach to achieve broader objectives. (Austin and Seitanidi discuss in depth the potential for creating value through collaborative strategies in Chapter Fifteen of this *Handbook*.)

Less common but also reasonable to consider is the option to acquire or merge with another organization. This is less common in nonprofits, yet there are many examples of how nonprofits have been successfully acquired or merged. The merger of the Points of Light Foundation and HandsOn Network is an interesting example. The Points of Light Foundation was by all indications the historical infrastructure organization in volunteer management; it represented the national network of volunteer centers. Points of Light employed a fairly traditional model to facilitate volunteer placements with partner nonprofits. In contrast, HandsOn Network was a younger organization that framed volunteer engagement slightly differently; they were more about organizing projects and developed "make-a-difference" day. Each of these partner organizations brought a slightly different orientation toward supporting volunteers, and together they have integrated multiple approaches in an effort to enhance their sustainability and impact. This illustrates how two different types of organizations interested in the same cause (supporting volunteerism) strategically joined forces to address real challenges in the field.

Political Engagement and Lobbying

In addition to direct service collaborations to achieve program goals, nonprofits can seek to influence broader political forces. Indeed, as Avner explains in Chapter Fourteen, many nonprofits have determined that advocacy is an essential element of their strategy. The classic parable of babies floating down the river helps illustrate this concept.

> There is a fisherman who lives in a town along a river and one day he discovers a baby floating down the river. Through heroic effort he pulls the baby from the river. The town decides they need to watch the river on a regular basis. As more and more babies come floating down the river, the town develops an elaborate system to pull the babies from the water and get them placed in good homes. They have developed a sophisticated

service delivery system that saves the babies, cleans them up, and places them with adoptive parents. At some point the town realizes they can't keep raising these babies. So someone goes upstream to see if they can stop the flow of babies. They find an ogre stealing babies and tossing them into the river. The downstream town joins forces with the upstream town and they kill the ogre, thereby ending the need for saving babies from the river.

The downstream town changed the system so that now it is unnecessary to save babies from the river. Nonprofits, consequently, need to provide services, but they should also work to change the system so their services are no longer needed. It is not just about finding a need, securing resources, and developing an amazing service delivery system: it is also about changing the system to limit the need for services altogether. In many instances this means changing the laws and rules to help eliminate the problem. MADD (Mothers Against Drunk Driving) is an example of a nonprofit that set out to change the rules about drunk driving. By organizing and campaigning, they helped change the way Americans thought about drinking and driving. MADD wasn't just about victim services and supporting mothers who had lost children. They were about changing the system so that there were fewer grieving mothers (MADD, 2005).

Performance and Control

The third component of the strategic cycle is related to control and performance (see Figure 8.4). This section considers how organizations monitor and control the various aspects of the organizational system. This aspect of strategy considers learning and knowledge to guide organizational participants. How do we improve our practices? It is also about performance and impact. What value or benefit do we create for significant stakeholders? Performance is a critical concern for nonprofits because it is often difficult to know the effectiveness of service initiatives. It is also why the strategic management cycle is particularly relevant; it identifies the instrumental function that control and performance play in nonprofit organizations (Moore, 2000).

There are many organizational effectiveness assessment systems available to nonprofits (for example, balanced scorecard and total quality management), and Chapter Ten discusses this concept in more depth. Closely related are program evaluation systems designed to assess the impact of specific program initiatives (and Chapter Sixteen addresses the process of outcome assessment and program evaluation). The strategic management challenge is to determine

FIGURE 8.4. Issues to Consider in Performance and Control

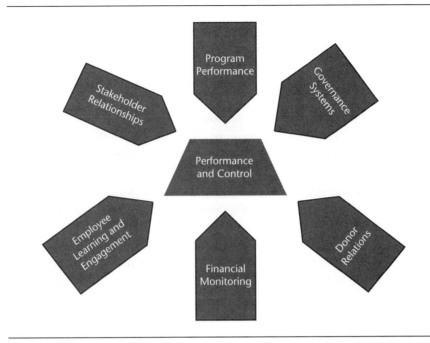

how much of an administrative bureaucracy is necessary for monitoring and evaluating organizational activities. As executives make decisions about staffing or about which programs to expand or discontinue, there need to be logical and objective criteria behind the decision. Unfortunately, it doesn't always work that way. It is complicated because there are multiple constituents who seek information about performance and operations. Developing and using effective performance assessment systems is a major concern. Donors, volunteers, and service providers can be resistant to organizational control strategies; executives, too, may resist utilizing control processes. Consequently, this is an important part of the strategic management system that might not receive enough attention. Performance and control are not just about counting numbers and objective indicators. It also is about monitoring relationships with key stakeholders.

Issues in Control and Performance

The nonprofit context suggests several performance and control issues that warrant consideration, and Figure 8.4 depicts the key areas nonprofits to monitor. Other chapters in this *Handbook* address each of these topics in detail, so our goal in this section is to highlight some of the key strategic management dimensions of each.

Financial Stewardship. Monitoring financial indicators through effective budgeting and reporting consumes a significant amount of time for nonprofit managers. With just concern, nonprofits often operate with limited reserve capabilities and stewardship expectations that require high-quality practices in this area. Donors and granting entities expect resources to be used judiciously. Frivolous expenditures, excessive compensation, or, heaven forbid, fraudulent practices can have a detrimental impact on an organization and the entire sector (Greenlee, Fischer, Gordon, and Keating, 2007). Like so many of the management challenges confronted by nonprofit executives, financial management is a paradox. Take, for example, the discussion about how much money is kept in reserves: too much and some contend the money is not being put to "good use"; not enough and the nonprofit runs the risk of falling short and being unable to meet obligations. Financial performance often becomes a proxy for organizational health, and executives need to consider how "the numbers" are reflective of other key operational issues such as program performance and donor relationships.

Governance. Governing board oversight is critical for nonprofit organizations in a number of ways. The board sets the tone and, more important, seeks to ensure consistency in organizational practices so as to achieve success across the organization. Boards help guide the organization and keep it on track. The board helps identify priorities related to strategic inputs and operational practices. The board does not meddle in the details of how services are delivered, but approves major initiatives and ensures management is moving forward to achieve priorities. Furthermore, the board monitors information that enables it to assess progress on these priorities.

The board helps keep management accountable but also partners in helping management overcome challenges and alter course as necessary. Executives look to the board to provide guidance and direction about operational gray areas. By staying attuned to the priorities of the organization and progress reports in these areas, boards can become active partners while fulfilling the most important function they have—oversight. The board also serves as intermediary to the market and key stakeholders. It exists to verify that the organization is operating honestly and according to the purposes. The role is not as an outsider, critical and confrontational, but as a partner to help achieve the priorities and objectives. The board is critical to effective strategic management because, with so many activities, opportunities, and challenges confronting nonprofits, managers need regular guidance on strategic priorities and decisions. This can only be accomplished with regular feedback and conversation.

Board effectiveness is central to organizational success, and regular self-assessment is an important and valuable tool for the board to employ (Harrison and Murray, 2015). Self-assessment provides information on key aspects of board activities and informs the board and organizational leadership about areas to improve. As Chapter Six on executive leadership explains, it is part of the chief executive's responsibility to help develop and support the work of the board activities so it can effectively perform this function. There is important evidence that, without a coordinated effort and a shared sense of importance, most boards lack the capacity to operate effectively (Renz and Andersson, 2013, pp. 32–33). It is an interesting paradox that the oversight body within the organization often depends on the goodwill and competence of its executives to operate effectively. Boards need to be partners in the strategic leadership of the organization that asks tough questions about performance.

Program Evaluation and Performance. Managers confront many challenges when trying to implement evaluation systems. In many cases it is difficult, if not impossible, to know exactly the benefit that programs create for service beneficiaries. Furthermore, using rigorous evaluation methodologies is often beyond the scope of many nonprofits. The principle is to encourage learning among providers, while being realistic about the quality of evaluation of activities. The value of evaluation is when it is part of the culture of the organization. It should be natural for program providers to boast about program successes that emphasize the beneficiaries, but they also should discuss and identify program weaknesses. It is not easy, but nonprofits need to stay attuned to the needs and perceptions of program beneficiaries, and good evaluation practices are critical.

Managing Relationships. Finally, it is essential that a strategic manager maintain a regular process by which to monitor the tone and quality of relationships with each of three key stakeholder groups: donors, paid and unpaid employees, and key decision makers in the external operating environment (such as regulators, political officials, and other service providers). Each of these constituencies plays a significant role in the strategic management choices of the organization, and the processes by which to develop and maintain these relationships are discussed in some depth in subsequent chapters of this book.

Conclusion

This chapter examines the decisions and processes nonprofit managers employ as they work to think and act strategically to accomplish their organization's goals and outcomes. Strategic management in nonprofit organizations is the ability to understand external opportunities and challenges while weaving together service delivery systems to address the needs and interests of the multiple stakeholders of the organization. Effective strategic managers guide, strengthen, and modify their programs and operations according to learning that is based on objective quantifiable information and the best guidance and intuition of the organization's leadership. Using the adaptive cycle developed by Miles and Snow (1978), the chapter discussed three key strategic "problems" for nonprofit managers: (1) understanding service and resource opportunities, (2) creating service delivery systems that utilize organizational capabilities, and (3) building control and performance management systems that foster learning.

Strategic management is informed by the desire to achieve alignment and coherence among organizational processes and practices. A fundamental element of strategic management is to ensure there is a framework to guide decision making and that the framework is discussed, evaluated and modified according to operational conditions. Even organizations that have been successful run the risk of losing their relevance and impact as circumstances change if they fail to practice effective strategic management.

References

Akingbola, K. Strategy and HRM in Nonprofit Organizations: Evidence from Canada. *International Journal of Human Resource Management*, 2006, 17(10), 1707–1725.

Altschuld, J. W., and Kumar, D. D. *Needs Assessment: An Overview*. Thousand Oaks, CA: Sage, 2010.

Andreasen, A. R., and Kotler, P. *Strategic Marketing for Nonprofit Organizations* (7th ed.). Upper Saddle River, NJ: Prentice Hall, 2008.

Andrews, R., Boyne, G. A., Law, J., and Walker, R. M. Strategy, Structure and Process in the Public Sector: A Test of the Miles and Snow Model. *Public Administration*, 2009, 87(4), 732–749.

Backman, E. V., Grossman, A., and Rangan, V. K. Introduction: New Directions in Nonprofit Strategy. *Nonprofit and Voluntary Sector Quarterly*, 2000, 29(1), 2–8.

Brown, W. A. *Strategic Management in Nonprofit Organizations*. Burlington, MA: Jones & Bartlett Learning, 2014.

Brown, W. A., Andersson, F. O., and Jo, S. Dimensions of Capacity in Nonprofit Human Service Organizations. *Voluntas: International Journal of Voluntary and Nonprofit Organizations*, 2015, 1–24.

Brown W. A., and Iverson, J. O. Exploring Strategy and Board Structure in Nonprofit Organizations. *Nonprofit and Voluntary Sector Quarterly,* 2004, 33(3), 377–400.

Brown, W. A., and Yoshioka, C. Mission Attachment and Satisfaction as Factors in Employee Retention. *Nonprofit Leadership and Management,* 2003, 14(1), 5–18.

Brown, W. A., and Yoshioka, C. A New Service Delivery Model to Support Volunteer Mentoring Relationships. *Journal of Volunteer Administration,* 2005, 23(3), 44–46.

Bruce, I. Do Not-for-Profits Value Their Customers and Their Needs? *International Marketing Review,* 1995, 12(4), 77–84.

Checkland, P. Soft Systems Methodology: A Thirty Year Retrospective. *Systems Research and Behavioral Science,* 2000, 17(S1), S11.

Chew, C., and Osborne, S. P. Identifying Factors That Influence Positioning Strategy in U.K. Charitable Organizations That Provide Public Services. *Nonprofit and Voluntary Sector Quarterly,* 2009, 38(1), 29–50.

Chan, A. Volunteer Center Shuts Doors After 45 Years. *Arizona Republic,* October 17, 2007. Accessed at www.azcentral.com, 1-7-2010.

Courtney, R. *Strategic Management for Voluntary Nonprofit Organizations.* New York: Routledge, 2002.

Delfin, F. G., and Tang, S. Y. Foundation Impact on Environmental Nongovernmental Organizations. *Nonprofit and Voluntary Sector Quarterly,* 2008, 37(4), 603–625.

Eikenberry, A. Refusing the Market: A Democratic Discourse for Voluntary and Nonprofit Organizations. *Nonprofit and Voluntary Sector,* 2009, 38(4), 582–596.

Frumkin, P., and Andre-Clark, A. When Missions, Markets, and Politics Collide: Values and Strategy in Nonprofit Human Services. *Nonprofit and Voluntary Sector Quarterly,* 2000, 29(1), 141–163.

Goodstein, J., and Boeker, W. Turbulence at the Top: A New Perspective on Governance Structure Changes and Strategic Change. *Academy of Management Journal,* 1991, 34(2), 306–330.

Greenlee, J., Fischer, M., Gordon, T., and Keating, E. An Investigation of Fraud in Nonprofit Organizations: Occurrences and Deterrents. *Nonprofit and Voluntary Sector Quarterly,* 2007, 36(4), 676–694.

Grønbjerg, K. A. *Understanding Nonprofit Funding: Managing Revenues in Social Service and Community Development Organizations.* San Francisco: Jossey-Bass, 1993.

Harrison, Y. D., and Murray, V. The Effect of an Online Self-Assessment Tool on Nonprofit Board Performance. *Nonprofit and Voluntary Sector Quarterly,* 2015, 44(6), 1129–1151.

Hitt, M. A., Ireland, R. D., and Hoskisson, R. E. *Strategic Management* (7th ed.). Mason, OH: Thomson South-Western, 2007.

Jeavons, T. *When the Bottom Line Is Faithfulness.* Bloomington, IN: Indiana University Press, 1994.

Jennings, K. N. Which Came First, the Project or the Fundraising? *The Bottom Line,* 2004, 17(3), 108.

Ketchen, D. J., Combs, J. G., Russell, C. J., Shook, C., Dean, M. A., Runge, J., et al. Organizational Configurations and Performance: A Meta-Analysis. *Academy of Management Journal,* 1997, 40, 223–240.

Kong, E. The development of strategic management in the nonprofit context: Intellectual capital in social service non-profit organizations. *The International Journal of Management Reviews.* 2007, 10(3), 281-299.

Lake, K. E., Reis, T. K., and Spann, J. From Grant Making to Change Making: How the W. K. Kellogg Foundation's Impact Services Model Evolved to Enhance the Management and

Social Effects of Large Initiatives. *Nonprofit and Voluntary Sector Quarterly,* 2000, 29(1), 41–68.

Lencioni, P. M. Making Your Values Mean Something. *Harvard Business Review,* July 1, 2002, 6.

Lynk, W. J. Non-Profit Hospital Mergers and the Exercise of Market Power. *Journal of Law and Economics,* 1995, 38(2), 437–461.

MADD. Secrets to Success. *Driven,* Fall 2005, 22–25. Accessed at www.madd.org/About-us/About-us/History.aspx.

Macedo, I. M., and Pinho, J. C. The Relationship Between Resource Dependence and Market Orientation: The Specific Case of Non-Profit Organization. *European Journal of Marketing,* 2006, 40(5/6), 533–553.

Mason, D. E. *Leading and Managing the Expressive Dimension.* San Francisco: Jossey-Bass, 1995.

Mclaughlin, T. A. *Nonprofit Strategic Positioning.* Hoboken, NJ: John Wiley & Sons, 2006.

Miles, R. E., and Snow, C. C. *Organizational Strategy, Structure and Process.* New York: McGraw-Hill, 1978.

Miles, R. E., Snow, C. C., Mathews, J. A., Miles, G., and Coleman, H. J., Jr., Organizing in the Knowledge Age: Anticipating the Cellular Form. *Academy of Management Review,* 1997, 11, 7–24.

Mintzberg, H. T. *The Structuring of Organizations.* Englewood Cliffs, NJ: Prentice Hall, 1979.

Moore, M. H. Managing for Value: Organizational Strategy in For-Profit, Nonprofit and Governmental Organizations. *Nonprofit and Voluntary Sector Quarterly,* 2000, 29(1), 183–204.

Pavicic, J., Alfirevic, N., and Mihanovic, Z. Market Orientation in Managing Relationships with Multiple Constituencies of Croatian Higher Education. *Higher Education,* 2009, 57, 191–207.

Pearce, J. L. *Volunteers: The Organizational Behavior of Unpaid Workers.* New York: Routledge, 1993.

Porter, M. E. *Competitive Strategy.* New York: The Free Press, 1998.

Preston, B. J., and Brown, W. A. Commitment and Performance of Nonprofit Board Members. *Nonprofit Management and Leadership,* 2005, 15(2), 221–238.

Pynes, J. E. *Human Resources Management for Public and Nonprofit Organizations.* San Francisco: Jossey Bass, 2004.

Quinn J. B. Strategic Change: "Logical Incrementalism." *Sloan Management Review,* 1989, 30(4), 45–60.

Renz, D. O., and Andersson, F. O. Nonprofit Governance: A Review of the Field. In C. Cornforth and W. Brown (eds.), *Nonprofit Governance: Innovative Perspectives and Approaches.* Abingdon, Oxon, UK: Routledge. 2013.

Ritchie, W. J., Kolodinsky, R. W., and Eastwood, K. Does Executive Intuition Matter? An Empirical Analysis of Its Relationship with Nonprofit Organization Financial Performance. *Nonprofit and Voluntary Sector Quarterly,* 2007, 36(1), 140–155.

Rodwell, J. J., and Teo, S.T.T. The Influence of Strategic HRM and Sector on Perceived Performance in Health Service Organizations. *International Journal of Human Resource Management,* 2008, 19(10), 1825–1841.

Schiemann, W. A. Aligning Performance with Organizational Strategy, Values, and Goals. In J. W. Smither and M. London (eds.), *Performance Management,* 45–87. San Francisco: Jossey-Bass, 2009.

Sowa, J. E. The Collaboration Decision in Nonprofit Organizations. *Nonprofit and Voluntary Sector Quarterly,* 2009, 38(6), 1003–1025.

Starkeather, D. B. Profit Making by Nonprofit Hospitals. In D. Hammack and D. Young (eds.), *Nonprofit Organizations in a Market Economy*, 105–137. San Francisco: Jossey Bass, 1994.

Stone, M. M., Bigelow, B., and Crittenden, W. Research on Strategic Management in Nonprofit Organizations. *Administration & Society*, 1999, 31(3), 378–423.

Weisbrod, B. A. The Nonprofit Mission and Its Financing: Growing Links Between Nonprofits and the Rest of the Economy. In B. A. Weisbrod (ed.), *To Profit or Not to Profit*, 1–22. New York: Cambridge University Press, 1998.

Zaleski, P. A., and Esposto, A. G. The Response to Market Power: Non-Profit Versus For-Profit Hospitals. *Atlantic Economic Journal*, 2007, 35, 315–325.

CHAPTER NINE

STRATEGIC PLANNING AND THE STRATEGY CHANGE CYCLE

John M. Bryson

This chapter presents an approach to strategic planning for nonprofit organizations and collaborations. The process, called the Strategy Change Cycle, does what Poister and Streib (1999, pp. 309–310) assert strategic planning should do. Specifically, they believe strategic planning should

- Be concerned with identifying and responding to the most fundamental issues facing an organization
- Address the subjective question of purpose and the often competing values that influence mission and strategies
- Emphasize the importance of external trends and forces as they are likely to affect the organization and its mission
- Attempt to be politically realistic by taking into account the concerns and preferences of internal, and especially external, stakeholders
- Rely heavily on the active involvement of senior level managers, and in the case of nonprofits, board members, assisted by staff support where needed
- Require the candid confrontation of critical issues by key participants in order to build commitment to plans
- Be action oriented and stress the importance of developing plans for implementing strategies
- Focus on implementing decisions now in order to position the organization favorably for the future

The Strategy Change Cycle becomes a *strategic management* process—and not just a *strategic planning* process—to the extent that it is used to link planning and implementation and to manage an organization in a strategic way on an ongoing basis (Poister and Streib, 1999, pp. 311–314). The Strategy Change Cycle draws on a considerable body of research and practical experience, applying it specifically to nonprofit organizations.

Two quotations help make the point that strategic thinking, acting, and learning are more important than any particular approach to strategic planning. Consider first the humorous statement of Daniel Boone, the famous 18th and 19th Century American frontiersman: "No, I can't say as I ever was lost, but once I was bewildered pretty bad for three days" (Faragher, 1992, p. 65). When you are lost in the wilderness—*bewildered*—no fixed plan will do. You must think, act, and learn your way to safety. Boone had a destination of at least a general sort in mind, but not a route. He had to wander around reconnoitering, gathering information, assessing directions, trying out options, and in general thinking, acting, and learning his way into where he wanted to be. In Weick and Sutcliffe's words (2007), he had to "act thinkingly," which often meant acting first and then thinking about it (Weick, 1995). Ultimately—but not initially, or even much before he got to there—Boone was able to establish a clear destination and a route that worked to get him there. Boone thus had a strategy of purposeful wandering, and it is true that he was not exactly lost; rather, he was working at finding himself where he wanted to be. So wandering with a purpose is an important aspect of strategic planning, in which thinking, acting, and learning clearly matter most.

Next, consider this from poet and essayist Diane Ackerman: "Make-believe is at the heart of play, and also at the heart of so much that passes for work. Let's make-believe we can shoot a rocket to the moon" (Ackerman, 1999, p. 7). She makes the point that almost anything is possible with enough imagination, ambition, direction, intelligence, education and training, organization, resources, will, and staying power. We have been to the moon, Mars, Venus, and a host of other places. We as citizens of the world have won world wars and cold wars, ended or avoided depressions, virtually eliminated smallpox, unraveled the human genome, watched a reasonably united and integrated Europe emerge, and seen democracy spread where it was thought unimaginable. But there obviously is much more to do, and previous triumphs are never permanent.

So let's think about joining others already focused on thinking, doing, and learning about how to have a good job for everyone, adequate food and housing for everyone everywhere, universal health care coverage, drastically reduced crime, effective educational systems, secure pensions and retirements, a dramatic reduction in greenhouse emissions, the elimination of terrorism and weapons of mass destruction, the elimination of HIV/AIDS, the realization in practice of the Universal Declaration on Human Rights, and so on. We can create institutions, policies, projects, products, and services of lasting public value by drawing on our diverse talents—and have done so again and again throughout history (Boyte, 2005), and clearly nonprofit organizations have an important role to play (Light, 2002; Powell and Steinberg, 2006). We can use strategic planning to help us think, act, and learn strategically—to figure out what we should want, why, and how to get it. Think of strategic planning as organizing hope, as what makes hope reasonable.

A Ten-Step Strategic Planning Process

Now, with the caution that strategic thinking, acting, and learning matter most, let us proceed to a more detailed exploration of the ten-step Strategy Change Cycle. The process, presented in Figure 9.1, is more orderly, deliberative, and participative than the process followed by an essayist such as Ackerman, or a wanderer like Boone. The process is designed to "create public value" (Moore, 2000) through fashioning an effective mission, meeting applicable mandates, organizing participation, creating ideas for strategic interventions, building a winning coalition, and implementing strategies. The Strategy Change Cycle may be thought of as a *processual model of decision making* (Barzelay, 2001, p. 56), or a *process strategy* (Mintzberg, Ahlstrand, and Lampel, 2005), where a leadership group manages the process, but leaves much of the content of what the strategies will be to others. The ten steps (or designed set of occasions for dialogue and decision) are as follows:

1. Initiate and agree on a strategic planning process.
2. Identify organizational mandates.
3. Clarify organizational mission and values.
4. Assess the external and internal environments to identify strengths, weaknesses, opportunities, and threats.
5. Identify the strategic issue facing the organization.
6. Formulate strategies to manage the issues.
7. Review and adopt the strategic plan or plans.
8. Establish an effective organizational vision.
9. Develop an effective implementation process.
10. Reassess strategies and the strategic planning process.

FIGURE 9.1. The Strategy Change Cycle

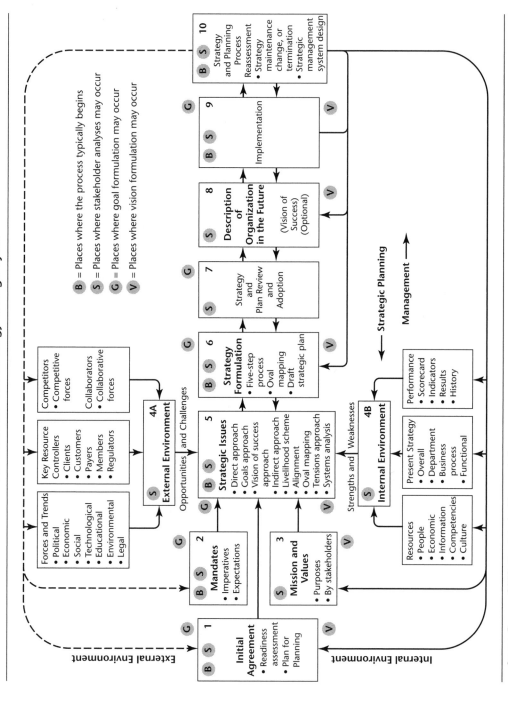

Source: Bryson, 2010. Reprinted with permission.

These ten steps should lead to actions, results, evaluation, and learning. It must be emphasized that actions, results, evaluative judgments, and learning should emerge at each step in the process. In other words, implementation and evaluation should not wait until the "end" of the process, but should be an integral and ongoing part of it.

The process is applicable to nonprofit organizations and collaborations. The only general requirements are a "dominant coalition" (Thompson, 2003), or at least a "coalition of the willing" (Cleveland, 2002), able to sponsor and follow the process, and a process champion willing to push it. For small nonprofit organizations, many well-informed strategic planning teams that are familiar with, and believe in, the process should be able to complete most of the steps in a two- or perhaps three-day retreat, with an additional one-day meeting scheduled three to four weeks later to review the resulting strategic plan. Responsibility for preparing the plan can be delegated to a planner assigned to work with the team, or the organization's chief executive may choose to draft the plan personally. Additional reviews and signoffs by key decision makers might take more time. Additional time also might be necessary to secure information or advice for specific parts of the plan, especially its recommended strategies. For large organizations, however, more time and effort are likely to be needed for the process. And when applied to a collaboration, the effort is likely to be considerably more time consuming in order to promote the involvement of substantial numbers of leaders, organizations, and perhaps members or citizens (Bryson, Crosby, and Stone, 2015; Huxham and Vangen, 2005).

Note that in practice the Strategy Change Cycle bears little resemblance to the caricature of strategic planning occasionally found in the literature as a rigid, formal, detached process (see, for example, Bryson, Crosby, and Bryson, 2009, and Mintzberg, Ahlstrand, and Lampel, 2005). Instead, the Strategy Change Cycle is intended to enhance strategic thinking, acting, and learning; to engage key actors with what is, as well as with what can be; to engage with the important details while abstracting the strategic message in them; and to link strategy formulation with implementation in wise, technically workable, and politically intelligent ways. You might think of the Strategy Change Cycle as identifying and helping organize a *deliberative pathway* to promote mutual persuasion and learning among stakeholders about what to do, how, and why in order to fulfill an organization's mission and meet its mandates (Garsten, 2006; Moynihan and Landuyt, 2009).

Step 1: Initiating and Agreeing on a Strategic Planning Process

The purpose of the first step is to negotiate agreement among key internal (and perhaps external) decision makers or opinion leaders about the overall strategic planning effort and the key planning steps. The support and commitment of key decision makers are vital if strategic planning in an organization is to succeed. Further, the involvement of key decision makers outside the organization usually is crucial to the success of nonprofit programs if implementation will involve multiple parties and organizations (Bryson, 2011; Light, 1998, 2002).

Obviously, some person or group must initiate the process. One of the initiators' first tasks is to identify exactly who the key decision makers are. The next task is to identify which persons, groups, units, or organizations should be involved in the effort. These two steps will require some preliminary stakeholder analysis, which is discussed in more detail below. The initial agreement will be negotiated with at least some of these decision makers, groups, units, or organizations. In practice, a *series* of agreements typically must be struck among various parties as support for the process builds and key stakeholders and decision makers sign on. Strategic planning for a nonprofit organization or collaboration is especially likely to work well if an effective policymaking body is in place to oversee the effort.

The agreement itself should cover

- The purpose of the effort
- Preferred steps in the process
- The form and timing of reports
- The role, functions, and membership of any group or committee empowered to oversee the effort, such as a strategic planning coordinating committee (SPCC)
- The role, functions, and membership of the strategic planning team
- The commitment of necessary resources to proceed with the effort
- Any important limitations or boundaries on the effort

As noted, at least some stakeholder analysis work will be needed in order to figure out whom to include in the series of initial agreements. A *stakeholder* is defined as any person, group, or organization that can place a claim on an organization's (or other entity's) attention, resources, or output or that is affected by that output. Examples of a nonprofit organization's stakeholders include clients or customers, third-party payers or funders, employees, the board of directors, members, volunteers, other nonprofit organizations providing complementary services or involved as co-venturers in projects, banks holding mortgages or notes, and suppliers.

Attention to stakeholder concerns is crucial: *the key to success in nonprofit organizations and collaborations is the satisfaction of key stakeholders* (Bryson, 2011; Light, 1998, 2002). A stakeholder analysis is a way for the organization's decision makers and planning team to immerse themselves in the networks and politics surrounding the organization. An understanding of the relationships—actual or potential—that help define the organization's context can provide invaluable clues to identifying strategic issues and developing effective strategies (Bryson, 2011; Patton, 2008). In this regard, note that the definition of stakeholder is deliberately quite broad for both practical and ethical reasons. Thinking broadly, at least initially, about who the stakeholders are is a way of opening people's eyes to the various webs of relationships within which the organization exists (Feldman and Khademian, 2002) and of assuring that the organization is alerted to its ethical and democratic accountability responsibilities, since they always involve clarifying *who* and *what* count (Lynn and Hill, 2008; Mitchell, Agle, and Wood, 1997).

For many nonprofit organizations, the label "customer" will be given to their key stakeholder. The customer label can be useful, particularly for organizations that need to improve their "customer service." In other situations, the customer language actually can be problematic. One danger is that focusing on a single "customer" may lead these organizations inadvertently to ignore other important stakeholder groups. Another danger is that the customer label can undermine the values and virtues of active citizenship that many nonprofit organizations are trying to promote (Boyte, 2005; deLeon and Denhardt, 2000). In addition, many community-based nonprofit organizations and those relying on government funding also face very complex stakeholder environments (Stone and Sandfort, 2009).

The organizers of the planning effort should count on using several different techniques, including as a starting point what I call the Basic Stakeholder Analysis Technique (Bryson, 2004, 2011). This technique requires the strategic planning team to brainstorm a list of the organization's stakeholders, their criteria for judging the performance of the organization (that is, their "stake" in the organization or its output), and how well the organization performs against those criteria *from the stakeholders' points of view*. If there is time, additional steps (perhaps involving additional analysis techniques) should be considered, including understanding how the stakeholders influence the organization, identifying what the organization needs from its various stakeholders (money, staff, political support), and determining in general how important the various stakeholders are. Looking ahead, a stakeholder analysis will help clarify whether the organization needs to have different missions and perhaps different strategies for different stakeholders, whether it should seek to have its mandates changed, and in general what its strategic issues are. (A variety of other useful techniques will be found in Bryson [2004, 2011].)

Step 2: Identifying Organizational Mandates

The formal and informal mandates placed on the organization consist of the various "musts" it confronts, meaning the requirements, restrictions, and expectations it faces. Actually, it is surprising how few organizations know precisely what they are (and are not) formally mandated to do. Typically, few members of any organization have ever read, for example, the relevant legislation, policies, ordinances, charters, regulations, articles, and contracts that outline the organization's formal mandates. Many organizational members also do not understand the informal mandates—which are typically political in the broadest sense—that the organization faces. It may not be surprising, then, that most organizations make one or more of three fundamental mistakes. First, by not articulating or knowing what they must do, they are unlikely to do it. Second, they may believe they are more tightly constrained in their actions than they actually are. And third, they may assume that if they are not explicitly told to do something, they are not allowed to do it.

Step 3: Clarifying Organizational Mission and Values

An organization's mission, or purpose, in tandem with its mandates, provides the organization's raison d'être, the social justification for its existence. An organization's mission and mandates also point the way toward the ultimate organizational end of creating public value. For a nonprofit organization, this means there must be identifiable social or political demands or needs that the organization seeks to fill in a way that accords with its nonprofit status (Bryce, 2000). Viewed in this light, nonprofit organizations must always be seen as a means to an end, not as an end in and of themselves. For a collaboration, it means identifying the "collaborative advantage" to be gained by working together, that is, what can be gained together that creates public value that cannot be achieved alone (Huxham and Vangen, 2005).

Identifying the mission, however, does more than merely justify the organization's existence. Clarifying purpose can eliminate a great deal of unnecessary conflict in an organization and can help channel discussion and activity productively (Nutt, 2002; Thompson, 2001). Agreement on purpose also defines the arenas within which the organization will collaborate or compete and, at least in broad outline, charts the future course of the organization. Agreement on purpose thus serves as a kind of taken-for-granted framework that bounds the plausibility and acceptability of arguments (Bolman and Deal, 2013). Agreement on purpose can go even further and provide a kind of premise control that constrains thinking, learning, and acting (Perrow, 1986; Weick, 1995) and even legitimacy (Suchman, 1995). Moreover, an important and socially justifiable mission is a source of inspiration and guidance to key stakeholders, particularly employees (Kouzes and Posner, 2008). Indeed, it is doubtful whether any organization ever achieved greatness or excellence without a basic consensus among its key stakeholders on an inspiring mission (Collins and Porras, 1997; Light, 2002).

Some careful stakeholder analysis work should precede development or modification of an existing mission statement so that attention to purpose can be informed by thinking about purpose *for whom*. If the purposes of key stakeholders are not served, then the organization may be engaging in what historian Barbara Tuchman (1984) aptly calls folly. The mission statement itself might be very short, perhaps not more than a paragraph or a slogan. But development of the mission statement should grow out of lengthy dialogue about the organization's identity, its abiding purpose, desired responses to key stakeholders, its philosophy and core values, and its ethical standards. These discussions may also provide a basic outline for a description of the organization in the future, or its "vision of success," described in Step 8. Considerable intermediate work is necessary, however, before a complete vision of success can be articulated.

Step 4: Assessing the Organization's External and Internal Environments

The planning team should explore the environment outside the organization to identify the opportunities and threats the organization faces (Step 4a). It should explore the environment inside the organization to identify strengths and weaknesses, and particularly existing or needed organizational competencies (Step 4b). Basically, "outside" factors are those not under the organization's control, while "inside" factors are those that are. Opportunities and threats usually (though not necessarily) are more about the future than the present, whereas strengths and weakness are about the present and not the future (Nutt and Backoff, 1992).

Monitoring a variety of forces and trends, including political, economic, social, educational, technological, and physical environmental ones, can help planners and decision makers discern opportunities and threats. Unfortunately, organizations all too often focus only on the negative or threatening aspects of these changes, and not on the opportunities they present, so care must be taken to assure a balanced view. In other words, attending to threats and weaknesses should be seen as an opportunity to build strengths and improve performance (Ackermann, Eden, and Brown, 2004; Weick and Sutcliffe, 2007).

Besides monitoring trends and events, the strategic planning team also should monitor various important external stakeholder groups, including especially those that affect resource flows (directly or indirectly). These groups would include customers, clients, payers or funders, dues-paying members, regulators, and relevant policy bodies. The team also should attend to competitors, competitive forces, and possible sources of competitive advantage, as well as to collaborators, collaborative forces, and potential sources of collaborative advantage.

The organization might construct various scenarios to explore alternative futures in the external environment, a practice typical of much strategic planning in large private-sector organizations. Scenarios are particularly good at demonstrating how various forces and trends are likely to interact, which are amenable to organizational influence, and which are not. Scenarios also offer an effective way of challenging the organization's "official future" when necessary. The "official future" is the presumed or taken-for-granted future that makes current strategies sensible (Schwartz, 1991). Organizations unwilling to challenge this future are the ones most likely to be blindsided by changes (Marcus, 2009).

Members of an organization's governing body (particularly if they are elected) may be better at identifying and assessing external threats and opportunities (particularly present ones) than are the organization's employees. This is partly due to a governing board's responsibility for relating an organization to its external environment and vice versa (Bryce, 2000; Carver, 2006). Unfortunately, neither governing boards nor employees usually do a systematic or effective job of external scanning. As a result, most organizations are like ships trying to navigate troubled or treacherous waters without benefit of human lookouts, global positioning systems, radar, or sonar. All too often the result is a very unwelcome surprise (Weick and Sutcliffe, 2007).

Because of this, both employees and governing board members should consider relying on a somewhat formal external assessment process to supplement their informal efforts. The technology of external assessment is fairly simple, and allows organizations to cheaply, pragmatically, and effectively keep tabs on what is happening in the larger world that is likely to have an effect on the organization and the pursuit of its mission. Clip services, Internet alerts, discussion groups and listservs, regular participation in professional conferences, and periodic retreats, for example, might be used in part to explore forces and trends and their potential impact. The key, however, is to avoid being captured by existing categories of classification and search, since they tend to formalize and routinize the past, rather than open one to the surprises of the future (Mintzberg, Alstrand, and Lampel, 2005; Weick and Sutcliffe, 2007).

Attention to opportunities and threats, along with a stakeholder analysis, can be used to identify the organization's "critical success factors" (Johnson, Scholes, and Whittington, 2008). These may overlap with mandates, in the sense that they are the things the organization must do, or criteria it must meet, in order for it to be successful in the eyes of its key stakeholders, especially those in the external environment. Ideally, the organization will excel in these areas, and must do so in order to outperform or stave off competitors.

To identify internal strengths and weaknesses, the organization might monitor resources (inputs), present strategy (process), and performance (outputs). Most nonprofit organizations, in my experience, have information on many of their inputs, such as salaries, supplies, physical plant, and full time equivalent (FTE) personnel. Unfortunately, too few organizations have a very clear idea of their philosophy, core values, distinctive competencies, and culture, a crucial set of inputs both for ensuring stability and managing change.

Organizations also tend to have an unclear idea of their present strategy, either overall, by subunit, or by function. Typically, they cannot say enough about their outputs, let alone the effects, or outcomes, those outputs create for clients, customers, or payers, although this, too, is changing. However, some nonprofit organizations have been able to pull their input, process, and outcome measures together in the form of a Balanced Scorecard (BSC) that shows, in effect, the organization's "theory of action" and allows it to monitor how it is doing in terms of the theory's predictions (Niven, 2008). BSCs attempt to show the linkages and achieve a "balance" among measures of customer or stakeholder satisfaction, financial performance, internal management or production process performance, and accomplishments in the areas of employee and organizational learning and growth. BSCs are likely to become far more widely used in the future by nonprofit organizations.

A lack of performance information presents problems both for the organization and its stakeholders. Stakeholders judge an organization according to the criteria *they* choose, which are not necessarily the same criteria the organization would choose. For external stakeholders in particular, these criteria typically relate to performance. If an organization cannot effectively meet its stakeholders' performance criteria at a reasonable cost, then regardless of its "inherent" worth, the stakeholders are likely to withdraw their support.

An absence of performance information may also create—or harden—major organizational conflicts. Without performance criteria and information, there is no way to reasonably and objectively evaluate the relative effectiveness of alternative strategies, resource allocations, organizational designs, and distributions of power. As a result, organizational conflicts are likely to occur more often than they should, serve narrow partisan interests, and be resolved in ways that don't further the organization's mission (Flyvbjerg, 1998; Gerzon, 2006). The difficulties of measuring performance are well known (Moynihan, 2008; Radin, 2006). But regardless of the difficulties, organizations are continually challenged to demonstrate effective performance to their stakeholders.

A consideration of the organization's strengths and weaknesses can also lead to an identification of its "distinctive competencies" (Selznick, 1957), or what have been referred to more generally as "core competencies" (Johnson, Scholes, and Whittington, 2008; Prahalad and Hamel, 1990) or "capabilities" (Stalk, Evans, and Shulman, 1992). These are the organization's most important abilities or practices on which it can draw routinely to perform well. What makes these abilities "distinctive" is the inability of others to replicate them easily, if at all, because of the way they are interlinked with one another (Ackermann and Eden, 2011). Nonprofit organizations should seriously consider taking the time to identify the existing and/or needed competencies and distinctive competencies necessary to achieve their aspirations (Bryson, Ackermann, and Eden, 2014). A clear statement that focuses solely on identifying and linking the existing or needed competencies and distinctive competencies to the nonprofit organization's mission and goals is sometimes referred to as its "livelihood scheme" and can provide the core logic of a strategic plan (Ackermann, Eden, and Brown, 2004). A livelihood scheme can also facilitate the identification of strategic issues (see next section).

Step 5: Identifying the Strategic Issues Facing an Organization

Together the first four elements of the process lead to the fifth, the identification of strategic issues. *Strategic issues* are fundamental policy questions or critical challenges affecting the organization's mandates, mission, and values; product or service level and mix; clients, users or payers; cost, financing, organization, or management. Finding the best way to frame these issues typically requires considerable wisdom, dialogue, and deep understanding of organizational purposes, operations, stakeholder interests, and external demands and possibilities. The first four steps of the process are designed deliberately to slow things down so that there is enough information and interaction for the needed wisdom to emerge. The process is designed, in other words, to "unfreeze" people's thinking (Dalton, 1970; Lewin, 1951) so that knowledge exploration, development, and learning might occur (Crossan, Lane, and White, 1999; March, 1991). This knowledge will be exploited in this and later phases.

Strategic planning focuses on achieving the best "fit" between an organization and its environment. Attention to mandates and the external environment, therefore, can be thought of as planning from the outside in. Attention to mission and organizational values and the internal environment can be considered planning from the inside out. Usually, it is vital that pressing strategic issues be dealt with expeditiously and effectively if the organization is to survive and prosper. An organization that does not respond to a strategic issue can expect undesirable results from a threat, a missed opportunity, or both.

The iterative nature of the strategic planning process often becomes apparent in this step when participants find that information created or discussed in earlier steps presents itself again as part of a strategic issue. For example, many strategic planning teams begin strategic planning with the belief that they know what their organization's mission is. They often find out in this step, however, that one of the key issues their organizations faces is the need to clarify exactly what its mission ought to be. In other words, the organization's present mission is found to be inappropriate, given the team members' new understanding of the situation the organization faces, and a new mission must be created.

Strategic issues, virtually by definition, involve conflicts of one sort or another. The conflicts may involve ends (what); means (how or how much); philosophy (why); location (where); timing (when); and who might be advantaged or disadvantaged by different ways of resolving the issue (who). In order for the issues to be raised and resolved effectively, the organization must be prepared to deal with the almost inevitable conflicts that will occur. Conflict, shifts in understanding, and shifts in preferences will all evoke participants' emotions (Gerzon, 2006; Heifetz, Grashow, and Linsky, 2009; Weick, 1995). It is therefore in this stage that the importance of emotion will become dramatically apparent, along with the concomitant need for emotional intelligence on the part of participants if the emotions are to be dealt with effectively (Goleman, 1995; Goleman, Boyatzis, and McKee, 2002; Heifitz, Grashow, and Linsky, 2009).

A statement of a strategic issue should contain three elements. First, the issue should be described succinctly, preferably in a single paragraph. The issue should be framed as a question that the organization can do something about. If the organization cannot do anything about it, it is best not to think of it as an issue for the organization; it is simply a condition. An organization's attention is limited enough without wasting it on issues it cannot address effectively. The question also should have more than one answer, as a way of broadening the search for viable strategies. Too often organizations "jump to solutions" without fully understanding what else might be possible, and without learning more about the issue by understanding more about the range of possible answers (Ackermann, Eden, and Brown, 2004; Burton, 2008; Nutt, 2002).

Second, the factors that make the issue a fundamental challenge should be listed. In particular, what is it about the organization's mandates, mission, values, or internal strengths and weaknesses, and external opportunities and threats that make this a strategic issue for the organization? Listing these factors will become useful in the next step, strategy development. Every effective strategy builds on strengths (and especially competencies and distinctive competencies) and takes advantage of opportunities, while minimizing or overcoming weaknesses and threats. The framing of strategic issues is therefore very important because it will provide much of the basis for the issues' resolution (Crosby and Bryson, 2005; Eden and Ackermann, 1998; Nutt, 2002).

Finally, the planning team should prepare a statement of the consequences of failure to address the issue. This will help organizational leaders decide just how strategic, or important, various issues are. If no consequences will ensue from failure to address a particular issue, then it is not a strategic issue. At the other extreme, if the organization will be destroyed or will miss a valuable opportunity by failing to address a particular issue, then the issue is clearly *very* strategic and is worth attending to immediately. Thus, the step of identifying strategic issues is aimed at focusing organizational attention on what is truly important for the survival, prosperity, and effectiveness of the organization.

Once statements of the issues are prepared, the organization will know what kinds of issues it faces and just how strategic they are. There are several kinds of strategic issues:

- Those that alter the organization and especially its "core business" and for which there is no real organizational precedent (or what might be called *developmental* issues), and those that do not (or what might be called *nondevelopmental* issues) (Nutt, 2001). Developmental issues involve a fundamental change in products or services, customers or clients, service or distribution channels, sources of revenue, identity or image, or some other aspect of the organization for which there is no real organizational precedent.

Nondevelopmental issues involve less ambiguity because most of the aspects of the organization's overall strategy will not change. Nondevelopmental issues therefore may still be very important, but are more operational than strategic.

- Those that require an immediate response and therefore cannot be handled in a more routine way.
- Those that are coming up on the horizon and are likely to require some action in the future, and perhaps some action now. For the most part, these issues can be handled as part of the organization's regular strategic planning cycle.
- Those where no organizational action is required at present, but which must be continuously monitored.

Nine basic approaches to the identification of strategic issues will be discussed. The *direct* approach goes straight from a discussion of mandates, mission, and SWOTs (strengths, weaknesses, opportunities, and threats) to the identification of strategic issues.

The *goals* approach starts with goals (or performance indicators) and then identifies issues that must be addressed before the goals (or indicators) can be achieved. Sometimes a careful goals clarification exercise is necessary in order to be clear just what the goals-in-practice are (Patton, 2008, pp. 97–149). The *vision of success* approach starts with at least a sketch of a vision of success in order to identify issues that must be dealt with before the vision can be realized. This approach is probably necessary in situations involving developmental decisions, where fundamental change is needed but the organization lacks a precedent (Nutt, 2001).

The *indirect* approach begins with brainstorming about several different kinds of options before identifying issues. Each option is put on a separate card or self-adhesive label. The sets of options include actions the organization could take to meet stakeholders' performance expectations, build on strengths, take advantage of opportunities, and minimize or overcome weaknesses and threats, as well as incorporate any other important aspect of background studies or reports or present circumstances. These options are then merged into a single set of potential actions that are then clustered according to potential themes or issue categories.

The *oval mapping* approach involves using oval-shaped cards (but they can be other shapes as well) to create word-and-arrow diagrams in which statements about potential actions the organization might take, how they might be taken, and why, are linked by arrows indicating the cause-effect or influence relationships between them. In other words, the arrows indicate that action A may cause or influence B, which in turn may cause or influence C, and so on; if the organization does A, it can expect to produce outcome B, which in turn may be expected to produce outcome C. These maps can consist of dozens, and sometimes hundreds, of interconnected relationships, showing differing areas of interest and their relationships to one another. Important clusters of potential actions may comprise strategic issues. A strategy in response to the issue would consist of the specific choices regarding actions to undertake in the issue area, how to undertake them, and why (see following; also see Bryson, Ackermann, Eden, and Finn, 2004; and Eden and Ackermann, 1998).

The approach is particularly useful when participants are having trouble making sense of complex issue areas, time is short, the emphasis must be on action, and commitment on the part of those involved is particularly important. Participants simply brainstorm possible actions, cluster them according to similar themes, and then figure out what causes what and which statements count as actions, issues, strategies, and goals or mission. Beyond that, the idea of causal mapping—that is, of placing statements on a page, flipchart sheet, or wall and linking them with arrows to indicate cause-effect relationships—can be used in tandem with the other approaches to indicate whatever logic is being followed.

The *livelihood scheme* approach makes use of a causal map that focuses specifically on aspirations (for example mission, goals, critical success factors, important performance indicators) and links these to competencies and distinctive competencies (Bryson, Ackermann, and Eden, 2014). The issues then relate to what might be necessary to take advantage of existing or needed links between aspirations and competencies. In other words, if a livelihood scheme outlines the core logic of a strategic plan, it thereby helps clarify what issues might need to be addressed in order to bring that logic to life in practice. The approach can be paired with the goals approach.

The *alignment* approach focuses on clarifying the issues involved in aligning mission, goals, resource deployments, strategies, and operations. In its simplest form, it involves just asking the planning team and/or key stakeholders what issues of organizational or stakeholder alignment, or both, need to be addressed for the mission and goals to be better achieved and for existing strategies and operations to be more effective. The approach may also make use of a balanced scorecard strategy map to help outline possible areas of misalignment among stakeholder desires or expectations, financial measures, production processes, and organizational competencies and learning needs (Kaplan and Norton, 2006; Niven, 2008).

The *tensions* approach was developed by Nutt and Backoff (1992) and elaborated in Nutt, Backoff, and Hogan (2000). These authors argue that there are always four basic tensions around any strategic issue. These tensions involve human resources and, especially, *equity* concerns; *innovation and change*; maintenance of *tradition*; and *productivity improvement*; and their various combinations. The authors suggest critiquing how issues are framed by using these tensions separately and in combination in order to find the best way to frame the issue. The critiques may be used in tandem with any of the other approaches and may need to run through several cycles before the wisest way to frame the issue is found. Finally, *systems analysis* can be used to help discern the best way to frame issues when the system contains complex feedback effects and must be formally modeled in order to understand it (Senge, 1990; Sterman, 2000).

By stating that there are nine different approaches to the identification of strategic issues, I may raise the hackles of some planning theorists and practitioners who believe you should *always* start with either issues, goals, vision, or analysis. I argue that what will work best depends on the situation and that the wise planner should choose an approach accordingly.

Step 6: Formulating Strategies and Plans to Manage the Issues

A *strategy* is defined as a pattern of purposes, policies, programs, actions, decisions, or resource allocations that define what an organization is, what it does, and why it does it. Strategies can vary by level, function, and time frame. Strategies are developed to deal with the issues identified in the previous step.

This definition is purposely broad, in order to focus attention on the creation of consistency across *rhetoric* (what people say), *choices* (what people decide and are willing to pay for), *actions* (what people do), and the *consequences* of those actions. Effective strategy formulation and implementation processes link rhetoric, choices, actions, and consequences into reasonably coherent and consistent patterns across levels, functions, and time (Eden and Ackermann, 1998). The reasoning behind and argumentation for the links should be clear and practical (Garsten, 2006; Heinrichs, 2007). They also will be tailored to fit an organization's culture, even if the purpose of the strategy or strategies is to reconfigure that culture in some way (Johnson, Scholes, and Whittington, 2008). Draft strategies, and perhaps drafts of formal strategic plans, will be formulated in this step to articulate desired patterns. They may also be reviewed and adopted at the end of this step if the strategic planning processes is relatively simple, small-scale, and involves a single organization. (Such a process would merge this step and Step 7.)

A Five-Part Strategy Development Process. There are numerous approaches to strategy development (Bryson and Anderson, 2000; Holman, Devane, and Cady,

2007). I generally favor either of two approaches. The first is a five-part, fairly speedy process based on the work of the Institute of Cultural Affairs (Spencer, 1996). The second can be used if there is a need or desire to articulate more clearly the relationships among multiple options to show how they fit together as part of a pattern.

The first part of the five-part process begins with identification of practical alternatives and dreams or visions for resolving the strategic issues. Each option should be phrased in action terms; that is, it should begin with an imperative, such as "do," "get," "buy," "achieve," and so forth. Phrasing options in action terms helps make the options seem more "real" to participants.

Next, the planning team should enumerate the barriers to achieving those alternatives, dreams, or visions, and not directly on their achievement. Focusing on barriers at this point is not typical of most strategic planning processes. But doing so is one way of assuring that any strategies developed deal with implementation difficulties directly rather than haphazardly.

Once alternatives, dreams, and visions, along with barriers to their realization, are listed, the team develops major proposals for achieving the alternatives, dreams, or visions directly, or else indirectly through overcoming the barriers. (Alternatively, the team might solicit proposals from key organizational units, various stakeholder groups, task forces, or selected individuals.)

After major proposals are submitted, two final tasks remain in order to develop effective strategies. Actions that must be taken over the next two to three years to implement the major proposals must be identified. And finally, a detailed work program for the next six months to a year must be spelled out to implement the actions. These last two tasks shade over into the work of Step 9, but that is good, because strategies always should be developed with implementation in mind. As Mintzberg explains (1994, p. 25), "Every failure of implementation is, by definition, also a failure of formulation." In some circumstances, Steps 6 and 9 may be merged—for example, when a single organization is planning for itself. In addition, in collaborative settings, implementation details must often be worked out first by the various parties before they are willing to commit to shared strategic plans (Bardach, 1998; Huxham and Vangen, 2005; Innes, 1996). In situations such as these, implementation planning may have to precede strategy or plan adoption.

Structuring Relationships Among Strategic Options to Develop Strategies. The second method is based on the Strategic Options Development and Analysis (SODA) method developed by Colin Eden, Fran Ackermann, and their associates (Bryson, Ackermann, Eden, and Finn, 2004; Eden and Ackermann, 1998, 2001). The SODA method builds on the oval mapping method discussed above and involves listing multiple options to address each strategic issue, where each option again is phrased in imperative, action terms. The options are then linked by arrows indicating which options cause or influence the achievement of other options. An option can be a part of more than one chain. The result is a "map" of action-to-outcome (cause-effect, means-to-an-end) relationships; those options toward the end of a chain of arrows are possible goals or perhaps even mission statements. Presumably, these goals can be achieved by accomplishing at least some of the actions leading up to them, although additional analysis and work on the arrow chains may be necessary to determine and clearly articulate action-to-outcome relationships. The option maps can be reviewed and revised and particular action-to-outcome chains selected as strategies. (Additional detail and numerous examples will be found in Bryson, Ackermann, Eden, and Finn, 2004.)

An effective strategy must meet several criteria. It must be technically workable and politically acceptable to key stakeholders, and must fit the organization's philosophy and core values. Further, it should be ethical, moral, and legal, and should further the creation of public value. It must also deal with the strategic issue it was supposed to address. All too often I have seen otherwise desirable strategies that were technically, politically, morally, ethically, and legally workable but did not deal with the issues they were presumed to address. Effective strategies thus meet a rather severe set of tests. Careful, thoughtful dialogue—and often bargaining and negotiation—among key decision makers who have adequate information and are politically astute are usually necessary before strategies can be developed that meet these tests. Some of this work typically must occur in this step; some is likely to occur in the next step.

Step 7: Reviewing and Adopting the Strategies and Plan

Once strategies have been formulated, the planning team may need to obtain an official decision to adopt them and proceed with their implementation. The same is true if a formal strategic plan has been prepared. This decision will help affirm the desired changes and move the organization toward "refreezing" in the new pattern (Dalton, 1970; Lewin, 1951), where the knowledge exploration of previous steps can be exploited (March, 1991). When strategies and plans are developed for a single organization, particularly a small one, this step actually may merge with Step 6. But a separate step will likely be necessary when strategic planning is undertaken for a large organization, network of organizations, or community. The SPCC will need to approve the resulting strategies or plan, relevant policymaking bodies; and other implementing groups and organizations are also likely to have to approve the strategies or plan, or at least parts of it, in order for implementation to proceed effectively.

In order to secure passage of any strategy or plan, it will be necessary to continue to pay attention to the goals, concerns, and interests of all key internal and external stakeholders (Borins, 2000). Finding or creating inducements that can be traded for support can also be useful. But there are numerous ways to defeat any proposal in formal decision-making arenas. So it is important for the plan to be sponsored and championed by actors whose knowledge of how to negotiate the intricacies of the relevant arenas can help assure passage (Crosby and Bryson, 2005).

Step 8: Establishing an Effective Organizational Vision

In this step, the organization develops a description of what it should look like once it has successfully implemented its strategies and achieved its full potential. This description is the organization's "vision of success." Few organizations have such a description or vision, yet the importance of such descriptions has long been recognized by well-managed companies, organizational psychologists, and management theorists (Collins and Porras, 1997; Kouzes and Posner, 2008). Such descriptions can include the organization's mission, its values and philosophy, basic strategies, its performance criteria, some important decision rules, and the ethical standards expected of all employees.

The description, to the extent that it is widely circulated and discussed within the organization, allows organization members to know what is expected of them, without constant managerial oversight. Members are freed to act on their own initiative on the organization's behalf to an extent not otherwise possible. The result should be a mobilization of members' energy toward pursuing the organization's purposes, and a reduced need for direct supervision (Moynihan and Landuyt, 2009; Nutt, 2001).

Some might question why developing a vision of success comes at this point in the process rather than much earlier. There are two basic answers to this question. First, it does not have to come here for all organizations. Some organizations are able to develop a clearly articulated, agreed-upon vision of success much earlier in the process. And some organizations start with "visioning" exercises in order to develop enough of a consensus on purposes and values to guide issue identification and strategy formulation efforts. Figure 9.1 therefore indicates the many different points at which participants may find it useful to develop some sort of guiding vision. Some processes may start with a visionary statement. Others may use visions to help them figure out what the strategic issues are or to help them develop strategies. And still others may use visions to convince key decision makers to adopt strategies or plans, or to guide implementation efforts. The further along in the process a vision is found, the more likely it is to be more fully articulated.

Second, most organizations typically will not be able to develop a detailed vision of success until they have gone through several iterations of strategic planning—if they are able to develop a vision at all. A challenging yet achievable vision embodies the tension between what an organization wants and what it can have (Rughase, 2007; Senge, 1990). Often, several cycles of strategic planning are necessary before organizational members know what they want, what they can have, and what the difference is between the two. A vision that motivates people will be challenging enough to spur action, yet not so impossible to achieve that it demotivates and demoralizes people. Most organizations, in other words, will find that their visions of success are likely to serve more as a guide for strategy implementation than strategy formulation.

Further, for most organizations, development of a vision of success is not necessary in order to produce marked improvements in performance. In my experience, most organizations can demonstrate a substantial improvement in effectiveness if they simply identify and satisfactorily resolve a few strategic issues. Most organizations simply do not address often enough what is truly important; just gathering key decision makers to deal with a few important matters in a timely way can enhance organizational performance substantially. For these reasons the step is labeled optional in Figure 9.1.

Step 9: Developing an Effective Implementation Process

Just creating a strategic plan is not enough. The changes indicated by the adopted strategies must be incorporated throughout the system for them to be brought to life and for real value to be created for the organization and its stakeholders. Thinking strategically about implementation and developing an effective implementation plan are important tasks on the road to realizing the strategies developed in Step 6. For example, in some circumstances direct implementation at all sites will be the wisest strategic choice, whereas in other situations some form of staged implementation may be best (Crosby and Bryson, 2005, pp. 312–339).

Again, if strategies and an implementation plan have been developed for a single organization, particularly a small one, or if the planning is for a collaboration, this step may need to be incorporated into Step 7, strategy formulation. However, in many multi-organizational situations, a separate step will be required to assure that relevant groups and organizations do the action planning necessary for implementation success.

Action plans should detail the following:

- Implementation roles and responsibilities of oversight bodies, organizational teams or task forces, and individuals
- Expected results and specific objectives and milestones
- Specific action steps and relevant details
- Schedules
- Resource requirements and sources
- A communication process
- Review, monitoring, and midcourse correction procedures
- Accountability procedures

It is important to build into action plans enough sponsors, champions, and other personnel—along with enough time, money, attention, administrative and support services, and other resources—to assure successful implementation. You must "budget the plan" wisely to assure implementation goes well. In interorganizational situations, it is almost impossible to underestimate the requirements for communications, the nurturance of relationships, and attention to operational detail (Huxham and Vangen, 2005).

It is also important to work quickly to avoid unnecessary or undesirable competition with new priorities. Whenever important opportunities to implement strategies and achieve objectives arise, they should be taken. In other words, it is important to be opportunistic as well as deliberate. And it is important to remember that what actually happens in practice will always be some blend of what is intended with what emerges along the way (Mintzberg, Ahlstrand, and Lampel, 2005).

Successfully implemented and institutionalized strategies result in the establishment of a new "regime," a "set of implicit or explicit principles, norms, rules, and decision-making procedures around which actors' expectations converge in a given area" (Krasner, 1983, p. 2; see also Crosby and Bryson, 2005; Crossan, Lane, and White, 1999). Regime building is necessary to preserve gains in the face of competing demands. Unfortunately, regimes can outlive their usefulness and must be changed, which involves the next step in the process.

Step 10: Reassessing Strategies and the Strategic Planning Process

Once the implementation process has been under way for some time, it is important to review the strategies and the strategic planning process as a prelude to a new round of strategic planning. Much of the work of this phase may occur as part of the ongoing implementation process. However, if the organization has not engaged in strategic planning for a while, this will be a separate phase. Attention should be focused on successful strategies and whether they should be maintained, replaced by other strategies, or terminated for one reason or another. Unsuccessful strategies should be replaced or terminated. The strategic planning process also should be examined, its strengths and weaknesses noted, and modifications suggested to improve the next round of strategic planning. Effectiveness in this step really does depend on effective organizational learning, which means taking a hard look at what is really happening and being open to new information, and designing forums within which knowledge can be developed and shared (Moynihan and Landuyt, 2009). As Weick and Sutcliffe (2007, p. 18) say, "The whole point of a learning organization is that it needs to get a better handle on the fact that it doesn't know what it doesn't know." Viewing strategic planning as a kind of action research can help embed learning into the entire process and make sure the kind of information, feedback, and dialogue necessary for learning occur (Eden and Huxham, 1996).

Tailoring the Process to Specific Circumstances

The Strategy Change Cycle is a general approach to strategic planning and management. Like any planning and management process, it therefore must be tailored carefully to specific situations if it is to be useful (Johnson, Langley, Melin, and Whittington, 2007; Wenger, 1998). A number of adaptations, or variations on the general theme, are discussed in this section.

Sequencing the Steps

Although the steps (or occasions for dialogue and decision) are laid out in a linear sequence, it must be emphasized that the Strategy Change Cycle, as its name suggests, is iterative in practice. Participants typically rethink what they have done several times before they reach final decisions. Moreover, the process does not always begin at the beginning. Organizations typically find themselves confronted with a new mandate (Step 2), a pressing strategic issue (Step 5), a failing strategy (Step 6 or Step 9), or the need to reassess what they have been doing (Step 10) and that leads them to engage in strategic planning. Once engaged, the organization is likely to go back and begin at the beginning, particularly with a reexamination of its mission. Indeed, it usually does not matter where you start, you always end up back at mission.

In addition, implementation usually begins before all of the planning is complete. As soon as useful actions are identified, they are taken, as long as they do not jeopardize future actions that might prove valuable. In other words, in a linear, sequential process, the first eight steps of the process would be followed by implementing the planned actions and evaluating the results. However, implementation typically does not, and should not, wait until the eight steps have been completed. For example, if the organization's mission needs to be redrafted, then it should be. If the SWOT analysis turns up weaknesses or threats that need to be addressed immediately, they should be. If aspects of a desirable strategy can be implemented without awaiting further developments, they should be. And so on. As noted earlier, strategic thinking *and* acting *and* learning are important, and all of the thinking does not have to occur before any actions are taken. Or as Mintzberg, Ahlstrand, and Lampel (2005, p. 71) note, "Effective strategy making connects acting to thinking, which in turn connects implementation to formulation. We think in order to act, to be sure, but we also act in order to think." And learn, they might add. Strategic planning's iterative, flexible, action-oriented nature is precisely what often makes it so attractive to public and nonprofit leaders and managers.

Making Use of Vision, Goals, and Issues

In the discussion of Step 8, it was noted that different organizations or collaborations may wish to start their process with a vision statement. Such a statement may foster a consensus and provide important inspiration and guidance for the rest of the process, even though it is unlikely to be as detailed as a statement developed later in the process. As indicated in Figure 9.1, there are other points at which it might be possible to develop a vision statement (or statements). Vision thus may be used to prompt the identification of strategic issues, guide the search for and development of strategies, inspire the adoption of strategic plans, or guide implementation efforts. The Amherst H. Wilder Foundation of St. Paul, Minnesota, for example, has been guided for years by the following vision (with only minor word changes from time to time) (Amherst H. Wilder Foundation, 2016)

> *The greater Saint Paul area will be a vibrant community where all individuals, families and neighborhoods can prosper, with opportunities to work, to be engaged in their communities, to live in decent housing, to attend good schools and to receive support during times of need. It uses the vision to help identify issues to be addressed and to develop strategies to be used to realize the vision. The decision to develop a*

vision statement should hinge on whether one is needed to provide direction to subsequent efforts; whether people will be able to develop a vision that is meaningful enough, detailed enough, and broadly supported; and whether there will be enough energy left after the visioning effort to push ahead.

Similarly, as indicated in Figure 9.1, it is possible to develop goals in many different places in the process. Some strategic planning processes will begin with the goals of new boards of directors, executive directors, or other top-level decision makers. These goals embody a reform agenda for the organization or collaboration. Other strategic planning processes may start with goals that are part of mandates. For example, government agencies often require nonprofit organizations on which they rely for legislated policy implementation to develop plans that include results and outcome measures that will show how the intent of the legislation is to be achieved. A *starting* goal for these nonprofits, therefore, is to identify results and outcomes they want to be measured against that which are also in accord with legislative intent. The goal thus helps these organizations identify an important *strategic issue*—namely, what the results and outcomes should be. Subsequent strategic planning efforts are then likely to start with the desired outcomes the organization thinks are important.

Still other strategic planning processes will articulate goals to guide strategy formulation in response to specific issues or to guide implementation of specific strategies. Goals developed at these later stages of the process are likely to be more detailed and specific than those developed earlier in the process. Goals may be developed any time they would be useful to guide subsequent efforts in the process *and* when they will have sufficient support among key parties to produce desired action.

In my experience, however, strategic planning processes generally start neither with vision nor with goals. In part, this is because in my experience strategic planning rarely starts with Step 1. Instead, people sense something is not right about the current situation—they face strategic issues of one sort or another, or they are pursuing a strategy that is failing, or about to fail—and they want to know what to do (Ackermann, Eden, and Brown, 2004; Borins, 1998; Nutt, 2001). One of the crucial features of issue-driven planning (and political decision making in general) is that you do not have to agree on goals to agree on next steps (Crosby and Bryson, 2005; Huxham and Vangen, 2005). You simply need to agree on a strategy that will address the issue and further the interests of the organization or collaboration and its key stakeholders. Goals are likely to be developed once viable strategies have been developed to address the issues. The goals typically will be strategy-specific.

Articulating goals or describing a vision in this way may help provide a better feeling for where an agreed strategy or interconnected set of strategies should lead (Ackermann, Eden, and Brown, 2004; Nutt, 2001). Goals and vision are thus more likely to come toward the end of the process than the beginning. But there are clear exceptions and process designers should think carefully about why, when, and how—if at all—to bring goals and vision into the process.

Applying the Process Across Organizational Subunits, Levels, and Functions on an Ongoing Basis

Strategic thinking, acting, and learning depend upon getting key people together, getting them to focus wisely and creatively on what is really important, and getting them to do something about it. At its most basic, the technology of strategic planning thus involves deliberations, decisions, and actions. The steps in the Strategy Change Cycle help make the process reasonably orderly to increase the likelihood that what is important is actually recognized and addressed, and to allow more people to participate in the process. When the process is applied to an organization as a whole on an ongoing basis (rather than as a one-shot deal), or at least to significant parts of it, usually it is necessary to construct a *strategic planning system.* The system allows the various parts of the process to be integrated in appropriate ways, and engages the organization in strategic *management,* not just strategic planning (Poister and Streib, 1999). In the best circumstances, the system will include the actors and knowledge necessary to act wisely, foster systems thinking, and prompt quick and effective action, since inclusion, systems thinking, and speed are increasingly required of nonprofit organizations (Bryson, 2003; Moynihan, 2008).

The process might be applied across subunits, levels, and functions in an organization as outlined in Figure 9.2. The application is based on the "layered" or "stacked units of management" system used by many corporations. The system's first cycle consists of "bottom up" development of strategic plans within a framework established at the top, followed by reviews and reconciliations at each succeeding level. In the second cycle, operating plans are developed to implement the strategic plans. Depending on the situation, decisions at the top of the organizational hierarchy may or may not require policy board approval (which is why the line depicting the process flow diverges at the top). The system may be supported by a set of performance indicators and strategies embodied in a Balanced Score Card (BSC) (Niven, 2008).

Strategic planning systems for nonprofit organizations usually are not as formalized and integrated as the one outlined in Figure 9.2. More typical is

FIGURE 9.2. Strategic Planning Systems for Integrated Units of Management

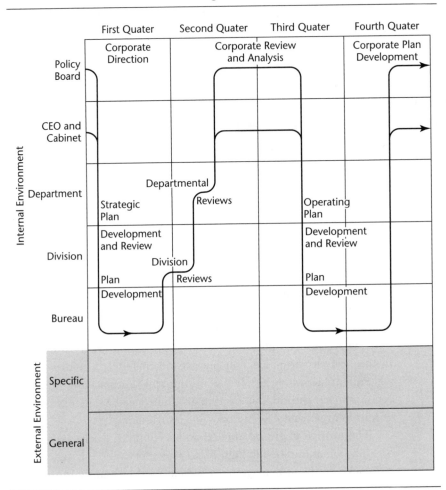

Adapted from Bryson and Roering (1987), p. 16.

a "strategic issues management" system, which attempts to manage specific strategic issues without seeking integration of the resultant strategies across all subunits, levels, and functions. Tight integration is not necessary because most issues do not affect all parts of the organization, are subject to different politics, and are on their own time frame. Other common public and nonprofit strategic planning systems include the "contract model," in which there is a contract or agreement between a "center" and related units, such as between a headquarters organization and local affiliates; "goal model," in which there are goals, but little else to assure implementation; and "portfolio model," in which organizational subunits or programs are managed as part of an overall organizational portfolio.

If the organization is fairly large, then specific linkages will be necessary in order to join the strategic planning and implementation process to different functions and levels in the organization so that it can proceed in a reasonably orderly and integrated manner. One effective way to achieve such a linkage is to appoint the heads of all major units to the strategic planning team. All unit heads can then be sure that their units' information and interests are represented in strategy formulation, and can oversee strategy implementation in their unit.

Indeed, key decision makers might wish to form themselves into a permanent strategic planning committee or cabinet. I certainly would recommend this approach, if it appears workable for the organization, as it emphasizes the role of line managers as strategic planners and the role of strategic planners as facilitators of decision making by the line managers. Pragmatic and effective strategies and plans are likely to result. Temporary task forces, strategic planning committees, or a cabinet can work; but whatever the arrangement, there is no substitute for the direct involvement of key decision makers in the process.

Applying the Process to Collaborations

When applied to a collaboration, the process probably will need to be sponsored by a committee or task force of key decision makers, opinion leaders, "influentials," or "notables" representing important stakeholder groups. Additional working groups or task forces probably will need to be organized at various times to deal with specific strategic issues or to oversee the implementation of specific strategies. Because so many more people and groups will need to be involved, and because implementation will have to rely more on consent than authority, the process is likely to be much more time consuming and iterative than strategic planning applied to an organization (Agranoff, 2007; Bardach, 1998; Huxham and Vangen, 2005).

Roles for Planners, Decision Makers, Implementers, and Citizens

Planners can play many different roles in a strategic planning process. In many cases, the "planners" are not people with the job title planner, but are in fact policymakers or line managers (Mintzberg, Ahlstrand, and Lampel, 2005).

The people with the title planner often act primarily as facilitators of decision making by policymakers or line managers, as technical experts in substantive areas, or both. In other cases, planners operate in a variety of different roles. Sometimes the planner is an expert regarding different kinds of expertise who can ease different experts in and out of the process for different purposes at different times. At still other times, they are "finders" of strategy, who do their job by interpreting existing actions and recognizing important patterns in the organization and its environment; "analysts" of existing or potential strategies; "catalysts" for promoting strategic thought and action; or, finally, "strategists" themselves (Mintzberg, 1994, pp. 361–396).

Since the most important thing about strategic planning is the development of strategic thought, action, and learning, it may not matter much which person does what. However, it does seem that strategic planning done by boards, executive directors, or line managers is most likely to be implemented. Exactly how people formally designated as planners contribute to that formulation is unclear. In any particular situation they should be involved in such a way that strategic thinking, acting, and learning are enhanced, along with commitment to agreed-upon strategies.

When a nonprofit organization is the principal focus of attention, for good or ill, there often is little participation by "outsiders" in the planning process other than that of board members. One reason may be that the organization may already possess the necessary knowledge and expertise in-house and therefore involvement by others may be redundant and excessively time-consuming. In addition, insiders typically are the chief implementers of strategies, so their ownership of the process and resultant decisions may be what is most crucial. Further, participation by outsiders may not be necessary to legitimize the process because the board is directly involved and its members are seen as legitimate representatives of a larger public. The absence of participation by ordinary outsiders would parallel much private-sector corporate planning practice. On the other hand, it is easy to be wrong about how much one "knows," or needs to know, and how much perceived legitimacy the process needs (Nutt, 2002; Suchman, 1995). Interviews, focus groups and surveys of outsiders, and external sounding boards of various sorts, such as advisory boards or councils, often are worth their weight in gold when they open insiders' eyes to information they have missed, add legitimacy to the effort, and keep insiders from reaching the wrong conclusions or making the wrong decisions (Nutt, 2002). So a word of caution is in order, and that is to remember, as the Greeks believed, that nemesis always walks in the footsteps of hubris!

Program-focused strategic planning appears to be much more likely to involve outsiders, particularly in their capacity as clients or customers. Outsiders' involvement in program planning thus is roughly analogous to extensive consumer involvement in private-sector marketing research and development projects. Finally, planning on behalf of a collaboration almost always involves substantial participation, but who is inside and who is outside can be difficult to determine (Huxham and Vangen, 2005).

Summary

This chapter has outlined a process called the Strategy Change Cycle for promoting strategic thinking, acting, and learning in nonprofit organizations and collaborations. Although the process is presented in a linear, sequential fashion for pedagogical reasons, it proceeds iteratively as groups continuously rethink connections among the various elements of the process, take action, and learn on their way to formulating effective strategies. In addition, the process often does not start with Step 1 but instead starts somewhere else and then cycles back to Step 1. The steps also are not steps precisely, but instead occasions for deliberation, decisions, and actions in part of a continuous flow of strategic thinking, acting, and learning; knowledge exploration and exploitation; and strategy formulation and implementation. Mintzberg, Ahlstrand, and Lampel (2005, p. 195) assert that "All real strategic behavior has to combine deliberate control with emergent learning." The Strategy Change Cycle is designed to promote just this kind of strategic behavior.

References

Ackerman, D. *Deep Play*. New York: Vintage, 1999.

Ackermann, F., and Eden, C. *Making Strategy: Mapping Out Strategic Success* (2nd ed.). London: Sage, 2011.

Ackermann, F., Eden, C., and Brown, I. *The Practice of Making Strategy: A Step-by-Step Guide*. London: Sage, 2004.

Agranoff, R. *Managing Within Networks: Adding Value to Public Organizations*. Washington, DC: Georgetown University Press, 2007.

Bardach, E. *Getting Agencies to Work Together*. Washington, DC: Brookings Institution, 1998.

Barzelay, M. *The New Public Management: Improving Research and Policy Dialogue*. Berkeley and New York: University of California Press and Russell Sage Foundation, 2001.

Bolman, L., and Deal, T. *Reframing Organizations*. (5th ed.) San Francisco: Jossey-Bass, 2013.

Borins, S. *Innovating with Integrity: How Local Heroes Are Transforming American Government*. Washington, DC: Georgetown University Press, 1998.

Borins, S. Loose Cannons and Rule Breakers, or Enterprising Leaders? Some Evidence About Innovative Public Managers. *Public Administration Review*, 2000, 60(6), 498–507.

Boyte, H. C. *Everyday Politics: Reconnecting Citizens and Public Life*. Philadelphia: University of Pennsylvania Press, 2005.

Bryce, H. J. *Financial and Strategic Management for Nonprofit Organizations*. San Francisco: Jossey-Bass, 2000.

Bryson, J. M. Strategic Planning and Management. In G. Peters and J. Pierre (Eds.), *Handbook of Public Administration*. Thousand Oaks, CA: Sage, 2003.

Bryson, J. M. What to Do When Stakeholders Matter: Stakeholder Identification and Analysis Techniques. *Public Management Review*, 2004, 6(1), 21–53.

Bryson, J. M. The Strategy Change Cycle: An Effective Strategic Planning Approach for Nonprofit Organizations." In D.O. Renz (ed.) *Jossey-Bass Handbook of Nonprofit Leadership and Management* (3rd ed.). San Francisco: Jossey-Bass. 2010, 230–261.

Bryson, J. M. *Strategic Planning for Public and Nonprofit Organizations* (4th ed.). San Francisco: Jossey-Bass, 2011.

Bryson, J. M., Ackerman, F., and Eden, C. *Visual Strategy: Strategy Mapping for Public and Nonprofit Organizations*. Hoboken, NJ: John Wiley and Sons, 2014

Bryson, J. M., Ackermann, F., Eden, C., and Finn, C. *Visible Thinking: Unlocking Causal Mapping for Practical Business Results*. Chichester, UK: Wiley, 2004.

Bryson, J. M., and Anderson, S. R. Applying Large-Group Interaction Methods in the Planning and Implementation of Major Change Efforts. *Public Administration Review*, 2000, 60(2), 143–162.

Bryson, J. M., Crosby, B. C., and Bryson, J. K. Understanding Strategic Planning and the Formulation and Implementation of Strategic Plans as a Way of Knowing: The Contributions of Actor-Network Theory. *International Public Management Journal*, 2009, 12(2), 172–207.

Bryson, J. M., Crosby, B. C., and Stone, M. M. "Designing and Implementing Cross-Sector Collaboration—Needed *and* Challenging." *Public Administration Review*, 2015, online.

Bryson, J. M., and Roering, W. D. "Applying Private Sector Strategic Planning to the Public Sector." *Journal of the American Planning Association*. 53(1), 1987, 9–22.

Burton, R. A. *On Being Certain: Believing You Are Right Even When You're Not*. New York: St. Martin's Griffin, 2008.

Carver, J. *Boards That Make a Difference: A New Design for Leadership in Nonprofit and Public Organizations*. San Francisco: Jossey-Bass, 2006.

Cleveland, H. *Nobody in Charge: Essays on the Future of Leadership*. New York: Wiley, 2002.

Collins, J. C., and Porras, J. I. *Built to Last: Successful Habits of Visionary Companies*. New York: HarperBusiness, 1997.

Crosby, B. C., and Bryson, J. M. *Leadership for the Common Good: Tackling Public Problems in a Shared-Power World*. San Francisco: Jossey-Bass, 2005.

Crossan, M. M., Lane, H. W., and White, R. E. An Organizational Learning Framework: From Intuition to Institution. *Academy of Management Review*, 1999, 24(3), 522–537.

Dalton, G. W. Influence and Organization Change. In G. Dalton, P. Lawrence, and L. Greiner (eds.), *Organization Change and Development*. Homewood, Il.: Irwin, 1970.

deLeon, L., and Denhardt, R. B. The Political Theory of Reinvention. *Public Administration Review*, 2000, 60(2), 89–97.

Eden, C., and Ackermann, F. *Making Strategy: The Journey of Strategic Management*. London: Sage, 1998.

Eden, C., and Ackermann, F. A Mapping Framework for Strategy Making. In A. S. Huff and M. Jenkins (eds.), *Mapping Strategic Knowledge*. London: Wiley, 2001, 173–195.

Eden, C., and Huxham, C. Action Research for Management Research. *British Journal of Management*, 1996, 7, 75–86.

Faragher, J. M. *Daniel Boone: The Life and Legacy of an American Pioneer*. New York: Henry Holt, 1992.

Feldman, M. S., and Khademian, A. M. To Manage Is to Govern. *Public Administration Review*, 2002, 62(5), 541–554.

Flyvbjerg, B. *Rationality and Power: Democracy in Practice* (new ed.). Chicago: University of Chicago Press, 1998.

Garsten, B. *Saving Persuasion: A Defense of Rhetoric and Judgment*. Cambridge, MA: Harvard University Press, 2006.

Gerzon, M. *Leading Through Conflict*. Cambridge, MA: Harvard Business School Press, 2006.

Goleman, D., Boyatzis, R., and McKee, A. *Primal Leadership: Realizing the Power of Emotional Intelligence*. Boston: Harvard Business School Press, 2002.

Goleman, D. *Emotional Intelligence*. New York: Bantam, 1995.

Heifetz, R. A., Grashow, A., and Linsky, M. *The Practice of Adaptive Leadership*. Boston: Cambridge Leadership Associates, 2009.

Heinrichs, J. *Thank You for Arguing*. New York: Three Rivers Press, 2007.

Holman, P., Devane, T., and Cady, S. *The Change Handbook: Group Methods for Shaping the Future*. San Francisco: Berrett-Koehler, 2007.

Huxham, C., and Vangen, S. *Managing to Collaborate: The Theory and Practice of Collaborative Advantage*. New York: Routledge, 2005.

Innes, J. E. Planning Through Consensus Building: A New View of the Comprehensive Planning Ideal. *Journal of the American Planning Association*, 1996, Autumn, 460–472.

Johnson, G., Langley, A., Melin, L., and Whittington, R. *Strategy as Practice: Research Directions and Resources*. New York: Cambridge University Press, 2007.

Johnson, G., Scholes, K., and Whittington, R. (eds.). *Exploring Corporate Strategy* (8th ed.). London: Prentice Hall, 2008.

Kaplan, R. S., and Norton, D. P. How to Implement a New Strategy Without Disrupting Your Organization. *Harvard Business Review*, 2006, 84.

Kouzes, J. M., and Posner, B. Z. *The Leadership Challenge* (4th ed.). San Francisco: Jossey-Bass, 2008.

Krasner, S. D. Structural Causes and Regime Consequences: Regimes as Intervening Variables. In S. D. Krasner (ed.), *International Regimes*. Ithaca, NY: Cornell University Press, 1983.

Lewin, C. W. *Field Theory in Social Science*. New York: Harper, 1951.

Light, P. C. *Sustaining Innovation: Creating Nonprofit and Government Organizations That Innovate Naturally*. San Francisco: Jossey-Bass, 1998.

Light, P. C. *Pathways to Nonprofit Excellence*. Washington, DC: Brookings Institutions Press, 2002.

Lynn, L. E., Jr., and Hill, C. J., *Public Management: A Three-Dimensional Approach*. Washington, DC: CQ Press, 2008.

March, J. G. Exploration and Exploitation in Organizational Learning. *Organization Science*, 1991, 2, 71–87.

Marcus, A. *Strategic Foresight: A New Look at Scenarios*. New York: Palgrave Macmillan, 2009.

Mintzberg, H. *The Rise and Fall of Strategic Planning: Reconceiving Roles for Planning, Plans, Planners*. New York: The Free Press, 1994.

Mintzberg, H., Ahlstrand, B., and Lampel, J. *Strategy Safari: A Guided Tour Through the Wilds of Strategic Management*. New York: The Free Press, 1998, 2005.

Mitchell, R. K., Agle, B. R., and Wood, D. J. Toward a Theory of Stakeholder Identification and Salience: Defining the Principle of Who and What Really Counts. *Academy of Management Review*, 1997, 22(4), 853–886.

Moore, M. H. Managing for Value: Organizational Strategy in For-Profit, Nonprofit, and Governmental Organizations. *Nonprofit and Voluntary Sector Quarterly*, 2000, 29(1), 183–204.

Moynihan, D. P. *The Dynamics of Performance Management*. Washington, DC: Georgetown University Press, 2008.

Moynihan, D. P., and Landuyt, N. How Do Public Organizations Learn? Bridging Structural and Cultural Divides. *Public Administration Review*, 2009, 69(6), 1097–1105.

Niven, P. R. *Balanced Scorecard Step-By-Step for Government and Nonprofit Agencies* (2nd ed.). Hoboken, NJ: John Wiley & Sons, 2008.

Nutt, P. C. Strategic Decision-Making. In M. A. Hitt, R. E. Freeman, and J. S. Harrison (eds.), *Blackwell Handbook of Strategic Management*. Malden, MA: Blackwell Business, 2001.

Nutt, P. C. *Why Decisions Fail: Avoiding the Blunders and Traps That Lead to Debacles*. San Francisco: Berrett-Koehler, 2002.

Nutt, P. C., and Backoff, R. W. *Strategic Management of Public and Third Sector Organizations: A Handbook for Leaders*. San Francisco: Jossey-Bass, 1992.

Nutt, P. C., Backoff, R. W., and Hogan, M. F. Managing the Paradoxes of Strategic Change. *Journal of Applied Management Studies*, 2000, 9, 5–31.

Patton, M. Q. *Utilization-Focused Evaluation* (4th ed.). Thousand Oaks, CA: Sage, 2008.

Perrow, C. *Complex Organizations: A Critical Essay*. New York: Random House, 1986.

Poister, T. H., and Streib, G. Strategic Management in the Public Sector: Concepts, Models, and Processes. *Public Productivity and Management Review*, 1999, 22, 308–325.

Powell, W. W., and Steinberg, R. (eds.). *The Nonprofit Sector: A Research Handbook* (2nd ed.). New Haven, CT: Yale University Press. 2006.

Prahalad, C. K., and Hamel, G. The Core Competence of the Corporation. *Harvard Business Review*, 1990 (May–June), 79–91.

Radin, B. A. *Challenging the Performance Movement: Accountability, Complexity and Democratic Values*. Washington, DC: Georgetown University Press, 2006.

Rughase, O. *Identity and Strategy*. Northampton, MA.: Edward Elgar, 2007.

Schwartz, P. *The Art of the Long View: Planning for the Future in an Uncertain World*. New York: Doubleday Currency, 1991.

Selznick, P. *Leadership in Administration: A Sociological Interpretation*. Berkeley: University of California Press, 1957.

Senge, P. M. The Leader's New Work: Building Learning Organizations. *Sloan Management Review*, 1990, Fall, 7–23.

Spencer, L. *Winning Through Participation*. Dubuque, IA: Kendall/Hunt, 1996.

Stalk, G., Evans, P., and Shulman, L. E. Competing on Capabilities: The New Rules of Corporate Strategy. *Harvard Business Review*, 1992, 70 (Mar.-Apr.), 57–69.

Sterman, J. *Business Dynamics: Systems Thinking and Modeling for a Complex World*. New York: Irwin/McGraw-Hill, 2000.

Stone, M. M., and Sandfort, J. R. Building a Policy Fields Framework to Inform Research on Nonprofit Organizations. *Nonprofit and Voluntary Sector Quarterly*. 2009, 38, 1054–1075.

Suchman, M. C. Managing Legitimacy: Strategic and Institutional Approaches. *Academy of Management Review*, 1995, 20(3), 571–610.

Thompson, J. D. *Organizations in Action*. Edison, NJ: Transaction, 2003.

Thompson, L. *The Mind and Heart of the Negotiator*. Upper Saddle River, NJ: Prentice Hall, 2001.

Tuchman, B. *The March of Folly: From Troy to Vietnam*. New York: Knopf, 1984.

Weick, K. E. *Sensemaking in Organizations*. Thousand Oaks, CA: Sage, 1995.

Weick, K. E., and Sutcliffe, K. M. *Managing the Unexpected: Resilient Performance in an Age of Uncertainty*. San Francisco: Jossey-Bass, 2007.

Wenger, E. *Communities of Practice: Learning, Meaning, and Identity*. Cambridge, UK: Cambridge University Press, 1998.

Amherst H. Wilder Foundation. "Mission, Vision, and Values." *Amherst Wilder Foundation*. Accessed January 29, 2016. http://www.wilder.org/AboutUs/Impact/Pages/Misson-Vision-Values.aspx

CHAPTER TEN

UNDERSTANDING NONPROFIT EFFECTIVENESS*

David O. Renz and Robert D. Herman

In an era of heightened concern for nonprofit performance, results, and accountability, we hear more and more about organizational effectiveness and our need to ensure it. Nonprofit leaders and funders all feel increased pressure to guarantee results, and it seems that the mantra of "effectiveness" has become the standard answer. Who can be against effectiveness? But what are we really talking about? Are we all talking about the same thing? Nonprofit organizational effectiveness continues to be an elusive and contested concept. The reality is that most nonprofit leaders and researchers, lacking the simple criterion of bottom-line profit or loss, struggle with the concept of nonprofit organization (NPO) effectiveness and how to make it meaningful in their own organizations. Confronted with these growing pressures to enhance nonprofit organization impact and accountability, they are exploring questions such as:

- What is nonprofit organizational effectiveness? And is program effectiveness the same as organizational effectiveness?
- Is there some "real" effectiveness out there just waiting to be discovered?
- Can those of us trying to explain effectiveness agree on what it is?

---

*This chapter is from an article first published by the authors in *Nonprofit Leadership and Management,* in Summer 2008; adapted and reprinted with permission.

- And if we found it, would we be able to agree on what we have identified?
- Do certain management practices generally promote greater organizational effectiveness? Are there "best practices" and, if so, what are they?

These are just a few of the important questions that confront those interested in studying and improving nonprofit organizational effectiveness. In this chapter we synthesize into key themes the results of recent research on nonprofit organizational effectiveness and explore the implications of these for practice and further study.

Theoretical Perspectives on Nonprofit Organizational Effectiveness

Organizational effectiveness has long been a challenging and contested concept in the world of organizational theory and research. For many, the obvious perspective to use in understanding organizational effectiveness is what theorists call the rational "goal attainment model." This pervasive and common-sense view considers organizations to be rational instruments—mechanisms to achieve something. Thus, the goal approach assesses nonprofit organization effectiveness by the degree to which the organization accomplishes its goals. This perspective is quite appealing. After all, most people join nonprofit organizations because they want to help them accomplish their missions. Yet, while the goal model makes intuitive sense, it often is inadequate to help us understand the real-life complexities of our organizations and what it takes for them to be successful. For example, is an organization truly effective if it accomplishes its goals for the year but must close because it has failed to raise adequate funds? Is a nonprofit effective if it accomplishes its goals by setting those goals so low that they are easily accomplished? And how effective is the organization that sets goals that are irrelevant to the needs of its clients? The reality is that nonprofit organization effectiveness is more complicated.

Given these concerns, some scholars and researchers have developed and tested alternatives or modifications to the goal model of effectiveness. One approach is the "system resource" approach (Yuchtman and Seashore, 1967). This perspective considers effectiveness to be the ability of an organization to acquire scarce and valued resources. This approach justifies the use of measures of resource acquisition, especially financial measures such as total revenues generated or fundraising success, as indicators of organizational effectiveness. Some studies of effectiveness have used this approach, such as the Pfeffer

(1973) study of hospitals that used the percentage increase in number of beds occupied and percentage increase in budget over a five-year period as measures of organizational effectiveness. Some others (for example, Provan, 1980) have used the percentage change in funding as the measure of success.

Certainly, resource acquisition is an aspect of effectiveness. Indeed, it may be the most important criterion for some chief executives or board members (although we doubt they would ever say so). But it seems unlikely to be very important to clients or other key stakeholders. Most leaders of nonprofits tend to emphasize the importance of mission and progress toward mission accomplishment, not increases in the budget, when talking about effectiveness. In fact, emphasis on financial growth in itself would threaten many organizations' legitimacy with their community if that were reported as their primary measure of effectiveness.

Some others, in recognition of the challenge of using the goal attainment model with its emphasis on the "ends" of the organization, will instead identify and measure performance on a variety of management practices (that is, "means," as opposed to the "ends") that they believe will result in organizational effectiveness. This is known as the "internal process approach" to organizational effectiveness (Steers, 1977). It often manifests itself as an assessment of an organization's use of "best practices."

In our own research on nonprofit effectiveness, we have found it important to draw on two contemporary theoretical perspectives to help us understand organizational effectiveness—the multiple constituency perspective and the social constructionist perspective. The multiple constituency perspective is supported by the work of Kanter and Brinkerhoff (1981), who observe that organizations have various constituencies, or stakeholders, and that each constituency is likely to evaluate an organization's effectiveness by using criteria important to that constituency. They argue that organizational effectiveness is not a single reality but rather a more complicated matter of addressing differing interests and expectations. This understanding makes sense to us. We too accept that nonprofits have multiple constituencies or stakeholders who may be likely to differ in how they evaluate the effectiveness of an organization.

The additional perspective we find useful, social constructionism, is not a specific model of organizational effectiveness but rather a general ontological perspective. Proponents of social constructionism explain that reality or some parts of reality are created by the beliefs, knowledge, and actions of the people who are involved. Thus, reality is not something independent of people and the judgments they make, even though people may believe that what they are examining exists as an independent, objective reality. It is a function of their perceptions. The "new institutional school" in organization theory (see Scott, 1995, for a summary) takes a social constructionist approach to analyzing many aspects of organizations, including effectiveness. Our approach to understanding organizational effectiveness builds on these two perspectives. In short, we have come to embrace the view that overall nonprofit organizational effectiveness *is* whatever its relevant multiple constituents or stakeholders judge it to be.

We recognize that nonprofit organizations have multiple constituencies, such as clients, employees, funders (both individual donors and organizations such as grant-making foundations and United Ways), licensing and accrediting bodies, boards of directors, and vendors. These different constituencies are likely to use different criteria, even when evaluating the effectiveness of the same nonprofit organization. This is not to say that such judgments of effectiveness are capricious or arbitrary—they simply differ from constituency to constituency. For example, clients may pay the most attention to changes in their personal condition (are they improving, achieving what they want from their relationship?), while funders may pay more attention to the degree to which the organization follows the correct management procedures (such as strategic planning or outcomes assessment) or provides consistently accurate client and financial reports. Individuals within constituencies, and no doubt to some extent across constituencies, are likely to communicate with one another about the nonprofit and how they think it is doing. They are also likely to see and hear communications from people in the organization about how well they and the organization are doing. In such ways, judgments of effectiveness are developed and even changed. It is not inevitable that constituencies differ in their judgments—we just know that they often do. We also have learned that their views of nonprofit effectiveness may change over time—it is not necessarily stable (even if organizational conditions do not change). In some situations, these social processes that result in judgments of nonprofit effectiveness may even lead to different constituencies using the same criteria and evaluating information about an organization in the same way. However, as we have learned from our own and others' research, it is not uncommon for different constituencies to differ in their judgments of the same organization's effectiveness.

Key Insights on Organizational Effectiveness

As we consider the findings of the research conducted since the early 1990s, we have identified some fundamental themes that help us understand nonprofit organization effectiveness, what it is, and how we might better understand it.

It's a Matter of Comparison

It is essential that we recognize that judgments on organizational effectiveness are, by logical requirement, always a matter of comparison. The key question, often left unasked, is to what are we comparing any particular organization's effectiveness? Is it comparison with the same organization at earlier times, or to similar organizations at the same time, or to some ideal model, or something else? And are others using the same basis for their comparisons? The basis for the comparison is a key to understanding varying judgments of effectiveness, and it often is hidden or unknown (sometimes even to those doing the judging).

Effectiveness Is Multidimensional

Nonprofit organization effectiveness is multidimensional. Most management practice models, as well as the models underlying much of the research on nonprofit organizations, expect that nonprofit organizations should have a number of different criteria by which to judge their effectiveness, and these criteria often are independent of one another. Models that reflect this characteristic include the competing values framework of Quinn and Rohrbaugh (1981), the balanced scorecard technique advanced by Kaplan and Norton (1992), and many other studies on nonprofit effectiveness (see reviews by Forbes, 1998; and Stone and Cutcher-Gershenfeld, 2002).

Baruch and Ramalho (2006), in their analysis of 149 studies published between 1992 and 2003 on organizational effectiveness (in all kinds of organizations), found that the criteria used to assess effectiveness varied significantly by types of organizations in the studies. For example, in studies of businesses, a slight majority used multiple criteria, but 42 percent used *only* financial criteria. In studies of nonprofits, virtually all used nonfinancial (for example, employee satisfaction, customer orientation, quality, public image) as well as financial criteria. However, they note that the most commonly used criterion in the nonprofit studies was efficiency (conceived as an input/output ratio), although nonfinancial criteria had been used almost as often.

This recognition that nonprofit effectiveness is multidimensional has fundamental implications for both research and practice. One of the most important implications: if nonprofit effectiveness is multidimensional, then it cannot legitimately be assessed by using only one single indicator. Thus, models that focus on helping nonprofits enhance effectiveness by maximizing a single criterion (for example, surplus, growth, total revenues) are inadequate. This also means that it is equally inappropriate to assess organizational effectiveness using only the results of individual program performance.

Effectiveness Is a Social Construction

Our research results reinforce our view that NPO effectiveness is "socially constructed." That is, effectiveness is whatever significant stakeholders think it is, and there is no single objective reality "out there" waiting to be assessed. This perspective challenges many because they want effectiveness to be an objective condition that can be seen, measured, and understood in the same way by everyone. It is not that simple. We recognize that the social construction perspective challenges many taken-for-granted understandings about the social world. Nonetheless, many parts of the social world are "real" only because people have believed and acted in ways that are consistent with that reality. This is not to deny that they have significance or consequence. For example, many scientists have observed that the idea and categories of "race" are social constructions. Of course, as our experience with "race" makes all too clear, once a social construction is perceived as real, it can become real in its consequences.

To illustrate how nonprofit effectiveness is socially constructed, we share a baseball story. As the story goes, three umpires are describing how they call balls and strikes. The first says "I call 'em as they are." The second says "I call 'em as I see 'em." The third, the social constructionist of the group, says "They ain't nuthin' 'til I call 'em." In the world of nonprofits, there are activities and accounts of activities, such as annual reports, program outcome reports, stories told by CEOs to board members, funders, and others, and so on. These activities, like pitches in the baseball story, are nothing until someone calls or interprets them. That is, they are not significant until someone forms judgments of effectiveness from them (and, usually, communicates those judgments) and acts on the judgments. Unlike in baseball, for most nonprofits there is no single umpire—all stakeholders are permitted to "call" or judge effectiveness. Some stakeholders will be more credible than others, and some will be more influential than others, and this will make a practical difference. As yet, there is no commonly agreed basis for judging NPO effectiveness, much less a single, objectively "real" measure.

Boards of Directors and Nonprofit Effectiveness

Many studies, using different kinds of nonprofits and different models and measures of board and organizational effectiveness, have found a relationship between board effectiveness and organizational effectiveness. The common assumption is that board effectiveness causes organization effectiveness. But it may not be this clear or unidirectional. Only one study to date (Jackson and Holland, 1998) provides any solid evidence in support of the assertion that board effectiveness is a cause of organizational effectiveness, and several others have failed to affirm this.

We conducted a study in which we compared changes in ratings of board effectiveness and organizational effectiveness for a group of human services organizations over a period of time (Herman and Renz, 2004a), and found that only slightly more than half of the organizations increased their use of recommended board practices during this time; some actually decreased their use of these recommended practices. Interestingly, we found that both chief executives and board members considered the financial condition of the organization as a significant measure of the *board's* effectiveness. We also found, in the case of funders, that perceptions of the prestige of the members of the board had some impact on funders' judgments of board effectiveness (completely separate from any information about the boards' actual practices or other measurable results).

There is some interesting research on the relationship between board performance and organizational performance. William Brown (2005) found that, for chief executives, certain dimensions of board performance (as judged by those executives) are related to organizational performance (as judged by board members). In fact, he also found (using the six board performance dimensions developed by Jackson and Holland [1998]) that board performance is related to organizational performance. In particular, he found that "interpersonal" board competence was significantly related to organizational performance, and both "interpersonal" and "strategic" board competence were significantly related to organizational performance. Further, in separate research by Preston and Brown (2005), there is evidence that board member emotional commitment, as well as members' length of membership, frequency of board attendance, and hours spent on organizational activities all are positively related to a higher level of board performance. Thus, recent research provides support for the view that (in at least some ways) board effectiveness is related to organizational effectiveness. But there is much more to learn.

Effectiveness and Management Practices

The idea that the use of certain board and management practices leads to improved organizational effectiveness is currently in favor. Perhaps this should not be a surprise. In general, the research indicates that nonprofits that are more effective are more likely to use correct management practices. And, as would be predicted by those of the institutional school of organization theory (for example, DiMaggio and Powell, 1983; Meyer and Rowan, 1977), when outcomes are difficult to measure or there is substantial uncertainty about the methods for achieving the desired outcomes, organizations are likely to emphasize the use of approved procedures to achieve or maintain their legitimacy. Thus, use of the "right practices" becomes a de facto indicator of effectiveness.

But does the use of correct management practices equate to organizational effectiveness? Some research suggests a relationship between the use of various management practices (often some part of the strategic planning process) and some measure of overall organizational performance. Several studies (Crittenden, Crittenden, and Hunt, 1988; Odom and Boxx, 1988; Siciliano, 1997) find relationships between the use of certain planning practices (such as financial analysis, stakeholder analysis, environmental trend analysis, goal setting, action plans, and monitoring of results) and higher levels of organizational performance. Among the varying kinds of measures of organizational performance that were used in these studies were membership numbers, growth in membership, growth in contributions, and ratio of total revenues to total operating expenditures. (Unfortunately, in a review of research on strategic planning in nonprofit organizations, Stone, Bigelow, and Crittenden [1999] found that little can be reliably said about exactly which elements of the strategic planning process could be used by nonprofit organizations to improve their overall effectiveness.)

In our research, we, too, have compared the practices of highly effective organizations with those of less effective organizations (effectiveness was based on the aggregate judgments of all of the organizations' key stakeholders). We identified the management practices through the deliberations of focus groups of experienced practitioners whom we convened to identify the practices they considered to be relevant to organizational effectiveness. The practices they considered to be indicators of effectiveness included the presence of a mission statement, a recent needs assessment, a planning document, a system to measure client satisfaction, a formal CEO and employee appraisal process, an independent financial audit, and a statement of organizational effectiveness criteria. We found, for funders, board members, and senior managers, that the organizations rated as more effective did in fact use more of these "correct" management practices, and that greater use of more of these correct practices was positively correlated with higher ratings of organizational effectiveness for all three groups.

Several studies support aspects of this thesis. For example, Galaskiewicz and Bielefeld (1998) report that increased use of selected managerial tactics led to increased organizational growth (in expenditures and number of employees). We could argue that increases in organizational size or growth are not necessarily appropriate indicators of organizational effectiveness, yet it also is certainly arguable that some stakeholders might regard growth in size as an indicator of effectiveness. We (Herman and Renz, 2004a) have found that board members judged organizational effectiveness in relation to the extent of use of correct management practices, but funders and senior managers did not. This illustrates the variation that can exist among different stakeholders, even when judging the same organization. Such results raise concern about the merit of the increasingly common trend to claim there is some validated set of practices that are "best." In relation to both nonprofit board management and organizational management, we must question the assumption that there is "one best way" of doing board work or managing NPOs.

We also have studied whether organizations that increase their use of correct management practices over time are viewed as more effective. Of the forty-four organizations we studied over a nine-year time frame, 55 percent increased their use of the proportion of recommended board practices, 14 percent made no changes, and 32 percent actually reported using fewer of the recommended board practices. This also suggests that assertions with regard to what constitute best practices will change over time. Our experience is that nonprofits are likely to find that certain influential stakeholders (foundations, United Ways, accrediting bodies) will change their beliefs about "best practices" because, as more and more nonprofits adopt the preferred "best practices" over a given period of time, those best practices will no longer seem to them to differentiate the more-effective from the less-effective. So they start looking at new practices and lists. However, this needs further investigation.

The Lure of "Best Practices"

In recent years, the concept of "best practices" has become something of a holy grail for nonprofits seeking to enhance effectiveness. It has been very widely invoked and applied. There is an argument to be made for valuing certain practices, as we discussed in the previous section. And yet, the promise of best practices should be viewed with skepticism. The evidence suggests it is unlikely that there are any universally applicable "best practices" that can be prescribed for all NPO boards and management. In our research (Herman and Renz, 2004a), the evidence does not support the claim that any particular board and management practices are automatically best or even good (that is, that using them leads to increased effectiveness for boards and organizations).

What evidence is required to support a claim of best practice? Keehley, Medlin, Longmire, and MacBride (1997) write that "best practices" should meet seven criteria: be successful over time; show quantifiable gains; be innovative; be recognized for positive results (if quantifiable results are limited); be replicable; have relevance to adopting organizations; and not be linked to unique organizational characteristics (in other words, they need to be generalizable). We have not found any "best practice" that comes close to meeting these criteria. Interestingly, in the business world, studies of what have been promoted as "best practices" for corporation boards also have found no relation between recommended practices and corporate performance (see Heracleous, 2001). We prefer to talk in terms of "promising practices" to describe those approaches that warrant consideration because, at best, it may be said only that they are worth consideration and must be judged in the context of the specific organization. Further, as noted in the previous section, practices that are considered to be "best" at one point in time are likely to change. There is much yet to be studied and understood regarding the assertion that more effective NPOs are likely to use correct management practices.

Effectiveness and Organizational Responsiveness

One of the realities of most research on organizational effectiveness is that researchers (and organizations) focus on specific objective criteria to measure or test. But our collective inability to identify any specific measures suggests that this may not be useful. Instead of telling the respondents exactly what criteria should be used, perhaps we should employ an alternate approach—and leave it to the judge or survey respondent to determine for themselves what criterion or criteria are to be used. In fact, this might offer a way to embrace the social construction of effectiveness yet still allow for aggregating stakeholders' judgments of effectiveness. To this end, we employed a measure of nonprofit effectiveness in our work that emphasizes responsiveness as a way to address the challenge of aggregating the ratings of the various stakeholder groups offering their differing judgments of effectiveness. Adapting the approach of Anne Tsui (1984), in which she measured co-workers' judgments of the effectiveness of individual managers, we asked various constituencies to assess how well the organization is doing on whatever they deem important. We did not tell the respondents what to use as a basis for their judgment.

We (Herman and Renz, 2004a) found that all stakeholder groups rated organizational responsiveness as strongly related to organizational effectiveness. Our work showed that responsiveness is positively related to effectiveness (for all stakeholder groups), and we also found that each stakeholder group's rating of organizational responsiveness was highly related to the average rating of effectiveness for all groups. This suggests to us that an averaged rating of responsiveness can be used as an indicator of effectiveness or, at least, one kind of effectiveness.

It is our hope that others engaged in nonprofit effectiveness research will conduct further study using this concept and instrument. For executives and board leaders, this simple tool (see the resource website for this book for a copy of the tool) may be used as one useful way to assess various stakeholders' judgments of their organization's effectiveness.

Type of Organization Makes a Difference

As many have observed, the (U.S.) legal category that has often been used to define and identify "nonprofit organizations" includes very disparate organizations—in terms of activities, size, scope and other characteristics. What such organizations have in common at a minimum is that they cannot distribute earnings to anyone (the non-distribution constraint) and that they must receive certain proportions of their revenues from various public sources (that is, public support).

Research indicates that it can be useful to differentiate among different "types" of nonprofit organizations as we assess the merits of different approaches to understanding nonprofit effectiveness. One limited but conceptually useful approach is to distinguish among publicly supported charities by general revenue orientation. Specifically, with a growing interest in social entrepreneurship and nonprofit commercial enterprise, we have found it useful to distinguish between "donative" and "commercial" charities (a distinction apparently first proposed by Hansmann, 1980). In other words, it is useful to compare characteristics of conventional nonprofits that operate largely on donations (thus, they are called "donative" organizations) versus nonprofits that engage in commercial activity to generate income. Some who advocate that nonprofits become more commercial certainly see such organizations as importantly different from donative nonprofits. Are they different from an effectiveness perspective?

One study that distinguished organizations by primary revenue source (private donations, government contracting, and commercial) found that chief executives of donative organizations reported using significantly more board involvement practices, compared to commercial and government-dependent organizations (Hodge and Piccolo, 2005). In our research (Herman and Renz, 2002; 2004b) we also investigated whether classifying nonprofits into donative and commercial categories would make a difference.

This kind of distinction is useful for both theoretical and practical perspectives. Neo-institutional theory suggests that organizations will use larger numbers of prescribed board and management practices as a way of showing that they are legitimate (that is, demonstrating to funders and other interested stakeholders that a nonprofit does the right things). The goal model, on the other hand, would lead us to believe that such practices are used as a rational means to achieve organizational goals. But if the use of these practices was focused on seeking legitimacy, then we would expect donative nonprofits to use a greater proportion of both prescribed board and management practices. We did find that, over time, the donative nonprofits increased their use of correct practices to a greater degree than did the commercial nonprofits.

We also compared whether financial management outcomes (surplus and change in revenues) were more strongly related to use of correct management practices in donative than in commercial nonprofits, and we found that, for donative nonprofits, the more they used both prescribed management practices and formal performance management over time, the larger their surplus. For commercial nonprofits, neither of these "good management" indicators was related to change in surplus. Similarly, for donative nonprofits, the more they used both prescribed management practices and formal performance management, the greater their increase in total revenues. For commercial nonprofits, neither good management indicator was related to financial growth. Galaskiewicz and Bielefeld (1998) found similar results in their research, although they focused on organizational growth (measured by revenues and numbers of employees and volunteers) rather than effectiveness itself.

We (Herman and Renz, 2004a) also examined whether stakeholders regarded either form of nonprofit, commercial or donative, to be more effective, and found no substantive differences for any stakeholder group. There were clear differences in the extent to which organizations relied on commercial versus donative or public sources of income, but this distinction was not consistently related to the use of board or management practices, managerial tactics, or stakeholder judgments of effectiveness. In other words, these and other studies indicate it is useful to examine how management practice and effectiveness differ in terms of this commercial-donative distinction, but not all have a relationship to effectiveness.

Differentiating Program, Organization, and Network Effectiveness

Nonprofit effectiveness, despite its elusiveness, is so important to so many stakeholders that it is not surprising that managers have done their best to measure and use whatever effectiveness results they can find to improve management practices. Yet, too often these assessments focus on the measurement and use of *program* outcomes. Nonprofit organizational effectiveness is related to, yet distinct from, effectiveness at both program and network levels of effectiveness. It is important to understand that difference in level of analysis makes a difference in understanding effectiveness; it is important to differentiate effectiveness at program, organization, and network levels.

The recent emphasis on the assessment of program outcomes as a way to assess organizational effectiveness suggests that some stakeholders (especially funders) consider program effectiveness to be more important or of greater interest than other kinds of effectiveness. And nonprofit organization effectiveness is sometimes treated merely as the sum of the effectiveness of an agency's programs. But research and practice both affirm that organizational effectiveness is not identical to program effectiveness and, similar though they are, each must be understood and assessed separately.

Sawhill and Williamson (2001) have argued that nonprofit missions (which certainly are closer to the organizational level of effectiveness) could be measured, yet they ultimately back away from that assertion and focus on the value of setting specific and fairly difficult goals. They also extol the marketing and public relations advantages of communicating performance goals. Such approaches may well be useful for managing, yet they do not provide a systematic basis for generating evidence relevant to general nonprofit effectiveness.

Likewise, it is becoming increasingly important to understand nonprofit effectiveness from the perspective of networks, especially in an era when "collective impact" approaches are becoming more popular with many foundations and other community funders. (Collective impact initiatives are initiatives that integrate the work of a large number of nonprofits to address a complex community or system challenge; see Kania and Kramer, 2011, for further explanation.) An emphasis on the effectiveness of nonprofits as separate and clearly distinct entities can easily lead to the conclusion that an organization creates its own effectiveness. However, in many ways, the perceived effectiveness of an organization often depends on the effectiveness of other organizations and people with which it is interconnected. As more nonprofits deliver services through networks of service delivery (including collective impact initiatives), network effectiveness will become increasingly important to understand in relationship to organizational effectiveness.

For example, Provan and Milward (1995) investigated how network characteristics (among community mental health service providers) were related to assessments of client outcomes. They found that client and family assessments of client outcomes were closely correlated, although staff assessments were not correlated (illustrating the thesis that stakeholders often evaluate program outcomes differently). They found network centralization was most clearly related to positive client and family assessments. Studies of program effectiveness may often need to go beyond an organizational focus to an understanding of networks (Provan and Milward, 2001).

Implications

The strong interest of NPO managers, board members, funders, and NPO regulators in finding clear answers to the question "How can an NPO be effective?" compels us to articulate some of the practical implications of the information we have presented. We do so in this final section.

Implications for Organizational Practice

Important stakeholders frequently are not clear about their bases for assessing a nonprofit's effectiveness. Like art, they may know effectiveness when they see it, but what do they look for? Further, over time, many stakeholders will change their implicit criteria for assessing effectiveness. It is essential that NPO leaders regularly interact with key stakeholders to ensure that they understand their criteria and how they may be changing. And if the NPO leaders find that stakeholder criteria are off base, they must help them refine them.

Research by Balser and McClusky (2005) supports the importance of managing stakeholder relations. In an in-depth qualitative study they find that organizations identified as highly effective by a panel of knowledgeable observers differed from much less effective organizations in the ways and extent to which the effective organizations engaged stakeholders. They suggest that effective stakeholder engagement is more than mere frequency of communication—effective nonprofits exhibit a consistent thematic approach to engagement. We believe it is crucial for the organization's managers to understand what stakeholders expect and move the organization toward more fully responding to and meeting its stakeholders' expectations (including, when appropriate, to respond to and honestly challenge or debate those expectations).

Some are uncomfortable with the notion that nonprofit effectiveness is a social construction; they worry that this means that nonprofit effectiveness is arbitrary. It is not. And even though effectiveness is socially constructed, there are useful dimensions of effectiveness (such as financial condition, fundraising performance, or program outcomes) that can be grounded in "hard" data. For example, use of generally accepted accounting principles provides solid evidence about revenues, costs, and surplus. Other dimensions of effectiveness, such as those related to community collaboration or working with volunteers, are likely to be less amenable to "hard" evidence. We support and encourage the use of "hard" evidence to the extent legitimately possible, but we also know that nonprofit leaders should not expect that all of their stakeholders will interpret and use that evidence the same way or combine it with other kinds of evidence in the same ways.

The popularity of "best practices" attests to the hope of finding a pot of gold at the end of the search. One key assumption of the best practices approach is that a particular technique or process that works well in one setting can and should be incorporated into other different settings. This may be true for certain rather standard administrative functions, for example, the adoption of procedures to improve billing. However, in many instances a practice that enhances effectiveness in one organization may be a poor choice for another.

We do *not* conclude that practices and procedures are unimportant. Undoubtedly, every organization must discover and continually seek to improve its practices, consistent with its values, mission, and stakeholders' expectations. But these practices must fit together to enhance effectiveness.

Implications for Boards and Governance

Board members need to understand that NPO effectiveness is socially constructed, that it is not a stable construct, and that different stakeholders will judge it differently. Likewise, board effectiveness is socially constructed and changeable. Thus, a critical role that board members may serve on behalf of a nonprofit is that of a monitor and sensor—a vital link to help the agency remain in touch with the potentially changing effectiveness judgments of key stakeholders.

Just as with management practices, we do not believe that the research suggests that board process management is unimportant. But not only is there no "silver bullet" (that is, one practice that ensures effectiveness)—but there is no "silver arsenal" for board success. Boards, perhaps with the help of executive or other facilitative leadership, need to identify those processes that will be most useful to them. Do not use a practice just because others say it is useful. Ask some key questions: Does the practice fit this board's circumstances? Does the practice actually help the board reach good decisions? Does the practice contribute to the organization's success?

Implications for Program Evaluation and Outcomes Assessment

We have explained the need to be careful about using program outcome assessments to judge nonprofit effectiveness. We see only a very few (rather unlikely) circumstances under which program outcomes could legitimately be considered to equal organizational effectiveness. (Such a conclusion would be valid, for example, in situations in which the nonprofit conducts only one program and there are no other explanations for outcomes, such as the effect of other programs or events.) These circumstances are so unusual that, for the typical nonprofit, program outcomes assessments must be regarded as relevant but limited indicators of organizational effectiveness.

Certain approaches to program evaluation may be uniquely useful. For example, qualitative forms of program evaluation that emphasize the engagement of key stakeholders in the process (see, for example, Patton, 1997) may more closely align with the realities of organizational effectiveness and be more likely to help all stakeholders to work toward mutually valued results.

Implications for Capacity Building and Capacity Builders

Given that we lack evidence for "best practices," those who fund or provide capacity building support should avoid advocating for one best way or set of ways for doing things. Ideally, they will recognize and support an array of promising practices and provide process skills and knowledge to help nonprofits assess the match of the practices to their environment, circumstances and stakeholders. (See Wing, 2004, for more on the dilemmas facing those funding and doing organizational capacity building.) Further, capacity building should go beyond the internal organization and help nonprofit leaders create processes by which to identify and understand the interests and expectations of key stakeholders, and to create constructive strategies by which to engage them. As noted earlier, some promising practices will differ depending on the domain or field of service of the organization. Therefore, capacity builders should research and help nonprofits identify the practices that are considered fundamental or "absolutely required" as matters of ethical practice, as well as the emerging and promising practices that will be relevant to effectiveness, given a nonprofit's particular domain and environment.

Conclusion

There is little doubt that readers will find some of these propositions and implications more compelling than others. We offer these observations and suggest these implications not because we have "the answers," but because we want to encourage further thoughtful examination of the construct of effectiveness and how we can better understand, measure, and develop it. We invite executives, scholars, and practitioners alike to test these observations and consider their implications for their work. Only as a community will we be able to develop useful understandings of nonprofit organization effectiveness and how we can build the sector's capacity to achieve meaningful results.

References

Abzug, R., and Simonoff, J. S. *Nonprofit Trusteeship in Different Contexts*, Burlington, VT: Ashgate, 2004.

Balser, D., and McClusky, J. Managing Stakeholder Relationships and Nonprofit Organization Effectiveness. *Nonprofit Management and Leadership,* 2005, 15(3), 295–315.

Baruch, Y., and Ramalho, N. Communalities and Distinctions in the Measurement of Organizational Performance and Effectiveness Across For-Profit and Nonprofit Sectors. *Nonprofit and Voluntary Sector Quarterly,* 2006, 35(1), 39–65.

Bloom, H. S., Hill, C. J., and Riccio, J. A. Linking Program Implementation and Effectiveness: Lessons from a Pooled Sample of Welfare-to-Work Experiments. *Journal of Policy Analysis and Management,* 2003, 22(4), 551–575.

Brown, W. A. Exploring the Association Between Board and Organizational Performance in Nonprofit Organizations. *Nonprofit Management and Leadership,* 2005, 15(3), 317–339.

Crittenden, W. F., Crittenden, V. L., and Hunt, T. G. Planning and Stakeholder Satisfaction in Religious Organizations. *Journal of Voluntary Action Research,* 1988, 17(2): 60–73.

DiMaggio, P. J., and Powell, W. W. The Iron Cage Revisited: Institutional Isomorphism and Collective Rationality in Organizational Fields. *American Sociological Review,* 1983, 48, 147–160.

Forbes, D. P. Measuring the Unmeasurable: Empirical Studies of Nonprofit Organization Effectiveness from 1977 to 1997. *Nonprofit and Voluntary Sector Quarterly,* 1998, 27(2), 183–202.

Galaskiewicz, J., and Bielefeld, W. *Nonprofit Organizations In an Age of Uncertainty,* New York: Aldine de Gruyter, 1998.

Hansmann, H. The Role of Nonprofit Enterprise. *Yale Law Journal,* 1980, 89, 835–901.

Heinrich, C. J., and Lynn, L. E., Jr. Governance and Performance: The Influence of Program Structure and Management on Job Training Partnership Act (JTPA) Program Outcomes. In C. J. Heinrich and L. E. Lynn, Jr. (eds.), *Governance and Performance: New Perspectives,* Washington, DC: Georgetown University Press, 2000.

Heracleous, L. What Is the Impact of Corporate Governance on Organisational Performance?" *Corporate Governance,* 2001, 9(3), 165–173.

Herman, R. D., and Renz, D. O. Multiple Constituencies and the Social Construction of Nonprofit Organization Effectiveness. *Nonprofit and Voluntary Sector Quarterly,* 1997, 26(2), 185–206.

Herman, R. D., and Renz, D. O. Theses on Nonprofit Organizational Effectiveness. *Nonprofit and Voluntary Sector Quarterly,* 1999, 23(2), 107–126.

Herman, R. D., and Renz, D. O. Effectiveness in Commercial and Donative Nonprofit Organizations. Paper presented at the Annual Meeting of the Association for Research on Nonprofit Organizations and Voluntary Action, Montreal, Canada, Nov. 14–16, 2002.

Herman, R. D., and Renz, D. O. Doing Things Right: Effectiveness in Local Nonprofit Organizations, a Panel Study. *Public Administration Review,* 2004a, 64(6), 694–704.

Herman, R. D., and Renz, D. O. Investigating the Relation between Financial Outcomes, Good Management Practices, and Stakeholder Judgments of Effectiveness in Nonprofit Organizations. Paper presented at the Annual Meeting of the Association for Research on Nonprofit Organizations and Voluntary Action, Los Angeles, Nov. 18–20, 2004b.

Herman, R. D., and Renz, D. O. Advancing Nonprofit Organizational Effectiveness Research and Theory: Nine Theses. *Nonprofit Management and Leadership,* 2008, Summer, 18(4), 399–415.

Hodge, M. M., and Piccolo, R. F. Funding Source, Board Involvement Techniques and Financial Vulnerability in Nonprofit Organizations. *Nonprofit Management and Leadership,* 2005, 16(2), 171–190.

Jackson, D. K., and Holland, T. P. Measuring the Effectiveness of Nonprofit Boards. *Nonprofit and Voluntary Sector Quarterly,* 1998, 27(2), 159–182.

Kania, J., and Kramer, M. "Collective Impact." *Stanford Social Innovation Review,* 2011, 36–41.

Kanter, R. M. and Brinkerhoff, D. W. Organizational Performance: Recent Developments in Measurement. In R. H. Turner and J. F. Short, Jr. (eds.), Palo Alto, CA: *Annual Review of Sociology: Annual Review,* 1981, 321–349.

Kaplan, R. S., and Norton, D. P. The Balanced Scorecard: Measures That Drive Performance. *Harvard Business Review,* 1992, 70(1), 71–79.

Keehley, P., Medlin, S., Longmire, L., and MacBride, S. A. *Benchmarking for Best Practices in the Public Sector: Achieving Performance Breakthrough in Federal, State, and Local Agencies.* San Francisco: Jossey-Bass, 1997.

Meyer, J. W., and Rowan, B. Institutionalized Organizations: Formal Structure as Myth and Ceremony. *American Journal of Sociology,* 1977, 83(2), 340–363.

Odom, R. Y., and Boxx, W. R. Environment, Planning Processes, and Organizational Performance of Churches. *Strategic Management Journal,* 1988, 9(2): 197–205.

Patton, M. Q. *Utilization-Focused Evaluation: The New Century Text* (3rd ed.). Thousand Oaks, CA: Sage, 1997.

Pfeffer, J. Size, Composition and Function of Hospital Boards of Directors: A Study of Organization-Environment Linkage. *Administrative Science Quarterly* 1973, 18: 349–364.

Preston, J. B., and Brown, W. A. Commitment and Performance of Nonprofit Board Members. *Nonprofit Management and Leadership,* 2005, 15(2), 221–238.

Provan, K. G. Board Power and Organizational Effectiveness among Human Service Agencies. *Academy of Management Journal,* 1980, 22(2): 221–236

Provan, K. G., and Milward, H. B. A Preliminary Theory of Interorganizational Network Effectiveness: A Comparative Study of Four Community Mental Health Systems. *Administrative Science Quarterly,* 1995, 40(1), 1–33.

Provan, K. G., and Milward, H. B. Do Networks Really Work? A Framework for Evaluating Public-Sector Organizational Networks. *Public Administration Review,* 2001, 61(4), 414–423.

Quinn, R. F., and Rohrbaugh, J. A Competing Values Approach to Organizational Effectiveness. *Public Productivity Review,* 1981, 5(2), 122–141.

Sawhill, J. C., and Williamson, D. Mission Impossible? Measuring Success in Nonprofit Organizations. *Nonprofit Management and Leadership,* 2001, 11(4), 371–386.

Scott, W. R. *Institutions and Organizations.* Thousand Oaks, CA: Sage. 1995.

Siciliano, J. I. The Relationship between Formal Planning and Performance in Nonprofit Organizations. *Nonprofit Management & Leadership,* 1997, 7(4): 387–403

Steers, R. M. *Organizational Effectiveness: A Behavioral View.* Santa Monica, CA: Goodyear. 1977.

Stone, M. M., Bigelow, B., and Crittenden, W. Research on Strategic Management in Nonprofit Organizations. *Administration & Society,* 1999, 31(3): 378–423.

Stone, M. M., and Cutcher-Gershenfeld, S. Challenges of Measuring Performance in Nonprofit Organizations. In P. Flynn and V. A. Hodgkinson (eds.), *Measuring the Impact of the Nonprofit Sector.* New York: Kluwer Academic/Plenum, 2002.

Thomas, J. C. Outcome Assessment and Program Evaluation. In R. D. Herman (ed.), *The Jossey-Bass Handbook of Nonprofit Leadership and Management* (3rd ed.). San Francisco: Jossey-Bass, 2010.

Tsui, A. S. A Role Set Analysis of Managerial Reputation. *Organizational Behavior and Human Performance,* 1984, 34, 64–96.

Wing, K. T. Assessing the Effectiveness of Capacity-Building Initiatives: Seven Issues for the Field. *Nonprofit and Voluntary Sector Quarterly,* 2004, 33(1), 153–160.

Yuchtman, E., and Seashore, S. E. A System Resource Approach to Organizational Effectiveness. *American Sociological Review,* 1967, 32: 891–903.

PART THREE

MANAGING NONPROFIT OPERATIONS

Effective nonprofit leaders and managers understand that their organizations develop, grow, and thrive because they have developed an important mutually beneficial relationship with the world they exist to serve. Similar to all organizations, nonprofits succeed because they offer value and make a valuable difference in the communities and societies they emerge to serve. The chapters of Part Three of this *Handbook* build on the foundational information of Part Two to explain how nonprofit organizations start, develop, grow, and (sometimes) disappear. Many nonprofit leaders assume their roles when their organizations are relatively mature, but no nonprofit starts life as a fully formed organization. In Chapter Eleven, Matthew T. A. Nash helps us understand various ways that nonprofits and other social ventures get their start and how those with socially innovative ideas hone and develop them to become functioning organizations that make a difference—that achieve a social impact. This is the realm of the increasingly popular but oft-misunderstood topic of "social entrepreneurship." Nash explains how successful socially entrepreneurial ventures evolve from ideas to plans to actions to results and what we are learning about what it takes to succeed at this unique kind of entrepreneurial activity.

Scott T. Helm, in Chapter Twelve, builds on the concepts presented in Nash's chapter with practical information about the ingredients and elements of the process by which nonprofit leaders can develop their nonprofit or other social venture into a viable enterprise that has greater potential for becoming sustainable and successful. Helm offers a thorough explanation of the process of business planning for social ventures, including how nonprofits can use the concepts and practices of business planning to effectively operationalize their visions for community service and impact.

Each of the last four chapters in this part of the *Handbook* explains a specific element of the larger process of leading and managing a nonprofit organization, including how each links to longer-term nonprofit success. In Chapter Thirteen, Brenda Gainer explains nonprofit marketing, the discipline that enables us to understand how to effectively develop and manage relationships and engage in the exchanges that every enterprise (nonprofit and for-profit) must develop with its key constituents, clients, and stakeholders to survive. Gainer describes the key elements of nonprofit marketing and explains the most important ways in which nonprofits can use marketing concepts and practices to advance their impact.

One of the most important and underutilized of exchange relationships in the nonprofit world is that of advocacy. In Chapter Fourteen, Marcia A. Avner explains the advocacy process, including but not limited to the practice of lobbying, and discusses the most effective approaches that nonprofits can employ to engage constituents and exercise influence in governmental policy processes to have an impact on legislation and policy that will affect their work and, often, their clients' lives. In Chapter Fifteen, James E. Austin and M. May Seitanidi offer a new perspective on collaboration and how nonprofits can understand and develop valuable collaborative relationships and alliances—alliances that have the greatest potential for generating additional benefit and impact for all partners. In a world where it takes collaborative and collective action to achieve some of the most important of social outcomes, Austin and Seitanidi's framework offers useful guidance for how to assess and develop the most productive and valuable options.

Of course, the press for nonprofits to show that the work they and their programs do makes a difference requires that nonprofit leaders and managers understand how to assess and communicate about the performance and impact of these programs. With the widespread and growing demands for nonprofits to be highly accountable and provide evidence of performance (as Ebrahim discusses in Chapter Four), nonprofit organizations must develop and maintain systematic ways to analyze and report on program and organizational effectiveness, and this work is addressed in the final chapter of Part Three, Chapter Sixteen by John Clayton Thomas. Program evaluation represents work at the intersection of management and accountability. Thomas explains the core principles of program evaluation, offers guidance for how nonprofits can most pragmatically assess program effectiveness and results, and discusses the basic approaches that agencies often employ to assess outcomes and evaluate programs.

CHAPTER ELEVEN

SOCIAL ENTREPRENEURSHIP AND SOCIAL INNOVATION*

Matthew T. A. Nash

What business entrepreneurs are to the economy, social entrepreneurs are to social change. They are the driven, creative individuals who question the status quo, exploit new opportunities, refuse to give up, and remake the world for the better.

DAVID BORNSTEIN, HOW TO CHANGE THE WORLD: SOCIAL ENTREPRENEURS
AND THE POWER OF NEW IDEAS

Few concepts in the social sector have caught on as quickly and have captured the imagination of so many, or have been the subject of such intense debate, as has social entrepreneurship. For the first time in human history, within just a few keystrokes on a computer and from the embarrassing comfort of our homes, we have the ability to witness the horrors of widespread hunger, intractable and epidemic disease, gripping poverty, entrenched conflicts, global climate change, unimaginable natural disasters, and inevitable economic turbulence and

---

*I am indebted for the definition of social entrepreneurship and for the formulation of much of the material on social entrepreneurship theory to my colleague, the late J. Gregory Dees, who was professor of the practice of social entrepreneurship and founding faculty director of the Center for the Advancement of Social Entrepreneurship (CASE) at Duke University's Fuqua School of Business, and who was widely recognized as the pioneer of social entrepreneurship research and education. This chapter draws heavily on his work and that of our current and former colleagues at CASE, especially Paul N. Bloom, Beth Battle Anderson, and Catherine Clark.

dislocation. Against this sobering backdrop have emerged a new generation of "social entrepreneurs"—those some have called "new heroes" (Byker, Stuart, Cohen, et al., 2005) or "unreasonable people," possessed of a relentless drive to pioneer breakthrough approaches to some of the world's most pressing problems (Elkington and Hartigan, 2008). Many of these social entrepreneurs draw upon and adapt principles, practices, and models from the business world, blurring the traditional boundaries between the public, private, and social sectors.

Although the concept of social entrepreneurship started to gain serious attention in the mid-1990s, the field has gained the momentum of a social movement over the past ten years. Social entrepreneurs have garnered public attention as recipients of prestigious prizes such as the MacArthur "genius awards," the Presidential Medal of Freedom, and even the Nobel Peace Prize; and stories about social entrepreneurs now appear regularly in newspapers and magazines such as *The New York Times, The Economist,* and the *Financial Times.* By many accounts, David Bornstein's 2004 book, *How to Change the World: Social Entrepreneurs and the Power of New Ideas,* and his subsequent focus on "solutions journalism" may deserve the greatest credit for inspiring the public's admiration of these social innovators.

Since the first known course on social entrepreneurship was offered by J. Gregory Dees at Harvard Business School in the early 1990s, scores of other universities have offered courses or started research initiatives on social entrepreneurship. Networks such as Ashoka's Changemaker Campus Consortium bring together faculty, administrators, and faculty to share promising practices in education and research. New academic journals such as the *Stanford Social Innovation Review, Innovations* (MIT) and the *Journal of Social Entrepreneurship* (Oxford) have emerged to provide a much needed forum for academic discourse. Numerous innovation competitions have emerged to challenge college students to pursue innovative solutions to social problems, such as the Hult Prize, Berkeley Big Ideas, VentureWell, and the Clinton Global Initiative University program, and new kinds of student organizations such as Net Impact, Compass Fellows, StartingBloc, and Design for America inspire their young members to pursue careers that achieve a social and environmental impact in addition to financial returns.

As some social entrepreneurs experiment with business models that aim to achieve a "blended value" of social, environmental, and economic impact, entirely new forms of corporate structure are being advanced, such as the "community interest company" in the United Kingdom, the "social business" proposed by Muhammad Yunus, and the low-profit limited liability company (L3C) and for-benefit "B corporation" in the United States.

The embrace of social entrepreneurship has crossed boundaries into the business sector, where a growing number of companies engage in partnerships with social entrepreneurs—some as a more fundamental approach to philanthropy and "corporate citizenship" that is strategically aligned with their corporate missions and values, some as a strategy to develop new business models and access new markets at the base of the economic pyramid (Chesbrough, Ahern, Finn, and Guerraz, 2006), and some to pursue other opportunities that may generate social and economic value (Austin, Leonard, Reficco, and Wei-Skillern, 2006).[1] Rising social entrepreneurs regularly rub elbows with top corporate executives and government leaders at the World Economic Forum at Davos.

Perhaps the most influential vote of confidence in the promise of social entrepreneurship came from President Barack Obama, who established in 2009 the White House Office of Social Innovation in fulfillment of a campaign pledge to identify the most promising, innovative, results-oriented social innovations and support their replication across the country. Committed to investing in "what works," the Office, in partnership with the Corporation for National and Community Service, launched in 2010 the Social Innovation Fund to deliver growth capital needed to enable programs with demonstrated results to scale their impact. Under the Obama Administration, agencies across the federal government embraced social entrepreneurship, innovation, and human centered design, with exemplars such as the Investing in Innovation Fund at the Department of Education and the Global Development Lab at the U.S. Agency for International Development.

Social Entrepreneurship Is Responding to the "New Realities"

For those who believe that social entrepreneurship represents an important new lens through which to view social change, these developments are encouraging, perhaps even exhilarating. However, the concept of social entrepreneurship did not arise in a vacuum.

One important historical shift that may be contributing to the ascent of social entrepreneurship, at least within the United States, is a widespread recognition of the limits of top-down government solutions to social problems. In the social sector, philanthropy and development aid continue to move away from simple charity and toward more pragmatic, results-oriented strategies, perhaps driven in turn by an engaged citizenry that increasingly demands lasting solutions.

Over the past two decades, as nonprofits competed for limited dollars from government and philanthropic funders, a growing number of organizations began to adopt market-driven approaches and experiment with practices drawn from the business sector, including the launch of earned-revenue ventures, (both mission-related social enterprises and unrelated businesses).[2]

As societies seek to harness private initiative, ingenuity, and investment to find new and better ways to solve social problems, the concept of social entrepreneurship captures the spirit of that search. It reflects broader and deeper social trends that are driving change in how we approach social problems. The rapid growth in popularity of social entrepreneurship can be seen, at least in part, as one response to these trends. Whether it will grow into a significant expression of a new mindset remains to be seen. It depends, in part, on the ability of proponents of social entrepreneurship to capitalize on these propitious circumstances (CASE at Duke, 2008).

What Is Social Entrepreneurship?

The concept of "social entrepreneurship" is relatively new, even if the practice arguably has been around for a very long time. As with many new concepts, its definition is open to debate. Different people and organizations use the term differently, and the number of academic definitions escalates each year as scholars endeavor to refine and clarify the concept. This discourse is healthy, as definitional disputes are common in many fields. Indeed, the term *entrepreneurship* has been around for more than two hundred years, but dozens of definitions circulate in scholarly literature, contributing to the debate within the field of social entrepreneurship.

Reviewing the development of the field of social entrepreneurship, Dees and Anderson trace the evolution of two major schools of thought and practice—*social enterprise*, which tends to focus on the application of business practices in the social sector, including the generation of earned revenue to serve a social mission, and *social innovation*, which is focused on establishing novel and more effective ways to address social problems or meet social needs. "While these schools are often conflated in popular discourse, they reflect different perspectives, priorities, and, to some extent, values. At times, their proponents have been at odds. But both schools have been critical to the growth of the field of social entrepreneurship" (Dees and Anderson, 2006, p. 41).

The Social Enterprise School of Thought

Typifying the "social enterprise school" of thought are those who subscribe to the conventional definition of entrepreneurship as the act of starting a business. Indeed, the Merriam-Webster dictionary online defines "entrepreneur" as "one who organizes, manages, and assumes the risks of a business or enterprise" (www .merriam-webster.com). Columbia Business School Professor Amar Bhide concurs: "Following common usage, I call individuals who start their own businesses entrepreneurs. Theorists attribute a variety of functions to entrepreneurs, such as coordination, risk-taking, innovation, and arbitrage.... I refrain from debating which of these roles are truly 'entrepreneurial'" (2000, pp. 25–26).

The rise of social enterprise in the 1980s and 1990s came about as a result of an increasing interest among nonprofit organizations in finding new sources of revenue to supplement donor and government funding, as well as by a desire among some business executives to promote the provision of human social services by for-profit companies (Dees and Anderson, 2006). An important emphasis among adherents of the social enterprise school is the blurring of the lines between the business and social sectors, often through experimentation with market-based solutions to social problems that seek to align economic and social value creation. One example is the launch of earned revenue ventures, both mission-related enterprises that aim to create social and economic value and enterprises unrelated to the mission and with the main purpose of making money to subsidize more direct social purpose activities.

The Social Innovation School of Thought

Although it may be commonplace to think of an entrepreneur as someone who starts and runs a business, many scholars contend that the definition of social entrepreneurship should be grounded in a more robust interpretation drawing upon the rich tradition of scholarly research and writing on the concept of entrepreneurship.

The Nature of Entrepreneurship. The term *entrepreneur* was first introduced in the 18th Century by French economists, who drew upon the word *entreprendre* from Old French, meaning "to undertake." According to Jean-Baptiste Say (1803), "entrepreneurs" are value creators who shift resources from areas of lower into areas of higher productivity and yield. Although the precise definitions of the terms *entrepreneur* and *entrepreneurship* have been debated ever since, these terms have almost always been reserved for the business context. Writing in the first half of the 20th Century, Austrian economist Joseph Schumpeter (1934) suggested that entrepreneurs perform their value-creating function through innovations, the carrying out of "new combinations" (pp. 65–66), including the creation of a new good or service as well as producing and delivering an existing good or service in a new way or to a new market. Schumpeter declared: "the function of entrepreneurs is to reform or revolutionize the pattern of production" (p. 132).

More recently, leading management scholar Peter Drucker pointed out that entrepreneurs constantly search for and exploit the opportunities created by change (in technology, consumer preferences, social norms, etc.) (Drucker, 1985). Put another way, entrepreneurs have a mindset that sees the possibilities rather than the problems created by change. Howard Stevenson carried this idea further, observing that entrepreneurs pursue these opportunities without being limited by the resources they have in hand; instead, entrepreneurs mobilize resources from others to achieve their objectives (Stevenson and Gumpert, 1985).

Although these scholars were writing about business entrepreneurs, their theories—and the skills, practices, and mindset of an entrepreneur—apply equally as well in the social sector. In this way, a social entrepreneur can be thought of as one type of entrepreneur. Simply put, social entrepreneurs are entrepreneurs whose "business" (or mission) is to achieve social impact. A business entrepreneur may seek to create economic value for private benefit, whereas social entrepreneurs seek above all to create social value for the benefit of society; they measure their productivity in terms of social impact and seek a social return on investment.

Social Innovation. Proponents of the "social innovation school" assert that social entrepreneurs combine the opportunity orientation identified by Drucker, the innovation as revolutionary change agents as described by Shumpeter, and create value through new and better ways of doing things, as described by Say, although the value that the social entrepreneur seeks to create and sustain is social value. According to this view, social entrepreneurs are individuals who reform or revolutionize the patterns of producing social value, shifting resources into areas of higher yield for the benefit of society. Adherents to the social innovation school do not restrict their definition of social entrepreneurship to the nonprofit sector. Instead, the selection of legal form of incorporation—nonprofit, for profit, cooperative, or hybrid—is seen as an important tactical decision that the social entrepreneur must make when crafting the strategy for attracting resources and when considering various restrictions associated with each form of incorporation.

In a similar spirit, and building on the scholarly literature on entrepreneurship, in the widely cited "The Meaning of Social Entrepreneurship" (1998b, rev. 2001), Dees elaborates on the proposition that social entrepreneurs play the role of change agents in the social sector, seeking to create systemic changes and sustainable improvements, by:

- Adopting a mission to create and sustain social value (not just private value)
- Recognizing and relentlessly pursuing new opportunities to serve that mission
- Engaging in a process of continuous innovation, adaptation, and learning
- Acting boldly without being limited by resources currently in hand
- Exhibiting a heightened sense of accountability to the constituencies served and for the outcomes created

Social Entrepreneurship Is About Innovation and Impact, Not Income

Having worked in this field for a while, I am always delighted to find that people are increasingly familiar with the term *social entrepreneur*. Too often, however, they identify social entrepreneurship with nonprofits generating earned income. When the Schwab Foundation for Social Entrepreneurship named Linda and Millard Fuller of Habitat for Humanity and Wendy Kopp of Teach for America, among others, as outstanding social entrepreneurs, it must have confused many people. Both organizations are well known, but neither of them is known for its earned income strategies. They rely heavily on grants and donations. In fact, these social entrepreneurs are masterful at attracting philanthropic donations. What makes them entrepreneurial is that each of them has pioneered creative ways of addressing social problems and marshaled the resources to support their work. Habitat mobilizes volunteers to build affordable houses for the poor. Teach for America recruits talented college graduates to teach in economically distressed schools. Schwab was following a view long endorsed by Bill Drayton at *Ashoka* that social entrepreneurship is about innovation and impact, not income. This view is well grounded in entrepreneurship theory (see my paper on "The Meaning of Social Entrepreneurship" [Dees, 2001]) but not sufficiently.

Despite efforts to spread an innovation-based definition, far too many people still think of social entrepreneurship in terms of nonprofits generating earned income. This is a dangerously narrow view. It shifts attention away from the ultimate goal of any self-respecting social entrepreneur, namely social impact, and focuses it on one particular method of generating resources. Earned income is only a means to a social end, and it is not always the best means. It can even be detrimental—taking valuable talent and energy away from activities more central to delivering on the organization's social mission. Though it is very popular right now, it is just one funding strategy among many and must be assessed on a case-by-case basis. The key is finding a resource strategy that works.

Focusing on earned income leads people to embrace the problematic idea of a "double bottom line." Profits should not be treated with equal importance to social results. No amount of profit makes up for failure on the social impact side of the equation. Any social entrepreneur who generates profits, but then fails to convert them into meaningful social impact in a cost-effective way has wasted valuable resources. From a management point of view, the financial "bottom line" is certainly important, but it is not on the same level as social impact. Social entrepreneurs have only one ultimate bottom line by which to measure their success. It is their intended social impact, whether that is housing for the homeless, a cleaner environment, improved access to health care, more effective education, reduced poverty, protection of abused children, deeper appreciation of the arts, or some other social improvement.

Many activities that generate earned income are not entrepreneurial at all. Earned income has become commonplace. In fact, if religious congregations are excluded, earned income has exceeded donations as a source of funds for public charities in the United States for many years now. Hospitals charge fees for medical services; private schools charge tuition; performing arts groups sell tickets; many museums charge admission and often have gift shops in their lobbies. No one thinks of these practices as examples of "social entrepreneurship" even though they all involve generating earned income. It would be absurd to give a social entrepreneurship award, for instance, to a major hospital simply because of its extremely high percentage of earned income from patient fees and the record profits at its gift shop and parking garage. Yet, this would be a logical implication of taking earned income as the yardstick of social entrepreneurship. High levels of earned income are often not innovative and may not be correlated with high levels of social impact.

Any form of social entrepreneurship that is worth promoting broadly must be about establishing new and better ways to improve the world. Social entrepreneurs implement innovative programs, organizational structures, or resource strategies that increase their chances of achieving deep, broad, lasting, and cost-effective social impact. To borrow from J. B. Say, the eighteenth century French economist who first popularized the term *entrepreneur,* they shift resources into areas of higher productivity and yield. Habitat persuades volunteers to shift their time from recreational activities to building a house. Teach for America persuades bright college graduates who did not major in education to devote two years of their careers to teaching in schools that have a difficult time finding teachers. This resource-shifting function is essential to progress. As Peter Drucker (1985) has said, "What we need is an entrepreneurial society in which innovation and entrepreneurship are normal, steady, and continuous."

Of course, some exciting forms of social entrepreneurship use earned income strategies to achieve social impact. We should encourage social sector leaders to explore innovative financial strategies that make their organizations more effective in serving social needs while leveraging social assets. Creative efforts to harness business methods to serve social objectives are often entrepreneurial in the best sense of that term. Consider Grameen Bank that was built around an innovative approach of using peer groups to improve the economics and effectiveness of micro-enterprise lending as a tool to fight poverty in Bangladesh. Or consider Delancey Street Foundation, a residential community of hardcore substance abusers in San Francisco that runs several businesses to provide productive employment to community members and generate funds for the organization. These are powerful examples of how social sector leaders can blend business methods with social objectives. What makes them entrepreneurial is not the source of income, but their innovations and their impact.

Earned income ventures are socially entrepreneurial only when they have a social purpose beyond simply making money. If social entrepreneurship is to be distinctive in any way, it must be because social objectives matter in how the venture is organized and managed. If the only way a venture serves your mission is by generating funds, it may be business entrepreneurship, but it is not social entrepreneurship. If I start a bakery to make money that will be used to support my sailing hobby, we do not call the bakery a "sailing venture." Likewise using the proceeds of the bakery for a social purpose does not make it into a "social" venture. It is a social venture only if social considerations are integrated into its objectives and management. A purely moneymaking venture can be managed using straight business principles. It makes no difference if the owner intends to use the cash generated by the venture to buy a bigger sailboat or to serve the homeless. True social ventures often require a more complex skill set than straight business ventures.

Only if we can embrace a definition of social entrepreneurship that focuses on innovation and impact can we put funding strategies in their proper perspective. It is not surprising that people are drawn to the earned income definition of social entrepreneurship. Resources are scarce and social needs are great. Everyone wants to explore new avenues for generating resources and earned income seems promising. Unfortunately, some social sector leaders appear to be more concerned about attracting resources and sustaining their organizations than they are about assessing, sustaining, and improving their social impact. They assume they are doing a great job on the social side and that they deserve the additional funding, often without much systematic evidence. These are risky assumptions. Finding ways to sustain organizations that are not cost-effectively delivering social value is a terrible waste of energy and resources. Social sector leaders should look for creative resource strategies that enhance their impact, rather than simply sustain their organizations. By embracing a definition of social entrepreneurship that focuses on innovation and impact, we can assure that social objectives are taken seriously in the entrepreneurial process. In the end, social entrepreneurship must be about creating social value, not simply about making money.

J. Gregory Dees, Adjunct Professor and Faculty Director, Fuqua School of Business Center for the Advancement of Social Entrepreneurship (CASE), Duke University. This article originally appeared on The Skoll Foundation's Social Edge in September 2003. It is reprinted here by permission.

The Imperative of Systemic Change. One important tenet of the social innovation school is that social entrepreneurship aims to effect large scale, sustainable, and systemic change. Writing in the *Stanford Social Innovation Review* in 2007, Martin and Osberg argued that social entrepreneurship is characterized by three fundamental components:

- Identifying a stable but inherently unjust equilibrium that causes the exclusion, marginalization, or suffering of a segment of humanity that lacks the financial means or political clout to achieve any transformative benefit on its own
- Identifying an opportunity in this unjust equilibrium, developing a social value proposition, and bringing to bear inspiration, creativity, direct action, courage, and fortitude, thereby challenging the stable state's hegemony
- Forging a new, stable equilibrium that releases trapped potential or alleviates the suffering of the targeted group, and through imitation and the creation of a stable ecosystem around the new equilibrium ensuring a better future for the targeted group and even society at large (p. 35)

Martin and Osberg draw a strong distinction between social entrepreneurship and two other forms of social engagement—social activism and social service provision—noting that the former is an indirect form of social engagement and arguing that the latter does not set out to achieve and sustain a new equilibrium (see Figure 11.1). Acknowledging the distinctive value that each form of social engagement brings to society, Martin and Osberg note that social activists, social service providers, and social entrepreneurs may borrow and adapt one another's strategies and develop hybrid models.

The emphasis on transformational systems change, at the core of this definition of social entrepreneurship, has long been championed by Bill Drayton, who is arguably the primary driving force advancing the social innovation school of thought. In 1980, Drayton founded Ashoka, the global network of leading

FIGURE 11.1. Pure Forms of Social Engagement

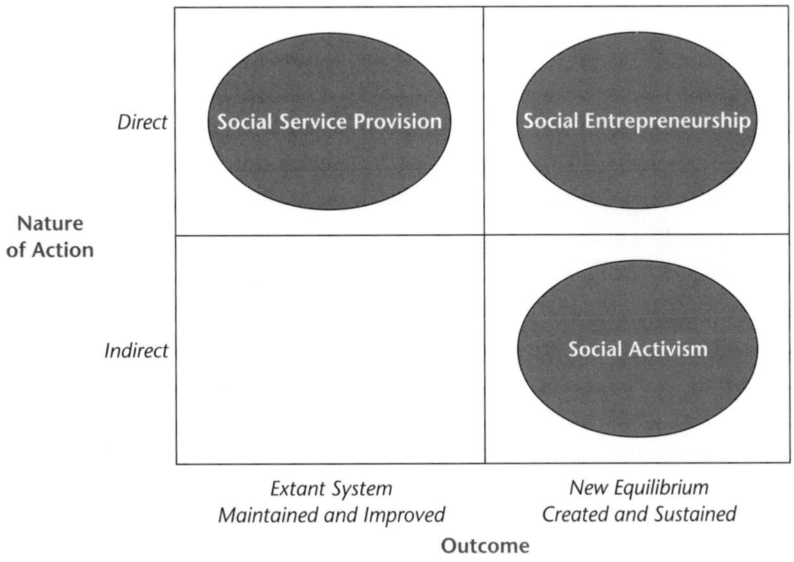

Source: Martin and Osberg, 2007. Reprinted with permission.

social entrepreneurs, and he framed its mission to find and support "outstanding individuals with pattern setting ideas for social change" (Drayton & MacDonald, 1993, p. i). Setting a high standard for those who would consider themselves social entrepreneurs, Drayton asserts: "The job of a social entrepreneur is to recognize when a part of society is stuck and to provide new ways to get it unstuck. He or she finds what is not working and solves the problem by changing the system, spreading the solution and persuading entire societies to take new leaps. Social entrepreneurs are not content just to give a fish or teach how to fish. They will not rest until they have revolutionized the fishing industry" (Leviner, Crutchfield, and Wells, 2006).

Toward a Shared Theory of Social Entrepreneurship

It is easy to see how these points of difference can lead to significant confusion over what "counts" as social entrepreneurship and what does not. Shared definitions will likely emerge from a give-and-take process among thought leaders in the field and the media outlets that popularize the term. In order to propel this field forward, we must find definitional solutions that increase precision and clarity while allowing healthy disagreements, respecting different perspectives. Too broad a definition will dilute the focus of the community, but too narrow a definition could exclude too many and result in a field that is "too special" for mainstream attention.

A vibrant and diverse community of practice is emerging, including those who embrace all the different definitions mentioned above. In order to maintain the interest, commitment, and participation of key players, while also allowing for academic discourse to advance the state of knowledge within the field, we should pursue a path forward that balances increased clarity with openness and respect for differences and that frames this emerging field of inquiry in a way that builds upon the rich work of reflective practitioners and scholars who have led the way thus far.

For those in the field with a vested interest in resolving the confusions about definitions, CASE has suggested the following guidelines (CASE at Duke, 2008):

- Clearly distinguish "social entrepreneurship," focused on innovation in social value creation, from "social enterprise," focused on the use of business methods to generate income.
- For the foreseeable future, define the community of practice and knowledge to include both social entrepreneurship and social enterprise.
- Find a vocabulary to distinguish the different forms of socially entrepreneurial behavior (that is, to distinguish independent start-ups led by one or two people from organizations engaged in finding innovative solutions to social problems) and the revolutionaries, aiming for major systemic change, from the reformers, aiming for more incremental improvements.
- Recognize the importance and legitimacy of all these forms of entrepreneurial behavior, and acknowledge that they have enough problems, concerns, and passions in common to be part of a shared community of practice and knowledge.
- Respect that it is healthy for key community participants to focus their work on forms of socially entrepreneurial behavior that they deem most important, interesting, and a good fit for them.

These guidelines should allow for the development of a diverse and vibrant community with some critical mass but without all the confusion that currently exists in the field. Participants need to respect honest differences while working together to help find new and better solutions to social problems.

As in many fields, consensus on a basic definition of the field may not emerge for some time. However, the critical need for rigorous research and high-quality teaching requires the field to make advances in the absence of full consensus. Observing encouraging signs of convergence between the two main schools of thought, CASE proposes a way of framing this new field of inquiry that raises a distinctive set of intellectual questions that cut across disciplinary boundaries. Dees and Anderson contend that the most promising arena for academic inquiry lies at the intersection of social enterprise and social innovation, which they identify as "enterprising social innovation, "defined as "carrying out innovations that blend methods from the worlds of business and philanthropy to create social value that is sustainable and has the potential for large-scale impact" (Dees and Anderson, 2006, p. 50). This framing forces scholars and practitioners to acknowledge the intimate connection between social and economic realities and the role of markets in the social sector. "In order to be considered 'enterprising,' the innovation must involve some business-inspired elements, whether through the adaptation of business methods to create or enhance social value, the operation of a social-purpose business, or the formation of cross-sector partnerships" (p. 51).

This framing on ventures that blend business and philanthropic methods has the potential to raise theoretically interesting questions and engage a broad range of scholars working in diverse disciplines and domains. Selected areas of academic inquiry could include:

- Aligning market dynamics with social outcomes
- Strengths and limits of different economic strategies (philanthropic and commercial)
- Role of different legal forms of organization
- Bias toward commercial market solutions
- Competitive advantage of social orientation
- Market discipline and accountability
- Efficiency in the social sector capital markets

Observing the accelerating trend of blurring of the boundaries between the public, private, and social sectors, Dees and Anderson call upon academics and thoughtful practitioners to seek to understand better what may lie ahead for the field of social entrepreneurship. "If we do not deepen our knowledge of these kinds of approaches, we are likely to fumble around in the dark, making more mistakes than necessary. Success will depend on a better understanding of how to effectively combine elements from the business world and the social sector, and how to recognize the limits and risks. This arena is where we should focus most of our limited time and resources. Doing so will not only serve both schools of thought and academia well; more importantly, it will be of great value to society." (p. 61)

The Process of Social Entrepreneurship: Creating Worthy Opportunities

All acts of entrepreneurship start with the recognition of an attractive opportunity (Stevenson and Gumpert, 1985). All entrepreneurs, whether business or social entrepreneurs, must uncover or create new opportunities through a dynamic design process of exploration, innovation, experimentation, and resource mobilization (Dees, 2007). The difference for the social entrepreneur is an opportunity worthy of serious pursuit must have sufficient potential for positive social impact in order to justify the investment of time, money, and energy required to pursue it seriously. Social entrepreneurs must have the same commitment and determination as a business entrepreneur, plus a deep passion for the social cause, minus an expectation of significant financial gains.

Drawing extensively upon the work of Guclu, Dees, and Anderson (2002), in the following pages we will discuss a useful process framework that social entrepreneurs may use to guide the discovery or creation of such an opportunity. This process is illustrated in Figure 11.2.

Step 1: Generate Promising Ideas

For entrepreneurs, whether business entrepreneurs or social entrepreneurs, the entrepreneurial journey begins with a promising idea. Although ideas commonly have their roots in personal experience, in identifying, exploring, and developing promising ideas, the social entrepreneur may also draw upon his or her understanding of social needs, social assets, and relevant changes in society.

Personal Experience. Personal experience often motivates, inspires, or informs the idea generation process. Not surprising, many successful new venture ideas arise from the entrepreneur's education, work experience, and hobbies (Vesper, 1979). It is important to note that relevant experience does not have to be in the same field in which the new venture would operate. Sometimes experience and knowledge of practices in other fields can help the social entrepreneur see new ways of doing things.

FIGURE 11.2. The Opportunity Creation Process

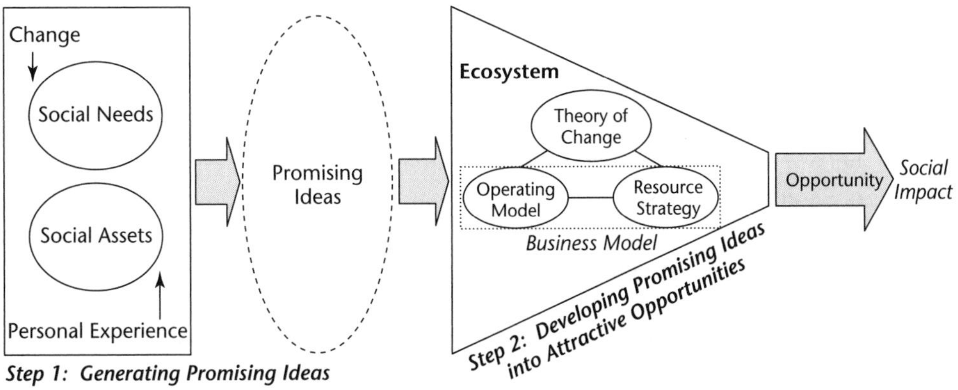

Source: Adapted from Guclu, Dees, and Anderson, 2002.

Dissatisfaction with the status quo often spurs entrepreneurial creativity, prompting social entrepreneurs to look for new approaches to problems and frustrations they have encountered personally, witnessed among family or friends, or seen on the job. Some social entrepreneurs point to a "moment of obligation" a time when they were confronted by a problem or issue and realized that they had to take action, whereas other social entrepreneurs undertake an intentional, systematic search for a problem to address.

Social Needs. Sound entrepreneurial ideas respond to genuine needs. For business ventures, these are unmet or poorly met consumer needs. Likewise, social entrepreneurs would be wise to look beyond their personal preferences in the search for promising ideas, basing them on an understanding of social needs, gaps between socially desirable conditions and the existing reality. They rest on some vision of a better world and are grounded in personal values. These values can provide a sense of moral imperative that may serve as a powerful motivator for social entrepreneurs and their ideas. Calling to mind the famous quote from Robert Kennedy, social entrepreneurs are unwilling to settle for the status quo; instead, they "dream of things that never were, and ask why not?"

Although the impetus for some ventures can be traced back to an accidental discovery or serendipitous occurrence, an exciting development in the field of social entrepreneurship has been the increasing incorporation of the principles and practices of *human-centered design* to identify needs and wants experienced by stakeholders and to co-create appropriate solutions that are desirable, feasible, and viable given the local context. These interactive methods of needs-finding emphasize contact, observation, and empathy with end-users to develop insights that will lead to more effective solutions. In particular, the design firm IDEO and the Hasso Plattner Institute of Design at Stanford University (also known as the "d.school") have been leading proponents of this approach that has been embraced by organizations as large as UNICEF and as small as local, grassroots initiatives.

Social Assets. Understanding the tangible and intangible assets in a community—local knowledge, social networks, cultural norms, and other resources—can lead to the development of promising ideas. Although it is important to ground ideas for new ventures in a plausible diagnosis of social needs, there is a danger of over-emphasizing the negative. Some argue that the social sector concentrates too much on needs and that better ideas emerge out of an appreciative focus on assets. The latter presents the community in a new light and may inspire creative new ideas that would not be visible if social entrepreneurs looked only at needs or "problems."

Change. It is common to think of entrepreneurs as creating change, but entrepreneurs are often inspired by the changes all around them. Peter Drucker has argued entrepreneurs "always search for change, respond to it and exploit it as an opportunity" (Drucker, 1985). In framing their ideas, social entrepreneurs may be stimulated by changing demographics, values, cultures, technologies, industry structures, economies, knowledge, public policies, and preferences. These changes can create new needs, new assets, or both, opening up new possibilities and prompting social entrepreneurs to generate promising new ideas.

Step 1 Summary. Personal experience, social needs, social assets, and change can stimulate promising ideas, but only if the social entrepreneur also adopts an opportunity-oriented mindset, actively looking for new possibilities to have significant positive social impact. Successful social entrepreneurs embody this "how can" attitude, particularly in the idea generation phase, as they ask themselves and the communities in which they seek to engage:

- How can we draw upon our personal experiences in seeking to achieve broad social impact?
- How can we address a particular social need or make the most of existing social assets to improve society?

- How can we capitalize on recent changes to seize new opportunities for social impact?
- How can we frame the root problems or underlying issues in a way that could lead to solutions that are desirable, feasible, and viable?
- What have others already done to attempt to address these issues, and what can we learn from those efforts?

Effective social entrepreneurs carry this orientation into the opportunity development process, engaging in continuous innovation, adaptation, analysis, and learning along the way.

Step 2: Develop Promising Ideas into Attractive Opportunities

The second step for the aspiring social entrepreneur is to convert an initially appealing idea into a worthwhile opportunity, combining rigorous analysis with creative adjustment as the social entrepreneur tests and refines the ideas through a mixture of research, innovation, and action. The chances of success are significantly increased if the envisioned social venture idea is grounded in a set of plausible, testable hypotheses about the underlying *theory of change* and a plausible *business model*, consisting of an effective operating model describing the activities, structures and systems required by the theory of change, and a viable strategy for attracting the necessary human and financial resources required by the operating model. The most attractive opportunities have strong theories of change and business models that fit with the ecosystem, or operating environment, and the personal characteristics of the social entrepreneur.

Theory of Change. As we have seen, social entrepreneurs are driven by a desire to achieve results—to create social value for their primary constituents or beneficiaries, society, and the world. Underlying any promising new social venture is a carefully conceived and testable hypothesis about how the venture will achieve its intended social impact. Expressing the cause-and-effect logic by which the venture's operating model connects inputs, activities, and outputs to generate desired outcomes, this "theory of change"—also known as a "development hypothesis" in the field of international development, and variously referred to as a "social impact theory" or "theory of action"—is central to the venture's strategy and generally embodies the organization's mission and values (Guclu, Dees, and Anderson, 2002). The articulation of this theory linking action to results should include a "convincing statement of how program inputs will produce a sequence first of intermediate and then ultimate outcomes, ... and some indication of the bases, in experience, for expecting a cascade of results" (Szanton quoted by Grossman and Curran, 1990). By clearly defining the venture's intended outcomes and means for achieving them, the theory also provides a precise description of the ultimate social impacts for which the organization will hold itself accountable (Campbell and Haley, 2006).

A well-articulated theory of change should also identify the critical assumptions underlying the hypothesis. We can think of these assumptions as the necessary preconditions that should hold in order for the theory of change to lead to achieving the intended impact. Considered alongside the intermediate outcomes that will jointly cause the intended impact, these assumptions complete the "if/then" logic inherent in the theory of change. Whenever possible, critical assumptions should be identified and tested prior to launching a venture by comparing the theory of change to existing relevant knowledge in the field or by doing new research and analysis. Despite their need and bias for action, social entrepreneurs should structure their actions carefully in such a way that they can test as many critical assumptions as feasible before making major, irreversible investments (McGrath and MacMillan, 1995).

To aid in developing and refining his or her theory of change, the social entrepreneur may wish to create a simple logic model that clearly identifies the specific resources or "inputs" required, the major activities of the venture, the "outputs" produced by those activities, and the "outcomes" resulting from the activities. Another useful tool is the "outcomes framework"—an inductive logic tree that illustrates the hypothesis implicit in the theory of change, the causal logic among the intermediate outcomes and ultimate intended impact, and any critical assumptions that should hold in order for the theory of change to lead to achieving the intended impact. When paired with carefully defined and objective performance measures for each intended output and outcome, logic models and outcome frameworks can become valuable tools for planning, communications, and management and should be reviewed and updated regularly.

Defining and refining a theory of change is a dynamic process that blends creativity and out-of-the-box thinking with concrete analysis and assessment of results. Social entrepreneurs should regularly test and, if necessary, revise their theory of change to assure they are pursuing a worthwhile opportunity and are on track to achieving their ultimate intended impact. Since social impact is so hard to measure and many social entrepreneurs aim for long-term, sustainable lasting impact, the testing process can take significant amounts of time. Having a clearly articulated theory of change and performance measures helps make the testing process more systematic and timely.

Business Model. In addition to a compelling theory of change, every worthwhile opportunity needs to be supported by a plausible business model. Every venture—whether commercial or social—has an implicit business model that indicates how the venture creates, distributes, and captures value. In many cases, social entrepreneurs are most creative and add the greatest value in the design of their business model—they employ a wide range of options for structuring their ventures, acquiring capital, pricing their services, paying their workers, and coming to terms with suppliers—all in the pursuit of creating and maximizing social value.

For the social entrepreneurial venture, the business model includes two key elements:

1. An *operating model* that includes internal organizational structure, activities, and external partnerships that are crucial for creating the organization's intended impact
2. A *resource strategy* that defines where and on what terms the organization will acquire needed resources (financial and human capital, facilities, equipment, supplies, technology, and other tangible or intangible resources)

These two elements of the business model work closely together to bring the theory of change to life. In this sense, the business model is essentially the conduit through which a social entrepreneur converts inputs into outcomes. It determines the organization's financial and talent needs, the extent and nature of dependence on different resource providers, and the efficiency with which resources are converted into impact, which factors into the social return on investment.

Regardless of how effective an innovation is at achieving impact, the business model must be "sustainable" over the period of time required to achieve widespread, lasting impact. If the business model is not capable of being scaled or replicated, widespread impact will be impossible to achieve. If the business model is not aligned with the mission and intended impact of an organization, the organization may be sustained and it may scale, but its ultimate impact will be undermined. This can even be a problem for for-profit social ventures that discover their mission impact would be better served through activities and costs that cannot be adequately covered by their revenues.

Operating Model. A fundamental component of the business model, the operating model describes how the theory of change will be implemented in practice.

FIGURE 11.3. The Simplified Social Value Chain

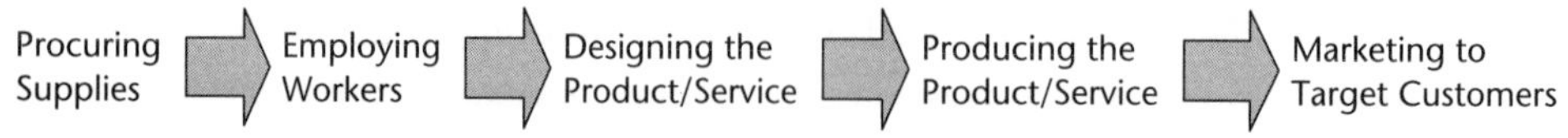

Procuring Supplies ➡ Employing Workers ➡ Designing the Product/Service ➡ Producing the Product/Service ➡ Marketing to Target Customers

Source: Guclu, Dees, and Anderson, 2002. Used with permission.

It is a combination of specific activities, structures, and support systems that are designed to work together to bring about the intended impact.

In developing an operating model, the first step is to trace a chain of activity from inputs to outcomes, identifying every step that is necessary in between. These direct productive activities will usually need to be supported by administrative functions, such as accounting, human resources, fundraising, and so on. When all of these elements are put together, the result looks similar to the "value chain" in a business (see Figure 11.3), a concept introduced by strategist Michael Porter (1985) as a tool for analyzing potential sources of competitive advantage for a firm.

This framework can be used to identify the major activities through which a social entrepreneurial venture can create or enhance social value. Social entrepreneurs may create social value at any of the steps in this process. For example, microfinance institutions such Grameen Bank create social value by making loans to people who otherwise would not have access to the capital they need. Perhaps Muhammad Yunus's most important innovation was to eliminate the requirement of assets as collateral for loans, an insurmountable barrier to the poor; instead Yunus created peer-lending groups, small groups of women borrowers from the same village who meet regularly, support each other, and share responsibility for repayment of loans made to anyone in the group, thus pooling risk and increasing return.

Fair trade organizations such as Ten Thousand Villages create social value in how and from whom they purchase the goods they sell. Other social ventures, such as Greyston Bakery and Homeboy Industries, create value through employing disadvantaged populations. Some, such as Triangle Residential Opportunities for Substance Abusers (TROSA) engage their beneficiaries in earned revenue ventures as a form of rehabilitative therapy and to foster job skills needed for reintegration in the community, thus increasing likely social impact. With hospice care, the social value is inherent in the design of the value or service. Through their distribution chains, both KickStart and VisionSpring harness the powerful incentives of small business ownership to sell foot-operated water pumps and deliver eye care services and products in rural villages in developing countries.

Once the social entrepreneur has identified all key activities in the value chain, she must make structural decisions, such as choosing a form of incorporation and defining the division of labor and coordination of activities. Social entrepreneurs may choose to incorporate their venture as a nonprofit organization, a for-profit social venture, or a hybrid that may combine two or more corporate entities; this decision may be based on a number of factors, including the desired sources of capital. A for-profit form of incorporation (proprietorships, partnerships, corporations, limited liability companies, and cooperatives) will be necessary if the social entrepreneur seeks to tap into private capital markets for investment funds, whether at or below market rate of return (Dees and Anderson, 2003).

The major labor division question concerns what the new venture should do and control versus what could be left to affiliates, partners, suppliers, contractors, or providers of complementary services. This decision should be driven largely by the importance of the activity, the presence or lack of competencies and efficiencies within the organization, and the value of maintaining control over it.

Finally, social entrepreneurs should consider the support systems that may need to be in place to assure effective and efficient social value creation, including systems for monitoring organizational performance and assessing outcomes, as well as intangible support systems such as the organization's culture.

With these pieces in place, the operating model should allow social entrepreneurs to trace a plausible and specific causal path through a chain of activities, structures, and support systems to the intended social impact. As with the theory of change, any proposed operating model will rest on assumptions that may be tested before anyone can say that the operating model is likely to be effective.

Resource Strategy. Whether in business or in the social sector, an operating model cannot begin to create value unless it is aligned with and supported by a viable resource strategy. At the most fundamental resource level, the social entrepreneur needs *people* (including their skills, knowledge, contacts, credentials, passions, and reputations) and *things* (including everything from office space to patents). Unlike business entrepreneurs, in the social sector, entrepreneurs may acquire both people and things with or without using money.

In developing a resource strategy, social entrepreneurs must first identify resource requirements; these may be deduced from the proposed operating model, along with performance and growth objectives. Resource needs cannot be determined without a specific operating model in mind that converts the resources into the capabilities necessary to create the intended social impact efficiently and effectively. Of course, as the idea is refined and tested, the original operating model may need to be adjusted to fit the realities of resource mobilization.

Next, social entrepreneurs must determine how best to mobilize the resources required through one or more of the following options: *building partnerships or alliances, attracting donations,* and *paying for the resources.*

Although some partnerships may be desirable as part of the operating model, others are driven more by resource considerations. When resources are scarce or hard to mobilize, as is often the case during the start-up stage, it may be wise to build resource-based partnerships with others that have (perhaps underutilized) resources of the kind required. However, social entrepreneurs should carefully consider benefits, costs, and risks of any partnership, particularly if it is not ideal from the operations point of view.

Social entrepreneurs may also attempt to acquire resources through volunteers and in-kind donations, which can reduce the cash needed to achieve social impact. Some organizations, such as Habitat for Humanity, rely heavily on volunteers and in-kind donations for core activities. Other social entrepreneurs have decided that operational effectiveness requires paying for key resources. For example, whereas most youth mentoring organizations typically rely on volunteers, Friends of the Children, winner of the Purpose Prize for 2009, has challenged that model, arguing that the use of paid mentors for at-risk kids leads to better social outcomes.

Even for those things that are purchased, social entrepreneurs can sometimes offer below-market compensation or seek discounts. For example, many organizations have been able to attract and retain high-quality workers with below-business-market wages, perhaps due to the personal satisfaction that people get from working for a cause that is deeply meaningful to them. Also, social ventures may qualify for discounted prices on equipment, supplies, services, professional fees, and so on, although the pool of available resources may be limited and the quality of services provided at reduced cost may be lower than desirable.

Finally, when considering the acquisition of costly equipment and facilities, social entrepreneurs must also decide whether they will purchase outright or whether they will simply rent or lease. When risk is high, renting or leasing is typically the optimal option.

Based on these decisions, social entrepreneurs should estimate the cash needs for their ventures and begin to identify plausible sources of funding. Although many social entrepreneurs would love for their ventures to be "self-sufficient," charging customers enough to cover all the operating costs (as occurs in the private sector) is often not optimal from the point of view of creating social impact. Although third-party payers (such as government agencies or corporations) may be found to cover costs, in many domains in which social entrepreneurs operate, revenues gained from service fees and contracts will fall short of what is needed to have the desired impact. In these cases, the resource strategy must include a plausible fundraising plan. However, social entrepreneurs must be vigilant about selecting cash income streams that do not pull the venture away from its core mission.

In summary, the social entrepreneur should craft the resource strategy based on assumptions about resource requirements and methods of meeting them, asking questions such as:

- How many staff and volunteers will be necessary for successful service delivery?
- Can the venture attract and retain staff with the requisite skills at the proposed levels of compensation? Can it recruit, train, and effectively manage the required volunteers?
- Will projected in-kind donations come with too many strings attached or have serious operating costs?
- Who may pay for the venture's activities? Who may be willing to donate to subsidize it? Will revenue sources be aligned with the mission?

Although some of the assumptions embedded in the model may be highly plausible based on past experience, social entrepreneurs should carefully identify those uncertain assumptions to which the resource strategy is most sensitive and make sure they are tested and adjusted as the venture rolls out. The various dimensions of nonprofit finance and resource development are addressed by the chapters in Part Four of this volume, and the chapters in Part Five address the challenges of recruiting, retaining, and motivating both staff and volunteers.

As with the rest of the process of social entrepreneurship, developing an attractive resource strategy requires creativity, especially given the intense competition for funding in the social sector. In some instances, an innovative resource strategy might even drive, or significantly impact, the social venture's operating model. However, a resourceful approach does not undermine the effectiveness of the business model and ultimate social impact of the venture. In fact, the most attractive resource strategies actually enhance social impact.

FIGURE 11.4. The Social Enterprise Spectrum

	Purely Charitable	⟵————————⟶	Purely Commercial
Motives, Methods, and Goals	Appeal to goodwill Mission-driven Social value creation	Mixed motives Balance of mission and market Social and economic value	Appeal to self-interest Market-driven Economic value creation
Key Stakeholders			
Targeted Customers	Pay nothing	Subsidized rates, and/or mix of full payers and those who pay nothing	Pay full market rates
Capital Providers	Donations and Grants	Below-market capital and/or mix of donations and market rate capital	Market rate capital
Work Force	Volunteers	Below-market wages and/or mix of volunteers and fully paid staff	Market rate compensation
Suppliers	Make in-kind donations	Special discounts and/or mix of in-kind and full price	Charge full market prices

Source: Dees and Anderson, 2006.

Business Model Summary. There are numerous ways by which a social entrepreneur may create social value. In designing a social venture, the social entrepreneur has a wide range of options for structuring their ventures, acquiring capital, pricing their services, paying their workers, and coming to terms with suppliers. In exploring these various options, it may be helpful to consider the Social Enterprise Spectrum illustrated in Figure 11.4 (Dees 1996, 2001).

This spectrum describes the full range of options available to social entrepreneurs, from purely philanthropic to purely commercial, with many variations in between. Philanthropic methods are involved anytime an organization falls short of the far right side on at least one dimension of the spectrum, indicating some form of subsidy or sacrifice. Excluding purely philanthropic or purely commercial ventures is not a major sacrifice in scope because very few social-purpose organizations exist at either extreme (Dees and Anderson, 2006).

Ultimately, the selection of a business model should be made upon careful reflection on the following questions:

- Does the business model use resources efficiently and effectively?
- Will it attract sufficient resources to achieve the intended social impact?

- How well does it fit with the ecosystems in which you want to operate?
- Is it sufficiently robust and scalable?
- Are the incentives in the business model aligned with your theory of change?

It is important to note that no single business model is best for all social entrepreneurs in all settings. Potential trade-offs and risks have to be assessed on a case-by-case basis, and the operating model may need to be adjusted accordingly. However, designing an effective business model is an essential part of the creative learning process of crafting, testing, and refining the hypotheses and assumptions inherent in the social entrepreneur's theory of change. This process of learning and refinement should continue well after the launch of the venture as the social entrepreneur gains experience and as the venture is affected by changes in the ecosystem in which it operates.

Ecosystem (or Operating Environment)

Drawing on the science of biology, scholars of strategy and management have begun to study and apply ecosystems theory to reveal lessons for business and entrepreneurship. So, too, social entrepreneurs hoping to create significant and sustainable social impact should also develop an understanding of, and may endeavor to alter, the broad environment in which they operate. This is true especially if they seek to leverage complex systems of interacting players in rapidly evolving political, economic, physical, and cultural environments. Indeed, changes in these conditions may determine whether and when a window of opportunity is open or closed to the social entrepreneur.

Ecosystem Players. Just as biological ecosystems are made up of complex webs of interrelated organisms, social ecosystems operate in much the same way. Social entrepreneurs get help from some individuals and organizations, give help to others, fend off threats from others, and compete with still others. To assist social entrepreneurs in identifying and mapping all of the relevant ecosystem players and the roles that they play, Bloom and Dees (2008) recommend dividing the players into six roles:

- *Resource providers,* including providers of financial, human, knowledge, networking, and technological resources, and any brokers or intermediaries that channel these resources to those who want them. Resource provides may include third-party payers, donors, volunteers, and workers, anyone who must voluntarily participate in the venture in order for it to be successful.

Social entrepreneurs must have a plausible value proposition for each group of resource provider.

- *Competitors*, including organizations that compete with the social entrepreneur's organization for resources as well as those that compete to serve the same beneficiaries.
- *Complementary organizations and allies*, including organizations or individuals who facilitate a social entrepreneur's ability to create impact, such as partners who perform critical steps in the social entrepreneur's theory of change, individuals and organizations supporting the same cause, and those providing important complementary services.
- *Beneficiaries and customers*, including clients, patients, customers, and others who benefit from social entrepreneurs' activities, whether or not the ultimate beneficiaries interact directly with the organization.
- *Opponents and problem makers*, including organizations and individuals who contribute to the problems social entrepreneurs are addressing, undermine the ability of the organizations to achieve and sustain their intended impact, or oppose their efforts politically.
- *Affected or influential bystanders*, including players who have no direct impact now, but who are affected by the social entrepreneur's efforts—especially those who could be harmed if the social entrepreneur succeeds and those who can be turned into allies or resource providers if convinced of the benefits of the social entrepreneur's efforts—or those who could influence her success, either positively or negative, such as members of the media.

Bloom and Dees note that these categories of ecosystem players are dynamic and not mutually exclusive (2008). Organizations may play more than one role or may switch over time; paradoxically, the same organization can be both an ally (for example, when it comes to advocating for legislation to serve the same cause) yet also a competitor (for example, when vying for limited funding). As in for-profit industries, new players may enter the ecosystem at any time, posing new threats or presenting opportunities for the social entrepreneur and her venture to benefit.

Environmental Conditions. Biological ecosystems are made up not only of other organisms, but also of environmental conditions (such as soil, weather, sunlight, and water) that have a significant impact on the type of organisms that can exist, as well as on their relationships with one another. So, too, with social ecosystems, although organizations and people can, in turn, influence the environmental conditions and bring about change within the social ecosystems of which they are a part. To aid social entrepreneurs in identifying relevant changes or trends that can influence their ability to create and sustain the intended social impact, Bloom and Dees (2008) identify four sets of environmental conditions that should be considered by the social entrepreneur:

- *Politics and administrative structures*, including rules and regulations—and the processes and procedures for adopting, enforcing, and reforming these rules—along with the political dynamics of the jurisdictions in which social entrepreneurs operate, including potential sources of public support or resistance.
- *Economics and markets*, including the overall economic health of the regions in which social entrepreneurs operate and seek resources, as well as the region's distribution of wealth and income, economic prospects, levels of entrepreneurial activity, and relevant markets.
- *Geography and infrastructure*, including not only the physical terrain and location, but also the infrastructure that social entrepreneurs count on for transportation, communication, and other operating needs.
- *Culture and social fabric*, including the norms and values, important subgroups, social networks, and demographic trends of the people living in the area. For example, many microfinance institutions and global health initiatives target women in hopes of achieving greater social and economic impact for the women and their families. However, local cultural norms about the role of women in the economy may pose significant challenges and present promising opportunities for the social entrepreneur.

Mapping the Ecosystem. Although the relevant features of the ecosystem will vary from venture to venture and will depend on the specifics of the venture idea, including the theory of change and the business model, most social entrepreneurs will make crucial assumptions about their markets, the industry structure, the political environment, and the culture. In studying and making assumptions about the ecosystem in which they operate, social entrepreneurs may choose to construct a simplified ecosystem map illustrating the key ecosystem players and environmental conditions, noting key relationships and trends, and anticipating potential changes that may positively or negatively affect their ability to achieve the desired social impact. Mapping the ecosystem in this way is a dynamic process that may yield significant strategic insights (Bloom and Dees, 2008).

In summary, an ecosystems framework can help social entrepreneurs in many ways, including:

- Imparting a deeper understanding of an organization's theory of change by making the environmental conditions and relationships on which the organization depends more visible, possibly leading to a revision of that theory

- Mapping the resource flows into and within the ecosystem, revealing constraints, bottlenecks, and underused sources, perhaps suggesting alternative resource strategies for the organization
- Identifying new operating partnerships, perhaps with complementary organizations, that fall short of systemic change but that promise to enhance the social entrepreneurs' impact by increasing the coordination of otherwise independent players
- Determining the minimum critical environmental conditions required for an organization's operating model to be successful and using that information to guide the social entrepreneur's efforts to take the model into new areas
- Developing different operating models for different ecosystems, or a more robust operating model that works in a variety of different ecosystems (Bloom and Dees, 2008, p. 53)

As social entrepreneurs flesh out the three core elements of their opportunities, they will inevitably make assumptions about their ecosystem or operating environment. The potential success of the venture depends largely on whether the assumptions accurately represent the context. Thus, a promising opportunity must fit with the characteristics of its environment. However, in the social sector as in the business world, windows of opportunity may close as quickly as they open.

Windows of Opportunity. Since ecosystems are dynamic, it is also helpful for social entrepreneurs to be sensitive to the window of opportunity, the time frame in which conditions are expected to be favorable for pursuing a given opportunity. In studying the conditions necessary for social entrepreneurship, respected nonprofit scholar Paul Light has asserted that such windows of opportunity are rare, cannot be predicted, tend to occur in great punctuations when the demand for change reaches a tipping point, emerge when entry costs are low, open and close quickly, favor competition over collaboration, and appear to the special few (Light, 2008, p. 203).

Social entrepreneurs may have better chances of success if they can take advantage of windows that are opening and that will stay open long enough for the venture to have its intended impact. Changes in the ecosystem or other external conditions may increase or decrease receptivity to new ideas, or may affect the viability of a proposed business model, thus opening or closing the window of opportunity. Such changes include the growth or decline of the social need being addressed, the number of people affected by the need, the visibility of the need and expected media coverage, perceptions of urgency or relative importance by key resource providers, levels of satisfaction with existing approaches, technological changes, changes in public policy, and popular trends or fashions in relevant fields (Guclu, Dees, and Anderson, 2002).

Personal Fit. As social entrepreneurs develop their ideas into worthwhile opportunities, they also have to be sensitive to personal fit. Even if they have identified an attractive opportunity, it may not be a good opportunity for them when assessed in relation to other options. Before seeking to launch a social venture, aspiring social entrepreneurs should conduct an honest self-assessment, asking themselves:

- Do I have the time, energy, fortitude, commitment, and determination required to coordinate ambitious social impact goals with scarce income sources and to satisfy excess need for services with an over-stretched staff and limited time?
- Do I have healthy support systems and strong personal and professional networks that can help me forestall and/or handle the burnout that not infrequently accompanies launching and managing an entrepreneurial venture?[3]
- Do I have the skills, expertise, credibility, credentials, contacts, and assets needed to launch this venture? Can I attract a strong team to help compensate for any critical shortcomings?
- Is this the right time in my life to pursue this kind of opportunity? Are there career and family or other personal considerations that must be taken into account?

New ventures of any sort are tremendously demanding. Social ventures are even more so. Ultimately, aspiring social entrepreneurs would be wise to pursue only opportunities that fit their personal commitment, qualifications, income requirements, and stage in life, embarking on their entrepreneurial journey with full awareness of the risks involved.

Step 2 Summary. In order to determine whether a promising idea can be transformed into an opportunity worthy of serious pursuit, it is essential for the social entrepreneur to articulate a compelling theory of change and a plausible business model. Developing a plausible business model requires designing an effective operating model and crafting a viable resource strategy. These pieces must fit together, and the assumptions embedded in them must be credible given the environment in which the social entrepreneur intends to operate. Finally, the requirements of the venture must fit the commitment, qualifications, and life stage of the entrepreneur considering it. When all these elements are feasible and aligned, the chances for success are relatively high and those involved can make a more informed estimate of the potential for social impact.

Strengthening the "Ecosystem" of Social Entrepreneurship

With the support of the Skoll Foundation, the Center for the Advancement of Social Entrepreneurship (CASE) at Duke University launched a groundbreaking project to identify opportunities for further building the field of social entrepreneurship, both as a field of practice and as a field of inquiry, knowledge, and learning related to that practice. The CASE team conducted in-depth interviews with eighty-five social entrepreneurs, funders, academics, consultants, journalists and authors, and others knowledgeable about the field. As a result of this study, CASE recommended a set of critical initiatives for strengthening the ecosystem in which the practice of social entrepreneurship takes place (CASE at Duke, 2008). By the term *ecosystem* at the field-wide level, we refer to the key resource providers and environmental factors that affect the ability of social entrepreneurs to achieve their intended social impacts.

To inform its research, CASE developed a simplified framework to describe the key elements of this ecosystem. Figure 11.5 presents this framework, illustrating the richness and complexity of the environment in which social entrepreneurs operate and the various determinants of their effectiveness.

The elements of the ecosystem are presented in two broad categories. The first category consists of the resources, or types of "capital," social entrepreneurs depend on to do their work, including financial capital, human capital, intellectual capital, and social/political capital. Although social entrepreneurs can, to some extent, develop these forms of capital through their operations, most social entrepreneurs rely on outside organizations to help them get or build the capital they need. Note that these subcategories are broadly defined, including capital creators, providers, and related intermediaries. The second broad category includes the context-setting factors, or external conditions, that could support or undermine the practice of social entrepreneurship. These conditions are divided into four subcategories: policy and politics, media, economic and social conditions, and related fields. These factors tend to have their influence indirectly, and they are highly diverse. Each of these factors has the potential to affect social entrepreneurs, various players in the capital infrastructure, and the other context-setting factors.

FIGURE 11.5. Ecosystem of Social Entrepreneurship

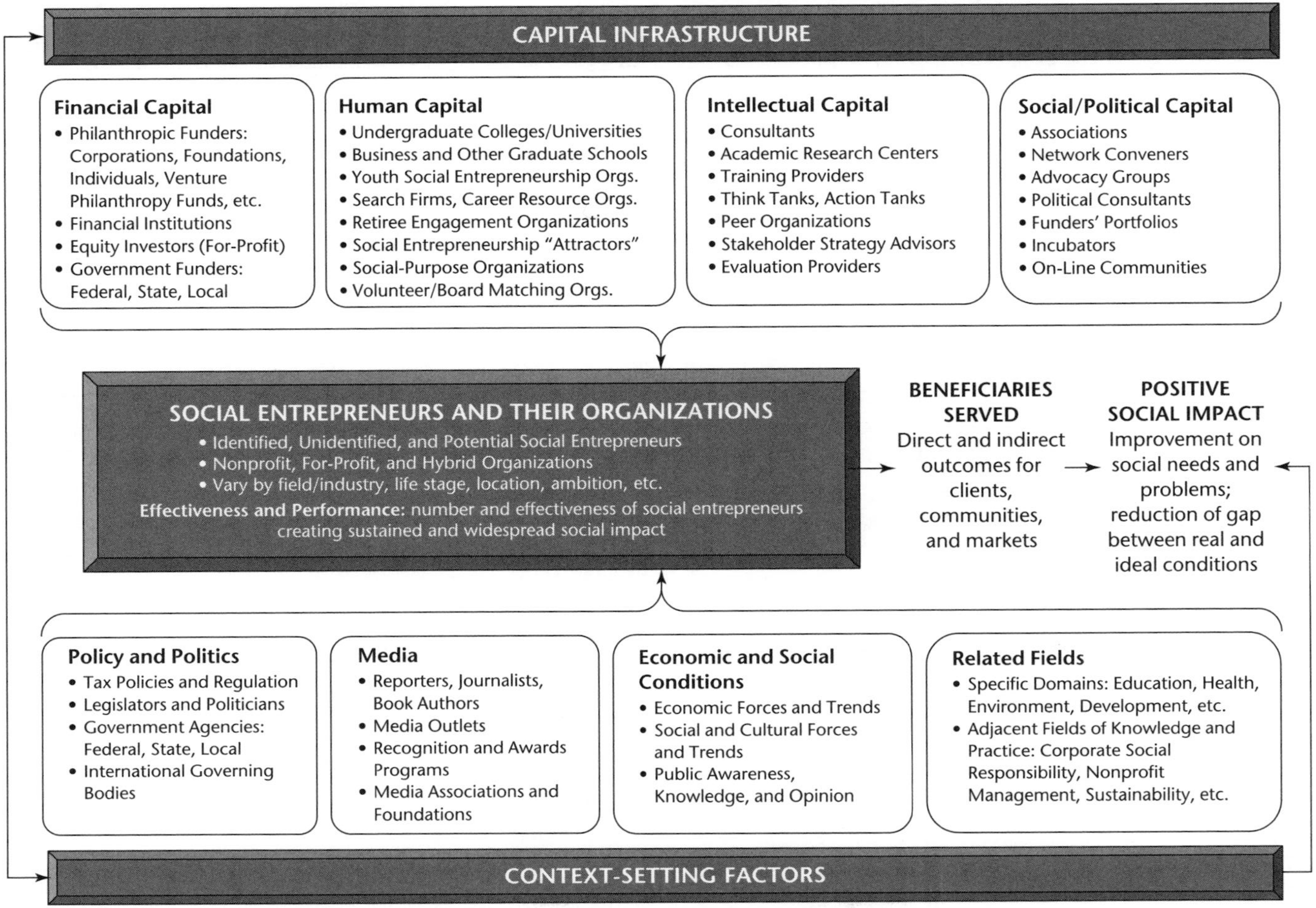

Source: Center for the Advancement of Social Entrepreneurship, Duke University, 2008. Reprinted with permission.

Finding Key Leverage Points in the Ecosystem

During the CASE field-building study, nearly all interviewees identified inefficiencies and obstacles in the ecosystem and discussed how these might be remedied so that the potential of social entrepreneurship may be more fully realized. While all agreed that serious challenges exist for those who want to improve the ecosystem, most interviewees felt optimistic that these challenges could be met with creative solutions, dedicated attention, and increased collaboration. Based largely on suggestions made by participants in the field research, the CASE team identified five potential leverage points that are particularly crucial to address in order for the field to advance, and offered suggestions for moving forward on each of them.

Making Financial Markets More Efficient and Responsive

In almost every interview for the CASE field-building study, participants identified the financial markets as a critical challenge for the field, agreeing that social sector capital markets are deficient in many ways. Funding is insufficient, especially to achieve scale, and the funding that is available often does not flow to its best uses (that is, the highest social return relative to the risk). Funders often do not know which use will produce the greatest benefits, and they seem to make their decisions based on factors that are not clearly related to performance. The financial markets for social ventures are full of inefficiencies. The search costs—the time and energy it takes to make the right match between social entrepreneurs and financiers—are high. The financial products, services, and terms of engagement often do not fit the needs of social entrepreneurs at different stages of development, or they impose burdensome conditions on the social entrepreneurs. Overall, social financial markets tend to be fragmented (often around different causes or interests), disjointed (different funders with different standards and requirements), and relatively small (compared to mainstream capital markets).

Those who want to strengthen the ecosystem for social entrepreneurs should consider doing or supporting the following:

- Develop specialized financial intermediaries who have the expertise to make sound funding decisions and the marketing skill to attract funding
- Create new financial "instruments" or "deal structures" designed to address the different kinds of business models and different stages of development

- Support high-quality, independent "analysts" to assess social ventures and provide platforms to distribute their reports to funders who would find them useful
- Experiment with more collaborative funding models in which major funders invest in each other's "deals," sharing the risks and the lessons
- Work toward common grant applications, requests for proposals, and reporting requirements for foundation funding
- Establish standardized tools for social entrepreneurs to track the information that would be relevant to funders
- Organize online information marketplaces to make it easier for social entrepreneurs and suitable funders to find each other more easily

Refining and Standardizing Performance Measurement Tools

Reliable, timely, and cost-effective measures of social value are crucial for demonstrating success, providing better information to the financial markets, and informing the strategic decisions of social entrepreneurs. Yet, social value is notoriously difficult to measure and to attribute to a specific intervention and many of the most important ways in which social entrepreneurs can make the world a better place are long-term, intangible, qualitative, not easily reduced to any single common metric. Funders, who have a crucial role in developing suitable systems and standards, and others seeking to drive progress in this area, may consider the following suggestions:

- Make social entrepreneurs aware of the different tools currently available, as well as the pros and cons of each.
- Encourage use of and continued experimentation with impact-oriented performance measures by social entrepreneurs, making sure to include qualitative elements as well as signs, symptoms, and indicators of intangible and long-term impact.
- Favor measurement systems that produce information that is valued by and useful to social entrepreneurs (usually including process measures as well as outcome measures for learning purposes).
- Distinguish what is publicly reported from what is available for internal, managerial use.
- Reward candor, learning, and informed strategic adjustments, not just raw outcome performance.
- Avoid the situation in which different funders impose significantly different and demanding measurement methodologies on a single organization.

- Use intermediaries to design and implement external reporting standards in a way that provides the information that capital providers want in forms that are meaningful and engaging.
- Make the values and assumptions behind any measurement scheme transparent and open to challenge.
- Recognize that judgment is required and make sure performance data are accompanied by information that helps users make sensible judgments and comparisons.

Helping Social Entrepreneurs Find Effective Pathways to Scale

In the CASE field research, nearly all interviewees seemed to agree that success for this field requires that social entrepreneurs ultimately achieve significant "scale" relative to the magnitude of the problems they are tackling. The successful spread of innovations and the growth of social ventures in the past indicates that it is possible to achieve considerable impact, even in this flawed ecosystem. Proponents need to help social entrepreneurs find viable paths to scale and widespread impact.

Those who wish to improve the ability of social entrepreneurs to scale may want to:

- Identify and document successful paths to achieving scale in an imperfect world, analyzing success stories and drawing on the best strategic thinking.
- Encourage innovation in the scaling process and capture the lessons from the experiments.
- Recognize that no one path fits all social ventures—each strategy needs to be designed for the circumstances at hand.
- Provide social entrepreneurs and their teams with knowledge about different scaling strategies, frameworks for designing their own, and opportunities for learning with and from others struggling with the same issues.
- Capture and share lessons learned along the way.
- Refrain from overemphasizing the need to scale quickly, which may result in premature efforts to scale.
- Acknowledge that not every "successful" local innovation or venture is scalable or worthy of scaling.
- Acknowledge that the role of the founding social entrepreneur may change through the scaling process and that other talented individuals may be needed to play a leading role.

Building New Talent Pipelines

In the business world, it is widely recognized that talent is the key to success. Venture capitalists know the importance of investing in high performing management teams. Business leaders see themselves in a "battle for talent." Human capital is no less important for the success of social entrepreneurs. The ecosystem needs new talent pipelines and development programs to prepare social entrepreneurs and their teams for the challenges of sustainability, scale, and the creation of new equilibria. Those who want to strengthen this part of the ecosystem should consider the following:

- Invest in programs that increase "hybrid" management and leadership skills, particularly those that address the needs of social entrepreneurs to scale their impact and sustain their ventures.
- Support team-building efforts and educational programs that work with teams, rather than just individuals.
- Facilitate peer learning, not only among social entrepreneurs, but also among members of the senior teams working with the social entrepreneurs.
- Explore emerging talent pools such as those embarking on second careers.
- Experiment with new approaches to draw on motivated talent from the business sector, adapt it to the needs of social entrepreneurs, and use it to develop internal capabilities.
- Find ways to reward talented people who work in this field, through reasonable compensation and attractive (but rarely offered) benefits, such as pensions, health care, insurance, training, and paid sabbaticals.
- Encourage suitable undergraduate and graduate programs (in business, public policy, education, social work, public health, environment, and engineering schools, or others) to offer tracks that make it possible for students to develop hybrid skills.

Providing Better Guidance on Effective Business Models

Social entrepreneurs will be successful only if their innovations are supported by sufficiently sustainable, scalable, and aligned business models. Greater attention to business model design could also force social entrepreneurs to think about how to mobilize the talent and knowledge they need on favorable and sustainable terms, perhaps through partnerships. Proponents of social entrepreneurship who want to strengthen the field should consider taking the following steps to strengthen social entrepreneurs' ability to develop robust and effective business models:

- Recognize that no single business model will work for all social entrepreneurs and that models drawn from the world of business may not be appropriate.
- Support research efforts to develop better knowledge of alternative business models for social entrepreneurs and to frame some design principles.
- Encourage experimentation with different business models, capturing the lessons from the experiments.
- Provide strategic assistance to social entrepreneurs who have attractive innovations but business models that limit their potential in serious ways.
- Develop funding schemes for foundations and social investors that encourage resource-smart business model redesign and help recipients make the transition to the new business models.

These five issues—financial markets, performance measurement, scaling strategies, talent development, and business models—emerged as priorities as the CASE team analyzed the data from interviews and conversations. Addressing these issues could go a long way toward strengthening the ecosystem, assuring greater success of social entrepreneurs, and building the field.

Ecosystem Summary: Providing Support with Discipline

It is essential to create a supportive ecosystem for social entrepreneurs if the field is to thrive. By contrast, business entrepreneurs benefit from a very supportive ecosystem, particularly in the United States. Yet there is an important difference between business entrepreneurship and social entrepreneurship that should not be neglected—business entrepreneurs face significant market discipline from both customer markets and financial markets. Customers determine whether the good or service provided creates more value for them than it costs to produce. Investors determine whether the venture is likely to provide sufficient returns to justify their investments. For social entrepreneurs, the ultimate test is social impact, and that value is not guaranteed by market discipline. We need other mechanisms.

If the ecosystem is to do its job of enhancing chances of success for the field as a whole, we must mimic this kind of market discipline, using the best measures and judgments available at the time. We need to create a healthy, vibrant ecosystem that supports innovative social entrepreneurs, but with appropriate discipline to assure that capital is directed to its best uses. Without some devices to filter out the underperformers, scarce forms of capital and other support will be spread among those who put it to good use and those who do not. Fortunately, a number of innovative and exciting efforts are under way to address these issues. Many in this field cautiously hope that the coming years will bring about significant advances in the development of the field of social entrepreneurship. These advances could have a beneficial impact on the social sector as a whole.

Conclusion

"New concepts are introduced all the time. Some never catch on. Others experience great popularity for a period, but then decline and are viewed as passing fads. A few concepts have staying power and sustained impact. In rare cases, a new concept serves as a foundation for a whole new field of practice and knowledge. Social entrepreneurship has the potential to be one of those rare field-creating concepts" (CASE at Duke, 2008, p. v).

As elaborated in this chapter, social entrepreneurship is about crafting innovative and sustainable solutions to social problems. Fundamentally, effective social entrepreneurship is a learning process that combines a valid theory of change with a supportive business model. Social entrepreneurs are innovative, resourceful, and results-oriented. They draw upon the best thinking in both the business and nonprofit worlds to develop strategies that maximize their social impact. These entrepreneurial leaders operate across a broad spectrum of organizations: large and small; new and old; nonprofit, for-profit, and hybrid.

We are at an undeniably exciting time for the field of social entrepreneurship. Having experienced dramatic growth in recent years, social entrepreneurship has attracted strong interest from policymakers, philanthropists, aid agencies, and academics, despite the fact that it is still being developed and researched. However, many thoughtful observers, including advocates, are concerned that the recent momentum could fade or be undermined before a solid foundation is laid for the future of this emerging field. As described earlier, success for the field will require a healthy institutional and social environment to support the practice. We refer to this as the "ecosystem of social entrepreneurship." Indeed, a vibrant ecosystem that supports innovative social entrepreneurs, but with appropriate discipline to assure that capital is directed to its best uses, could have a beneficial impact on the social sector as a whole.

Notes

1. We accept as the definition of corporate social entrepreneurship "the process of extending the firm's domain of competence and corresponding opportunity set through innovative leveraging of resources, both within and outside its direct control, aimed at the simultaneous creation of economic and social value" (Austin, Leonard, Reficco, and Wei-Skillern, 2006).

2. For the purpose of this chapter, we have adopted the definition of "social enterprise" advanced by Kim Alter: "a socially oriented venture (nonprofit/for-profit or hybrid) created to solve a social problem or market failure through entrepreneurial private sector approaches that increase effectiveness and sustainability while ultimately creating social benefit or change" (Alter, 2005).

3. For an insightful discussion on building strong support networks, see Gergen and Vanourek, 2008, pp. 111–128. The authors draw upon extensive interviews of successful business entrepreneurs and social entrepreneurs.

References

Alter, K. Social Enterprise Definition. Washington, DC: Virtue Ventures, 2005.

Austin, J., Leonard, H., Reficco E., and Wei-Skillern, J. Social Entrepreneurship: It Is for Corporations, Too. In A. Nicholls (ed.), *Social Entrepreneurship: New Models of Sustainable Social Change*. New York: Oxford University Press, 2006.

Bhide, A. V. *The Origin and Evolution of New Business Ventures*. New York: Oxford University Press, 2000.

Bloom, P. N., and Dees, J. G. Cultivate Your Ecosystem. *Stanford Social Innovation Review*, 2008, Winter, 6(1), 46–53.

Bornstein, D. *How to Change the World: Social Entrepreneurs and the Power of New Ideas*. New York: Oxford University Press, 2004.

Byker, C., Stuart, C., Cohen, B., et al. (producers). *The New Heroes*. Video series. Portland, OR: Oregon Public Broadcasting, 2005.

Campbell, K., and Haley, B. Business Planning for Nonprofits: What It Is and Why It Matters. Boston, MA: The Bridgespan Group, 2006.

CASE at Duke. Developing the Field of Social Entrepreneurship. Durham, NC: Center for the Advancement of Social Entrepreneurship, Duke University, the Fuqua School of Business, 2008.

Center for the Advancement of Social Entrepreneurship (CASE). Developing the Field of Social Entrepreneurship: A Report from the Center for the Advancement of Social Entrepreneurship (CASE), Duke University, the Fuqua School of Business. Durham, North Carolina: Duke University. June 2008. p. 14.

Chesbrough, H. M., Ahern, S., Finn, M., and Guerraz, S. Business Models for Technology in the Developing World: The Role of Non-Governmental Organizations. *California Management Review*, 2006, 48(3).

Dees, J. G. *The Social Enterprise Spectrum: Philanthropy to Commerce*. Boston: Harvard Business School Publishing, Case # 9–396–343, 1996.

Dees, J. G. *The Meaning of Social Entrepreneurship*. Self-published essay. Revised May 2001. Available at www.caseatduke.org/documents/dees_sedef.pdf.

Dees, J. G. Taking Social Entrepreneurship Seriously. *Society*, 2007, 44(3), 24–31.

Dees, J. G., and Anderson, B. B. For-Profit Social Ventures. In M. L. Kourilsky and W. B. Walstad (eds.), *Social Entrepreneurship*. Dublin, Ireland: Senate Hall Academic Publishing. A special issue of the *International Journal of Entrepreneurship Education*, 2, 1–26, 2003.

Dees, J. G., and Anderson, B. B. Framing a Theory of Social Entrepreneurship: Building on Two Schools of Practice and Thought. In R. Mosher-Williams (ed.), *Research on Social Entrepreneurship: Understanding and Contributing to an Emerging Field*. Indianapolis, IN: Association for Research on Nonprofit Organizations and Voluntary Action, ARNOVA Occasional Paper Series, 2006, 1(3), 41.

Drayton, W., and MacDonald, S. *Leading Public Entrepreneurs*. Arlington, VA: Ashoka: Innovators for the Public, 1993.

Drucker, P. *Innovation and Entrepreneurship*. New York: Harper & Row, 1985.

Elkington, J., and Hartigan, P. *The Power of Unreasonable People: How Social Entrepreneurs Create Markets That Change the World*. Boston, MA: Harvard Business Press, 2008.

Gergen, C., and Vanourek, G. *Life Entrepreneurs: Ordinary People Leading Extraordinary Lives*. San Francisco: Jossey-Bass, 2008.

Guclu, A., Dees, J. G., and Anderson, B. B. The Process of Social Entrepreneurship: Creating Opportunities Worthy of Serious Pursuit. Center for the Advancement of Social Entrepreneurship, Duke University, the Fuqua School of Business, 2002.

Grossman, A., and Curran, D. F. quoting Peter Szanton in, *EMCF: A New Approach at an Old Foundation*. Boston: Harvard Business School Publishing, Case # 9–302–090, 1990, p. 4.

Leviner, N., Crutchfield, L., and Wells, D. Understanding the Impact of Social Entrepreneurs: Ashoka's Answer to the Challenge of Measuring Effectiveness." In R. Mosher-Williams (ed.), *Research on Social Entrepreneurship: Understanding and Contributing to an Emerging Field*. Indianapolis, IN: Association for Research on Nonprofit Organizations and Voluntary Action, ARNOVA Occasional Paper Series, 2006, 1(3), 93.

Light, P. *The Search for Social Entrepreneurship*. Washington, DC: Brookings Institution Press, 2008.

Martin, R., and Osberg, S. Social Entrepreneurship: The Case for Definition. *Stanford Social Innovation Review*, 2007, Spring, 29–39.

McGrath, R., and MacMillan, I. Discovery-Driven Planning. *Harvard Business Review*, 1995, July-August.

Porter, M. E. *Competitive Advantage: Creating and Sustaining Superior Performance*. New York: The Free Press, 1985.

Say, J. B. (1803). Traité d'économie politique, ou simple exposition de la manière dont se forment, se distribuent et se consomment les richesses (1st ed., 1803, Paris: Deterville).

Schumpeter, J. A. *The Theory of Economic Development: An Inquiry into Profits, Capital, Credit, Interest, and the Business Cycle* (trans. by Redvers Opie). Cambridge, MA: Harvard University Press, 1934.

Stevenson, H. H., & Gumpert, D. E. The Heart of Entrepreneurship. *Harvard Business Review*, 1985, 63(2), 85–95.

Vesper, K. New Venture Ideas: Do Not Overlook the Experience Factor. *Harvard Business Review*, 1979, December, 57.

CHAPTER TWELVE

SOCIAL ENTERPRISE AND NONPROFIT VENTURES

Scott T. Helm

Interest in social enterprise has grown substantially since 2010, in the United States and around the world. Books on the topic are seemingly infinite in number, and their topics range from social enterprise and construction (such as Loosemore and Higgon, 2015) to social impact measurement (for example, Patton, 2003) to an exceptional range of "how-to" books (such as Social Enterprise Alliance, 2010). The attention to social enterprise has developed as part of the larger interest in the overall phenomenon of social entrepreneurship (for example, Nash, 2010) and reflects the interaction of several significant forces and challenges. Central is the impact of the growing competition for limited funding from both governmental and philanthropic sources, and, as Nash describes, the search for alternative sources of revenue has encouraged a growing number of nonprofits to "explore market-driven approaches and experiment with practices drawn from the business sector, including the launch of earned-revenue ventures, both mission-related social enterprises and unrelated businesses" (2010, p. 264). Similarly, Lester Salamon (2010, p. 91) has observed that one of the drivers of growth of the U.S. nonprofit sector has been "the vigor with which nonprofit America embraced the spirit and the techniques of the market." He suggests that a clear indication of the success of this approach is the substantial rise in non-profit income from fees and charges, which he characterizes as "indicative of the success with which nonprofit organizations succeeded in marketing their services to a clientele increasingly able to afford them" (Salamon, 2010). Social enterprise continues to grow in practice, even as its legitimacy is challenged by some, and it promises to play a significant role in the 21st Century nonprofit sector.*

Many nonprofits generate significant commercial revenues in the course of their everyday activities. Salamon reports "fees and charges accounted for nearly half (about 47 percent) of the growth in nonprofit revenue between 1977 and 1997—more than any other source." McGeever and Pettijohn (2014) report that health care organizations and educational institutions, the two largest income-generating nonprofit classifications, comprise 30 percent of all public charities yet account for 70.5 percent of public charity revenue. They also report that more than 73 percent of all public charity revenue was generated from fees-for-service or government contracts.

A related trend among nonprofit organizations is the growth in unrelated business income. Unrelated business income refers to income generated from any nonprofit business activity that is outside the scope of the charitable purpose for which the organization received its tax-exempt status. Unrelated business income is reported separately and, because it is generated from activity outside the scope of the organization's tax-exempt mission, it is subject to income tax (and social enterprises that involve unrelated business fall in this category, too). According to the U.S. Internal Revenue Service (IRS), the number of nonprofits filing unrelated business income tax (UBIT) returns increased 59 percent between 1990 and 2011. Further, the amount of unrelated business income reported over the same period increased 187 percent (IRS, 2015). This growth is especially interesting in light of the fact that U.S. nonprofit law limits the amount of unrelated business income that a nonprofit may generate without jeopardizing its tax exempt status.

As the statistics illustrate, the lure of social enterprise can be very enticing to nonprofit leaders. In times of economic stress, such as that experienced by many parts of the nonprofit sector from 2008 until recently, the development of a social enterprise can appear to be a panacea. Especially to a financially desperate non-profit leader, social enterprise may seem to be a sure-fire way to stabilize financials and maintain programming. Unfortunately, nonprofit leaders past and present can tell many tales of ill-conceived enterprises that exhausted already-limited funds. Foster and Bradach, for example, tell the story of a nonprofit organization that decided to make and sell salad dressing (2005). The intent was to develop revenues that could subsidize the nonprofit's mission-relevant operations.

---

* Consistent with the definitions of Nash (2010), "social enterprise" and "social entrepreneurship" are *not* used as synonymous terms in this chapter.

However, a failure to recognize or account for indirect costs and an inaccurate assessment of direct costs led the organization to severely underestimate total costs of salad dressing production. Using the inaccurate numbers, the organization set the price for the dressing with the expectation that each bottle of salad dressing would earn $0.35—a nice profit for the organization. In fact, their later assessment determined each bottle cost the organization approximately $86.50 to produce—a terrible and dramatic loss! Not every case of financial failure is this dramatic, yet such mistakes illustrate the need for nonprofits to fully understand the implications (financial and otherwise) of operating social enterprises. This is especially true when the social enterprise is expected to be a profit generator.

Horror stories notwithstanding, many nonprofits have generated significant benefits from their enterprise activities. Consider, for example, Support Kansas City, which is regionally recognized as a successful enterprising nonprofit organization. Originally fostered into existence by Bank of America, Support Kansas City provides back office solutions for small- to medium-sized nonprofits in the Greater Kansas City community. Recognizing that many nonprofit organizations with excellent client services lacked necessary capacity in accounting, Bank of America created this support organization to bolster area nonprofits by allowing them to focus on meeting mission. The design of the new organization would bring together financial management expertise akin to a for-profit accounting firm with a price structure that would be affordable for nonprofit organizations. Since their inception in 2001, Support Kansas City has added technology support, fundraising strategy support and strategic management support. In 2014, this suite of services generated almost 84 percent of all of the organization's revenue.

The purpose of this chapter is not to promote or discourage the use of social enterprise strategies but to provide nonprofit leaders with a broader understanding of the issues and opportunities associated with social enterprise and help them prepare to examine them. Rather than duplicate the content of the many existing "How-to" volumes on social enterprise, this chapter is designed to serve as an orientation to help nonprofit leaders make sense of key elements of the overwhelming volume of literature on the topic and understand key concepts that will be important to consider as they explore options for enterprise development. I encourage every nonprofit leader considering social enterprise options to discuss the relevant issues identified in this chapter with their board and executive colleagues and collaborators. This *Handbook*'s Internet resource site includes a number of tools and resources that may be helpful to nonprofit leaders as they facilitate such conversations and weigh their options. Many of the important elements of the social enterprise development process fall under the bailiwick of other chapters in this *Handbook*, and it will be important to link the insights of this chapter with the discipline-specific methods and tools presented in the associated chapters (e.g., Chapter Nine for further information on the strategy and planning process, and Chapter Thirteen for specific information about market research and planning).

Social enterprises develop within the larger context of the nonprofit organization and even the nonprofit sector, and this context differs from region to region of the world. Therefore, I begin this chapter with a brief discussion of the cultural context of social enterprise. Culture shapes and influences the ways we perceive and understand the value of a strategy such as pursuit of social enterprise. Next, I address the questions: Who should launch a social enterprise? What are the implications of this choice? I describe knowledge acquisition and resources likely to be useful in the process of enterprise development. I then discuss who ventures into social enterprises, and the options that exist for engaging in a social enterprise. Finally, I discuss planning, the planning process, and the relationship between planning and social enterprise.

Culture and the Context of Social Enterprise

Analysis of social enterprise in 2016 is a global pursuit. The abundance of non-profit (and more important for our discussion) social enterprise activity worldwide provides important insights into the role that culture and national context play in the creation of various forms of nonprofit enterprise. This is illustrated by the variation in the types of social enterprises described in the European literature versus those described in the American literature. There are several differences of interest and relevance and, taken together, they offer important insights into the reasons and ways that such enterprises develop and function.

Generally speaking, European scholarship describes social enterprise as it develops in the context of a strong welfare state. A 2014 study underwritten by the European Commission sought to provide the first continental mapping of social enterprises in twenty-nine countries (Wilkinson, Medhurst, Henry, Wihlborg, and Braithwaite, 2014). The study defined social enterprises by the following characteristics:

1. The organization must engage in economic activity: this means that it must engage in a continuous activity of production and/or exchange of goods and/or services;
2. It must pursue an explicit and primary social aim: a social aim is one that benefits society;

3. It must have limits on distribution of profits and/or assets: the purpose of such limits is to prioritize the social aim over profit making;
4. It must be independent, that is, organizational autonomy from the state and other traditional for-profit organizations, and
5. It must have inclusive governance (that is, characterized by participatory and/ or democratic decision-making processes).

U.S. social enterprises, which develop in the context of capitalism, differ in some relatively significant ways. Typically, U.S. social enterprise exhibits the following characteristics:

1. Social enterprise is a strategy, not an organization category.
2. It comprises both for-profit and nonprofit organizational forms (Dart, 2004).
3. It focuses on revenue generation as well as social benefit (LeRoux, 2005).
4. It operates in many different service niches or "industries" (Kerlin, 2006).
5. It is privately funded (Kerlin, 2006).

This chapter focuses on U.S. social enterprises and, as such, the reader will note a strong emphasis on the purpose of commercial revenue generation. Equally important from this perspective is that social enterprises are often funded privately (that is, by foundations, individuals, nonprofit lenders, and banks). Both of these have important implications for how U.S. social enterprises are planned and implemented.

Who Should Establish a Social Enterprise?

Unlike Hamlet's quandary "To be or not to be, that is the question," the decision to establish a social enterprise venture is less existential and more pragmatic. As noted earlier, in many European countries social enterprise is a special class of organization designed to serve particular purposes; in the United States it is a strategy. Therefore, in the United States, the choice to operate a social enterprise (like any strategy choice) is available to any nonprofit organization regardless of its particular mission niche.

Social enterprise may be an option to any nonprofit, yet that does not mean every nonprofit should launch a commercial venture. Then how should a nonprofit begin to decide? The answer to this question requires significant deliberation, particularly regarding four core areas of deliberation:

- Mission impact and relevance
- Characteristics of the nonprofit's operating environment

- Financial and revenue implications
- Organizational capacity to implement the enterprise

Each of these four areas offers a different and complementary lens through which to examine your enterprise's possibilities.

At the core, it is essential to have clarity regarding who you are as an organization and how a potential enterprise strategy might relate to this. Typically, when asked to define their organization, nonprofit leaders will recite their mission. Mission is important, so this is an important starting point, but I would assert that mission only begins to describe the true nature of a nonprofit. Equally important is the unique value a nonprofit provides for the community. In what ways might a potential enterprise be relevant to mission? Will the potential enterprise boost value creation or might it interfere? What are the organization's core values or guiding principles and what guidance do they offer when it comes to exploring enterprise options? Will the development of an enterprise add value to the organization's core services or might it distract? It is essential that nonprofit leaders develop a shared sense of why they might explore an enterprise option, the results they seek, the risks they are willing to incur as a part of the process (and why they would be warranted), and whether an enterprise option will, in fact, offer appropriate benefits and results.

The second of the key areas of consideration and deliberation is that of operating environment. Later in this chapter, I discuss the implications for assessment of the operating environment as it relates to planning. At this early phase in exploring enterprise ideas, there are two basic areas to examine with regard to operating environment. First is the category of legal environment; the second is that of normative environment. When nonprofits take actions that conflict with either the legal or normative expectations of their environments, the ramifications can be grave—and both environments place constraints on the options that will be acceptable for nonprofit enterprise. In the United States, for example, legal environment parameters include constraints on

- The amount (or percentage) of unrelated earned income an organization can generate
- The use of funds for (mission) unrelated activities
- The demonstration of charitable purpose in the normal business of the organization

Normative elements are less formal and usually vary by the mission of the organization, the location of the organization, and the constituencies of the organization. Normative elements are primarily about expectations and the sense of what is and is not acceptable for a nonprofit to do, and it is essential that nonprofit leaders consider these dimensions at the very outset of their exploration of enterprise options. Even though a given enterprise option may be legal, it may be dangerously inconsistent with the expectations and values of an organization's key stakeholders. It may be inconsistent with (or even threaten) the overall culture of the nonprofit itself. For example, the decision of a volunteer center to charge people for their volunteer placement might conflict with the values of traditional volunteer center operations or the norms of the communities in which they operate. These are critical issues that have great potential to damage the legitimacy, credibility, and even sustainability of the nonprofit.

The third area of initial deliberation focuses on the business model or revenue model of the nonprofit and how it may change (or need to change) if an enterprise is developed. At core, the idea of the revenue model involves understanding the sources of revenue for the organization and why and how they provide financial resources. Nonprofits need to make explicit and informed choices about the potential of various types of revenue sources that might be available to finance their operations. This topic is fundamentally a marketing and economics discussion—beginning with an understanding of the demand for the nonprofit's services and the nonprofit's relationships with its current customers, and consideration of alternative ways that customers might be willing to engage in commercial exchanges with the organization. The topic of markets and market relationships is thoroughly examined in Chapter Eleven of this volume; the focus of this chapter is to underscore that these central choices must be examined again by a nonprofit considering the development of an enterprise.

Similarly, in Chapter Nineteen of this volume, Young and Soh discuss non-profit finance and examine another facet of the revenue model—the critical relationship between source of revenue and beneficiary of the provision of ser-vices. Framing revenue generation in economic terms, Young's model connects commercial revenues with the value a client places on a service. The question is one of value and the overall value proposition: Do potential clients consider the value commensurate to the cost? This is central to any consideration of social enterprise. For example, an opera house may provide multiple programs to their community. The main line of business is the production of operas. Opera enthu-siasts view purchasing a ticket to a show as a value transaction. The consumer receives a good (in this case the ticket to the opera) and is willing to pay a price commensurate to the value he or she places on an experience. In economic parlance, this is the essence of private good markets; social enterprises must operate successfully in private good markets.

More generally, nonprofits providing a good or service that directly benefits the client and only that client may be well-advised to examine that relationship as social enterprise. A few examples of this type of venture include:

- Counseling
- Medical care
- Education
- Business consulting
- Fitness services
- Performance art productions

Each of these types of services has individual clients (even though some may involve third parties, such as insurance companies) who pay for the value they receive for the respective service.

An emerging area of financial implications to consider involves the impact that commercial revenue may have on philanthropic donations. Smith, Cronley and Barr (2012) explored what happens with donation levels when an existing nonprofit launches a social enterprise. Their findings suggest donations decrease marginally when the social enterprise has good mission fit and more significantly when the donor does not perceive mission fit between the new enterprise and the mission. More studies will need to further our understanding of this relationship, but it is important to note that social enterprise may have a negative impact on donor behavior.

Finally, nonprofits exploring social enterprise will be well served by an analysis of organizational capacity and assets. Similar to environmental and revenue model issues, capacity issues are examined in great depth as part of the enterprise planning process, but they must be given initial general consideration at an early stage in any dialogue about the potential to develop an enterprise. In addition to financial capacity, the organization's leaders need to assess the organization's capacity with regard to the knowledge and competence required to move forward with enterprise development and the availability of other key resources needed to develop the enterprise—particularly human capital and assets.

Each of these "lenses" provides nonprofit leaders with a framework to help initiate an assessment of their organization and their enterprise options. Because social enterprise is a strategy that, at least in principle, can be employed by any type of nonprofit, the insights that you can gain from this examination will not necessarily encourage or discourage your decision to develop an enterprise. But it is important to understand these dimensions of your organization; having a better understanding of who you are as an organization will make it easier to recognize future obstacles and opportunities if you choose to develop an enterprise.

Access to Knowledge and Expertise About Social Enterprise

Google the phrase "social enterprise" and you will find there is no shortage of information on the topic. The sheer volume of social enterprise information may present a different problem for the busy nonprofit executive, since sifting through the many sources may seem an insurmountable task. However, nonprofit leaders beginning to explore social enterprise options may need to do so as an internally developed process. These "Do-It-Yourselfers" will probably seek resources for two types of information: the enterprise planning process and options for enterprise strategies. The vast range of literature derives from one of three general categories: social enterprise management books, information websites, and planning templates.

Management books on social enterprise target the nonprofit practitioner. As a whole, the genre introduces nonprofit leaders to key social enterprise concepts and provides instruction on how to use these concepts. Topics include market analysis, organization structure, and financial management. Some are organized as workbooks with exercises for the nonprofit to complete as they plan their enterprise (such as Barreiro and Stone, 2014); others are more conceptual and help nonprofit leaders frame their enterprise (for example, Lynch and Wall, 2009). In addition to these volumes, which take a holistic approach, practitioners can draw on the wisdom of books on specific functional areas of social enterprise management (technology, marketing, financial management).

Finally, a growing number of new books penned by successful veterans of social enterprise have begun to emerge (see a list compiled in 2013 by Stanford Social Innovations Review at http://ssir.org). Such books provide a director's eye view of social enterprise and can offer more intimate insights about the often-undulating path of new venture start-up. (When selecting specific books, remember that books of different nations are unlikely to work from a consistent definition of social enterprise. Therefore, select books that are relevant to the nation where you wish to develop the enterprise.)

New Internet sources also provide an abundance of information for the Do-It-Yourselfers. Using the Internet as a research medium has both positives and negatives, of course, but there is much that the careful user can glean.

Among the promising are information websites with enterprise case studies (for example, Social Enterprise Alliance), reference materials on legal and managerial considerations (National Center for Nonprofit Enterprise and Social Enterprise Magazine-Online), and interactive venues such as chats and blogs (such as hosted by The Skoll Foundation). There is also a variety of planning tools and templates available on the Internet. Of course, Internet sources also have shortcomings. The most significant shortcoming is the reliability of some information sites. (References and links to useful Internet sites and resources are provided to readers via this *Handbook*'s resource site.)

Nonprofit leaders considering the development of a social enterprise may debate whether to go it alone or work with a consultant. When making this decision, the questions and observations may help clarify the answer:

1. Do you have the time to plan in addition to your existing workload? Many nonprofits hire consultants as a time management tactic—their leaders simply do not have time to do all that is needed. The saying "The urgent crowds out the important" speaks to the potential danger of trying to develop a social enterprise internally: Will the process of developing the enterprise create interference that undermines other leadership or management work? Consultants can offer process organization, process facilitation, research assistance, and guidance. All of these services can reduce the time demands on executives and board leaders.

2. Do the existing information resources (books, electronic materials, and templates) provide adequate support to equip you and your team with the knowledge you need to implement the enterprise development process?

3. Will the absence of a consultant hamper full involvement by all necessary parties? Effective planning processes are contingent on diverse participation. Each member of the planning team brings a unique perspective. If a current leader assumes the role of facilitator, one of two potentially negative scenarios may occur. One, the facilitator dominates planning, essentially creating their own plan instead of a plan that draws upon the full range of diverse expertise in the room; or two, the facilitator takes care to remain in the facilitation role and therefore does not provide information or input, even when he or she has important information to share. As a result, the plan may lack the insights of a key organization leader (often the executive director or a board member).

4. Can you afford the cost of assistance? Although consultants may bring important value to the social enterprise development process, they also

bring cost. Consultant fees vary by region and expertise. When investigating consultants, consider their background with social enterprise and familiarity with your industry in addition to their price tag. It may be useful to do a cost-benefit analysis to compare the cost of a consultant to the cost of internal development.

5. Do you have start-up experience? Starting a new venture has many peculiar aspects that are different from running an ongoing venture. As you enter planning stages, it will be critical that you understand and can accurately estimate start-up costs, sunk costs, capital needs, and management challenges of starting a new venture. If your team lacks start-up experience, you can purchase it from a consultant. Of course, if experience is the critical issue, you will want to find a consultant with either experience leading other organizations during start-up or managing his or her own nonprofit start-up.

Structure Options for Social Enterprises

One of the first questions many nonprofit leaders consider when organizing a social enterprise is, How should I structure it? Structures need to be chosen based on the purpose and conditions under which the enterprise will operate, and the appropriate answer will be influenced by a number of factors:

- Who is to be served by the enterprise?
- Will the enterprise be implemented within an existing organization or will the enterprise be established as a new nonprofit?
- What are the social, political, and other environmental considerations?

Social enterprises typically take one of three general forms (Alter, 2009):

- The social enterprise is constituted as a discrete organization.
- The social enterprise is part of the organization.
- The social enterprise is a subsidiary or affiliate of the organization.

I describe each of these forms in the following sections (based on the typology of Alter, 2009). At the outset, it is important to note that no form is inherently superior to another and each form offers potential merits (and drawbacks). Further, no model is automatically consistent with an organization's external environment. Instead, these organizational forms should be evaluated as strategic options.

Discrete Organization

Nonprofit organizations that implement their sole or core "business" as a revenue-generating social enterprise are common throughout the sector. Hospitals, day care centers, and schools all charge fees-for-services and use these fees to finance the cost of providing their services. Operating in environments with norms (and laws) supportive of the generation of earned income, these organizations implement earned-income programs that are completely aligned with their charitable missions. Their enterprise programs are central to their organization's charitable purpose, so the organization does not need to be concerned with questions of mission relevance or the threat that the enterprise might lead to mission drift.

When a social enterprise constitutes the organization's primary business, it is most likely to be implemented as a new organization. (Existing nonprofit organizations that are not already social enterprises are unlikely to appear in this category since they obviously have revenue sources other than fees-for-service.) When an existing nonprofit chooses to shift its design to make a social enterprise its primary business, one of two scenarios is likely to have caused the change:

1. The organization's operating environment changed and, for whatever reason, the primary enterprise now can be (or maybe even needs to be) funded by fees-for-service.
2. The nonprofit has chosen to discard its previous primary program design and create a new social enterprise business.

Part of the Organization

A second structural arrangement is the operation of a social enterprise as one part or unit of an organization. Unlike the first structural form, these social enterprises are considered related but not necessarily central to mission fulfillment. Depending on the relevance of the enterprise to the organization's mission, the earnings of this form of social enterprise may be subject to unrelated business income tax (UBIT). However, more often than not, a program's activities will be sufficiently related to mission to avoid this. For example, a typical program of a sheltered workshop includes work activities to be implemented by their developmentally disabled clients. The workshop then sells the products of their work to the public. For the sheltered workshop, the work opportunities for the developmentally disabled population are central to the mission. Therefore, the earnings of the work products are directly related to the mission and thus not subject to UBIT. We often see this second structural form in existing organizations. A nonprofit may realize there is a revenue generation opportunity, closely related to their mission, that they could implement. Consequently, they establish this mission-relevant program to generate additional revenues

Subsidiary or Affiliated Organization

Social enterprises structured as subsidiaries or affiliates of the nonprofit are a third structural option. The subsidiary structure allows a nonprofit to achieve legal separation between an enterprise and the parent organization. This may be useful or even essential as the nonprofit implements an enterprise that may not be feasible or appropriate to operate internally, usually for reasons of tax or other legal liability. The subsidiary organization may take either the nonprofit or for-profit form of organization. I discuss the implications of both next.

Nonprofit Subsidiaries. Social enterprise subsidiaries that take a nonprofit form often exist because an organization wants to pursue a charitable purpose without opening itself to UBIT or other legal liability (see Chapter Two of this volume for further discussion of legal and related risk management issues). For example, this option might be chosen because a nonprofit wishes to address a new need or opportunity that is tax-exempt and charitable but is not within the scope of its own tax exemption as granted by the IRS. Or it might be chosen to ensure a legal separation so that risks and liabilities associated with the new venture could not result in losses of the new venture being assessed against the parent organization (for example, a church that creates a low-income housing redevelopment agency and wants to keep its church assets separated from the riskier work of the redevelopment agency). The subsidiary is a separate nonprofit corporation with its own legal status. The subsidiary organization will have a separate governing board, but it will be under the control of the parent nonprofit (for example, the parent organization board would appoint or approve the membership of the subsidiary organization's board). Therefore, the board of the parent organization will be the primary governing body for the parent nonprofit *and* will either oversee or itself serve as the board of a subsidiary.

For-Profit Subsidiaries. The for-profit subsidiary approach appears more often in the U.S. social enterprise literature. Prescribed as a revenue-generation model, the for-profit subsidiary is a taxable entity that can pursue financial opportunities outside of traditional charitable constraints. Since its earnings are taxable but it pays tax on them just as any other for-profit would do, it has no limits associated with tax-exempt status. Of course, the use of the for-profit subsidiary status can bring some of its own problems. Thus, prior to creating or spinning off a for-profit subsidiary, a nonprofit would be wise to consider the implications of the following potential issues:

- *New places, new faces:* Entering a profit-oriented marketplace means a different set of competitors. In particular, when nonprofits enter for-profit markets they will be met by competition from for-profit organizations already in that market. These for-profits may well have more experience in this operating environment, giving them certain competitive advantages. Further, it is likely existing organizations in this new market will have developed at least some form of an established customer base. In order to be profitable in such an environment, nonprofits will need to make up significant ground in both of these areas.
- *Capacity 2.0:* Management and staff of the parent nonprofit organization may need to develop new or additional skills that will be required to succeed in the new business in the new operating environment. The extent of the adjustment will be partially dictated by staffing decisions for the subsidiary. If staff and management of the parent will be redeployed to work in the new subsidiary, they will need to adjust to the orientation of working in a for-profit environment—and this may be a major adjustment. The employees of the for-profit will need to have the capacity to address what are likely to be different marketing techniques, financial management systems, and sales processes.

Of course, the specific skills needed for each of these areas will be determined by the subsidiary's type of business; some will be highly transferable and others will not. Further, if staff members are redeployed from the nonprofit to the subsidiary, will important functions in the parent organization be in danger of being shortchanged or ignored? I have seen nonprofit executive directors invest so much time in their new subsidiaries that their core nonprofit activities have suffered from inattention and neglect—to the detriment of the parent's performance. If new staff are hired and will run the new venture autonomously, top management also should determine how the two entities will connect and coexist. Will the subsidiary develop a unique culture or adopt the parent organization's culture? How will compensation and benefits need to differ? How much, if any, collaboration or coordination is to take place between the nonprofit and for-profit subsidiary? Appropriate answers to these questions will be critical to success.

The specific sector of incorporation is not an arbitrary decision. When weighing whether the subsidiary should be for-profit or nonprofit, management must consider the capital needs, the profit potential and the input markets of the subsidiary. Ventures with significant capital needs and profit potential tend to be suitable for for-profit forms. Ventures with low capital demands and inefficiencies in either customer or input markets often are better suited for nonprofit forms.

Other Enterprise Options

Nonprofit social enterprises are not confined to program activities. Many non-profit social enterprises have successfully generated revenues from activities that are not directly involved with their programming. Three increasingly common enterprise opportunities of this type are

- Cause-related marketing (CRM)
- Licensing
- Asset reappropriation

Each of these strategies involves the utilization of an organization's assets in a new way. CRM and licensing leverage a nonprofit's brand through relationships with for-profit organizations. Asset reappropriation involves the use of organizational assets for commercial revenue generation. Each of these is described below.

Cause-Related Marketing (CRM)

How many times have you visited a grocery store around Thanksgiving or another holiday and, at the checkout counter, the cashier asks if you would like to make a donation to the local food pantry? If you answered more than zero, then you have experienced a form of CRM. The question for a nonprofit leader is: When does CRM make sense?

Cause-related marketing is defined as, "a mutually beneficial collaboration between a corporation and a nonprofit in which their respective assets are combined to: create shareholder and social value, connect with a range of constituents,...and communicate the shared values of both organizations" (Foundation Center, 2010). Research on CRM has validated the potential value of a mutual-benefit relationship as described in the definition and, more specifically, research has found that CRM between organizations with similar purposes improves customer perceptions of the for-profit organization (Barone, Miyazaki, and Taylor, 2000; Pracejus & Olsen, 2004).

Cause-related marketing has become a big business in the United States. The IEG sponsorship report estimates corporate cause sponsorships will hit $1.92 Billion in 2015 (n.d.). There are a multitude of examples of CRM success. The initial example cited by the Foundation Center was between American Express and the Statue of Liberty. American Express launched a campaign in 1983 that donated to the restoration of the Statue of Liberty one cent for every purchase on one of their credit cards. As a result, usage increased 28 percent (Foundation Center, 2010). In a more recent CRM type of collaboration, telecommunications firm Sprint Nextel donated $2 to the Nature Conservatory for each Samsung reclaimed phone that was sold (http://causerelatedmarketing.blogspot.com/).

These examples demonstrate two critical points for nonprofits considering a CRM strategy. First, to attract for-profit partners, the nonprofit needs strong brand identity. A strong brand is critical so the for-profit's customers identify (and value) the nonprofit cause. Second, it is more useful for a nonprofit to seek for-profit partners whose businesses have some mission or service commonality. For example, the link between recycled telephones and an environmental organization offered such synergy for the Sprint-Nature Conservancy relationship. The key here is that not every for-profit will be a good CRM partner. A mutually beneficial relationship is contingent on some form of common purpose.

Brand Licensing

Let's go back to the grocery store setting we described in the CRM section. As you fill your cart with your favorite items you recognize that some of the items you have selected have the American Heart Association brand and logo. This is illustrative of another form of partnership, brand licensing. Under such relationships, nonprofits license the use of their brand in a business's marketing for a fee.

Similar to CRM, the success of brand licensing is contingent on a strong nonprofit brand and consistency between the nonprofit's mission and the for-profit product. This may appear to be a sure-fire social enterprise strategy, but it is important to remember that connecting your nonprofit brand and identity with a for-profit organization can open the door to problems. If the for-profit product performs poorly or the business misrepresents an aspect of a product that carries the nonprofit brand, the damage affects the nonprofit. Even in cases of no impropriety, failure of the nonprofit to conduct due diligence may lead to a partnership that conflicts with the core values of the nonprofit. In these cases, the nonprofit appears to "sell out" for money and the result can be loss of trust, credibility, or worse. Chapter Thirteen of this book offers a useful framework for examining the relative merit and value of various collaborative approaches.

Asset Reappropriation

Unlike CRM and brand licensing, which are enterprising strategies using a nonprofit's soft assets, asset reappropriation involves finding alternative uses for tangible assets. Too often, nonprofits look at their assets through overly narrow lenses: a building, for example, is only a place to implement core mission activities, or land is merely green space that adds to the aesthetic quality of the campus.

A strategic look at these same assets may uncover a possible revenue opportunity or stream not previously considered. For example, Drumm Farm is a Missouri nonprofit originally started as a boys' home in the early 1900s. As the founding family passed away and perceptions of the roles of boys' homes in society changed, Drumm experienced a significant decline in clients. What at one point was a robust campus with extensive acreage and buildings full to capacity began to wither away. Hampered with severely depreciating assets leading to ever-greater cash flow problems, the Drumm Farm executive director and board of directors revaluated their use and began to redeploy their property assets. Instead of leaving their buildings empty, they created a social service campus and rented the buildings to local nonprofits. Further, realizing their greatest asset was property, they developed a lease agreement with a local golf course management company. The management company converted a segment of the Drumm Farm land into a golf course, operates the new course, and pays the nonprofit an annual fee (lease). This venture has provided a significant source of new income that Drumm has been able to use to help fund its core mission operations.

Of course, not every nonprofit has an abundance of land and empty buildings. But almost all nonprofits do have some assets that may have potential as a source of additional revenue. It is important to ensure that redeployment of the assets should generate income that will exceed (by some significant margin) the expense involved in redeploying the asset. For example, if it takes $1,000 of time to negotiate the use of the asset, you should require the venture to generate profit exceeding that $1,000 by an appropriate margin. Further, you may not need to manage the use of the asset to generate revenues. In the Drumm Farm example, Drumm staff did not manage the golf course or the organizations in the buildings. Lease agreements included management responsibilities. This allowed Drumm Farm to earn revenues without incurring the expense of management or oversight.

Enterprise Planning

Thus far, this chapter has discussed in relatively broad terms some of the options for social enterprise. Of course, to take these options and develop them into a useful social enterprise that benefits the nonprofit organization requires additional planning and development, and that is the focus of this section of the chapter. It is important to understand that effective enterprise planning and development flows from and builds on the broader organizational strategizing and planning processes explained by Brown in Chapter Eight and Bryson in Chapter Nine of this *Handbook*. In many cases, the development and implementation of a new enterprise would constitute a strategy in the context of a nonprofit's overall strategic plan. The planning and development process explained in this chapter will be most useful if it is implemented as an outgrowth of such a strategic plan.

Before elaborating on our discussion of planning, it is important to note an alternative approach to enterprise start-up has gained significant attention since 2010—the so-called "Lean Start-Up." As Steve Blank explains in his *Harvard Business Review* article, a Lean Start-Up "favors experimentation over elaborate planning, customer feedback over intuition, and iterative design over traditional 'big design up front' development" (2013). Many nonprofits have picked up on this trend that preaches a less elaborate innovation path. However, it is important to recognize that lean start-up approaches apply only to process, not outcomes. As Peter Murray and Steve Ma point out in their 2015 article in *Stanford Social Innovation Review*, "No form of rapid experimentation, for instance, can test whether an intervention aimed at kids in preschool will affect high school graduation rates."

Time and experimentation will help us assess the utility of lean models for nonprofit organization social enterprise. In some ways, the tenets of the lean approach are reminiscent of the work of Senge and other organization innovation theorists who have wrestled with the question of how to encourage organizational learning and innovation (Senge, Kleiner, Roberts, Ross, Roth, and Smith, 1999). More detailed resources on the practice of the lean start-up approach are available in the resource website for this *Handbook*.

The more traditional approach to enterprise planning demands that nonprofit leaders recognize the preconceptions and commitments associated with the process. A quick survey of any group of individuals who have participated in planning exercises in the past is likely to reveal that many have had less-than-positive experiences. Common among planning complaints are "It's a lot of talk with no action" and "There are more important things I could do with my time." It is essential that the planning process be planned and organized well, and that it make effective use of participants' time and input. As discussed earlier in the chapter, the amount of time demanded of participants and (especially) executives will be influenced by the decision to use a consultant or process facilitator. However, even with external help, it is essential to recognize that a well-developed process will require that key participants devote an adequate amount of time to the process, time that will be in addition to their existing work responsibilities.

The enterprise planning process must begin with consideration of the current state of the organization. Organization leaders must have the answer to the question Where are we today? In an earlier section of this chapter, I outlined the key elements of this type of initial discussion—discussion about mission impact and relevance, characteristics of the nonprofit's operating environment, financial and revenue implications, and organizational capacity to implement the enterprise. The decision to proceed with enterprise planning assumes that those initial deliberations resulted in a conclusion that the context for enterprise development is positive and that a social enterprise strategy has potential for benefiting the nonprofit.

Overall, there are three levels of planning that are germane to the process of evaluating and planning a social enterprise: strategic planning, feasibility assessment, and business planning. A summary of the three levels is provided in Table 12.1. Each of these levels of planning has its own focus, and each adds its own unique value to the development of the enterprise.

The remainder of this section of the chapter explains the sequence and key elements that comprise the seven stages of activity that will be important to a successful enterprise planning process. These seven stages or elements are

1. Planning your planning
2. Organizational assessment
3. Environmental assessment
4. Strategy design
5. Financial considerations
6. Implementation
7. Evaluation

Planning Your Planning

The beginning of the planning process starts with an organizing stage. Consistent with the recommendations Bryson presents in his Chapter Nine outline of the planning-to-plan process, critical questions to address during this stage include

TABLE 12.1. Linking Enterprise Process and Practice

Planning Type	Purpose	Role in Enterprise Development Process
Strategic Planning	Disciplined effort to produce fundamental decisions and actions shaping the nature and direction of an organization's (or other entity's) activities within legal bounds (see Bryson, Chapter Nine of this volume).	An organization with no specific direction would begin with strategic planning. This comprehensive approach would identify multiple organizational strategies, including options for social enterprise.
Feasibility Study	Assess the viability of an opportunity, and usually serves as a precursor to a business plan.	Explore an enterprise idea (usually from the strategic planning process) and assess how well it would fit and operate within the organization (or link to the organization, if developed as a subsidiary). The idea is formed and needs to be examined through a feasibility process.
Business Planning	The final type of planning that leads to implementation, the business plan specifies in relatively great detail how the enterprise will be organized, managed, financed, staffed, and operated. It specifies goals and provides time-based projections of financial, market, and operational performance for the enterprise.	Assuming the feasibility study process suggests that the idea is viable and attractive, the nonprofit would develop a business plan for the enterprise. This will serve as a guiding document for the initial three to five years of operation.

1. Who will be on the planning team?
2. What is the purpose and goal(s) of the planning process?
3. What is the time line and what are the target dates for the process?
4. How often will the planning team meet?

The composition of the planning team is critical to the overall success of the process. The key is to bring to the table the people who have important knowledge to inform the planning of the potential enterprise. Inclusion of executive leadership plus a mix of board and staff is important because it combines the strategic leadership and perspective of the board and senior executive(s) with the operational and tactical organizational knowledge of staff. The exact mix will vary by organization and opportunity. Regardless, board members provide a valuable perspective and should be included in the planning process; often board members bring knowledge, skill sets, and experiences that staff do not possess. In addition to board and staff, some organizations also invite selected key stakeholders to participate on the planning team. These stakeholders may be previous board members, past clients, or close collaborators. It should be noted that involving individuals outside the organization may require additional norming processes to ensure the team comes together and is "pulling" in the same direction.

After the planning team is created, the plan-to-plan shifts focus to aligning the intentions of all the members. The first step in this process is developing a goal. The goal of the planning process will be defined by the purpose of the proposed social enterprise. For example, if the process is the result of a collaborator approaching your organization with a social enterprise idea, the planning process goal would be to assess the viability of the idea. Alternatively, if the process is the result of a strategic plan strategy that directs the organization to create a new earned-income enterprise, the planning process goal would be to develop enterprise options and then proceed to viability assessment. The key purpose of the goal definition is to provide a standard by which planning progress can be assessed and to help ensure all team members are working toward a common purpose.

Based on the planning goal, the planning team should establish milestones and time lines for the planning process. The planning process as a whole should have a finite end point. One pitfall many nonprofits encounter as they plan a social enterprise is perpetual planning. Seeking a level of certainty not feasible, some nonprofits continue to plan with no end date. Planning team fatigue eventually sets in and the process fizzles with no outcome. The long-term impact of these endless processes is evident when the organization begins to plan again. Team members and other stakeholders will be reticent to engage in a process they fear will have no end.

In order to avoid this trap, establish decision-making deadlines at the beginning. The deadlines should include the timing of a final decision on whether or not to pursue the enterprise, as well as intermediate deadlines for completion of stages such as the situational analysis. When considering time lines, it is important to achieve a balance between enough time to complete your work and time frames short enough to maintain planning momentum. No rule of thumb exists on how long an enterprise planning process should last. However, your plan will be built on certain assumptions and if your processes extend for too long those assumptions may change.

Finally, the plan to plan addresses the frequency of team meetings. The number of team meetings is not as important as how the meeting time is spent. Research should be conducted and summarized outside of meetings. This allows meeting time to focus on interpretation and analysis of the data. After broad enterprise strategies are developed, it may be useful to break the full team into a set of smaller sub-project work teams. These work teams (composed of fewer members) will investigate specific areas of a strategy and bring information back to the full planning team for further analysis and planning. The work team model may be useful for making effective use of specialized skill sets of individual planning team members.

Organizational and Environmental Assessments

The foundation of successful planning is research. Research enables nonprofit leaders to have a full understanding of the organization's capacities, effectiveness, and efficiencies. In an organizational context, research is often referred to as assessment. During a social enterprise planning process, assessment has dual foci: internal and external. Because the motivations for each are unique I will deal with them separately.

Internal Assessment. Internal assessment, sometimes taking the form of an organizational audit, is designed to identify organizational capacity and assets and identify organizational weaknesses. Operating a social enterprise requires specific capacities, capacities unique from traditional nonprofit activity. It is important that these capacity needs be clearly identified at the outset of this process. Then the organizational assessment should take care to assess whether the necessary organizational capacities and systems are in place to support the enterprise.

There are a multitude of assessment tools available to nonprofit organizations, and some will be more relevant or useful than others (for an overall discussion of various tools available for organization capacity assessment, see Bartczak, 2005). Assessment value needs to be judged on the basis of the information the organization needs to know in order to evaluate its capacity for the specific enterprise in question. Some types of enterprise call for very specific capacity, others do not. General assessments, such as the McKinsey Capacity Assessment (Bartczak, 2005), focus on an overall set of organizational capacity elements. The McKinsey assessment provides a vehicle for an organization's leaders to assess seven general categories:

1. Organization mission and vision (aspirations)
2. Strategy
3. Organizational skills
4. Human resources
5. Systems and infrastructure
6. Organizational structure
7. Culture

Tailoring an assessment such as McKinsey to a social enterprise process often requires a nonprofit leader to add additional assessment areas. However, every process should provide a systematic basis by which to assess each of the following capacity elements:

- *Financial management:* Social enterprise management requires cost accounting, break-even analysis, and revenue projections. Running a social enterprise involves accounting for transaction revenues. Unlike grants and donations, transaction revenues are collected directly from the client (or a third party in some cases). Consequently, your assessment should examine whether or not staff members are knowledgeable about transaction receivables management, break-even analysis, and unit cost analysis (see the chapters of Part Four of this *Handbook,* especially Chapter Twenty-One, for a substantive discussion of these and related processes).
- *Customer relationships:* Traditional nonprofit management has a focus on quality that at least equals that of a for-profit business. However, equal does not mean the same. The relationship with and behavior of a client who seeks services from a soup kitchen is different from the relationship and behavior of a free-market customer who may purchase services. The free-market customer presumably has options from which to choose, and this creates a need for the supplier (that is, the enterprise) to develop a relationship with the customer. The assessment process for a nonprofit considering a social enterprise must evaluate existing capacities for customer relationship management. In addition, it will be very important to determine staff's ability to engage in market research and analysis (for example, to collect and synthesize information about customer characteristics; see Chapter Thirteen of this volume for in-depth discussion on markets, market research, and market decision making).

- *Human resources:* The human resource functions of a nonprofit focus on recruiting, retaining, and motivating qualified personnel, board members, and volunteers. Comparable to the comments regarding the financial management and customer relationship topics, social enterprise makes demands relevant to the field of human resources. Enterprise planners should consider the ability of human resource personnel and systems to attract new employees for the enterprise with backgrounds in transactional businesses. For example, a social enterprise program director should have some background in financial management and marketing, and the agency's human resources systems will have to become proficient in adapting the human resource system to meet the needs for people with these (potentially) new capabilities. (See the chapters in Part Five of this *Handbook* for substantive discussion of the functions and capacities of human resource systems.)
- *Strategic leadership:* Even as it implements a social enterprise, mission must be the primary focus of a nonprofit organization. Nonetheless, the elevated importance of transactional revenues in the social enterprise process demands that members of the nonprofit's executive leadership team (executive and key board leaders) have some capacity in this area. Related to this, at least some members of this group should have knowledge of and experience in providing oversight of commercial activities of the type that would be central to the proposed enterprise.

These four capacity areas do not constitute an exhaustive list. Other areas of concern will relate to the focus of the proposed enterprise. For example, will the enterprise operate in an area governed by professional regulatory or licensure authorities (for example, admission to practice law or medicine)? It is essential to identify the additional areas of capacity that are likely to be relevant to your enterprise and implement relevant assessments in these areas.

External Assessment. An external organizational assessment for a social enterprise does not vary dramatically from external assessments any nonprofit would conduct, although a new enterprise idea may require a nonprofit to go back and redefine its relevant "external environment." During an external assessment the planning team will collect data on competitors (often similar service providers), pricing models and practices, client characteristics, key stakeholder perspectives, and other factors (such as legislation) that are relevant to the venture. The goal of the external assessment is to identify and understand the implications of the opportunities and threats in the new enterprise environment. In order to develop a successful strategy, the planning team must be apprised of environmental influences that will support or mitigate performance of the new venture.

Following the completion of both assessments, the planning team will analyze the information by using practices similar to those Bryson discusses in Chapter Nine. Many nonprofits will use processes such as SWOT (strengths, weaknesses, opportunities, and threats) analyses for the analysis process. Such analyses provide the initial sense of the implications for enterprise viability or acceptability, and development of this information into strategic decisions is the essence of the next stage of the enterprise planning process. The most promising venture ideas will capitalize on synergies between existing organizational capacities and environmental opportunities. Of course, the real world rarely affords us such utopian scenarios. More likely, analysis will reveal a couple of options where some capacity exists and potential threats are minimized. The next stage of planning, strategy formulation, takes these ideas and develops plans to move forward.

Strategy Formulation

Strategy formulation is the stage during which key strategic choices are made—choices about which options to pursue and how best to organize and pursue them. In the context of enterprise planning, this is the point in the process at which the nonprofit's decision makers weight the relative merits of the enterprise options and determine whether or how to proceed. In the previous stage the planning team identified a couple of possible broad directions or opportunities. During strategy formulation the planning team develops broad programmatic maps to guide the new enterprise.

Other chapters in this book explain in significant depth the key facets of strategy development, so little space will be allocated to those topics in this chapter. For example:

- The legal and regulatory implications of social enterprise options are discussed in Chapter Two
- The processes for strategy development and strategy decision making are discussed in two chapters in Part Two of this book, Chapter Eight on strategic management (by William Brown) and Chapter Nine on the strategy cycle (by John M. Bryson);
- The processes by which nonprofit leaders examine and make decisions about market opportunities (including issues of market positioning and pricing

issues) are explained in detail by Brenda Gainer (Chapter Thirteen), and key questions associated with portfolio analysis and enterprise development also are explored in a special section of Jeanne Bell and Shannon Ellis's chapter on financial leadership (Chapter Seventeen).

- The overall topic of social entrepreneurship and the range of entrepreneurship options that exists for nonprofit organizations are discussed by Matthew Nash in Chapter Eleven.

Financial Implications Planning

The next stage in the enterprise planning process involves aligning the financial dimensions of the enterprise with the strategic choices to be made. Far too many nonprofits adopt courses of action without ever making any systematic assessment of the financial implications of their choices—choices about where and how revenues are generated, and choices about where and how these resources are managed. The results of ignoring these financial aspects of our choices can range from underperformance on important mission-centric projects to an outright diversion of resources from mission to a relatively less-valued activity. This stage of the planning process calls for the nonprofit's leaders to examine and prepare to make decisions regarding three key areas:

- Financing the start-up of the social enterprise, including determination of the amount of money needed to effectively start and capitalize the initial phases of operation of the new enterprise and also assessing the costs and implications of securing these essential financial resources from various sources (banks, key donors, foundations, government funders, etc.)
- Financing the ongoing operations of the enterprise, including covering all ongoing operating costs, securing sources of additional operating capital, managing the costs of ongoing operations, and servicing the debt as you repay the sources of the start-up financing
- Documenting and accounting for the financial operations of the enterprise and ensuring the necessary levels of accountability and transparency for both the social enterprise and its relationship (overlap and separation) with the host nonprofit

The actual methods by which these assessments, plans, and decisions are made are explained in Part Four of this book. The essential point I wish to make in this chapter is that these all are important elements of the initial social enterprise planning process, and there are critical decisions to be made—decisions that can have lasting implications for both the social enterprise *and* the larger nonprofit organization that is the host or parent entity for the enterprise.

Financial discussions can be difficult for nonprofit leaders. Because mission is (and must be) the central focus for a nonprofit organization's executives, financial discussions often end up being of secondary concern (if they even receive that much consideration). However, when it comes to social enterprises, ignoring financial matters can have disastrous results. At worst, social enterprise financial problems can end up undermining all that the organization is doing to maximize mission accomplishment! I previously related the story of a nonprofit organization that decided to make salad dressing and the terrible costs the organization incurred because it failed to account for indirect costs and inaccurately understood its direct costs. Such mistakes underscore the need for nonprofits to ensure careful financial planning as they evaluate prospective social enterprises. This is especially true when the social enterprise is expected to be a profit generator.

A critical financial concern for a new social enterprise and its host organization is that of "capital structure." A nonprofit's capital structure is the mix and distribution of an organization's assets, liabilities, and net assets (Miller, 2003); a nonprofit's capital structure can create significant problems with a nonprofit's ability to develop a viable social enterprise. Capital structure essentially defines the ability of a nonprofit to undertake new projects and absorb risks (both conventional projects and potential enterprises). Stated plainly, organizations with more liquidity have more flexible capital structures that are going to be more flexible in accommodating the financial dimensions of a new social enterprise. Analysis of capital structure helps the planning team appraise fixed assets available for the new enterprise (and if there is no one on the planning team with the ability to assess this aspect of the nonprofit's capacity, the organization should secure external talent to ensure that this can be done). Significant insights into this aspect of financial planning and management are also discussed by Bowman in Chapter Twenty-One of this *Handbook*.

In the enterprise planning process, it is essential to acknowledge that all new ventures require start-up capital. Social enterprise planning must plan for start-up funding, including attention to the amount needed to initiate the venture and to the debt service necessary to recover start-up costs. Flexible budgets (which map multiple scenarios) and break-even analysis can provide organization leaders with insights that inform necessary cash-reserve decisions. Armed with this information, the planning team can identify potential funders for their new enterprise. When it comes to nonprofit social enterprises, the most common start-up funders tend to be the nonprofit hosts themselves (using cash reserves), individual donors, and charitable foundations. On a less frequent basis, nonprofits may find start-up support from government grants or banks.

Strategy Implementation Plan

Moving from strategy development and financial implications to strategy implementation planning can be much more involved than many nonprofits expect. At this stage, the process moves from one of assessment to one of decision and—assuming that the decision to proceed is affirmative—to the creation of the actual operational or business plan that will take the information from the earlier stages of the planning and integrate it into an operational document. The process of evaluating the feasibility of an enterprise strategy and, ultimately, creating the implementation plan requires decisions on the key issues that have been examined throughout the process, including the following:

- What services will you provide? This is an obvious question, but one that requires detail and specificity. In addition to describing the services, you must also outline the service delivery pattern. At what times of the day will you provide the services? Will the services be provided on site or at a remote location?
- To whom will you sell this? Who is the target market for the program? Understanding the demographics of the target market will inform marketing strategies, pricing, and service delivery. For example, if you will be providing clinical services, your price will be influenced by reimbursement schedules of third-party payers. In addition, it is important to clarify whether the target market demands the services or whether you are providing services that will require you to create awareness. The two scenarios will require differing marketing approaches.
  - How will these services be delivered and sold? Is this place-based, Internet-based, or some combination? Where will the actual business be located and what kinds of facilities will be needed?
  - How will the program be structured? Will the venture be a program of the existing organization or will the venture be a separate subsidiary?
  - Who will manage and who will staff the enterprise? This decision is grounded in the internal assessment. How many people will you need, and will you hire new staff or use (or redeploy) existing staff? Implicit in this discussion is the issue of capacity. If you use existing staff, what additional capacities will you need to develop? If you hire new staff, what will you pay them (for example, comparable to nonprofit salaries or to for-profit market rates)?

- What are the financial plans for the enterprise? For example, what are the revenue projections for the first three years? What is your profit estimate for the first three years? When will the enterprise break even? How much money do you need, and why? How will the money be repaid?

In order to develop the strategy implementation plan, the planning team may need to involve other key staff members (if they are not already on the planning team). Knowledgeable input from key staff is critical in this process.

The strategy implementation plan often is created in the form of a business plan for the new social enterprise. Business plans are documents that bring all of this information together and present it in a well-organized and complete manner—one single place that leaders and managers can use as the key reference point as they proceed with the implementation process. There are many formats for business plans, and the Internet resource site for this *Handbook* provides examples and a number of resources and links. A typical business plan will include the following specific information (drawn from Massarsky, 2005; the following list could serve as the table of contents for such a document):

- Executive summary
- Description of the business (including a mission statement)
- Industry and market analysis (including forecast of demand)
- Marketing plan
- Governance and management plan
- Operations plan (including staffing)
- Financial plan (including projections and forecasts)
- Risk assessment and contingency plan
- Appendix (supporting documents)

A number of books and guides have been written specifically for nonprofit enterprises. These can be especially useful because they contain sections that are not typically found in traditional for-profit business plans, such as a description of the mission of the nonprofit, its purpose and goals for the social enterprise, and the operational, financial, and legal relationships between the nonprofit and the new enterprise (Massarsky, 2005).

Evaluation

Similar to any planning process, the enterprise planning process should include a process for evaluation and refinement of plans and operations. It is important to note that evaluation plans should be developed before the social enterprise planning process concludes. In addition to program metrics, metrics of enterprise financial performance also must be included (examples of financial metrics are profit and loss, marginal costs, and unit costs for both outputs and outcomes). Program evaluation is addressed in depth by John Clayton Thomas in Chapter Sixteen of this volume, with important guidance regarding processes that are appropriate to enterprise evaluation. The reader is encouraged to incorporate this information as they develop the evaluation part of the enterprise plan.

Moving Forward

Social enterprise continues to be a source of both excitement and intimidation to nonprofit leaders as they explore the most useful ways to ensure that their organizations remain viable and responsive for years to come. Implemented effectively in appropriate contexts, social enterprise is another important strategy that the nonprofit sector has to use to address the needs of its clients and communities. Used less appropriately, social enterprise has the potential to derail an organization and undermine the trust it has earned. As discussed throughout this chapter, social enterprise simply is one unique strategic option among many strategic options.

Nonprofits should not begin their consideration of enterprise strategies with the assumption that they "ought to" create a social enterprise. Legitimate enterprise development requires thorough and thoughtful assessment and deliberation and due diligence by nonprofit governing boards and executives. The process begins with an accurate assessment of the organization's mission and critical issues, and a thorough understanding of markets, structure, and culture is imperative to the successful development of a viable social enterprise.

The content of this chapter serves two purposes. First, the framework of social enterprise is intended to be useful to academics and practitioners as they pursue their equal yet diverse interests. For both groups, the discussion of markets, structure, and strategy is intended to help organize the diverse aspects of social enterprise in a meaningful way that will enhance understanding. Second, the chapter is designed to serve as a reference tool to guide thinking as practitioners consider social enterprise options.

As we, academics and practitioners alike, continue to grow and develop with the sector, we have much to learn and share regarding social enterprise. Academics will continue to explore issues of structure, finance, markets, and culture through carefully constructed research. Practitioners will also conduct their own form of research and development as they explore enterprising new ways to fulfill their missions and sustain their organizations. Together we can add to the growing knowledge of the sector as we help ensure that nonprofits remain vital and viable as they provide the critical services their clients and communities need.

References

Alden, K. Green Up Your Cause Marketing. Retrieved February 10, 2010, from http://causerelatedmarketing.blogspot.com/, 2010.

Alter, K. *Social Enterprise Typology*. Retrieved February 5, 2010, from www.virtueventures.com/setypology, 2009.

Barone, M. J., Miyazaki, A. D., and Taylor, K. A. The Influence of Cause-Related Marketing on Consumer Choice: Does One Good Turn Deserve Another? *Journal of the Academy of Marketing Science*, 2000, 28(2), 248–262.

Barreiro, T. D., and Stone, M. M. *Social Entrepreneurship: From Issue to Viable Plan*. New York: Business Expert Press, 2014.

Bartczak, L. (ed.) *Funder's Guide to Organizational Assessment: Tools, Processes, and Their Use in Building Capacity*. St. Paul, MN: Fieldstone Alliance, 2005.

Blank, S. Why the Lean Start-Up Changes Everything. *Harvard Business Review*, 2013, 91(5), 2013.

Dart, R. The Legitimacy of Social Enterprise. *Nonprofit Management and Leadership*, 2004, 14(4), 411–424.

Dees, J. G., Emerson, J., and Economy, P. *Enterprising Nonprofits*. Hoboken, NJ: John Wiley & Sons, 2005.

Foster, W., & Bradach, J. "Should nonprofits seek profits?" *Harvard Business Review* 83(2), 2005.

Foundation Center. Frequently Asked Questions." Retrieved February 10, 2010, from http://foundationcenter.org/getstarted/faqs/html/cause_marketing.html, 2010.

Grau, S. L. Study: Nonprofits Put Brand at Risk in Corporate Partnerships. Retrieved February 10, 2010, from www.eurekalert.org/pub_releases/2009-11/djc-snp111309.php, 2010.

IEG. Sponsorship Spending Report. Retrieved from www.sponsorship.com/IEG/files/4e/4e525456-b2b1-4049-bd51-03d9c35ac507.pdf, n.d.

Internal Revenue Service (IRS). Retrieved from www.IRS.gov, 2015.

Kerlin, J. Social Enterprise in the United States and Europe: Understanding and Learning from the Differences. *International Journal of Voluntary and Nonprofit Organizations*, 2006, 17(3), 247–263.

LeRoux, K. M. What Drives Nonprofit Entrepreneurship? A Look at Budget Trends of Metro Social Service Agencies. *American Review of Public Administration*, 2005, 35(4), 350–362.

Loosemore, M., and Higgon, D. *Social Enterprise in the Construction Industry: Building Better Communities*. London, UK: Routledge, 2015.

Lynch, K., and Wall, J. *Mission, Inc.: The Practitioners Guide to Social Enterprise*. San Francisco: Berrett-Koehler, 2009.

Massarsky, C. W. Enterprise Strategies for Generating Revenue. In R. D. Herman (ed.), *The Jossey-Bass Handbook of Nonprofit Leadership and Management* (2nd ed.). San Francisco: Jossey-Bass, 2005.

Massarsky, C. W., and Beinhacker, S. L. *Enterprising Nonprofits: Revenue Generation in the Nonprofit Sector*. New Haven, CT: Yale School of Management–the Goldman Sachs Foundation Partnership on Nonprofit Ventures, 2002.

McGeever, B. S., and Pettijohn, S. L. Retrieved December 10, 2015, from www.urban
.org/sites/default/files/alfresco/publication-pdfs/413277-The-Nonprofit-Sector-in-
Brief.PDF, 2014.

Miller, C. Hidden in Plain Sight: Understanding Nonprofit Capital Structure. *The Nonprofit Quarterly,* 2003, Spring, 1–8.

Murray, P., and Ma, S. The Promise of Lean Experimentation. *Stanford Social Innovations Review,* 2015, Summer.

Nash, M.T.A. Social Entrepreneurship and Social Enterprise. In D. O. Renz (ed.), *The Jossey-Bass Handbook of Nonprofit Leadership and Management* (3rd ed.). San Francisco: Jossey-Bass, 2010.

Patton, R. *Managing and Measuring Social Enterprise.* London: Sage, 2003.

Pracejus, J. W., and Olsen, G. D. The Role of Brand/Cause Fit in the Effectiveness of Cause-Related Marketing Campaigns. *Journal of Business Research,* 2004, 57(6), 635–640.

Salamon, L. M. *America's Nonprofit Sector.* New York: The Foundation Center, 1999.

Salamon, L. M. The Changing Context of Nonprofit Leadership and Management. In D. O. Renz (ed.), *The Jossey-Bass Handbook of Nonprofit Leadership and Management* (3rd ed.). San Francisco: Jossey-Bass, 2010.

Senge, P., Kleiner, A., Roberts, C., Ross, R., Roth, G., and Smith,. B. *The Dance of Change: The Challenges to Sustaining Momentum in a Learning Organization.* New York: Doubleday, 1999.

Smith, B. R., Cronley, L., and Barr, T. F. Funding Implications of Social Enterprise: The Role of Mission Consistency, Entrepreneurial Competence, and Attitude Toward Social Enterprise on Donor Behavior. *Journal of Public Policy & Marketing,* 2012, 31(1), 142–157.

Social Enterprise Alliance. *Succeeding at Social Enterprise: Hard-Won Lessons for Nonprofits and Social Entrepreneurs.* San Francisco: Jossey-Bass, 2010.

Wilkinson, C., Medhurst, J., Henry, N., Wihlborg, M., and Braithwaite, B. W. *A Map of Social Enterprises and Their Eco-Systems in Europe: Executive Summary.* Brussels, Belgium: European Commission, 2014.

CHAPTER THIRTEEN

MARKETING FOR NONPROFIT ORGANIZATIONS

Brenda Gainer

Marketing has long been defined as the science of exchange (Bagozzi, 1975). In the for-profit sector, marketing is the management discipline that is focused on developing and maintaining exchange relationships with customers. In the nonprofit sector marketing pertains not only to customers or clients but also to exchange relationships with a wide range of donors, funders, supporters, users, suppliers, partners and adherents—as well as taxpayers and public opinion. Although the facilitation of exchanges with many of these groups is called by names other than "marketing" in nonprofit organizations (for example, fundraising, grant writing, volunteer and employee recruitment, program development, communications, or public relations), the marketing paradigm articulates an approach to value creation and exchange as being at the heart of an organization's interaction with and responsiveness to the individuals and institutions in its environment.

The conceptual framework upon which strategic marketing is based asserts that satisfying the needs and wants of key target groups through exchange results in organizational "success" (the achievement of the organization's goals). Research in the private sector has demonstrated that higher levels of organizational orientation toward the market are associated with performance outcomes such as return on investment (Narver and Slater, 1990). Of course, in the nonprofit sector organizational goals comprise many complex ambitions beyond the simple goal of profitability that is paramount in the for-profit sector. Research on nonprofit organizations has shown that market orientation not only predicts success in attracting financial resources but is also associated with other important mission-based outcomes such as higher degrees of client satisfaction (Gainer and Padanyi, 2002). This supports the notion that a focus on value creation with respect to all the different stakeholder groups with which the organization interacts is at the heart of realizing its ambitions.

Because marketing theory was developed in the private sector and focuses directly on profitability derived from customers, controversy has existed for years among marketing scholars about the "boundaries" of marketing and whether its concepts and tools can be applied to the nonprofit sector (Parson, Maclaran, and Tadajewski, 2008). Hutton (2001) has argued that the customer metaphor is fundamentally incompatible with an organization charged with the mission of social value creation. Nevertheless, prominent marketing scholars have argued that the marketing paradigm is extremely relevant to conceptualizing the relationship of the nonprofit organization to its environment (Andreasen and Kotler, 2008; Sargeant and Wymer, 2007).

Despite the acceptance of marketing in nonprofit organizations, there often remains a very limited view of what marketing entails. Marketing is often implemented primarily in terms of a few key sub-fields such as sales, communications or public relations and associated with information, education and persuasion processes. As a result of this narrow conceptualization of marketing, the value that a strategic marketing "mindset" can contribute at the leadership level to overall organization performance and success is often less than it could be.

In the for-profit sector, marketing is associated with both resource attraction and resource allocation—marketing is used to influence customers to buy products and services (resource attraction) and it is also the functional area that ultimately decides which products and services will be developed in order to attract those sales (resource allocation). Perhaps because of this reciprocal relationship between the resource attraction and resource allocation functions of marketing in the private sector, acceptance of marketing as a component of high-level strategic management and leadership in the nonprofit sector has been controversial. There has been an assumption that organizations that respond to "market forces" will drift away from a focus on their mission because they will begin to allocate funds to the development of "market-driven" programs associated with resource attraction in preference to "mission-driven" programs associated with resource allocation.

However, even though conflict may occasionally arise in nonprofits over decisions with respect to the "market" for resources and the "mission" associated with expenditures, these constructs are not dichotomous opposites nor mutually exclusive. The adoption of a strategic marketing mindset in a nonprofit organization does not mean that financial considerations will take precedence over operations or that devoting resources to marketing will erode spending on programs. Instead the implementation of the marketing concept and the development in the nonprofit sector of what has been called a "market orientation" in the private sector will mean that the nonprofit organization becomes more responsive to the wants and needs of the multiplicity of stakeholder groups with which it interacts—as well as to society more generally (Sargeant, Foreman, and Liao, 2002).

Key Concepts in Nonprofit Marketing

In the for-profit sector, marketing is the means through which firms engage in transactions with customers that are based on an exchange of value. Successful firms are those that are able to understand the needs and wants of their customers better than their competitors. In the nonprofit sector, marketing is based on a similar notion, although vastly more complicated in execution.

First, those who provide revenues to the firm are not often "customers" who buy goods or services. Therefore, the value exchange is often nonmonetary—though nonetheless valuable. For example, in exchange for financial contributions, labor (paid and unpaid), political support or behavioral change, a nonprofit organization may provide achievement, inclusion, sociability, status, skills, social networks, advocacy, enactment of public policy and—extremely difficult to measure but nonetheless very "real" in terms of value—better communities and a better world.

Second, in nonprofit marketing, the idea of multiparty as opposed to dyadic, or two-party, exchange is critical. There are many more constituencies with which a nonprofit organization engages in exchange transactions than simply "customers." Those for whom programs are designed are not always those who support the organization and even if earned revenues are substantial, resources are almost always attracted from a variety of sources (Young, 2006). The key concept here is that in each of the markets in which a nonprofit organization transacts, the notion of value exchange applies—government funders are looking for a means of implementing public policies while volunteers are looking for skill development, social engagement, or a way to contribute meaningful activity to their community. If a nonprofit organization wants to be successful in attracting resources, it will have to deliver sufficient value to the providers of those resources—while providing value to the different constituencies that "consume" those resources.

Of course, in practice, as an organization attempts to devote limited financial and human resources to the creation of value for all of the various constituencies that form the context in which it is embedded, conflict may emerge. A strategic marketing approach will not dictate that resources go to the market as opposed to the mission but it will provide a logical and defensible framework for analysis and planning that can lead to the most efficient *and* effective use of resources to build organizational success, defined as the organization's ability to achieve its mission over the long term. A marketing approach is based on the recognition that nonprofit organizations must be responsive to many different constituencies, understand the unique needs and wants of each, and take steps to create the tangible and intangible value that will form the basis of stable, sustainable, long-term exchange relationships.

The long-term quality of the relationship between an organization and its exchange partners is coming to be recognized as more important than using marketing techniques and tools to trigger isolated transactions (Conway, 1997). It is becoming increasingly important to consider the lifetime value of a client in the nonprofit sector because long-term relationships are associated with lower costs over time (Brennan and Brady, 1999). It is particularly difficult to continue investing in long-term relationships when organizations have revenues that are unpredictable from year to year and, moreover, are under substantial pressure to spend as much money as possible on programs and services and not on fundraising or recruitment or other kinds of administrative expenses. A marketing analysis based on value exchange would suggest, however, that investments in long-term relationships pay off not only in terms of cutting costs that come from losing clients after one transaction and then having to pay more later to attract new ones, but also from the ability to move long-term relationships to higher levels of value exchange.

A strategic approach to marketing goes beyond a focus on the relationships between an individual organization and the many client groups to which it directly offers services or advocacy or from whom it gathers financial and other resources. Nonprofit organizations are embedded in large market systems that operate the same way that for-profit market systems work. Market systems consist of many producers or programs and services and many potential clients who "consume" the programs and services in different ways—as well as many indirect players and forces such as regulators, suppliers, umbrella groups, credentials, qualifications, reputations, and others. Market systems can be based on a system of production (settlement programs for new immigrants, symphony concerts, opposition to an oil pipeline) or can cut across producers (such as the market for volunteer labor or fundraising). Understanding the totality of the market systems in which an organization participates will determine how well it is able to innovate, adopt new technologies and ideas, obtain financial support and achieve its goals (Giesler, 2015).

In the next section I examine the three direct components of the market systems in which nonprofit organizations are embedded and introduce concepts and theories that underpin a strategic approach to nonprofit markets and marketing. The three elements of this framework are the clients or customers for whom the organization develops programs and services, the "competitors" or rival organizations appealing to clients, and the particular competencies or strengths of the marketing organization in terms of producing its programs or services. In the final section of the chapter, I examine the four main types of decisions that an organization must make in order to develop the "marketing mix" that it will use to participate in a marketing system. In this section some of the key models, tools, and techniques of marketing are presented and adapted for nonprofit organizations and systems.

A Strategic Approach to Marketing

Figure 13.1 outlines a step-by-step hierarchy of decisions that must be made about which groups to serve or to target given the competitive situation, the human and financial resources that are available, and the organization's particular competencies and expertise. Once these strategic choices have been made, an organization can develop a marketing mix of appropriate programs and services, communications, pricing and delivery systems that will maximize its potential to achieve its mission. All of the inputs to the decision processes mapped in this chart should be based on analysis of concrete data.

It should be noted that the analytical process outlined in Figure 13.1 can be used to develop marketing strategies that will be applied to each "market system" in which a nonprofit organization is embedded—for example, a segmentation strategy, the first decision point at the top of the chart, will be different for the fundraising market than for the client services market.

FIGURE 13.1. The Strategic Marketing Process

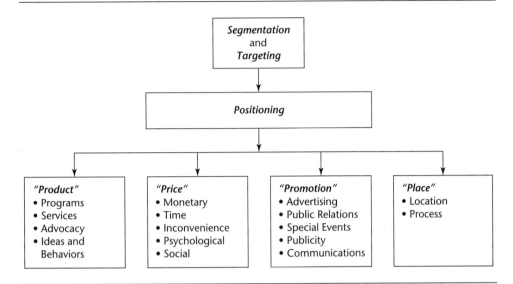

The Role of Data Analysis in Decision Making

Formal market research in nonprofit enterprises is quite rare and usually limited to the larger fundraising organizations (universities, colleges, hospitals, and some of the large medical research and service organizations). The cost of research is often prohibitive, but there are other reasons that nonprofits are reluctant to undertake research. One is that many nonprofit organizations are convinced that they already understand their markets and what they need, a notion that results from the fact that many nonprofits offer services provided by highly trained and specialized professionals such as social workers, psychologists, educators, artists, scientists, or medical personnel. Market studies may appear unwarranted because the service deliverer seems to be in a better position than the user to specify the appropriate service or program. The service deliverer may see it as a duty to prescribe what services the other party should receive. Other reasons that many nonprofit organizations fail to see value in research is that they often operate on a small scale and know the individuals with whom they interact personally, and they often deal with end-users directly, as opposed to through intermediaries. However, organizations that make an organized effort to collect and analyze data to answer specific questions with regard to resource allocation and attraction will not only be more effective in their markets but also be more accountable to their stakeholders as a result of evidence-based decision making.

"Big data" is a new term that pertains to the growing proliferation of data generated by digital technology in many areas of human endeavor (for example, science and the environment, business and finance, health and hospitals). The nonprofit sector is far behind the business and public sectors in using big data to help manage their operations. There are several reasons for this: data pertaining to social issues are relatively unstructured, can lack variety, and may be unreliable; there is little sharing of data about social issues between agencies or with the public as relevant data are often buried in administrative systems; effective data governance systems are lacking; and finally, the data can often be misinterpreted or even manipulated when it comes to public issues and thus be misleading and/or lead to unintended consequences (Desouza and Smith, 2014). Large intersectoral collaborative networks formed around complex social problems such as poverty, homelessness, or human migration may be the first to use big data, partly because the owners and analysts of the data will come from the public or for-profit sectors. It remains to be seen, however, what contribution big data can make to addressing the "wicked" questions individual organizations face as they grapple with messy and complex social issues.

However, as for-profit business moves toward big data to support marketing decision making, new and small-scale techniques are emerging in the social sector that allow individual and relatively small organizations to collect their own data relatively quickly, cheaply, and effectively. Recently, Acumen, an organization interested in social impact measurement, has developed a direct approach to data collection that they call "lean data." The lean data approach is based on a shift away from surveys that collect data for reporting to and enabling compliance with outside agencies, funders, investors, and regulators. Instead it is designed to provide value to the organization itself. It is affordable and easily managed by nonexperts because it is based on familiar mobile phone technology and simple customer feedback instruments. As opposed to simply measuring outcomes "after the fact," the lean data approach can also be used to help marketers decide about program and product development, understand clients' and customers' needs better, and test hypotheses about the behavioral outcomes of various approaches. This approach can be adopted by almost any nonprofit organization, regardless of size or expertise in data analysis (Dichter, Adams, and Ebrahim, 2016).

Regardless of how simple or small the investigation, it is increasingly important that nonprofit organizations undertake some form of data-based analysis before making decisions about their programs. On the management side, the collection and analysis of reliable data can combat organizational myopia that stems from being too close to an issue and, more important, to a particular organizational culture that has defined the external environment in a particular way. Data analysis is a way to engage in "critical thinking" about an issue and the people involved with it; it allows managers and leaders to look at questions from different perspectives and reframe issues. It has been suggested that because clients and funders are separate constituencies in nonprofit organizations, there is no direct feedback loop as exists in the business sector to ensure good service (Connor, 1999). Moreover, when nonprofit clients are ill-served, their remedies may be few and frail. Clients of many social or community service organizations are more likely to be disadvantaged and vulnerable, to have less opportunity to switch to other providers, and to be more afraid of complaining than in for-profit marketing situations. Anonymous, confidential, and simple data collection can give these important stakeholders opportunities to provide information that should be part of every nonprofit organization's decision processes.

Segmentation and Target Marketing

Target marketing is the process whereby decisions are made about which groups an organization will choose to serve within specific market systems. For example, in the market for donations, an organization may divide individual donors into several groups, each of which responds differently to a nonprofit organization's appeals, such as board members, current or former clients (such as students, audience members, patients), people who may be affected personally by the cause in the future, prominent and known philanthropists, and well-to-do members of the community who are aging and perhaps considering legacy gifts. Moreover, because organizational resources are limited and may not allow a nonprofit to target all of these segments at once, decisions need to be made about which market segments best fit the organization's objectives and abilities, and then about how to tailor marketing programs to create the most value for each of the chosen segments. All of these decisions about whether and how to segment a market need to be made for each of the separate constituencies or market systems within which a nonprofit organization acts (Rupp, Karn, and Helmig, 2014).

Choosing to "target" certain groups while ignoring others may seem a questionable, if not unacceptable, approach in the nonprofit sector. Choosing some segments means that an organization will focus on some people and that may mean not serving or communicating with others. In a field in which turning no one away or achieving mass social change is often a cherished norm, neglecting some possible clients as a matter of policy can seem to degrade fundamental organizational values.

However, the case for target marketing is both strong and responsible. In an environment in which human needs are escalating while resources are constrained and shrinking, no organization can reach all possible constituencies. The question then is not whether the enterprise will constrain its domain but how. Market segmentation allows nonprofit organizations to control whom they serve by choosing where they will be most effective, based on their competencies, or where it is most important for them to act, or according to organizational mandate or mission, and then to spend limited resources efficiently, rather than letting the limits of their funding arbitrarily decide which markets they cannot serve when they run out of funds. Segmentation helps an organization focus its resources on the clienteles that best fit its mission, capabilities, and aspirations.

The first step in segmentation is to divide the market into meaningful groups. Segments are considered meaningful when they are "homogeneous within, heterogeneous without." This means that the people or organizations within a segment are considered to behave the same way in response to particular marketing programs and to behave differently from people in other segments. There are a number of variables that may be used to define segments. The most conventional segmentation criterion is *socio-demographic*, a term coined to represent a wide variety of easily observable characteristics (for example, geographic residency; "social class" as measured by education, profession, or income; or age). These variables are convenient because available data are most often arrayed along these lines, and they can serve as useful surrogates for deeper psychological and behavioral motivations that marketers cannot always access. For example, fundraisers are becoming more and more interested in segmenting on the basis of age since research indicates that Generation Y donors behave differently than older ones; they are motivated much more by "sharing" as opposed to "giving" and are therefore more likely to respond to appeals based on social network ties and that emphasize pleasure as opposed to duty, which may be more relevant to older segments (Urbain, Gonzalez, and Le Gall-Ely, 2013).

However, despite the convenience of using socio-demographic segmentation, it does not always stand as an effective surrogate for behavior. Other data, although more difficult to collect and interpret, can often provide a more nuanced approach to segmentation. Psychographics, based on information about lifestyles, values, attitudes, and opinions, can be particularly important in segmenting for social marketing efforts designed to change attitudes and behaviors. Personality variables such as empathy and self-esteem have been suggested as useful segmentation variables for recruiting volunteers (Wymer, 1997). Benefit segmentation is efficacious because, being rooted in the fundamental notion of market exchange, it not only identifies homogeneous client clusters but also is suggestive of the most relevant offer for each. Benefit segmentation is useful in volunteer marketing and is also used to good effect in fundraising. Behavioral segmentation (for example, heavy versus light users) is relevant to many causes; heavy users are especially propitious targets. Fundraisers have now begun to segment their markets on the basic of financial value, calculating the worth of a potential target group over the course of a long-term relationship (Rupp, Kern, and Helmig, 2014).

Once potential segmentation criteria have been formulated for a particular market, the marketer must calculate whether the value of using these specific criteria is worthwhile. For example, if some potential donors are moved by sympathy for people who have a given disease while others react to a warning that they may contract it, a segmentation scheme that identifies that these groups respond positively to different messages and develops two different marketing programs to solicit donations may be warranted. In a case such as this, the decision will be made on the basis of whether the expected reward from appeals tailored more specifically to the needs of individual groups will outweigh the costs associated with developing multiple campaigns.

In choosing which segments to target, several criteria come into play. The first, of course, is whether a particular segment fits the mission of the enterprise. Just because a particular segment is easiest to reach, for example, may not mean it will be the most important group to target. A second criterion is whether the segment aligns with the organization's capabilities. In appraising the goodness of fit of a potential target market with an organization's capabilities, organizations must be careful not to overvalue their own capabilities and underestimate the strengths and competencies of competitors.

A third criterion is whether the segment is sufficiently large to justify a special marketing treatment. Arriving at an answer to this question can be complicated in the nonprofit sector. In a commercial firm, the projected value of a superior return from an investment in a unique marketing program is usually the only arbiter of acceptable segment size. In a charitable enterprise, financial considerations may be overridden. This may be acceptable if the organization is able to cross-subsidize special programs through revenues from more "profitable" segments, but not if the loss associated with serving the small segments endangers the survival of the organization.

A final consideration in target selection is whether particular segments can be accessed by special marketing programs. Often targets are difficult to estimate and the members are hard to reach through specialized marketing programs. Ideally, the idea of targeting specific markets is to use a narrow approach in which only the specified clients are reached by specialized media, messages, pricing, and so forth—it is through targeting specific segments that the cost savings are realized that make segmentation so efficient. However, if a segment is not easily reachable, it is often necessary, and more economical, to use a "mass market" approach, which leaves it to members of the target population to choose to "come into the market" through a process of self-selection. Social media now achieve some of the benefits of both strategies; it is a cheap way to distribute messages to many people, but the messages are somewhat restricted to those who participate in particular social networks. It can be suitable for large target markets for whom personal contact is not required and the message can be tailored to appeal to specific groups. For important small target markets where personal contact is paramount, other methods of reaching the target will be necessary.

Competition, Positioning, and Branding

Competition is an idea that is often troubling in the nonprofit sector. Adherents of economic theories of the nonprofit sector who consider these organizations to have developed out of market failure argue that nonprofit organizations respond to need and do not compete. Often there is a philosophical aversion to the idea of competition on the part of those who work in the nonprofit sector, who would prefer to think of the sector as being engaged in cooperative, as opposed to competitive, behavior.

Nevertheless, competition is a reality in the nonprofit sector (Oster, 1995). In many countries the number of nonprofit organizations has exploded, and many of them have been founded specifically because they intend to provide alternative programs or philosophies to the offerings of existing organizations in the same market system. Moreover, many nonprofit organizations are trying to influence attitudes and behavior, and their target markets always have choices about how they think and behave—even if it means continuing with their old habits and patterns. In this sense, even "doing nothing" can be considered "competition."

Positioning refers to the place that an agency occupies in the minds of the individuals in its target market (Trout and Rivkin, 1997). It is always related to how an organization and its offerings are evaluated in terms of a known set of alternatives (or competition). The first step in developing a positioning strategy

FIGURE 13.2. Positioning Map for Hypothetical Immigrant-Serving Agencies

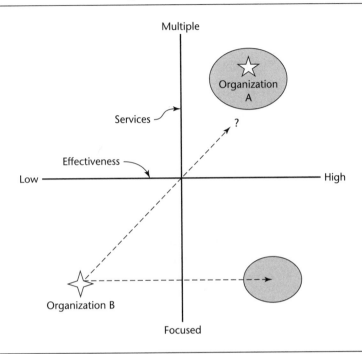

involves understanding the dimensions that the target market uses to compare organizations and alternatives, and the second seeks to place the alternatives, relative to each other, in a "space" defined by those dimensions. For example, if potential clients evaluate immigrant-serving organizations along the dimensions of "multiple service offerings" and "effectiveness in service outcomes," they would place different settlement organizations in different positions on a grid formed with the two dimensions as axes (see Figure 13.2).

One of the troubling realities of positioning in the nonprofit sector is that the multiple constituencies with which organizations interact often evaluate both the dimensions that they use to compare agencies and the position of individual agencies along those dimensions differently. For example, wealthy potential donors may compare arts organizations in terms of the service and opportunities for recognition that they provide to their major patrons, while government granting agencies that support artistic work may compare the same organizations on different dimensions, such as originality or creativity. It may also happen that different market constituencies use the same dimensions but evaluate competitors differently. For example, both clients and foundation officials may evaluate and compare social service agencies in terms of their effectiveness. However, clients may evaluate a particular agency as highly effective in personal terms, while a funder may rate the same agency as low on effectiveness because they don't see large-scale change in a community. The key point is that positioning refers to the dimensions and the relative positions along those dimensions that are in the minds of *each* clientele with which the marketing organization interacts. A nonprofit organization that serves several clienteles (for example, donors, users, government grantors) will develop a unique positioning map for each market system, and this in turn will dictate a unique marketing strategy for each separate clientele.

Of course, the grids cannot be mapped unless the perceptions of the target markets are known, and the best way to collect this information is through some form of concrete data analysis. However, even a dispassionate and objective "back of the envelope" grid can be mapped without expensive data if managers are willing to talk to their potential audiences and listen to what they say about the evaluative dimensions that matter to them and how they see the alternatives before them in terms of these dimensions.

Once an organization has determined its positioning, the next step is to develop a positioning strategy. Positioning is based on the key marketing idea of *differentiation*—in other words, an organization is positioned on the grid on the basis of how it differs from its competitors on the dimensions of interest. The important thing to notice about Figure 13.2 is that, even if an organization has given no thought to positioning and is not interested in the process, it is still positioned on the grid in the minds of its target market!

An organization may choose to maintain its current position by continuing to emphasize those factors that differentiate it in positive ways, or it may choose to emphasize characteristics that would differentiate it in more positive ways by using elements of the marketing mix to move to a more advantageous position on the grid. In either case, it is important to keep in mind that not all competitors should plan to locate themselves in the same position on the grid (different segments will be located in different places in accordance to their particular preferences). The trick is to find a market group of sufficient size, that wants a particular combination of attributes the organization has the capacity to provide—and is able to provide them better (faster, cheaper, with better outcomes) than other organizations. If an organization can do something better than a competitor, it will not be in the same place as a competitor on the grid—it will be in a better one.

In Figure 13.2 the shaded circles represent the size of market segments and their preferences. We can see Organization A is well positioned and Organization B is not. What should Organization A's strategy be? It should continue to emphasize the fact that it offers "one-stop shopping" (multiple services) and that it is effective in delivering desired outcomes. What should Organization B's strategy be? This organization has two choices: it must definitely improve the public perception of its effectiveness, but instead of adding more programs and services in order to move up and serve the segment located in the upper right quadrant, where it would have to compete directly with Organization A, it would be better off to target the segment in the lower right quadrant interested in, say, effective language training but who are not particularly looking for job training, child counseling, or computer training. It should also be noted that there may be several ways that it could "move" to the right on the grid and target the segment we see there. It may be that this organization is, in fact, highly effective but that is not well known. In that case a communications or advertising strategy would be effective in "moving" the organization to the right. If, on the other hand, the organization has not had a record of high achievement in language training, it will need to change or improve its programs in order to increase the perception of its effectiveness in this area.

Branding in the Nonprofit Sector

An important marketing idea related to positioning is *branding*. A brand is a shortcut means of identifying an organization, program, or cause in a way that differentiates it from alternatives. It is much more than a logo, a tagline, or a document that outlines a set of desired organizational characteristics. A brand is a psychological construct held in the minds of those aware of it. It embodies a set of characteristics that external communities believe will be delivered consistently. It can convey the organization's position in the market, build trust between the organization and its clienteles, raise an organization's profile and provide insulation from competition (Ritchie, Swami, and Weinberg, 1999).

In the nonprofit sector, branding was considered for many years to be an expensive extra, and it is true that the typical approach to branding in the nonprofit sector could absorb considerable financial resources as new logos and taglines were developed and advertised with little obvious return. Because this work was often instigated and managed by only one department, usually the fundraising department, there was little buy-in across the organization and certainly no sense that all functional areas needed to support the brand and possibly even change service delivery modes and program elements to be consistent with the brand image. It was often seen as a notion that pertained to "market-driven" organizations and had no relevance to organizations dedicated to social change. The branding process in many organizations led to skepticism and even resistance. This was exacerbated by the problems that developed in global or large national organizations with multiple branches with a high degree of local autonomy. It can be very difficult to standardize not only advertising materials, but also organizational cultures and decision making around the values inherent in the brand (Quelch and Laidler-Kylander, 2006).

Despite these difficulties, nonprofit branding is experiencing a renewal in nonprofit organizations as they come to realize that a brand is a psychological construct that is based on trust—and that an organization is likely to be "branded" in the public's mind whether the organization has taken a direct hand in that process or not. Recently it has been argued that a new, explicitly nonprofit, branding paradigm is emerging, which views the development of a nonprofit brand as a strategic effort to create greater social impact through sparking public discourse on issues and to build support for an explicit theory of change, both externally and internally (Kylander and Stone, 2012). Kylander and Stone characterized this new brand paradigm as the "Nonprofit Brand IDEA," which incorporates four elements relevant to the nonprofit sector, specifically integrity (social mission), democracy (a participatory process), ethics (shared values within an organization and among its stakeholders), and affinity (key partnerships with those who buy into the theory of change).

Managing the Marketing Mix

Having chosen target markets through a thoughtful approach to segmentation and determined a positioning strategy on the basis of dispassionate competitive analysis, the marketing organization is in a position to use the four major tactical elements of the marketing mix to facilitate exchange relationships with its chosen targets by offering them better "value" than alternatives. Value is the ratio of benefits to costs, and in the nonprofit sector this, of course, includes not only material benefits and financial costs but also intangible benefits (for example, experience, status, social networks) and costs (time, inconvenience, hard work). In other words, value is a perceptual construct, not simply an economic one.

Marketers, in an excessive devotion to alliteration, sometimes define the elements of the marketing mix as the "four Ps": product, place, price, and promotion. None of these is a very exact term. In the nonprofit sector, the *product* construct is the element of the marketing mix that refers to services, programs, advocacy, or ideas for which the organization wants to find users or supporters. *Place* refers to choices about distribution channels; *price* refers to all of the costs, tangible and intangible, that are considered by potential exchange partners; and *promotion* extends well beyond advertising to include all marketing communications (paid and earned, planned and unplanned).

Product Marketing in the Nonprofit Sector

The marketing of physical products, while it occurs in the nonprofit sector, is relatively uncommon. Instead most nonprofit organizations are engaged in service marketing and/or social marketing (behaviors and ideas). Physical products such as items in a thrift store, baked goods in a sheltered kitchen, or merchandise offered to those who buy membership is relatively easy for potential clients to evaluate. The same is not true of services such as literacy programs or home care for senior citizens, and it is even more difficult for potential supporters to evaluate such intangibles as anti-racism, a political candidate, or recycling.

Programs, Services, Behaviors, and Ideas

Some of the key differences between marketing products and marketing services are documented in the marketing literature. Services, for example, are generally considered to be harder for users to evaluate and harder for producers to control, in terms of standardization of quality, and impossible to inventory. Recently, scholars have also defined some of the key features that distinguish social marketing from product and service marketing: social marketing is often controversial (safe sex, gay and lesbian rights, the banning of "obscene" art), it is often deeply embedded in individuals' lives, cultures, and psyches (racial prejudice, overeating, corporal punishment of children), and it often involves target markets that are entire populations (changing to the metric system) or subsets of populations that are pitted against each other (ownership of handguns, support of political parties) (Andreasen, 2006; Kotler and Lee, 2007).

All of this suggests that the markets in which most nonprofit organizations typically engage are the most complex and challenging in which to succeed. Further challenges to making effective decisions about program marketing are posed by the internal circumstances of most nonprofit organizations. First, because competition is often considered to be weak or nonexistent, it is difficult to make a case for spending resources to collect data about market preferences or about new programs or services. In addition, where a case can be made for upgrading, downgrading, or eliminating a program, internal deliberations can be complicated by the attachment of founders, directors, funders, staff, or volunteers to preserving or protecting certain programs at the expense of other priorities. Underlying all of these obstacles to timely and rational planning of the "product line" is the absence of a market mechanism to arbitrate disagreements as to the proper adding, dropping, or changing of nonprofit programs. This can lead to extreme waste of resources, as sentiment about heritage programs can outweigh a focus on overall organizational effectiveness in terms of goal attainment. Most nonprofit organizations, especially larger ones but even small ones to some extent, are an assemblage of enterprises. Such organizations confront decisions not unlike those of a corporation that must determine which product lines to promote, maintain, or drop.

Portfolio analysis is a formal analytical process that is useful in allocating limited resources for maximum effectiveness in a nonprofit organization. Essentially, portfolio analysis identifies the main programs of an organization, establishes a set of criteria for judging the relative importance of these units, and evaluates each program against those criteria. Matrix models are often used to conceptualize and manage the decision processes inherent in portfolio analysis. Individual criteria can be clustered to produce a summary evaluation of the contribution of each program to the organization's goals on two or three key dimensions. In a nonprofit situation, one of the dimensions used to evaluate a particular program is "contribution to (or centrality of) mission," and others may be such factors as the size and growth of the market it serves, its quality and reputation, community need, contribution to revenue or the likelihood of breaking even. The summary appraisals are often mapped visually in a grid that yields a convenient visual representation (MacMillan 1983) or fitted into a table in which "scores" are assigned to each program on each dimension and then summed.

The Product Life Cycle

Programs, services, and policies need to be continually reappraised over the course of their lives as the environment in which they are developed changes. Important changes that affect nonprofit sector "products" are the entry of new services or service providers, the emergence of new community needs, and the loss of a major source of funding. A tool that has been useful in terms of understanding and managing the lifecycles of nonprofit causes, organizations, and specific programs and services is the product life cycle, based on the similarity of a marketplace to an ecological environment. The product life cycle (PLC) is visually represented as an "S" shaped curve mapped against two axes:

in a nonprofit context the curving line represents the number of "exchanges" (usage occasions, changes in behavior, and so forth) that take place as a program or service or organization engages in market relationships over time. Verbal models divide this evolution into stages of introduction, growth, maturity, and decline, and the curve rises rapidly in the introductory and growth stages but flattens dramatically in the mature stage of the life cycle.

Each phase of the PLC not only describes changes in both clients and competitors at different stages of evolution but also prescribes useful changes in marketing strategies to maximize the number of marketing exchanges at each phase. As shifts in the awareness, demand, and behavior of clients and the pressures of competitors emerge over time, nonprofit organizations need to change the elements of their marketing mix in order to achieve maximum effectiveness in terms of mission achievement. One of the most important insights from the PLC for nonprofits is that an organization that is offering a relatively new program may grow quickly in the early stage with little investment in communications or strategic positioning. However, as its success attracts more clients and competitors into the market system and the market reaches maturity, nonprofits will have to devote more resources to competing for clients and funding, and can expect the ratio of revenues to costs to decline substantially. In the for-profit sector this would lead to a "shake out" in which some firms collapse and leave the market; in the nonprofit sector this may suggest that mergers or partnerships are indicated (Gainer, 1989).

Adoption and Diffusion

In guiding products through their life cycles, particularly the education and advocacy programs characteristic of social marketing, nonprofit organizations can also take advantage of what is known about how innovations are adopted and then diffused throughout populations. Sociologists have discovered that new ways of thinking and behaving are accepted by certain groups of people within a population first, and that subsequent groups join in only after these initial "innovators" have gone ahead. This diffusion process is represented visually by a "bell curve" diagram, with "time" represented on the horizontal axis. Innovators or opinion leaders are represented by the small tail on the left, followed, as time passes, by a larger group of people known as "early adopters." As the curve rises toward its peak, more and more people adopt the behavior or ideas, eventually constituting the majority of the population. As the curve slopes downward again, the late adopters, and finally the laggards, are converted.

The implications of a model like this for nonprofit organizations are clear. One of the aspects of diffusion is that special interest should be directed toward finding and persuading those who are likely to be active and influential at the outset of the life cycle of a new idea or behavior. Rogers (1995) has suggested that compared to those who "get on board" later, early adopters in a social system tend to be younger, of higher social status, financially better off, more plugged into impersonal and cosmopolitan information sources, and in closer contact with the origins of new ideas. The model not only suggests that it is important to reach these people early in the process of developing new programs or behavior but also that it is a waste of organizational resources to target people who are more likely to be in the majority or late adopter categories—even if these are the people who ultimately are particularly important to reach. Even if the target market most closely aligned with organizational mission is older, more conservative, and of lower socioeconomic status, it is unlikely that a new idea or behavior will be adopted by this group until it has become more widely diffused in the general population. Nonprofit organizations often have a tendency to begin a program by targeting those who need it most. Although this can appeal to funders and board members, it can be a waste of organizational resources if the new ideas or behavior are not widely accepted by society at large.

Pricing in the Nonprofit Sector

Too often in nonprofit organizations, prices (including a decision to deliver goods or services at no fee, as in, say, a food bank or a crisis center) are set in arbitrary and casual ways. Moreover, prices are often set on the basis of attitudes or beliefs such as that services of a nonprofit organizations should always be delivered free or that the target market cannot afford to pay anything, when this is not necessarily the case. Many nonprofit organizations need to revisit their pricing policies on the basis of objective research into the needs and means of the target markets and decide whether they are accepting an unnecessary loss of revenue and, as a result, perhaps accepting a diminution of available benefits to their clients. Moreover, as more and more nonprofits address the revenue crises they face through activities associated with social enterprise, they are going to be setting prices in a competitive marketplace. For these reasons, pricing decisions in the nonprofit sector need to be made in a logical and analytical manner.

Understanding Nonfinancial Costs: A "Value" Approach to Pricing. Before describing useful approaches to setting monetary prices, it is worthwhile considering that the "price" of using a service or accepting an idea or adopting a behavior will include nonfinancial costs. Such nonfinancial costs might include awkwardness or embarrassment, time costs such as missing work or having to travel to remote and difficult locations, ancillary financial costs such as having to pay for parking or childcare, or psychological costs associated with giving up familiar or pleasurable habits.

A marketing perspective would put forward the idea that before putting resources into promoting a service or a behavior, one should search out opportunities to reduce each of these nonfinancial costs. A "value" approach to pricing would suggest that customers compare the benefits they receive for the costs they incur. Lowering the costs to the clientele, including nonfinancial costs, can thus increase the value of the offering substantially. Increasing the value of a product by cutting social, psychological, and time costs may be particularly important in a situation in which the organization is about to start charging for a service that has previously been free.

Pricing Objective. If an organization has made the decision to set a financial price for the first time or to revisit existing pricing policies, one of the first considerations is to get a clear sense of the organization's pricing objectives. There are a number of pricing objectives; for enterprises that are designed to raise money to cross-subsidize mission-based programs (such as museum shops), profit maximization may be the dominant goal. In other cases the goal may be cost recovery—in other words, instead of aiming for profits that can be used to subsidize other programs or services, the goal is to be able to offer services or programs so that their costs are covered by the people who use them. Cost recovery is used in situations in which an organization does not have the capacity or the desire to raise funds for certain programs from grants or donations. Setting prices according to "ability to pay" is also a scheme used by many nonprofits that use sliding scales based on income; objectives here are cost recovery but also social justice. Other considerations that may lead some nonprofits to modify pricing schemes that otherwise would focus solely on the basis of profit maximization or cost recovery are considerations such as not wanting to discourage use; not to be considered elitist or exclusive; not thought insensitive; or incur charges of unfair competition from private sector suppliers of similar services.

Pricing Strategies. *Cost-based pricing.* One of the easiest pricing strategies to understand and implement is cost-based pricing. The only complication in calculating the costs of services or programs is when an organization has a portfolio of multiple programs and decisions need to be made about the allocation of costs that are incurred jointly to individual programs (such as the rent paid for common facilities or the executive director's salary). As when diverse products come out of a single factory, an organization needs to arrive at a basis for allocating charges that seems rational under the circumstances (see Chapter Twenty-One and associated resources on the *Handbook* Internet website for information about cost allocation methods). Once a method of cost allocation has been developed, it is a simple matter to calculate the total cost of providing a particular program within an organization.

However, setting the price to charge each client who accesses that program is a more complicated matter. One of the most crucial pieces of information needed for this decision is a break-even analysis. This analysis takes into account how many "units" would have to be "sold" at a given price in order to cover all costs to produce it. One begins by separating expenses that vary with the number of clients (*variable costs*) from costs that are fixed regardless of how many people access the service or program (*fixed costs*).

For example, if we think of a language class for new immigrants, it is clear that printing costs for handout materials will vary according to how many people sign up for the class (these are variable costs), whereas the cost for the instructor's salary and the cost for the classroom space and heat and light are the same regardless of how many people are in the class (these are fixed costs).

A second important pricing concept is that of "contribution per unit." To develop a concrete example, consider that the class described above has variable printing costs of $200 per person for handouts and fixed costs of $1,750 for the teacher and $750 allocated for the room, light, and heat. The contribution per unit will be calculated by comparing the expected revenue per student (say we are considering a price of $250) and the variable cost per student (which is $200 for printing). The difference between these two amounts is how much we get from each student that will go to covering the fixed costs. Here our contribution per student is $50.

When using cost-based pricing, both the break-even volume (how many users we need to cover all of the fixed and variable costs) and the contribution per unit (how much each individual contributes to the fixed costs) must be considered. If it appears that the price that needs to be charged to recover the full costs is out of reach of the majority of users for whom the service is designed, then a decision can be made to reduce the variable costs (use cheaper accommodation, eliminate lunches, and so on) or to charge less than "cost" and subsidize the costs through grants or donations.

Demand-based pricing. Note that whereas the organization began with costs to calculate the break-even price, it then led to considerations about how prospective clients would respond to that price. This example demonstrates that it is critically important to understand the concept of *break-even* in order to plan fundraising or grant writing efforts, and that it is equally important to understand that cost analysis is linked to demand analysis when actually setting prices. A useful concept in analyzing demand is that of *elasticity*. Price elasticity is the responsiveness of demand to changes in price. When a large change in price causes little change in demand, demand is said to be "price inelastic." When a small change in price causes big changes in demand, the demand curve is said to be "elastic" at that point. In general, inelastic demand means that an organization can increase revenues by raising prices, whereas elastic demand means that it is best to avoid price increases and, if the goal is to expand the number of users of a product or service, to lower prices. Clearly, knowledge of the elasticity of demand can be helpful in deciding whether to initiate user fees and at what level to set them.

Elasticity of demand may vary dramatically across market segments. That variability invites different prices for different segments. The differential pricing of seats in a theater, the offering of lower-priced services for students or seniors, and the subsidization of some children in a camp all represent pricing schemes that recognize and respond to differing demand elasticities. Of course, differential pricing involves ethical as well as economic decision making, which nonprofit leaders must recognize, resolve, and defend.

Demand-based pricing requires that the price-setting organization knows or is able to estimate accurately the value of the offer as perceived by the "buyer." This has important implications for nonprofit leaders. Those who are insulated from their markets may substitute their own beliefs about their clients for facts and thereby invent inaccurate pricing data. This can lead nonprofit organizations to price their services too low based on beliefs about clients considering nonprofit programs to be "second rate" or on beliefs about what clients will want to or be able to pay.

Competitive pricing. Pressed to keep up with the demand for services, nonprofit organizations often react as though they have no competition and dismiss competitive analysis as irrelevant. Yet the intended clienteles of most nonprofit enterprises do have alternatives for their patronage. End-users often define relevant competitors as those that offer similar benefits, rather than just similar-looking products or services delivered by similar-looking nonprofit agencies. Appraising competition can be useful in several ways. First, it will help identify the ceiling—the highest price that can be charged. Studying competitors' prices, both monetary and nonmonetary, can also reveal ways in which service deliverers can offer better products at lower prices. However, nonprofit managers must also consider the ethical implications of competitive pricing. Sometimes competitors, particularly in the private sector, are able to offer low prices through extremely low wage policies or by hiring less qualified service deliverers than nonprofit agencies are comfortable with. Moreover, private-sector firms in high-demand markets may choose to serve only those segments with high-profit potential, whereas nonprofit agencies may feel ethically bound to make their services available to those market segments with more limited means. However, for-profit companies may feel that nonprofits are unfairly undercutting their prices because they are not subject to the same tax demands as for-profit companies. Thus, competitive analysis is a useful and essential input to the pricing process, but it must be employed in conjunction with costs, market demand, and social and ethical considerations.

Designing Marketing Channels

Decisions about how best to distribute an offering to a market can have a major effect on the fortunes of the offering itself. In some respects, the choice of channels can be more critical in the third sector than in the private sector. When the product is a service, it is often consumed at the same time and place that it is produced, thereby putting the nonprofit employee in direct contact with end-users. Religious, psychological, health, and educational services tend to be of that sort. The buyer-seller contact may be inherently sensitive and intrusive, making the quality of the channel offering unusually critical to a satisfactory outcome and requiring that the nonprofit marketer is a client-oriented channel manager. It follows from this that the first step in channel design should be to analyze the requirements of the end-user and a basic building block in building a market channel is the user's specification of acceptable performance.

In designing service facilities, management may find it useful to invoke a categorization common in retailing: that of convenience, shopping, and specialty goods. Convenience products are those that the shopper will not exert much effort to investigate; at the other extreme, specialty goods are those that call forth considerable effort. Shopping goods lie somewhere in between. These definitions, derived from clients, have implications for logistics: convenience products must be readily accessible, while specialty products can be successfully distributed through few and more remote channels. Thus, social marketing messages that advocate changes in behavior will not be sought out by the target market and must be readily accessible and ubiquitous in order to reach the target because people will not seek out this information or put effort into finding it. Yet, an organization that provides specialized home care for a unique market segment can probably expect that their services will be sought out.

When alternative suppliers are absent, as they often are in the nonprofit sector, suppliers are inclined to design distribution systems that suit their convenience more than the end-user's in order to save costs. Nevertheless, the organization has to balance the client's desire for convenience with the service deliverer's need for operating efficiency. There are several ways to manage this trade-off (Lovelock and Weinberg 1989). One is to decentralize the client contact function while centralizing the technical operations—this is the Red Cross model of blood collection in which blood is collected where it is convenient to the donors but processed centrally. This model is also used by international and national charities that centralize direct mail fundraising, for example, but have many local and regional offices that provide "high touch" engagement of volunteers who raise funds through special events and social networks. A third variation of this solution is to offer more limited services at branches than at the main site, and a fourth is to join with other providers of compatible products to offer a larger meaningful assortment at a local site—information agencies or entertainment ticket agencies are examples of this channel strategy.

Related to a channel's accessibility is the question of the kind and quality of the experience it will deliver. In the past, museums and hospitals have attracted critical comment for their forbidding atmosphere. In contrast, an immigrant settlement agency may record its answering message in many different languages in order to communicate a multilingual and multicultural atmosphere for callers contacting the agency for the first time.

Finally, although there are often advantages for the short, controlled distribution channels that are characteristic of most nonprofit organizations, it is sometimes necessary or advisable to use channel intermediaries. These channels may be cheaper, more quickly activated, more expert, or more accessible to end-users. Nonprofit organizations also use channel collaborators in order to achieve their goals. To illustrate, advocacy alone may persuade some smokers that they should quit, but their behavior is more likely to change if it is validated by medical judgments, mandated by laws, and supported by workplace regulations. No organization acting alone can deliver all of these components, but out of such imperatives come marketing partnerships among hospitals, cancer societies, medical associations, school boards, industry associations, and government department.

Where there are interinstitutional relationships, however, there will also be conflict. Even institutions that want to collaborate will bring to the table, in addition to complementary knowledge and skills, potentially competing values, goals, and priorities. Because charitable enterprises are highly value-driven, imprinted with founders' visions, protective of their turf, and in competition for scarce funds, they are just as likely as business firms to experience conflict in the distribution chain. Third-sector organizations need to be assiduous about forming partnerships that work to the advantage of the distribution system as a whole, including the end-user, and recognizing the need for continuous attention to the power relationships and their management that a complex channel requires. In the field of early intervention services for children with disabilities, for example, it has been suggested that neutral brokers may help parents or caregivers access the best services by resolving some of the channel conflict that clients may lack the power to resolve on their own (Fugate, 2000).

Marketing Communications

The marketing communications program must flow logically from, and fit consistently with, the other elements of the overall strategic approach to an organization's multiple markets. Additionally, as we see rapid changes in the fragmentation of media with more specific media usage and a huge growth in online usage, it is increasingly important to integrate marketing communications across all the different media and contact points through which the various clienteles of interest interact with a nonprofit organization.

Marketing communications in contemporary organizations consist of three types of messages. Planned messages are the most obvious—the traditional form of controlled communications comprising advertising, public relations, direct response marketing, licensing, websites and Internet marketing. However, communication does not only consist of messages that organizations send out to their audiences, but also what messages are actually received by target markets of interest. Recently it has come to be understood that unplanned (and uncontrolled) messages play an equally important part in terms of organizational communications. Employee behavior, media stories and investigations, chat groups and social network sites, government investigations, blogs, and Twitter all convey information about an organization, its programs and services, its policies and advocacy, and its brand. And there is a third, "unconsidered" aspect of communications as well—factors such as service, facilities, and the other elements of the marketing mix such as pricing, distribution channels, and programs, and services communicate volumes about an organization and its brand. These unconsidered elements of marketing communications are, in fact, controllable and serve to underline the point that not only do the formal elements of the communications mix (such as advertising and direct mail and public relations) need to be integrated, but that all of the messages through which an organization communicates to its target markets need to be considered, planned, and controlled in so far as possible.

Simply coordinating the look of marketing communications does nothing to integrate the fragmented messages that contemporary clients receive, however. To truly "brand" an organization so that it represents a clear, differentiated, and trusted place in clients' minds, the messages that they receive must be integrated and consistently delivered—and not only across the different media an organization uses to get its messages out but also across all the different aspects of the organization with which clients interact.

The traditional elements of the marketing communications mix used by for-profit organizations are advertising, publicity, public relations, direct response, sales promotions, and personal selling. Increasingly, new media, especially the Internet, and sponsorships and events are coming to be seen as important channels of communication as well. More and more marketing communications take place in the street or online, as opposed to in the home through advertising, mail, telephone, and news media. This shift represents not only the emergence of new communications technology but also the emergence of a new trend in marketing communications, namely participation. As people become less and less inclined to simply "receive" marketing communications and more engaged in participating in the creation of communications through events and social media, nonprofit organizations need to recognize that, although marketing communication still occurs through commercial channels, it is also delivered through cultural and community contexts (Hanna and Middleton, 2008). For example, research indicates that a "social network effect" results in a different set of giving determinants; online donors give for different reasons and to different causes than those who give through traditional media (Saxton and Wang, 2014).

This is both good news and bad news for the third sector. On the one hand, it means that unplanned and uncontrolled communications abound about organizations that have traditionally already been subject to a very high degree of public scrutiny and misinformation. On the other hand, it means that a sector, deprived of the resources necessary to undertake expensive, advertising campaigns and media buys, can, through strategic communications planning, capitalize on one of its greatest assets—the engagement and participation of citizens embedded in the social networks that constitute communities. Social networks coupled with social communications technology appear to be leading to a new resource for nonprofit organizations: that of "social media capital" (Saxton and Chao, 2014).

Summary

Marketing is the management discipline charged with facilitating exchanges with key constituencies. The marketing concept posits that organizational success is achieved through satisfying the needs and wants of exchange partners better than competitors do. In large nonprofits, particularly in those that deliver services in return for payment or create programs that attract large donations, we have seen the adoption of sophisticated marketing systems and thinking across organizational departments and levels, sometimes characterized as a "market orientation." In many other organizations, particularly those that are most reliant on grant income (transfer payments), the importance of external constituencies is much less evident to leaders, and marketing is still considered to be limited to the fields of communications and public relations. A value-based approach to clients (both providers and users of resources), a strategic approach to competitors, and an analytical approach to organizational programs, services, and competencies is lacking in many nonprofits. Moreover, in some nonprofit organizations, a fear persists that a "marketing approach" to decision making will derail an organization from its mission.

In part this is because marketing theory as applied to the for-profit sector dictates that the marketing department has control over all of the "four Ps," whereas this notion is rejected almost universally in the nonprofit sector. In fact, in many organizations there is a "dual leadership" function that is designed precisely to separate decision making that pertains to operations and programs from that which pertains to income development. In some arts organizations, this is formalized by having two "equal" leaders at the top of an organizational hierarchy (Reid and Karambayya, 2009), whereas in other nonprofit settings the duality may reside in one senior leader who takes advice on programs from different experts than those who offer marketing advice. For example, in a live performing arts company, the repertoire is largely chosen by the artistic director; in a family service agency, the programs to be mounted are primarily determined by professional social workers or psychologists; in a university, the curriculum is mostly shaped by the faculty; in a public arts gallery, decisions about acquisitions lie primarily with curators; and in a hospital, the type and quality of care are governed largely by physicians, nurses, and other health care workers.

These customary organizational arrangements are highly significant for nonprofit marketing. They testify to the fact that in many parts of the nonprofit sector, key decisions about the most pivotal parts of the "marketing mix" are made by experts who, in their training and their experience, have little exposure to or regard for marketing. Whereas the primary purpose of for-profit organizations is to make money for their owners or shareholders, and thus it is appropriate for marketing managers to have control over much of the production of these organizations, the primary purpose of nonprofit organizations is to serve the public good through the production of goods, services, and ideas that are generated on the basis of expert knowledge and not necessarily on the basis of demand.

However, while marketing experts in the nonprofit sector must understand and accept that "subject matter" expertise is critical to achieving the mission of nonprofit organizations, it is equally important for others to recognize that facilitating mutually advantageous exchanges between the organization and its environments is critical. Nonprofit organizations achieve their mission not merely through producing services and advocacy but also by ensuring that this production is adequately funded and that their services and ideas reach those for whom they are produced.

Marketing is the aspect of management in nonprofit organizations that is most often to be found advocating for responsiveness to external clienteles and environments. For-profit organizations have unambiguous feedback from a conventional market mechanism, but nonprofit organizations must find other ways to ensure that they respond effectively to clients' wants and needs. Marketing facilitates this responsiveness, not by developing programs and ideas that are within the domain of subject-matter experts, but by monitoring the environment, undertaking market research, communicating changing wants and needs of key client groups, participating in portfolio analysis, suggesting suitable segmentation schemes and target markets, creating and maintaining a consistent brand internally and externally, establishing differentiation, and most important, by fostering the relationships that are crucial to the long-term survival of the organization. It is particularly important to recognize that, although many of these relationships may provide financial resources that contribute to sustainability, many others provide equally important "nonfinancial" support—attitudinal and behavioral change, public trust, political pressure, or volunteer commitment and engagement.

Progressive nonprofit organizations realize that in an era of increasing emphasis on notions of transparency, accountability, participation, engagement, equity, and democracy, a more systematic and strategic approach to both understanding and responding to the needs of the multiple constituencies with an interest in the organization is necessary. Organizations need to pay more than lip service to the notion of including the needs of key constituencies, both internal and external, in their decision making and activities and to the need for increasing participation in and engagement with civil society organizations. Marketing is the discipline of management that is charged with "boundary spanning" activities and bringing the perspectives and ideas of external constituencies inside the nonprofit organization. Incorporating the insights and analysis of marketing into decision making at all levels of the nonprofit organization is thus a critical aspect of a new third-sector leadership that is focused not only on increasing the resource base and visibility of the third sector but also on enhancing its role in building connected communities and an active and engaged citizenry.

References

Andreasen, A. R. *Social Marketing for the 21st Century*. Thousand Oaks, CA: Sage, 2006.

Andreasen, A. R., and Kotler, P. *Strategic Marketing for Nonprofit Organizations* (7th ed.). Upper Saddle River, NJ: Prentice Hall, 2008.

Bagozzi, R. P. Marketing as Exchange. *Journal of Marketing*, 1975, 39, 32–39.

Brennan, L., and Brady, E. Relating to Marketing? Why Relationship Marketing Works for Not-for-Profit Organisations. *International Journal of Nonprofit and Voluntary Sector Marketing*, 1999, 4, 327–337.

Connor, R. How Responsive Are Charities to Market Needs? *International Journal of Nonprofit and Voluntary Sector Marketing*, 1999, 4, 338–348.

Conway, T. Strategy vs. Tactics in the Not-for-Profit Sector: A Role for Relationship Marketing? *International Journal of Nonprofit and Voluntary Sector Marketing*, 1997, 2, 42–51.

Desouza, K. C., and Smith, K. L. Big Data for Social Innovation. *Stanford Social Innovation Review*, 2014, 12(3), 38–43.

Dichter, S., Adams, T., and Ebrahim, A. The Power of Lean Data. *Stanford Social Innovation Review*, 2016, 14(1), 36–41.

Fugate, D. L. Channel Design for Early Intervention Services: Is There a Role for Brokers? *Journal of Nonprofit and Public Sector Marketing*, 2000, 7(4), 3–15.

Gainer, B. The Business of High Art: Marketing the Performing Arts in Canada. *Service Industries Journal*, 1989, 9, 143–161.

Gainer, B., and Padanyi, P. Applying the Marketing Concept to Cultural Organizations: An Empirical Study. *International Journal of Nonprofit and Voluntary Sector Marketing*, 2002, 7, 182–193.

Giesler, M. The Secret to Bird Feeding (and Innovation Success). *Tedx YorkU*, 2015.

Hanna, J., and Middleton, A. *Ikonica: A Fieldguide to Canada's Brandscape*. Vancouver: Douglas and McIntyre, 2008.

Hutton, J. G. Narrowing the Concept of Marketing. *Journal of Nonprofit and Public Sector Marketing*, 2001, 9(4), 5–24.

Kotler, P., and Lee, N. *Social Marketing: Influencing Behaviors for Good* (3rd ed.). Thousand Oaks, CA: Sage, 2007.

Kylander, N., and Stone, C. The Role of Brand in the Nonprofit Sector. *Stanford Social Innovation Review*, 2012, 2, 36–41.

Lovelock, C., and Weinberg, C. B. *Marketing for Public and Nonprofit Managers* (2nd ed.). Redwood City, CA: Scientific Press, 1989.

MacMillan, I. C. Competitive Strategies for Not-for-Profit Agencies. *Advances in Strategic Management*, 1983, 1, 61–68, reprinted in S. M. Oster (ed.), *Strategic Management for Nonprofit Organizations: Theory and Cases*. New York: Oxford University Press, 1995.

Narver, J. C., and Slater, S. F. The Effect of a Marketing Orientation on Business Profitability. *Journal of Marketing*, 1990, 54, 20–35.

Oster, S. M. *Strategic Management for Nonprofit Organizations: Theory and Cases*. New York: Oxford University Press, 1995.

Parson, L., Maclaran, P., and Tadajewski, M. (eds.). *Nonprofit Marketing* (3 vols.). Thousand Oaks, CA: Sage, 2008.

Quelch, J. A., and Laidler-Kylander, N. *The New Global Brands: Managing Non-Government Organizations in the 21st Century*. Mason, OH: Southwestern, 2006.

Reid, W., and Karambayya, R. Impact of Dual Executive Leadership in Creative Organizations. *Human Relations*, 2009, 62(7), 1073–1112.

Ritchie, R., Swami, S., and Weinberg, C. B. A Brand New World for Nonprofits. *Journal of Nonprofit and Voluntary Sector Marketing*, 1999, 4(1), 26–42.

Rogers, E. *The Diffusion of Innovations* (4th ed.). New York: The Free Press, 1995.

Rupp, C., Karn, S., and Helmig, B. Segmenting Nonprofit Stakeholders to Enable Successful Relationship Marketing: A Review. *International Journal of Nonprofit and Voluntary Sector Marketing*, 2014, 19(2), 76–91.

Sargeant, A., Foreman, S., and Liao, M. Operationalizing the Marketing Concept in the Nonprofit Sector. *Journal of Nonprofit and Public Sector Marketing*, 2002, 10(2), 41–45.

Sargeant, A., and Wymer, W. *The Routledge Companion to Nonprofit Marketing*. Oxford, UK: Routledge, 2007.

Saxton, G., and Chao, G. Online Stakeholder Targeting and the Acquisition of Social Media Capital. *International Journal of Nonprofit and Voluntary Sector Marketing*, 2014, (4), 286–300.

Saxton, G., and Wang, L. The Determinants of Giving Through Social Media. *Nonprofit and Voluntary Sector Quarterly*, 2014, 43(5), 850–868.

Trout, J., and Rivkin, S. *The New Positioning: The Latest on the World's #1 Business Strategy*. New York: McGraw-Hill, 1997.

Urbain, C., Gonzalez, C., and Le Gall-Ely, M. What Does the Future Hold for Giving. An Approach Using the Social Representations of Generation Y. *International Journal of Nonprofit and Voluntary Sector Marketing*, 2013, 18(3), 159–171.

Wymer, W. W., Jr., Segmenting Volunteers Using Values, Self-Esteem, Empathy, and Facilitation as Determinant Variables. *Journal of Nonprofit and Public Sector Marketing*, 1997, 5(2), 3–28.

Young, D. R. (ed.). *Financing Nonprofits: Putting Theory into Practice*. Lanham, MD: AltaMira Press, 2006.

CHAPTER FOURTEEN

ADVOCACY, LOBBYING, AND SOCIAL CHANGE

Marcia A. Avner

Nonprofit advocates and lobbyists have been involved in nearly every major public policy accomplishment in the country—from civil rights to environmental protection to health care. These are not abstract issues. Tens of thousands of lives have been saved by passing laws that improve car safety and reduce drunk driving. Hunger and disease for millions of children have been reduced by passing laws that advance public health as well as food and nutrition programs.... In other words, nonprofit advocacy is an honorable tradition, a peon to our American heritage, the First Amendment, and free speech.

GARY BASS, OMB WATCH (2009), "ADVOCACY IN THE PUBLIC INTEREST"

Charities make an enormous contribution to our national life, and a good share of that is accomplished through direct services. The challenges that we face, in our communities and as a nation, call for continued support for needed services, and they call for more: they call for policy solutions that address root problems and the growing promise of new opportunities. As nonprofits increase their recognition that policy matters, they fulfill a need identified by the late Bob Smucker, a pioneer in nonprofit advocacy, who asserted that "the right of citizens to petition their government is basic to our democracy, and charities are one of the most effective vehicles for allowing citizen participation to shape public policy. Our democratic system can only be strengthened by charities and their volunteers telling public officials about the needs as they see them—firsthand" (2005, p. 231).

Emmett Carson, CEO of the Silicon Valley Community Foundation, underscored these ideas in a 2013 keynote address at a meeting of nonprofit leaders and philanthropists hosted by Independent Sector, saying that "Our advocacy is essential to a well-functioning democratic process." Carson writes, in *Power in Policy:*

> Only public policy engagement can affect the laws that determine how people will be treated, what services will be provided, what behaviors are acceptable, and the incentives and disincentives to compel compliance. . . . Status quo mission statements often focus on providing direct human services and do not include a philosophy for social change. Such mission statements are an implicit endorsement that the current socio-economic system of providing opportunity is essentially fair at allocating scarce resources. Status quo mission statements hold the view that there is no need for a fundamental reordering of any aspect of the existing system. The status quo is not enough. If we are to realize the promise of a democratic society, we need to meet the enormous challenges in our economy, our environment, our infrastructure. (Arons, 2007)

Carson also asserts: "Democratic society is healthier when the public is exposed to and engaged in debating the kind of society in which we want to live and our mutual obligations to each other."

This chapter introduces the topic of nonprofit advocacy and civic engagement and provides readers an understanding of what constitutes public policy advocacy, why nonprofits are uniquely positioned to be effective advocates, the potential benefits, and how to make this an integral part of a nonprofit's strategy for meeting mission. We urge nonprofits to recognize the importance of their role in public life in addressing the economic and social challenges of our times by including advocacy and civic engagement in their missions. In an era of income inequality, needed reforms in the criminal justice system, threats to voting rights and human rights, and major debate about the role of government in health care, education, social services, housing, climate change, jobs, wages, and other keystones of our society, nonprofits have a responsibility to be involved.

Nonprofits are in the unique position to both serve as experienced experts, advocating for policies that they believe will benefit the people they serve and vehicles for engaging the community in the public dialogue about issues. It is a fundamental tenet of our democracy that people who are affected by decisions should have a voice in those decisions. Nonprofits can and should make sure that our organizations and the people in our communities meet that civic obligation.

Why Should Nonprofits Advocate?

Nonprofits have the potential to create public policy changes that have a profound impact on peoples' lives. Imagine the power and the reach of the nonprofit sector, given the experience, expertise, intellect, and commitment of boards, staff, volunteers, participants, and donors! Nonprofits connect to essentially all members of our society. More and more nonprofits recognize that the combination of knowledge, community involvement, and a broad base of support position this sector to lead the way in shaping policy strategies that address our local, state, and national problems in sound and responsible ways.

How Do We Know That Nonprofits Make a Difference?

There is a long history of nonprofit achievement in shaping policy. In a short period of time, starting at the local level, nonprofits dedicated to preventing cancer, lung disease, heart disease, and unhealthy workplaces have built a "smoke free" movement that has achieved nationwide changes in indoor environments. These organizations' advocacy efforts have led to changes in the laws and, most important, changes in personal behavior and cultural norms. In an additional example, through the efforts of a diverse group of nonprofits working consistently over many decades, nonprofit advocacy has led to creative solutions to family violence. We now address that violence with policies that mandate anti-bullying programs in schools, protections for victims of abuse, services for survivors, and sanctions and treatment for perpetrators. The Violence Against Women Act would not have advanced without the determined work of countless nonprofits and citizen advocates. Advocacy works. Community organizing and engagement work.

What Do We Mean by Advocacy, Lobbying, Organizing?

Advocacy is general support for an idea or issue, and *direct lobbying* is a specific form of advocacy. Nonprofit lobbying involves asking an elected official to take a particular position on a specific legislative proposal. For instance, asserting that "We have 7,000 homeless people a night in our city and we need more affordable housing" is an advocacy position. Moving to the specific opportunity and asking a state legislator "Will you vote yes on Senate Bill 6643, which ensures that all publicly subsidized housing requires eligible tenants to pay less than 30 percent of their income in rent," is direct lobbying. Lobbying is asking for a particular action on a discrete proposal. *Organizing* is the ability to understand who has an interest in the issues and positions that you champion and to engage those people and institutions in working with you, in becoming part of your base of support. Grassroots organizing, which engages people who are likely to be directly affected by the decisions that are under consideration, builds the power and resources of your organization and your community. Constituents in their communities have unique access to elected officials, and when they are involved in your advocacy and lobbying, they expand your impact through their relationships and numbers. A nonprofit that advocates through organizing and lobbying can achieve change.

What is *civic engagement*? This broad term applies to organizing efforts that inform people about issues and create opportunities for them to have a voice on issues that matter to them. It includes involving people in the electoral process. For nonprofit organizations in the United States, this work must be scrupulously nonpartisan. Within that constraint, nonprofits can lead and support voter registration, voter education, candidate education, and voter turnout.

An emergent trend in the nonprofit and philanthropic domains is to integrate issue-based advocacy and lobbying with civic engagement to ensure community voices have power in shaping policies and holding decision makers accountable. Some groups refer to this as "Integrated Voter Engagement."

FIGURE 14.1. The Advocacy Cycle

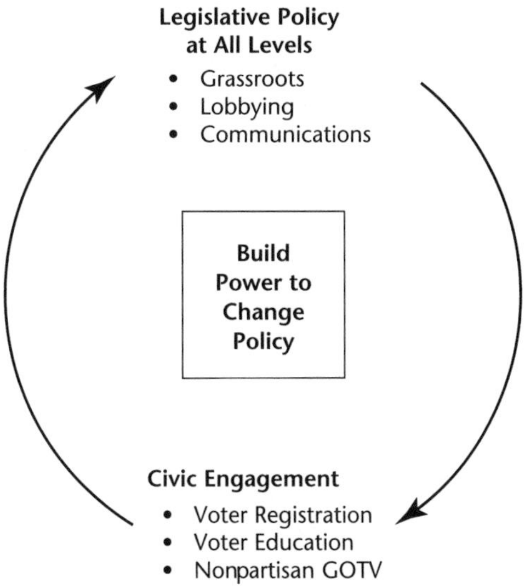

Legislative Policy at All Levels
- Grassroots
- Lobbying
- Communications

Build Power to Change Policy

Civic Engagement
- Voter Registration
- Voter Education
- Nonpartisan GOTV

Source: Grassroots Solutions. Used with permission.

Others describe it as a "virtuous circle" that includes educating candidates and elected officials on issues and positions using the experience and expertise in the community, and then working to advance work on issues in legislative and executive branch arenas (Figure 14.1). This chapter invites readers to consider how this integrated approach builds and sustains community involvement in important policy work.

So Why Don't More Nonprofits Advocate, Lobby, and Promote Civic Engagement?

The call to advocacy is clear. Yet recent research on nonprofit participation in advocacy and lobbying (Arons, 2002, 2007) makes clear that many 501(c)(3) public charities, especially those dedicated to providing social and human services, are not engaging in or maximizing their potential to fulfill their mission because they are meeting needs but not addressing the reason that so many basic needs exist.

Bob Smucker sheds light on the reluctance of some nonprofits to advocate and lobby, noting:

> The importance of government decisions on nonprofit programs and the government funding of those programs argues strongly for the development by nonprofits of lobbying skills and knowledge of the laws governing nonprofit lobbying. However, managers of nonprofits and their boards of directors have been slow to recognize and act on this point. Many still doubt that lobbying is a proper and legal nonprofit activity.... The law is absolutely clear about the legality of lobbying.... In 1976 legislation was passed that clarified and vastly expanded the amount of lobbying nonprofits can conduct. Equally important, on August 31, 1990, the Internal Revenue Service promulgated regulations that support both the spirit and the intent of the 1976 law. Together the law and the regulations provide more lobbying leeway than 99 percent of all nonprofits will ever need or want. (2005, pp. 231–232)

Civic engagement is also an area where the lack of understanding of rules for nonprofit electoral activity stymies nonprofits. A critical rule to guide nonprofits in elections is that they may not do anything to influence the outcome of an election by supporting any candidate or party. As nonprofits active in elections for many decades report, engaging people because they and their community need to be part of the process—without influencing HOW they should vote—is relatively easy and valued by eligible voters who want to know how to participate and are tired of pressure from candidates and parties. People value information from trusted community partners. They want to know how to register, know about candidates, know when and where to vote, know how to navigate local election rules and practices, and know how to protect their voting rights.

Even when a nonprofit organization's leaders understand that lobbying is legal and that it is, in fact, a responsible activity for nonprofits to undertake, many are still uncertain about how to build an advocacy and lobbying effort. Put doubts to rest. The following pages offer a practical understanding of how to plan and act to impact public policy debates. We begin with the role of nonprofits in advancing their cause through public policy advocacy.

The Role of Nonprofits in the Public Dialogue

Nonprofit public policy advocacy strategies are essential to mission accomplishment. Nonprofits in a diverse array of activity areas share a common commitment to meeting the interests and needs of people and communities. Their work on programs, services, and excellence in management are directed to the changes they want to make in society. The work of nonprofits is different from the work of political and business institutions, and nonprofits advance goals, ideas, movements, and programs separate from governmental and market priorities. Nonprofits bring values, information, and the voices of the community to their work with government. Often nonprofits are a countervailing force to the influence of the marketplace on governmental decisions at all jurisdictional levels. Because of their unique and essential role in ensuring a full, informed public dialogue, nonprofits need to fulfill their key role in decisions about government programs, policies, and priorities.

Nonprofits often work with people at the individual and community level. Public charities often have the most far-reaching, trusted, and comfortable of relationships with people in their communities. Based on those ongoing and respected relationships, nonprofits have the potential to encourage individuals and groups to step up to their place in a healthy democracy. And nonprofits provide public leaders with insights about community interests. These organizations hold government accountable to a broad public, present the diverse values reflected in society, and advance issues that are not otherwise addressed. And they are a vehicle through which many members of the society have a voice in the policy and political process.

Public policy need not be mysterious. Nonprofits need to recognize that, at the core, *public policy embodies the decisions we make about how we will care for one another, our communities, and the land.* Regardless of whether a particular organization's issues are addressed at the federal, state, or local level, nonprofits have the opportunity and the responsibility to shape policies. Without policy work, nonprofits might never have seen an Americans with Disabilities Act provide access to countless spaces and resources for people whom they may serve. Without public policy work, nonprofits could not have shaped some responses to welfare reform that enable people to get out of poverty, not just off welfare. Without public policy, nonprofit arts organizations would not have resources to play their role in building quality of life and serving as economic engines in communities. Without public policy, nonprofits would have lost their sector's rights to lobby, to engage in voter registration, benefit from tax exemptions, and secure what funding exists for the programs and services they offer.

Their public policy work is essential to nonprofit mission, but it is also essential to policymakers. Elected officials must be generalists. Nonprofits bring to them expertise and experience that is needed for a fully informed public policy debate. Charities have information: research, data, stories, measures of support. Since policy decisions will be made with or without nonprofit input, the choice to enrich the policy dialogue with our knowledge and point of view becomes an imperative.

It long has been the role of the sector to engage people in the decisions that affect their lives; this is yet another dimension of a nonprofit's role in a democratic society. Through nonprofit information and organizing efforts, individuals who would otherwise be silent add their ideas, interests, and insights to the policy debate. Through nonprofit, nonpartisan political activity, people who are not engaged in the public life of the community may become voters, participate in community and public sector decision making, and exercise their potential to work for their communities' interests.

Nonprofit advocacy work is not abstract. It is a concrete component of an organization's work to identify and meet needs, protect community resources, and ensure that individuals are using the power they have to be a voice on issues. Collectively, nonprofits promote, protect, and support policies and reforms that impact quality of life, community vitality, economic security, and justice.

> Americans have a long-standing tradition of association and expression on political issues . . . they largely organize their voices through a variety of nonprofit organizations. In fact, nonprofit organizations are a familiar institutional force in American politics on almost every side of every issue. They promote the interests, values, and preferences of a diverse civic culture that includes the mainstream and minority, social service providers

and their clients. . . . Along with elected officials and formal institutions of government, nonprofits are part of the system of representation in American democracy. (Reid, 2006, p. 343–344)

What Constitutes Advocacy?

Advocacy is general support for an idea or issue. We are all advocates. As individuals and as organizational leaders, managers and staff, we embrace causes and work to persuade others to support our issues and our point of view.

Lobbying is a very specific form of advocacy. Lobbying is explicitly defined by the IRS in its regulation of nonprofit organizations. Details about what constitutes lobbying and how nonprofits report such activity are included later in this chapter and in extensive online resources. Basically, lobbying involves you, or those whom you organize and mobilize, asking elected officials or others who can make policy decisions to act in a particular way on a specific policy proposal. Although advocacy includes broad promotion, education, persuasion, and lobbying, lobbying is that limited component of advocacy that includes a request for a particular action on a specific policy.

Organizing involves building, engaging, preparing, and mobilizing a base of supporters. Included in organizing is the ability to understand who is likely to support the issues and positions that you champion and to engage those people and institutions in working with you on behalf of an issue. Grassroots organizing, which engages people who are likely to be affected by the decisions that are on the table, builds the power and resources of your organization. Constituents in their community have unique access to elected officials and, when constituents are involved in your advocacy and lobbying, they expand your impact through their relationships and numbers. A nonprofit that advocates through organizing and lobbying can achieve change.

Building and Contributing to Social Change Movements

While it is great to "win" on single specific issues, nonprofits have the knowledge, leaders, power base, and regional and national networks to inspire, implement, build, and sustain *social change movements*. In so doing, nonprofits shape the broad political will to remedy societal problems. Social change movements have revolutionized the way Americans understand and respond in values and policies to an exceptional array of issues, including domestic violence, food safety, substance abuse, abuses of corporate power, human rights, poverty alleviation, public art, medical care, early childhood education, and so much more. Individually and collectively, movements work to change systems, rules, and regulations in ways that improve conditions for programs and services that people count on in their communities.

An Example

Imagine a nonprofit that provides shelter and programs for the homeless. They are also advocates for more shelters to meet existing and future needs and for increased units of affordable permanent housing. This nonprofit, Coalition for the Homeless, engages in a wide range of activities. Staff works with local university faculty to research the numbers of people experiencing homelessness, the diverse reasons for individuals and families to be homeless, the numbers and effectiveness of services for the homeless, and the unmet needs in the community. In sharing that information and their concern that more be done to alleviate homelessness, the coalition's nonprofit advocates communicate with all those connected with their organization, with allied organizations and coalitions, with the media, with Facebook friends, and probably include what they know and are passionate about in most conversations. They may have general discussions with elected officials about the problem as they understand it.

In preparing to be effective advocates, the organization carries out a well-planned organizing campaign. It identifies those who are already on board with their work, those who have an interest in the success of the work, and those who will be most directly affected by the proposed changes. In reaching out, often on a one-to-one basis, they learn about the individual or organization's specific interests and capacity to support an advocacy campaign. As they target, recruit, educate, prepare, and mobilize the supporters whom they can win over, the nonprofit builds a powerful community base that can leverage change.

As they work for particular reforms or laws as part of the solution to the problem of homelessness, their advocacy effort has a lobbying component. Lobbying is the work that the organization does to prepare for the "ask"— the request, for instance, to the head of the State House of Representative's Housing Committee to support a particular proposal. The lobbying component builds on all of the advocacy that the coalition has done and is the step that focuses on the effort to get decision makers to "Vote to stop the bill that cuts funding for the homeless," or "Vote 'yes' for House File 220 to fund three hundred units of affordable housing at scattered sites in Santa Fe."

Because affordable housing is a nationwide need, nonprofit networks and coalitions combine their efforts to do public education, organizing, and advocacy. They work to build a movement, to raise public awareness and inspire broad public support for making housing a priority in communities across the nation. Countless groups working at the local level change attitudes and reach deeply into the community. The work at the local level connects to similar efforts in other places, often through nonprofit networks and national associations. As values change, as the issue becomes a national priority, as increasing numbers of political leaders and officials take up the issue to satisfy the needs of their constituents and communities, an affordable housing movement expands and elevates the issue in public and political life.

Nonprofits that have been effective in winning housing victories and building a movement at the national, state, and local levels keep their supporters involved by sustaining their engagement. From policy advocacy in legislative arenas, they turn to civic engagement activities. Nonprofits and supporters of housing policy, for example, talk to potential voters about the importance of learning and influencing candidates' positions on housing issues and voting for those whose interests match their own. They encourage people who care about the issue to participate in the public life of their community, promoting housing in many ways—from voting, to serving on task forces and boards, to participating in media opportunities that advance the issue.

Civic engagement is one of many terms used to describe efforts to sustain and expand participation in all forms of activities that relate to democratic society. Some nonprofits increase civic engagement by convening groups to understand an issue. For example, they hold "Eggs and Issues" breakfasts or community town hall meetings to encourage people to understand and become involved in issues of concern, from the placement of a stop light at a dangerous intersection to the elements of national health care reform. Many nonprofits encourage the people with whom they work to be active with advocacy groups that are working to address an issue or to volunteer to serve on the citizen task forces and committees that inform governmental activities.

For increasingly large numbers of nonprofits, nonpartisan voter mobilization builds on the organization's trusted role in the community to encourage those eligible to vote to learn the election process, register to vote, know about issues and candidates, and vote. These activities have drawn many people into exercising their proper role in democracy in the interests of themselves and their communities. Engaging nonprofit constituents in both issue advocacy and electoral activity increases the impact of community and nonprofit voices.

Nonprofit Activism and the Law[1]

Nonprofits have the opportunity and responsibility to engage in democracy-supporting activities as discussed here. Nonprofit executives and board members need to recognize that lobbying is legal and, within limits, encouraged.

In the United States, the Internal Revenue Service (IRS) regulates lobbying activities. At this federal level, the oldest standard for lobbying limits has been the 1934 "insubstantial part test," which states that "no substantial part of a charity's activities . . . may be carrying on propaganda or otherwise attempting to influence legislation." This dangerously vague standard frustrated and intimidated proponents of nonprofit lobbying and led to successful pressure for the passage of the 1976 Lobby Law, which establishes a "bright line test" for the limits of permissible lobbying. (See Chapter Two of this *Handbook* for more on all facets of U.S. nonprofit law.)

The IRS developed rules under the 1976 law that establish a clear expenditure test for 501(c)(3) lobbying. This bright line test requires nonprofits to file IRS Form 5768, known as the "h" election because it refers to Section 501(h) in the Internal Revenue Code. The "h" election provides a generous allowance for lobbying activity, capped at $1 million in lobbying expenditures and calculated as follows:

- Twenty percent of the first $500,000 of exempt purpose expenditures, plus
- Fifteen percent of the next $500,000 of exempt purpose expenditures, plus
- Ten percent of the next $500,000 of exempt purpose expenditures, plus
- Five percent of the remaining exempt purpose expenditures up to $1 million

More of the expenditures allowed under the "h" election may be used for direct lobbying than for grassroots lobbying. Direct lobbying, in which the nonprofit and its members ask legislators to vote or act in a particular way on a specific issue, may be used for the full amount of the allowed expenditure. If the nonprofit reaches out to the broader public, which constitutes grassroots lobbying, only 25 percent of the allowable expenditure may be dedicated to that work.

Many activities are not counted as lobbying, thus making the lobby limits even more generous. Activities *not* counted as lobbying include:

- Contact with elected officials on executive branch officials on proposed regulation (as opposed to legislation);
- Lobbying by volunteers (because no money is expended; only reimbursement for travel or meals for volunteers is counted); and
- Response to written requests to testify before legislative bodies.

Lobbying activity is reported as a component of a nonprofit's Form 990 filing with the IRS. Nonprofits that have taken the "h" election have a much simpler expenditure report than those that choose not to use the "h" election. Those not choosing the "h" election need to provide detailed descriptions of all lobbying activity. It is recommended that nonprofits that are comfortable with the $1 million cap on the lobby limits file for the "h" election.

In spite of the clarity of the bright line expenditure test option, studies of two thousand organizations were conducted by Jeff Berry and David Arons in 2003. They concluded that most view the rules as overly complex. For this reason, the rules and reporting requirements have had a chilling effect on nonprofit lobbying.

Individual nonprofit board and staff leaders need to take advantage of the resources available to help them understand the rules that govern lobbying and assure that their organizations choose to elect as appropriate, and then have in place, the simple systems required for tracking time and expenditures that need to be reported.

More detailed information about the lobby law itself and action steps for nonprofits that choose the "h" election are available on the Internet resource site for this book. There readers will find samples of IRS form 5768, sample forms to enable a nonprofit to track time and expenditures for lobbying activity, and samples of 990 reporting. Organizations that provide information, training, and work for lobby law reform are easy to access from this resource site, as well.

Nonprofit Nonpartisan Election Activities and the Law

Nonprofits are prohibited from participating in partisan political activity, and they may not take any steps to influence the outcome of an election by supporting individual candidates or parties. Nonetheless, nonprofits (while taking care to be rigorously nonpartisan) have an important role to play in elections.

Nonprofit VOTE, a national online resource center for nonprofit nonpartisan election activity, studied the impact of nonprofits in the 2012 U.S. elections (2012). Their report, "Can Nonprofits Increase Voting Among Their Clients, Constituents, and Staff" presents evidence that nonprofit service providers, using personal contact with the people in their community, increased voter turnout among low propensity voters. They reported that nonprofits had several important impacts:

1. They reached clients and constituents who were more diverse, lower income, and younger than other registered voters in the twenty-seven states studied.

2. The eligible voters nonprofits contacted personally voted at a higher rate than the average turnout for voters in their states.

3. Those traditionally underrepresented in the voting population increased participation in voting significantly when nonprofits engaged them, and this closed the usual gap in voter turnout based on race, ethnicity, income, and age.

Checklist: Preparing Your Organization for Nonprofit Advocacy Engagement

Nonprofit advocacy and nonpartisan voter engagement are legal. But what steps do nonprofits need to take to do this work well? Here is a checklist of preparatory steps:

- ☐ Formalize the organization's commitment to advocacy.
- ☐ Know the laws governing nonprofit lobbying and election activity.
- ☐ Develop a strategic plan for advocacy work.
- ☐ Identify capacity needs and plan to build the capacity needed.
- ☐ Be issue experts: conduct and prepare research and communications.
- ☐ Learn about policy arenas where you will be working.
- ☐ Target and recruit allies and partners.
- ☐ Study and prepare to respond to opponents.
- ☐ Build advocacy and organizing skills.

Build Advocacy Capacity

While it is easy to identify many nonprofits that have an ongoing commitment to public policy advocacy and to celebrate their accomplishments, most small and mid-sized nonprofits have engaged in little intentional planning for advocacy as a key strategy. Nonprofit leaders, good stewards for their organizations, step forward when there is an immediate threat of cuts in government funding, but they don't build the commitment, capacity, or skills to sustain their advocacy efforts. To advance their ability to use advocacy as a tool for shaping change, nonprofits would benefit from the following specific steps:

Make a Commitment. The board and staff of a nonprofit need to agree that advocacy is a key component of their work. Organizations that do so often design board-level policy committees or policy councils that include program participants, sister organizations, and community leaders to ensure there is good counsel and focused attention to policy work.

Plan. Advocacy should be included in an overall strategic plan, or an advocacy plan can be developed and integrated into the organization's overall strategic plan. Sample planning guides are available on this chapter's section of the *Handbook*'s Internet resource site. Among the core planning questions: Is our organization making a short-term or long-term commitment to advocacy? What are our near- and long-term policy goals? What systems do we need to develop to support issue selection, timely decision making, and securing the resources and skills needed for the work? Who will shape and implement the advocacy plan and serve in the role of policy coordinator?

Build Capacity. The organization needs to identify needs and current capacity. There are guides available to support nonprofits in assessing their capacity needs (see the Internet resources). In addition to a strong strategic plan for advocacy, nonprofits can rely on a growing field of publications to determine:

- The organization's decision making processes;
- Criteria for issue selection;
- Processes and protocol in targeted executive and legislative arenas of influence at the local, state, or national level;
- Commitments of staff time and resources to advocacy at levels that are carefully matched to advocacy goals; and
- Communication systems for internal and external information dissemination.

Strengthen the Knowledge Base. Conduct research. Collect information. Format the data and stories that your organization has built over time. Understand where there are additional informational resources. Nonprofits add value to the policy dialogue because of the experience and information that they bring to the table. Be sure that you make a strong case for your position by having user-friendly data and well-developed and presented stories.

Know the Arenas for Change. At all levels of government, Internet-based information is available about how policies and budgets progress through a policy process, time lines for action, and the roles and background of key decision makers. Often the elected officials who champion the issues that you are working on and those elected in the areas that you serve can be your guides. Staff for individual elected officials and for committees that work with your issues can provide essential information about the process and the history of the issues. It is also useful to understand the culture of the legislative arenas to recognize how to shape your nonprofit's work. In the highly polarized political landscape that dominates much of our national and state work, nonprofits can be nonpartisan bridge makers, bringing people together around issues that have broad reach.

Identify Partners. Many issues are important to multiple nonprofits and the people they serve. A nonprofit new to advocacy rarely has to discover and do this work alone. It is often most productive to work with existing or emerging alliances and coalitions with which your organization has a common agenda. It is useful to find partners and mentors, and state or national organizations can be helpful matchmakers. The National Council of Nonprofits can identify state-level associations of nonprofits; these associations can facilitate connections to like-minded organizations. National organizations that focus on your issues can be especially helpful with materials, model advocacy efforts, and identification of allies.

Understand the Opposition. Knowing who opposes your position and why enables your nonprofit to prepare responses to other points of view. Elected officials appreciate knowing what you know about all "sides" on an issue. In addition, knowing the opposition's case allows you to preempt their key messages by addressing them in your own case statements.

Build Skills. Much nonprofit advocacy depends on relational skills, and nonprofits can gain training in the key components of advocacy, lobbying, and civic engagement from state or national infrastructure organizations. State associations of nonprofits usually provide training and materials to their members and others, and entities like the Bolder Advocacy Campaign at the Alliance for Justice, Independent Sector, the National Council of Nonprofits, and universities with leadership programs all offer training and skill-building programs.

Framework for Advocacy: A Pragmatic Approach to Advocacy and Lobbying

---

Checklist: Steps in Developing and Implementing a Lobbying Plan

The following are essential to do as you develop and prepare to implement your lobbying plan.

❑ Understand the framework for an advocacy action plan presented as follows and apply it to your issue and our planning process.

❑ Set your policy issue goals.

❑ Prepare your key messages and materials.
❑ Include messages about your organization as well as your issues.
❑ Identify and prepare your key messengers: lobbyists and organizational spokespersons.

Once nonprofits understand that advocacy is part of their work and have made a commitment to implement advocacy strategies, it is important to understand how to act on policy issues. Whether the objective is to propose a new policy, to join efforts to pass legislation, or to stop a proposal deemed harmful, nonprofits can be rapid responders to immediate needs and can build effective advocacy and lobbying strategies with a pragmatic and systematic approach.

The Advocacy Triangle presented in Figure 14.2 poses four key questions that a nonprofit should be able to address with a high level of specificity:

1. What is the problem or opportunity?
2. What do you want to have happen?
3. Who decides?
4. How do you influence them?

Once the nonprofit decides on what it wants to happen and how to talk about it, there are three core tactics to be considered: direct lobbying, grassroots organizing, and media advocacy.

Set Goals: What Do You Want to Happen?

Advocacy and lobbying are heavily influenced by external factors that the nonprofit cannot control. While nonprofits do this work to create sound policies by

FIGURE 14.2. Advocacy Triangle

passing laws and ensuring that they are implemented, there are many objectives to be met along the way to achieving a "win." It is important to set goals and specific objectives related to the policy result to be achieved, but also aim to:

- Establish your organization as a trusted resource to elected officials and staff.
- Insert your experience, expertise, and point of view into the policy dialogue.
- Build support from likely and unexpected sources.
- Establish ongoing connections to the base of supporters to build power for the long term.
- Build positive working relationships with decision makers, staff, and media.
- Position your work to be covered favorably in traditional and social media.
- Strengthen internal capacity, including board capacity for engagement in advocacy (including an active policy committee).

Focus on Position and Power

Remember, nonprofit advocacy is most effective if it is based on a long-term, sustained effort to work for change that is grounded in your organization's values, vision, and mission. In setting goals, place a premium on *positioning your organization* to be a resource and a valuable leader in the public dialogue and *building power* to work for the changes that are needed.

Prepare Key Messages and Messengers

Nonprofits need to be able to provide clear and compelling case statements. What is the problem or opportunity? What is the proposed solution and why? What is your organization and what is your expertise and position?

Once these questions are addressed in thoughtful message development, they become the background for consistent messaging throughout an advocacy campaign. The core message should be used internally, in building and expanding the base, in conversations with elected officials and other leaders, and in media messages. The challenge is to present the core message in a way that is effective with the intended audience. Once the case statement is prepared, short versions of the key themes work well with introductory meetings with all target audiences.

Match the depth of detail in the message, the tone of the message, and the medium for moving the message to the intended audience. What do they care about? How do you connect your cause to their interests? What do they need to know about the issue and your position, even if they have only a brief amount of time with you?

It is useful to assess each audience by asking: What do they need to know? Who do they need to hear from? The messenger and the media are as important as the message. The organization should determine who manages the message as it adapts to the evolution of the dialogue and who prepares the messengers. Then develop ways to ensure they deliver a consistent and disciplined message while reaching out to many audiences.

Nonprofits can be highly effective at reaching target audiences—their supporters, opinion shapers, and elected officials—when they use both traditional and social media. Some audiences respond to coverage of issues by traditional newspaper, radio, and television outlets. A nonprofit media plan should identify the journalists and outlets that cover the issues, build strategic working relationships with those media, and use all the tools needed to reach them. This work might include letters to the editor, opinion editorials, news conferences, press releases, placement of features articles, editorials, and columns. Some elected officials and members of the public will follow these sources regularly, often relying on their websites as well as printed editions of papers and television or radio broadcasts. In an era of media fusion, nonprofits can approach the multiple formats used by traditional media to advance their issue as we "read" the radio news and "watch" newspaper stories online.

Because social media have become central to our public dialogue as well as our social lives, nonprofit communications strategies need to maximize their strategic use of these tools, too. By "social media," we mean online tools and sites that allow for two-way communication between you and your audiences. The most common types of social media employed in advocacy include (1) online communities, such as Facebook, Google+, and Pinterest, and (2) blogs and articles with comment sections, especially micro-blogs like Twitter. Social media often connect people to your website, and the participants in social media become part of your contact list, people whom you can target and recruit to work with you on issues and activities.

In most organizations, members of the board and executive staff are important candidates for the formal role of organizational spokesperson. These are the people whom the press and public expect to hear from on your key issues. Lobbyists can be these same people, but it is usually wise to include among those who are doing direct lobbying the issue experts and grassroots advocates who are constituents of the elected official whom you are approaching. Develop a strategy of matching the messenger to the audience.

Primary Advocacy Actions: Direct Lobbying, Grassroots Organizing, and Media Advocacy

Effective nonprofit advocacy comprises a number of specific processes and activities, including direct lobbying, grassroots organizing, and media advocacy. Each offers its own unique leverage and value in the advocacy process, and the choice to employ one or more is an important strategic decision.

Checklist: Steps in Direct Lobbying

The following are essential to do as you prepare to engage in direct lobbying:

❏ Identify and learn about the decision makers whom you need to influence and whose support you need to win.
❏ Establish strong working relationships with key elected officials as early as possible.
❏ Identify the elected officials who are your champions and work closely with them.
❏ Present your information to targeted elected officials and their staff.
❏ Ask decision makers to support your position.
❏ Respond to decision makers based on their level of agreement with you.

Direct Lobbying

Lobbying, and the relationship building, education, and advocacy that lead to lobbying, are most effective when organizations begin to work with policy decision makers prior to the time when the "ask" is for a "yes" or "no" vote on specific legislation.

Target. Early in an advocacy effort, determine which elected officials you need to work with most closely. This can be determined by where you have the most power because your organization and the people you serve are constituents. It is prudent to build the best possible relationships with those who are designated representatives for your area and where the official is held accountable at election time by those in the district. Other priority targets should be based on the power, position, and passion of the elected official. Identify:

- Who has cared about this or similar issues and is likely to share our values and position? Who serves on the committees that will hear our policy issue?

- Who is a champion for our cause who is in the political majority and has a power advantage?
- Who will demonstrate broad support if added to our list of allies based on geography, ethnicity, gender, political party, leadership within the city council, legislature, or congress?
- Who will work well across party lines and between legislative bodies—House and Senate, for example.

Build Strategic Relationships. If your organization is to be a trusted resource for elected officials and in a position to influence them, it is important that they know your organization and that you articulate common interests. Research helps. Check websites, blogs, and press coverage to learn about officials you wish to influence. Examine what they have supported in the past. Understand the issues that are key in the official's district and to her political party. And then begin to meet.

Some meeting options:

- Meet at your organization's site. This is especially appropriate for the officials who represent the district, but anyone interested in your issues should be invited to a "kitchen table" meeting with a few people (board, staff, program participants) who can explain who you are, what you care about, and why. These site meetings are often the best venue for listening to the elected official. Ask her to share her goals, expectations, and hopes for the work ahead. Understand where there is shared experience—perhaps with illness in the family or an experience with an injustice or a shared frustration with a system that isn't meeting its public purpose.
- Convince the elected official that you can be or are a resource in your issue areas, and provide information and "real people" who can tell their stories as part of the policy debate.
- Invite elected officials to tell you how they prefer to receive communications with you (Which e-mail address? Which phone number? In their offices or at home in the community?).
- Stay in touch. Consider your advocacy to be an ongoing conversation with those whose support you have and want. Information updates, a presence at their community meetings—all strengthen relationships.
- Maintain the trust. Always tell the truth, get information that is requested, and deliver what you promise.

Identify Elected Officials Who Are Your Champions. Early in your lobbying effort, identify the elected officials who are likely to be your strongest supporters and who are also in a position to advance your cause. It is useful to have champions who are passionate about your issue, respected by their peers and able to garner bi-partisan support, and in positions of power on the committees that will carry primary responsibility for your issue area. Your champions may turn out to be authors of the bills that you propose or support. The policy leaders with whom you work in partnership have the ability to guide you through the intricacies of legislative processes as they advance the issue. And they will count on you to be a good partner. The nonprofit organization's role is to ensure that the legislative champions for the issue had accurate and compelling information, visible and broad support in the community, and people who will work in support of the issue.

And Let the Lobbying Begin. Present your ideas to elected officials you have identified as the decision makers whom you need to influence. The messages, messengers, and materials that you prepared early in your planning and preparation swing into action mode now.

Prepare elected officials by communicating with them about your issue and position. Nonprofits often take advantage of the time before elected officials are in decision-making mode to meet with them at the nonprofit site, in the district, or at their offices to introduce the organization and the issue. Preliminary meetings establish your presence on an issue and can encourage the elected official to recognize you as a resource on the issue as well as an organization that wants to be at the table as the issue is addressed. The more time spent educating and persuading elected officials with meetings, letters, e-mails, and calls before they have to make a decision the better. Nonprofits sometimes create events, including legislative forums or a "Day on the Hill." Such events may attract media attention and become a forum for both explaining your position and demonstrating how many people support your position.

As the time nears for decision making, be sure to build on early contacts and work hard to persuade elected officials to commit to supporting you or to letting you know how you might win their support. Grassroots advocacy, discussed below, is one component of persuasion. In direct lobbying, however, nonprofits are best served by having a small group meet with the targeted elected officials. These are most often leaders on the issue, members of the committee who will hear the bill, and legislative leaders.

The nonprofit should have a small group participate in the meeting, including a person with expertise on the issue, a constituent when possible, someone with a story to tell to illustrate the importance of the position that you are advocating. People learn from stories, and elected officials like to have facts and illustrative examples to use in their thinking and in their own discussions about the issue.

Set up meetings by contacting the staff person who schedules the elected official's appointments. Be sure to identify the nonprofit, the issue, and indicate whenever possible that a constituent will be part of the small group at the meeting. Keep a few tips in mind for your meeting with an elected official:

- Be on time and be prepared. It is a good idea to "rehearse" legislative meetings when you are new to this effort.
- Identify yourself to the staff and tell staff a little about your issue. Offer thanks for setting up the meeting and provide contact information to the staff in case he or she or the elected official needs to reach you at a future time.
- Greet the official warmly and introduce the members of your team by identifying their role in your organization and on the issue. It is effective to have one person on the team serve as the key facilitator for your team.
- Verify the amount of time that the official has for the meeting so that you can get to your key points in a timely way.
- Remind the official of your previous discussions or contacts.
- Be direct and clear. Explain why you are there and what you want.
- Provide brief, clear, materials.
- Provide an opportunity for the official to ask questions.
- Make a direct ask: Do you support us and will you vote for our position?
- Next steps depend on the elected official's answer.

Be clear when you ask an elected official for support for your position. What do you want? Why? What is your counter to opposing arguments? And who cares? If constituents, other elected officials, your base, and allies care, then share that information.

The answer is yes. When an elected official supports your position, thanks are in order. Push to understand how much the elected official is willing to do in addition to voting in the way that you have requested. Will she talk to other legislators? Author an ordinance or bill? Ask for a hearing? Talk to the press? And be sure to provide elected officials who are your advocates with the information and insights that will help them.

The answer is "I don't know yet." This is the time to ask: What do you need to know? Who do you need to hear from? And then follow through to the extent possible with information and contacts.

And "absolutely not!" It isn't worth spending too much time with those who clearly oppose your position and tell you that they are immovable. It is worth asking if anything would change that position. But a strong tactic is to avoid an unnecessarily negative exchange. The opponent on one issue can surface as the supporter on another. "Thank you for meeting with us. We hope we can work together on issues in the future" is an exit line that prevents you from making an enemy.

In all exchanges with elected officials, it is helpful to have brief and compelling materials, back-up documents for those who want to delve into the issue, and a list of contact people whom the official can reach with questions and requests.

A word about officials' staff members: When elected officials have staff who work for them, those staff should be included in your relationship-building approach. Often the staff person maintains the information files, contact lists, and requests that you make. More important is the reality that staff facilitates everything from your access to an individual elected official to who is on the agenda when a policy proposal is being heard. Respect the time pressures and responsibilities of staff, but recognize their importance to the process. Distinguish your organization by thanking them for their help!

Lobbying includes meetings, calls, letters, e-mails, testimony, press events, and other communication formats that request support. Be strategic in matching your approach to the interests and styles of the officials and staff as you get to know them and as you demonstrate that you add value to the public policy debate. Purely public charities are often trusted because of the information and people they bring to the table. Nonprofits can position themselves to be seen as the ethical voice of the community, in contrast with the self-interest of private-sector lobbyists. Maintain the trust.

Grassroots Organizing

Grassroots organizing is the most essential of the strategies central to effective nonprofit advocacy to achieve short-term and long-term policy reforms. Grass-roots community-based organizing is the process through which people plan and build shared efforts to work for the changes that they want on their issues. Organizing enables people to build the power they need to advance issues, challenge failed systems, and become respected participants in decisions that affect their lives.

Nonprofits are often quite effective at mobilizing those who support them for a short-term effort. But mobilizing is only one component of organizing. Organizing builds a sustainable base, builds power, and builds leadership. Mobilizing is one tool that organizers use to activate their base at strategic points. Nonprofits are well served if they focus on organizing, building an ever-growing and regularly engaged base.

Marshall Ganz, now at Harvard's Kennedy School, has developed theories of leadership and organizing that provide helpful background to nonprofits moving into this arena of advocacy. He underscores that "Organizers identify, recruit, and develop leadership; build community around leadership; and build power out of community" (Ganz, 2009, pp. 16–17)

Short-term and long-term advocacy initiatives benefit from effective organizing, base building, and advocacy. Nonprofits working on issue campaigns are most likely to achieve desired policies if they build, sustain, and activate a base of support that is able to use its collective power to influence public awareness, political will, and decision makers.

Organizing is especially important in the highly polarized political landscape that dominates policy dialogues at the federal, state, and local level. Elected officials are demonstrating high levels of loyalty to partisan agendas. To override the demands for disciplined support for political party agendas, nonprofits have to rely on the individual values of a particular legislator or build enough pressure in the elected official's district to persuade her or him that the community has placed a high priority on your issue and position. Good organizing includes holding decision makers accountable, and community voices have a keen influence in many instances.

Organizing support for public policy issues will require each organization to determine its particular approach to this work. For organizations already working with an activated constituency, the ongoing engagement and expansion of the base is important. For organizations new to this work, starting within the organization and reaching out to potential allies, both organizations and individuals, will be a starting point. The common components of nonprofit grassroots organizing are targeting supporters, recruiting supporters, engaging supporters, mobilizing the base, evaluation of activities, and reengagement.

Checklist: Key Organizing Actions

❑ Identify existing supporters.
❑ Develop a list of potential supporters. These are your "targets."
❑ Recruit. Reach out to have conversations with potential supporters. Understand their interests and allow those interests to influence your organizing and advocacy strategies.
❑ Engage supporters and make them an integral part of your team. Provide information, gather their knowledge and stories, include them in planning and strategy sessions, and be responsive in dialogue with them.
❑ Prepare your base so that people have training in the skills that you are asking them to use and know what they will be asked to do and when.

❑ Mobilize the base when the time is ripe for their advocacy, from e-mails to meetings to events.
❑ Debrief and evaluate your collective efforts. Celebrate accomplishments and the rewards of working collectively.
❑ Reengage for the next tier of action on your issues.

Analysis of Potential Supporters. A nonprofit has rarely reached all those who care about the success of its policy efforts. Mapping stakeholder potential allows a nonprofit to be strategic in targeting outreach and organizing. Who cares about the issue? Within that broad potential, which individuals and organizations add the most value to your effort, based on everything from the strength of their numbers to their status in the policy debate? Whom can you reach easily within the complement of groups who would be valuable supporters?

Cycle of Organizing. The ongoing work of building a base, building power, ensuring that people have a voice on issues, requires an ongoing cycle of activity. Figure 14.3 illustrates the nature and flow of this cycle. In organizing for public

FIGURE 14.3. The Cycle of Organizing

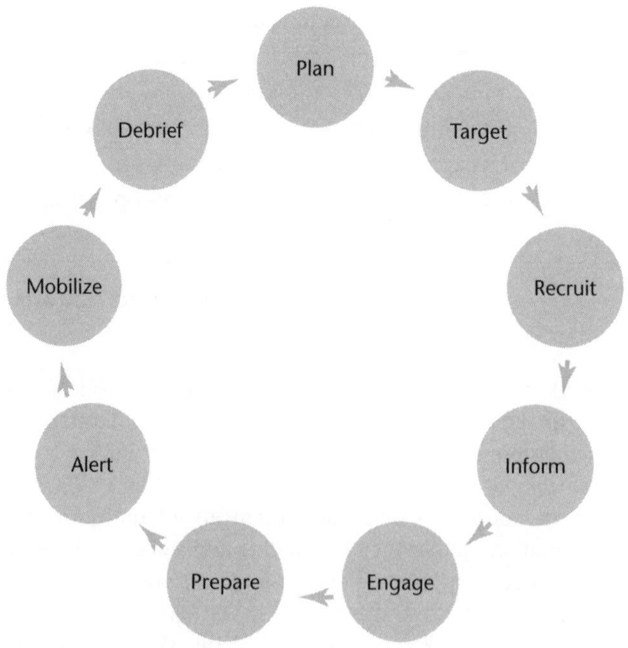

policy advocacy and in organizing for civic engagement, nonprofits target those who will support and advance their work, recruit supporters, often with initial personal contact, ensure that supporters are engaged, informed, and trained for their role. Once supporters have been engaged, then it is possible to do authentic grassroots mobilizing, calling upon people to do the work that you have been getting ready for over time. The action is not the end. It is a step along the way. Every action deserves a debriefing session and evaluation. Each support can be applauded and thanked. And then: reengage.

Media Advocacy

Public policy advocacy, lobbying, and civic engagement depend on building solid working relationships, and this is true in media advocacy. Nonprofits strive to have their issues and activities portrayed positively in all media forms. Often having an editorial or feature story about the value of your organization's issues and programs provides a spotlight that will gather the attention that you seek from supporters.

Checklist: Elements of Media Advocacy

❏ Learn about the media available to you (traditional and social media).
❏ Identify and build working relationships with members of the traditional media who cover your issue area, government, and politics.
❏ Present your organization as a resource to the media on issues in which you have expertise.
❏ Prepare your key messages and adapt them for many media: letters to the editor, opinion editorials, YouTube videos, podcasts, Facebook postings, web postings, and other available outlets.
❏ Provide journalists covering your issues with contacts 24/7. Their deadlines may not coincide with your usual working hours.
❏ Build and maintain good media lists and communications systems for reaching media.

Nonprofits work with both earned media and paid media. In all instances, the challenge is to convey key messages to target audiences using media that they use and respect. For elected officials, newspaper coverage matters. Most political leaders pay close attention to opinion pieces, editorials, letters to the editor, online or in newspapers, especially in their districts. Supporters are encouraged by supportive news coverage and excited by the opportunity to participate in the public debate on the radio or TV. Social media can be especially effective in providing up-to-date information, commentary, and calls to action to the base, giving them knowledge and building momentum for their action.

Message development and media strategies are key components of advocacy, and much has been written to guide nonprofits. Large coalitions often work with media consultants who can shape the messages and media used in an advocacy or organizing campaign. Polling and focus groups can strength message development. In an information-overloaded society, selecting the most compelling and user-friendly ways to reach target audiences is a priority.

Regardless of the scale of the effort, relationships with target audiences matter. To gain media attention, to be consulted by the media for your point of view on your issues, to establish your organization as an interesting and reliable source of news and feature stories, study the media available to you. Who covers your issues? Who vets opinion pieces for news and radio outlets? Which blogs have legitimacy with target audiences? Which radio producers program policy debates? Once you identify the media useful for your effort, introduce your organization to members of the press and producers in brief meetings that demonstrate that you are a resource to them.

Plan media components to your advocacy work as part of your overall advocacy strategy and prepare the groundwork so that you have access when needed and your role in the public debate and promotion of civic engagement is elevated.

Evaluating Public Policy Advocacy, Lobbying, and Civic Engagement

As with all initiatives, policy, lobbying, and civic engagement work should be evaluated relative to the project goals and objectives to the extent possible. For all forms of advocacy, however, many projects move slowly and in increments. Some work—engaging the broad public in increased civic activity—is never done. Some issue-related work advances only when the political landscape and public will are ready. Therefore, *nonprofits should rely on quantitative and qualitative tools to assess progress.*

Questions to consider include measures of gains and continuing needs in organizational capacity, the extent of base building in progress, the quality and nature of relationships with elected officials and the media, progress on increasing voter turnout or moving the needle on an issue in decision-making areas, and the satisfaction of those organizations and individuals in their experience with your organization.

Design evaluation as part of the initial work plan and capture stories as well as data throughout the work. The sector needs case stories from which to learn more about this ever-growing field of advocacy, and your organization and others will benefit from what you can measure and what you learn from stories about signs of progress or concern. Your assessment of this work is ongoing and can direct your organization to make timely and strategic course corrections as well as to build on your strengths.

Advancing Advocacy as a Field

No significant social change has ever taken place without the energy and perseverance of movements and advocates.

Gara LaMarche, Atlantic Philanthropies

Nonprofits are increasingly a force for change as more and more of them engage in civic life and draw their constituencies into the public decisions of our society. Collective action, collective power, commitment to sustained effort in advocacy, lobbying, and civic engagement strengthen the nonprofit sector and position it for increasing power.

As nonprofits become increasingly aware of the power of advocacy, they are building this key component of their mission-related work. Take care to include advocacy and civic engagement activities in your strategic planning. They are relevant to your excellence in meeting mission. The information included here will provide you with a sound starting place, and there are an increasing number of information resources, training opportunities, and partners available to support nonprofit advocacy. As you initiate or enhance your nonprofit's work in advocacy, these key lessons should drive your work:

1. Advocacy and lobbying are legal nonprofit activities, encouraged by the Congress and expected by elected officials.
2. Nonpartisan nonprofit election activity is a component of broad civic engagement and organizing work, and is a permissible and important activity for 501(c)(3) organizations.

3. Nonprofits need to be part of the public policy dialogue. The sector and its specific activity areas have the expertise and experience needed for a fully informed policy dialogue. In this sense, nonprofits are a critical resource for policy shapers and for the community. Those who count on nonprofit programs and services also count on nonprofits to be a voice in shaping decisions in public arenas.

4. Nonprofit advocacy requires strategy and planning. A basic framework for advancing issues allows you to define a need, propose a specific solution, determine where the issue is decided, and influence those decisions.

5. The three primary tools for nonprofit advocacy are organizing, lobbying, and media advocacy. Your organization can build its capacity in these skill areas with existing talent, the advocacy training materials available in the sector, and through training.

6. Nonprofits are a vehicle through which people participate in public life. One key role for nonprofits is to engage people through organizing and civic engagement initiatives. Doing this work on an ongoing basis builds power for your organization, your issue, and the people you represent and serve.

In a democratic society, nonprofits have important potential to help level the playing field in policy arenas. Nonprofits have information and organized power that can offset the influence of other powerful groups in setting policies that have an impact on people and communities. Advocacy work also can position your nonprofit as the lead organization in an issue area, and it can help secure your organization's place in leadership circles. Most important, advocacy can make an enormous difference in your organization's ability to serve your community well for the long term. Advocacy can help address the root causes of basic social problems and, over time, redefine the context within which people and communities strive for fairness, equity, and an acceptable quality of life.

For dedicated nonprofit leaders and managers, public policy engagement is an extraordinary leadership opportunity. And there are increasing opportunities for policy-oriented jobs in the sector. Academic institutions that support undergraduate and graduate nonprofit management programs include policymaking among their core competencies for nonprofit excellence. Many philanthropic organizations also have or are beginning to recognize that education, advocacy, and organizing are essential strategies for ensuring that nonprofits can effect the changes that are needed in communities. In the spectrum of mission-related work that ranges from research to lobbying and organizing, advocacy planning, capacity, and impact are highly valued.

Change sometimes takes a long time. The dedicated and determined leaders in the nonprofit sector who are committed to change need to be advocates for needed change. There has rarely been a more important time for nonprofits to insist that the voices of people in communities are heard. It is important for nonprofits to recognize the value of their deep knowledge of issues and people's needs and experience. And it is important for nonprofits to insist that that knowledge be included in public dialogue.

Begin now to do your part. Start the conversation. Help to plan the work. Join with others to build a strong base of support and prepare to play a meaningful role in shaping public policies. Advocacy and civic engagement are important and exciting. We encourage you to be the person to encourage the nonprofits with which you work to begin or expand their commitment to a robust cycle of advocacy. When the choices are between angst and action, nonprofits are charged with being the steady hand and the strong voice that speaks to community needs and advocates for change.

Note

1. It is important to keep in mind that the nonprofit law explained in this chapter applies to active 501(c)(3) charitable organizations. Community foundations are permitted to lobby in similar ways. But other nonprofits and foundations are governed by different rules. Bolder Advocacy, The Alliance for Justice, Independent Sector, and the Council of Foundations are good resources for the rules applicable to foundations and other nonprofit organizations that are not public charities.

References

Alliance for Justice. *The Rules of the Game: An Election Year Guide for Nonprofit Organizations.* Washington, DC: Alliance for Justice, 1996.

Alliance for Justice. *Worry-Free Lobbying for Nonprofits: How to Use the 501(h) Election to Maximize Effectiveness.* Washington, DC: Alliance for Justice, 2003.

Amidei, N. *So You Want to Make A Difference: Advocacy Is the Key.* Washington, DC: OMB Watch, 2002.

Arnstein, S. R. A Ladder of Citizen Participation. *Journal of the American Institute of Planners,* 35, 1969, July, 216–224.

Arons, D. F. Lobbying, Advocacy, and Nonprofit Management. In V. Futter, J. Cion, and G. W. Overton (ed.), *Nonprofit Governance and Management* (2nd ed.). Chicago: American Bar Association Section of Business Law and American Society of Corporate Secretaries, 2002.

Arons, D. F. (ed.). *Power in Policy: A Funder's Guide to Advocacy and Civic Participation.* New York: Fieldstone Alliance, an Imprint of Turner Publishing Company, 2007.

Avner, M. with Josh Wise, Jeff Narabrook, Jeannie Fox, and Susie Brown. *The Lobbying and Advocacy Handbook for Nonprofit Organizations* (2nd ed.). New York: Fieldstone Alliance, an Imprint of Turner Publishing Company, 2013.

Avner, M. *The Nonprofit Board Member's Guide to Lobbying and Advocacy.* St Paul, MN: Wilder Foundation, 2004.

Bass, G. D. Advocacy in the Public Interest. *Essays on Excellence: Lessons from the Georgetown Nonprofit Management Executive Certificate Program.* Washington, DC, Georgetown University Press, 2009.

Bass, G. D., Arons, D. F., Guinane, K., and Carter, M. *Seen But Not Heard: Strengthening Nonprofit Advocacy.* Washington, DC: Aspen Institute, 2007.

Berry, J. M., and Arons, D. F. *A Voice for Nonprofits.* Washington, DC: Brookings Institution Press, 2003.

Carson, E. "On Foundations and Public Policy: Why the Words Don't Match the Behavior." In D.F. Arons (ed.) *Power in Policy: A Funder's Guide to Advocacy and Civic Participation.* St. Paul, MN: Fieldstone Alliance an Imprint of Turner Publishing Company, 2007, 11–21.

Ganz, M. Organizing. In G. R. Goethals, G. L. Sorenson, and J. M. Burns (eds.). *Encyclopedia of Leadership.* Thousand Oaks, CA: Sage, 2004, pp. 1134–1144.

Ganz, M. *Why David Sometimes Wins.* New York: Oxford University Press, 2009.

Gibson, C. M. *Citizens at the Center: A New Approach for Civic Engagement.* Washington, DC: Case Foundation, 2006.

Gulati-Partee, G., and Ranghelli, L. *Strengthening Democracy, Increasing Opportunities: Impacts of Advocacy, Organizing, and Civic Engagement in Minnesota.* Washington, DC: NCRP, 2009. (Part of a series on the states. See www.ncrp.org.)

Libby, P., and Associates. *The Lobbying Strategy Handbook: 10 Steps to Advancing Any Cause Effectively.* Thousand Oaks, CA: Sage, 2012.

Minieri, J., and Getsos, P. *Tools for Radical Democracy: How to Organize for Power in Your Community.* San Francisco: Jossey-Bass, 2007.

NonprofitVOTE. Can Nonprofits Increase Voting Among Their Clients, Constituents and Staff?: Executive Summary, Washington D.C.: NonprofitVote, 2012.

Piven, F. F., and Cloward, R. *Poor People's Movements: How They Succeed, Why They Fail.* New York: Random House, 1977.

Reid, E. J. Advocacy and the Challenges It Presents for Nonprofits. In E. T. Boris and C. E. Steuerle (eds.), *Nonprofits and Government: Collaboration and Conflict* (2nd ed.). Washington, DC: The Urban Institute Press, 2006.

Sen, R. *Stir It Up: Lessons in Community Organizing and Advocacy.* San Francisco: Jossey-Bass, 2003.

Smucker, B. Nonprofit Lobbying. *The Jossey-Bass Handbook of Nonprofit Leadership and Management.* San Francisco: Jossey-Bass, 2005, pp. 230–253.

Smucker, B. *The Nonprofit Lobbying Guide* (2nd ed.). Washington, DC: Independent Sector, 1999.

Stone, D. *Policy Paradox: The Art of Political Decision Making* (rev. ed.). New York: W.W. Norton & Co., 2001.

Wellstone Action. *Politics the Wellstone Way.* Minneapolis: University of Minnesota Press, 2005.

CHAPTER FIFTEEN

VALUE CREATION THROUGH COLLABORATION

James E. Austin and M. May Seitanidi

We are in the Age of Alliances. And this is because greater value can be created for organizations, individuals, and society through collaboration. This chapter focuses on the co-generation of value by partnering between nonprofits and businesses, a phenomenon that has exhibited explosive growth since the 1990s. Almost all successful nonprofits and businesses, big or small and all around the world, are engaged in multiple alliances. Such collaboration is no longer just a nice thing to do; it is a strategic necessity for generating greater value. Many of the conceptual and analytical aspects of the nonprofit-business collaboration framework we will present are also applicable to other types of cross-sector collaborations and even intra-sector alliances.

We define collaborative value as "the transitory and enduring multidimensional benefits relative to the costs that are generated due to the interaction of the collaborators and that accrue to organizations, individuals, and society" (Austin and Seitanidi, 2012a, 2012b). While there has been significant advancement in our collective understanding of cross-sector collaboration, our exhaustive review of the research literature and practice literature (Austin and Seitanidi, 2012a, 2012b) revealed that there is an inadequate understanding of the sources and types of value, of the value drivers as partnering relationships evolve, of the processes that create value, and who receives the benefits. These deficiencies can

FIGURE 15.1. The Collaborative Value Creation Framework

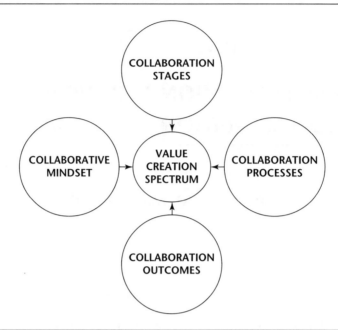

Source: J. Austin and M. M. Seitanidi, *Creating Value in Nonprofit-Business Collaboration,* p. 6. Jossey-Bass, 2014. Used by permission.

lead to a failure to realize the full potential value and an undercounting of the true value of such collaborations.

The Collaborative Value Creation (CVC) Framework[1] remedies these weaknesses and provides an analytical and managerial tool to enable a deeper understanding and more systematic approach to co-generating collaborative value, highlighting the potential multidimensional and multilevel benefits that can accrue during and as a result of the collaboration process.

The CVC Framework consists of five interrelated components. They are depicted in Figure 15.1 and explained in the remainder of this chapter. These five components are:

- Value Creation Spectrum
- Collaborative Value Mindset
- Collaboration Stages
- Collaboration Processes
- Collaboration Outcomes

The Value Creation Spectrum

Collaborations can produce a wide range of value depending on how they are designed and managed. Collaboration underachievers leave value on the table, and that constitutes collaborative negligence. The core leadership and managerial issue is how to create more value, to drive the value creation to higher levels on the value creation spectrum. This requires a deeper understanding of two fundamental questions:

- Where does value come from (that is, what are the sources of value)?
- What kinds of value get created (that is, what the types of value generated are for each partner, for both of them, but also for society)?

We address these two questions as follows.

Sources of Value

There are four key sources of value in a collaboration. Each can be addressed by a basic analytical question:

1. *How good is our resource fit?* The basic motive for partnering is to obtain resources that we need and others have, in order to achieve *resource complementarity*. Each partner provides a resource that fills a gap in the other partner's resource portfolio. The more significant the gaps that can be filled, the greater the potential for value creation.

2. *Who provides the resources and how?* It is important to understand the direction and magnitude of the resource flows between the partners in order to assess the r*esource directionality*. If one partner provides almost all of the resources, that is a unilateral flow that creates an imbalance that is often not sustainable; a one-way street does not permit two-way collaboration. If both partners are swapping valued resources, that is a parallel and more sustainable exchange. If both partners are fusing their resources in order to create a new constellation of complementary resources, then even greater value creation potential arises.

3. *What kinds of resources are deployed?* Different types of resources have different potential for value; this is associated with the *resource nature*. In collaborative value creation we highlight two types of resources: generic resources and organization-specific resources. Generic resources are those commonly available. For example, all companies have money; all nonprofits deliver some socially desirable good or service. These are desirable, yet resources that

FIGURE 15.2. The Collaborative Value Creation Spectrum and Sources of Value

	LOW VALUE ──────────────▶ HIGH VALUE
Resource Directionality	Sole ───────▶ Dual Creation ───────▶ Co-Creation
	Unlateral ─▶ Bilateral and Parallel ─▶ Conjoined
Resource Complementarity	Unconnected ─▶ Connected ───────▶ Complementary
	Misfit ───────────▶ Compatible ───────▶ High Fit
Resource Nature	Generic ─▶ Organization Specific ─▶ Key Success Assets
	Common ───────▶ Differentiated ───────▶ Distinctive
Linked Interests	Narrow ───────▶ Moderate ───────▶ Broad
	Shallow ───────▶ Moderate ───────▶ Deep

Source: J. Austin and M. M. Seitanidi, *Creating Value in Nonprofit-Business Collaboration,* p. 24. Jossey-Bass, 2014. Used by permission.

are specific to the particular organization, such as a brand or technology or clients, are more valuable. Even more valuable are the organization-specific resources that are the key success determinants of a partner's performance. The complication is that the more valuable the resource, the scarcer its availability.

4. *What are our shared interests?* The greater that the partners' perceived interests are tied together, the greater the motivation to partner due to their *linked interests.* Partners often seek different objectives; this highlights the importance of understanding what the other party values in order to identify value connections. There are two key dimensions to assessing linked interests: breadth and depth. The more points of connection, the greater the potential value linkages. But many trees with shallow roots can be blown down in a storm. A single key connection with very deep roots can create stability. But a lightning strike can topple a single tree. The goal is to have multiple and deep linkages.

By scrutinizing each of these potential sources of value, collaborators can identify where greater value can be co-generated. Figure 15.2 illustrates the set of sources of value in a collaboration and how, depending on the nature of the sources, they can vary across the Value Creation Spectrum.

Types of Value

The sources of value discussed in the previous section give rise to types of collaborative value generated, which are commonly expressed in terms of economic, social, and environmental benefits. Whereas these general categories are important, it also is significant to analyze value in terms of more specific precursor types. This allows for comparison beyond content and context differences. Four types of value are particularly useful: associational, transferred asset, interaction, and synergism. Not all types of value are equally important to all kinds of partners. Identifying and analyzing each of these more specifically enables one to have a more complete view and understanding of the potential for or actual creation of different types of value. Too often, the full significance of collaboration is undervalued due to lack of specificity.

Associational Value. This is the value that accrues to each partner due to being associated with the other. In this sense, it is intrinsic to collaboration, but what is important is to identify the multiple manifestations of such value. When chosen as a partner by a well-known, prestigious organization, the partner may harvest the halo effects of the association with its stakeholders, leading to the following benefits:

- Reputation
- Credibility
- Desirability
- Legitimacy
- Visibility
- Employee recruitment, retention, motivation, and productivity
- Clients' patronage and loyalty
- Community support
- Governmental support
- Attractiveness to investors and donors

Of course, there also exists the risk of negative associational value. If, for example, one partner takes actions or experiences situations that adversely affect its own reputation, there are likely to be negative spillover effects on its partners.

Transferred Asset Value. Value is also manifested by the type and magnitude of the resources transferred from one partner to the other. It is useful to distinguish types of assets. *Depreciable* assets are those that get used up readily; a cash donation gets spent and a social service gets delivered. *Durable* assets last for a longer period; equipment, buildings, or skills, for example, can continue to produce benefits over years. What is particularly important to recognize is that once an asset has been transferred, it is no longer part of the ongoing value exchange. For the value proposition to sustain the partnership, it must be regularly renewed, either by transferring more of the same assets or transferring a different type of desired asset. Asset renewability is essential to collaboration longevity.

Interaction Value. This value emerges from the process of partner interactions that produce a variety of intangibles, such as trust or communication skills. These, in turn, become inputs to the value creation partnership process, as well as capabilities that can be valuable to a partner beyond the collaboration. Economists would label interactions as transaction costs; we consider them an important type of value. Examples of interaction intangibles include the following:

- Relational capital
- Trust building
- Access to networks
- Diversity management
- Empathy and solidarity
- Joint problem solving
- Conflict resolution
- Communication
- Coordination
- Collaborative leadership
- Risk reduction

Synergistic Value. The fourth type of value emerges from the fundamental judgment or rationale that combining partners' complementary resources will enable more to be accomplished together than working separately. The basic premise is that collaboratively creating social or environmental value can give rise to economic value which, in turn, can enhance social or environmental value, and so on. This can become a synergistic relationship, whereby the generation of one type of value gives rise (sequentially or simultaneously) to other types of value, and this creates a "virtuous value circle." Innovation fuels the synergism and also opens up new avenues for value creation. Figure 15.3 summarizes the four different types of value and how they vary.

Collaborative Value Mindset

Effective co-generation of value is fundamentally shaped by the mental frameworks or mindsets that partners have regarding both collaboration and value. Since the 1990s, thinking by business and nonprofit leaders about both of these concepts has undergone significant evolution. We have identified two sets of mindset dimensions, and how a potential collaborator thinks about each can either impede or foster collaborative value creation. The first set focuses on how

FIGURE 15.3. Value Creation and Types of Value

	LOW VALUE		HIGH VALUE
Associational Value	Intrinsic to Partnership → Specific ———→		Deep Identificatior
Transferred Resource Value	Depreciable ————————→ Durable ——→		Renewable
Interaction Value	Infrequent ——————→ Selective ——→		Multiple
Synergistic Value	Basic ————————→ Partial ——→		Innovation

Source: J. Austin and M. M. Seitanidi, *Creating Value in Nonprofit-Business Collaboration,* p. 36. Jossey-Bass, 2014. Used by permission.

one thinks about value. The second set focuses on how one thinks about collaboration itself.

Value Mindset

Seven dimensions are relevant to understanding the value mindset. Consideration of each of the following dimensions will enable each partner in a collaboration to assess its own value mindset and also to better recognize and understand the mindset of potential collaboration partners. In effect, this allows potential collaborators to assess the compatibility of their mindset patterns. Figure 15.4 lists the seven dimensions, and each is summarized in the following section of this chapter.

Breadth. How broad is each potential collaborator's view of the value offered by a prospective collaborator? Some potential collaborators think about value quite narrowly (for example, the view that a business produces only economic value or that a nonprofit generates only social value). Increasingly, however, leaders and even society more generally believe it is possible for and expect all sectors to produce multiple types of value.

Interrelatedness. What is each potential collaborator's view of the relatedness of all of the potential types of value offered by a prospective collaboration? Even as one recognizes that there are different types of value, it is more powerful to consider them as an integrated constellation of value rather than segregated or individual elements.

Compatibility. How compatible and holistic are the views of the potential collaborators with each other? A holistic approach is rooted in a recognition that one

FIGURE 15.4. Value Mindset Dimensions

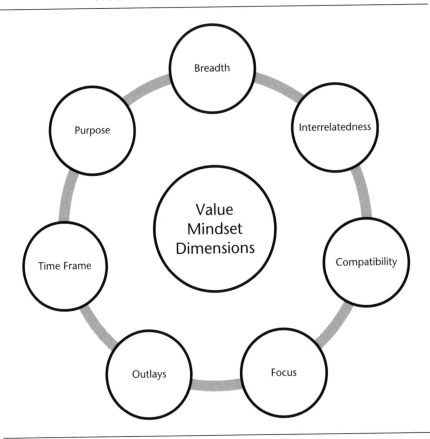

need not, for example, trade off economic value to obtain social value, or vice versa. Rather, the generation of these different types of value can be synergistic.

Focus. How narrow or broad is the perspective of each of the potential collaborators? In a successful value-generating collaboration, the focus on benefits goes beyond that of the value accruing to the partnering organizations and stresses the value generated for external beneficiaries, too.

Outlays. How are the resources in a social purpose collaboration viewed? In a successful value-generating collaboration, resources are viewed as investments aimed at generating multiple-value returns, rather than thinking of resources deployed in a social purpose collaboration as expenses. This investment orientation reflects a difference in the potential collaborators' investment framework, moving away from a cost-cutting mentality to an impact-enhancing perspective.

Time Frame. What is the expected time frame for results to begin to accrue from the collaboration? While one may well aspire to realize results and achieve some impact as soon as possible, the collaborators of a successful value-generating collaboration recognize that complicated societal problems require longer-run efforts and expectations and are worth taking the time needed to realize the desired impacts.

Purpose. How do the prospective collaborators perceive the purpose of the potential collaboration? If the partners view the undertaking as charitable giving and fundraising activity, then the value-creation frontier will be significantly constrained; whereas seeing the collaboration as strategically important to maximizing multiple value creation expands the frontier of possibilities.

Collaboration Mindset

In addition to understanding the value mindset of the potential collaborators, it is important to understand the mindset of prospective collaborators with regard to the *process* of collaboration. We have identified six particular dimensions that are relevant to a collaborator's mindset (see Figure 15.5). Assessing the mindset with regard to each of these six dimensions is useful to understanding both your own collaboration mindset as well as that of your potential collaborator. Incompatibility between or among collaborators on one or more of these dimensions is important to recognize and consider. When identified in advance, such assessment presents opportunities for discussion and clarification between the parties before proceeding to develop a partnership strategy.

- *Attitude.* Some business and nonprofit managers harbor adversarial, suspicious, or deprecating attitudes toward each other, and this is likely to breed conflict. Co-generation of value requires mutually cooperative and respectful views.
- *Dependency.* Perceiving sectors as independent of each other blinds a potential collaborator from identifying the multiple points of interdependence and capitalizing on these linked interests that can be sources of collaborative value.
- *Compatibility.* There is value in looking beyond mere acknowledgment of the interdependencies that exist; there is growing evidence that the business and nonprofit sectors are converging in terms of goals, activities, and competencies and that this has potential value.

FIGURE 15.5. Collaborative Mindset Dimensions

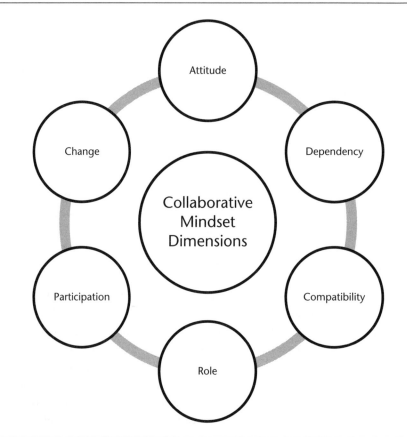

- ***Role.*** Collaborations involve the creation and capture of value. In the more successful undertakings, the partners give first priority to creating value for their partners rather than extracting it for themselves. This tends to create a virtuous reciprocity dynamic in which the receiving partner in turn tries to add yet more value to the other partner.
- ***Participation.*** If partners have greater openness about options for organizational engagement on multiple levels and alternatives to resource integration, then more opportunities for value creation will emerge. Boundary permeability fosters value discovery.
- ***Change.*** If the partners seek and welcome significant change, then the possibilities will be greater for generating innovative and more impactful collaborative undertakings.

Collaboration Stages

The third component of the CVC Framework focuses on how value creation can change depending on the nature of the evolving partnering relationships. These can be viewed as a Collaboration Continuum that consists of four stages: philanthropic, transactional, integrative, and transformative; the potential for value creation increases at each stage. There are *value drivers* that affect each stage, and these value drivers can be analyzed in terms of alignment, engagement, and leverage. Perceiving this as a continuum recognizes that each stage is not necessarily discrete; we must recognize that collaborations can exhibit some aspects that are characteristic of one stage and yet others may be more characteristics of aspects of a subsequent stage. Whereas relationships will often evolve from one stage to another, some can leapfrog; a relationship might start, for example, as a transactional relationship rather than a philanthropic relationship. Furthermore, there is nothing automatic about progressing along the continuum; to progress is dependent on the actions (and inactions) of the collaborating partners. In fact, it is possible to regress rather than progress (for example, to regress from an integrative stage to a transactional stage).

The Collaboration Continuum

In the following section, we will describe each of these stages and then examine how each of the three value drivers, *alignment, engagement,* and *leverage,* change across the continuum.

- *Philanthropic Stage.* This is the traditional and most common stage, characterized by nonprofits seeking and businesses giving donations to further the nonprofit's causes. It is frequently a check-writing relationship. These donations can be quite valuable, but even greater value can be added as one moves into the other stages.
- *Transactional Stage.* This stage involves activities that are more specific, with clearer objectives, defined time periods, and an explicit exchange of resources and value. Examples include cause-related marketing, sponsorships, highly structured employee volunteer programs, certification labeling, and similar projects.
- *Integrative Stage.* At this stage, the missions, strategies, organizations, and resources merge, and the collaboration takes on the characteristics of a joint venture more than a transactional deal.

- *Transformational Stage.* The primary focus of the collaborators operating at the transformational stage is on a larger (that is, societal) problem, with the collaboration goal aimed at creating innovative solutions that transform systems, institutions, processes, or attitudes to produce significant societal value. At this stage, organizationally, more institutions and multiple sectors engage in the collaboration.

Value Drivers

- *Alignment.* As the relationships progress across the continuum (that is, from philanthropic to transactional to integrative to transformative), the alignment among collaborators increases, creating more value. These shifts in alignment draw on linked interests and occur in multiple areas. The collaboration's relevance to the partners' *missions* moves from peripheral at the philanthropic stage to central at the transformational stage. The *strategic importance* of the collaboration grows from insignificant to vital. The connection between the partners' core organizational *values* deepens greatly. The *knowledge* of the societal problem being addressed moves from a state in which only one partner understands it to a level of understanding that is shared equally by both. Their *frameworks* for understanding how maximum value is co-generated merge. The focus on *benefits* shifts from the individual partners to society.
- *Engagement.* Progression through the stages toward higher value is propelled by a deeper and more multifaceted form of engagement that deepens partner commitment and strengthens collaborative sustainability. Further the *emotional connections* of the partners with the societal cause and between collaboration members deepens. Partners' *interactions* shift from procedural activities (for example, grant making) to more substantive involvement (for example, actual problem solving). The *involvement* grows from a few individuals to become organization-wide top to bottom participation, with an increasing frequency of *interactions.* This enables *trust* to build and deepen. The partners discover additional opportunities to broaden the *scope* of their collaborative value creating activities. As the problems addressed become more complex in higher stages, the *structure* of the collaboration encompasses more entities. Also, the *managerial demands* of the collaboration grow as the complexity of creating higher value increases.
- *Leverage.* This driver is rooted in making the most from available resources. The *magnitude* of resources deployed grows with progression through each stage, and the *type of resources* change from generic (at the philanthropic stage)

to organization-specific to key success assets (at the transformative stage). The *resource link* between the partners is not only two-way but increasingly conjoined. The *synergism* between partners' resources and actions becomes ever stronger with progression through the stages. This is propelled in part by ever more robust *continual learning*, giving rise to greater *innovation*. *Internal change* propels ever greater levels of *external change*.

Collaborative Value Creation Processes

Organizational processes are the engines that create value. They are the mechanisms that tap into the four sources of value and convert them into associational, transferred asset, interaction, and synergistic value, thereby giving rise to economic, social, and environmental value. These value creation process pathways can be examined in each of the four phases that any collaboration may pass through: (1) Formation, during which one is searching for possible partners; (2) Selection, during which a single partner is assessed and chosen; (3) Implementation, during which the collaboration becomes operational; and (4) Institutionalization, during which collaboration is solidified. Each of these phases is discussed in the following section.

Formation

The first step of this phase is to clearly articulate the problem that the collaboration is to address so as to be able to screen candidates as to their likely interest. Then, one can examine possible candidates' experiences in order to assess likely intentions for addressing the problem and doing so collaboratively. Next, one should assess candidates' visibility relative to one's own desire for visibility. It is also helpful to identify individuals who might champion such collaboration. Finally, one can create a map of the possible candidates to assess the fit with one's existing portfolio of collaborations.

Selection

The next phase in the assessment and selection of a specific collaborator candidate should be guided by a set of explicit criteria rooted in the specific organizational needs and characteristics one seeks. Given the importance of fit, an initial point of analysis involves mapping the linked interests. One must assess the candidates' resources, particularly their distinctive capabilities and assets, in terms of their complementarity to one's own resource set. Last, one should weigh the possible risks of the association. Some of these steps involve engaging in a form of due diligence, such as by examining publicly available information or consulting with other collaborators of the candidate. However, significant direct interaction and discussion with the candidate is essential to achieving the mutual understanding and motivation that will be essential to a strong partnership. Taking time to get to know one another is a good investment.

Implementation

This phase involves the joint design and operation of the collaboration. It is useful to acknowledge that there will be initial experimentation and adaptation as the collaboration partners refine the design and smooth out operating procedures. It is useful to incorporate an ongoing operational evaluation process into this phase, to secure feedback aimed at continual improvement.

Institutionalization

Over time one strives to embed the collaboration into the partnering organizations. Indicators of successful institutionalization include surviving a change of leadership at the operating level or at the top of either organization. Another is when the partners talk in terms of "we" rather than "us" and "them." This institutionalized unity is also manifested by a fusion of the partners' value creation frames. All of this must be grounded in governance processes that involve collective decision making and equitable power sharing.

Collaborative Value Outcomes

The final component of the CVC Framework focuses on the outcomes produced by the collaboration. We address three questions related to value outcomes: (1) Who benefits? (2) What value is produced? and (3) What are key measurement issues?

Who Benefits?

It is important to identify the full range of beneficiaries from a collaboration. The value recipients should encompass three levels: individuals, organizations, and society (also referred to as the micro, meso, and macro levels). It is also helpful to distinguish between the benefits internal to the collaboration (that is, benefits to the partnering organizations and the individuals in them) and the benefits external to the partnership (that is, benefits to the individual clients or beneficiaries receiving the social service or good, external stakeholders of the businesses and nonprofits, and society in general).

Types of Value

The CVC Framework recognizes the importance of using the general categories of economic, social, and environmental value. However, we must stress the utility of specifying the previously described four types of value: associational, transferred assets, interaction, and synergism, each with their multiple manifestations. Such specificity enables a more analytical assessment of the value generated accruing to different beneficiaries from the collaboration.

Assessment Perplexities

Assessing outcomes of collaborations is fraught with complications. To address these complications, it is important that the partners work with a shared mindset that seeks to evaluate the collaboration's ongoing value creation. A second necessity is to have clear objectives for the collaboration, with corresponding performance indicators by which to assess their accomplishment. Accompanying these objectives should be a statement of the collaboration's theory of change and value creation pathways. The partners need to ensure that the resources required to carry out the assessment are available. Too often, funders demand evaluation but do not provide the resources to do it. Measurement is often complicated by the intangible nature of a collaboration's intended benefits, which means that qualitative measures should be employed as well as quantitative measures. Attribution of results to the collaboration's actions may be complicated because of other possible influencing factors. The rigorous approach to dealing with this problem is to employ randomized control trial groups, but this approach often is too costly or not feasible. This is where the theory of change and value creation can provide supportive evidence, as can the use of evaluation studies for similar interventions.

Smart Collaborative Value Creation Practices

To summarize the foregoing, we offer the following list of twelve smart practices that will contribute to maximizing value creation through collaboration:

1. Understand value creation in terms of sources and types of value.
2. Achieve a collaborative value mindset.

3. Advance through the collaborative stages by using the alignment, engagement, and leverage value drivers.

4. Manage value-creation pathways in the formation-selection-implementation-institutionalization phases.

5. Assess outcomes in terms of the separate types of value created for individuals, for organizations, and for society, internal and external to the collaboration.

6. Seek partners who fit in terms of mission, strategy, values, and complementary resources.

7. Bond with your partner through understanding, empathy, emotional connection, and commitment.

8. Govern and organize the collaboration through clear roles and responsibilities, shared planning and decision making, constructive conflict, and equitable power management.

9. Communicate effectively between the partners, within each partnering organization, and to external stakeholders.

10. Build trust by keeping your word, being dependable, sharing key resources, and respecting confidentiality.

11. Learn continuously about better collaboration processes and how to co-create greater value.

12. Transform the partners and society.

Conclusion

The Collaborative Value Creation (CVC) Framework we have described in this chapter provides an analytical and practical vehicle for answering the following question: *How can collaboration between businesses and nonprofit organizations most effectively co-create significant economic, social, and environmental value for society, organizations, and individuals?* Each of the five CVC Framework components deepens one's understanding of the interactions that contribute to value creation, while providing guidance to researchers and practitioners who wish to assess the collaboration's generation of value. The framework also aims to promote consistency and maximize comparability between processes and outcomes of collaboration. The goal is to offer a roadmap on the possible pathways to maximize value creation across all levels of social reality rather than to prescribe a fixed approach to value creation. Partnering organizations can adapt the framework according to their partnership circumstances and researchers can employ either elements of or the complete CVC Framework to examine the value creation spectrum, the relationship stages, processes, and outcomes.

In summary, the first CVC component examines the sources of value employed, how they are used, and to what effect by the partners; the second component unpacks the value and collaboration mindset of each partner; the third component positions partners' cross-sector interactions within the collaboration continuum's stages and examines the nature of the relationship according to value descriptors; and the fourth component examines how partnership processes contribute to the value co-creation of the partners. The final component, partnership outcomes, assesses the value of each partner on the different levels of analysis to facilitate the assessment of the benefits and costs. To conclude, we set forth a set of smart practices that can be used to maximize value creation.

Understanding more deeply the virtuous circle of value creation facilitates a paradigm change to enable equal prioritization of social and environmental value creation with that of economic value creation, and it also highlights the significance of each of the processes at the same time. The partnership literature is in the early stages of addressing the challenges of mapping the value creation "road" on different levels of analysis. Thus, additional research will certainly lead to further elaboration, revision, and refinement of the CVC Framework and its theoretical constructs.

Note

1. The Collaborative Value Creation (CVC) Framework is more fully elaborated with over one hundred illustrative collaboration examples in J. E. Austin and M. M. Seitanidi, *Creating Value in Nonprofit-Business Collaborations: New Thinking and Practice.* San Francisco: Jossey-Bass (2014).

References

Austin, J. E., and Seitanidi, M. M. Collaborative Value Creation: A Review of Partnering Between Nonprofits and Businesses: Part I. Value Creation Spectrum and Collaboration Stages. *Nonprofit and Voluntary Sector Quarterly*, 2012a, 41(5), 231–246.

Austin, J. E., and Seitanidi, M. M. "Collaborative Value Creation: Partnerships Processes." *Nonprofit and Voluntary Sector Quarterly.* 2012b, 41(6), 230–240.

Austin, J. E., and Seitanidi, M. M. *Creating Value in Nonprofit-Business Collaborations: New Thinking and Practice.* San Francisco: Jossey-Bass, 2014.

Reference Resources

An extensive set of CVC Framework-related readings, references, and resource materials is available at the Internet resource website that offers supplementary premium content for this *Handbook.*

CHAPTER SIXTEEN

OUTCOME ASSESSMENT AND PROGRAM EVALUATION

John Clayton Thomas

Nonprofit organizations need to know how effectively they are performing their jobs. Are their programs achieving the desired results? How could programs be modified to improve those results? Because the goals of nonprofit programs are often subjective and not readily observable, the answers to these questions may be far from obvious.

These questions have grown in urgency in recent years as a consequence of new external pressures. As perhaps the watershed event, "the Government Performance and Results Acts of 1993 ... placed a renewed emphasis on accountability in federal agencies and nonprofit organizations receiving federal support" (Stone, Bigelow, and Crittenden, 1999, p. 415). More specific to nonprofit organizations, funders increasingly demand evidence of program effectiveness, as exemplified by the United Way of America's outcome measurement initiative of recent decades and its more recent Outcome Measurement Resource Network (see, for example, United Way of America website for the Outcome Measurement Resource Network). As Ebrahim describes in Chapter Four of this volume, there is today a major press for nonprofit organizations to be highly accountable in all sorts of ways. Yet research on contemporary practice indicates that many nonprofit agencies still perform relatively little assessment of program performance (Carman, 2007; Morley, Hatry, and Cowan, 2002).

To address these needs nonprofit organizations need, at a minimum, to engage in systematic outcome assessment—that is, regular measurement and monitoring of how well their programs are performing relative to the desired outcomes. (The terms *outcome assessment* and *performance assessment* will be used interchangeably in this chapter.) Nonprofit executives may want, in addition, to employ the techniques of program evaluation in order to define the specific role their programs played in producing any observed beneficial changes. Used appropriately, outcome assessment and program evaluation inform a wide range of decisions about whether and how programs should be continued in the future and satisfy funder requirements.

This chapter introduces the techniques of outcome assessment and program evaluation as they might be employed by nonprofit organizations. These techniques are not designed for more general evaluations of organizational effectiveness which, as Herman and Renz (2008, p. 411–412) have observed, seldom "could be legitimately considered to equal" program effectiveness (see Chapter Ten in this volume for a detailed discussion of organizational effectiveness). The emphasis here is on how these tools can be useful to organization executives by providing information that speaks to decisions those executives must make. To make that case, we will first provide a step-by-step description of how to conduct outcome assessment, before turning to how that assessment can be incorporated into more advanced program evaluations processes.

Planning the Process for Outcome Assessment

For outcome assessment to have maximum value, the process for that assessment must be well planned and executed. The first step in that regard is for the organization's leaders to be committed to the effort. Ideally, an initiative of this kind will begin with the chief executive of the nonprofit organization but, in any event, the chief executive and the organization's board should understand and support the initiative. Support includes recognizing and accepting that outcome assessment could uncover unwelcome truths about program performance. There is no point in taking the time to develop and obtain performance data if those in charge are not committed to using the data.

Assuming this support is assured, outcome assessment should be undertaken on a program-by-program basis. For a nonprofit organization with multiple programs, that guideline means that each program will require separate outcome assessment planning. A specific individual should be assigned primary responsibility for that planning for each program, preferably as part of a small team.

(The discussion that follows will use the term *decision makers* to encompass both possibilities.)

Regardless of whether a team is used, the planning process should entail extensive involvement of staff and perhaps even clients who are involved with the program. That involvement serves at least two functions. First, it assists in information gathering. Since those who are involved with a program know it from the inside, they can provide valuable intelligence on the program's desired outcomes and possible means for measuring their achievement. Second, involvement can build ownership in the outcome assessment process. If program staff and clients have the opportunity to speak to how the program will be assessed, they are more likely to buy into the eventual results of the assessment.

Finally, the process should also be linked to the organization's information technology. Improved information technology, by facilitating the recording and analysis of performance data, is a major factor underlying the recent push for better performance assessment in both the nonprofit and public sectors. Building a strong performance assessment system requires that the system be planned in conjunction with the organization's technology.

Defining Program Goals

Outcome assessment is a goals-based process; programs are assessed relative to the goals they are designed to achieve. Defining those goals can prove to be a difficult task since the project leader or team must define and differentiate several types of goals while navigating the often-difficult politics of goal definition. This section first explains several goal types and then discusses how to define them in a political context.

Types of Goals

A first type of goal refers to the ultimate desired program impact. United Way of America, in its outcomes assessment website, defines *outcome goals* as "benefits or changes for individuals or populations during or after participating in program activities." Here we prefer a broader definition of outcome goals as the final intended consequences of a program for its clients and/or society. An outcome goal has value in and of itself, not as a means to some other end, and is usually people-oriented because most public and nonprofit programs are designed ultimately to help people. This broader definition probably fits better the new United Way interest in measuring the success of programs based on both "client-level outcomes" and "achievement of measurable community outcomes" (Minich et al., 2006, p. 183).

Activity goals, by contrast, refer to the internal mechanics of a program, the desired substance and level of activities within the program. These specify the actual work of the program, such as the number of clients a program hopes to serve. How the staff of a program spend their time—or are supposed to spend their time—is the stuff of activity goals.

The distinction between outcome and activity goals can be illustrated through a hypothetical employment-counseling program. An activity goal for this program might be "to provide regular employment counseling to clients," with an outcome goal being "to increase independence of clients from public assistance." The activity goal refers to the work of the program, the outcome goal to what the work is designed to achieve. As this example also suggests, outcome goals tend to be more abstract, conceptual, and long term; activity goals are more concrete, operational, and immediate.

Understanding the distinction is crucial if outcome assessments are to resist pressures to evaluate program success in terms of activity rather than outcome goals. Program staff often push in that direction for several reasons. First, activity goals are easier for them to see; they can more readily see the results of their day-to-day work than what that work is designated to achieve sometime in the future. Second, activity goals tend to be more measurable; it is easier to measure the "regularity" of counseling than "independence from welfare." Finally, activity goals are usually easier to achieve. Police working in a crime prevention program, for example, can be much more confident of achieving an activity goal of "increasing patrols" than an outcome goal of "reducing crime."

Outcome assessment planning often can sidestep pressures of this kind by including both types of goals in the goal definition. As a practical matter, both outcome and activity goals must be examined in most outcome assessments in order to know how different parts of a program link to eventual program outcomes.

Sometimes a program will have so many activity goals that it could be too much work to attempt to define much less measure all of them as part of the outcome assessment system. A good guideline in such cases is to define activity goals only for key junctures in the program, that is, only at the major points in the program sequence where information is or might be wanted (see also Savaya and Waysman, 2005, p. 97).

Falling between activity and outcome goals are *bridging goals,* so named because they supposedly connect activities to outcomes (Weiss, 1972, pp. 48–49).

Bridging goals, like outcome goals, relate to intended consequences of a program for society, but bridging goals are an expected route to the final intended consequences, rather than being final ends in and of themselves. In an advertising campaign designed to reduce smoking, for example, a bridging goal between advertising (activity) and reduced smoking (outcome) might be "increased awareness of the risks of smoking." That increased awareness would be a consequence of the program for society but, instead of being the final intended consequence, it is only a bridge from activity to outcome.

Bridging goals can be important for outcome assessment systems for a variety of reasons. For one thing, because they are often essential linkages in a program's theory of change—the hypothesized process by which program inputs lead to outcomes—their achievement may be a prerequisite to demonstrating that program activities have produced the desired outcomes. Thus, to confirm that a program works, it may be necessary to establish first that the bridging goal is achieved before any change on the outcome goal would even be relevant. Bridging goals also may provide a means to obtain an early reading on whether a program is working. Effects may be observable on a bridging goal when it is still too early to see any impact on final outcome goals.

Outcome assessment systems may also occasionally incorporate *side effects*. Side effects, like outcome and bridging goals, are also consequences of a program for society, but *unintended* consequences. They represent possible results other than the program's goals. For example, a neighborhood crime prevention program might displace crime to an adjacent neighborhood, producing the side effect of increased crime there. A side effect can also be positive, as when a neighborhood street cleanup program induces residents to spruce up their yards and homes, too.

Given the potential for any given program to have a wide range of side effects, where should an assessment draw the line? An outcome assessment for a non-profit agency program should incorporate side effects only to the extent that the chief executive, staff, and/or other key stakeholders view specific possible side effects as important program aspects. Is there an interest in examining a possible negative side effect, perhaps with an eye to changing the program so as to reduce or eliminate that result? Agency decision makers must make that judgment based on whatever data they believe are necessary for a full outcome assessment. In most cases, given a principal interest in activity and outcome goals, the executive may not want to spare limited resources to monitor possible side effects, too. On occasion, though, possible side effects may loom as so important that they must be addressed.

Whatever the type of goal, its definition should satisfy several criteria:

1. Each goal should contain only one idea. A goal statement that contains two ideas (for example, "increase independence from welfare through employment counseling") should be divided into two parts, with each idea expressed as a distinct goal.
2. Each goal should be distinct from every other goal. If goals overlap, they may express the same idea and so should be differentiated.
3. Goals should employ action verbs (for example, "increase, improve, reduce"), avoiding the passive voice.

Goal definitions can be derived from two principal sources: (1) program documentation, including initial policy statements, program descriptions, and the like, and (2) the personnel of the program, including program staff, the organization's executive, and possibly other key stakeholders such as clients. These personnel should always be asked to react to draft goals before they are finalized.

The Politics of Goals Definition

Understanding the different types of goals and where to find them may be the easy part of goal definition. The difficult part can be articulating those definitions in a manner that satisfies all important stakeholders. To do that may require navigating the perilous politics of goal definition.

As a first difficulty, many programs begin without clearly defined goals. Initial program development focuses on where money should be spent to the neglect of defining what the program is expected to achieve. Second, as programs adapt to their environments, goals sometimes change and, in the process, depart from the program's original intent. "Policy drift" can result wherein programs move away from that original intent, and once-distinct goals become fuzzy or inconsistent (for an example, see Kress, Springer, and Koehler, 1980).

More difficulties can arise when planning for outcome assessment begins. The commonly perceived threat from any kind of assessment may prompt some program staff or other stakeholders, when they are asked, to be evasive about goals. Or, those staff or other stakeholders from their different vantage points inside and outside the program may simply have different views, resulting in conflicting opinions about a program's goals.

A variety of techniques is available to cope with these problems. Fuzzy or inconsistent goals may be accommodated by including all of the different possible goals in a comprehensive goals statement. If some perspectives appear too contradictory to fit in the same statement, a goals clarification process might be initiated (for an illustration, see Kress, Springer, and Koehler, 1980). Working with staff and stakeholders to clarify the goals of a program could be the most important contribution of an outcome assessment planning process since it may build a cohesiveness previously lacking in the program.

Disagreement over goals can also sometimes be sidestepped as irrelevant. Patton (2008, pp. 238–241) recommends asking stakeholders what they see as the important *issues* or questions about the program. These issues, because they represent areas where information might be used, should be the focus of most eventual data analysis anyway. And, there may be more agreement about issues than about goals. Decision makers might then be able to express these issues in terms of the types of goals outlined earlier.

The agency's chief executive can play any of several roles in the definition of program goals. At a minimum, the executive should oversee the entire process to ensure the necessary participation, lending the authority of her or his position as necessary. Ideally, the executive should review proposed goals as they are defined, both for clarity and for conformity to the agency's overall focus. Finally, if conflicts over goals arise, the executive may need to intervene to achieve resolution.

The Impact or Logic Model

As part of the process of goal definition, a program's various goals should be combined into a visual *impact* or *logic model*—an abstracted model of how the various goals are expected to link to produce the desired outcomes (see Savaya and Waysman, 2005; McLaughlin and Jordan, 2015; W. K. Kellogg Foundation, 2004). Such a model should have several characteristics. First, it should be an abstraction, removed from reality but representing reality, just as the goals are. Second, the model should simplify matters, reducing substantially the detail of reality. Third, as the "logic" component, the model should make explicit the significant relationships among its elements, showing for example how activity goals are expected to progress to outcome goals. Fourth, the model may involve formulation of hypotheses—the suggestion of possible relationships not previously made explicit in program documents or by program actors. Indeed, a principal benefit of model development often lies in how program stakeholders are prompted to articulate hypotheses they had not previously recognized. Exhibit 16.1 shows an impact model for a hypothetical nonprofit training program.

The model links the various goals from the initial activity goals through the bridging goals to the ultimate outcome goal. As the model illustrates, bridging goals sometimes fall between two activity goals, but still serve as links in the chain

---

EXHIBIT 16.1. AN IMPACT MODEL FOR A TRAINING PROGRAM FOR EXECUTIVES OF LOCAL BRANCHES OF A NATIONAL NONPROFIT

1. Determine developmental needs of local executives (AG).
2. Develop training materials to address these needs (AG).
3. Screen and select executives for training (AG).
4. Conduct training of executives (AG).
5. Executives formulate individualized plans for development of their organizations (BG).
6. Executives attend follow-up training (AG).
7. Local organizations increase volunteer membership (OG).
8. Local organizations increase volunteer giving (OG).

Key: AG = activity goal

BG = bridging goal

OG = outcome goal

---

from activity goals to outcome goals. This model may be atypical in that the goals follow a single line of expected causality, where the more common model may fork at one or more points (as, for example, if different types of executives received different kinds of training). Should staff and/or stakeholders disagree about the likely impact model, decision makers must determine whether the disagreement is sufficiently important to require resolution before further outcome assessment planning can proceed.

Development of an impact model can help staff and stakeholders clarify how they expect a program to work and the questions they have about its operation, in the process perhaps suggesting how to use assessment data once it becomes available. As Savaya and Waysman (2005, pp. 85–86) have documented, impact models can be useful for a variety of other purposes, too—from "assessing the feasibility of proposed programs" to "developing performance monitoring systems." To date, however, these models still appear to be used only infrequently by nonprofit organizations (Carman, 2007, p. 66).

Measuring Goals

Once the goals have been defined, attention must turn to how to measure them. Before thinking about specific measures, decision makers should become familiar with some basic measurement concepts and with the various types of measures available.

Concepts of Measurement

Measurement is an inexact process, as suggested by the fact that social scientists commonly speak of "indicators" rather than measures. As the term implies, measurement instruments indicate something about a concept (that is, about a goal), rather than provide perfect reflections of it. So, crime reported to police constitutes only a fraction of actual crime; and scores on paper-and-pencil aptitude test reflect the test anxiety and/or cultural backgrounds of test takers as well as their aptitudes.

The concepts of *measurement validity* and *measurement reliability* rest on recognition of the inexactness of measurement. Measurement validity refers to whether or to what extent a measure taps what it purports to measure. More valid measures capture more of what they purport to measure. Measurement reliability refers to a measurement instrument's consistency from one application to another. Reliability is higher if the instrument produces the same reading (a) when applied to the same phenomenon at two different times or (b) when applied by different observers to the same phenomenon at the same time. Obviously, the better measures are those that are more valid and reliable.

Executives and staff of nonprofit agencies need not become experts on how to assess the validity and reliability of measures, but they should know to keep at least two points in mind. First, given the fallibility of any particular measure, multiple measures—two or more indicators—are desirable for any important goal, especially any major outcome goal. (One measure each may prove sufficient for many activity goals.) Once data collection begins, the different measures should then be compared to see if they appear to be tapping the same concept. Second, if there are concerns about reliability, taking multiple observations is recommended. Any important measure should, if possible, be applied at a number of time points to see if and how readings might fluctuate. (Multiple observations are also useful for other aspects of research design, as explained as follows.)

Decision makers must also consider *face validity;* that is, whether measures appear valid to key stakeholders. Measurement experts sometimes discount the importance of face validity on the grounds that measures that appear valid sometimes are not. However, the appearance of validity can be crucial to the acceptance of a measure as really reflecting program performance. As a result, decision makers should be concerned for whether recommended measures appear valid, but they must try to avoid using any seemingly attractive measures that may *not* actually tap the relevant goal.

In selecting measures, the ability of program staff to assess measurement validity should not be underestimated. By virtue of their experience with the program, staff often have unique insights into the merits of specific measures, insights that trained outside experts might miss.

Types of Measures

Outcome assessments can employ several types of measures, and to achieve the benefit of multiple measures, will typically utilize two or more of the types. The different types are briefly introduced below in terms of what nonprofit executives and staff may need to know about each.

Program Records and Statistics. An obvious first source for data is the program itself. Records can be kept and statistics maintained by program staff for a variety of measures. Almost every evaluation will employ at least some measures based on program records (for a detailed treatment, see Hatry, 2015).

These measures must be chosen and used with caution, however. For one thing, program staff ordinarily should be asked to record only relatively objective data such as numbers of clients served, gender and age of clients, dates and times services are delivered, and the like. Staff usually can record these more objective data with little difficulty and high reliability; they should not be expected, without training, to record more subjective data such as client attitudes, client progress toward goals, and so on.

In a similar vein, although program records can serve as an excellent source of measures of activity goals—the amount of activity in the program—they should be used only sparingly as outcome measures and probably never as the *sole* outcome measures. Program staff are placed in an untenable position if they are asked to provide the principal measures of their own effectiveness, especially if those measures include subjective elements.

That concern not withstanding, the staff who will record the measures should be involved in defining the measures. In addition to offering insights about measurement validity, staff can speak to the feasibility of the proposed record keeping and help ensure that the record keeping process will not be so onerous that staff must choose between spending their time on the evaluation or on the actual program. If that were to happen, either the evaluation would interfere with the program because staff give too much time to record keeping, or the measures will produce poor data because staff slight record keeping in favor of working on the program's activities.

Client Questionnaire Surveys. Any program serving client populations, including most nonprofit programs, should include some measures of client perceptions and attitudes. These perceptions could include ratings of the program's services and service providers, client self-assessments, and other basic client information. The obvious means for obtaining these measures is a questionnaire survey, of which there are several forms. Each has its own advantages and disadvantages (see also Newcomer and Triplett, 2004; Rea and Parker, 2014).

Phone surveys can produce good response rates (that is, responses from a high proportion of the sample), assuming respondents are contacted at good times (usually in the evening) and interviewed for no more than ten to fifteen minutes. However, phone surveys can be expensive due to interviewer costs and the need for multiple phone calls in order to reach many respondents.

The desire for a lower-cost procedure often leads to consideration of *mail surveys*. Here questionnaires are mailed to respondents, who are asked to complete and return by mail. Any reduction in costs through using a mail survey can be more than offset, however, by the frequent poor response rate, typically lower and less representative than with a phone survey. Questions on mail surveys must also be structured more simply since no interviewer is available to guide the respondent through the questionnaire. Mail surveys work best when sent to groups that are both highly motivated to respond (as sometimes with clients of nonprofit programs) and willing and able to work through written questions independently. Even then, obtaining a high response rate usually requires sending one or two follow-up mailings to nonrespondents.

E-mail surveys represent a contemporary variation on the mail survey. Relatively inexpensive online options are now available, too, for recording and summarizing responses. Obviously, though, this technique will work only with a computer-literate population, and, as with mail surveys, the population must be motivated to respond. As another alternative, e-mail surveys might be combined with traditional mail surveys, an approach that can often produce excellent response rates (see, for example, Thomas, Poister, and Ertas, 2010).

The best choice for many programs will be the so-called *convenience survey*, a survey of respondents who are available in some convenient setting such as when they receive program services. A program can capitalize on that availability by asking clients, while on site, to complete and return a brief questionnaire. As with mail surveys, the questionnaires must be kept simple and brief to permit easy and rapid completion. To reassure respondents about the confidentiality of their responses, ballot-box-like receptacles might be provided for depositing completed questionnaires. A well-planned convenience survey can produce a good response rate at a cost lower than that of any of the alternatives.

Construction of any kind of questionnaire requires some expertise. Agency executives wishing to economize might share the construction process with an outside consultant. The outcome assessment planners might draft initial questions for the consultant to critique before another review by staff and again by the consultant. This collaborative procedure can both reduce the organization's costs and provide training in questionnaire construction to program staff.

Formal Testing Instruments. With many programs, the outcomes desired for clients—self-confidence, sense of personal satisfaction—are sufficiently common that experts elsewhere have already developed appropriate measurement instruments. Some formal testing instruments are available free in the public domain; others may be available at a modest per-unit cost. In either case, it is sometimes wiser to obtain these instruments than to develop new measures.

Trained Observer Ratings. These ratings can be especially useful "for those outcomes that can be assessed by visual ratings of physical conditions," such as physical appearance of a neighborhood for a community development program (Hatry and Lampkin, 2003, p. 15). As that example suggests, these ratings work best for subjective outcomes that are not easily measured by other techniques. These ratings can be expensive in terms of both time and money, however, since their use necessitates development of a rating system, training of raters, and a plan for oversight of the raters. It may also be difficult in a small or moderate-sized nonprofit agency to find raters who do not have a personal stake in a program's effectiveness.

Qualitative Measures. Outcome assessment will typically be enhanced by use of some qualitative measures, measures designed to capture nonnumerical in-depth description and understanding of program operations. After long disdaining these measures as too subjective to be trusted, most experts now recognize that programs with subjective goals cannot be evaluated without qualitative data.

Qualitative measures can be obtained through two principal techniques, observation and in-depth interviews. Observation can provide a sense of how a process is operating, as, for example, in evaluating how well group counseling sessions have functioned. By observing and describing group interaction, an evaluator could gain a sense of process unavailable from quantitative measures.

In-depth interviews have a similar value. In contrast to questionnaire surveys, relatively unstructured interviews are composed principally of open-ended questions designed to elicit respondent feelings about programs without the constraints of the predefined multiple-response choices of structured question-naires. These interviews can be extremely useful as, for example, in assessing the success of individualized client treatment plans.

Still, nonprofit agencies should use qualitative measures with caution, taking care to avoid either over- or underreliance on them. Evaluation of most nonprofit programs calls for multiple measures, including both quantitative and qualitative measures. Outcome assessment planners should be sure that both perspectives are obtained.

Finally, outcome assessment planners should be prepared for the possibility that discussion of measures may rekindle debate about goals. Perhaps staff paid too little attention to the earlier goal definition, or maybe thinking about measures prompts staff to see goals differently. When that happens, planners should be open to a possible need to re-formulate goals.

Data Collection, Analysis, and Reporting

Once the necessary measures have been defined, decision makers should plan for data collection, analysis, and reporting. They must ensure first that procedures are established for recording observations on the measures. They must also determine how the new data collection process will be integrated with the agency's information technology, including evaluating whether new software will be needed for the effort.

Before putting the full outcome assessment in place, the agency should pilot test the measures and the data collection procedures to see how well they work. Measures sometimes prove not to produce the anticipated information. Convenience surveys, for example, sometimes elicit only partial responses from program clients, which could require either improving or abandoning that instrument. Problems can also arise in the recording of data, perhaps necessitating rethinking the recording procedures.

Decision makers, certainly including the agency's chief executive, should also establish a schedule for regular reporting and review of the data. Depending on agency preferences and perceived needs, reviews might be planned as frequently as weekly or as infrequently as annually. Or, less intensive reviews might be planned more often with more intensive reviews scheduled only occasionally (e.g., on a quarterly or annual basis).

The details of the schedule are probably less important than that a schedule is established and implemented. Judging from the findings of one study (Morley, Hatry, and Cowan, 2002, p. 36), many nonprofit agencies that collect outcome information do not systematically tabulate or review the data, instead "leaving it to supervisors and caseworkers to mentally 'process' the data to identify patterns and trends." Agencies unnecessarily hamstring themselves when they make such choices. If systematic outcome data are available, agencies should ensure that the data are tabulated and reviewed.

Growing numbers of governments and some nonprofit agencies (see Carman, 2007, p. 65) are taking the additional step of putting program effectiveness and efficiency data into comprehensive performance management systems and then reporting the data through summary "scorecards" or "dashboards." Popularized by Kaplan and Norton (1996), the so-called "balanced scorecards" are designed to present a 360-degree picture of an organization's performance at any given time. With their growing popularity among governments (see, for example, Edwards and Thomas, 2005), these scorecards seem likely to become increasingly common among nonprofit agencies in the coming years.

Actual review of the data can go in a number of directions depending on what the data look like and what questions the agency has about the programs. At the outset, initial data on any new measures can be at once the most interesting, yet the most difficult to interpret. Novelty accounts for the likely high interest: agency executives and staff may be looking at outcome readings they have only been able to guess at before. However, with initially only one data point to analyze, those readings may seem uninterpretable. Interpretation becomes easier as readings accumulate over time, permitting comparisons of current performance to past performance.

To increase interest and potential utilization of the data, agencies should consider asking key staff to predict results in advance. Poister and Thomas (2007) have documented that asking for such predictions (albeit on a limited number of measures) increased interest among state administrators in the results of stakeholder surveys. Prediction questions can be asked relatively simply, too (e.g., "what proportion of program clients will say they are satisfied with the program?").

The focus of the interpretation depends on a variety of factors. If the data show an unexpected trend or pattern—such as an unanticipated decline on an outcome measure from one quarter to the next—attention may focus on explaining that pattern. More generally, though, the analysis of the data should be driven by the questions and concerns of the agency. Is there a concern about whether a program is working at all? Or, might the concern instead be whether a new program component is achieving desired improvements?

At the same time, care should be taken not to *over-interpret* outcome data. In particular, outcome data should not by themselves be read as implying causality—that is, to conclude that any observed changes resulted from a specific program or programs. Such changes could have resulted from other factors (a change in the economy, for example) that are wholly independent of the program. Outcome assessment data by themselves speak to important questions of whether progress is being made on key agency objectives, but cannot explain the part the agency has played in inducing those changes.

When questions about program performance turn toward these issues of causality, agency executives must move a step beyond outcome assessment to conduct a full program evaluation. Program evaluations, in essence, start from a foundation of strong outcome assessment and add the techniques of comparison and control necessary to speak more definitively to the role of specific programs in producing desired outcomes.

Two Approaches to Program Evaluation

Program evaluation can seem a frightening prospect, raising the specter of outside experts "invading" the organization, seeking information in a mysterious and furtive manner, and ultimately producing a report that may contain unexpected criticisms. Such fears are not ungrounded. The traditional approach to program evaluation, sometimes termed the *objective scientist* approach, often proceeds along those lines.

Borrowed from the natural sciences, the objective scientist approach entails several elements. To begin with, objectivity is valued above all else. To achieve objectivity, the evaluator seeks to maintain critical distance from the program being evaluated in order to minimize possible influence by program staff, who may be biased in the program's favor. The objective scientist also strongly prefers quantitative data, recognizing qualitative data to be subjective by nature—the antithesis of objectivity. Finally, the usual purpose of an evaluation for the objective scientist is to determine whether or to what extent the program has achieved its goals. Is the program sufficiently effective to be continued, or should it be terminated? The objective scientist takes little interest in how a program's internal mechanics are functioning.

Two decades of experience have revealed shortcomings to this approach. Evaluators who insist on keeping their distance miss the unique insights staff often have about their programs. Disdaining qualitative data further limits the ability to assess a program because the goals of most public and nonprofit programs are too subjective to be measured only by quantitative techniques. Finally, the insistence on critical distance combined with an exclusive focus on program outcomes can result in evaluations that fail to answer the questions decision makers have.

Recognition of these problems led to the development of an alternative, the approach that Michael Quinn Patton has termed *utilization-focused evaluation*. As Patton (2008, pp. 451–452) has explained, this approach begins with the goal of balance rather than objectivity. Where objectivity implies taking an unbiased view of a program by observing from a distance, balance recommends viewing program operation from up close as well as from afar, thus to discern important details as well as broad patterns. Achieving balance also requires qualitative as well as quantitative data because the latter are unlikely to capture all that is important about programs whose goals are subjective. A balanced assessment necessitates multiple perspectives.

The balanced approach also rejects outcome assessment—"did the program work?"—as the only purpose of an evaluation. A utilization-focused evaluation seeks information for use in modifying and improving programs, too. Getting close to the program helps by putting the evaluator in contact with the program administrators who have questions about how programs should be modified as well as the authority to implement those modifications.

The balanced approach is not appropriate for every program, every evaluator, or every nonprofit executive. In getting close to a program, an evaluator can risk being "captured" by the program and, at the extreme, becoming only a "mouthpiece" for those who are vested in the program. For that reason, if there are serious questions about the quality of a program or about the competence of its staff, the nonprofit executive may prefer an evaluation performed from the critical distance of the objective scientist.

For the most part, though, nonprofit executives will find that the utilization-focused evaluation approach promises both a more balanced assessment and information more likely to be useful in program development. As a consequence, the discussion that follows assumes a utilization-focused approach to evaluation.

Who Does the Evaluation?

A first question, when planning a program evaluation, is who should conduct the evaluation. Here the principal options are (a) an internal evaluation performed by the organization's staff, (b) an external evaluation performed by outside consultants, and (c) an externally directed evaluation with extensive internal staff assistance.

An internal evaluation is possible only if the organization has one or more staff members with extensive training and experience in program evaluation. Unlike outcome assessment, full-scale program evaluation is too technical a task to attempt without that expertise. An internal evaluation also requires that the nonprofit executive give essentially a free rein to the evaluation staff. Since inside evaluators may face strong pressures to conform their findings to the predispositions of program staff, standing up to those pressures is possible only if the nonprofit executive has made an unequivocal commitment to an unbiased evaluation.

As a practical matter, although many nonprofit organizations prefer to conduct evaluations internally (e.g., Carman, 2007, p. 70), most appear to lack sufficient in-house expertise to produce high-quality evaluations. They are probably better advised to seek outside assistance from United Way or private-sector consulting firms, management assistance agencies for the nonprofit sector, or university faculty (often found in public administration, education, or psychology departments).

Hiring an outside consultant carries its own risks. Perhaps the greatest risk is that the external evaluators, perhaps trained in the objective scientist tradition, may resist getting close to the program and consequently conduct the evaluation with insufficient concern for the organization's needs. A preference for critical distance may blind them to the questions and insights the agency has about the program.

To minimize this risk, the nonprofit executive should discuss at length with any prospective evaluators how the evaluation should be conducted, including whether they are capable of taking a utilization-focused approach. It is also wise to negotiate a contract that specifies in detail how the nonprofit organization will be involved in the evaluation.

Perhaps the best means for conducting an evaluation is through a combination of outside consultants and internal staff. In this mode, outside consultants provide technical expertise plus some independence from internal organizational pressures while internal staff perform much of the legwork and collaborate with the consultants in developing the research design, collecting data, and interpreting findings. The idea, as documented in one study of successful evaluations (Minich et al., 2006, p. 186), is to "not expect program staff to be researchers" and, in that spirit, to "shift measurement tasks to full-time evaluators."

There are several advantages to this approach. First, it provides the necessary technical expertise without sacrificing closeness to the program. Second, greater staff involvement should produce greater staff commitment to the findings, increasing the likelihood that findings will be utilized. Third, the evaluation can be used to train staff to serve a greater role in future evaluations. Finally, having staff implement much of the legwork could reduce the out-of-pocket costs for the outside consultants. This reduction is possible, however, only if care is taken that working with the staff does not require too much of the consultants' time.

That time commitment can be limited by creating a small advisory team to oversee the evaluation. This team should include the outside evaluators, the nonprofit executive (or the executive's representative), and at least one to three other staff members in the nonprofit organization. The team should serve as the central entity to which the evaluator reports, reducing the time necessary for working with program staff. Keeping its size small (in the range of three to five members) facilitates the team ability to provide clear and prompt feedback to the evaluation process. A team of this kind is probably desirable for wholly internal or external evaluations, too.

The only way to assure that the chief executive's concerns about the program are addressed is for that executive to be personally involved in the evaluation, optimally as a member of the evaluation advisory team. In addition, as the literature on organizational change attests (see, for example, Fernandez and Rainey, 2006), programmatic change is unlikely to occur through an evaluation unless the chief executive is involved and committed to the process.

The goal of this involvement should not be to obtain the "right" answers—answers that conform to the executive's predispositions—but to ensure that the right *questions* (the questions crucial to the program's future) are asked. The chief executive should emphasize this distinction to the evaluator(s) up front, and then monitor to be sure the distinction is observed as the evaluation proceeds.

Determining the Purpose of the Evaluation

The first task of an evaluation is to define its purpose. That is, what sort of information is desired and why? How will the information be used? Answers to these questions will be crucial in determining the other elements of the evaluation.

Discussion of evaluation purposes typically begins with a dichotomy between *summative* and *formative* purposes (see Rossi, Lipsey, and Freeman, 2004, pp. 34–36). A *summative* purpose implies a principal interest in program outcomes, in "summing up" a program's overall achievements. A *formative* purpose, by contrast, means that the principal interest is in forming or "re-forming" the program by focusing the evaluation on how well the program's internal operations function. In reality, though, the purposes of evaluations are much more complex than a dichotomy can convey. Saying an evaluation has a formative purpose, for example, does not indicate which of the program's internal mechanisms are of interest.

An evaluation's purpose should reflect the concerns key stakeholders have about the program. The process of defining this purpose thus should begin with the nonprofit organization's executive: What questions does he or she have about how the program is working? What kinds of information might speak to anticipated decisions about the program? Opinions of other stakeholders, including funders, may also be solicited.

In the end, a number of purposes is possible, depending on the perceptions of stakeholders and the specific program. An evaluation performed primarily for funders, who may be most interested in whether the program is having the desired impact, is likely to have a summative purpose. By contrast, a program that has only recently been implemented may be a good candidate for an *implementation assessment*—an evaluation of how well a program has been put into operation—but a poor candidate for a summative evaluation because the program has not been operating in the field long enough to expect an observable impact. Evaluations designed mainly for program staff are likely to have principally formative purposes to help staff modify and strengthen the program.

Because this purpose will guide decisions at all subsequent steps in the evaluation, a mistake at this stage can hamper the entire effort. The nonprofit executive should consequently review this purpose and make certain it reflects his or her concerns as well as the concerns of other key stakeholders. It is also true, though, that an evaluation's purpose may become clearer as the evaluation progresses. Stakeholders may be able to articulate their questions about programs only as they consider program goals and measures. Evaluators should be open to this possibility.

Evaluators and nonprofit executives must also be alert to the possibility of so-called *covert purposes,* unvoiced hidden purposes for an evaluation (Weiss, 1972, pp. 11–12). Program managers, for example, sometimes have an unspoken goal of "whitewashing" a program by producing a favorable evaluation. The responsible chief executive will reject such an evaluation as unethical as well as incapable of producing useful information.

It is at this stage that the evaluator and the organization's chief executive should also consider whether the evaluation is worth doing. Revelation of a dominant covert purpose would provide one reason to bow out. Or, it may be impossible to complete an evaluation in time to inform an approaching decision about the program. The resources necessary for a program evaluation are difficult to justify unless the results can be meaningful and useful.

Outcome Evaluation Designs

Most program evaluations will be concerned to some extent with assessing program impact—whether or to what extent a program has produced the desired outcomes. To achieve that end, evaluators can employ a number of outcome evaluation designs. Nonprofit executives and staff usually will neither need nor desire to become experts on these designs. However, to participate intelligently in the evaluation process, they need to understand at least their basic structure and underlying principles. This section will explain those principles and then briefly survey the most important of the designs. (For a more detailed discussion of the designs, see Rossi, Lipsey, and Freeman, 2004, Chapters 8–10.)

Causality

The goal of any outcome evaluation design is to assess causality—whether a program has caused the desired changes. To do so, the evaluation design must satisfy three conditions:

1. *Covariation*: Changes in the program must covary with changes in the outcome(s). Changes in outcome measures should occur in tandem with changes in program effort.
2. *Time order*. Since cause must come before effect, changes in the program must *precede* changes in the outcome measures.
3. *Nonspuriousness*. The evaluator must be able to rule out alternative explanations of the relationship between the program and outcome. The evaluator must demonstrate that the relationship is not spurious, that it is not the result of a joint relationship between the program, the outcome, and some third variable.

An evaluation design has *internal validity* to the extent that it satisfies these three conditions. Internal validity, in other words, refers to how accurately the design describes what the program actually achieved or caused.

Evaluation designs can also be judged for their *external validity*: the extent to which findings can be generalized to contexts beyond that of the program being evaluated. Ordinarily, nonprofit organizations will have little or no concern for external validity; nonprofit executives usually will be interested only in how their own program works, not with how it might work elsewhere. External validity becomes a major concern only if, for example, a program is being run as a pilot to test its value for possible broader implementation. Even then, internal validity must still take first priority. We must be sure that findings are accurate before considering how they might be generalized.

Threats to Internal Validity

The difficulties of satisfying the three conditions for causality can be illustrated relative to three so-called pre-experimental designs, designs that are frequently but often carelessly used in program evaluations:

1. One-shot case study: X 01
2. Posttest only with comparison group: X 01 02
3. One-group pretest/posttest 01 X 02

In each case, X refers to treatment, 01 to a first observation, and 02 to a second observation (on the comparison group in item 2, on the experimental group in item 3).

The one-shot case study satisfies none of the conditions of causality. As the most rudimentary design, it provides no mechanism for showing whether outcomes and program covary, much less for demonstrating either time order or nonspuriousness.

The posttest only with comparison group design can establish covariation since the comparison of a program group to a nonprogram group will show whether outcomes and program covary. However, this design can tell us nothing about time order; we cannot tell whether any outcome differences occurred *after* the program's inception or were already in place beforehand.

The one-group pretest/posttest design can satisfy the first two conditions for causality since taking observations before and after a program's inception tests for covariation and time order. The weakness of the design—and it is a glaring weakness—lies in its inability to establish nonspuriousness.

Take, for purposes of illustration, a rehabilitation program for substance abusers as evaluated by the one-group pretest/posttest design. This design can establish covariation, whether substance abuse decreases with program involvement, and it can establish time order, since substance abuse is measured both before and after the program intervention. But it does not control for such threats to nonspuriousness as the following:

1. *Maturation:* Decreased substance abuse could have resulted from the maturing of participants during the time of the program, a maturation not caused by the program.

2. *Regression*: Extreme scores tend to "regress toward the mean" rather than become more extreme. If program participants were selected on the basis of their extreme scores (that is, high levels of substance abuse), decreased abuse could be a function of irrelevant statistical regression rather than a program effect.

3. *History:* Events concurrent with but unrelated to the program can affect program outcomes. Perhaps a rise in the street price of illegal drugs produced a decline in substance abuse, which could mistakenly be attributed to the program.

These flaws make the pre-experimental designs undesirable as the principal design for most evaluations. Stronger designs are necessary to provide reasonable tests of the conditions of causality.

Experiments

Experimental designs offer the strongest internal validity. The classic experimental design takes this form:

$$R \ 01 \ X \ 02$$
$$R \ 03 \ \ \ \ 04$$

R refers to *randomization,* meaning that subjects are assigned by chance—for example, by lot or by drawing numbers from a hat—to the experimental or control group in advance of the experiment.

Randomization is a crucial defining element of experimental designs. With the inter-group and across-time components of this design testing for covariation and time order, randomization establishes the final condition of causality, nonspuriousness, by making the experimental and control groups essentially equivalent. As a consequence of that equivalence, the control group provides a test of "change across time"—the changes due to maturation, regression, history, and so forth, which could affect program outcomes. Comparing the experimental and control groups can thus separate program effects from other changes across time, as this simple subtraction illustrates:

Program effects + change over time $(02 - 01)$

$-$ Change over time $(04 - 03)$

= Program effects

Unfortunately, many practical problems work against the use of experimental outcome designs in evaluations. In particular, randomization poses a number of difficulties. First, it must be done prior to the beginning of an intervention; participants must be randomly assigned before they receive treatment. Second, ethical objections may be raised to depriving some subjects of a treatment that other subjects receive, or political objections may be raised to providing treatment on anything other than a "first come, first served" basis. Experiments can also be costly, given the need to establish, maintain, and monitor distinct experimental and control groups. Since many programs are still changing as they begin operation, it sometimes proves impossible to (as an experiment requires) maintain the same program structure throughout the length of the experiment.

But the possibility of conducting an experiment should not be dismissed too quickly. The need for prior planning can sometimes be surmounted by running an experiment not on the first cohort group of subjects, but on a second or later cohort group, such as a second treatment group of substance abusers. Ethical and political objections often can be overcome by giving the control group a traditional treatment rather than no treatment. That choice may make more sense for the purpose of the evaluation anyway, since the ultimate choice is likely to be between the new treatment and the old, not between the new treatment and no treatment.

Quasi-Experiments

If an experimental design cannot be used, the evaluator should consider one of the so-called *quasi-experimental designs*. These designs are so named because they attempt, through a variety of means, to approximate the controls that experiments achieve through randomization. The strongest of these designs come close to achieving the rigor of an experiment.

A first quasi-experimental design is the *nonequivalent control group*:

$$01 \quad X \quad 02$$
$$03 \qquad 04$$

Here, in lieu of randomization, a comparison group is matched to the experimental group in the hope that the pre-post comparison of the two groups will furnish an indication of program impact.

This design is as strong—or weak—as the quality of the match. The goal of matching is to create a comparison group that is as similar as possible to the experimental group, except that it does not participate in the program. A good match can be difficult to achieve because the available comparison groups often differ in crucial respects from the experimental group.

Consider a hypothetical job-training program for the unemployed that takes participants on a first come, first served basis. The obvious candidates for a comparison group are would-be participants who volunteer *after* the program has filled all of the available slots. The evaluator might select from those late volunteers a group similar to the experimental group in terms of race, sex, education, previous employment history, and the like—similar, in other words, on the extraneous variables that could affect the desired outcome of employment success.

The difficulty arises in trying to match on all of the key variables at once. Creating a comparison group similar to the experimental on two of those variables—say, race and gender—may be possible, but the two groups are unlikely then also to have equivalent education levels, employment histories, and other characteristics. In addition, the two groups may differ on some unrecorded or intangible variable. Perhaps the early volunteers were more motivated than late volunteers, accounting for why they volunteered sooner. If that difference were not measured and incorporated in the analysis, the program could erroneously be credited for employment gains that actually stemmed from the differences in motivation. In cases such as this, no match is preferable to a bad match.

A second kind of quasi-experimental design is the *interrupted time series design*, diagramed as follows:

$$01 \quad 02 \quad 03 \quad X \quad 04 \quad 05 \quad 06$$

The defining elements of this design are three or more observations recorded both before *and* after the program intervention. Multiple observations are important because they provide a reading on trends, thereby controlling for most changes over time (maturation, regression, and so on), which experimental designs achieve through randomization. Those controls give this design relatively good internal validity.

History is the principal weakness of this design, with respect to internal validity. There is no control for any event that, by virtue of occurring at the same time as the program, could affect program impact. A program to improve the situation of the homeless could be affected, for example, by an economic upturn (or downturn) that began at about the same time as the program.

Obtaining the necessary multiple observations can also prove difficult. On the front end, preprogram observations may be unavailable if measurement of key outcome indicators began only when the program itself began. On the back end, stakeholders may demand evidence of program impact before several post-program observations can be obtained.

One of the strongest of the quasi-experimental designs is the *multiple interrupted time series*:

$$01 \quad 02 \quad 03 \quad X \quad 04 \quad 05 \quad 06$$
$$07 \quad 08 \quad 09 \quad \quad 010 \quad 011 \quad 012$$

The strength of this design results from combining the key features of the interrupted time series and the nonequivalent group design. The time series dimension controls for most changes across time; the nonequivalent control group dimension controls for the threat of history.

The problems with this design derive from the possible weakness of its component parts. A bad match can provide a misleading comparison; the lack of longitudinal data can rule out use of this design at all.

Other Designs and Controls

The realities of many programs preclude the use of either experimental or quasi-experimental designs. Perhaps no one planned for an evaluation until the program was well under way, thereby ruling out randomization and providing no preprogram observations. Finding a comparison group may also prove too difficult or too costly. Under these conditions, the evaluator may be forced to rely on one or more of the pre-experimental designs as the principal outcome evaluation design, leaving the evaluation susceptible to many threats to internal validity.

Fortunately, means are available to compensate for if not to eliminate these design weaknesses. A first possibility is to use *statistical controls*. If their numbers and variability are sufficient, the subjects of a program can be divided for comparison and control. For example, a one-group pretest/posttest might be subdivided into those receiving a little of the program (x) and those receiving a lot (X). The resulting design becomes more like the stronger nonequivalent control group design:

$$01 \quad X \quad 02$$
$$03 \quad x \quad 04$$

There remains the question of whether the two groups are comparable in all respects other than the varying program involvement. If that comparability can be established, the design can provide a reading on whether more program involvement produces more impact, substituting for the unavailable comparison of program versus no program. The option to strengthen designs through statistical controls can also be useful with quasi-experimental and experimental designs. When a nonequivalent control group design is used, the evaluator may want to subdivide and compare subjects on variables on which the matching was flawed. If the two groups were matched on race and gender but not on education, the experimental and control groups might be compared while statistically controlling for education. Or, where a time series design is employed, additional data might be sought to control for threats of history. In a study of how the 55-mile-per-hour speed limit affected traffic fatalities, researchers examined data on total miles traveled to test an alternative explanation that fatalities declined as a consequence of reduced travel (amid the 1974–1975 energy crisis), not as a consequence of reduced speed (Meier and Morgan, 1981, pp. 670–671). The data added to the evidence that reduced speed was the cause.

Combining several outcome evaluation designs can also add to the strength of the overall design. Many evaluations will employ multiple designs, each for a different measure. Stronger designs on some measures might then help to compensate for the weaker designs necessary for other measures.

Assuming an outside evaluator is involved, these design decisions will be made principally by that individual. Still, to the extent that executives and staff understand these basic principles of evaluation design, they will be able to advise evaluators on these decisions. The nonprofit executive can perform an even more important role by monitoring the design planning to assure its fit to the purposes of the evaluation. The most rigorous design will be of no use unless it speaks to the issues of concern to the organization's board, executive and/or stakeholders. It is up to the executive to ensure that the evaluation remains relevant and appropriate to the organization's needs.

Process Evaluation

With most program evaluations, nonprofit executives will want to evaluate the program process as well as its ultimate impact. Outcome evaluation designs usually indicate only whether a program is working, not why. Process evaluation may be able to discern what steps in a program's process are not working as intended, perhaps pointing to how a program can be changed to increase its effectiveness. These suggestions will often prove the most useful.

The techniques of process evaluation are both simpler and less systematic than those for outcome evaluations (see also Thomas, 1980). In essence, process evaluation entails examining the internal workings of a program—as represented largely through activity goals—both for their functioning and for their role in producing the desired outcomes. It usually begins with the development of a good logic model (see Savaya and Waysman, 2005), then progresses to an examination of specific parts of that model.

The executives and staff of nonprofit organizations should be key actors in any process evaluation. To begin with, they should attempt to define at the outset the specific questions they have about the program's process. Conceivably, they may already feel adequately informed about performance as it pertains to some activity goals, and so may not desire new information there. They will then want to be certain that the evaluation includes the questions they do have about program process.

The basics of a process evaluation can be illustrated by the case of an affirmative action program designed to increase the hiring of minority firefighters by a municipal government. The activity goals of interest in this evaluation included the following:

1. Increase the number of minority applicants.
2. Increase the success rate of minority applicants on the written examination.
3. Increase the success rate of minority applicants on the physical examination.

These activity goals are designed to lead to this outcome goal (among others):

4. Increase the proportion of minority firefighters in the fire department.

The several activity goals can illustrate how a process evaluation can be useful. Data on these various activities could indicate where, if at all, the program might be failing. Are too few minorities applying? Or are minorities applying only to be eliminated disproportionately by written or physical exams? Answering these questions could help a program administrator to decide whether, or how, and where to change the program.

A good process evaluation often can help to compensate for weaknesses in the outcome evaluation designs. When the difficulty of controlling for all threats to internal validity in an outcome evaluation design leaves unanswered questions about the linkage of program to outcomes, the process evaluation could provide an additional test of this linkage by documenting whether the program activities have occurred in a manner consistent with the observed outcomes. If an impact evaluation shows significant gains on the outcome measures *and* the process evaluation shows high levels of program activities, the evaluator can argue more convincingly that the program caused the impact. By contrast, evidence of low activity levels in the same scenario would cast doubts on the possibility that the program is responsible for outcome gains.

Most program evaluations should contain some form of process evaluation. Though less systematic than outcome designs, process evaluation techniques will often provide the more useful information for nonprofit executives.

Data Development, Report Writing, and Follow-Up

Nonprofit executives should plan to involve themselves and the program staff extensively in analysis and review of evaluation findings. This involvement is necessary first for accuracy: staff review of data and reports minimizes the risk of outside evaluators reporting inaccurate conclusions. Staff members also are more likely to utilize findings and implement recommendations that they helped to develop.

When outside evaluators are used, the best approach to this involvement may be to ask for the opportunity to review and comment on interpretations and reports while still allowing the evaluators to retain final authority on the substance of reports. Most evaluators should welcome this arrangement for self-protection; no evaluator wants to go public with conclusions that are subsequently shown to be erroneous. Staff might also be involved in basic data interpretation as, for example, by meeting with evaluators to review data printouts. As suggested earlier, interest among staff might be heightened by asking them to predict some of the results before the findings are in (Poister and Thomas, 2007).

The chief executive must also decide what final written products to request. A comprehensive evaluation report is usually desirable, both for the historical record and as a reference in case questions arise, along with a brief executive summary of one to three pages for broader distribution and readership. Other reports may be desirable for particular types of clients.

The job of the outside evaluator customarily concludes at this point, but the agency's chief executive and program staff should consider if and how the program should be changed in light of the evaluation. A program evaluation can provide both a direction and an impetus for change, but often with a limited window of opportunity to achieve any change. The agency's chief executive should take advantage of that window by discussing the evaluation with staff and, where appropriate, developing plans for what changes to make and how. Since the evaluation data presumably came from the agency's outcome assessment system, this is also a good time to consider any need to change that system. Only through such efforts can a nonprofit agency gain the full value of a program evaluation.

Summary

Nonprofit agencies today confront increasingly strong demands to demonstrate that their programs work. To meet these demands, contemporary nonprofit agencies must engage in systematic outcome assessment, measuring and monitoring the performance of their programs.

Outcome assessment data can speak to important questions of whether progress is being made on key agency objectives. As a result, every nonprofit agency, if it has not already done so, should consider if and how it can develop, collect, and analyze these data on a continuing basis.

Outcome assessment data alone can *not* speak to issues of causality, that is, to whether any observed changes resulted from a specific agency program or programs. Agency executives who wish to investigate those kinds of causal connections should consider taking a step beyond outcome assessment to conduct a program evaluation, too. Program evaluations build from a foundation of strong outcome assessment, adding the techniques of comparison and control necessary to speak to the role of specific programs in producing desired outcomes.

Success in these efforts may not come easily. For one thing, nonprofit agencies often need to find additional funds to support new initiatives in either outcome assessment or program evaluation. Yet as Carman (2007, p. 71) has observed, "although funders and other stakeholders may be asking [nonprofit agencies] to report on evaluation and performance information, most are not receiving separate funds or additional grants to collect this information." In the long term, the solution may lie in these agencies "investing in their own evaluation capacity," as Carman (2007, p. 73) recommends, but that strategy offers no help in the near term.

Even if the necessary funding can be found, success in either outcome assessment or program evaluation also requires a delicate balance of analytic and scientific expertise with group process skills. On the analytic side, nonprofit executives and staff should acquire at least a basic expertise, which can be supplemented as necessary with the talents of skilled consultants. On the group process side, nonprofit executives must ensure that any outcome assessment planning or program evaluation includes extensive participation of the agency's stakeholders, including at least the program staff and funders. Achieving that balance can give the executives and staff of nonprofit organizations the knowledge necessary to provide better programs and services.

References

Carman, J. G. Evaluation Practice Among Community-Based Organizations: Research into the Reality. *American Journal of Evaluation*, 2007, 28(1), pp. 60–75.

Edwards, D. J., and Thomas, J. C. Developing a Municipal Performance Measurement System: Reflections on the *Atlanta Dashboard*. *Public Administration Review*, 2005, 65(3), 369–376.

Fernandez, S., and Rainey, H. G. Managing Successful Organizational Change in the Public Sector. *Public Administration Review*, 2006, 66(2), 168–176.

Hatry, H. P. Using Agency Records. In K. E. Newcomer, H. P. Hatry, and J.S. Wholey (eds.), *Handbook of Practical Program Evaluation* (4th ed.) San Francisco: Jossey-Bass, 2015 325–343.

Hatry, H., and Lampkin, L. *Key Steps in Outcome Management*. Washington, D.C.: The Urban Institute, 2003.

Herman, R. D., and Renz, D. O. Advancing Nonprofit Organizational Effectiveness Research and Theory: Nine Theses. *Nonprofit Management & Leadership*, 2008, 18(4), 399–415.

W. K. Kellogg Foundation. Logic Model Development Guide. Battle Creek, Michigan: Author, 2004.

Kaplan, R. S., and Norton, D. P. *The Balanced Scorecard: Translating Strategy into Action*. Boston: Harvard Business School Press, 1996.

Kress, G., Springer, J. F., and Koehler, G. Policy Drift: An Evaluation of the California Business Enterprise Program. *Policy Studies Journal*, 1980, 8, 1101–1108.

McLaughlin, J. A., and Jordan, G. B. Using Logic Models. In K. E. Newcomer, H. P. Hatry, and J.S. Wholey (eds.), *Handbook of Practical Program Evaluation* (4th ed.) San Francisco: Jossey-Bass, 2015. 62–87.

Meier, K. J., and Morgan, D. P. Speed Kills: A Longitudinal Analysis of Traffic Fatalities and the 55 MPH Speed Limit. *Policy Studies Review*, 1981, 1, 157–167.

Minich, L., Howe, S., Langmeyer, D., and Corcoran, K. Can Community Change Be Measured for an Outcomes-Based Initiative? A Comparative Case Study of the Success by 6 Initiative. *American Journal of Community Psychology*, 2006, 38, 183–190.

Morley, E., Hatry, H., and Cowan, J. *Making Use of Outcome Information for Improving Services: Recommendations for Nonprofit Organizations*. Washington, D.C.: The Urban Institute, 2002.

Newcomer, K. E., and Triplett, T. Using Surveys. In K. E. Newcomer, H. P. Hatry, and J. S. Wholey (eds.), *Handbook of Practical Program Evaluation* (4th ed.) San Francisco: Jossey-Bass, 2015, 344–382.

Patton, M. Q. *Utilization-Focused Evaluation*, 4th ed. Thousand Oaks, Calif.: Sage, 2008.

Poister, T. H., and Thomas, J. C. The 'Wisdom of Crowds': Learning from Administrators Predictions of Citizen Perceptions. *Public Administration Review*, 2007, 67(3), 279–289.

Rea, L. M., and Parker, R. A. *Designing and Conducting Survey Research: A Comprehensive Guide*, (4th ed.) San Francisco: Jossey-Bass, 2014.

Rossi, P. H., Lipsey, M. W., and Freeman, H. E. *Evaluation: A Systematic Approach* (7th ed.) Newbury Park, CA.: Sage, 2004.

Savaya, R., and Waysman, M. The Logic Model: A Tool for Incorporating Theory in Development and Evaluation of Programs. *Administration in Social Work*, 2005, 29(2), 85–103.

Stone, M., Bigelow, B., and Crittenden, W. Research on Strategic Management in Nonprofit Organizations: Synthesis, Analysis, and Future Directions. *Administration & Society*, 1999, 3, 378–423.

Thomas, J. C. 'Patching Up' Evaluation Designs: The Case for Process Evaluation. *Policy Studies Journal*, 1980, 8, 1145–1151.

Thomas, J. C., Poister, T. H., and Ertas, N. Customer, Partner, Principal: Local Government Perspectives on State Agency Performance in Georgia. *Journal of Public Administration Research and Theory*, 20(4), 2010, 779-799.

United Way of America. *Outcome Measurement Resource Network.* http://www.liveunited.org/outcomes/. Visited December 17, 2009.

Weiss, C. H. *Evaluation Research: Methods of Assessing Program Effectiveness*. Englewood Cliffs, N. J.: Prentice-Hall, 1972.

PART FOUR

DEVELOPING AND MANAGING NONPROFIT FINANCIAL RESOURCES

E ssentially all nonprofit managers and leaders understand the importance of financial resources to the success of their organization. And yet, all too often, the way nonprofit leaders and managers view the financial aspects of the nonprofit enterprise are too narrow and constricted. The chapters of Part Four collectively address the multiple facets of the process of securing, allocating, using, and accounting for financial resources, all with the orientation of maximizing the potential for mission impact and results. Jeanne Bell and Shannon Ellis set the tone for Part Four with their discussion in Chapter Seventeen of strategic financial leadership—a critical yet generally overlooked dimension of successful nonprofit financial performance. Bell and Ellis explain how the strategic orientation of effective financial leadership has the potential to open the door to new possibilities for nonprofit development, and they discuss how this work serves as the foundation for the operational work of financial management.

Of course, raising money through philanthropic channels is a time-honored approach to securing funds for nonprofits, and fundraising has become more competitive and sophisticated. Many consider philanthropic fundraising to be the heart of nonprofit finance and, in Chapter Eighteen, Sarah K. Nathan and Eugene R. Tempel outline the key elements of an effective fundraising program for a typical nonprofit and explain some of the key options that exist for nonprofits that seek gifts and donations, with an emphasis on the need to engage in the fundraising process in a way that aligns well with the mission and culture of the organization. In Chapter Nineteen, Dennis R. Young and Jung-In Soh approach the financial resource question from a broader and more strategic perspective, with a framework they recommend be used by nonprofit financial leaders to assess their revenue options. This chapter offers a relatively comprehensive discussion of the range of options for securing financial resources and explains how nonprofit leaders can use the framework to make decisions about the critical question of revenue mix. Of course, one of the most common revenue sources for many nonprofits is governmental funding, which often involves contracting with government. In Chapter Twenty, Steven Rathgeb Smith examines the nature and implications of nonprofit-government contracting and how this has evolved in the United States, discusses the key benefits, challenges, and dynamics associated with it, and offers advice for ways that nonprofits might maintain an appropriate level of engagement and autonomy when engaged in this common yet potentially problematic nonprofit revenue relationship.

Nonprofit organizations, of course, do not exist to raise money. They exist to pursue their missions and causes. Central to mission accomplishment, however, is effective and responsible financial management, a process that enables the thoughtful and responsible stewardship and utilization of the financial resources of the organization. This is the focus of Woods Bowman's Chapter Twenty-One. Bowman explains in pragmatic terms the fundamental tools and techniques that are integral to effective nonprofit financial management. In his discussion about the challenges of financial sustainability and the need for mission-based decision making, Bowman provides practical financial management advice that is relevant to and usable by both financial and general managers of nonprofit organizations of any size, as they work to ensure that they are good stewards who are using the financial resources of the organization to achieve the greatest benefit and impact.

CHAPTER SEVENTEEN

FINANCIAL LEADERSHIP IN NONPROFIT ORGANIZATIONS*

Jeanne Bell and Shannon Ellis

In the financial realm, there is an important and often overlooked distinction between management and leadership. Financial *management* is about *producing* accurate reporting; financial *leadership* is about *interpreting* financial reporting and putting it in context with a wide mix of internal and external factors to make strategic decisions that strengthen the organization over time. Increasingly, we recognize these strategic decisions to be necessary year-round, not just during formal planning processes. In "The Strategic Plan Is Dead. Long Live Strategy" (*Stanford Social Innovation Review*, 2013), O'Donovan and Flower write that traditional strategy and decision making were characterized by "predictions, data collection, and execution from the top down," while today's adaptive strategy and decision making are characterized by "experiments, pattern recognition, and execution by the whole." As the sector moves away from long-term, predicative strategic plans, it becomes even more critical that financial leadership be distributed well beyond the executive office. Strong ongoing analysis and decision making by all staff and board—rather than mere implementation

---

*The focus of this chapter is explicitly on public charities, although the concepts will apply to other types of tax-exempt organizations as well. Some of the key themes and concepts presented in this chapter are drawn from the author's book with Steve Zimmerman on financial leadership and strategy, *The Sustainability Mindset: Using the Matrix Map to Make Strategic Decisions* (2014) and reprinted here with permission.

of a plan—is dependent upon shared understanding of how the organization and its key activities work financially.

Thus, it is incumbent upon an executive director to ensure that the organization has the culture, systems, and skills in place to support financial leadership by the many rather than the few. Practically, that means:

1. Ensuring that the annual budgeting process is thoughtful, inclusive, and reflective of staff's best current sense of the business model and strategic direction.
2. Providing *all* staff and board with timely and accurate financial reporting.
3. Continuously training staff and board to be good consumers of financial reporting.
4. Transparently engaging all staff and board in assessing the organization's financial performance and making adjustments to plans as necessary.

Organizational Culture, Systems, and Skills to Support Financial Leadership

The foundational tenet of a healthy culture of money is transparency: the consistent sharing of meaningful financial reporting with *all* staff and board. Among the most toxic problems that can plague an organization is a leader who won't share financial information. The motivation is often one of two things, or both at once: financial illiteracy or the fear of how people will react to the financial truth. Some executives are not as financially literate as they need to be to skillfully play the interpretive leadership role, and thus are uncomfortable sharing and discussing financial information. This is easily corrected through an intentional investment in their own professional development. Some executives worry that sharing less than optimal financial results with staff will scare them unduly and hurt morale. But staff members have the right to know when an organization is struggling financially, even if it means they will opt to leave. In fact, staff members may have good ideas for ways to improve the situation if only they were engaged in the problem solving.

Further, morale is never maintained when layoffs and program cuts happen in a seemingly sudden fashion because staff members weren't informed along the way of financial trouble. Some executives don't want to share full financial information with their boards because they fear they will be judged or blamed for poor financial results. Of course, they very well may be. Yet, it is delaying the inevitable (not to mention unethical) to keep a board in the dark about serious financial problems. Again, how can the board help if it doesn't understand the problem? Financial transparency is fundamental to a healthy culture of money. Given the choice, executives should over-share rather than under-share financial information. In so doing, they educate and empower their staff and board colleagues to share responsibility for the financial health of the organization.

In order to be transparent, leaders have to have something of quality to share. This is where strong systems and skills complement healthy culture. Nonprofit tendencies to under-invest in administrative infrastructure can yield inadequate financial systems. The result is late, inaccurate, or unhelpful financial reporting, leaving staff and board members with little to go on as they make decisions. Poor systems also create chronic inefficiencies and frustration among staff. Taking two weeks rather than two hours to cobble together a grant report to a funder because expenses have not been well coded to the grant all year is the kind of frustrating recurrence that drives talented people to leave poorly led nonprofits. Quality financial information also needs to be shared with funders, auditors, the Internal Revenue Service (IRS), and other regulators. The results of non-compliance in these cases range from reputation damage to loss of tax-exempt status.

Systems are often dependent on the skills and initiative of the finance staff. Whether financial employees, contract bookkeepers, or consulting CPAs, the most important question to answer is: "Do they understand and have experience with *nonprofit* accounting?" In particular, the rules and regulations around managing contributed income, including tracking donors' programmatic-use restrictions on gifts, make nonprofit accounting quite distinct from for-profit accounting. We have found it helpful to consider finance staffing in three categories: strategic, operational, and transactional skills and competencies. Table 17.1 defines these categories and provides examples of the tasks and qualifications for each category.

It's certainly critical that the people *producing* financial reporting have the appropriate skills and that their professional development—too often overlooked in nonprofit organizations—be invested with the same commitment as that of program or other executive staff. But for *financial leadership* to be truly distributed, all staff and board need ongoing support in developing their financial literacy skills. Executives should ensure that a meaningful orientation to the organization's budget and financial statements is part of recruitment and on-boarding for *all* staff and board members, for instance. They may include a refresher on reading and engaging with the annual budget when it is adopted each year. They may encourage financial literacy-related professional development goals for program and development staff. And again, they must themselves model interest in and comfort with all of the organization's financial reporting.

TABLE 17.1. Finance Functions, Tasks, and Qualifications

Finance Functions	Specific Tasks	Qualifications
Strategic Perform the planning and oversight role for the finance department; guide accounting activities as needed	• Conduct general financial planning and provide oversight • Develop a cost-allocation framework • Analyze financial reports on a monthly basis and submit reports to the board and executive director on a monthly basis • Monitor financial activities; conduct a periodic comparison to the budget • Lead the annual budgeting process • Serve as the main point of contact with the auditor	• Strong analytical skills • Excellent communication skills • Exposure to nonprofit financial statement analysis • Program planning and nonprofit budgeting
Operational Pay bills, invoice contracts, follow up on accounts receivable, prepare bank deposits, process payroll, and perform other accounting duties as assigned	• Prepare A/P, A/R, and 1099 forms • Make cash disbursements • Complete contract invoicing (including the preparation of monthly reports to funders) • Report hours by program to the payroll processing agency • Perform journal entries • Assist with budget and financial statement preparation • Monitor cash flow • Allocate all expenses (code checks) to the appropriate programs and grants based on the established cost-allocation methodology • Respond to ad hoc analytic requests from the finance director	• Strong skills in Microsoft Excel • Strong nonprofit accounting experience (A/R, A/P), and experience in accounting for restricted grants • Experience in preparing financial statements from an accounting software system • Quick, accurate worker
Transactional Support the accounting function by performing clerical and administrative tasks	• Write checks once they are coded • Distribute financial statements to program managers • Photocopy checks, invoices, and other documents as required, and maintain check and invoice files • Make bank deposits • Maintain grant binders (obtain grant agreements, copies of monthly reports, and other necessary grant documentation) • Maintain personnel files	• Exposure to basic accounting principles • Strong attention to detail

As culture, systems, and skills are intentionally developed and nurtured, more and more people on staff and board will be skillful interpreters of financial information and strong communicators about the information's implications. Communicating about finance across an organization is a high art. It requires engaging people who are untrained in finance in meaningful financial discussions, sharing financial information that may at times be uncomfortable or unflattering, and demonstrating financial accountability to the people and institutions that use, fund, and regulate your work as a nonprofit. But the most important outcome of ongoing, clear communication is the ability of the executive director, the board, and the staff to anticipate financial challenges, revise plans, and avoid uninformed or ill-informed decisions that could lead the organization into financial weakness or crisis.

Leading with a Long-Term Wealth Frame

Even in organizations with a healthy culture of money and well-distributed financial leadership, the conversation is typically dominated by annual performance to budget. Reporting and metrics are nearly always tied to a single fiscal year. But nonprofits—and our funders and donors—are facing a significant shift in how we think about, and therefore plan for and monitor, the resources that fuel our work. This is the financial corollary of the profound shift in the sector from a focus on programs and services (the activities we do) to an emphasis on impact (the results we achieve). When we apply this shift as financial leaders, we recognize a need to move from an operations frame, focused narrowly on financial management and accountability, to a wealth frame, focused on financial resilience and the creation of social value and impact over time. The changes that this requires in our thinking, our systems, our habits, and in our communications are not insignificant. When we act within an operations frame, we are limiting our thinking and decision making to income and expense, most often focused on meeting the needs of the present and short-term future. Shifting to a wealth frame requires that we think more deeply about how we are developing and deploying our resources to achieve longer-term goals and more significant impact.

Leading within the wealth frame, ultimately, is about fulfilling purpose. It is a reorientation from building and preserving a set of programs to aligning people and resources around a clear social purpose. It necessarily requires that we broaden our way of thinking and talking about financial health and well-being. Relying solely on the familiar language of nonprofit finance—restricted funding, functional expenses, allocation methodologies—keeps us in an operations frame that is primarily defined by accounting and legal compliance. While it's important to understand and be comfortable with that language, it is not the language that will lead us to significant social value creation.

The starting place for leaders making this paradigm shift is in naming and claiming the full array of capital necessary to achieve powerful social impact. A formal definition of capital is *wealth in the form of money and other assets that generate value over time to serve the organization's purpose.* This definition specifically invites us to explore two elements that are often neglected when we act in the operations frame: (1) the value of the "other assets" that fuel our work and (2) the recognition that organizations "generate value over time." Thinking beyond the dollars to our "other assets" opens a broader discussion about how we attract, manage, and invest in the noncash resources that are most critical to achieving our impact. The list below identifies six forms of capital that are essential to the work of nonprofits:

1. *Financial capital* is the money used by the nonprofit to buy what it needs to fuel campaigns, provide services, or generate the artistic expression that create its particular social value.
2. *Human capital* is the value of the knowledge, skills, and creativity of the nonprofit's staff, volunteers, and board allowing them to effectively perform the work that creates its particular social value.
3. *Political capital* refers to the trust, goodwill, and influence the nonprofit has with the public and with political figures. This goodwill is a type of invisible currency that nonprofits can use to mobilize people or public officials in relation to the issue.
4. *Social capital* is the value created across organizations and networks; transactions are marked by reciprocity, trust, and cooperation, and people come together in service of a common good.
5. *Intellectual capital* includes the intangible assets provided to a nonprofit by its employees' efforts and also knowledge assets such as patents, trademarks, copyrights, and other results of human innovation and thought.
6. *Physical capital* focuses on physical assets such as facilities or equipment that are used in the nonprofit's operation. This includes any kind of real physical asset with an enduring contribution to the organization's work.

Tending with intention to these forms of capital has direct financial implications: nurturing relationships with donors (social capital) or providing salaries that attract and retain talent (human capital), for instance. Other kinds of capital development have an indirect impact on the organization's finances: developing longstanding relationships with city council members or a robust membership base (political capital) that can activate policy change in line with the organization's mission over time, for instance. When we think about our resources in this way, our discussions around financial planning broaden significantly from "How much money can we raise next year?" to "Given the social impact we intend to have, which of our assets do we need to nourish?" And further, when we think of impact and value creation as ongoing rather than bound by fiscal year budgeting and reporting time lines, we ask: "If we invest in this staff person, this new facility, or this leading technology today, how will that generate additional human, physical, or intellectual capital in years to come?"

A Dynamic Modestly Profitable Program Portfolio

The aforementioned shift underway in the sector from a focus on programs and services (the activities we do) to an emphasis on impact (the results we achieve) means that relevant organizations will be in continuous reflection about the portfolio of activities they are using at any given time to achieve impact. They will hold on tightly to intended impact, but loosely to any particular program; programs are simply the organization's best recent thinking about how to achieve impact. Programs must change over time as context, assumptions about best practices, and numerous other forces require them to. Rather than scaling programs as is just to grow the organization, leaders are students of what is working particularly well in their program portfolios and what is waning in relevance or excellence. And they consider their impact results alongside the financial results so that they are making bold but pragmatic pivots that strengthen rather than weaken the organization over time. The program portfolio's contents will vary along the impact and money continua. By design, not everything a nonprofit does has high mission impact, just as not everything has high financial return. Figure 17.1— a dual bottom line matrix—captures this idea.

For instance, a $1.5 million youth services organization might have seven core activities in its current portfolio: tutoring, arts, sports, a gala fundraising dinner, an annual donor campaign, general fundraising, and administration. From a financial *management* perspective, an accountant creates a cost center for each of these and reports financial results monthly. From a financial *leadership* perspective, the executive and her team must ensure that each activity is financed as well as it can be—in most nonprofits not every activity will be self-sustaining—and that together the seven-activity portfolio results in both high mission impact and financial health.

FIGURE 17.1. The Dual Bottom Line Matrix

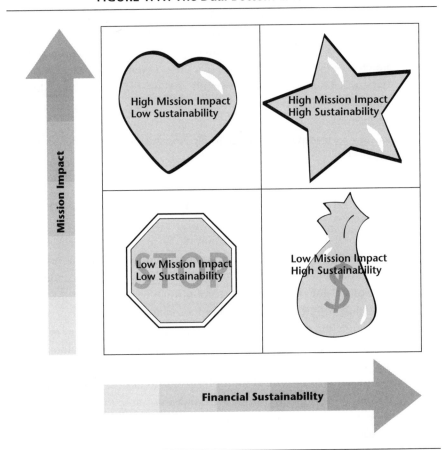

For the youth services organization, their tutoring program is a "star." They have the evaluation data to demonstrate its impact on kids finishing high school, and a school district contract combined with loyal foundation support result in the program covering all of its costs. On the other hand, the arts program is a "heart." It, too, has measurable impact on youth social and academic outcomes, but the program has no dedicated funding source, so it is being subsidized by the annual dinner gala. In turn, the annual dinner gala is a "money bag." Despite the inclusion of youth art in the silent auction and moving client stories during the program, it is a classic fundraiser with modest mission impact. However, it nets $125,000 a year for the organization, partially offsetting the arts program losses. And so it goes in most nonprofit business models: an alchemic mix of money losers and money makers leveraging one another to achieve the organization's overall programmatic and financial position.

A note of caution: Although many nonprofits receive large programmatic grants and contracts from foundation and government agencies, it is critical to recognize that these funding sources are *not* core activities. Again, the three programmatic core activities in the hypothetical youth services organizations are tutoring, arts, and sports. The tutoring program has three funding sources: a school district contract and two foundation grants. A very common mistake that nonprofit leaders make is to treat each of these sources as its own core activity rather than having them all "roll up" to one core activity, which is tutoring. Each source does need to be tracked and reported on the financial *management* system, yet the *leadership* should be analyzing whether tutoring as an activity is delivering exceptional impact and—with its three funding sources—meeting financial objectives. In other words, grant and contract tracking is financial management, analyzing the mission and money performance of core activities is financial leadership.

The nonprofit activity portfolio is dynamic rather than static. Strong financial leadership involves continuously monitoring and, to the degree possible, anticipating the migration of activities along the dual bottom line axes. The tutoring program is a "star" now, but next year's state budget cuts could mean a 30 percent reduction in the school district contract. Suddenly a "star" becomes a "heart" through no fault of staff and board. Will leadership immediately cut expenses and services by 30 percent? Will it quickly seek an additional foundation grant? Will it raise gala dinner prices to increase the event's net to $175,000 for greater subsidy of its programs? If they choose to maintain services and increase income, will it work? What if they continue spending as if the increased income plan will work, but then it doesn't? These are the questions and anxieties of nonprofit financial leadership.

From Planning to Deciding

For too long in the nonprofit sector there has been an over-emphasis on planning, to the neglect of decision making and execution. Making matters worse, much of the strategic planning that goes on in the sector lacks any real financial basis; nonprofit leaders and their consultants define strategies and goals and objectives, but nowhere in the planning do they do the hard work of determining how they will actually fund or finance them. The last economic recession has proved again, as all recessions do, that predicting the future is a very dicey proposition. Periodic organizational planning, wherein board and staff work together to ensure that everyone shares an understanding of the current operating context and the essential direction of the organization, is certainly valuable. Nonetheless, the day-to-day work of financial leadership involves making the best business decisions possible given the information at hand at the relevant time. Three-year strategic plans are very unlikely to anticipate a recession, or an employee lawsuit, or a market opening caused by the closure of a competitor, or even the resignation of a long-time leader. These unplanned factors mandate real-time decision making, and the leaders who get more of those decisions right than wrong are the ones who sustain and grow mission impact over time.

The practice of business planning is gaining traction in the nonprofit sector, yet it too often focuses only on earned income strategies instead of holistically on the entire business model that the vast majority of nonprofits employ. Further, it tends to downplay mission impact as a critical component of the nonprofit business model. That is, it does not assume nor plan for the dual bottom line reality in which nonprofits operate. And finally, it too tries to predict the future and assure people that documented plans are somehow highly likely to come true. Thus, just like traditional strategic planning, it runs the risk of providing a false sense of security and "doneness" (that is, all the big decisions have been made and now staff "simply" has to implement the plan).

It's not overstating the case to say that leadership is to a great degree about decision making. Further, all-important decisions have some kinds of financial implications, whether immediate or eventual. What does it look like to shift from a predominantly planning orientation to a predominantly financial decision-making and execution orientation? Of great importance is that all decision making is based on an explicit consideration of mission and money factors. If the organization is trying to decide whether to have a live receptionist or just a voicemail system, for instance, executive leaders should frame the mission and money factors for the decision-making group's consideration. On the mission side: Will the youth clients, including those for whom English is a second language, navigate a voicemail system or will they be discouraged and hang up (thus limiting our impact with them)? On the money side: Exactly how much (with full benefits) does a live receptionist cost us? Is there a way we could deploy those dollars in service of mission with greater return, or is this expenditure essential? Perhaps the group could consider using youth volunteer receptionists as employment training. On the other hand, what would it cost to recruit, train, and supervise these volunteers, and who on staff would do that and at what opportunity cost? The point here is that no executive should be allowed to make mission-only or money-only decisions; the factors must be considered holistically. In the end, judgment will be required to make a decision; there is always subjectivity. Financial leadership is about framing the decision in mission and money terms and about a focus on decisive execution.

Conclusion

Like all leadership, financial leadership is a *process* not a single position or positions. That said, the executive director has a responsibility to attend to the culture, systems, and skills development that allow for successfully distributing financial leadership. Strong financial management is absolutely essential, but it is what leaders *do* with that information each and every day that leads to sustained mission impact, or not. Strategic plans and business plans can help to clarify and document direction, but in the end it's the decisions that leaders make in real time that are the difference between financial weakness and strength over time. Those decisions will be stronger when they favor long-term value creation over short-term compliance and achieving intended impact over program preservation.

References

Bell, J., and Schaffer, E. *Financial Leadership: Guiding Your Organization to Long-term Success.* St. Paul, MN: The Fieldstone Alliance, 2005.

O'Donovan, D., and Flower, N. *The Strategic Plan Is Dead. Long Live Strategy. Stanford Social Innovation Review,* 2013, January 10.

Zimmerman, S., and Bell, J. *The Sustainability Mindset: Using the Matrix Map for Making Strategic Decisions.* San Francisco: Jossey-Bass, 2014.

CHAPTER EIGHTEEN

PHILANTHROPY AND FUNDRAISING

The Comprehensive Development Program

Sarah K. Nathan and Eugene R. Tempel

Philanthropic fundraising is essential to charitable nonprofit organizations in the United States. By virtue of their 501(c)(3) legal status, charitable nonprofits are the only type of nonprofit organization that offers donors a tax deduction in exchange for a donation. Much deeper than this seemingly simple transaction, however, is an ethical relationship rooted in a philosophy of philanthropy. It is in this relationship between an organization's mission and its donors that an approach to integrating philanthropic fundraising into all facets of an organization's life is presented.

Philanthropy serves both instrumental and expressive purposes in nonprofit organizations. Likewise, fundraising is also an instrumental and expressive management process for nonprofit professionals. For donors, prospective donors, volunteers, and community members at large, fundraising presents an opportunity to engage one's personal philanthropy. It is through philanthropy that individuals express their values, believes, and hopes for the future. For organizations, fundraising is an opportunity to engage its supporters in its mission. And, as an instrumental management process, fundraising is an essential source of resources necessary to enact its programs, services, and mission.

We emphasize fundraising within the context of voluntary action for the public good, Robert *Payton's* (1998) conception of philanthropy. According to

Payton, it is through philanthropy—the voluntary giving of time and resources—that individuals, foundations, and corporations support efforts that benefit society. Consistent with this conception, as fundraising sage Hank Rosso, said, "Fundraising is the servant of philanthropy" (Rosso, 1991). Rosso's philosophy of fundraising has withstood the test of time. In other words, fundraising is more than the application of technical skills or processes—it is a transformational relationship rooted in an organization's mission.

Rosso's philosophy guides this chapter's examination of fundraising as an integrated management function that extends across a nonprofit organization, from the highest levels of board leadership to all members of its staff. No doubt fundraising for organizations in the 21st Century is a sophisticated operation, but it also must be one that substitutes pride for apology (Tempel, Seiler, and Burlingame, 2016). And because charitable contributions make up about 15 percent of all the revenue in the nonprofit sector (McKeever, 2015), it is essential that all nonprofit professionals, no matter their position, understand and participate in the fundamentals of a fundraising operation.

The manager of a nonprofit organization must understand the role that philanthropy plays in the organization and in society at large. This manager also must understand, as Rosso expressed, that fundraising is essential to building philanthropy. It is both essential and a means, not an end in itself. Fundraising is the difficult work of engaging potential donors and donors with the mission of the organization. It is a long-term process. The program of fundraising described in this chapter can enable an organization to reach its full potential. To achieve success, fundraising must be integrated into the central management of the organization, as well as its planning, communications, program delivery, evaluation processes.

There is much written and discussed about the importance of adopting or developing a culture of philanthropy. Typically, practitioners writing on the topic describe a culture of philanthropy as the acceptance of fundraising responsibility by the entire staff and the board of the organization (Joyaux, 2015). It long has been considered a best practice for fundraising to be integrated within the organization's management structure and viewed as an activity in which the entire staff and board participate. A culture of philanthropy, however, is more foundational to nonprofit organizations. It begins with an acceptance of philanthropy as a legitimate source of funds for a nonprofit to carry out its mission, just as are fees for service and government grants (Tempel, 2016). And when fundraising is a legitimate activity to generate philanthropic support, everyone has an important role to play.

The Philanthropic Environment and Context

After a dip during the Great Recession between 2007 and 2009, giving by Americans has shown a healthy rebound. In 2014, charitable contributions totaled an estimated $358.38 billion in the United States (*Giving USA*, 2015), a 7.1 percent increase from the previous year. Contributions to recipient categories is presented below in Figure 18.1. Individual giving makes up the great majority of all giving in the United States, equal to 72 percent of contributions. When added with bequest giving (gifts following an individual's passing) and foundation

FIGURE 18.1. Contributions by Recipient Category

GIVING USA THE NUMBERS

2014 contributions: $358.38 billion by type of recipient organization
(in billions of dollars—all figures are rounded)

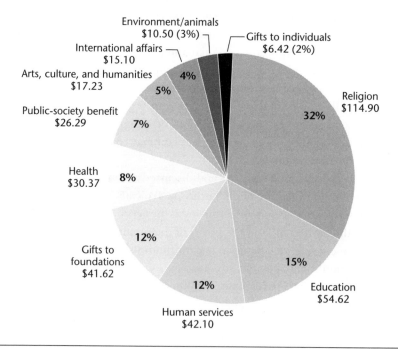

Source: Giving USA: The Annual Report on Philanthropy for the Year 2014. Chicago: Giving USA Foundation. Reprinted by permission.

giving, which is composed mostly of individual and family foundations, giving by individuals accounts for 95 percent of all philanthropy—approximately $340 billion. Although giving has surpassed pre-recession levels, it is important to note that giving as a percentage of Gross Domestic Product (GDP) has remained relatively flat—hovering around the 2 percent mark—in the fifty years that *Giving USA* has documented giving (*Giving USA*, 2015). That said, projections for philanthropy are encouraging, with contributions expected to increase 4.1 percent in 2016 and 4.3 percent in 2017 (Indiana University Lilly Family School of Philanthropy, 2016).

Volunteering time is another type of philanthropy and often supports an organization's fundraising function. Approximately 62.8 million Americans (25 percent) volunteer each year, equal to eight billion hours and worth an estimated $184 billion (O'Neil, 2015). When individuals volunteer, they see the direct impact of the organization's mission and take greater ownership of it. By far the most common volunteer activity is fundraising, with 25 percent of volunteers engaged in fundraising efforts (Corporation for National and Community Service, 2015). Volunteers are twice as likely to contribute to a nonprofit organization as other donors, making volunteers doubly important for their gifts of time and money.

Americans of all ages, races, faiths, and economic backgrounds and capacities give of their time and money. According to the Philanthropy Panel Study, a long-running, longitudinal study, approximately 65.4 percent of Americans donate in any given year, and the average household gives about $2,300 a year (Indiana University Center on Philanthropy, 2009).

Not surprisingly, high net worth individuals (those with an income of more than $200,000 or a net worth of at least $1,000,000 or both) are even more likely to give, and to give more than the general public does (Rooney and Osili, 2016). High net worth donors are particularly intentional about their giving and are impact driven (Indiana University Lilly Family School of Philanthropy, 2014). A growing body of research now informs our understanding of donor characteristics, preferences, and motivations. Much of this research is now freely available, enabling all fundraising professionals to have a basic understanding of donor dynamics. Advanced professionals may wish to examine closely the available research to benchmark their organizations' donors and prospective donors. Research also suggests that high net worth donors also distribute their philanthropy differently than donors in general, as Figure 18.2 shows. The largest share of their philanthropy goes to education, in contrast to donors in general, who give more by far to religion.

FIGURE 18.2. Percentage of High Net Worth Households Who Gave to Charity in 2009, 2011, and 2013, Compared to the U.S. General Population (in Percent)

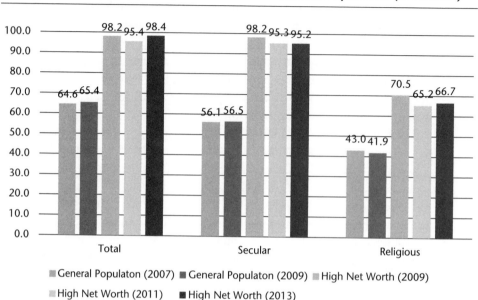

Note: Sources for the U.S. general population are the Philanthropy Panel Study 2007 and 2009 waves, the latest year available. High net worth figures are for 2009, 2011, and 2013 giving and are based on the Bank of America Merrill Lynch (BAML) Study of High Net Worth Philanthropy. Reprinted by Permission. (The difference between general population and high net worth results was found to be statistically significant).

The Total Development Program

Any fundraising program begins with the organization's mission. The mission must be based on the organization's benefit to society; it is the organization's reason for existence and the foundation of its fundraising efforts. From it, an organization may build a total development program or comprehensive development operation that encompasses a range of functions—including an annual fund, capital campaigns, major giving, and planned giving—and the numerous vehicles for solicitation that support each. The total development program is important because it has an impact on the philanthropic gift potential of an organization, as well as on its fundraising costs (and return on fundraising investment).

The emphasis here will be on building the case for support and implementing the fundraising cycle with a focus on individual donors.[1] Once an organization's mission is established, the fundraising cycle begins. Fundraising needs to be understood as a cycle because of its ongoing, continuous nature. Supporting the fundraising cycle is a carefully designed plan that is based on the organization's overall plan for fulfilling its mission. Organizations that have invested the time and energy in creating fundraising plans generally raise more money than those that have not (Nonprofit Research Collaborative, 2014). In fact, recent research reveals that, for small organizations (that is, with budgets less than $2 million), having a fundraising plan is strongly related to fundraising success (Yandow, 2015). A defined plan not only gives the fundraising team a strategic direction, but it helps justify investments in the fundraising operation over time.

The fundraising cycle is a multi-step guide on which to develop one's plan. The complete fundraising cycle, as illustrated in Figure 18.3, consists of fourteen steps. For brevity's sake here, we emphasize the cycle's planning and action steps. The first planning step in the fundraising cycle is developing the case for

FIGURE 18.3. The Fundraising Cycle

Awareness of Marketing Principles

Strategic Checkpoint:
Demonstrate Stewardship and Renew the Gift

Planning Checkpoint:
Examine the case

Planning Checkpoint:
Analyze Market Requirements

Action Checkpoint:
Solicit the Gift

Planning Checkpoint:
Prepare Needs Statement

Action Checkpoint:
Activate Volunteer Corps

Planning Checkpoint:
Define Objectives

Planning Checkpoint:
Prepare Communications Plan

Action Checkpoint:
Involve Volunteers

Planning Checkpoint:
Prepare Fundraising Plan

Planning/Action Checkpoint:
Validate Needs Statement

Planning Checkpoint:
Identify Potential Giving Sources

Planning Checkpoint:
Select Fundraising Vehicle

Planning Checkpoint:
Evaluate Gift Markets

Source: Adapted from Henry A. Rosso and Associates, *Achieving Excellence in Fund Raising* (2nd ed.), p. 24. Copyright © 2003 Jossey-Bass Inc., Publishers. Reprinted by permission of Jossey-Bass Inc., Publishers, a subsidiary of John Wiley & Sons, Inc.

support. The case for support is a summary of all the reasons why an individual, foundation, or corporation might give to or volunteer for the organization. Fundraising begins with the case for support because it is the ethical basis for the organization to seek philanthropic support. The case is both an internal and external articulation of the organization's mission and needs, supported by evidence. The internal case may take the form of a more technical document used by fundraisers to inform their communications with donors and potential donors. The external case for support often takes the form of brochures, short booklets, and various types of digital media. Regardless of the medium, the case for support must clearly make a compelling argument for supporting the organization.

Additional planning is done when the case for support is tested in the market. Individual donors, corporations, and grantmaking foundations each compose a market. The case for support and the importance of the organization's needs must resonate with each market, or fundraising will not be successful (Seiler, 2016).

The first action step is to engage volunteers in the fundraising process. Volunteers include board members and other well-known volunteers whose own philanthropic support for the organization brings credibility to the fundraising effort. Volunteers can assist fundraising efforts in many ways, from providing feedback on the case for support to hosting donor engagement events, and from directly soliciting prospective donors to supporting all kinds of back office activities. Whatever their role, volunteers lend credibility to the organization's mission and can be powerful advocates for its work (Freeman and Hermanson, 2016).

The final three steps in the cycle are critical. We must solicit the gift, whether we are asking someone to join us in making an annual fund contribution through a letter or on Facebook, or whether we are writing a grant proposal to a foundation, or soliciting a leadership gift in the capital campaign via a face-to face visit. Then we must not only thank the donor who has made a gift (at any level) but demonstrate good stewardship of gifts given to the organization. Finally, we must renew the gift or solicit another gift from the donor, as the cycle begins anew. Every donor is a prospect for another gift, and a donor at one level is a prospect for a gift at a higher level.

Organizations typically have four different uses for funds: (1) ongoing operations, (2) special projects, (3) major equipment or facility updates, and (4) to add to their endowments (that is, investment funds that generate income, typically without using the corpus). Individuals, foundations, and corporations all may be prospective donors for operating, project, and capital funds. Typically, only individuals are prospective donors for an endowment. The total development program is based on the assumption that many donors will make small gifts

FIGURE 18.4. The Donor Pyramid of Fundraising Strategies

Source: Indiana University The Fund Raising School, *Principles and Techniques of Fund Raising,* pp. iv–8. Reprinted with permission.

to the organization, fewer will make larger gifts, and fewer yet will make very large or planned gifts. Each level and type of gift we solicit requires a different form of communication, ranging from a special event invitation to an e-mail or social media *#GivingTuesday* note to personal solicitation for a planned gift. In essence, as the amount of a donor's donation increases, the degree of personalization for the interaction increase as well. Figure 18.4 illustrates the relationship among donors, fundraising strategies, and the form of donors' gifts; this commonly is known as the "Donor Pyramid."

Components of the Development Program

Various functions or programs compose the comprehensive development operation. As part of the planning for the fundraising efforts, attention must be given to each function and careful planning done to implement each of the fundraising strategies described in this section. The successful fundraising operation will use, analyze, test, and evaluate each of the methods.

The annual fund is the foundation of the total development program. It is through these smaller, ongoing contributions (annually, quarterly, or monthly) that individual donors test the organization. Through this ongoing relationship, the donor learns more about the organization's operations and impact. If the organization meets expectations, the donor is more likely to increase his or her giving over time. Within the annual fund operations, there are a variety of solicitation vehicles that are used, most often including a combination of direct mail, digital solicitation, and phone solicitation (short- or long-term telephone campaigns). In addition to soliciting contributions, annual fund communications offer opportunities to thank donors and provide updates on how the organization has utilized previous donations.

A comprehensive campaign, traditionally called a "capital campaign," is a fundraising strategy that is centered on capital needs such as a new building or major renovation, or technology or equipment upgrades. Today, the comprehensive campaign is just as likely to be organized around special projects (such as student scholarships) or endowment building. In short, a comprehensive campaign is a multi-year fundraising effort with a publicly defined goal, with the objective of raising funds to take an organization "to the next level" in its physical or programmatic capacities. Whatever form it takes, a comprehensive campaign must be supported by and integrated into an organization's overall strategic plan. In other words, the strategic plan justifies the needs for which the campaign raises money (Conley, 2016). Campaigns require intensive planning on the front end and stewardship management upon their completion.

Major gift fundraising is at the heart of a comprehensive campaign, but it serves an important component of an organization's fundraising efforts, even when it is not part of a campaign. There is no one definition or dollar amount considered "standard" for a "major gift." Rather, what constitutes a major gift depends on an organization's size and history. One organization may consider gifts over $5,000 as a major gift while, for another, only gifts of more than $50,000 will garner the attention and resources of an organization's major gift officer. Because of their size and potential to transform the organization's work, major gift fundraising is the most intensive and takes the most time—often many years—to realize results. Major gifts are generally made through an ongoing dialogue with a donor during which his or her interest is expressed and matched with an organization's mission. As illustrated in the Donor Pyramid (Figure 18.4), such solicitation is highly personalized and done in person. It is important to note that, for smaller organizations, adding more prospective donors to its cultivation does not necessarily mean more major gifts will be secured. Alternatively, though, the longer a major gift fundraising professional for a small organization has been on the job and the more specialized training they have received, the more successful they are likely to be (Joslyn, 2016).

Planned giving, like major gift fundraising, involves a longer time horizon and requires a highly personalized approach. "Planned giving" is an umbrella term for the various financial and investment vehicles that leave a gift to the organization after a donor's passing. Because of their complexity, planned gift fundraising requires specialized expertise in various legal and investment practices such as charitable gift annuities, trusts, and wills. At the same time, however, a fundraiser soliciting planned gifts must be extremely sensitive when speaking with prospective donors about these matters. Donors are more likely to give bequests or other planned gifts to organizations with which they have been engaged for some time; donors are less likely to choose an organization spontaneously as a planned gift beneficiary. There are diverse motivations for planned gifts but, in many ways, a planned gift extends the donor's identity, offering him or her a sense of immortality upon his or her death (Routley and Sargeant, 2015). The Partnership for Philanthropic Planning, a national professional association, maintains many excellent resources and research to assist organizations and fundraising in developing a planned giving program.

While the focus of this chapter has been on fundraising from individuals, it is worth noting that fundraising from corporations and grantmaking foundations requires the same kind of relational, personalized approach as has been discussed for individuals. According to *Giving USA* (2015), giving by both corporations and foundations increased in 2014 over 2013. U.S. grantmaking foundations gave $53.97 billion (15 percent of all giving) in 2014; they hold approximately $715 billion in assets (Foundation Center, 2014). Corporations gave the least in 2014, equal to $17.77 billion or 5 percent of all giving (Giving USA, 2015). Fundraising from either entity requires the fundraisers to know and understand the specific funder's process for grantmaking. Such processes may or may not include a letter of inquiry, submission of a formal grant application or proposal, site visits, extensive expectations for documenting outcomes, and processes for reporting results. Matching the prospective donor's—in this case a foundation or corporation—interests and priorities with the nonprofit's mission and needs is often done in a detailed, evidence-driven process involving a case for support or a formal grant application. In a larger fundraising office, the work of fundraising from each or both corporations and foundations may be done by a dedicated staff member with expertise in each area.

Today's sophisticated fundraising operation is supported by a robust database. There are countless commercial products an organization may choose to develop its database, each with its own advantages and limitations. The right choice for a database really depends on the organization's size, complexity, budget, and a wide variety of other considerations. At the most basic level, a fundraising database should enable the organization to record information to ensure that donors are identified and thanked promptly, gift data is secure, contact information is kept updated, and donor preferences are noted. The possibilities for data collection and analysis are almost limitless, as long as a staff member assigned to database management has the expertise and training necessary to make full use of a database's potential. When choosing a new database or considering a switch from one to another, allow for significant time to solicit demonstrations from several providers, test a variety of products, train employees once the database has been chosen, and integrate it with all the rest of the organization's management processes. While there is no one perfect database, there are many options to find best fit for an organization's needs.

Stewardship and Accountability

Organizations today operate in an environment in which donors have high expectations for an organization to demonstrate impact. A recent study of high net worth households by the Indiana University Lilly Family School of Philanthropy (2014) found that donors would give more if only they could be assured that their gifts would make a difference. Stewardship is both the practical process of and ethical principles for upholding the public's trust in the organization and, more specifically, honoring the donor's wishes. It begins by thanking a donor for her gift, followed by sharing information about the outcomes or results gained from the use of that gift, and then extends into the organization's careful use and management of all its resources.

Organizations can operate in a transparent way by posting their audited financial statements, plus the Form 990 and other government documents on their websites, and by e-mailing copies to all donors (or at least major donors). Websites are also a good way to make members of the organization's staff, board of directors, and donors (but only with their permission) known to the public. Budgets, financial audits, program evaluations, and other evidence of program outcomes and results can also be made easily available this way.

The website is also a good tool for stewardship. The organization's annual report should be accessible on the website. It might be e-mailed or otherwise distributed to donors, but the general public should have ready access to the annual report as well. Solicitation letters to renew gifts, and progress and final reports to individuals, foundations, and corporations at the completion of special projects are examples of more personalized stewardship. (A more complete discussion of stewardship and accountability can be found in Chapter 34 of *Achieving Excellence in Fundraising* [4th ed.], by Tempel, Seiler, and Burlingame, 2016). As explained earlier in the chapter, more personalized approaches are required as are appropriate to the level of engagement and support for a donor.

Ethical behavior toward donors is an important organizational responsibility. Fundraising executives often help guide the organization toward ethical behavior by sharing the Donor Bill of Rights, presented in Exhibit 18.1, which explains the organization's responsibilities for stewardship, accountability, and ethical behavior toward its donors. But it is essential for the chief executive, the chief financial officer, and the members of the board of directors all to recognize that they have primary responsibilities, as well.

Ethical philanthropic fundraising represents the ideals of practicing fundraising as servant to philanthropy and fundraising based on mission. Professional fundraisers typically follow a code of ethics as a foundation for building trust. Three associations in the field of fundraising, the Association for Fundraising Professionals (AFP), the Association for Healthcare Philanthropy (AHP), and the Council for Advancement and Support of Education (CASE), have adopted codes of ethics specific to the practices of their members. AFP has the broadest membership base of all three, representing the entire nonprofit sector and fundraisers around the globe, so we include the AFP Code of Ethics presented in Exhibit 18.2 as one example of the ethical codes that are critical to the field of fundraising.

EXHIBIT 18.1. THE DONOR BILL OF RIGHTS

Philanthropy is based on voluntary action for the common good. It is a tradition of giving and sharing that is primary to the quality of life. To ensure that philanthropy merits the respect and trust of the general public, and that donors and prospective donors can have full confidence in the nonprofit organizations and causes they are asked to support, we declare that all donors have these rights.

I. To be informed of the organization's mission, of the way the organization intends to use donated resources, and of its capacity to use donations effectively for their intended purposes.

II. To be informed of the identity of those serving on the organization's governing board, and to expect the board to exercise prudent judgment in its stewardship responsibilities.

III. To have access to the organization's most recent financial statements.

IV. To be assured their gifts will be used for the purposes for which they were given.

V. To receive appropriate acknowledgement and recognition.

VI. To be assured that information about their donation is handled with respect and with confidentiality to the extent provided by law.

VII. To expect that all relationships with individuals representing organizations of interest to the donor will be professional in nature.

VIII. To be informed whether those seeking donations are volunteers, employees of the organization or hired solicitors.

IX. To have the opportunity for their names to be deleted from mailing lists that an organization may intend to share.

X. To feel free to ask questions when making a donation and to receive prompt, truthful and forthright answers.

The Donor Bill of Rights was created by the Association of Fundraising Professionals (AFP), the Association for Healthcare Philanthropy (AHP), the Council for Advancement and Support of Education (CASE), and the Giving Institute: Leading Consultants to Non-Profits. It has been endorsed by numerous organizations. Reprinted with permission.

EXHIBIT 18.2. ASSOCIATION OF FUNDRAISING PROFESSIONALS (AFP) CODE OF ETHICAL PRINCIPLES AND STANDARDS OF ETHICAL PRACTICE

ADOPTED 1964; AMENDED SEPT. 2007

The Association of Fundraising Professionals (AFP) exists to foster the development and growth of fundraising professionals and the profession, to promote high ethical behavior in the fundraising profession and to preserve and enhance philanthropy and volunteerism.

Members of AFP are motivated by an inner drive to improve the quality of life through the causes they serve. They serve the ideal of philanthropy, are committed to the preservation and enhancement of volunteerism; and hold stewardship of these concepts as the overriding direction of their professional life. They recognize their responsibility to ensure that needed resources are vigorously and ethically sought and that the intent of the donor is honestly fulfilled.

To these ends, AFP members, both individual and business, embrace certain values that they strive to uphold in performing their responsibilities for generating philanthropic support. AFP business members strive to promote and protect the work and mission of their client organizations.

AFP members both individual and business aspire to:

- practice their profession with integrity, honesty, truthfulness and adherence to the absolute obligation to safeguard the public trust
- act according to the highest goals and visions of their organizations, professions, clients and consciences
- put philanthropic mission above personal gain
- inspire others through their own sense of dedication and high purpose
- improve their professional knowledge and skills, so that their performance will better serve others
- demonstrate concern for the interests and well-being of individuals affected by their actions
- value the privacy, freedom of choice and interests of all those affected by their actions
- foster cultural diversity and pluralistic values and treat all people with dignity and respect
- affirm, through personal giving, a commitment to philanthropy and its role in society
- adhere to the spirit as well as the letter of all applicable laws and regulations
- advocate within their organizations adherence to all applicable laws and regulations
- avoid even the appearance of any criminal offense or professional misconduct
- bring credit to the fundraising profession by their public demeanor
- encourage colleagues to embrace and practice these ethical principles and standards
- be aware of the codes of ethics promulgated by other professional organizations that serve philanthropy

ETHICAL STANDARDS

Furthermore, while striving to act according to the above values, AFP members, both individual and business, agree to abide (and to ensure, to the best of their ability, that all members of their staff abide) by the AFP standards. Violation of the standards may subject the member to disciplinary sanctions, including expulsion, as provided in the AFP Ethics Enforcement Procedures.

Member Obligations

1. Members shall not engage in activities that harm the members' organizations, clients or profession.
2. Members shall not engage in activities that conflict with their fiduciary, ethical and legal obligations to their organizations, clients or profession.
3. Members shall effectively disclose all potential and actual conflicts of interest; such disclosure does not preclude or imply ethical impropriety.
4. Members shall not exploit any relationship with a donor, prospect, volunteer, client or employee for the benefit of the members or the members' organizations.
5. Members shall comply with all applicable local, state, provincial and federal civil and criminal laws.
6. Members recognize their individual boundaries of competence and are forthcoming and truthful about their professional experience and qualifications and will represent their achievements accurately and without exaggeration.
7. Members shall present and supply products and/or services honestly and without misrepresentation and will clearly identify the details of those products, such as availability of the products and/or services and other factors that may affect the suitability of the products and/or services for donors, clients or nonprofit organizations.
8. Members shall establish the nature and purpose of any contractual relationship at the outset and will be responsive and available to organizations and their employing organizations before, during and after any sale of materials and/or services. Members will comply with all fair and reasonable obligations created by the contract.
9. Members shall refrain from knowingly infringing the intellectual property rights of other parties at all times. Members shall address and rectify any inadvertent infringement that may occur.
10. Members shall protect the confidentiality of all privileged information relating to the provider/client relationships.
11. Members shall refrain from any activity designed to disparage competitors untruthfully.

Solicitation and Use of Philanthropic Funds

12. Members shall take care to ensure that all solicitation and communication materials are accurate and correctly reflect their organizations' mission and use of solicited funds.

13. Members shall take care to ensure that donors receive informed, accurate and ethical advice about the value and tax implications of contributions.
14. Members shall take care to ensure that contributions are used in accordance with donors' intentions.
15. Members shall take care to ensure proper stewardship of all revenue sources, including timely reports on the use and management of such funds.
16. Members shall obtain explicit consent by donors before altering the conditions of financial transactions.

Presentation of Information

17. Members shall not disclose privileged or confidential information to unauthorized parties.
18. Members shall adhere to the principle that all donor and prospect information created by, or on behalf of, an organization or a client is the property of that organization or client and shall not be transferred or utilized except on behalf of that organization or client.
19. Members shall give donors and clients the opportunity to have their names removed from lists that are sold to, rented to or exchanged with other organizations.
20. Members shall, when stating fundraising results, use accurate and consistent accounting methods that conform to the appropriate guidelines adopted by the American Institute of Certified Public Accountants (AICPA)* for the type of organization involved. (*In countries outside of the United States, comparable authority should be utilized.)

Compensation and Contracts

21. Members shall not accept compensation or enter into a contract that is based on a percentage of contributions; nor shall members accept finder's fees or contingent fees. Business members must refrain from receiving compensation from third parties derived from products or services for a client without disclosing that third-party compensation to the client (for example, volume rebates from vendors to business members).
22. Members may accept performance-based compensation, such as bonuses, provided such bonuses are in accord with prevailing practices within the members' own organizations and are not based on a percentage of contributions.
23. Members shall neither offer nor accept payments or special considerations for the purpose of influencing the selection of products or services.
24. Members shall not pay finder's fees, commissions or percentage compensation based on contributions, and shall take care to discourage their organizations from making such payments.

25. Any member receiving funds on behalf of a donor or client must meet the legal requirements for the disbursement of those funds. Any interest or income earned on the funds should be fully disclosed.

The AFP Code of Ethics prescribes a basic level of ethical behavior upon which fundraisers can build trust with donors and the public. Several components of the code are of particular import to nonprofit leaders. First, fundraisers pledge to exercise leadership inside their organization to make sure the organization obeys local, state, and national laws. Second, they pledge to assure that all gifts are used for the purposes for which they were given (Standards 14 and 15).

Nonprofit executives should be aware that fundraisers agree to work on behalf of the organization, and all relationships established with donors should be connected to the organization and its mission. Importantly, these relationships are not to be used for the personal benefit of the fundraiser (Standard 4).

Nonprofit executives and boards sometimes make two mistaken assumptions about approaching and compensating fundraising executives. First, they assume that the fundraisers will bring relationships and donor information with them from previous positions. However, both the Donor Bill of Rights, which requires confidentiality, and the AFP Code of Ethics (Standards 17 and 18) declare this as unethical. We must assume donor confidentiality across the philanthropic sector. And we must uphold the notion that all relationships established by fundraisers on behalf of an organization belong to the organization. Second, many nonprofit board members who come from the corporate world believe that basing compensation on a commission or percentage of money raised will create an environment in which fundraisers will be more productive. This is a misunderstanding of the complexity of the fundraising process as described earlier. And it puts fundraisers in direct conflict with donors' interests because, under such conditions, the fundraiser's livelihood depends on securing gifts without respect for donor time lines, interests, and financial conditions. This is also a violation of the AFP Code of Ethics (Standards 21 and 22).

Organizational Issues Impacting Fundraising

Two organizational issues have a direct impact on fundraising success: (1) the engagement of the board of directors and other volunteers and (2) understanding fundraising costs.

Hank Rosso's maxims about successful fundraising are very wise. They have also been substantiated by subsequent research. One maxim is "Fundraising begins with the board" (Rosso, 1991). His premise was twofold: (1) the board, through its stewardship of the organization, must plan for fundraising and the development of the board and (2) because the board is closest to and most fully engaged with the organization, its members should make the first gifts and assist in the fundraising process as it goes forward. Both have proven to have a positive impact on fundraising (Board Source, 2015; Herman and Renz, 2000).

Unfortunately, many organizations recruit board members without openly stating their expectations for their involvement in fundraising, including expectations for members to make a generous gift and to be engaged in some way in fundraising. It is important to note that board members can become involved in fundraising in a variety of ways, including (but not limited to) personally soliciting gifts. They should be asked to make a commitment to engage in those activities with which they are most comfortable. Exhibit 18.3 provides a list of possible ways board members can be helpful in the process of fundraising.

The other issue with which organizations must deal is that of fundraising costs. Like all other aspects of operating a nonprofit organization, it costs money to raise money. Nonprofit executives and boards must understand and be committed to this so they can properly invest in fundraising to enable the organization to reach its full philanthropic potential. The issue of fundraising costs (now often referred to as return on investment, especially by business-oriented executives and boards) is a major challenge in building public trust. And there are many problems. They are difficult to calculate, they vary by organization type, they are often used by one organization competing with another ("our fundraising costs are lower than your fundraising costs"), and they may exceed public expectations for what is appropriate.

There are more important principles for nonprofit executives and boards to keep in mind in addition to "it costs money to raise money." Cost per dollar raised is higher for first-time gifts than for renewed gifts. Smaller gifts are more expensive to raise than larger gifts (even though small gifts form the basis for

---

EXHIBIT 18.3. BOARDS OF DIRECTORS' AREAS OF INVOLVEMENT IN FUNDRAISING

The following list highlights many ways for board members to be involved in the fundraising process (listed in order of level of direct involvement)

- Make a personal contribution
- Write thank you notes for gift acknowledgement
- Participate in strategic and development planning
- Provide prospective donor information
- Add names to mailing lists
- Write personal notes on solicitation letters
- Introduce potential donors to members of the organization
- Write a support letter to a government agency, foundation or corporation
- Seek out donations for a special event or help plan a special event
- Cultivate relationships with potential donors
- Make a solicitation call with other volunteers or board members

Source: Tempel, Eugene, R. 2004. *Development Committee.* Washington, DC: Board Source. Reprinted with Permission.

---

tomorrow's larger gifts). Human service organizations have higher fundraising costs than higher education programs. And organizational size, type, and age all impact fundraising costs (Hager, Pollak, and Rooney, 2001).

There are two ways organizations can show themselves accountable to the public on fundraising costs. First, they can report and compare their fundraising costs with organizations of the same type and size (for example, a regional theater in the Midwest should report its expenses compared to other regional theaters in the Midwest). Second, they should monitor and assess the appropriateness of fundraising costs over time. The goal of the fundraising staff should be to lower fundraising costs over time as gift sizes grow larger and donor development strategies become more effective.

Conclusion

Hank Rosso (1991) said, "Fundraising is the gentle art of teaching people the joy of giving." Like so many of his approaches to and maxims about fundraising, this notion has been substantiated by research. Recent cutting-edge research from experimental psychology and other fields have shown that there is joy in giving. Konrath (2016) has shown that giving and volunteering have a positive effect on the donor's and volunteer's health and well-being. These findings should help shape and energize our attitudes toward fundraising. When organizations integrate philanthropy into their management philosophy and processes, there is great potential to improve the organization's health as well as that of its donors and volunteers.

Note

1. Training programs, such as those offered by Indiana University The Fund Raising School, and practical guides, such as *Achieving Excellence in Fund Raising*, 4th edition, (Conley, 2016), offer in-depth examinations of each function and approach.

References

Association of Fundraising Professionals (AFP). Association of Fundraising Professionals (AFP) Code of Ethical Principles and Standards of Ethical Practice. Adopted 1964, revised 2007. Arlington, Virginia: Association of Fundraising Professionals. 2007.

Board Source. *Leading with Intent: A National Index of Nonprofit Board Practices.* Washington, DC: Board Source, 2015.

Conley, A. Capital Campaigns. In E. R. Tempel, T. L. Seiler, and D. F. Burlingame (eds.), *Achieving Excellence in Fundraising* (4th ed.). Hoboken, NJ: John Wiley & Sons, 2016.

Corporation for National and Community Service. Volunteering and Civic Engagement in the United States: Trends and Highlights Overview, 2015. Retrieved December 3, 2015, from www.volunteeringinamerica.gov/.

Foundation Center. Key Facts on U.S. Foundations (2014 ed.), 2014. Retrieved from http://foundationcenter.org/gainknowledge/research/keyfacts2014/.

Freeman, T. M., and Hermanson, E. Volunteer Management. In E. R. Tempel, T. L. Seiler, and D. F. Burlingame (eds.), *Achieving Excellence in Fundraising* (4th ed.). Hoboken, NJ: John Wiley & Sons, 2016.

Giving USA. *The Annual Report on Philanthropy for the Year 2014.* Chicago: Giving USA Foundation, 2015.

Hager, M. A., Pollak, T., and Rooney, P. Variations in Overhead and Fundraising Efficiency Measures: The Influence of Size, Age, and Subsector. Overhead Cost Study Working Paper, presented (revised title) at the 2000 AFP and 2001 ARNOVA meetings, 2001. Retrieved from https://philanthropy.iupui.edu/files/research/variations_in_overhead_and_fundraising_efficiency_measures.pdf.

Herman, R. D., and Renz. D. O. Board Practices of Especially Effective and Less Effective Local Nonprofit Organizations. *American Review of Public Administration,* 2000, 30(2), 146–160.

Indiana University Center on Philanthropy. Overview of Overall Giving. Philanthropy Panel Study, 2009. Retrieved from https://scholarworks.iupui.edu/bitstream/handle/1805/6075/2009PPSKeyFindings.pdf?sequence=1&isAllowed=y.

Indiana University The Fund Raising School. *Principles and Techniques of Fund Raising.* Indianapolis, IN: The Trustees of Indiana University, 2009.

Indiana University Lilly Family School of Philanthropy. *The 2014 U.S. Trust Study of High Net Worth Philanthropy.* Indianapolis, IN: The Trustees of Indiana University, 2014.

Indiana University Lilly Family School of Philanthropy. *The Philanthropy Outlook: 2016 & 2017.* Indianapolis, IN: The Trustees of Indiana University, 2016.

Joslyn, H. Big Gifts, Small Charities: Fundraising Success Secrets. *The Chronicle of Philanthropy,* 2016, January 5.

Joyaux, S. Building a Culture of Philanthropy in Your Organization. *Nonprofit Quarterly,* 2015, March 27.

Konrath, S. The Joy of Giving. In E. R. Tempel, T. L. Seiler, and D .F. Burlingame (eds.), *Achieving Excellence in Fundraising* (4th ed.). Hoboken, NJ: John Wiley & Sons, 2016.

McKeever, B. S. *The Nonprofit Sector in Brief 2015.* Washington, DC: Urban Institute, 2015.

Nonprofit Research Collaborative. Nonprofit Fundraising Study Covering Charitable Receipts at Nonprofit Organization in the United States and Canada in 2013, 2014. Accessed December 7, 2015, at www.afpnet.org/files/ContentDocuments/2014NRCWinter.pdf.

O'Neil, M. Volunteerism Rate Inches Downward to New Low. *The Chronicle of Philanthropy,* 2015, December 8.

Payton, R. L. *Philanthropy: Voluntary Action for the Public Good.* New York: American Council on Education/Macmillan, 1998.

Rooney, P., and Osili, U. Understanding High Net Worth Donors. In E. R. Tempel, T. L. Seiler, and D. F. Burlingame (eds.), *Achieving Excellence in Fundraising* (4th ed.). Hoboken, NJ: John Wiley & Sons, 2016.

Rosso, H. A. *Achieving Excellence in Fund Raising* (1st ed.) San Francisco: Jossey-Bass, 1991, 2003.

Routley, C., and Sargeant, A. Leaving a Bequest: Living on Through Charitable Gifts. *Nonprofit and Voluntary Sector Quarterly,* 2015, 44(5), 869–885.

Seiler, T. L. Developing and Articulating a Case for Support. In E. R. Tempel, T. L. Seiler, and D. F. Burlingame (eds.), *Achieving Excellence in Fundraising* (4th ed.). Hoboken, NJ: John Wiley & Sons, 2016.

Tempel, E. R. *Development Committee.* Washington, DC: Board Source, 2004.

Tempel, E. R. 2016. A Philosophy of Fundraising. In E. R. Tempel, T. L. Seiler, and D. F. Burlingame (eds.), *Achieving Excellence in Fundraising* (4th ed.). Hoboken, NJ: John Wiley & Sons, 2016.

Tempel, E. R., Seiler, T. L. and Burlingame, D. F. (eds.). *Achieving Excellence in Fundraising* (4th ed.). Hoboken, NJ: John Wiley & Sons, 2016.

Yandow, Heather. To Boost Individual Donor Giving, Nonprofits Need a Plan. Stanford Social Innovation Review, December 1, 2015.

CHAPTER NINETEEN

NONPROFIT FINANCE

Developing Nonprofit Resources

Dennis R. Young and Jung-In Soh

Nonprofit organizations finance themselves through a wide variety of sources that provide both monetary and in-kind resources. This is one way in which nonprofits distinguish themselves from business or government organizations. Nonprofit sources include fee revenues, charitable contributions, government funding, returns on investment, and volunteer and in-kind contributions. Thus nonprofit finance involves much more than traditional charitable fundraising. Rather, it requires cultivation of several of these sources, as well as finding the right mix of sources for organizations in different fields of service, with different missions, and in different circumstances. This chapter explores the conditions under which nonprofits can pursue these alternative sources, as well as the factors that may determine their proportions of total income. The discussion is guided by economic theory, especially the idea of public and private goods and the notion of economic benefit that can be tied to finance through the concept of demand by individuals, groups, and organizations that are willing to pay for nonprofit services.

Sources of Nonprofit Income

We use the term *income* to include both monetary and in-kind sources of support. However, most available data are confined to monetary support that is commonly referred to as "revenue." In this chapter we distinguish between these two terms,

509

but primarily focus on revenue for which data are most readily available and with which nonprofit management practice is most heavily concerned. Data on nonprofit finance are generally aggregated into broad categories. For example, data from the IRS Form 990 distinguish broadly between charitable contributions (called public support), government grants, program revenues, and investment returns. These categories blur important distinctions among individual versus institutional philanthropy, government grants versus contracts, and fee revenue from sales versus government reimbursements. In this chapter we make finer distinctions among alternative sources of revenue. Still, a review of the broad categories of income provides a useful general picture of finance of U.S. nonprofit organizations in different fields of service. Table 19.1, for example, shows that among broad fields of service, as reported by nonprofits that file IRS 990 forms for the year 2010, there is considerable variation among sources of support. (Note that these data do not include churches or nonprofits with annual income less than $25,000. Moreover, these data apply only to charitable nonprofits under section 501(c)(3) of the IRS code, not to various other categories of nonprofit corporations and associations.)

Table 19.1 demonstrates that over broad fields of service, the revenue bases of nonprofit organizations vary substantially. Education and health nonprofits are most heavily dependent on fee revenue, whereas arts, environmental, and international nonprofits depend more substantially on charitable contributions. The human services subsector is the only field that is primarily dependent on government revenue, which includes grants and fees derived from insurance and reimbursement programs such as Medicare and Medicaid. Investment income tends not to dominate any particular field, but is quite important in education and the arts.

TABLE 19.1. Sources of Revenue for Alternative Nonprofit Subsectors

	Fee (%)	Private Gifts (%)	Government (%)	Investment Income (%)	Other (%)
All	50.3	13.3	31.9	2.8	1.7
Arts	34	44.5	13	5.4	3
Education	61.1	17.2	14	5.8	1.9
Environment	30.2	49.1	14.6	3.2	3
Health	56.3	4.4	35.9	1.9	1.5
Human Services	27.5	20.2	48.5	2	1.9
International	8	69	20	1.6	1.4

Source: Roeger, Blackwood, and Pettijohn, 2012.

TABLE 19.2. Selected Arts and Culture Nonprofits in Atlanta

	Fee (%)	Private Gifts (%)	Government (%)	Investment Income (%)	Other (%)	Total Revenue ($ Millions)
Zoo	50.3	40.9	1.6	1.1	6	$20.6
Botanical Garden	35	61	0.6	2.2	1.1	$22.1
Children's Museum	30.8	66.5	2	0.8	0	$3.8
Ballet	72.4	25.8	0.4	1.4	0	$8.3

Source: Computed from 2013 IRS 990 forms; nccsweb.urban.org.

TABLE 19.3. Selected Human Service Nonprofits in Atlanta

	Fee (%)	Private Gifts (%)	Government (%)	Investment Income (%)	Other (%)	Total Revenue ($ Millions)
Atlanta Habitat	45.5	52.8	1.6	0.1	0	$16.6
Families First	27.2	38	30.8	3.9	0.2	$9.4
Georgia Justice Project	0	99.8	0	0.1	0.1	$1.8
Traveler's Aid	5.4	4.8	89.8	0	0	$4.1

Source: Computed from 2013 IRS 990 forms; nccsweb.urban.org.

The aggregate numbers of Table 19.1 obscure considerable variation within broad categories of nonprofits. For example, Tables 19.2 and 19.3 display a few well-known organizations in the city of Atlanta that are broadly categorized within the fields of Arts and Culture and Human Services, respectively. While these are not representative samples, they illustrate the wide variation for each source of income in both of these fields of service even in the same city. Similar variation obtains for most other nonprofit subfields. Such data clearly demonstrate that, although field of service is an important determinant of the sources of nonprofit income, variations are substantial and many other factors come into play.

Another way in which aggregate data can be misleading is the implication that particular types of income—for example, fee income, charitable gifts, or government funding—are homogeneous in nature. This is far from true, although it is often analytically convenient or necessary to treat them as such. To illustrate, charitable contributions may consist of gifts from individuals or from institutions such as foundations or corporations, they may come in the form of annual giving or gifts for capital projects, they may be gifts from living donors or bequests from estates, or they may derive from income from special fundraising events such as golf tournaments or running or bicycling marathons. So, too, earned (fee income) may come in the form of fees for service, royalties, and license fees for intellectual property or from rental income. A particularly interesting category of revenue is memberships, which may represent fee income (such as the cost of belonging to a YMCA) or essentially a charitable contribution with some benefits (such as membership in a museum) (Steinberg, 2007). Similarly, government income may come in the form of grants (which are essentially gifts), contracts (which are essentially fee for service), and insurance reimbursements, credits, and vouchers (which is revenue routed through clients and looks like fee income). Even investment income is multifaceted. It may take the form of returns on permanent endowment funds, interest on operating accounts, returns on commercial ventures, or returns on so-called "program-related investments" designed to produce both social benefits and financial returns (for example, microloans to social enterprises designed to employ challenged populations).

Finally, in-kind income can be particularly important to nonprofits in various circumstances. In arts institutions such as museums, for example, contributions of works of art are critical to success. And in many human services, such as homeless shelters, food banks, youth organizations, or emergency relief, volunteering is critical. Organizations such as the Girl Scouts and the Red Cross depend overwhelmingly on volunteer labor, more so than on paid staff. For that matter, many of the smaller nonprofit organizations that fly under the radar of the datasets that we have available are based primarily on volunteer effort. Some scholars characterize the part of the nonprofit sector that we can count and measure and whose finances we can analyze as only the tip of an iceberg that may include vastly more entities in the United States than those we know about (Smith, 1997).

Given the wide variations in financing of nonprofit organizations, it is clear that nonprofits require some integrating concepts to guide how they should be financed in any particular case. In this chapter, we examine each source of potential finance from the viewpoint of microeconomic theory, focusing on the benefits, beneficiaries, and beneficiaries' willingness to pay that characterize alternative nonprofit services, leading to different combinations of finance appropriate to particular circumstances. First, we delineate the economic concepts that will aid in this analysis. Then we examine each potential source of nonprofit finance individually. Finally, we discuss the considerations that go into combining different sources of income into a mix or portfolio appropriate for a given organization.

Economic Concepts Underlying Nonprofit Finance

The economic concept of "demand" is tied to the notion of "willingness to pay" (Young and Steinberg, 1995). In the commercial marketplace, consumers express their demand for private goods and services by paying the market price. This price represents the marginal benefit they receive from purchasing the good. Some nonprofits produce goods that are largely private in nature (that is, goods or services for which consumers receive personal benefits not shared by others and from which they can be excluded if they refuse to pay for them). Attendance at a concert, enrollment in a training program, or treatment for an illness are illustrations. In these cases, consumers receive personal benefits for which they may be willing to pay some direct fees.

Nonprofits also produce goods and services that are public in nature (that is, goods whose benefits are shared widely by others and for which it is difficult to exclude people if they are unwilling to pay). Such goods include research, public art, and advocacy for a social cause. In this case, there is some group of people who intrinsically value the good and would theoretically pay for it, but they have no market incentive to do so through fees. In economists' terms, there is a "free rider" problem, since the goodwill presumably would be available to them whether or not they pay for it. Thus, financing depends on another mechanism, for example charitable contributions made by members of the beneficiary group who feel particularly strongly about its provision or are driven by other motives such as a sense of social responsibility or pressure or a "warm glow" from the act of giving. Alternatively, if the benefits of the public good are particularly widespread and diffused among a large group of beneficiaries, it may be necessary for government to finance the good through taxation (Olson, 1965).

In addition, many nonprofits produce goods or services that are mixtures of public and private. Such goods may be characterized as having significant "positive externalities." For example, inoculating a child to prevent contraction of a contagious illness provides direct private benefits to that child and her family, as well as widespread benefits to the community because of the smaller likelihood that the disease will spread to others. In such cases, there are two groups of beneficiaries: direct recipients of the good who are probably willing to pay something for the personal benefits through fees, and a wider community that should be willing to subsidize the good through charitable contributions or government support.

Moreover, nonprofits also produce goods that may be characterized as "redistributional" in nature. That is, they produce private goods that are deemed desirable or necessary for the recipients to consume, whether or not they are able to pay for them. Distributions from a food bank, vaccinations for children from low-income families, work training for former felons, and homeless shelters fit this description. For all practical purposes, redistributional goods may be treated as public goods. They depend on the charitable motivations of groups of people who care about particular distressed populations and they may be considered to be of such widespread importance to society as to warrant government support.

Finally, let's consider another variation on private and public goods with which nonprofits are commonly involved—"transactions goods" that produce "trade" or "exchange" benefits. For example, nonprofits often enter collaborations or partnerships with other organizations or groups with which services and benefits are exchanged. These goods can be peripheral to a nonprofit's mission, but they may be integral to its ability to garner the financial or material support to carry out that mission. For example, in partnership with Dell, the American Red Cross opened three digital centers that help the American Red Cross monitor disasters and increase blood donations by using social media. American health charities have also entered licensing partnerships with major pharmaceutical companies to support products such as tobacco patches or toothpaste that are considered beneficial to the cause the nonprofits promote (such as smoking reduction or dental hygiene). In such arrangements, the corporate partners are willing to support the nonprofits through grants and in-kind services (such as enhanced publicity or employee volunteer hours) because they receive strategic corporate benefits such as increased product sales and improved public relations.

The concepts of private, public, redistributional, and transactions goods, and the associated mechanisms through which to pay for private, public, redistributional, and trade benefits, support the rationales under which nonprofits can pursue particular forms of income support. These are considered in greater depth in the next section.

The Role of Different Forms of Nonprofit Income

There are many forms of income that a nonprofit could employ, including fee or earned income, individual gift income, institutional gifts, governmental support, investment income, and volunteer and in-kind support. Each form has unique characteristics, benefits, and challenges that must be considered.

Fee (Earned) Income

It comes as a surprise to many that fee income is the dominant source of revenue for reporting charitable nonprofits in the United States, given the traditional association between charities and gifts. However, the United States is not alone in this pattern; many other countries' third sectors are dependent primarily on fee income (Salamon, Sokolowski, and Associates, 2004). Nor does this pattern hold for all nonprofit subsectors, as previously noted. Still, fee income is sufficiently dominant as to warrant its examination for most operating nonprofit organizations in the course of their resource development and planning deliberations. The issue of fees breaks down into several parts. For any given service offered by a nonprofit, one can ask whether a price should be charged at all. If the answer is positive, then the question becomes how to appropriately design the price structure. The latter question is contingent on the nature of the service itself. If the service entails public as well as private benefits, then the price will need to reflect that, perhaps only partially covering the cost of the service in order to ensure that an efficient level of externalities or distributional benefits are produced. However, if the service produces fully private benefits, and is perhaps even intended solely for financial support rather than mission impact, then prices should be designed to maximize net revenue.

Given a salience of private benefits, the issue of whether to charge a fee involves several considerations (Oster, Gray, and Weinberg, 2004). First, implementing a fee for a previously free service will entail investment in what economists call "transactions costs"—a new cost of doing business. An historically free museum will need to build and staff ticket booths, implement a system to collect, track, and reconcile these new revenues, and implement fraud prevention measures, or contract with an outside firm that knows how to do these things. Thus, the nonprofit needs to determine if the additional net fee revenue would offset the additional transactions costs associated with putting in place a fee system.

In addition, the museum may have to overcome cultural resistance from a community or donor base that feels entitled to free access or believes that open access is historically mandated or required by the original benefactors. Cooper Union, a New York City college that provided free tuition for students since 1902, is a prime example of this cultural resistance. In 2012, the college announced that it would begin charging tuition to graduate students and that in 2014, undergraduate students would begin paying tuition (Mytelka, 2012;

Vilensky, 2015). Although Cooper Union stated it had to charge tuition to prevent financial insolvency, there were outcries against the college's decision. A group of individuals comprised by students, graduates, and a professor of Cooper Union sued the board of directors to stop tuition charges and, in 2015, the New York Attorney General began investigating Cooper Union's past financial decisions to understand the school's decision to charge tuition (Vilensky, 2015). The resistance to the tuition charges stems in part from disagreements over the founder's original goals and whether he intended for all students to attend tuition-free (Harris, 2015).

The question of how fees will affect the ability of the nonprofit to accomplish its mission is, of course, central to the decision. In the case of a museum, one has to ask whether the fee system would reduce usage by those people the organization is intended to serve. This is partly a matter of *how* the fee system is implemented. For example, sliding scales or special periods of time when access is made free (for example, free Wednesdays at the museum) can allow fee revenues to be collected without seriously impinging on mission impact. In fact, properly designed fees can sometimes increase mission impact. In particular, aside from providing more revenue, fees can create constructive incentives. In the case of Cooper Union, tuition charges are meant to prevent financial insolvency by generating funds from students who are able to pay while the neediest students are still eligible for scholarships. In other cases, a fee can add a dignity factor that may make it more likely for targeted populations to participate. For example, a free transport service for elderly residents to travel to their senior center might be viewed as "charity," whereas a nominal fee might preserve self-respect and increase usage.

Once a decision to implement a fee is reached, there are a variety of considerations that go into determining the fee structure. Much stems from the goals of the service involved. If the service is purely a commercial venture intended to generate maximum profit for the organization, which can then be devoted to support mainline mission-related services, then prices should be set for that purpose. If, however, the service addresses a mission-related social purpose, the fees must be gauged to what targeted recipients are willing to pay for the private benefits they receive. Here is where sliding scales and other approaches can be helpful. In such cases, the goal is not full cost recovery or the generation of net financial surpluses but rather some level of off-setting revenues that can help pay for the service, or extend its volume or reach, in combination with other forms of support.

Finally, it is worth addressing the option of "membership" fees or dues in connection with overall fee revenue alternatives (Steinberg, 2007). One conception of membership dues is that they are a form of "package pricing" under which it may be more effective to charge consumers for several services under a single price than to charge them separately for each component service. For example, memberships in YMCAs are more efficient than charging clients separately for the weight room, the swimming pool, and towels. Savings accrue in the form of convenience and lower transaction costs. In addition, package pricing can help advance the mission of the organization by inducing clients to use included services that they might not otherwise use if they had to pay separately. Thus, clients of the Y are more likely to use the diet counseling service if it is included in the membership price, thus advancing the Y's mission to improve personal health.

Overall, the key to determining whether fee revenue should be a component of a nonprofit's revenue mix is to assess whether there is a strong component of private benefit to an identifiable beneficiary group to whom prices can be feasibly and effectively charged. For a variety of reasons, many nonprofits produce services for which there is a strong private benefit component. One reason is that they are capable of offering certain commercial products at a profit because of some competitive advantage, the revenues from which can support the charitable mission. Universities are good at offering public lecture programs and arboreta are well suited to provide attractive facilities for private weddings and bar mitzvahs. Moreover, nonprofits' mainline missions often justifiably entail private goods and benefits because of their competitive advantage in producing sensitive services, such as child day care or elderly care, in which consumers can comfortably place their trust. In such cases, it is entirely sensible for nonprofits to pursue fee income as an important component of their revenue portfolios.

Gift Income Contributed by Individuals

When nonprofits offer services that entail a significant component of public or redistributional goods or externalities, it makes sense to look for other sources to supplement fee revenues. This is because the benefits associated with these goods are such that beneficiaries can enjoy them without paying for them. For example, it is difficult to charge people in a community for the benefits of lower contagion risk associated with inoculating their neighbors' children. Similarly, the benefits of cleaner air, lower crime, or more informed citizens that may result from the programs of particular nonprofit organizations accrue collectively to various groups of beneficiaries whose individual members would be difficult to identify or charge. As a result, substantial "free riding" occurs when people are asked to pay voluntarily.

Nonetheless, people do contribute voluntarily to nonprofits for services they care about. The challenge to nonprofits is to find ways to overcome free riding as much as possible so that beneficiary and donor groups come as close to contributing levels commensurate with the benefits they receive. Those benefits, related to the reasons that people do give, are several-fold. Research shows that people are both altruistic and self-serving in their giving behavior, that is, they value both public and private benefits from giving (Vesterlund, 2006). To the extent that donors care directly about the level of output a nonprofit provides, they are being altruistic, giving simply to ensure that those services are provided in sufficient quantity. Donors also receive personal satisfaction from the act of giving itself, sometimes called "warm glow." In this case, donors give irrespective of the nonprofit's level of service in amounts that reflect their personal satisfaction (Andreoni, 1990).

In order for nonprofits to be effective in raising charitable contributions from individual donors, they must build strategies based on these diverse motivations. They can appeal to altruism by measuring, describing, and communicating the level, quantity, and effectiveness of the services they perform, and they can appeal to warm glow by communicating the virtue of their work, the good reputation of the organization, the good feelings associated with giving, and by recognizing donors' particular contributions. Long ago, Mancur Olson (1965) identified several distinct strategies for overcoming free riding in the case of public goods. One of these strategies, which he called "selective incentives," would appeal to the warm glow and other selfish motives of donor and beneficiaries by tying private rewards (special gifts, naming rights, membership privileges, and so on) to gift giving. Another strategy, social pressure, would exploit the power of small groups and public exposure to encourage, perhaps intimidate, donors and beneficiaries to give their fair share. Such strategies are common in church congregations and on boards of directors of prestigious or well-respected nonprofit institutions. The social network effect associated with online giving and crowdfunding, when fans of organizations on social networking sites encourage each other to give (Saxton and Wang, 2014), is also an example of social pressure.

In sum, there are several steps nonprofit managers and development officers can take in order to enhance individual giving as much as possible. These include identifying those groups of beneficiaries and potential donors who care about the collective (public and redistributional) benefits the organization is producing, understanding and appealing to the motivations of these groups, and devising strategies to overcome the tendency to free ride on the contributions of others. Just as fee revenue has its transactions costs, development efforts to secure contributions involve fundraising costs. A sensible way for a nonprofit to view its fundraising program is to conceive of it as a profit-making business whose purpose is to maximize net revenues. Like any business, this entails some investment in the form of fundraising expenses to identify and communicate with current and potential donors. An important question is how much a nonprofit should spend on its fundraising operation. Viewed as a profit-maximizing business, an economist would say: continue to invest until the last dollar of expense produces at least a dollar in raised revenue (Young and Steinberg, 1995). Spending any less would forfeit potential additional net contributed revenue; spending any more would entail spending some (marginal) dollars for less than a dollar in return.

As simple as the above rule is, nonprofits commonly violate it because of certain commonly accepted practices. One such practice is to set an arbitrary fundraising goal and spend whatever it takes to reach that goal. Obviously, if that goal is not carefully calibrated, it can cause the nonprofit to over- or under-spend on fundraising, perhaps even spend more on fundraising than the goal itself. Another practice is to adhere to specified ratios of fundraising expenses to total expenses (sometimes identified as "good practice" by watchdog agencies such as Charity Navigator or the Wise Giving Alliance) or, worse, to attempt to minimize average fundraising cost within some range of revenue generation. The problem here is that the point of maximum net revenue generation does not necessarily correspond to the point at which specified ratio standards are met. Indeed, the level of optimal fundraising expense will vary widely with the circumstances (for example, field of service, age, size, location) of the nonprofit in question. Thus, nonprofit managers need to use careful judgment and basic economic principles to determine how much they can raise in the form of individual charitable contributions, rather than strictly adhere to arbitrarily specified goals or ratios.

Institutional Giving

According to Giving USA, 80 percent of charitable giving comes from individuals, yet the remaining 20 percent from foundations and corporations can be very important to nonprofit organizations. Although there are more than one hundred thousand foundations in the United States, and many additional corporate giving programs not formalized as separate foundations, the largest of these institutional philanthropies are the most visible, focused, and assertive in their giving. Thus, they are the natural targets for nonprofits seeking charitable support. However, institutional givers are not entirely similar to individual donors, although there are some common attributes. In particular, the many small foundations (including family foundations) and some larger ones are essentially the institutional personifications of their benefactors, who have found it to be efficient to channel their giving through the foundation structure. Moreover, much of the funding by community foundations takes place through "donor-advised funds" that essentially manifest the giving preferences of their individual donors. The same observation applies even more strongly to giving by the charitable funds administered by securities firms such as Fidelity or Schwab.

One variety of institutional philanthropy takes the form of foundations that can be viewed essentially as nonprofit organizations with their own articulated missions, but which have chosen to pursue those missions by making grants. In some sense, these are nonprofits that simply outsource the implementation of their missions through operating nonprofit grantees. As a consequence, nonprofits seeking support from such philanthropies need to propose projects and programs that promulgate those missions, one hopes without distorting their own missions. Many institutional funders, however, have broad missions and programs that may accommodate a wide variety of nonprofit proposals. Nonetheless, there are again serious transactions costs associated with searching for appropriate potential institutional funders, cultivating relationships with program officers, staff consultants, or board members and engaging in the procedures, negotiations, and implementation and evaluation processes required by those funders. These costs vary widely from funder to funder.

Given the relatively small role that institutional philanthropy plays in the overall financing of nonprofit organizations in the United States (20 percent of the approximately 13 percent of nonprofit funding that is accounted for by charitable giving, or 2.6 percent of the total), it is not surprising that institutional funders prefer to make strategic grants rather than be relied upon as sources of ongoing operational support. Thus, foundation grants tend to be time limited and focused on particular project initiatives and contingent on an overall plan for the nonprofit to sustain the initiative over the longer run from other sources. There are many exceptions to this pattern, of course, and foundations have been criticized for failing to provide ongoing infrastructure support for nonprofits. One variant that addresses some of this criticism is an approach called "venture philanthropy" under which institutional funders make intensive and ongoing investments in selected nonprofit organizations, and then maintain intensive oversight and support of those organizations, at least until it is clear that they can make it effectively on their own or are judged to have failed.

An important distinction should be made between funding by private independent foundations or public charities, such as community foundations on the one hand, and corporate philanthropy on the other. Internal corporate giving programs and many separately incorporated corporate foundations that maintain close ties to the mother corporation must be understood within the overall context of corporate strategy. Corporations can derive many benefits from their relationships with nonprofits and charitable causes, and most corporations have these in mind as they engage in charitable giving. Such benefits include improved public and community relations, enhanced employee morale, greater effectiveness in marketing their products and services, opportunities to cultivate new markets among nonprofit stakeholders, obtaining access to expertise and knowledge that the nonprofit may harbor, and tax benefits. These are the kinds of "exchange" benefits corporations can derive for themselves by supporting nonprofits.

The trick to securing corporate support is to find a corporate relationship with the right "strategic fit" wherein the needs of the nonprofit and those of the corporation are both met (that is, a mutually satisfactory exchange of benefits can be arranged). Nonprofits may receive monetary and valuable in-kind support, including, for example, valuable public exposure through a corporation's marketing program, in exchange for some combination of the above-mentioned benefits to the corporation. In this negotiation, the nonprofit needs to think about what exchange benefits are of value to the corporation and to pitch its proposals accordingly. There is risk in this exchange, of course, if the negotiated arrangements damage the reputation of the nonprofit or somehow undermine its mission. For example, nonprofits must be wary of endorsing corporate products that may be harmful or fail to best serve their stakeholders. Thus, the American Cancer Society or the American Lung Association can be comfortable associating themselves with manufacturers of tobacco patches, but they would err by endorsing a particular brand because other brands may ultimately prove to be superior. In fact, SmithKline Beecham Consumer Healthcare, which licensed the American Cancer Society's name and logo for smoking cessation products in 1996, eventually settled with twelve state attorneys general in 1998 due to the misrepresentation that the nonprofit endorsed the products (Daw, 2006). Although there were no financial consequences for the American Cancer Society, this example suggests the possibility of negative reputational impacts from corporate support.

In summary, support from institutional philanthropy requires awareness of the needs and goals of the funders. In the cases of independent and community foundations, the issues are likely to be compatibility with the charitable missions of those institutions and planning for long-term sustainability once the initial grants are expended. For corporate funding, the objective is to find the appropriate strategic partnership that serves the purposes (provides the exchange benefits) to both parties in the transaction.

Government Funding

Approximately one-third of nonprofit funding derives from government in the form of contracts and grants of various kinds. Like charitable giving, the rationale for government funding derives from the public or redistributional nature of some of the goods and services delivered by nonprofit organizations. In particular, a third strategy for overcoming the free rider problem in providing collective goods is for the government to apply coercion through taxation. For goods and services that entail widespread public benefits or widely supported redistributional goals, there may be a political consensus for government to support these services through legislation. Ultimately, government may choose either to deliver these services itself or to outsource them to private delivery agents, commonly nonprofit organizations. This is the American system of "third-party government" described by Salamon (1987), which permits government to exploit efficiencies and diversity in private provision while assuring adequate resource support. Chapter Twenty of this volume addresses the issues of government contracting in great depth.

From the nonprofit viewpoint, seeking government funding is appropriate for support of programs and services for which there are widespread public benefits and existing or potential statutory programs available for funding. This is largely the case in areas such as human services, education, health care, and environmental conservation, but less so for expressive activities such as the arts or religion, where there is less consensus.

As with other sources of funds, government support comes with certain risks, challenges, and costs. Substantial transaction costs are often associated with building and maintaining the necessary capacity, skills, and political acumen to navigate governmental systems of funding eligibility and maintaining mandated reporting and evaluation procedures. New governmental policies and changes to existing policies have the potential to significantly impact the funding and operations of nonprofits. For instance, the 2010 Affordable Care Act requires nonprofit hospitals to have explicit financial assistance policies, limit the amounts charged to financially needy patients, determine financial assistance of needy patients before taking collection actions, and to conduct community health needs assessments. If the hospitals do not meet these requirements, they face an excise tax (www.irs.gov). Governments also have a reputation for slow payment of their bills, requiring nonprofits to set aside working capital to manage cash flow.

A number of other, more subtle, risks are also sometimes associated with government funding. For example, given the substantial investment that nonprofits receiving government funding must make in administrative infrastructure and in meeting government service standards, there is the risk that a nonprofit will become heavily professionalized and lose some of its voluntary spirit and indeed become less attractive to volunteers or effective paid workers who lack the formal credentials that government may require. Moreover, government funding may "crowd out" private contributions if donors perceive that the recipient nonprofits no longer require as much in charitable assistance (Andreoni and Payne, 2003). There is also the possibility, however, that government funding, especially if it is properly structured in the form of matching requirements, can induce a "crowd in" of additional private contributions (Okten and Weisbrod, 2000). Finally, substantial dependence on government funding may run the risk of "mission drift" wherein the nonprofit essentially loses its own sense of direction and assumes the role of a government contractor, foregoing its own autonomy and independence (Smith and Lipsky, 1993). One manifestation of this may be increased reluctance of the nonprofit to engage in advocacy work if such activity causes friction with its government benefactors. In addition, dependence on government funding may cause financial problems for nonprofits as a result of government delays in payments and failure to cover full costs of contracts (Boris, de Leon, Roeger, and Nikolova, 2010).

Of course, the foregoing risks are likely to vary with the different forms of government support. The strings are looser on grants than contracts, and payments in the form of vouchers, tax credits, or per capita subsidies attached to service consumers are likely to be even less constraining. These constraints associated with each form of government support may positively or negatively influence program performance (Sandfort, Selden, and Sowa, 2008), so seeking government revenue should be a deliberate decision. In general, it makes sense for nonprofits to seek out government assistance when it provides services with widespread public or redistributional benefits or positive externalities that are supported by government programs, and where fee income and private charitable contributions are unlikely to support efficient levels of service provision.

Investment Income

Income from investments constitutes a category of support for nonprofits somewhat different from other sources because it is not generally directly associated with particular services and benefits. Investment income comes in the form of interest and dividends on nonprofit funds, ranging from interest on operating funds to investment returns on endowments or other restricted funds (Bowman, Keating, and Hager, 2007). As such, funds from investments provide flexibility for nonprofits because they do not generally require appealing to a particular beneficiary group or providing a particular kind of service or benefit. However, this statement requires a number of qualifications. First, the principals or corpuses of investment funds from which returns are derived must come from somewhere.

For example, they may accrue from accumulated operating surpluses derived from fee income and annual charitable contributions. Typically, endowments are put in place through capital gifts by living donors or through bequests. As such, the building of investment income requires appealing to the beneficiaries of these sources of capital, along the lines discussed earlier.

In addition, there are some forms of investment income that are tied more directly to services, benefits, and beneficiaries—namely program-related investments (PRIs). PRIs are generally the domain of grantmaking foundations. They entail loans or other investments of the corpus of foundation funds in activities that have a direct mission impact but that also provide a financial return. For example, a foundation can provide low-interest loans to nonprofits starting up a new commercial venture, say a restaurant, intended to employ inner-city youth. PRIs may also be appealing for larger operating nonprofits. For example, a large children's hospital may wish to loan funds to the local children's museum for a project that educates children and families about nutrition and preventive health practices, on the theory that such an investment contributes both revenue to the hospital and advances its mission of improving children's health. The use of PRIs dates back to the 1960s, but PRIs have increased in popularity since the late 1990s, although less than 1 percent of foundations make PRIs (Osili et al., 2013).

As discussed as follows, investment income can have an important role to play in a nonprofit organization's overall income portfolio by allowing for stable production of goods and services (Fisman and Hubbard, 2003). Investment income can aid risk management and help cover shortfalls due to potential instability of future revenue and costs. In particular, investment income can aid production smoothing when there are large fixed costs (Bowman, 2007). For example, costs associated with maintaining large physical plants or core staff may be difficult to fully finance from other forms of operating income that depend more directly on the level of output that the organization can produce. Frequently, nonprofits restrict use of returns on endowment funds to particular long-term fixed costs, such as building maintenance, student scholarship support, endowed chairs for professorships or curator positions, and so on. Nonprofits may also want to build endowments to assure benefits for future generations or to exploit tax incentives that yield higher investment returns for nonprofits compared to corporations (Hansmann, 1990).

Endowments intended to generate steady streams of operating income also entail some challenges and risks. First, as recent experience has shown, investment revenues, despite their presumed immunity from the day-to-day volatility of service provision, can exhibit substantial instability over time. They also entail transactions costs in the form of competent investment management, and they are subject to the systemic risks associated with downturns in the stock market and the economy at large, as experienced in the Great Recession of 2008–2010. Older and larger nonprofits, as well as private foundations, are more likely to earn higher investment returns compared to other nonprofit organizations, which speaks to the importance of investment management experience and financial know-how (Heutel and Zeckhauser, 2014). Moreover, endowments are often raised for specific projects and facilities that can involve significant additional operating costs. In particular, it is often attractive for donors to contribute endowments for a new building or program facility, or for hiring a prestigious new professorship named in their honor. These projects entail ongoing maintenance and support costs that the donor is often uninterested in covering. Indeed, sometimes donors prefer to give "challenge grants" that require nonprofits to raise additional capital from other donors and also cover the increased operating costs of the new project. For nonprofits, this is a matter of looking gift horses in the mouth. What can appear to be an attractive, prestigious, and generous gift can easily become an albatross that threatens the entire organization. Prudent negotiations with donors of endowment capital require that the ancillary fixed costs associated with capital projects are part of the financing package. The recent Kroc gift to the Salvation Army for the construction of a series of new community centers is an interesting case in point (Strom, 2009). The gift included endowments equal to the cost of construction of each center, intended to generate revenues to cover shortfalls between operating revenues and costs. However, the endowments proved inadequate and required the Salvation Army to raise additional funds.

Volunteer and In-Kind Contributions

A major portion of the income support for nonprofit organizations in the United States comes in the form of nonmonetary or in-kind contributions, most of that in the guise of volunteer labor. It is reasonably estimated that the value of such labor is roughly equal to the value of monetary charitable contributions to nonprofit organizations. The Urban Institute estimates the 2013 value of volunteer labor to be $163 billion, or 10 percent of total nonprofit revenue. Thus, although these forms of income do not normally appear in the financial statements or tax forms of nonprofit organizations, they do constitute significant resources that nonprofits should take into account in developing, managing, and planning their finances.

As with other sources of income, in-kind support entails substantial transactions costs. For material contributions such as art collections, real estate, automobiles, furniture, computers, or perishables such as food or supplies, there are several issues: maintenance and operating costs, compatibility of use in the organization's operations, and liquidity (Gray, 2007). In short, gifts-in-kind are not necessarily net gains to the organization unless their benefits exceed their maintenance or operating costs, or they can be easily used without excessive adjustment or loss of quality in operations, or they can be profitably sold for cash. Still, handled well, gifts-in-kind can be valuable contributions to nonprofit income.

Appropriate contributions of art can add substantially to a museum's mission, contributed real estate in areas where real estate values are rising can become an important part of an organization's asset portfolio or might contribute directly to the mission of an environmental organization wishing to protect a rural area from overdevelopment, and receipt of used cars can provide a source of resale income or economical replacements for cars in a nonprofit's existing fleet. Motivations of individual donors vary from needing to dispose of unwanted but functional items to seeking to preserve cherished collections to receiving tax benefits more or less equivalent to selling items directly. (As to the latter, it is important for nonprofits to be prudent in offering donors a fair market estimate of the value of the gift to avoid the taint of a tax scam.) For corporate gifts, there is the additional motivation for companies to provide visibility to their products, with the possible benefit of expanding future markets. Gifts of pharmaceuticals to health clinics or computers to schools allow manufacturers to expose future paying consumers to their products. In this sense, in-kind income, particularly from corporations, involves the generation of exchange benefits wherein both donor and recipient nonprofit purposes should be well served.

Similar considerations apply to volunteering (Leete, 2006). People volunteer with nonprofit organizations for a variety of reasons, and nonprofits must employ them prudently if volunteering is to be an effective addition to an organization's income. Here again, nonprofits may be viewed as exchanging various benefits to secure the resources that volunteers provide. For volunteers, these benefits may span the range from pure altruism in wanting to advance the charitable work of the organization to various private benefits, including warm glow, experience gained that may prove useful in future paid work, social benefits of interaction with other individuals in the workplace, free or reduced-cost access to the organization's services (such as the opportunity to hear concerts or attend classes), and nonmonetary recognition of a job well done.

The transactions costs associated with volunteering are also multidimensional. Resources must be devoted to managing volunteers, including their recruitment, screening, assignment to tasks, training, monitoring, evaluation, and coordination with other members of the workforce. (See Chapter Twenty-Four of this volume for a substantive discussion of the process of volunteer management.) Preston (2007) makes an interesting distinction between two classes of volunteers—those whose work complements those of paid workers and those whose work can substitute for that of paid workers. In the latter case, volunteers offer a financial savings to the organization and do not require extensive coordination with other (paid) workers. In the former case, volunteers can increase the productivity of paid workers; however, they may also generate extra costs associated with properly coordinating them with the paid work staff. (This can be problematic if volunteer schedules are irregular or unpredictable.) In short, volunteers are not free, and nonprofit managers must ensure that they are accepted and utilized prudently in order for their contributions to represent net additions to the organization's resources.

Portfolio Issues

Nonprofit organizations necessarily finance themselves with different mixes of fee, gift, government, investment, and in-kind income because, fundamentally, even nonprofits with very similar missions produce different combinations of public and private goods and services and their associated classes of benefits. If nonprofit finance is necessarily transactional (that is, that resource support is forthcoming in rough exchange for the kinds of benefits produced), then different missions, program and service combinations, and consequent benefits and beneficiaries will lead to different income portfolios. We argue here that a productive way to approach nonprofit finance is to begin with mission, analyze the programs and services that follow from this mission, consider the public and private benefits that are generated by these services, and develop a strategy for securing payments that exploit the willingness to pay of the various sets of beneficiaries.

The foregoing sounds very straightforward and logical and perhaps obvious. However, it tends to turn conventional nonprofit development strategy on its head. Rather than figure out how to increase one or another form of income, given a nonprofit organization's overall financial needs, a "benefits approach" to nonprofit finance emphasizes mission and program as the key to finance. Thus, ensuring adequate financing of a nonprofit organization necessarily involves two basic questions: (1) Are the benefits accruing to particular individuals and groups being captured through appropriate forms of finance, such as fees, contributions or government support? and (2) What adjustments in programs and services might lead to a stronger mix of benefits and beneficiaries and associated payments toward a stronger financial position for the organization?

It is the rare nonprofit that produces only one kind of benefit and is restricted to one source of income. Examples of such may include the following:

- A health charity that funds research on a rare disease and depends solely on charitable contributions from individuals at risk of contracting the disease or families and friends of the afflicted. If the disease is rare, it may not draw sufficiently widespread interest to warrant government support, volunteer involvement, or a market for any kind of fee income.
- An offender rehabilitation program entirely funded by government, reflecting its widespread public benefits of citizen safety and redistributional benefits to low-income communities, but which generates little empathy among potential donors and produces no particular marketable product or service.
- A church whose operations are financed solely on the basis of a Sunday collection plate to whom regular worshippers contribute.

Even in these cases, it is not hard to imagine additional sources of income tied to broader benefits and beneficiary groups. The health charity might emphasize the fundamental nature of its research (such as genetic), hence drawing on a wider pool of donations and possible corporate sponsors and government support. The offender rehabilitation organization might incorporate a social business enterprise, such as a restaurant or a landscaping service, as a means of teaching its clients market skills, thus drawing on fee income from consumers of that enterprise. The church could provide religious instruction or social programs for which fees could be charged, it could hold bake sales or other special events to generate additional contributions, or it could package its services into memberships for which dues can be charged.

More generally, nonprofits depend on multiple sources of income, prompting economists such as Estelle James (1983) to model them as "multi-product firms." Consider the following examples:

- A thrift shop that provides used clothing at low cost to needy citizens depends on a combination of in-kind donations, volunteer labor, and fee income from sales.
- A theater that offers experimental works of new artists depends on a combination of ticket revenues and charitable gifts from the local community of theater lovers.
- A preschool center that charges tuition for its services, perhaps on a sliding scale basis, and receives government support in recognition of the society-wide benefits (greater economic productivity, reduced crime, and so on) associated with early childhood education.
- An organization that monitors environmental quality receives government funding, reflecting its contributions to a cleaner and healthier environment, and charitable contributions from a community of nature lovers, scientists, and conservationists.
- A university that supports itself on tuition income, recognizing the private benefits accruing to its students, charitable contributions from alumni who care about the institution and benefit from its reputation, government funding that supports its research and contributions to a more informed and productive citizenry, and capital gifts from alumni who enjoy the special benefits of naming rights and prime seats at football games.

The possible combinations are manifold and particular to each institution. Moreover, any given institution can entertain a variety of ideas for additional sources of income. It does not follow, however, that every nonprofit should increase the number of its income sources without limit. In particular, as we have noted, each additional source of income comes with its own transaction costs. Hence, nonprofits must always consider the possible trade-offs between the transaction costs of pursuing an additional source of income and the potential net income benefits that might derive from the addition. There are also a number of other considerations that go into deciding the appropriate number and mix of income sources in a nonprofit portfolio.

Mission Effectiveness

The advantage of analyzing benefits and beneficiaries is that it will help nonprofits avoid leaving money on the table from beneficiaries who might provide the resources to allow them to expand to an optimal scale for providing maximum net social benefits. This applies to both the private and public benefits a nonprofit may produce and may finance through alternative mechanisms.

In theory a nonprofit should continue to expand as long as the marginal benefits, as reflected in additional revenues from beneficiaries, at least offset additional costs of expansion.

Solvency

As previously noted, some sources of support are more difficult to garner than others. In particular, free-rider effects may preclude a nonprofit from fully exploiting the willingness to pay of beneficiaries of the public benefits it provides. In order to finance those benefits, adjustments may be needed in its finance portfolio, such as the generation of investment revenues or the undertaking of commercial ventures that can compensate for free-rider losses. Essentially, nonprofits are private organizations producing a combination of private and public benefits. As such they must ensure that their financial bottom lines are sound.

One additional factor affecting solvency is the problem of cash flow. If the nonprofit depends on revenues that are episodic in nature, it will need ways to even the flow of income so as to be able to pay its expenses on a regular basis. There are various ways of addressing this issue, including prudent borrowing and building up a working capital fund that can be depleted and replenished as income flows permit. Another approach is to seek alternative sources of income with different time profiles. For example, tuition payments and alumni gifts may flow into a nonprofit school at different times, thus helping smooth the flow of income over the course of a year.

Income Interactions

By pursuing benefit-related income from one source, losses or gains may be incurred in another. This is the so-called "crowding out" or "crowding in" noted above in connection with government funding. Crowding effects may also manifest themselves with other combinations of income, such as fee revenues crowding out charitable contributions (Kingma, 1995). It is also possible for individual sources of fee revenue to cause different crowding effects on each other (Wicker, Breuer, and Hennigs, 2012). This requires awareness on the part of nonprofit managers as they pursue one source of income at the possible expense of another. As such it may limit the degree to which additional sources of income can be productively pursued, or it may require an educational initiative to explain to resource providers why substitutions are undesirable. Alternatively, revenue interactions may provide opportunities for synergy if, for example, donors are encouraged by organizational efforts to increase earned income, or if government programs match income from other sources.

Organizational Capacity

The seriousness of transaction-cost issues associated with administering different sources of income may depend on the maturity, size, and sophistication of the particular nonprofit organization. A small or young organization may not be capable of handling more than one type of income source. For example, it may know how to collect donations from individuals through an annual campaign or special event, but may be clueless in applying for a government grant. As organizations grow and mature, they can acquire additional capacities and skills to enable effective administration of multiple sources of income. In general, larger nonprofit organizations tend to have more diversified income portfolios, partly for this reason.

Risk Management

In the management of financial investments, diversification is a key strategy of risk management. So-called *unsystematic risk* can be reduced for any given level of investment return by diversifying investments whose fluctuations are uncorrelated or weakly correlated over time. The same principle applies to nonprofits, since fee, gift, government, investment, and in-kind income do not vary exactly in tandem over time (that is, they are imperfectly correlated). This can provide a measure of safety for nonprofits that would be at greater risk if they depended on only a single source. In particular, drawing on multiple streams of income can contribute to revenue stability (Mayer, Wang, Egginton, and Flint, 2012). Thus, within the parameters and limitations discussed earlier, it is desirable for nonprofits to diversify their sources of income, both among broad categories of income such as fees versus contributions, and also within categories, for example, by engaging a variety of different donors or corporate sponsors.

There are limits to this strategy, however. First, not all financial risk to nonprofit organizations is unsystematic. The economic downturn of 2008–2010 illustrates that when there is a fundamental deterioration of the overall economy, multiple sources of support can be affected deeply and simultaneously. This has been the case with charitable contributions, government funding and investment income, and to a certain extent earned income as well. However, these sources have not been perfectly correlated so that delays in reductions in foundation funding and other charitable contributions have helped ease the initial shocks to nonprofits. Moreover, the crisis has led to a rise in volunteering and to increases in certain manifestations of fee income, such as tuitions to lower-cost educational institutions as a result of people going back to school or moving from higher- to lower-cost colleges and universities. And although revenue diversification may help stabilize revenue, concentrated income portfolios may allow higher long-term revenue growth (Chikoto and Neely, 2013). The decision to diversify should then be based on stability, growth, and other considerations

For instance, diversification may undermine another source of potential stability for nonprofits—the development of deep relationships with funders. The premise here is that putting most of your eggs in the right basket, such as government social service programs that are unlikely to be diminished (such as Medicare or Medicaid) can be an effective risk management strategy (Grønbjerg, 1993). However, recent experiences with federal, state, and local governments struggling with their budgets raise doubts about the efficacy of this strategy.

In addition to income diversification, nonprofits can manage their financial risk in other ways. For example, developing various types of funds can help provide stability (Bowman, 2007). A reserve fund that socks away six months or a year's worth of operating income in anticipation of a future period of scarcity is a wise precaution assuming it is invested in safe securities. More generally, endowment funds, although they are intended for other purposes, can provide a modicum of stability. Endowments offer a steady source of income unconnected with the success of the nonprofit's program side (and sources of income associated with those programs). However, even a prudent investment strategy may not withstand the kind of market turmoil recently experienced. Even the financial investment wizards at Harvard and Yale experienced 30 to 40 percent losses of endowment value in the recent downturn. Still, endowments provide other safety features as well, including an increased capacity to borrow in hard times, given the asset value that endowments represent. In dire circumstances, it may be assumed that endowments can be invaded to secure debt or cover operating deficits. This is a dangerous practice, however, which has led to the demise, or severely threatened the viability, of once healthy and prestigious institutions such as the New York City Opera (Stewart, 2013)) and the New York Historical Society (Guthrie, 1996).

Conclusion

This chapter has focused on the various ways that nonprofit organizations finance their operations. We have not given particular attention to financing of capital needs, which would entail examination of a variety of technical strategies (including capital campaigns, tax-free bonds, and various other debt, equity, and governmental financing approaches). Nonetheless, with the exception of borrowing, the sources of nonprofit capital are mirrored by the main sources of nonprofit operating income support—charitable giving, government financing, and retained (earned) income. As such, the general approach that we have taken here—connecting the benefits of a nonprofit's programs to its sources of finance—applies as well to capital financing. In fact, the two dimensions of nonprofit finance are intimately related. In particular, the capital structure of a nonprofit, especially its degree of reliance on fixed assets, helps determine the kinds of operating income it needs to generate. Fixed costs associated with the maintenance of capital assets such as real estate and physical facilities, for example, require steady sources of income independent of service output, such as investment income or steady sources of charitable gifts, including capital gifts from donors who appreciate being associated with named facilities.

The main premise of this chapter is that nonprofits produce unique mixes of public and private and benefits, which through appropriate financial mechanisms can be paid for by the recipients of those benefits. By matching financing strategies to benefits and beneficiaries, nonprofits can approach efficient levels of financing that allow them to produce maximum net social benefits within acceptable bounds of organizational stability and remain true to the missions for which they are established.

References

Andreoni, J., and Payne, A. A. Do Government Grants to Private Charities Crowd Out Giving or Fund-Raising? *American Economic Review,* 2003, 93(3), 792–812.

Andreoni, J. Impure Altruism and Donations to Public Goods: A Theory of Warm-Glow Giving. *The Economic Journal,* 1990, 100(401), 464–477.

Boris, E. T., de Leon, E., Roeger, K. L., and Nikolova, M. *Human Service Nonprofits and Government Collaboration: Findings from the 2010 National Survey of Nonprofit Government Contracting and Grants.* Washington, DC: Center for Nonprofits and Philanthropy, The Urban Institute, October 2010.

Bowman, W. Managing Endowment and Other Assets. In D. R. Young (ed.), *Financing Nonprofits.* Lanham, MD: AltaMira Press, 2007, 271–289.

Bowman, W., Keating, E., and Hager, M. A. Investment Income. In D. R. Young (ed.), *Financing Nonprofits.* Lanham, MD: AltaMira Press, 2007, 157–181.

Chikoto, G. L., & Neely, D. G. "Building Nonprofit Financial Capacity: The Impact of Revenue Concentration and Overhead Costs. *Nonprofit and Voluntary Sector Quarterly,* 2013, 43, 570-588.

Daw, J. *Cause Marketing for Nonprofits: Partner for Purpose, Passion, and Profits.* Hoboken, NJ: John Wiley & Sons, 2006.

Fisman, R., and Hubbard, R. G. The Role of Nonprofit Endowments. In E. L. Glaeser (ed.), *The Governance of Not-for-Profit Organizations.* Chicago: University of Chicago Press, 2003.

Gray, C. M. Gift-in-Kind and Other Illiquid Assets. In D. R. Young (ed.), *Financing Nonprofits*. Lanham, MD; AltaMira Press, 2007, 227–241.

Grønbjerg, K. A. *Understanding Nonprofit Funding: Managing Revenues in Social Services and Community Development Organizations*. San Francisco: Jossey-Bass, 1993.

Guthrie, K. M. *The New York Historical Society: Lessons from One Nonprofit's Long Struggle for Survival*. San Francisco: Jossey-Bass, 1996.

Hansmann, H. Why do Universities Have Endowments? *Journal of Legal Studies*, 1990, 19(1), 3–42.

Harris, E. A. Cooper Union Offers to Let President Go as Part of Deal with State Attorney General. *The New York Times*, April 10, 2015. Retrieved from www.nytimes.com/2015/ 04/11/nyregion/cooper-union-offers-to-let-president-go-as-part-of-deal-with-state-attorney-general.html?_r=0.

Heutel, G., and Zeckhauser, R. The Investment Returns of Nonprofit Organizations, Part II: The Value of Focused Attention. *Nonprofit Management and Leadership*, 2014, 25(1), 59–75.

James, E. How Nonprofits Grow: A Model. *Journal of Policy Analysis and Management*, 1983, Spring, 2(3), 350–365.

Kingma, B. Do Profits "Crowd-Out" Donations or Vice Versa? The Impact of Revenues from Sales to Local Chapters of the American Red Cross. *Nonprofit Management and Leadership*, 1995, 6(1), 21–38.

Leete, L. Work in the Nonprofit Sector. In W. W. Powell and R. Steinberg (eds.), *The Nonprofit Sector: A Research Handbook* (2nd ed.). New Haven, CT: Yale University Press, 2006, 159–179.

Mayer, W. J., Wang, H. C., Egginton, J. F., and Flint, H. S. The Impact of Revenue Diversification on Expected Revenue and Volatility for Nonprofit Organizations. *Nonprofit and Voluntary Sector Quarterly*, 2012, 43(2), 374–392.

Mytelka, A. Cooper Union Will Start Collecting Tuition from Graduate Students. *The Chronicle of Higher Education*, April 24, 2012. Retrieved from http://chronicle.com/ blogs/ticker/cooper-union-will-start-collecting-tuition-from-graduate-students/ 42654.

Okten, C., and Weisbrod, B. A. Determinants of Donations in Private Nonprofit Markets. *Journal of Public Economics*, 2000, 75(2), 255–272.

Olson, M. *The Logic of Collective Action: Public Goods and the Theory of Groups*. Cambridge, MA: Harvard University Press, 1965.

Osili, U., Bhakta, R., Thayer, A., Hayat, A., Kalugyer, A. D., Hyatte, C.... Patterson, Z. Leveraging the Power of Foundations: An Analysis of Program-Related Investing. Lilly Family School of Philanthropy at Indiana University, 2013. Retrieved from www.philanthropy.iupui.edu/files/ research/complete_report_ final_51713.pdf.

Oster, S. M., Gray, C. M., and Weinberg, C. Pricing in the Nonprofit Sector. In D. R. Young (ed.), *Effective Economic Decision Making by Nonprofit Organizations*. New York: The Foundation Center, 2004, 27–45.

Preston, A. E., Volunteer Resources. In D. R. Young (ed.), *Financing Nonprofits*, Lanham, MD: AltaMira Press, 2007, 183–204.

Roeger, K., Blackwood, A., and Pettijohn, S. *The Nonprofit Almanac 2012*. Washington, DC: Urban Institute Press, 2012.

Salamon, L. M. Partners in Public Service: The Scope and Theory of Government-Nonprofit Relations. In W. W. Powell (ed.), *The Nonprofit Sector: A Research Handbook*. New Haven, CT: Yale University Press, 1987, 99–117.

Salamon, L. M., Sokolowski, S. W., and Associates. *Global Civil Society: Dimensions of the Nonprofit Sector* (Vol. 2). Bloomfield, CT: Kumarian Press, 2004.

Sandfort, J., Selden, S. C., and Sowa, J. E. Do Government Tools Influence Organizational Performance? Examining Their Implementation in Early Childhood Education. *The American Review of Public Administration,* 2008, 38(4), 412–438.

Saxton, G. D., and Wang, L. The Social Network Effect: The Determinants of Giving Through Social Media. *Nonprofit and Voluntary Sector Quarterly,* 2014, 43(5), 850–868.

Smith, D. H. The Rest of the Nonprofit Sector: Grass Roots Associations as the Dark Matter Ignored in Prevailing "Flat Earth" Maps of the Sector. *Nonprofit and Voluntary Sector Quarterly,* 1997, 26(2),114–131.

Smith, S. R., and Lipsky, M. *Nonprofits for Hire: The Welfare State in the Age of Contracting.* Cambridge, MA: Harvard University Press, 1993.

Steinberg, R. Does Government Spending Crowd Out Donations? Interpreting the Evidence. *Annals of Public and Cooperative Economics,* 1991, 62(4), 591–617.

Steinberg, R. Membership Income. In D. R. Young (ed.), *Financing Nonprofits.* Lanham, MD: AltaMira Press, 2007, 121–155.

Stewart. J. B. A Ransacked Endowment at New York City Opera. *The New York Times,* October 10, 2013. www.nytimes.com/2013/10/12/business/ransacking-the-endowment-at-new-york-cityopera.html?pagewanted=print.

Strom, S. Plan for Dozens of Salvation Army Centers Falters. *The New York Times,* June 14, 2009. www.nytimes.com/2009/06/15/us/15salvation.html?_r=0.

Vesterlund, L. Why Do People Give? In W. W. Powell and R. Steinberg (eds.), *The Nonprofit Sector: A Research Handbook* (2nd ed.). New Haven, CT: Yale University Press, 2006, 568–587.

Vilensky, M. New York Attorney General Eric Schneiderman Is Investigating Cooper Union. *The Wall Street Journal,* March 24, 2015. Retrieved from www.wsj.com/articles/new-york-attorney-general-eric-schneiderman-is-investigating-cooper-union-1427244617.

Wicker, P., Breuer, C., and Hennigs, B. Understanding the Interactions Among Revenue Categories Using Elasticity Measures—Evidence from a Longitudinal Sample of Non-Profit Sport Clubs in Germany. *Sport Management Review,* 2012, 15(3), 318–329.

Wing, K. T., Pollak, T. H., and Blackwood, A. *The Nonprofit Almanac 2008,* Washington, DC: The Urban Institute Press, 2008.

Young, D. R., and Steinberg, R. *Economics for Nonprofit Managers.* New York: The Foundation Center, 1995.

CHAPTER TWENTY

MANAGING THE CHALLENGES OF GOVERNMENT CONTRACTS*

Stephen Rathgeb Smith

During the last forty years, government contracting with nonprofit organizations for the delivery of important public services has risen sharply. The widespread interest, in the United States and in other countries, in contracting with nonprofit organizations reflects many factors: pressure to reduce the costs of public service; broad interest in voluntarism, social innovation, and citizen and community engagement; and public management reform which seeks to improve the efficiency and effectiveness of public services through privatization, more competition, individual choice, and decentralization (Phillips and Smith, 2011; Smith and Smyth, 2010). Nonprofits also represent diverse communities and local citizens, so policymakers may also turn to nonprofits to enhance the responsiveness and representativeness of public services. Government contracts also can be attractive from the perspective of the nonprofit organization, offering greater resources, improved legitimacy in the community and the potential to have broader and deeper impact on urgent social problems or concerns (De Hoog, 1984; Grønbjerg, 1993; Kramer, 1982; Smith and Lipsky, 1993).

Significantly, though, government contracting can have profound effects on nonprofit organization governance, program innovation, and the relationship of

*The author would like to gratefully acknowledge the excellent research assistance of Meghan McConaughey and the input of Putnam Barber in the preparation of this chapter.

agencies to their local communities and the citizens using their services (Smith, 2016; Smith and Lipsky, 1993). Moreover, political, economic, and organizational trends are creating much greater uncertainty for nonprofit organizations receiving such contracts than those that rely on other funding sources: competition for contracts among nonprofits and with for-profit firms is growing; government contract funds are scarcer; policymakers are expecting much higher levels of performance and accountability from nonprofits; and citizens are demanding more choice and responsiveness from nonprofits providing contracted services. In addition, governments at all levels are moving away from a reliance on contracts to support nonprofits and toward a more diverse set of financing tools, including vouchers, tax credits, tax-exempt bonds, and client-based fees for services such as Medicaid (Smith, 2016).

This chapter deals with the management challenges for nonprofit agencies created by contracting in an era of greater competition and environmental uncertainty. Potential strategies for nonprofit agencies to adopt to effectively cope with the higher accountability demands while successfully developing a sustainable, effective organization will also be discussed and highlighted. The chapter is based on extensive research on the impact of government contracting on nonprofit organizations, primarily in the fields of social services and health care, although many of the findings and management recommendations are applicable to other types of nonprofit organizations.

Background

Prior to the 1960s, nonprofit agencies in the United States were primarily dependent on private revenue from client fees, charitable donations, and endowment income. Some agencies such as child welfare organizations received public subsidies, but these agencies were nonetheless largely reliant on private funds. However, this funding mix changed dramatically in the 1960s with the rise of the federal role in social policy. As part of the War on Poverty, the federal government created a host of new programs and initiatives, including neighborhood health centers, community mental health centers, community action agencies, youth service agencies, and drug and alcohol treatment programs. Most of these new programs were implemented through government contracting with local nonprofit service organizations. Some of these agencies were entirely new; yet many existing agencies such as Catholic Charities and Lutheran Social Services also expanded their service offerings in response to the dramatic increase in federal funding support for social and health services (Smith and Lipsky, 1993).

Many nonprofit agencies were initially reluctant to accept government contracts due to concern that government funding might undermine their mission and autonomy (Kramer, 1982; Smith and Lipsky, 1993). However, most of these agencies eventually accepted government contracts. This shift occurred for several reasons. First, some federal programs were matching programs so a private agency might be able to use a 25 percent private match to obtain a 75 percent matching grant from the federal government. So at least initially, federal revenues essentially allowed the expansion of existing services. Second, some of the early federal grant programs had very loose accountability requirements, so nonprofit agencies could accept the funds without onerous compliance requirements, thus allowing substantial discretion by nonprofits on the management and implementation of their programs. Third, federal grants offered many agencies far more money than they could reasonably expect from private philanthropy and fees. Fourth, and relatedly, federal funding allowed nonprofit agencies to reduce their dependence on private donations and fees, allowing agencies in some cases to increase their services to disadvantaged and very needy clients. And fifth, many federal programs were structured as grants to state and local governments who then contracted with local agencies. Often, state and local government officials already had established relationships with local nonprofits agencies such as Catholic Charities. With the advent of federal funding, state government officials tended to simply continue these relationships and, at least initially, did not change the terms of the existing agreements between the nonprofit agency and government (Smith, 2016).

Federal spending on contracts soared in the 1960s and 1970s, through direct contracts with nonprofits and more indirectly through grants to the states which then contracted with local community organizations (Smith and Lipsky, 1993). Many state agencies relied almost exclusively on nonprofit agencies to provide services, especially new and innovative services such as community residential programs, respite care, and day treatment.

This increased federal role changed dramatically when the Reagan administration reduced federal spending on many community programs provided by nonprofits, and devolved more responsibility for federal grant programs to the states (Smith, 2012). Over time, though, federal spending rebounded, in part through the expansion of existing grant programs or via the enactment of new programs in areas such as child welfare, workforce development, and community residential programs for the homeless and disadvantaged. Through a variety of changes to existing law as well as new program initiatives, funds for social and health services provided by nonprofit agencies rose again in the late 1980s and 1990s.

Contracting with nonprofits grew in the aftermath of the landmark welfare reform legislation of 1996. As part of this legislation, the federal government created new funding for services and gave greater administrative discretion to state and local governments to spend the new money, including much greater flexibility by local administrators to shift money from cash assistance to services. At least initially, many states used the increased administrative discretion to increase contracting with local community agencies to provide various support services to individuals on welfare, including day care, welfare to work, job training, and counseling programs. Other federal programs reliant on contracting with nonprofits also increased in the late 1990s and early 2000s, including programs for at-risk youth, community service, drug and alcohol treatment, prisoner reentry, and home care.

Since the early 2000s, though, non-health spending on social programs has been in a long-term decline, especially after the 2008 recession (Gais, Dadayan, Bae, 2009; Lynch, 2014). Even before the recession, many federal social programs had essentially been either level-funded or incrementally reduced each year; for grant programs such as the Social Service Block Grant (SSBG) these resulted in a sharp drop in value over time in inflation-adjusted terms (Lynch, 2014). Federal funding for child welfare services has also declined (DeVooght, Fletcher, and Cooper, 2014, p. 2). Likewise, state government funding of key social programs declined during the 2000s after a period of sharp growth in the mid- to late-1990s (Gais, Dadayan, and Bae, 2009). With the onset of the recession of 2008, many state governments dramatically cut funding for social programs, resulting in often sharp cutbacks in staffing and services by community-based nonprofit agencies (Harrison, Eleveld, and Ahern, 2011; National Council of Nonprofits, 2010; Pettijohn and Boris, 2013). As the economy has recovered, states have been able to replace some of the lost funding; nonetheless, the recovery has been very uneven, with many states still struggling to fund their social and health programs (see, for example, Palmer and Robertson, 2016).

Two policy fields are the exception to this overall trend of cutbacks and slow recovery, albeit unevenly. First, Medicaid has emerged as a central funder for community-based, nonprofit social service programs—a trend that dates to the 1980s. But the cutbacks in federal and state funding programs like SSBG has accelerated this shift, particularly for services for the mentally ill, developmentally disabled, and at-risk youth. For instance, in 1980, most public funding for services for the developmentally disabled came from state dollars, but because of Medicaid's Home and Community Based Services waiver program, federal dollars (and the state match) through Medicaid are currently the primary funder for these services (Andrews, Grogan, Brennan, and Pollack, 2015;

Braddock, Hemp, Rizzolo, Tanis, Haffer, and Wu, 2015; Ng, Harrington, Musumeci, and Reaves, 2015).

Medicaid funding for community nonprofit health agencies has also increased sharply in the last few years because of the implementation of the Affordable Care Act (ACA). The high-profile legislation offers significant federal subsidies to states that decide to expand eligibility for Medicaid. As of 2015, over half of the states have taken advantage of these subsidies and increased eligibility and services for low-income and disabled individuals (Snyder and Rudowitz, 2015). This effort has, in turn, led to sharp rises in federal funding of community health centers and other related community health programs such as substance abuse clinics.

The second policy field with growth in government funding of nonprofit organizations is early childhood and kindergarten through grade twelve (K–12) education. As states have changed their laws in recent years, the number of charter schools—largely financed by government—has risen from 1,542 in 1999–2000 to 6,440 in 2013–2014 (Public Agenda, 2014). Many of these charter schools are independent nonprofit schools, while over 30 percent of the total number of charter schools are overseen by management companies, including large nonprofit management entities like the Knowledge Is Power Program (KIPP) (Miron and Gulosino, 2013). Importantly, the growth in nonprofit charters has occurred in the context of falling overall funding for K–12 education in many states (Leachman, Albares, Masterson, and Wallace, 2016). The result for local nonprofits, including charter schools, is often underfunding and intense competition for contracts and resources.

In sum, the funding environment for nonprofits with government contracts has been very turbulent: cutbacks have often occurred with relatively little notice; state and local governments continue to face fiscal scarcity, despite the recovery of the economy; and alternative sources of revenue for nonprofits such as private philanthropy and earned income are difficult for many nonprofits to raise. Moreover, significant changes have been under way in the form government funding takes via diversification of the tools of government funding, with profound effects on the management of nonprofit organizations and their relationship to government and their communities.

Ironically though, this competitive and austere funding climate is likely to encourage continued reliance on government funding for nonprofits through contracts and other funding tools. State and local governments, eager to save money, often view contracting as a less costly way of providing needed public services. The widespread interest in social innovation and social entrepreneurship is also fueling government support through contracts with nonprofits with novel but proven program models.

A Restructured Contracting Relationship

Even before the economic crisis, nonprofit agencies receiving government contracts were facing important shifts in their funding and their relationship with other government, nonprofit and for-profit organizations as well as their host communities. These developments have profoundly affected the contracting relationship, as well as the staffs and clients of nonprofit agencies. Significantly, even though it had increased such funding until 2008, government had moved away from the traditional contracts that were the hallmark of the initial period of widespread government contracting in the 1960s and 1970s. In this earlier period, most nonprofit agencies did not really compete with other agencies for contracts. Most contracts were cost-reimbursement contracts that paid agencies for their costs based on the contract terms and budget. Reimbursement was not linked to outcomes, and most agencies recovered their costs (at least as specified in the contract). Little incentive existed for agencies to compete with other agencies since contracts were unlikely to be moved from one agency to another unless egregious problems existed.

The current contracting environment is much more competitive, with higher levels of expectation based on performance. Many government contracts with nonprofits are performance-based, with government specifying the program targets that nonprofits are required to meet in order to receive reimbursement for their services (Desai, Garabedian, and Snyder, 2012; Fraser and Whitehill, 2014; Smith, 2016; Smith and Grinker, 2004). These performance-based contracts are now widely used in many different service fields, including child welfare, mental health, workforce development, and low-income housing.

These performance-based contracts are part of a broader movement affecting public and nonprofit management called "pay-for-success" (PFS) (Corporation for National and Community Service, 2015; In the Public Interest, 2015; Roman, Walsh, Bieler, and Taxy, 2014). A relatively recent innovation in performance-based contracting is the development of "social impact bonds" (SIBs) that depend on private investors loaning money to a third-party intermediary, which then subcontracts with a local nonprofit service agency on a performance contracting basis. The project is evaluated by independent researchers and government repays the loan to investors if the performance targets are met. Despite widespread publicity to SIBS, they remain quite limited in terms of their impact on services, in part because of their complexity and high transaction costs.

Performance contracts and "pay for success" models are especially consequential because they increase organizational and revenue uncertainty and because these contracts offer at least the threat of contract termination for poor performance (although, in practice, losing contracts remains infrequent). Nonprofit service agencies also have an incentive to compete with their fellow agencies since they could potentially grow through additional contracts. Also, performance contracts are usually structured so that agencies receive graduated payments as they hit their performance targets; thus, agencies may receive less revenue than planned, reducing their available cash flow.

Increased competition for funding is also a direct and indirect effect of the restructuring of government support itself. In the big build-up of government contracting with nonprofits, government funding primarily flowed to nonprofits through block contracts for a certain levels of service. However, many current forms of government support are tied to the client rather than the agency. The most vivid example is Medicaid, which functions like a "quasi-voucher" since eligibility is tied directly to the client (Steuerle, 2000). Agencies are reimbursed for providing qualifying services to eligible clients; their reimbursement rate is a vendor rate, whereby government will pay a certain amount for a specific service regardless of the actual costs incurred by the agency. In general, Medicaid vendor rates encourage competition for clients, since it may only be possible to generate surpluses at high levels of service volume (because each new Medicaid-eligible client is more revenue for the agency at only marginally more cost). This financing arrangement is dramatically different from the traditional cost-reimbursement contract. Under the latter, agencies actually faced disincentives for service expansion because additional services added to an agency's cost without any certainty that these costs would be reimbursed.

The diversification of government support—or policy tools (Salamon, 2002; Smith, 2016)—is also evident in the growing use of vouchers for child care and housing and tax-exempt bond money to support the capital needs of nonprofit agencies. Access to bond funding can be very competitive and subject to the state budget cycle; nonetheless it has become an important source of capital financing for many nonprofit agencies providing community-based services (Calabrese and Ely, 2015).

The scarcity of contract funding, the emphasis on performance, and the growth in the number of nonprofit agencies (McKeever, 2015) fueled growing competition from for-profit social and health services firms, especially in community-based services like home care, child care, early childhood education, and mental health. Many for-profits possess some notable advantages vis-à-vis nonprofits in competition for government contracts (and private fees). For example, for-profit chains have access to capital and operate at a sufficient size to enable substantial economies of scale, allowing them to operate at least some programs more efficiently. Further, since nonprofits are mission-based and many are small and unwilling to serve certain types of clients or certain regions, the opportunities for them to cross-subsidize their operations through growth or a diversified client mix are reduced. Many community-based nonprofits may also be very ambivalent about expansion (or even lack the capacity for expansion). For-profits typically do not have these types of mission constraints and are thus more willing or able to serve a more diverse mix of clients. Finally, larger for-profits may be able to use their size and bargaining power to obtain higher rates than the small community-based nonprofits. As a result of these factors, the percentage share of the market among for-profits has been rising for the last twenty years in these community services such as home care and child care (U.S. Census Bureau, 2015).

Contracting as a Regime

This turbulent and more competitive environment for contracting is disrupting (and has the potential to further disrupt) many longstanding relationships between government and nonprofit agencies. During the development of extensive contracting in the 1960s and 1970s, contracting tended to evolve through patterned relationships and expectations between government and nonprofit agencies that could be characterized as a "contracting regime" (that is, "a set of stable relationships that transcend simple common practice and reveal assumptions about the way the world works" [Smith and Lipsky, 1993, p. 43]). The historic nonprofit-government contracting relationship could be characterized as a "regime" for the following reasons. First, regimes tend to have accepted means of resolving disputes and addressing particular problems. This is evident in the tendency to rely upon nonprofit organizations funded by government to address current social problems, and in the existence of accepted norms governing the interaction between nonprofit organizations and government. Second, the regime concept is helpful in illuminating the regularized patterns of interaction between government and nonprofit agencies, even when these nonprofit organizations are opposed or resistant to particular government regulations and mandates. Third, regimes are marked by continuity, and participants in regimes are mutually dependent. If participants depart from the regime norms, they are penalized, either by the dominant party or by third parties. Fourth, regimes are usually sustained and dominated by a powerful party. For example, in international relations, this role is performed by a country whose policies and norms are accepted by other countries in the regime (Krasner, 1982). The government-nonprofit relationship is similar; despite the mutual dependency of government and nonprofit organizations, government tends to be the more powerful in the relationship. Thus, nonprofit organizations are often in the position of being forced to accept or follow the norms and policies of government (Considine, 2000; Smith and Lipsky, 1993).

The implications of the contracting regime for nonprofit management are profound. Managers of nonprofit agencies receiving government contracts are not free agents but are linked in an ongoing relationship with government, which at once constrains their behavior as well as provides certain incentives for organizational strategy, including a susceptibility to government influence. The vulnerability of nonprofit agencies receiving government contracts reflects the important characteristics of nonprofit finance, especially in the fields of social and health services. Nonprofit agencies, especially grassroots community organizations such as battered women's shelters, poverty agencies, and youth organizations, emerge through the collective efforts of like-minded individuals interested in addressing a particular social problem. Typically, these organizations are dependent on a mix of small cash and in-kind donations. As a result, they tend to be significantly undercapitalized. Overcoming the capitalization dilemma is hampered by the preference of private donors for specific programs and projects. This undercapitalization can be exacerbated by many banks' reluctance to lend money to nonprofits, especially smaller agencies. Such constraints on building an adequate capital base make it difficult to weather disruptions in cash flow. When nonprofit organizations are young, mostly volunteer, and small, a cash flow interruption may represent a minor problem. But when a nonprofit becomes involved in a contractual arrangement with government, the implications of cash flow disruptions often are more serious. Contracting typically requires more resources, such as more paid staff with higher salaries and greater levels of professionalization (Hwang and Powell, 2009), hence much higher cash flow demands. Thus, shortfalls in client censuses, management miscues, payment delays, or unexpected expenses are much more disruptive and problematic. For some agencies, cash flow problems in the current competitive contract environment can encourage mergers—or even the outright closure of some agencies.

Importantly, the uncertainty of contract revenue has been exacerbated by changes in the structure of the government-nonprofit contracting relationship. In the early years of widespread contracting, most contracts entailed a direct relationship between government and the nonprofit agency, such as a direct contract between state or federal government and a local nonprofit social service agency. But this relationship has evolved significantly through the involvement of a wide variety of intermediary organizations. Managed care organizations are one prominent example in health and social services, including child welfare and mental health (Courtney, 2000; McBeath and Meezan, 2010). In particular, many states contract with managed care organizations (MCOs) for their Medicaid spending; these MCOs then contract with local nonprofit and for-profit service providers. This increase in intermediary relationships is evident in various public-private partnerships that have become more common in the last twenty-five years. For example, a nationwide initiative called Funders Together to End Homelessness strives to bring together the resources and expertise of multiple funders in order to develop a more coordinated and effective strategy to end homelessness (Wertheimer, 2011). Many other similar public-private partnerships exist around the country in services such as early childhood education and workforce development.

Overall, the growth of these intermediary associations has created greater turbulence and less predictability in the contracting relationship from the perspective of the nonprofit agency, thus contributing to financial challenges and uncertainty. The cash flow problem, as well as the more general challenge of generating adequate revenue, is exacerbated by a common characteristic of the contracting regime: the inability to secure contracts that fully fund the agency's costs. Given the continuing budgetary volatility faced by many state governments, government officials across the country routinely set rates for nonprofit providers at levels insufficient to cover their costs. Multiple factors account for this shortfall: a contract may have declined in inflation-adjusted terms due to government budget cuts and austerity; a nonprofit manager may have underestimated the contract implementation costs; or government may saddle the agency with unexpected expenses or fail to provide the expected revenue. In this performance-based contracting environment, the latter is a much greater possibility than in the past. Also, agency expenses may rise unexpectedly and exceed contract revenues.

Underfunded contracts put nonprofit managers in a delicate position: relinquish the contract, with its implications for staff layoffs and shrinkage of the agency, or continue with the contract, albeit at an underfunded level. Since nonprofit executives are rarely rewarded for staff layoffs and the accompanying organizational turmoil, most nonprofit executives elect to keep the contract. To compensate for revenue shortfalls from contracts, nonprofit managers often try one or more of several strategies: (1) diversify their government contracts so they can obtain greater economies of scale and mitigate their risk from any one particular contract; (2) seek private donations from individuals or corporations;(3) obtain foundation grants; (4) increase earned income such as rental or technical assistance income; and (5) attempt to directly or indirectly tap fee income from government sources, including Medicaid, vouchers, or tax credits such as the Low Income Housing Tax Credit (LIHTC).

Obtaining additional revenue in the current economic climate is especially challenging though. Intense competition exists for private donations and government contracts, and many agencies lack the infrastructure and capacity to effectively compete for government contracts, raise private donations, or generate earned income. Consequently, large nonprofit agencies and for-profit firms have a decided competitive advantage, since they are more likely to have access to adequate credit lines or bank loans and possess the professional staff to raise private donations and launch commercial ventures.

The Challenges of Contract Renewal

The greater uncertainty of the contracting environment for nonprofits has exacerbated longstanding problems that may occur in the contract renewal process. Delays and problems in contract renewal occur for many reasons: a state legislature may be deadlocked, requiring that the state agencies suspend final action on contract renewals until the available funding for contracts is known; key government contract administrators may have left or been replaced; an election may be under way, generating funding uncertainty and job insecurity with resultant ripple effects on the contracting process.

Other reasons for delay may be more strategic. For example, government contract administrators may delay the process of contract renewal in order to gain greater compliance by nonprofit agencies with contract terms and expectations. Alternatively, government administrators may use their ability to expedite the contract-renewal process, to at least some degree, as a way of currying favor with nonprofit contract agencies. This assistance may then be remembered in future negotiations.

The uncertainties of the contract renewal process are masked somewhat by the relatively high rate of contract renewal, despite the increase in performance-based contracts. A domestic violence agency awarded a contract in 2005 is likely to still have a contract in 2015, barring egregious quality problems or major shocks to the provider system. Nonetheless, the renewal process can be highly frustrating. Nonprofit managers may be unclear as to the exact amount of the new contract. And, due to government funding cutbacks, a renewed contract might well be for a lower amount than the previous one. Also, government officials may decide to rewrite the contract upon renewal. For instance, a child welfare agency might have a contract for several years to provide counseling services to children. But a change in political priorities might lead state administrators to use contract renewal as an opportunity to restructure the agreement so that the child welfare agency, if it wants to keep the contract, would be required to provide (for example) intervention services to abused and neglected children. Other examples of substantive changes in contracts by state officials include requiring nonprofit agencies to serve a larger geographical area, giving part of a contract to another agency, reducing the administrative costs allowed on the contract, and adopting new policies on client referrals and reimbursement.

Nonprofit managers, at least theoretically, have the option of refusing to accept the terms of the contract or to abide the long delays often accompanying contract renewal. Yet, managers are often ill-positioned to challenge or refuse the contract. First, the proliferation of nonprofit (and for-profit) service agencies gives government administrators more service options (although the number of agencies varies tremendously across geographic areas). Thus, nonprofit managers know that if they resist the renegotiation of a contract, many other agencies are likely to be eager to take the contract on the terms stipulated by government. Second, competition for private charitable funds, which might serve as alternatives to contract funds, is fierce. Moreover, most foundation and United Way grants tend to be short-term and for much smaller amounts than government funds. And raising private funds with appeals to individuals is a long-term process that usually cannot substitute for lost government funds. Third, nonprofit agencies often find that the only way they can fulfill their mission to address a particular problem, such as juvenile delinquency or child abuse, is through government funding; private funding is either unavailable or inadequate for the agency's needs.

Strategic Management in an Era of Impact, Competition, and Accountability

Despite the increasingly uncertain and competitive environment for nonprofits contracting with government, many nonprofit executives are nonetheless able to develop sustainable, effective business models for their organizations. This strategic success requires sustained attention to agency governance, effective leadership, the development of broad and sustained community support, and ongoing advocacy on behalf of the agency and its clients.

Rethinking Agency Governance and Management

An effective board of directors of a nonprofit agency serves as a key connecting link between the organization and the local community. This board role is especially critical if community-based service agencies are to effectively represent their communities and service users. Yet, contracting poses complicated governance challenges for many boards. Most board members tend to be unfamiliar with contracting and the intricacies of the contracting process. Consequently, board members may be unable or unwilling to exercise effective oversight over agency contracts.

Significantly, contracting also requires the agency to develop and maintain effective new systems of accountability to document and report on expenditures and clients, almost inevitably requiring greater staff specialization and professionalization (Hwang and Powell, 2009), more formal organizational structure, and new investments in agency capacity and infrastructure. As the paid staff expands and the demands on the agency's resources grow, the board may not be well positioned to set the agenda for the agency, especially if they are highly dependent on contract revenues. The board may be relegated to a position of supporting the executive's initiatives, rather than the executive implementing the board's directives and policies. For the organization, the danger inherent in this kind of shift is that the board may encounter some unpleasant surprises. The executive, in the pursuit of contract revenues, may obligate the agency to contracts that are underfunded or ill-advised. Board involvement in the agency may wither as board members find that their governance roles are restricted. And as board involvement declines, management mistakes or morale problems may go undetected until a crisis develops.

Other types of management problems may develop due to conflicts over agency mission. For example, the board of a relatively young nonprofit may be comprised of the founding members of the organization who are deeply committed to a specific mission and vision. In some cases, to secure additional contract funds, an executive may try to steer the organization in a direction that is quite different from the board's vision for the agency. The result may be protracted negotiations between the board and staff about the agency's future. Sometimes, the outcome is the resignation of some board members or the ouster of the chief executive as the board and staff compete to define the agency's future mission. Alternatively, the executive may serve in the key role in agency governance until a crisis develops, such as inadequate cash flow, staff discontent, or lost contracts. Then, in response, the board may intervene to exert greater control and oversight over agency operations. Although the board often withdraws to its previous role as the crisis eases, in other cases the board simply may be unable to find an appropriate executive director and so the board will retain a major role in day-to-day agency management as well as the overall agenda setting for the organization.

Overall, a general tendency exists among nonprofits with substantial contracts to see a shift in influence from the board to the executive director and his or her staff, although the extent of this change will differ with organizations' individual circumstances. This change can be especially visible in new community-based organizations with roots in the informal sector of community members, neighbors, and social movements. For these organizations, professional management often represents values and policies at variance to the original purposes of the organization, and the result can be significant internal dissension

To an extent, the enhanced role of the executive and the professionalization of the staff is part of the natural process of the nonprofit organizational life cycle that entails greater formalization as a nonprofit evolves and grows (Carlson and Donohoe, 2010, pp. 119–126; Speakman Management Consulting, 2009). Thus, the challenge for nonprofits is to successfully adapt their organizations to the imperatives of professionalization and formalization attending to contracting (and organizational growth) while maintaining the commitment of staff and volunteers to their organizing mission. Critical to the successful adaptation of the organization is strengthening board governance and developing positive, productive board-staff relations. First, the board can recruit individuals with knowledge of contracting for board membership. Second, the board can develop a broad base of community support for the agency. A number of strategies exist to achieve this goal: regular community forums to engage citizen feedback; advisory committees of community members; more diverse board membership; participation by agency staff on other local committees and boards; and increased engagement with the policy process at the local, regional, or state level. And third, the board can support investments in infrastructure and capacity to help the agency to effectively manage the contracting development and implementation process. Chapter Five of this *Handbook* provides important additional information on organization, development, and maintenance of nonprofit governing boards.

Finding the Right Executive

Given the changing environment for contracting, the quality of executive leadership is more important than ever to the ability of nonprofits to provide effective and efficient programming. In the current era of budget scarcity, even a relatively small management mistake can create a financial crisis for the agency. Consequently, significant pressure exists on the executive director to effectively manage both the internal operations and the external network of public and private funders. Ideally, agency executives should be very knowledgeable of government contracting and financial management, as well as sensitive to the agency's mission. Given the multiple economic and organizational challenges facing executive directors, the process of selecting an executive director can often reveal underlying differences among members of the board and staff about the agency's future. Moreover, many individuals with the credentials necessary to cope with the management complexities of contracting may not be well attuned to the subtleties of the agency's relationship with its surrounding community or consumers. This situation can be exacerbated in the current era of funding cutbacks, when executive directors may need to make difficult programmatic or administrative decisions.

Given these leadership challenges, the ideal type of executive for a nonprofit service agency cannot be determined without understanding the particular characteristics and needs of the organization. And although it may no longer be sufficient to have a respected clinician with relatively little management training or experience as an executive, it is equally true that a board of directors would be in error if it simply sought an executive whose primary qualification was government contracting experience or a business management background. Instead, an agency needs to strike a balance between a concern for the efficient utilization of resources, due in part to the demands of the contracting regime, and sound financial management with a commitment to agency mission. Thus, agencies might choose executives from the government and business sectors who have also demonstrated support for the agency's mission through board and volunteer service.

Arguably, the current contracting environment also places a primacy on the ability of nonprofit executives to work collaboratively, both internally and externally. Competition and scarcity of funding mean that executive directors need to be able to work closely and productively with government contract administrators. In addition, agency executives need to be able to partner with local foundations, other nonprofits, and local businesses. Indeed, many government contracts now require agencies to collaborate with other agencies. Also, collaboration on back-office and benefit costs may help nonprofits become more efficient and better cope with funding scarcity.

The higher expectations for social impact and innovation also encourage nonprofit executives to build their internal organization to foster learning, effective problem solving, and new and creative strategies to achieve individual and "collective impact" (Kania and Kramer, 2011). This effort also calls for a strategic, forward-looking vision for the agency, rather than simply reacting to external demands or developments, including the expectations of government contract agency. Moreover, while it is certainly common for government contract administrators to specify in great detail the expectations for contracts, many contracts have vague or unclear performance expectations, at least initially, requiring that the government administrators and nonprofit leaders work together to develop appropriate performance expectations. Chapter Six of this volume presents an extensive discussion of the demands for effective executive leadership.

Broadening the Agency Constituency

Nonprofit agencies, as noted, typically represent, at their founding, the efforts of like-minded people to address a particular problem. Often these organizations are not representative of their community as a whole; many agencies are directed by people from a particular political, ideological, ethnic, or income group in a community. Indeed, many nonprofit organizations are valued for their ability to represent specialized or minority constituencies (Smith and Lipsky, 1993). This community of interest focus can become a handicap as an agency develops and obtains contracts from the government: the board may be small; broader community connections may be weak; political support may be lacking; and government priorities for the target population and clients may over time be at variance with the nonprofit's priorities.

Successful and sustainable nonprofits with government contracts are able to transcend the initial limited focus of the agency and relative lack of professionalization of the board and staff while retaining their strong mission commitment. Key to this is a diversification and broadening of the organization's constituency. Toward this end, an agency may create an affiliate organization that can help with fundraising, community support, and program visibility. Typically, these organizations are directed by the paid staff of the parent organization, but are operated primarily by volunteers. A nonprofit also may alter the composition of its board in order to engage key supporters in the oversight and governance processes of the organization. Further, an agency might join community organizations, such as the Chamber of Commerce. The regular presence of a nonprofit agency at Chamber meetings can go a long way toward creating a role for the agency as a vital and important member of the community.

An agency may also alter its rules for membership. As noted earlier, many nonprofit organizations were established by a relatively small number of people who formed the core of the initial board of directors; no official membership in the organization apart from the board and staff existed. Often, in these situations, the board of directors is self-perpetuating rather than elected by the membership. Such a board structure can work against wide and sustained community engagement. Thus, a nonprofit agency may be well served by rethinking the concept of membership and consider engaging community members and service users as members (voting or non-voting) of the organization. This approach can offer important friends of the organization a stake in the agency and help recruit new supporters and volunteers. Over time, these new members could be very helpful in mobilizing community and political support on behalf of the agency as well as promoting greater accountability. To be sure, this type of membership is not appropriate for all nonprofit agencies. Nonetheless, service agencies with roots in a local community might benefit from rethinking their membership structure.

One strategy to engage the community that may achieve some of the same goals as changes in membership is the use of advisory committees (or other more informal governance entities) as complements to the board of directors. Advisory structures can be especially helpful for specialized purposes such as strategic planning, advocacy, or a new capital campaign for the organization (Saidel, 1998; Smith, forthcoming).

Constituency development can also be achieved through strategic partnerships and collaborations with other nonprofit, public, and for-profit organizations. Partnerships with local businesses can help with private fundraising, political support for the agency, and the recruitment of volunteers and board members. Collaborations with other nonprofits can yield potential savings on administrative costs and potentially help win new grants and contracts, given the current emphasis of public and private funders on collaboration among nonprofit service agencies. The entire subject of nonprofit partnerships and collaboration is discussed in more depth in Chapter Fifteen of this volume.

It must be noted that enlarging an agency's constituency is not without risks. New members or supporters may try to change the agency's mission and lead it in new directions. An agency may trade dependency on state contract administrators for dependency on a powerful donor or group of donors. More community members may make the organization more risk-averse. Mobilizing community members can be complicated, and it is often difficult to organize a representative sample of local citizens in support of the organization. Nonetheless, greater community connections can be helpful in improving nonprofit programs despite these difficulties. Engaging with citizens in providing programmatic support can provide valuable information for program improvement and build social capital that can be a base to build donor and volunteer involvement in the agency.

Engaging the Policy Process

Prior to the advent of widespread government contracting, nonprofit service agencies tended to operate quite apart from the political process. Dependent primarily on private revenues, management decisions, and the fate of the organization were relatively disconnected from decisions made by state and local legislatures, the federal government, or governors and mayors. The practice of government contracting fundamentally changed this situation; nonprofit agencies with contracts are now inextricably connected to the political process.

Important political decisions, legislation, and administrative rulings can have a profound impact on the success of nonprofits and their leaders. For example, if a legislature refuses to allocate sufficient funds for a contract rate increase, the nonprofit may be forced to reduce staff, with the resultant implications for morale and program quality. Accountability requirements instituted by the legislature or government administrators may also have a major impact on staff priorities and activities. Contract requirements and/or funding cutbacks may require agencies to collaborate, merge, or go out of business entirely. Even relatively minor or technical changes to eligibility requirements or rate levels can have an enormous impact on the capacity of local nonprofit agencies to deliver quality services. Sometimes, nonprofits providing contract services may need special zoning permits in order to house their facilities. Often, local nonprofits receive cash and in-kind subsidies from municipalities. Special linkages with local government may also be required. For example, a nonprofit child welfare agency may need to work very closely with the local school districts, or the users of nonprofit services may need to use public transportation in order to receive agency services.

Importantly, government officials possess many tools to restructure or alter a contract in ways unfavorable to a nonprofit agency. Contract administrators may want to refer different types of clients to the agency. Or the state may want to restrict or curtail certain contract expenditures. The state may even want to end the contract altogether and award it to another agency. Personal appeals by the executive, the board of directors, or intervention by community political supporters may produce a reversal of unfavorable decisions, although many nonprofit agencies (especially smaller or newer agencies) frequently lack substantial political clout, creating a vulnerability to government influence. In short, the success of nonprofits now hinges, at least in part, on effective agency advocacy, especially at the state and local level. As a result, nonprofit executives and their boards need to be actively engaged with policymakers on an ongoing basis, including maintaining an agency's visibility and support. Thus, nonprofit boards and staff should enlist the support of local political figures, including municipal leaders and state legislators. This goal may be accomplished in part by selecting key community leaders to be agency board members. More routinely, nonprofit staff and boards should make local leaders aware of agency activities through the active use of social media, the agency's website, print mailings, and other local publications, including newspapers.

As nonprofit staff and volunteers engage in advocacy, they should also strive to represent the needs of their clients and communities, broadly defined. Nonprofit agencies receiving government contracts tend to be most involved in policy issues such as funding and regulations directly relevant to the agency itself (Mosley, 2014; Smith and Lipsky, 1993). Ideally, though, nonprofit agencies should also strive to advocate on behalf of broader user and community needs and issues, such as the lack of affordable housing, persistent poverty, and community economic development.

Despite these strong incentives for advocacy due to the dynamics of contracting, many nonprofit staff and board members are reluctant to engage in advocacy on behalf of their agency or their clients. They are wary because they fear that it might spur scrutiny from the Internal Revenue Service or other government regulators, perhaps leading to threats to their tax-exempt status or serious fines (Bass, Arons, Guinane, and Carter, 2007; Berry, 2003; Pekkanen, Smith, and Tsujinaka, 2014). Further, many agencies are quite small and lack the staff resources to actively engage in advocacy. The board members of many nonprofits tend to be attracted to board service due to their commitment to the agency's mission and services such as child welfare or homelessness. Most board members possess little formal advocacy experience. Relatedly, board members may be unfamiliar with regulations on permissible advocacy by nonprofits, especially 501(c)(3) charitable organizations. Nonprofit agencies can be effective advocates in spite of these obstacles, but to do so does require persistence and a multipronged strategy, including education of board and staff on legal issues; investment in staff with expertise on advocacy; and building positive network relationships with government officials. Chapter Fourteen of this volume provides a practical explanation of how nonprofits can effectively engage in such advocacy.

Importantly, nonprofits should work collaboratively with other nonprofits as well as through local and statewide associations and coalitions to influence government policy. Three important types of nonprofit associations and coalitions exist. The first type are mission- or service-specific associations, such as the North Carolina Association of Home Care Agencies and the Massachusetts Association of Community Mental Health Centers; these coalitions and associations tend to be quite homogeneous in terms of organizational type. The second category are statewide nonprofit associations representing all nonprofits in the state. Prominent examples include the California Association of Nonprofits and the Maryland Association of Nonprofits. Typically, these associations are heavily involved in various government contracting issues, including funding levels. These statewide associations are also represented at the national level by the National Council of Nonprofits, which advocates at the federal level and throughout the United States on important policy concerns of direct relevance to nonprofits and government contracting. Indeed, one of the top priorities of the National Council was the implementation in 2014 of a rule issue by the U.S. Office of Management and Budget (OMB) requiring that the federal government pay reasonable overhead and administrative costs to nonprofits that receive federal contracts (National Council of Nonprofits, 2016). A third type of association or coalition is a public interest organization dedicated to a particular policy cause, such as Medicaid expansion or ending homelessness. These coalitions typically attract a diverse membership and often have private foundation funding to support their goals and objectives (Boyarski, 2016). These coalitions can be quite helpful in pushing broader social policy goals as well as increased government funding—such as Medicaid expansion—that benefit nonprofit organizations and their local communities. Overall, each of these different types of associations and coalitions can help nonprofits develop broader networks in support of their agencies (Chandler and Kennedy, 2015). Statewide associations and coalitions can also assist member agencies with more operational concerns, such as insurance and liability issues, human resource problems, and bulk purchasing. To be sure, some associations are small and many may lack paid staff. Nonetheless, in an era of greater competition and funding scarcity, nonprofit associations and coalitions can be important resources for nonprofit agencies with government contracts.

Innovation and Reform in Contracting

The sharp expansion of contracting with nonprofits in the United States and beyond has been accompanied by persistent nonprofit complaints about the contracting process itself, including lack of transparency, overly burdensome regulations and reporting requirements, inappropriate performance targets, and underinvestment in infrastructure. In response, government and nonprofits have tried different types of reforms and innovations.

First, many performance-based contracts represent the imposition of specific outcome targets on nonprofit organizations with little input from these agencies. However, many performance-based contract negotiations begin with a decided lack of adequate information on the appropriate outcomes; thus, the construction of the contract can be a process of mutual discovery and problem solving. This point is another reason why nonprofits need to invest in their own capacity to manage and implement contracts; government officials may be looking to them for input. Second, a persistent lament among nonprofits is excessive regulation of nonprofit contract agency budgets, greatly limiting spending flexibility (Pettijohn and Boris, 2013). Further, the spread of performance-based contracts and "pay-for-success models" has often meant much greater attention to outcomes without a corresponding reduction in paperwork on accounting for specific line-item expenditures. Consequently, initiatives for innovation and reform in contracting have increasingly focused on identifying ways in which government can hold nonprofits accountable for expenditure of government funds while not imposing unnecessary restrictions. In many jurisdictions, officials and nonprofit agencies have been attempting to reduce regulatory burdens and at the same time achieve positive outcomes. For example, New York City has established the Health and Human Services Accelerator, which seeks to streamline the procurement process with local nonprofit (and for-profit) service providers. Many other jurisdictions have been exploring or implementing similar policies to reduce the regulatory burden of contracting (National Council of Nonprofits, 2014).

In addition, a wide variety of efforts are being devoted to more self-regulation by nonprofit service providers as a strategy to raise service standards while reducing the need for intensive government regulation. One example involves new initiatives in the area of accreditation, which typically specify a minimum standard of service that is detailed by the accrediting body. For example, nonprofit organizations in Herefordshire in the United Kingdom created their own accreditation system, which is administered by a third-party organization; government agrees to only contract with accredited agencies (Smith and Smyth, 2010). Other examples include the Commission on the Accreditation of Rehabilitation Facilities (CARF) and the Joint Commission (which accredits health care organizations). Increasingly, governments are looking to these accrediting bodies to certify minimum standards of quality in services provided by nonprofit (and sometimes for-profit) service providers in social and health care.

Also, growing interest exists in the United States and abroad in developing quality frameworks specifically tailored for nonprofit organizations. Thus, Maryland Nonprofits (2016) developed its Standards for Excellence program, which details ethical and quality guidelines for the governance and management of nonprofits. Similarly, the Charities Review Council (2014) in Minnesota has created a set of "Accountability Standards" and the Minnesota Council of Nonprofits (2014) has issued the "Principles and Practices for Nonprofit Excellence." Relatedly, efforts are under way to strengthen the self-regulation of fundraising by nonprofits (see NCVO, 2015a, 2015b).

Further, recognition is growing among policymakers and nonprofit leaders that investment in nonprofit capacity also is essential for the delivery of sustainable and quality programs (Gregory, A. G., 2009). Indeed, since so many nonprofit organizations are now "agents" of government, one could argue that government has an obligation to support training and education and, more generally, capacity building among nonprofit agencies providing public services. Government can provide funding to associations, coalitions, and other intermediary organizations such as Maryland Nonprofits to provide technical assistance to nonprofits. Government officials can also provide direct help to nonprofits through information sessions and direct capacity building assistance to nonprofits, and they can indirectly assist nonprofits by their willingness to work collaboratively with nonprofit organizations and their representative associations on issues of mutual concern (such as rates and regulations) (National Council of Nonprofits, 2014; NCVO, 2015b; Pettijohn and Boris, 2013). Of course, a sustained collaborative effort requires an ongoing commitment of resources by government.

In support of improved nonprofit capacity, government can structure contracts to include support for reasonable administrative costs. This is especially important given the constant challenge faced by nonprofits to find sufficient funds to support their administrative infrastructure. Underfunded infrastructure is a common problem, since many government and private funders focus on program-related funding. Lacking sufficient funds to pay for an adequate administrative structure, agencies are at a disadvantage when they seek to raise private funds and compete for public grants and contracts. Insufficient infrastructure also contributes to program instability, especially among smaller community-based organizations. More generally, state and local governments can strive to more fully fund contracts to reflect reasonable costs of nonprofits (National Council of Nonprofits, 2014; NCVO, 2015b). Importantly, the U.S. Office of Management and Budget in 2014 adopted a rule requiring that U.S. federal agencies pay for legitimate administrative expenses in addition to direct program expenditures (National Council of Nonprofits, 2016).

Government can also play an important role in directly and indirectly helping nonprofit contract agencies with their capital costs. Before the financial crisis hit in 2008, many states and localities expanded nonprofit contract agencies' access to tax-exempt bonds to help them with their capital needs, such as the purchase and renovation of their facilities and new equipment (Calabrese and Ely, 2015; Human Services Council, 2015; Smith, forthcoming). To the extent that nonprofits can improve their capital position, they will be in a better position to manage their cash flow effectively and be able to develop productive relationships with government contract officials.

Government administrators, especially at the state and local level, can also help improve governance and performance among nonprofit organizations through their support of appropriate mergers and collaborations. As discussed earlier, many nonprofits are small and struggle with capacity and funding issues, creating problems with board and executive leadership. Mergers of some of these organizations could be quite helpful in resolving some of these governance problems. Nonetheless, nonprofits are often resistant to mergers, so support from government (and private funders) is often essential if mergers are actually to occur.

Importantly, these steps to enhance performance in nonprofits will be insufficient to improve the overall quality and effectiveness of publicly funded services provided by nonprofit agencies unless government takes steps to invest in its own management team and structure. In the case of contracting with nonprofits, state and local government will most assuredly fail to realize the benefits of contracting if government contract administrators are unable to monitor nonprofit performance or work effectively with nonprofits. Consequently, government agencies need contract managers with skills in negotiation and bargaining, and knowledge of management, finance, budgeting, and the organization of nonprofits. Government managers could thus benefit from executive education and training opportunities focused on contract management, nonprofit management, financial management, program evaluation, and negotiation (National Council of Nonprofits, 2014; Smith and Smyth, 2010).

Government contract managers with these skill sets would also promote more effective relationships with nonprofits, as well as support working groups and more formal arrangements among nonprofits and government, to address important sector policy and management issues. Toward this end, government and nonprofit organizations in the United Kingdom negotiated a formal agreement, called "The Compact," outlining key principles and practices to guide their interactions at all levels of government (Compact Voice, 2010). The U.K. Compact has generated broad attention among governments and nonprofit organizations throughout the world. Some countries such as Australia have experimented with local level compacts (Casey and Dalton, 2006). Nonetheless, the basic principles of The Compact, such as regular communication and dialogue between government and the nonprofit sector and good standards of practice, can be developed through more informal relationships and partnerships at any level of government.

Nonprofits, for their part, should strive to invest in their administrative and programmatic infrastructure, including new technology and qualified administrative staff (Human Services Council, 2015; Light, 2004). The development of a private donor base can also be essential to building capacity, especially given the competition for scarce public contracts. Fundraising may not produce large benefits for the organization in the short term but, in the long term, may become very important as a way of cross-subsidizing programs inadequately funded by government contracts, and it may help build broader community support.

Conclusion

Government contracting with nonprofit agencies is in the midst of an important transition. The competition for government contracts is increasingly intense, reflecting growth in the number of agencies, coupled with the profound and broad-based interest of government and many private donors in accountability, efficiency, and results. Over time, this emphasis on performance and outcomes will produce more comparative analysis among nonprofit organizations, as well as between nonprofits and for-profits, particularly in service fields (such as home care) where these agencies directly compete. In the process, the monopoly now enjoyed by many nonprofits in their local communities is likely to be eroded or threatened by for-profit agencies or upstart nonprofit agencies. Moreover, larger nonprofit (and for-profit) contract agencies with proven track records and capacity are likely to have an edge in the competition for contracts. Further, government is likely to continue to shift at least some of its contract funding away from traditional contracts and into other, less direct funding vehicles such as vouchers, quasi-vouchers (such as Medicaid), and tax credits, further encouraging a more competitive, entrepreneurial contract culture. Amidst this competitive contracting environment, nonprofits will also need to engage in collaborative initiatives to enhance efficiency and program effectiveness, including the co-location of services; cooperative arrangements on benefits; sharing staff; and formal agreements to merge some services, yet retain separate organizations.

In short, the contracting environment is likely to remain relatively unpredictable and turbulent for the foreseeable future. Thus, nonprofits will need to adapt in ways that support both agency sustainability and program effectiveness. In the process, they will need to balance the imperative to be market-oriented in order to compete effectively for contracts with the imperative to stay true to their social mission and community orientation. Multiple revenue streams will become increasingly important, even for modest-sized agencies, and effective advocacy on behalf of the agency and its local constituencies will be vital for agency sustainability. Ongoing investments in their own capacity will be necessary for agencies, too. Nonetheless, government also needs to recognize its obligation to invest in nonprofit infrastructure and capacity and to support nonprofit contractors with equitable and fair funding. For nonprofit leaders and managers, such investments in agency capacity and good governance, coupled with sustained engagement of local citizens and stakeholders, will enable the sector to realize the promise that nonprofits offer as effective providers of vital public services in a new and dynamic environment.

References

Andrews, C., Grogan, C., Brennan, M., and Pollock, H. A. Lessons from Medicaid's Divergent Paths on Mental Health and Addiction Services. *Health Affairs*, 2015, 34, 7, 1131–1138.

Bass, G. D., Arons, D. F., Guinane, K., and Carter, M.F. *Seen But Not Heard: Strengthening Nonprofit Advocacy*. Washington, D.C.: Aspen Institute, 2007.

Berry, J. M. *A Voice for Nonprofits*. Washington, DC: The Brookings Institution Press, 2003.

Boyarski, L. M. *Whose Voice Is Being Heard? The Role of Nonprofit Coalitions in Policy Advocacy*. Unpublished doctoral dissertation. Washington, DC: Department of Government, Georgetown University, 2016.

Braddock, D. L., Hemp, R. E., Rizzolo, M. C., Tanis, E. S., Haffer, L., and Wu, J. *State of the States in Intellectual and Developmental Disabilities* (10th ed.). Washington, DC: AAIDD, 2015.

Calabrese, T. D., and Ely, T. L. Borrowing for the Public Good: The Growing Importance of Tax-Exempt Bonds for Public Charities. *Nonprofit and Voluntary Sector Quarterly*, 2015, 1–20.

Carlson, M., and Donohoe, M. *The Executive Director's Survival Guide: Thriving as a Nonprofit Leader* (2nd ed.). San Francisco: Jossey-Bass, 2010.

Casey, J., and Dalton, B. The Best of Times, the Worst of Times: Community-Sector Advocacy in the Age of "Compacts." *Australian Journal of Political Science*, 2006, 41(1), 23–38.

Chandler, J., and Kennedy, K. S. *A Network Approach to Capacity Building*. Washington, DC: National Council of Nonprofits, 2015.

Charities Review Council. *Accountability Standards*. St. Paul, MN: Charities Review Council, 2014.

Compact Voice. *The Compact: The Coalition Government and Civil Society Organisations Working Effectively in Partnership for the Benefit of Communities and Citizens in England*, 2010. www.compactvoice.org.uk/sites/default/files/the&uscore;compact.pdf.

Considine, M. Contract Regimes and Reflexive Governance: Comparing Employment Service Reforms in the United Kingdom, the Netherlands, New Zealand, and Australia. *Public Administration*, 2000, 78(3), 613–638.

Corporation for National and Community Service, Office of Research and Evaluation. *State of the Pay for Success Field: Opportunities, Trends, and Recommendations*. Washington, DC: author, 2015.

Courtney, M. E. Managed Care and Child Welfare Services: What Are the Issues? *Children and Youth Services Review*, 2000, 22(2), 87–91.

De Hoog, R. H. *Contracting Out for Human Services: Economic, Political, and Organizational Perspectives*. Albany, NY: State University of New York Press, 1984.

Desai, S., Garabedian, L., and Snyder, K. *Performance Based Contracts in New York City: Lessons Learned from Welfare-to-Work*. Albany, NY: Rockefeller Institute of Government, 2012.

DeVooght, K., Fletcher, M., Cooper, H. *Federal, State, and Local Spending to Address Child Abuse and Neglect in SFY 2012*, 2014. www.childtrends.org/wp-content/uploads/2014/09/2014-47ChildWelfareSpending2012.pdf.

Fraser, J., and Whitehill. E. *Introducing Performance-Based Contracts: A Comparison of Implementation Models*. Pittsburgh, PA: Allegheny County Department of Human Services, 2014.

Gais, T., Dadayan, L., and Bae, S. *The Decline of States in Financing the U.S. Safety Net: Retrenchment in State and Local Social Welfare Spending, 1977–2007*. Albany, NY: Rockefeller Institute of Government, 2009. www.rockinst.org/pdf/workforce_welfare_and_social_services/sws.pdf.

Gregory, A. G., and Howard, D. The Nonprofit Starvation Cycle. *Stanford Social Innovation Review*, 2009, Fall. http://ssir.org/articles/entry/the_nonprofit_starvation_cycle.

Grønbjerg, K. A. *Understanding Nonprofit Funding: Managing Revenues in Social Services and Community Development Organizations*. San Francisco: Jossey-Bass, 1993.

Harrison, D. S., Eleveld, J., and Ahern, P. *Resilient Nonprofits: How Western Washington Nonprofits Have Been Coping with the Impact of the Economic Downturn*. Seattle, WA: Nancy Bell Evans Center on Nonprofits and Philanthropy, Evans School of Public Affairs, University of Washington, 2011. http://evans.uw.edu/sites/default/files/public/ResilientNonprofits2011_0.pdf.

Human Services Council. *New York Nonprofits in the Aftermath of FEGS: A Call to Action*. New York: Human Services Council, 2015. www.capitalnewyork.com/sites/default/files/Nonprofits%20in%20the%20Aftermath%20of%20FEGS%202016.pdf.

Hwang, H., and Powell, W. W. The Rationalization of Charity: The Influences of Professionalism in the Nonprofit Sector. *Administrative Science Quarterly*, 2009, 54, 268–298.

In the Public Interest. *A Guide to Evaluating Pay for Success Programs and Social Impact Bonds*. Washington, DC: In the Public Interest, 2015. www.inthepublicinterest.org/wp-content/uploads/ITPI-Pay-for-Success-Guide-Dec-2015.pdf.

Kania, J., and Kramer, M. Collective Impact. *Stanford Social Innovation Review*, 2011, Winter. http://ssir.org/articles/entry/collective_impact.

Kramer, R. *Voluntary Agencies in the Welfare State*. Berkeley: University of California Press, 1982.

Krasner, S. D. Structural Causes and Regime Consequences: Regimes as Intervening Variables. *International Organization*, 1982, 36, 185–205.

Leachman, M., Albares, N., Masterson, K., and Wallace, M. *Most States Have Cut School Funding, and Some Continue Cutting*. Washington, DC: Center for Budget and Policy Priorities, 2016. www.cbpp.org/sites/default/files/atoms/files/12-10-15sfp.pdf.

Light, P. C. *Sustaining Nonprofit Performance: The Case for Capacity Building and the Evidence to Support It*. Washington, DC: Brookings Institution, 2004.

Lynch, K. E. *Social Services Block Grant: Background and Funding*. Washington, DC: Congressional Research Service, 2014. https://greenbook.waysandmeans.house.gov/sites/greenbook.waysandmeans.house.gov/files/CH%2010%2094-953_gb_0.pdf.

Maryland Nonprofits. *Standards for Excellence: An Ethics and Accountability Code for the Nonprofit Sector*. Baltimore, MD: Maryland Nonprofits, 2016. http://standardsforexcellence.org/home-2/code/.

McBeath, B., and Meezan, W. Governance in Motion: Service Provision and Child Welfare Outcomes in Performance-Based, Managed Care Contracting Environment. *Journal of Public Administration Research and Theory*, 2010, 20, Supplement 1: The State of Agents: A Special Issue (January), i101–i123.

McKeever, B. S. *The Nonprofit Sector in Brief 2015: Public Charities, Giving, and Volunteering*. Washington, DC: Urban Institute, 2015. www.urban.org/sites/default/files/alfresco/publication-pdfs/2000497-The-Nonprofit-Sector-in-Brief-2015-Public-Charities-Giving-and-Volunteering.pdf.

Minnesota Council of Nonprofits. *Principles and Practice for Nonprofit Excellence*. St. Paul, MN: Minnesota Council of Nonprofits, 2014. www.minnesotanonprofits.org/Principles Practices.pdf.

Miron, G., and Gulosino, C. *Profiles of For-Profit and Nonprofit Education Management Organizations* (14th ed.—2011–2012. Boulder, CO: National Education Policy Center, 2013. http://nepc.colorado.edu/files/emo-profiles-11-12.pdf.

Mosley, J. From Skid Row to the Statehouse: How Nonprofit Homeless Service Providers Overcome Barriers to Policy Advocacy Involvement. In R. J. Pekkanen, S. R. Smith, and Yutaka Tsujinaka (eds.), *Nonprofits and Advocacy: Engaging Communities and Governments in an Era of Retrenchment*. Baltimore, MD: Johns Hopkins University Press, 2014, 107–134.

National Council of Nonprofits. *State Budget Crises: Ripping the Safety Net Held by Nonprofits*. Washington, DC: National Council of Nonprofits, 2010. https://www.councilofnon profits.org/sites/default/files/documents/Special-Report-State Budget-Crises-Ripping-the-Safety-Net-Held-by-Nonprofits.pdf.

National Council of Nonprofits. *Toward Common Sense Contracting: What Taxpayers Deserve*. Washington, DC: National Council of Nonprofits, 2014. https://www.councilofnon profits.org/sites/default/files/documents/toward-common-sense-contracting-what-taxpayers-deserve.pdf.

National Council of Nonprofits. *OMB Uniform Guidance*. Washington, DC: National Council of Nonprofits, 2016. https://www.councilofnonprofits.org/omb-uniform-guidance.

National Council of Voluntary Organisations (NCVO). A *Bigger Difference: Realising the Potential of Voluntary Organisations and Volunteers*. London: NCVO, 2015a. https://www .ncvo.org.uk/images/documents/policy_and_research/ncvo-manifesto 2015.pdf.

National Council of Voluntary Organisations (NCVO). *Regulating Fundraising for the Future: Trust in Charities, Confidence in Fundraising Regulation*. London: NCVO, 2015b. https:// www.ncvo.org.uk/images/documents/policy_and_research/giving_and_philan thropy/fundraising-review-report-2015.pdf.

Ng, T., Harrington, C., Musumeci, M. B, and Reaves, E. L. *Medicaid Home and Community-Based Services Program: 2012 Data Update*. Menlo Park, CA: Kaiser Family Foundation, 2015. http://kff.org/medicaid/report/medicaid-home-and-community-based-services-programs-2012-data-update/.

Palmer, E., and Robertson, C. Mississippi Fights to Keep Control of Its Beleaguered Child Welfare System. *The New York Times*, January 16, 2016. www.nytimes.com/2016/01/18/us/mississippi-fights-to-keep-control-of-itsbeleaguered-child-welfare-system.html.

Pekkanen, R. J., Smith, S. R, and Tsujinaka, Y. (eds.). *Nonprofits and Advocacy: Engaging Communities and Governments in an Era of Retrenchment*. Baltimore, MD: Johns Hopkins University Press, 2014.

Pettijohn, S. L., and Boris, E., with DeVita, C. J. and Fyffe, S. D. *Nonprofit-Government Contracts and Grants: Findings from the 2013 National Survey*. Washington, DC: Urban Institute, 2013. www.urban.org/sites/default/files/alfresco/publication-pdfs/412962-Nonprofit-Government-Contracts-and-Grants-Findings-from-the-National-Survey.PDF.

Phillips, S. D., and Smith, S. R. (eds.). *Governance and Regulation of the Third Sector: International Perspectives*. London: Routledge, 2011.

Public Agenda. *Charter Schools in Perspective*. Chicago: Spencer Foundation and Public Agenda, 2014. www.in-perspective.org/.

Roman, J. K., Walsh, K. A., Bieler, S., and Taxy, S. *Pay for Success and Social Impact Bonds: Funding the Infrastructure for Evidence-Based Change*. Washington, DC: Urban Institute, 2014. www.urban.org/sites/default/files/alfresco/publication-pdfs/413150-Pay-for-Success-and-Social-Impact-Bonds-Funding-the-Infrastructure-for-Evidence-Based.PDF.

Saidel, J. R. Expanding the Governance Construct: Functions and Contributions of Nonprofit Advisory Groups. *Nonprofit and Voluntary Sector Quarterly*, 1998, 27, 421–436.

Salamon, L. M. (ed.). *The Tools of Government*. New York: Oxford University Press, 2002.

Smith, D. C., and Grinker, W. J. *The Promise and Pitfalls of Performance Based Contracting*. New York: Seedco, 2004. http://seedco.org/wp-content/uploads/2011/11/The-Promise-and-Pitfalls.pdf.

Smith, S. R. "The Political Economy of Contracting." In Y. Hasenfeld (ed.), *Human Services as Complex Organizations* (2nd ed.). Thousand Oaks, CA: Sage, 2010, 139–160.

Smith, S. R. Social Services. In L. M. Salamon (ed.), *The State of Nonprofit America*. Washington, DC: Brookings Institution, 2012, 192–228.

Smith, S. R. Cross-Sector Nonprofit-Government: Financing. In E. Boris and C. E. Steuerle (eds.), *Nonprofits and Government: Collaboration and Conflict* (3rd ed.). Washington, DC: Urban Institute, forthcoming.

Smith, S. R., and Lipsky, M. *Nonprofits for Hire: The Welfare State in the Age of Contracting*. Cambridge, MA: Harvard University Press, 1993.

Smith, S. R., and Smyth, J. The Governance of Contracting Relationships: "Killing the Golden Goose," a Third Sector Perspective. In S. Osborne (ed.), *The New Public Governance? Critical Perspectives and Future Directions*. London: Routledge, 2010.

Snyder, L. and Rudowitz, R. *Medicaid Financing: How Does It Work and What are the Implications?* Menlo Park, CA: Kaiser Family Foundation, 2015. http://files.kff.org/attachment/issue-brief-medicaid-financing-how-does-it-work-and-what-are-the-implications.

Speakman Management Consulting. *Nonprofit Organizational Life Cycle*. Atlanta, GA: Speakman Management Consulting, 2009. www.speakmanconsulting.com/go/speakman/resources/nonprofit-lifecycle-matrix.pdf.

Steuerle, C. E. Common Issues for Voucher Programs. In C. E. Steuerle, V. D. Ooms, G. E. Peterson, and R. D. Reischauer (eds.), *Vouchers and the Provision of Public Services*, Washington, DC: Brookings Institution, 2000, 3–39.

U.S. Census Bureau. *Economic Census*. Services Report. Washington, DC, Author, 2015.

Wertheimer, D. Maximizing the Impact and Amplifying the Voice of Philanthropy. *Responsive Philanthropy*, 2011, Fall, 1–6. www.ncrp.org/files/rp articles/Responsive%20Philanthropy_Fall11_Homelessness.pdf.

CHAPTER TWENTY-ONE

TOOLS AND TECHNIQUES OF NONPROFIT FINANCIAL MANAGEMENT*

Woods Bowman

Recessions and bad luck do not cause financial crises; incompetence and poor planning do. Recessions and bad luck merely expose weaknesses in financial management. Survival in bad times requires preparation in good times. Long run success requires planning and disciplined execution. This chapter introduces tools and techniques that nonprofit executives and financial managers can use to prepare for adversity and to plan for growth. After a brief introductory section highlighting a special feature of nonprofit finance that is of particular importance to financial management, the chapter progresses from short-term tactical issues to long-term strategic issues and governance, focusing on:

- How to avoid a cash shortage;
- How to prepare a budget;
- How to use a budget to manage;
- How to achieve long-run success; and
- How boards should oversee finance.

Italicized words and phrases generally are defined in endnotes to avoid interrupting the narrative, and supplementary information is available on this

*The author thanks Brianna Bingham, Sue A. Dahlkamp, Chris Einolf, and Francie Ostrower for many useful comments on earlier drafts. Some equations in this chapter may *not* apply to endowed organizations (that is, those having an investment portfolio that exceeds spending on operations). For more on these cases, see Bowman (2011).

Handbook's website (including a catalog of resource sites, "Websites Featuring Financial Data and Other Useful Information.")

A Special Feature of Nonprofit Finance

The United Nations (2003, p. 218) defines nonprofit institutions (NPIs) as:

> organizations that do not exist primarily to generate profits, either directly or indirectly, and that are not primarily guided by commercial goals and considerations. NPIs may accumulate surplus in a given year, but any such surplus must be plowed back into the basic mission of the agency and not distributed to the organizations' owners, members, founders, or governing board.

Mission primacy, protected by a prohibition against distributing any surplus to private persons, makes nonprofit organizations attractive to donors who share goals and objectives similar to the organization. Donors may give without specifying how the recipient should spend their gifts, or they may restrict their gifts to specific projects. Nonprofit organizations have a moral obligation and, in some cases, a legal duty, to honor donors' wishes. This complicates nonprofit financial management because every restricted gift and grant must be accounted for individually. The simplest and surest method of maintaining the integrity of restricted gifts and grants is to deposit them in a special bank account reserved exclusively for restricted cash pending satisfaction of restrictions.

How to Avoid a Cash Shortage

The key financial concept introduced here is liquidity, which refers to maintaining enough *cash and cash equivalents* free from donor restrictions to pay all obligations as they come due.[1] This section deals with the common situation in which cash inflows equal or exceed cash outflows in a given year but from time to time cash outflows exceed cash inflows (that is, *cash flow shortfalls*). The amount of cash needed at the beginning of each year to cover occasional shortfalls during the next twelve months is *working cash*.

Cash Flow Analysis

Table 21.1 presents a simplified description of cash flow for a hypothetical organization, which would enable a manager to anticipate the amount of cash needed for every month of a *fiscal year* (abbreviated *FY*).[2]

TABLE 21.1. Hypothetical Cash Flow Analysis
in dollars, for FY 20XX as of (insert preparation date here)

Income	Budget	Q1[a]	Q2	Q3	Q4	Sum[b]
Gifts & Grants	300,000	60,000	74,700	62,700	102,600	300,000
Fees & Charges	165,000	40,000	40,000	45,000	40,000	165,000
Released[c]	20,000	0	0	0	20,000	20,000
Cash In	485,000	100,000	114,700	107,700	162,600	485,000

Spending	Budget	Q1[a]	Q2	Q3	Q4	Sum[b]
Personnel	320,000	75,000	75,000	75,000	95,000	320,000
Occupancy	63,000	15,000	16,000	16,000	16,000	63,000
Other	100,000	25,000	25,000	25,000	25,000	100,000
Cash Out	483,000	115,000	116,000	116,000	136,000	483,000
Net Cash Flow[d]	2,000	(15,000)	(1,300)	(8,300)	26,600	2,000

Notes: [a]"Q1" is 1st quarter of the fiscal year.

[b] Sum of Q1 through Q4. At the beginning of a fiscal year "Sum" equals "Budget".

[c] Cash "released" from restrictions are withdrawals from a bank account reserved for restricted gifts and grants pending satisfaction of restrictions.

[d] "Cash In" minus "Cash Out."

It presents financial information according to the customary practices of finance professionals.

1. Tables should indicate the ending date of the fiscal year.
2. Because numbers change as new information becomes available, tables should always indicate a preparation date.
3. Parenthesis indicates negative numbers.
4. Inflows and outflows are recorded on a *gross* basis.[3]

An actual cash flow table would show more income and spending detail and be organized by months. Payments (cash outflow) and receipts (cash inflow) are tabulated when they are expected to occur. Restricted gifts and grants should not be tabulated as cash inflows until restrictions are satisfied (that is, *released from restrictions*).[4]

Table 21.1 shows a negative net cash flow in the first three quarters but a positive net cash flow in the last quarter and for the fiscal year. The hypothetical

TABLE 21.2. Hypothetical Cash Flow Projections
in dollars, for FY 20XX as of (insert preparation date here)

Available Income	Budget	Actual YTD[a]	Q3	Q4	Sum[b]
Gifts & Grants	300,000	128,000	62,700	102,600	293,300
Fees & Charges	165,000	85,000	45,000	40,000	170,000
Released	20,000	0	0	20,000	20,000
Cash In	**485,000**	**213,000**	**107,700**	**162,600**	**483,300**

Spending	Budget	Actual YTD[a]	Q3	Q4	Sum[b]
Personnel	320,000	150,000	75,000	95,000	320,000
Occupancy	63,000	31,000	16,000	16,000	63,000
Other	100,000	45,000	25,000	25,000	95,000
Cash Out	**483,000**	**226,000**	**116,000**	**136,000**	**478,000**

Net Cash Flow	**2,000**	**(13,000)**	**(8,300)**	**26,600**	**5,300**

Notes: [a]Actual YTD is Actual Year-to-Date data.
[b]Sum = Actual YTD + Q3 + Q4.

organization must begin the year with at least $24,600 cash ($15,000 + $1,300 + $8,300) to avoid a cash shortage before the fourth quarter. Cash could be withdrawn from the special account early to minimize the expected cash flow shortfall but only if the restrictions attached to a $20,000 grant are certain to be satisfied by the fourth quarter of the current year.

Table 21.2 illustrates a revision of Table 21.1 that assumes that two quarters have elapsed since Table 21.1 was created. It replaces estimated numbers for the first and second quarters with a single column of actual data year-to-date (YTD).

- Gifts and grants YTD were $128,000, $6,700 less than anticipated. Fees and charges YTD were $85,000, $5,000 more than anticipated. Total cash inflows were $1,700 less than anticipated.
- Personnel and occupancy costs are unchanged from their initial estimates but "other" costs were $5,000 less. So total cash outflow was $5,000 less than anticipated.
- Actual net cash flow is negative $13,000 instead of negative $16,300 that had been anticipated, representing an improvement of $3,300.

Borrowing would appear as a cash inflow on Tables 21.1 and 21.2.

Optimizing Liquidity

The solution to a cash shortage is to establish a fund consisting of *unrestricted* cash and cash equivalents that enables an organization to avoid borrowing from banks or other external lenders, that is, a *working cash fund*.[5] A popular rule of thumb is that working cash should not be less than an average month's cash outflow. However, a one-size-fits-all rule is unlikely to be optimal for all organizations.

While it is important to have adequate liquidity, too much is wasteful. Managing liquidity is like managing time: it is important to be punctual for every appointment, but being very early wastes time. An organization should find the minimum level of working cash it needs from its own experience. In other words, it should *optimize* its working cash. The optimal size for this hypothetical organization's working cash fund would be $25,000 (rounded).

In preparation to optimize, an organization should complete the following three-point checklist in Figure 21.1.

A line of credit (LOC) with a commercial bank guarantees ready access to enough cash to deal with a temporary cash shortage. A LOC that is never used is indicative of too much working cash. However, withdrawing from a LOC more than once or twice a year indicates insufficient working cash.

What to Do with Liquid Assets

Restricted gifts and grants and working cash should only be invested short term. The simplest and safest investment opportunity is an interest-bearing checking account at a federally insured commercial bank. The Federal Deposit Insurance Corporation (FDIC) insures accounts up to "$250,000 per depositor, per insured bank, for each account ownership category, including checking

FIGURE 21.1. Three-Point Checklist

✓ Restricted gifts and grants:	Should not be comingled with unrestricted cash; preferable deposited in a segregated account.
✓ Operating budget:	The operating budget must be balanced. Budgeting is covered the next section of this chapter.
✓ Payables/receivables:	Bills should be paid on time but not too early; debtors should be encouraged to pay on time.

accounts, savings accounts, money market deposit accounts, and certificates of deposit [CDs]" (FDIC, 2014). It does not insure other financial products and services that commercial banks may offer. Nor does it insure money market funds at non-bank institutions.

Diagnostic Tests for Liquidity

An organization's liquidity is the total of all of its liquid assets minus donor-restricted funds. Organizations should keep a continuous record of all bills to be paid (that is, *accounts payable*) and all of its own billings (that is, *accounts receivable*). On the same date of every month a financial manager should prepare reports of receivables and payables that tally open accounts, indicating the average length of time elapsed since the invoice dates. These reports are called *aging reports*. Two key rules of thumb for receivables and payables are

- Receivables should not exceed sixty days. Extra effort should be made to collect past due receivables. An increase in receivables indicates worsening liquidity; a decrease indicates improving liquidity.
- Payables should not exceed sixty days. Payables should not be allowed to become past due because they accrue late fees and interest. It would be cheaper to borrow the necessary cash.

How to Prepare a Budget

Budgeting is an essential management tool. It has a rich vocabulary, so this section begins with a few definitions before outlining general recommendations and issues that may arise during budget preparation. After defining the basic terms, I offer eight recommended practices for preparing a budget.

Definitions

A *budget* is an annual financial plan. There are two categories: *operating* budgets and *capital* budgets. When the word "budget" is used without a modifier it refers to an operating budget. Budgets are usually organized by *line items*, which are the categories of goods and services an organization plans to buy during the year. Once a board *adopts* a budget, the spending lines are called *appropriations*. *Debt* is the cumulative result of *borrowing*; *long-term debt* consists of loans an organization must pay off (that is, *retire*) more than one year hence.

An organization's budget is intimately related to its accounting system. Nonprofits use either of two types of accounting systems: cash-basis accounting or accrual-basis accounting. *Cash-basis accounting* enters a transaction into the record (that is, it recognizes it) only when cash changes hands. *Accrual-basis accounting* recognizes a transaction whenever it creates a financial obligation, regardless of when cash changes hands (which could be years into the future). Accrual-basis accounting rules in the United States are known as "generally accepted accounting principles" (GAAP), and they are promulgated by the Financial Accounting Standards Board. Other countries use a variant of "international financial reporting standards" (IFRS) promulgated by the International Accounting Standards Board.

Regardless of the accounting system, bookkeepers identify every financial transaction with a code number identifying the source of funds and purpose of spending. The set of such codes constitutes what is called a *chart of accounts.*

Recommended Budgeting Practices

Boards should adopt a budget policy to provide consistency in budget preparation from year to year. Supplements A and B of this *Handbook*'s website provide a sample budget policy and a sample budget, respectively, reflecting my recommendations for budgeting practices that are applicable to all organizations in all circumstances.

1. *A budget should be adopted before the next fiscal year begins.* A budget cannot effectively control spending when it is adopted after a new fiscal year begins. Maximum effectiveness requires that the board adopt it in advance. However, advance preparation requires estimating income and spending for the current year (see Recommendation 7, as follows).
2. *The operating budget should be separate from the capital budget.* An *operating budget* is a plan for mobilizing resources (income) to spend on services and goods that have a useful life of one year or less, in other words, "spending on operations." In general, the goods and services included in an operating budget are purchased every year, which are the result of an organization's ongoing commitments.

    A *capital budget* is a plan for mobilizing resources (restricted gifts and grants, loans, allocation of current income from operating accounts) to spend on *capital assets,* which are assets having useful lives exceeding one year.[6] Capital assets are expensive as compared to most items in an operating budget, and items in a capital budget are not purchased every year.

An organization should not merge operating and capital budgets because year-to-year comparisons of total income and total spending would be meaningless due to fluctuations in capital spending. However, capital assets that cost less than a minor amount—the *capitalization threshold*—are included in an operating budget without ill effect.[7] Supplement C on the book's website offers a typical organizational policy regarding capital assets.

Ideally, an operating budget should show allocations of current income to the capital budget based on specific financing needs. Some nonprofit organizations include depreciation in their budget. However, *depreciation* is a number that accounts for the fact that capital assets wear out. Depreciation is a cost, yet it is not paid out to anybody. Practically speaking, including depreciation in a budget is functionally equivalent to saving, and it allows the organization to set aside money that will help replace capital goods when they wear out. However, the amount listed for depreciation is based on original cost. When capital goods must be replaced, they will be more expensive than their original cost. Thus, allocations of current income to the capital budget should be based on specific financing needs that reflect current prices.

3. *An operating budget must be balanced without borrowing, whereas borrowing is an acceptable method for financing a capital budget.* Organizations should balance their operating budgets. By definition a balanced operating budget may show a surplus but never should show a deficit. Figure 21.2 presents the operating budget equation; it displays sources of funds on the left and uses of funds on the right.

Because operating budgets embody ongoing commitments, deficits (that is, negative surpluses) are unsustainable. Number 2 on a recently published list of "10 ways to kill your nonprofit" is "operate in the red" (Hager and Searing, 2014, p. 67).[8] A small surplus in the budget is useful because it provides a cushion against external shocks and internal stresses.

Borrowing is an acceptable method of financing capital assets, provided: (1) the repayment period does not exceed the useful life of the items being financed and (2) there is sufficient cash flow to retire the debt on schedule. Interest on the debt should be in an operating budget, not in a capital budget.

FIGURE 21.2. Operating Budget Equation

current income	+	released from restrictions	=	spending on operations	+	debt service	+	current income allocated to capital budget	+	surplus (to board-designated capital reserve)

FIGURE 21.3. Capital Budget Equation

allocation from operating budget $+$ released from restrictions $+$ from board-designated capital reserve $+$ borrowing $=$ capital spending

Figure 21.3 presents the capital budget equation. It shows sources of funds on the left and uses of funds on the right.

4. *The line items in an operating budget should correspond to the accounting system's chart of accounts.* A budget cannot effectively be used to control spending when it is organized into income and spending categories that are different from the categories used by the accounting system, namely the chart of accounts. Also, using accounting software with budgeting functionality is preferable to preparing a budget on a spreadsheet. When using one system for both, it ensures that income and spending categories will be the same in both the accounting reports and the budget document.

5. *An operating budget should not include restricted income, unless restrictions are expected to be satisfied during the fiscal year that the budget is in effect.* Organizations have a moral obligation to honor donors' restrictions and, in the United States, they have a legal obligation to do so as well. Therefore, an organization should not include a restricted gift in a budget unless it will be able to satisfy a donor's restrictions in the same year. Conversely, if an organization that received a restricted gift or grant in a prior year with restrictions it was unable to satisfy at the time and it now can satisfy them in the new year, this should be shown in the budget with the statement that it is "released" from restrictions.

6. *An operating budget should include no more than a small amount of non-recurring income.* Examples of non-recurring income are bequests and proceeds from asset sales. Because most line items in an operating budget recur every year, it is risky to rely on non-recurring income to balance an operating budget. It is wise for an organization to establish a policy limiting the amount of non-recurring income that will be included in its annual operating budget. Whenever a bequest exceeds this amount, the organization should spend it on capital or other non-recurring needs or designate it for a reserve fund.

7. *An operating budget for a new year should be based on the current year's estimated income and spending—not the current year's budget.* Some financial managers take the easy way out and use the current budget as the starting point for preparing the next year's budget. This habit is not only lazy, but it is also inefficient and unwise. The purpose of a budget is to provide just enough

financial resources—not too much and not too little—to buy needed items. Assuming that an organization does not allow its employees to spend more than the appropriated amount for any particular line item (an important requirement), there may be appropriations (funds) left at year's end for many line items. These are *lapsed appropriations* that may reflect inaccuracies in that budget. Thus, if a financial manager bases the next year's budget on the previous budget instead of on the actual spending for the year, he or she will be incorporating past errors into the next budget.

8. *A narrative is an integral part of a budget.* A budget is a plan based on assumptions about future events. It is meaningless without an accompanying narrative that explains key assumptions. During the implementation phase, an organization will be able to move quickly to respond to assumptions that are no longer valid even before an operating deficit becomes evident, if they have been made clear. In addition, a good budget narrative reviews the successes and failures of the current year and sets quantified goals and objectives for the upcoming year.

Budgeting Decisions

The preceding discussion features recommended practices that apply to every organization, large or small, located in this country or that. The following section highlights matters that are organization-specific and contingent on circumstances.

1. Cash or Accrual? A budget document should be compatible with the organization's accounting system. A critical decision for every organization is which basis of accounting to adopt. *Cash-basis accounting* is the same in every country and used by half of U.S. nonprofit organizations because it is very simple. It is generally satisfactory for organizations having incomes less than $250,000. However, *accrual-basis accounting* provides a more complete representation of an organization's financial condition. Use of an accrual accounting system requires a professionally trained financial manager. It is important to note that government purchasing regulations typically require vendors to submit audited financial statements based on accrual accounting, regardless of an organization's size.

2. Structure. A typical budget is organized by line item; a list of all types of anticipated "available" income from every source (gifts, sales, released from restrictions, and so forth) and spending authorization for all of the types of goods and services that will be purchased in the year (for example, personnel, supplies).

TABLE 21.3. Template for Line Item and Program Budgets Combined

Line Item	Program A	Program B	General & Unassigned	Totals	Current Year's Actual
Personnel					
Supplies					
Total Direct Costs[a]	Total (A)	Total (B)	Total (G)	Total All	
Earned Income + Funds Released from Restrictions					
Net Surplus or Deficit[b]					

Notes: [a]Total Direct Costs equals the sum of line items (personnel, supplies).
[b]Net Surplus or Deficit equals Total Direct Costs minus Program Income.

This format facilitates spending control during budget implementation. However, for organizations that operate more than one program, it is useful to have a budget structure that also identifies each of the programs of the organization, how much each program costs, and how much income each generates.[9]

Budgets can be prepared both ways simultaneously, as Table 21.3 shows. The shaded area is a conventional line-item budget for the entire organization. The last column is a benchmark for determining which line items have increased or decreased. A program budget shows the portion of budgeted spending applicable to each program, together with each program's earned income and any restricted gifts and grants intended for it alone. A program budget facilitates accountability because all the direct costs and earned income of the program are the undivided responsibility of that program's manager. Costs that are shared by more than one program should be divided by usage. Each program's share then is shown as another cost that is assigned to the program.

Budgeted spending authority for personnel and other resources that are not direct costs of any specific program are shown in "General & Unassigned." These costs are known by the name of *overhead*. Costs associated with governance, finance, and nonspecific public relations generally fall into this category. The full cost of a program equals the sum of its direct costs and its share of overhead. Each program's share of overhead equals its direct cost multiplied by the *overhead rate* of the entire organization. The overhead rate is the direct cost of "general and unassigned" cost divided by the sum of program direct costs. In Table 21.3 the overhead rate equals the Total (G) divided by the sum of Total (A) and Total (B).

Fundraising should be shown in a separate column, but it is omitted from Table 21.3 for purposes of simplicity. Fundraising is, in effect, a program that serves the organization instead of the public, so accountability demands separate treatment. The costs of fundraising are not included in overhead because fundraising pays for itself.[10]

Audited financial statements of health and welfare nonprofits in the United States always include a Statement of Functional Expenses that looks like Table 21.3. Other organizations may elect to have such a statement included in their audit, and many do so. Supplement D in this chapter's section of the *Handbook* website shows a sample Statement of Functional Expenses. With the addition of an income line, it can be used as a template for a program budget.

3. Special Problems of Budgeting for Fundraising.

There are three kinds of contributed resources: grants, gifts, and noncash (that is, *in-kind*) contributions. Budgeting should distinguish between those grants and gifts intended for supporting current spending and others contributed to a capital campaign.

Cash and in-kind contributions are not perfect substitutes, so budgets should segregate them. Consumption of contributed goods should be shown as spending. The value of volunteer time may be included in a budget. However, does not allow it to be included in financial statements, except in certain specific cases.[11]

Grants may hurt an organization's surplus more than they help. They hurt when they do not pay the full cost of the programs they support (see issue 2 earlier). An organization's grants should not only cover direct program costs, but they should cover the program's portion of overhead costs as well. For a grant to be helpful, the current year's portion of the grant minus the direct program cost must equal or exceed the grantee's overhead rate multiplied by direct program cost.

It is reasonable to pay the costs of soliciting grants and gifts in support of current spending with funds received in the same fiscal year. Capital campaigns, however, are episodic and may incur substantial initial costs before the first dollar is forthcoming, sometimes even several years in the future. The costs of capital campaigns should be paid from a special board-designated reserve set aside as seed money for the campaign. Neither working cash nor the operating reserve should be used for this purpose.

Development staff and budget staff typically use different metrics to account for funds raised; development typically includes pledges for funds but financial management staff typically do not.

TABLE 21.4. Characteristics of Nonprofit Income Sources

	Predictability	Autonomy
Investment Income	High	High
Government Contracts*	High	Moderate
Earned Income (3rd party payers)	High	Low
Federated Gifts and Grants	High	Low
Individual Contributions (small/many)	Moderate	High
Membership Dues	Moderate	High
Earned Income (individuals)*	Moderate	High
Individual Contributions (large/few)*	Low	Low
Foundation Grants	Low	Low

Sources: Pratt (2004) and *Froelich (1999) as adapted by author.

4. Special Problems Related to Estimating Income. Some sources of income are unpredictable and some, frequently, are restricted. Table 21.4 describes predictability for different types of nonprofit income, and shows the typical degree of accuracy of predictions and autonomy for each source. *Autonomy* in this table refers to the degree of freedom from restrictions that typically will be imposed by the source of income.

Organizations that anticipate a high proportion of their income will come from sources that rank low on either of the scales of unpredictability or autonomy should budget a little extra for surplus to compensate for possible error in their income estimates. Also, although the amount of income from government contracts is highly predictable, the timing of payments may be erratic. Organizations doing business with government may experience long delays during economic recessions. This possibility should be considered when optimizing an operating reserve and obtaining a line of credit. Additional important information about the characteristics and implications of government contracts is presented in Chapter Twenty of this *Handbook.*

Arithmetically, it is immaterial which part of the budget is prepared first. However, it is important to recognize that if the process of estimating spending precedes the process of estimating income, it can be too easy to indulge in wishful thinking and overestimate future income in order to avoid the painful necessity of reducing proposed spending. Unrealistically high estimates are worse than worthless; they are dangerous.

5. Program Deficits and Cross-Subsidy. Many nonprofits operate multiple programs. If one or more programs chronically spends more than it earns, it must find a reliable way to make up the difference. It can (1) use unrestricted gifts and grants, (2) take the surplus of a different program and use it to pay the bills of the deficit-plagued program (that is, *cross-subsidy*), or (3) use investment income. The first two options are covered here. A later section of this chapter explores the investment option.

As explained earlier, gifts and grants are not always predictable (issue 4) and some grants may hurt an organization's surplus more than they help (issue 3). Cross-subsidy is a risky long-term financing strategy because the surplus-generating potential of a popular program may become known to other nonprofit organizations and they will imitate it. In time, the effectiveness of cross-subsidy may erode because competition squeezes profits.

Furthermore, cross-subsidy creates short-term budget problems. Whenever it tries to balance its budget with across-the-board budget cuts, the organization will reduce positive cash flow from profit centers in tandem with reducing negative cash flow of deficit centers. Budgetary balance may not improve and could worsen as a result.

How to Use a Budget to Manage

The key financial concept of this section is *resilience*. Resilient organizations are able to withstand external shocks and internal stresses. Resilience requires regular budget surpluses *and* a "rainy day" fund (that is, an *operating reserve*). It can be useful to have other reserve funds, as well, especially reserves that can be used for capital acquisition or seeding a capital fundraising campaign.

The Goal for Surplus

The label *nonprofit* does not mean that an organization generates zero profit. It merely connotes that an organization has a purpose that transcends making a profit. Nonprofit organizations often eschew the term profit, preferring to talk in terms of *surplus* or *net income*. (The equivalent organizational label, *not-for-profit*, is more evocative but not as popular.) Every nonprofit organization must generate a surplus to keep its capital assets in good condition and to grow.

Financial performance of a nonprofit organization is measured by the excess of unrestricted income over spending on operations, usually known as an *operating surplus*. (A negative surplus is called a *deficit*.) Calculation of operating surplus depends on which accounting rules an organization follows—cash or accrual,

GAAP or IFRS. The following definitions of operating surplus are comparable measures for nonprofit organizations in the United States:

- The *cash-basis operating surplus* is the sum of (1) net unrestricted cash inflow, including cash released from restrictions and (2) spending to acquire capital assets.
- The *accrual-basis operating surplus* is change in unrestricted net assets *plus* depreciation and *minus* pledges. The calculation of this differs outside the United States.[12]

To avoid compromising its ability to deliver service, a nonprofit organization must maintain its assets at current market prices (that is, replacement cost), which naturally increase with inflation. Ideally, a U.S. organization that uses GAAP should have a minimum annual operating surplus equal to the product of the value of its assets (excluding land) and the long run rate of inflation of 3.4 percent.[13] Thus, an organization having capital assets of greater value than its spending on operations (for example, a museum) will need to have an operating surplus that exceeds the long-run rate of inflation (Bowman, 2011). Conversely, an organization having capital assets with a value that is less than spending on operations (for example, a legal services clinic) can survive comfortably with a surplus that is less than the long-run rate of inflation. Organizations with repeated annual surpluses that are less than the prescribed amount will find it necessary to conduct periodic capital campaigns to address the conditions created by deferred maintenance.

Exercising Control

Early every month, an organization's financial managers should search for areas of weakness in financial performance by comparing, line by line, actual income and spending to budgetary expectations. *Variances* should be calculated. A positive difference is favorable and a negative difference is unfavorable.

- Income variance = actual income − budgeted income
- Spending variance = budgeted spending − actual spending

Table 21.5 combines information from Tables 21.1 and 21.2 in a variance analysis to show how each item in the budget performed relative to expectations. It reports an unfavorable variance in gifts and grants but a favorable variance in fees, charges, and "other" costs. Gifts, grants, and "other costs" are both lower

TABLE 21.5. Hypothetical Variance Analysis
in dollars, for FY 20XX as of (insert preparation date here)

Available Income	Budget	Budget YTD	Actual YTD	Variance[a]
Gifts & Grants	300,000	134,700	128,000	(6,700)
Fees & Charges	165,000	80,000	85,000	5,000
Released	20,000	0	0	0
Income	465,000	214,700	213,000	(1,700)

Payments	Budget	Budget YTD	Actual YTD	Variance[b]
Personnel	300,000	150,000	150,000	0
Occupancy	63,000	31,000	31,000	0
Other	100,000	50,000	45,000	5,000
Spending	463,000	231,000	226,000	5,000

Net	2,000	(16,300)	(13,000)	3,300

Notes: [a]Variance = Actual Income YTD minus Budgeted Income YTD.
[b]Variance = Budgeted Spending YTD minus Actual Spending YTD.

than budgeted, but one variance is negative whereas the other variance is positive. The net difference is projected to be $3,300 higher than budgeted, which is favorable.

Early intervention in response to an incipient operating deficit can avert catastrophe. To illustrate: an actual operating deficit of 2 percent at the end of the first quarter may not seem like much, but it is worthy of immediate corrective action. Reducing spending by 2 percent for an entire year requires cutting quarterly spending by 2.67 percent to obtain the necessary savings over the three remaining quarters. If a financial manager waits until the last quarter to eliminate a projected 2 percent annual operating deficit, the total cuts will have to constitute 8 percent of projected spending.[14]

Reserves

Operating deficits are not sustainable. When confronted with an operating deficit, an organization can (1) cut expenses, (2) find new sources of income, or (3) wait until its economic situation improves. Assuming that it does not want to hurt its clientele by cutting expenses, the organization is left with two choices, but both tactics take time to implement. To buy the time it needs to supplement weak income, an organization must have a pool of unrestricted assets that can be converted into cash with little or no loss in value and without significant transaction costs (such as early withdrawal penalties). In other words, it needs an *operating reserve*. An operating reserve is similar to a working cash fund, except that its assets are slightly less liquid. An operating reserve should never be invested in stocks of individual corporations or in stock mutual funds.

Some executives do not want an operating reserve. Some say, "I can either serve one hundred more clients or have a reserve" (Sloan, Grizzle, and Kim, 2014), but this is wrong-headed. The purpose of a reserve is to *continue* service to *current* clients when income suddenly and unexpectedly becomes insufficient for an extended period of time. An operating reserve provides relief until circumstances improve or until managers find a new source of continuous funding. Once it is established, maintaining it at a constant level does not deduct from net income until replenishing it occurs.

Many organizations establish a target level for their operating reserve based on a rule of thumb, such as a minimum of three months of spending on operations (Nonprofit Operating Reserve Initiative, 2008). However, a one-size-fits-all rule is unlikely to be optimal. An organization can determine the minimum necessary reserve (that is, the *optimum reserve*) by learning from its own experience (that is, *optimizing*).

An organization with a history of conservative budgeting will need a smaller reserve than one with frequent unexpected operating deficits. To calculate the optimum reserve, subtract spending from unrestricted income in each of the past five years. Only the negative numbers (deficits) are cause for concern. After adjusting calculated deficits for inflation, add them. (Supplement E in the book's website shows how to adjust historical data for inflation.) Division by last year's spending on operations and multiplication by twelve converts this number to *months* of spending.

Whenever an organization withdraws funds from its operating reserve to finance an operating deficit, it should replenish the reserve in the first upcoming budget. If the organization cannot replenish the entire amount in one year, it should develop a plan to replenish it within a maximum of three years.

Investing Reserve Funds

Bills and notes issued by the U.S. government are an alternative to bank deposits for all reserve funds.[15] Individuals and nonprofit organizations can purchase these securities electronically at the most recent auction price through Treasury

TABLE 21.6. Yields on U.S. Securities and APRs on Bank-Issued CDs by Maturity (in Percent as of December 23, 2014)

	3 mo.	6 mo.	1 yr.	2 yr.	3 yr.	5 yr.
US Bills & Notes	0.03	0.14	0.26	0.73	1.17	1.76
Bank CDs	—	0.70	1.10	1.30	1.45	2.25

Note: APR is Annual Percentage Rate.
Source: US Department of the Treasury (2014b). The bank is not identified to avoid the appearance of product endorsement.

Direct (U.S. Department of the Treasury, 2014a, 2014b). Bank-issued certificates of deposit (CDs) are a higher-earning option. Table 21.6 shows the difference between market interest rates ("*yields*") at various maturities. Maturities should be staggered ("*laddered*") so some bills and notes mature every month. See Supplement F of this book's resource website for a sample investment policy.

Diagnostic Tests for Resiliency

Nonprofit organizations should consistently have surpluses. The method of calculating an operating deficit depends on an organization's basis of accounting. Comparable metrics were given in the discussion of financial performance, discussed earlier in this chapter. For organizations in the United States that use GAAP, the annual surplus should be no less than 3.4 percent multiplied by total assets, excluding land.

How to Achieve Long-Run Success

An organization can be liquid and resilient but still fail to thrive. It is the quality of robustness that enables nonprofit organizations to fulfill their mission to the maximum possible extent. The first part of this section discusses the theory and method of designing an income portfolio to achieve robustness. The second part discusses the two faces of long-term debt: How it can aid growth?, and How it can be a drag on growth.

The Income Portfolio

Commercial business firms derive nearly all of their income from sales of goods and services (that is, they have earned income). In addition to earned income, nonprofit income may include gifts, grants, and investment income.[16] Each type of income has advantages and disadvantages (Froelich, 1999). Conventional wisdom urges nonprofit organizations to diversify their income portfolios but Dennis Young's Benefits Theory of nonprofit income argues that every organization faces natural constraints on possibilities for exploiting diversification. The key to growth is finding the right combination of income sources. In Chapter Nineteen of this *Handbook*, Young and Jung-In Soh discuss a wide range of nonprofit funding sources. Benefits Theory posits "Sources of income should correspond with the nature of benefits conferred on, or of interest to, the providers of those resources" (Young, 2007, p. 341).

- *Private benefits* accrue from individuals who are willing to pay for the goods and services. Private benefits generate *earned income* (examples: ticket sales, tuition). Ideally, the market price of these goods and services covers their cost of production. If mission dictates that price should be below cost, the producing organizations must seek cross-subsidy, gifts, or endowment income.
- *Group benefits* benefit a subgroup of society to which donors belong or benefit a group that donors care about (examples: art lovers, homeless persons). The chief source of income to cover the cost of production is *gifts*.
- *Public benefits* accruing to a sufficiently large segment of the general public stimulate political support that can result in *government funding* (examples: libraries, privately owned historic sites). There may be overlapping interests with subgroups, such as assistance for homeless persons.
- *Trade benefits* are goods and services purchased by institutions or groups in commercial relationship with the producing nonprofit organization (examples: ads in trade publications and program booklets). Trade benefits also generate *earned income*.

Table 21.7 shows the composition of income portfolios of major nonprofit subsectors. Nonprofit organizations should diversify their income portfolios to the extent possible, recognizing that their efforts to develop new income sources are constrained by whom they benefit and who is interested in seeing that its beneficiaries are well-served.

Every nonprofit organization should occasionally compare the composition of its income portfolio to a relevant peer group. According to Benefits Theory, their income portfolios should be similar. Marked differences should raise questions. For example, if an inquiring organization's peers have income from government sources but it does not, there may be possibilities for it to obtain public funding. A peer analysis proceeds in three steps.

TABLE 21.7. Composition of Income Portfolio of Major Subsectors
in 2010 as a percent of subsector income

	Private Gifts	Earned Income	Government Grants	Investment Income
Arts, culture, humanities	45	35	12	5
Education	17	63	12	6
Environment, animals	49	31	14	3
Health care	4	90	3	2
Human services	20	53	23	2
International	69	9	19	2
Other reporting charities	44	32	16	5
Total	13	74	8	3

Note: Rows may not add to 100 percent due to rounding.
Source: Roeger, Blackwood, and Pettijohn, 2012, Tables 5.19–5.25.

- *Identify peers.* All U.S. tax-exempt organizations' Internal Revenue Service (IRS) Form 990 reports are publicly available on the Internet (GuideStar, 2014). An inquiring organization should look up its own report and find its National Taxonomy of Exempt Entities (NTEE) code number, then search for other organizations with the same NTEE code number, in the same geographic region, in the same size category, using the same basis of accounting (cash or accrual).
- *Calculate the percent of total income ("revenue" on the form) by income category.* The information is found on the IRS 990 form (page 9, part VIII, column A). Substitute zero for net gain from sales of assets other than inventory (page 9, line 7d) and all negative numbers. Calculate total income reflecting all substitutions. The sum of calculated percentages must be 100 percent, plus or minus rounding error.
- *Compare percentages in each category with the corresponding percentages of peers.* If the peer organization is able to derive substantially more support from a particular source than has been the case for the inquiring organization, Benefits Theory predicts that it should be able to improve its support from the same source or type of source.

Financing Deficit Centers Long Term

It is possible to finance deficit centers with surpluses from high market value programs (that is, cross-subsidy), but competition is likely to negate this tactic in the long run. A more reliable alternative than cross-subsidy for long-term financing of chronic deficit centers is an endowment which, in this context, means a portfolio of long-term investments that generate a cash flow of constant purchasing power in perpetuity.[17] A common misperception is that only interest and dividend income may be spent. In fact, the increase in market value also may be converted into cash for current spending.[18]

Long-term investments may have attractive returns but they are inherently riskier than short-term investments used to manage reserves. *Return* is the sum of an investment's interest, dividends, and capital gain. *Risk* is variability in return.[19] Table 21.8 shows three of the many ways to measure it: (1) return in the best year minus return in the worst year, (2) the worst annual return alone, and (3) the number of years returns were negative.

The goal of investing is to assemble an *efficient portfolio*—a collection of investments that maximizes return at an acceptable risk or, conversely, minimizes risk for an acceptable return. Efficiency is achieved by diversification, which is a process of investing in stocks and bonds with different returns and risks.[20]

A portfolio of long-term investments should be diversified at two levels: *between* asset categories and *within* asset categories. So in addition to allocating investments among stocks, bonds, cash equivalents, and possibly other asset categories, diversify within each asset category (that is, do not place all of your assets with one single investment). The SEC offers the following warning with regard to the use of mutual funds as an investment vehicle

Mutual funds make it easy for investors to own a small portion of many investments. A total stock market index fund, for example, owns stock in thousands of companies. That's a lot of diversification for one investment! . . . Be aware, however,

TABLE 21.8. Asset Allocation Models

Allocation

Stocks (%)	0	20	30	40	50	60	70	80	100
Bonds (%)	100	80	70	60	50	40	30	20	0

Performance

Avg. return (%)	5.5	6.7	7.4	7.8	9.3	8.9	9.2	9.6	10.2
Best year (%)	32.6	29.8	28.4	27.9	32.3	36.7	41.1	45.4	54.2
Worst year (%)	(8.1)	(10.1)	(14.2)	(18.4)	(22.6)	(26.6)	(30.7)	(34.9)	(43.1)
Loss years (#)	14	12	14	16	17	21	22	23	25

Source: Vanguard, https://personal.vanguard.com/us/insights/saving-investing/model-portfolio-allocations (accessed December 2014).

that a mutual fund investment doesn't necessarily provide instant diversification, especially if the fund focuses on only one particular industry sector. Investing in more than one mutual fund may be necessary to get the desired extent of diversification. (U.S. Securities and Exchange Commission, 2014, n.p.)

State law governs long-term investing and spending, usually modeled on the Uniform Prudent Management of Institutional Funds Act (UPMIFA). The 2010 Dodd-Frank Wall Street Reform and Consumer Protection Act requires charities to register with the U.S. Commodities Futures Trading Commission if they co-manage funds for private investors.

Most endowed organizations spend a fixed fraction of the average of the most recent three to five years of the market value of their endowment's portfolio. An alternative method, which sets a cap and a floor on the spending rate, is growing in popularity because it is less volatile and provides more predictability to operating budgets (Sedlacek and Jarvis, 2010). For example, Yale University uses a 6.0 percent cap and a 4.5 percent floor (Yale University, 2010).

An organization should optimize its working cash and operating reserve before establishing an endowment. Using cash flow from annual operating surpluses to form the nucleus of an endowment is difficult and/or time-consuming. The usual method of endowment building involves a combination of major gifts and a host of smaller ones. Common experience is for 10 percent of donors to account for 90 percent of gifts. Chapter Eighteen of this book offers an extensive discussion of the practices associated with fundraising and philanthropy.

Borrowing and Long-Term Debt

Organizations that do not invest in themselves do not grow. Capital assets (buildings and equipment) are productive resources. If they are allowed to deteriorate, the inevitable result will be less output or lower quality services. Because nearly everything becomes more expensive over time, average annual spending on capital should be equal to the long-term inflation rate (3.4 percent) multiplied by the value of existing assets. Growth requires greater spending on capital.

There are two ways to pay for capital projects—equity and debt. *Equity* in this context refers to major gifts and grants. The gift aspect of equity is appealing, but its downside is the cost of fundraising and the time it takes to accumulate enough equity to begin a project.[21] Debt is appealing because it can be acquired quickly, but it saddles an organization with ironclad financial obligations for years into the future.[22] At the top of a recently published list of "10 ways to kill your nonprofit" is to "overwhelm it with liabilities"—in other words, create a heavy debt load (Hager and Searing, 2014, p. 67). Capital project financing is a complex balancing act.

There are many good reasons for owning rather than renting, and they all are either a cause or an effect of growth:

- When a nonprofit organization needs more space for specialized activities (for example, laboratories, theatrical productions, museums), it faces a decision to spend its resources to improve its landlord's property or to acquire its own. Acquisition is preferable, provided it is cost-effective.
- Renters are vulnerable to losing their leases or being forced out when landlords raise rents to unaffordable levels. If doing business at a particular location is important, acquisition is preferable to renting, provided it is cost-effective.
- When the scale of a nonprofit's operations reaches a certain point it will be unable to rent sufficient space at a single location. If it is important that staff or consumers have face-to-face communication with all departments, then it becomes necessary to create a campus and acquisition is likely to be cost-effective.

The qualifier in every case is cost-effectiveness. Property acquisition, unlike renting, involves large initial costs and operating costs that may have been shared with neighbors in leased space. The economics of every project is different and each must be evaluated on its own merits.[23] There are some certainties, however: (1) only liquid and resilient organizations should consider borrowing and (2) estimates of fundraising and borrowing capacities should be realistic. It should be unnecessary to stress the last point, but the following cautionary tales suggest otherwise.

- When the Field Museum of Natural History in Chicago raised less money than the project budget required, it borrowed. The result was a crisis in its operating budget that forced the museum to cut deeply into its research program (Gillers and Grotto, 2013).
- The initial plan for creating a new August Wilson Performing Arts Center in Pittsburgh called for donations of $2 million. Cost overruns were $11 million, so the board amended the plan to increase the donation requirement. The original estimate of $2 million was a realistic fundraising goal, but $11 million was not. It defaulted and its creditors now have possession of the property (Bloom, 2014).

During a project's concept phase (that is, pre-planning), an organization should assess its capacity to fundraise and to borrow. Financing decisions determine the scale of a project, which is not easily changed after work commences. A project's budget should utilize as much equity as possible to minimize borrowing. As noted earlier, a general rule is that 10 percent of donors contribute 90 percent of the money (counting pledges) to a capital campaign. Before an organization decides on the scale of a project, it should canvass a large sample of the most generous 10 percent of likely donors to determine the depth of philanthropic support.

As a general rule, current cash flow must be sufficient to retire a long-term debt because estimates of future income growth for nonprofit organizations are notoriously unreliable. A commonly used test of ability to retire a debt is the *debt service ratio*—the average annual surplus before interest and depreciation divided by projected annual debt service payments.[24] Supplement G in this book's resource website offers more detail on this topic.

Diagnostic Tests for Robustness

There is no simple test to assess the robustness of an income portfolio; peer analysis is recommended instead. Average annual spending on capital should be equal to the long-term inflation rate multiplied by the value of existing assets. Growth requires greater spending. Total debt should not exceed 50 percent of total assets.

How Boards Should Oversee Finances

Organizations work best when neither staff nor board dominates the other party. In a word, the board should be independent of the organization's executive leadership—neither compliant nor domineering. I encourage a balanced division of labor between board and staff, emphasizing the role of a board's Finance and Audit Committee. (Some organizations have a separate Audit Committee.)

Chapter Five of this book discusses in broad scope the work of the governing board; here we address the specific aspects of a governing board's work with regard to financial oversight. The board's role in financial management is to ask questions, especially when important decisions are imminent. When undertaking a new project, the board should verify that the staff has considered all contingencies.

Executive and finance staff have primary responsibility for financial operations, but a governing board always shares culpability when an organization collapses or fails to thrive. All governing boards have a *fiduciary duty* to the public. That is, a board must act solely in the public's best interest. Of course, staff should do likewise, but the board's fiduciary duty is legally binding (Legal Information Institute, n.d.). Practically speaking, all organizations with income of $500,000 or more should have an annual financial audit and, in recognition of the board's role as a legal fiduciary, auditors should send the final audit and accompanying documents directly to the board chair to share with the board.

Members of a nonprofit's governing board, acting in their official capacity, have three individual duties:

- *Duty of Care.* Board members must be reasonably familiar with relevant laws and regulations. (See Supplement H of the website for a summary of U.S. federal law.) They must be reasonably informed about the organization's business and regularly participate in activities of the board and of the committees on which they sit. When making decisions they must: act in good faith, exercise prudence, and avoid conflicts of interest. Ignorance of finance is no excuse for failure to exercise these responsibilities. Board members have an ethical obligation to learn the rudiments.
- *Duty of Loyalty.* Board members must place the interests of the organization above their own and above the interest of other organizations they may also serve as director. The duty of loyalty precludes conflicts of interest. (Supplement I has a sample conflict of interest policy and a sample annual disclosure form.)
- *Duty of Obedience.* Board members must be committed to advancing the organization's mission. While the board may amend the mission statement in light of changing circumstances, it must follow procedures prescribed by the bylaws and law in order to do so. Losing focus on the mission is inappropriate; allowing "mission drift" is not only inappropriate, it is wasteful.

Boards are ultimately responsible for the *control environment* and *internal controls.* The control environment "includes the integrity, ethical values, and competence of the entity's people" (University of Delaware, 2014, n.p.). Internal controls are methods to ensure "the integrity of financial and accounting information, meet operational and profitability targets and transmit management policies throughout the organization" (Investopedia, 2014, n.p.). Internal controls vary considerably depending on the complexity of an organization and should be reviewed and revised as an organization grows.

Boards can forestall problems by adopting formal policies on budgeting, cash management, investing, and internal controls. Policies are often technical but always time-consuming to draft and implement, so every board should have a finance committee to take ownership of this work. (Supplement J has a sample Finance and Audit Committee Charter, together with an annual checklist of typical committee activities.) The annual cycle of committee responsibilities must include oversight of budgeting and auditing.

Dialogue between the finance committee and the staff during budget preparation is important and often can expose hazards and contingencies that staff, working alone, might overlook. Further, the finance committee should monitor budget implementation throughout the year by regularly reviewing a variance analysis. Finance committee members also should understand how common financial transactions are executed and by whom on behalf of the organization. As an organization grows, its finance committee should review its internal controls to be sure they align with changing needs and risks.

Finance committees often serve in the dual role of audit committee. The purpose of an audit is to verify the accuracy of information that an organization's financial managers present on its financial statements (subject to GAAS). It must be understood that auditors do not express an opinion on the financial health of an organization. They do, however, evaluate the control environment and the adequacy of internal controls. Undetected or unresolved material weaknesses are likely to result in one or more misstatements on financial statements that distort the picture of an organization's true financial strengths and weaknesses.

Finance committees should be alert to careless financial practices. For example, they should (1) never allow one person have sole custody of cash before it has been counted and recorded, (2) require at least two persons, working independently, to complete every transaction, and (3) require all persons who have financial responsibilities to be bonded.[25] Supplement K of the website offers a short list of issues that a policy on internal controls should address. Theft from nonprofits is not unusual. In the event of theft, boards should not hesitate to file a criminal complaint. Failure to prosecute sets a bad precedent and it may jeopardize an insurance claim.

A finance committee should never have responsibility for fundraising. The knowledge, skills, and abilities needed for each function differ significantly, and both areas of responsibility can consume entire meeting agendas. If finance and fundraising are combined, there is a constant danger that mundane but important aspects of finance will be neglected in favor of resource development, or vice versa, depending on the personal interests of committee members.

Conclusion

The chapter began with a discussion of short-term tactical issues and progressed to long-term strategic issues. However, successful executives and financial managers think in the reverse sequence. Their long-term goals form the basis for short-range plans that guide daily their activity.

The language and methods of financial management intimidate many, yet anyone can master these tools and techniques. Mastery is only a matter of study and practice. Successful financial managers may have modest technical skills, yet they are always disciplined. Only a disciplined individual can implement a painful solution to a problem. And it must be noted that postponing intervention narrows the range of options for addressing problems, and the last option available is often the most painful.

Discipline also helps financial managers avoid succumbing to wishful thinking, which is the principal cause of borrowing more than an organization can afford. Nonprofit organizations need dreamers, but they need disciplined dreamers most of all.

Reference Resources

An extensive set of financial management resource materials is available at the Internet resource website that offers supplementary premium content for this *Handbook*. This url address for this site is www.wiley.com/go/JBHandbook. Among the resources provided by the author are a white paper on "Managing Reserves and Investments" and supplements such as sample policies and assessment tools.

Notes

1. *Cash* consists of currency and demand deposits (checking accounts). *Cash equivalents* include savings accounts, money market funds, and, according to some authorities, certificates of deposit (CDs). Cash and cash equivalents are known as *liquid assets.*
2. A *fiscal year* is a twelve-month period that reflects the annual rhythm of an organization's financial operations, which may not coincide with the calendar year. Fiscal years ending June 30 are common because many state governments, which are important funding sources, have June 30 fiscal years. The U.S. federal fiscal year ends September 30.

3. *Gross* means that receipts and payments for a fundraising event would be recorded in the inflow and outflow categories, respectively. The alternative of *net* recording is where only the profit or loss of an event would be reported.

4. Performing arts organizations should treat subscription sales as restricted income and designate a fraction to each production in the series.

5. Working cash should not be confused with *working capital*, which includes obligations to pay (payables) and rights to be paid (receivables).

6. Accountants call capital assets "fixed assets" or "property, plant, and equipment." The IRS 990 Form refers to them as "land, building, and equipment."

7. There is no standard capitalization threshold for nonprofit organizations. Based on rules for businesses and government, it should be in the range of $500 to $5,000, depending on the size of an organization.

8. Number 1 is "burden it with liabilities [i.e., debt]." See the next section of the chapter for more.

9. A precondition for a program budget is a chart of accounts that includes programs in its coding scheme.

10. The overhead *ratio* is the fraction of total cost attributable to overhead. It is cited in debates about whether organizations spend enough of their resources on programs. These debates usually include fundraising costs in overhead.

11. An organization may include the value of a volunteer's time on its financial statements only if the volunteer performs a specialized skill and the organization would have purchased the same service in the absence of volunteer assistance.

12. IFRS for Small and Medium Enterprises (SMEs) treats nonprofit organizations the same as proprietary firms. A nonprofit organizations adhering to these rules should calculate their surplus as "net profit" (the IFRS term) *plus* depreciation and *minus* change in the balance in the bank account holding restricted gifts and grants pending satisfaction of restrictions, if withdrawn cash is used as intended.

13. The long-term U.S. inflation rate is from Bowman (2011).

14. Two percent is three-quarters of 2.67 percent and one-quarter of 8 percent.

15. *Bills* mature in less than one year; *notes* mature between one and ten years. An investment's *maturity* is the date when the investor, who is also the purchaser, is paid its face value.

16. Nonprofit organizations also receive in-kind contributions (discussed in the budgeting section of this chapter, that is, goods and volunteer time), but these do not affect cash flow.

17. The literature contains various definitions of endowment. The definition here is equivalent to the sum of *true endowment* (permanently restricted net assets) and *quasi-endowment* (board-designated unrestricted net assets that function like true endowment).

18. This assumes a donor does not explicitly restrict the capital gains on his or her gift.

19. Technically, it is variability *relative* to a so-called risk-free investment, like U.S. Treasury bills.

20. For diversification to be effective, risks must be uncorrelated, meaning that the return on one investment is unaffected by returns on other investments.

21. Gifts of real estate should be examined for environmental contaminants, which are very expensive to abate.

22. At the same time, creditors possess a claim on the organization that takes precedence over all other claims. Assets used as collateral become forfeit in case of default.

23. A common misperception is that nonprofit-owned property is exempt from property tax, whereas leased space is taxed. Actually, property tax exemption is a matter of state law and nonprofit ownership is never sufficient. Some states exempt rented space, and nonprofit lessees in this select group of states already receive benefits from exemption.

24. *Interest* in this context refers to interest paid on debt. "*Before interest and depreciation*" means that these costs are to be added to surplus. Explanation: depreciation does not use cash and the level of operations has no effect on interest payments but both reduce the size of a surplus. Adding them to surplus gives a metric of the profitability of operations.

25. A *bond* in this context is an insurance policy that protects the organization from loss due to *defalcation*—more commonly known as theft and fraud.

References

Bloom, E. The Rise and Fall of the August Wilson Center. *Pittsburgh Post-Gazette*. February 8, 2014.

Bowman, W. *Finance Fundamentals for Nonprofits: Building Capacity and Sustainability.* Hoboken, NJ: John Wiley and Sons, 2011.

Federal Deposit Insurance Corporation. *Understanding Deposit Insurance,* https://www.fdic .gov/deposit/deposits (accessed December 2014).

Froelich, K. A. Diversification of Revenue Strategies: Evolving Resource Dependence in Nonprofit Organizations. *Nonprofit and Voluntary Sector Quarterly*, 1999, 28(3), 246–268.

Gillers, H., and Grotto, J. Dinosaur-Size Debt. *Chicago Tribune*, March 8, 2013.

GuideStar. www.guidestar.org (accessed December 2014).

Hager, M. A., and Searing, E. A. M. 10 Ways to Kill Your Nonprofit. *Nonprofit Quarterly*, 2014, Winter, 66–72.

Investopedia. *Internal Controls.* www.investopedia.com/terms/i/internalcontrols.asp (accessed December 2014).

Legal Information Institute. *Fiduciary Duty.* www.law.cornell.edu/wex/fiduciary _duty.

Myers, S. C. Capital Structure, *Journal of Economic Perspectives*, 2001, 15(2), 81–102.

Nonprofit Operating Reserve Initiative. *Maintaining Nonprofit Operating Reserves: An Organizational Imperative for Nonprofit Financial Stability.* Washington, DC: Author, 2008.

Pratt, J. Analyzing the Dynamics of Funding: Reliability and Autonomy. *Nonprofit Quarterly*, 2004, 11(2), 8–13.

Roeger, K. L., Blackwood, A. S., and Pettijohn, S. L. *The Nonprofit Almanac, 2012.* Washington, DC: Urban Institute Press, 2012.

Sedlacek, V. O., and Jarvis, W. F. *Endowment Spending: Building a Stronger Policy Framework.* Danbury, CT: Commonfund, 2010.

Sloan, M. F., Grizzle, C., and Kim, M. You Say Potato...The Disconnect Between Academic Understanding of Operating Reserves and Executive Director Perceptions. Paper presented to the Annual Research Conference of the Association for Research on Nonprofit Organizations and Voluntary Action (ARNOVA) in Denver, Colorado, November 2014.

United Nations. *Handbook of Nonprofit Institutions.* Author: New York, 2003.

University of Delaware. *Internal Control.* www.udel.edu/Treasurer/intcntrldef.html (accessed December 2014).

U.S. Department of the Treasury. *Treasury Direct.* www.treasurydirect.gov/ tdhome.htm (accessed December 2014a).

U.S. Department of the Treasury. *Daily Treasury Yield Curve Rates.* www.treasury.gov/ resource-center/data-chart-center/interest-rates/Pages/TextView.aspx?data=yield (accessed December 2014b).

U.S. Securities and Exchange Commission. www.sec.gov/investor/pubs/assetallocation. htm (accessed December 2014).

Vanguard. https://personal.vanguard.com/us/insights/saving-investing/model-portfolio allocations (accessed December 2014).

Yale University. *The Yale Endowment 2010.* www.yale.edu/investments/Yale_Endowment_ 10.pdf (accessed December 2014).

Young, D. R. Toward a Normative Theory of Nonprofit Finance. In D. R. Young (ed.), *Financing Nonprofits: Putting Theory into Practice.* Lanham, MD: Rowman & Littlefield, 2007, p. 341.

PART FIVE

LEADING AND MANAGING PEOPLE IN NONPROFITS

There are no nonprofit leaders or managers with any significant experience who have any doubt that the single most critical contributor to a nonprofit's success is its people. Regardless of the mission, size, history, or geographic location of the organization, every nonprofit must be able to attract, retain, reward, and motivate its people. Unfortunately, experienced leaders also cannot deny that some of the most important yet vexing aspects of nonprofit leadership and management are directly related to the work of leading and managing people. When it comes to people, there are no magic bullets or special techniques that will make the process simple and easy. But there is a valuable body of knowledge about human resource management and how it can be handled effectively and (relatively) efficiently. The chapters of Part Five apply the insights of this field to the work of nonprofit managers, most of whom have little or no training in this aspect of their management work. These chapters provide an important foundation for understanding the basic elements of human resource and personnel management—for paid staff and for volunteers—and share useful insights for how nonprofit managers can make effective use of this information to motivate and mobilize their people to accomplish the results they seek.

Mary R. Watson and Rikki Abzug lead us into the topic in Chapter Twenty-Two, to explain the overall process of human resource management and detail the human resource systems, processes, and practices that are important to any well-functioning nonprofit organization. Building on the foundation presented by Watson and Abzug, Nancy E. Day explains in Chapter Twenty-Three how to approach one of the most challenging yet important of human resource management issues, the challenge of compensating work and rewarding performance. Day explains the orientation known as the Total Rewards approach to compensation and benefits from the perspective of the characteristics and expectations of people working in the nonprofit sector, and shares insights into some of the most useful ways that this approach can be employed. Finally, in Chapter Twenty-Four, Jeffrey L. Brudney discusses the segment of the human resource world that is most unique to the nonprofit sector—the volunteer. Brudney presents a comprehensive explanation of the effective volunteer management program, and how it should be developed and operated, and explains how a nonprofit can systematically and strategically implement a program that will enable it to attract, organize, lead, and manage the volunteers it needs and wants. Building on the insights shared by Jeavons in Chapter Seven, each of the chapters of Part Five gives careful attention to the ethical and legal aspects of working with people, employees, and volunteers alike, while emphasizing the importance of keeping the mission and people at the forefront of the leadership and management process.

CHAPTER TWENTY-TWO

EFFECTIVE HUMAN RESOURCE MANAGEMENT

Nonprofit Staffing for the Future

Mary R. Watson and Rikki Abzug

The attraction, selection, and retention of staff are among the most important processes managers in organizations undertake, especially in today's dynamic workforce conditions. Forecasts suggest that tomorrow's leaders are likely to have a dozen jobs or more over the course of a career, and effective organizations will need to align opportunities with dynamic career paths. The nature of work itself is rapidly changing, requiring more innovation, design, and data skills (Gillett, 2015). Millennials with these talents seek work with organizations with strong purpose and flexible work arrangements, and they are interested in working on important societal goals (Benko, Erickson, Hagel, and Wong, 2014). Forward-thinking nonprofit organizations hire staff whose talent set and education align with organizational roles, thus recruiting and keeping staff satisfied (Lee and Sabharwai, 2016). Yet designing these recruitment and retention processes requires expertise, time, and an eye toward future organizational needs, all of which can be difficult for nonprofit leaders to find given the pressures of the immediacy of running a nonprofit (Gregory and Howard, 2009). Straight out of the box human resource techniques, most of which were developed in for-profit businesses, can provide general guidance to leaders of nonprofits, but nonprofits benefit most from crafting a different kind of human resource system (Maier, Meyer, and Steinbereithner, 2016).

The purpose of this chapter is to help nonprofit executive directors and staff at all levels build a system of human resource practices that is both effective and realistic in the contexts of their own organizations. Toward this end, we have organized the chapter around two goals. Our first goal is to demonstrate the advantages of thinking systemically about the role that people play in organizations, showing how better human resource practice leads to better long-term outcomes. Not only is it possible to save time and effort in recruitment, selection, and staff retention programs, but building an effective human resource culture is key to long-term success. Our second goal is to provide an overview of the most critical human resource processes, demonstrating how they can be accomplished in settings without significant formal human resource structures and staff in place. We also discuss important legislation related to various aspects of finding and keeping the right people that enable each nonprofit to reach its own unique objectives. Although it is not possible to be comprehensive in every aspect of human resource management—volumes have been written on this subject—this chapter provides the essential knowledge necessary to find staff prospects, interview and evaluate applicants, retain and keep staff motivated, and manage the circumstances under which staff will ultimately leave the organization. The next chapter in this *Handbook*, prepared by Nancy Day, provides complementary information about the design and management of compensation and benefits programs.

Staff and leaders might wonder what is different about our approach to nonprofit human resources. In fact, one might simply pick up a current practitioner article on the "top ten tips for recruitment," for example, and conclude that the answers are stated there. The difference lies in our deliberate recognition that nonprofit organizations are values-driven, and so must be their approach to human resources (Ridder and McCandless, 2010). Yet there is no universal style of nonprofit human resource management because of the variety of contexts, structures, and conditions in which social sector organizations operate. Further, there are no simple rules: contingency approaches that argue a simple set of "if . . . then" recommendations (for example, if an organization is in a rural area, then it must have a local recruitment strategy) are not sufficient. Outcome measures like return on investment can be useful, but they are not sufficient unless systems are considered holistically and in context. Instead, we propose that "configurational" (Toh, Morgeson, and Campion, 2008) approaches are best because they recognize that there are unique synergies gained through human resource systems and that these synergies differ depending on the context in which they exist. Executives who capitalize on the relationships among human resource approaches, the organization's environment, the mission and goals of the organization, and knowledge management principles are the ones who are successful in building momentum toward the organization's desired state, especially when the organization considers its mission in the context of other similar organizations (Koch, Galaskiewicz, and Pierson, 2015). To aid in this endeavor, throughout this chapter, we remind executives of the key questions that should be asked regarding elements of the human resource system in their organizations.

Why Emphasize Recruitment and Retention?

Given the humanistic missions of most nonprofit organizations, it is paradoxical that nonprofit leaders need to be reminded of the importance of the people in the organizations. Yet across organizations and time, multiple constituencies demand attention from nonprofit leaders. Nonprofit mission statements typically do focus on people, but people who are external to the organizations—the clients—rather than internal staff. The attention paid to internal staff issues is scant in many nonprofit settings.

The primary goal of nonprofits is typically to ensure that the organization delivers on mission. Most staff are attracted to nonprofits because they are motivated by their organization's mission. Thus, compared to their for-profit counterparts, nonprofits have an extremely powerful advantage in all aspects of their human resource systems. Studying the nonprofit workforce, Paul Light (2004, p. 7) has suggested that "the nonprofit sector survives because it has a self-exploiting workforce: wind it up and it will do more with less until it just runs out." A 2006 American Humanics report underscored Light's findings that nonprofit employees are comparatively highly motivated, hard working, and deeply committed (Halpern, 2006), and a 2012 study by Park and Word confirmed that nonprofit employees were highly intrinsically motivated compared with both for-profit and public-sector employees. Even in treacherous economic times, the motivations of nonprofit staff are precisely what enable their organizations to thrive, if they avoid the pitfalls of adopting for-profit approaches without first considering their suitability for nonprofits (Beck, Lengnick-Hall, and Lengnick-Hall, 2008).

We emphasize here that the nature of nonprofits makes them ideally suited to maximize their outcomes through the people of the organizations. This focus on people results in additional organizational capacity, effective succession planning, engaged and motivated staff, and improved client service delivery. These are not just effectiveness outcomes; they are also the keys to the time, money, and information organizations need to survive and thrive. They also lead to reputation effects that attract staff and funders through positive profiles featured in outlets such as *The Nonprofit Times'* annual roundup of "Best Places to Work" (for 2015, see Hrywna) and awards given by entities like *The New York Times* with its Nonprofit Excellence Awards (www.npccny.org/info/awards.htm).

Successful nonprofit organizations recognize that organizational success lies in the creative engagement of the human resources of the organization. They regard human resources not as a staff function outside the organization's operation, but rather as the central conduit through which organizations succeed. They capitalize on the power of mission to attract and motivate staff. They recognize the critical nature of staff synergies in selecting new staff members. They leverage technology, where appropriate, to reduce recruitment costs and administer standardized human resource functions. They encourage diversity on many dimensions, and they enact cultures that are constituted by diverse groups working well together. They design motivation and retention systems that recognize both the intrinsic motivators that brought staff to the organization (such as mission focus or client focus) as well as the extrinsic motivators (such as pay, health care, or retirement) that are necessary for staff financial and physical health. They retain and develop talented staff whenever possible, and they manage terminations in humane and positive ways when layoffs are unavoidable.

Human Resources Is a System, Not a Set of Tasks

Our approach is a systems approach to human resources that considers the unique complement of the configuration of human resource practices. The activities of human resources cannot be thought about independent of one another, and effective leaders develop an overarching set of integrated human resource goals to guide their day-to-day decision making. Effective nonprofit managers avoid staffing decisions that come about as part of an immediate crisis, for example, needing to hire quickly to scale up and deliver on outcomes expected from additional funded projects or reacting to the sudden departure of a crucial staff person who needs to be replaced immediately. Instead, effective nonprofit organizations keep an eye on their future, anticipating stages where the mission will be broadened and additional talent will be needed, conducting succession planning to identify needs to develop internal staff before there is a crisis, and monitoring the external environment to determine what new funding sources will be coming its way.

Avoiding immediate crises can circumvent unintended long-term outcomes. For example, government contractors who consistently add and delete staff based on variable levels of program funding can inadvertently create a climate of insecurity and distrust. Organizations that vary staff levels can develop a reputation as an unstable employer, thus discouraging qualified and committed applicants to apply when new staff are needed. Individual human resource decisions, seemingly isolated, can cause reverberations inside and outside the organization, many of which may be unintended and unwanted.

Not only are human resource functions interconnected, but in the aggregate they also represent the experienced culture of the organization. The organization's human resource goals are very important because they define the day-to-day quality of work life enjoyed by staff. Because of their centrality, informed executives engage all staff in imagining their ideal collective human resource culture. In this way, they begin at the desired end. First they figure out, collectively in their organization, where they want to go. Then they do a needs assessment of their current culture of human resources, assess their planning needs, engage staff at all levels in designing human resource processes, and later evaluate their progress toward the desired end. All along the way, effective nonprofits keep in mind where they are trying to go as they take the small steps that will get them there.

Some examples will illustrate the point. Affirmative businesses (alternatively called *social firms* or *supported employment*), incorporated as or created by nonprofits, with goals of providing jobs and job training for mentally, physically, or economically disadvantaged individuals, often center human resources in their sustainability and growth plans (Bond, Drake, and Becker, 2012; Warner and Mandiberg, 2006). For vocational or training organizations serving the mentally ill or the homeless, for example, the line between clients and staff can be amorphous, and best practices suggest an integrated approach that emphasizes job design, career pathing, motivational compensation, and respect for individual choice. Organizations from New York's Housing Works Bookstore to Seattle's Boomtown Café find they can do good by doing well if they stand by all of their people.

If You Build It, They Will Come (and Stay)

There are two key concepts to keep in mind while imagining the end state of an effective nonprofit human resource system: fit and embeddedness. These two concepts make clear that, whereas successful executives design human resource systems, these systems are continually re-created by everyone associated with the organization. Therefore, in successful nonprofits, all staff are continually rebuilding their human resource culture. There is no true end result: human resource culture is a never-ending exercise in coevolution.

In two decades of studies on person-organization fit and person-job fit (Hoffman, Bynum, Piccolo, and Sutton, 2011), a consistent finding is that staff are attracted to organizations with which they perceive an alignment between the goals of the organization and their own values and objectives. This is one explanation as to why recruiting by internal referral is so successful: individuals who know insiders are much more likely to understand what the organization is about and accurately assess whether or not they would like to work there. Thus, self-selection on the part of prospective and current staff plays a huge role in shaping the ultimate human resource culture. This notion of perceived fit has been shown to apply to the person and the job, the person and the work group, and the person and the organization as a whole (Resnick, Baltes, and Shantz, 2007).

Nonprofit executives should keep in mind that these perceived fit processes are going on in all aspects of the human resource system (attracting, recruiting, selecting, retaining, and staff turnover). Perceived fit has been shown to be developed throughout the recruitment process, thus the ways in which nonprofits recruit staff is essential in attracting the right candidates (Swider, Zimmerman, and Barrick, 2015). One productive task is to engage all staff in a dialogue around what constitutes fit in their organization. Effective nonprofits work to make explicit what the fit dimensions are, beginning by examining the mission statement. A second task is to investigate perceptions of your organization held by those in similar and different organizations. Knowing how the culture of the organization is perceived by outsiders will provide key information about who might be attracted to the organization and who might be approaching staff to recruit them away. Once these dimensions are clearer, the human resource strategy of the organization can recognize the power and limitations of the notion of fit. Whether an organization makes it explicit or not, perceived fit (or lack thereof) is always an element of the human resource system success.

One important clarification needs emphasis here. Fit is not a synonym for homogeneity. Successful organizations tend to seek and engage diverse viewpoints. In fact, one might have as an element of the mission an explicit goal of nourishing a culture of diversity. In this case, fit means attracting staff who share the value of honoring difference, not attracting similar staff. Successful nonprofits shape their human resource systems around a broad and diverse set of views, using their historical, community, and mission contexts to define their diversity goals.

The second key element of an effective nonprofit human resource system is the notion of embeddedness. This refers to the extent to which the staff and their families are engaged in the organization and its community. Embeddedness is a broader concept than organization satisfaction and commitment, which have been argued to account for less than 5 percent of actual turnover. Drawing on Kurt Lewin's field theory (1951), research on embeddedness suggests that staff who are more embedded in their organizations are less likely to leave voluntarily. There are three dimensions to embeddedness: the extent to which individuals have links to other people, the extent to which their job and community fit with other aspects of their lives, and the perception of what would be lost if the individual left his or her job (Mitchell, Holtom, Lee, Sablynski, and Erez, 2001).

For successful nonprofits, embeddedness is a powerful concept. Nonprofit organizations can increase their human and social capital by remembering what embeds staff into their organizations (Holtom, Mitchell, and Lee, 2006). Not only is it desirable that staff share a passion for the organization's mission, but they must also be motivated by the way in which their role facilitates reaching part of that mission. Further, the more extensive the networks of relationships they and their families have within the organization and the community, the more likely they are to stay with the organization. Finally, the understanding of what would be lost if they left the organization ("sacrifice," in embeddedness terms) helps leaders guide human resource systems closer to the ideal state that staff would imagine. Here a good exercise for executive directors would be to encourage open dialogue around human resource systems, eliciting from staff a shared understanding of the really unique elements of the nonprofit and the community it serves. Note that discussion of human resources includes all aspect of work, including the design of jobs themselves.

In addition to shared values, it is also important to recognize individual needs of staff, which will differ from person to person and family to family, and vary considerably by generation (Johnson and Ng, 2015; Kunreuther, 2003; McGinnis, 2011). The quality of the relationship that staff members have with leaders is a key factor in their intention to stay with the organization. Informal dialogue, or more formalized 360-degree performance appraisals systems, in which staff give constructive feedback to the executive staff (and vice versa), can help keep positive communication open across levels. Staff families matter, too. Offering cafeteria style benefits, allowing staff to choose from an array of human resource benefits what best fits their family needs, is one example of engaging with the "whole person." Flexible work schedules might also help in this area. At a minimum, open dialogue between staff and managers must be encouraged to keep shared lines of communication open.

First Things First: Make It Legal

It is always wise to begin any discussion of the processes involved in human resource systems with a discussion of the existing law related to these human resource processes. Many nonprofit managers are unfamiliar with current legislative statutes, and the consequences of decisions that violate the law can be dire, particularly for smaller organizations without the resources to engage in lawsuits or absorb fines.

Despite a very rocky beginning at the dawn of the new Republic, The United States now has a century-long tradition of creating policy to protect workers. Starting around the turn of the 20th Century with the growth of the modern union movement, and following the 1912 shirtwaist workers' strike, the U.S. Congress created the Department of Labor ("The Labor History Timeline" of the AFL-CIO, www.aflcio.org/About/Our-History/Labor-History-Timeline). Employment law emerged in fits and starts from the Progressive Era, through the New Deal and ramped up during the civil rights movement of the 1960s around race and equity, and through advances in workplace safety in the 1970s. Employment law continues to evolve to try to keep pace with today's work issues, including expanded access to health care, religious exemptions, and the rights of transgender employees, family-friendly policies, and procedures to reduce terrorism. We shall review the essential laws that all nonprofit professionals must know, whether "human resources" is part of their job title or not.

It is important to note that nonprofits are typically held accountable for actions taken by their staff, vendors, clients, and contractors. In general, actions that managers knew about, as well as those the courts deem they should have known about, are the responsibility of the nonprofit's leadership, not the individual who committed the discriminatory action. The best defense against discrimination charges is the existence of clear policy that spells out the nature of discriminatory actions and a system through which all staff are educated about fair employment practice.

There are a variety of legislative frameworks around the world, made up of varying combinations of national, regional, and local legislation. Knowing how these levels of legislation interact in one's own country is important. For instance, the Canada Labor Code covers only 6 percent of the nation's employees, so most employment legal issues are determined by laws defined by the various provinces and territories (Labour Program, 2016: www.labour.gc .ca/eng/regulated.shtml). In the United States, by contrast, federal regulations apply to all organizations with staff above a certain size (which varies, depending on the particular law). There are also state and local laws that provide more stringent standards than the federal legislation, and each nonprofit must familiarize itself with the laws of its own state and the states in which it operates. Due to space limitations, we review only U.S. federal law here. State and local laws vary considerably, and nonprofit managers may want to keep abreast of ever-changing legal requirements both nationally and locally by following coverage in the *Chronicle of Philanthropy, Nonprofit Times, Nonprofit Quarterly's*

Online NPQ Newswire, and the newsletters and/or websites of state or local nonprofit associations.

This section provides a general overview of the U.S. federal legislative framework, with particular emphasis on discrimination law. Using this chapter as a starting place, you may find that a user-friendly legal guide to U.S. federal employment law (such as Guerin and DelPo, 2013) can help clarify key questions. However, general legal knowledge is not to be substituted for appropriate legal advice from qualified counsel. It is always necessary to consult an attorney for specific applications to your organization.

Title VII: The Civil Rights Act of 1964

Title VII of the Civil Rights Act, arguably the most influential piece of legislation regarding employee treatment, was passed into law in 1964. Building on energy from the civil rights movement that garnered more attention than previous civil rights bills, the Civil Rights Act was signed into law under Lyndon Johnson's administration. Title VII of that act focuses on employment, and it specifically prohibits employment discrimination based on race, skin color, religion, sex, and national origin. In addition, it established the Equal Employment Opportunity Commission (EEOC), a federal agency empowered with the enforcement of discrimination violations. Other sections of the Civil Rights Act relate to education and public facilities contexts. Here we focus only on the employment dimensions of the law specified in Title VII.

The prohibition of discrimination provided under Title VII applies to all aspects of the work relationship: recruiting, hiring, promoting, performance evaluation, access to training, discharging, and so on. A common misperception is that the coverage is narrowly applicable to hiring decisions. All organizations with fifteen or more employees are required to adhere to nondiscriminatory practices in all aspects of their treatment of employees. Furthermore, any organization of any size that receives substantial federal government funds or contracts (the dollar value varies by program) must comply. Also, any employment agency, labor organization, or joint labor-management committee controlling apprenticeship or other training or retraining must comply, regardless of size. Title VII was amended by the Civil Rights Act of 1991 to include the opportunity of compensatory and punitive damages for intentional discrimination, enable litigants to collect legal fees, and allow for jury trials.

There is one particularly notable exception to enforcement of anti-discrimination categories. In general, religious organizations have been considered exempt from the religion category and supported in their right to make employment decisions based on faith. Indeed, efforts by successive Congresses to pass an Employment Non-Discrimination Act (ENDA) have often blown up over the breadth of exceptions for religious and nonprofit membership-only clubs (Signorile, 2014). Further, the 2014 Supreme Court Decision in *Burwell v. Hobby Lobby*, enshrined private companies' religious rights in corporate decision making. However, some federal social programs (the Workforce Investment Act, for example) contain language explicitly prohibiting religious discrimination, others (such as community development block grants and Head Start) might be interpreted as prohibiting employment decisions based on religion, and some other states and localities require religious organizations not to discriminate on the basis of religion in order to be eligible for funding. Obviously, this is an area of employment law that is constantly evolving, and nonprofit managers are encouraged to familiarize themselves with media outlets that provide coverage of this turbulent legal arena.

Disparate Treatment Versus Adverse Impact. Understanding what human resource practices constitute as discrimination requires reading the legal text of Title VII. Discrimination, as defined under Title VII, falls into two categories. What is termed *disparate treatment* is sometimes also called deliberate or direct discrimination. Under a charge of disparate treatment, a litigant who is a member of a protected group (race, color, religion, sex, or national origin) would argue that he or she was treated differently because of his or her protected class. A litigant might argue that the interviewer indicated racial or national origin bias during the interview, for example. In addition to evidence of direct discrimination, disparate treatment charges require not only that the litigant has been denied access to the employment benefit but also that another person who is not a member of the protected class was chosen. Fortunately, most organizations have put human resource practices and staff training programs in place to alleviate many of the intentional discrimination charges.

Lesson

Make sure all staff members are aware of the organization's intolerance of deliberately discriminatory practices, and ensure that training around these issues is provided. Many issues are subtle.

Determining the much more common charge "adverse impact" is more complex. Sometimes called indirect or unintentional discrimination, adverse impact occurs when the aggregate outcomes for a protected group are less advantageous than for the majority group. The landmark case in this instance is *Griggs v. Duke Power* (401 U.S. 424, 1971). Griggs, an African American employee of the Duke Power Company in North Carolina, was denied promotion to a supervisory position because he did not hold a high school diploma. At that time in North Carolina, the high school graduation rates for blacks and whites were significantly different, with blacks earning diplomas at a lower rate (this disparity has since been corrected). The U.S. Supreme Court ruled that the high school diploma requirement discriminated against blacks because they had a lower graduation rate. Further, the organization failed to demonstrate why a high school diploma was necessary to do the job effectively. In fact, some supervisors promoted earlier did not have diplomas.

The *Griggs* case makes two things clear for nonprofit leaders. First, it is necessary to examine your own human resource practices to ensure that the outcomes for protected groups are not different from the outcomes for majority groups. Second, be certain that you can demonstrate the job-relatedness of any human resource criterion, regardless of whether you think it might be correlated with protected class. For example, imagine that you regularly select staff to attend a leadership development program. To encourage fairness, you make it a practice to choose individuals from across your organization's geographical locations to attend, and you make these decisions one by one over time. Imagine, however, that in compiling an analysis of your decisions in the past year, you discover that in the aggregate, women have been chosen less frequently than men, despite the fact that your workforce is balanced by gender. How would you know whether you have enacted a discriminatory selection for training?

The first test is to see whether you have what is called a *prima facie* ("on its face") case of discrimination. The legal test is what is called the four-fifths rule: Was the rate of selection of the women at least four-fifths (80 percent) of the rate of selection for the men? Assume that there are ten women and ten men from whom you might have chosen. If you have chosen five men, you must also have chosen at least four women to diffuse a prima facie case. In the event that there appears to be discrimination after application of the four-fifths rule (in this example, if you chose fewer than four women), can you defend the decisions you made by arguing that the criteria on which you based the selection of trainees are related to job performance? Numerous court decisions based on gender, including well-publicized ones argued by airlines to defend female-only flight attendant positions, have established that gender is not a valid job criterion.

Lesson

Remember that under Title VII, discrimination does not have to be intentional to be illegal. The aggregate outcome of your organization's decisions can be used as evidence of discrimination, even if it was not intentional.

Consider another example. Imagine you are choosing among applicants for a counseling position where the clients speak English. Among your applicant pool are ten U.S.-born native English speakers and ten Chinese-born immigrants with Mandarin as their native tongue. If five of the Americans pass the initial English language test you use for prescreening but only one of the Chinese applicants does, is there discrimination based on national origin? On the face of it, there is a prima facie case of discrimination (50 percent of the U.S.-born make the cut, compared to only 10 percent of the Chinese-born, which fails the four-fifths test). In this situation, however, you may be able to successfully muster a job-relatedness defense that the skill on which you screened (language) is essential to performing the job (counseling clients). Although there are other defenses in the case of prima facie discrimination (seniority system, bona fide occupational qualification), job-relatedness is the best defense (Fick, 2006). Nonprofits need to be careful to use selection criteria that are quantifiable and empirically proven to be related to job performance. General impressions of candidates and their attitudes do not hold up well in court.

Lesson

Use only human resource criteria that your organization can demonstrate are directly related to job performance. Do not rely on opinions or assumptions; collect hard data.

Interpretations of Title VII. An interpretation of Title VII surrounds the issue of sexual harassment. Although Title VII did not specifically identify sexual harassment as part of its domain, subsequent court cases have interpreted sexual harassment as discrimination based on gender. According to law, there are two kinds of sexual harassment. The first is called *quid pro quo*, Latin for "something in exchange for something." To meet the criteria under this category, a staffer (or in some legal findings, clients or board members) must have been the unwanted recipient of an advance that is sexual in nature, where the "submission to or rejection of this conduct explicitly or implicitly affects an individual's employment," including employment decisions (Equal Employment

Opportunity Commission, 2016). Most organizations have mechanisms in place to ensure that deliberate sexual harassment does not occur, as well as channels for safely reporting incidents.

The category of "hostile work environment" is more subtle. In general, a staffer must have been subjected to either sexual advances or other verbal or physical conduct of a sexual nature that either "unreasonably interfered with an individual's work performance" or created "an intimidating, hostile, or offensive working environment" (Equal Employment Opportunity Commission, 2016). Courts typically consider whether the staffer made it known to the alleged harasser that the advances or behaviors were unwelcome, and the advances or behaviors must have been repeated. However, in some circumstances, courts have interpreted an act as so egregious as to not warrant meeting the conditions of notice and readvance.

Supreme Court cases clarify that both men and women are protected, and harassment can be perpetrated by individuals of the same sex regardless of the sexual orientation of either party (for example, *Oncale v. Sundowner Offshore Services, Inc.*, 523 U.S. 75, 1998). Further, the harasser can be connected to the organization in many capacities: as a supervisor, employee, agent of the organization, co-worker, or nonemployee. Employers can be held liable even if the employee does not complain about the harassment (*Faragher v. Boca Raton*, 524 U.S. 775, 1998). Finally, the harassed does not need to be the direct recipient of the unwanted sexual behavior. A charge can be filed by anyone affected by the conduct. Court decisions on legal standards for behavior have shifted from those of a "reasonable person" to those of a "reasonable woman" or "reasonable victim."

Lesson

Make sure all staff members understand what constitutes sexual harassment, how to avoid harassing incidents, and the channels they should follow to report unwanted behaviors. Extend your training to clients, vendors, and other related staff.

Legislation Protecting the Disabled

Other legislation has extended nondiscriminatory practices to other protected groups. For example, the Age Discrimination in Employment Act of 1967 (and amendments in the Older Workers Benefit Protection Act) applies to employers with twenty or more employees and protects workers over age forty (younger in some states) against discrimination based on age. The Pregnancy Discrimination Act (an amendment to Title VII) protects women who are pregnant against refusals to hire, requires treatment of pregnancy that interferes medically with the employee's ability to work to be treated as any other disability, requires that any health insurance offered by the employer include pregnancy coverage (but not abortion coverage), and requires that employees be given leave, vacation calculation, and pay under the same practices that are afforded to other employees on leave.

One final group deserves special explanation: the disabled. The Council for Disability Rights estimates that forty-three million Americans have physical or mental disabilities (Council for Disability Rights, 2009). The employment rate of those with disabilities is half that of those without, despite the fact that two-thirds of those unemployed with disabilities say they would prefer to be working (National Council on Disabilities, 2007).

The Americans with Disabilities Act of 1990, and as amended in 2008, protects those with physical and mental disabilities, whether perceived or real, from discrimination in employment (and public access). The act covers all employers with more than fifteen employees, as well as all state and government programs and activities. The ADA defines a person with a disability as "someone with a physical or mental impairment that substantially limits a major life activity, has a record of such an impairment, or is regarded as having such an impairment" (Equal Employment Opportunity Commission, 2016).

Clarifications of the ADA by the EEOC indicate that the use of items like medications or prostheses does not disqualify a disabled person. Mental and emotional characteristics such as thinking and concentrating are covered, and short-term impairments are generally interpreted as less life-altering (Equal Employment Opportunity Commission, 2000). Active drug use is not a disability, although prior drug use can qualify if the person is discriminated against based on a record or perception of prior use. Although the ADA and its amendments do not specify the disabilities that qualify, case law has upheld such diverse conditions as mobility, vision, speech, and hearing impairments, asymptomatic HIV status, learning disabilities, and mental illness.

The passage of the ADA changed employment screening practices directly. Under the ADA, no employer may require a medical examination prior to extending a job offer. Further, where applicants or employees request "reasonable accommodation" of the physical workplace, the design of their jobs, or their benefits, employers are required to comply to the extent to which the accommodations do not cause the employer undue financial or logistical hardship. Examples of accommodations under ADA might include modifying work schedules, purchasing special equipment to facilitate reading or translation, physical alteration of the work site, or job reassignment.

> ## Lesson
>
> Be open to making accommodations to employees who might have disabilities. Encourage open dialogue so that staff members with "invisible" disabilities feel free to come forward to request accommodation. Do not screen based on disability; ask only if the employee can do the essential functions of the work required.

Legislation Protecting Individuals Based on Sexual Orientation and Gender Identity

Progress toward federal legislation that protects individuals from discrimination based on sexual orientation, gender identity, or transgendered status has been slow in its development. Although not detailed explicitly in Title VII, the EEOC interprets Title VII to prohibit discrimination based on sexual orientation or gender identity, interpreted to be a form of sex discrimination. The Employment Non-Discrimination Act (ENDA) has been considered by Congress many times since its introduction in 1994. ENDA would extend nondiscrimination based on sexual orientation in ways similar to the Title VII and the ADA. In 2009 a transgender-inclusive version of ENDA was introduced; in 2013 a version of the bill passed the Senate, but as of this writing the bill has not passed through the House of Representatives. Executive Order 13672, signed by President Obama in 2014, added gender identity as a protected category in the civilian federal workforce and sexual orientation and gender identity as protected groups for federal government contractors and subcontractors.

Some state and local level protection does exist based on sexual orientation, but the coverage is inconsistent across the United States. At the state level, twenty states and the District of Columbia have discrimination protection based on sexual orientation and gender identity in place, and twelve states and the District of Columbia have discrimination protection based on sexual identity. More than 250 cities and counties have added protections based on sexual orientation or gender identity.

> ## Lesson
>
> Although there is currently no federal law protecting individuals based on sexual orientation, state and local coverage exists in many locations. Ensure that your staff members are well versed in nondiscriminatory practices based on sexual orientation, sexual identity, and transgendered status.

Legislative Protection for Genetic Information

Title II of the Genetic Information Nondiscrimination Act of 2008 prohibits discrimination in employment based on genetic information. This protection extends to all conditions of employment (hiring, promotion, pay, firing, and so on), as well as prohibiting sharing of genetic information. Included in protected data is family medical history, which may be seen as a proxy for genetic predisposition. Harassment and retaliation based on genetic information are prohibited. Except in certain specific cases, the law prohibits the collection of genetic information. Among the exceptions are information needed to support Family Medical Leave (FMLA) requests, voluntary wellness programs, and information obtained inadvertently.

Role of the EEOC in Discrimination Cases

Under federal law, discrimination charges must be filed with the EEOC within 180 days of the incident or awareness that the incident might have caused discrimination. Most state laws allow up to three hundred days. Charges can be brought against an individual or any organization on behalf of the individual. No private lawsuit can be filed until the EEOC evaluates the case. Where EEOC investigation warrants, and where individuals request an EEOC "right to sue," private lawsuits can be started within a period of 90 days after the right to sue finding (Equal Employment Opportunity Commission, 2016).

Additional Legislation

In addition to the antidiscrimination legislation just described, there are many other major laws that affect your organization. Details about the key legal frameworks are listed here, and the U.S. government's official web portal (www .firstgov.gov) is a great place for nonprofit managers to find resources to answer questions.

- Fair Labor Standards Act (FLSA) of 1938, which covers wages and hours standards, as well as overtime, for employees who work interstate. This act covers large employers (with $500,000 in annual revenue) and small employers whose employees operate across state borders. Of particular interest in this legislation is the determination of which staff are exempt from overtime pay for work in excess of forty hours per week. "Professionals," "executives," and "outside salespeople" are the official exempt categories, but interpretations are more complex. Note: The US Department of Labor issued new FLSA regulations to take effect December, 2016, that will have important impact on certain nonprofits and their employment practices.

- Equal Pay Act of 1963, which prohibits sex-based wage discrimination and applies to most organizations with one or more employees. Exceptions include seniority, merit pay, and job performance. The Lilly Ledbetter Fair Pay Act of 2009 extended the time allowed for filing pay discrimination claims.

- Executive Order 11246, which requires nondiscrimination and affirmative action plans of federal government agencies and government contractors.

- Occupational Safety and Health Act of 1970, which was designed to reduce workplace injuries and illnesses and resulted in the creation of the Department of Labor's Occupational Safety and Health Administration.

- Immigration Reform and Control Act of 1986, which requires employers to verify employee identity and legal eligibility to work in the United States.

- Family and Medical Leave Act of 1993, which guarantees up to twelve weeks of unpaid leave to employees in organizations with more than fifty employees to welcome a natural or adoptive child into the family, to care for an immediate relative, or to recover from an illness.

- The Health Insurance Portability and Accountability Act of 1996 (HIPAA), which is designed to ensure that new staff can obtain health care benefits without being subjected to preexisting conditions clauses. This legislation is complex, and the reader can find details at the Health and Human Services website (www.hhs.gov).

- USA Patriot Act of 2001, which broadens government ability to review employment records, conduct surveillance of employees and employers, and monitor financial flows.

- Homeland Security Act of 2002, which contains provisions regarding the hiring of foreign workers. The act created the Department of Homeland Security and transferred the processing of work authorizations from the Immigration and Naturalization Service to the Bureau of Citizenship and Immigration Services, a division of the Department of Homeland Security.

- The Affordable Care Act of 2010 (Obamacare), which may even the playing field for small nonprofit organizations looking to recruit top talent. Because the act makes health insurance more accessible and affordable for more employees without requiring small employers to actually provide the insurance themselves, smaller nonprofits may be less disadvantaged than before as they compete for personnel.

- All state and local laws related to the workplace. Many of these follow the spirit of the federal laws but are likely to cover more organizations of smaller size. They may also cover groups not protected by federal legislation.

Make It Legal, Make It Fair

There is a sometimes a paradox in legality and fairness: What is legal is not always perceived as fair, and what is perceived as fair is not always legal. It is, of course, necessary to meet legal standards in all human resource decisions, and the law is relatively clear on what those specifics might be. However, a higher and more complex standard is establishing human resource approaches that are perceived by everyone inside and outside the organization as fair. Promoting antidiscrimination, following legal hiring procedures, and creating legal wages and benefits are all important signals of the centrality of human resources to the nonprofit.

Yet despite consensus on these concepts, implementation can often lead to staff feeling that they are not being treated fairly. In what has been, historically, rare, but may be increasing instances, nonprofit social service workers (following the lead of their compatriots in nonprofit hospitals and many nonprofit educational institutions) may consider creating or joining a union if nonprofit management does not proactively implement state-of-the-art human resource practices and cultures. Commentators have suggested that as the public sector (where union membership is the relatively highest) is shrunk, is increasingly hostile to unions, and/or is contracting out services to the nonprofit sector, the nonprofit sector, itself, may become an arena of the next big unionization push (Hill, 2013). However, observers also note that nonprofit managers may be in a relatively unique position to ensure that a unionization drive is a mutually beneficial exercise (Cohen, 2013). Indeed, as unions are, themselves, part of the nonprofit universe, the two sides in the intra-sectoral labor dispute may be more inclined to work in consonance rather than opposition. In any event, creating open communication channels to bring issues of fairness—and perceived unfairness—to everyone's attention is important. Finally, going beyond simply what is legal to embracing what staff feel is fair takes an organization a long way toward building trust and commitment.

This is especially true for small or religious organizations that may be exempt from the requirements of many of these legislative initiatives. Small or religious organizations that do not respect the spirit of the law (even if not required to respect the letter of the law) do so at their own risk. They run the risk of disengaging the funding community, government opportunities, and local labor markets and talent pools, as well as segments of the giving public. With exemptions for religion-based discriminatory hiring for faith-based organizations seeking public support currently under contention, all organizations need to weigh the mission fulfillment and community needs argument in favor of exclusionary human resource practices against legal and public norms and expectations of fairness and diversity.

Putting It All Together: The Processes of Human Resources

This section of the chapter reviews effective approaches to recruiting and retaining motivated nonprofit staff. We begin by reinforcing the idea of beginning with the desired end state, and we recall the concepts of fit and embeddedness. We discuss how recruitment and selection affect the culture of any nonprofit. We address legal pitfalls. Finally, we raise awareness about what elements of the organization's context must be taken into consideration.

The Human Resource Audit

Earlier in the chapter, we introduced the idea of "starting at the desired end," that is, figuring out where the organization stands with respect to human resources and where it wants to go. Every nonprofit organization should regularly engage in systematically evaluating where it stands with respect to human resources. Exhibit 22.1 suggests the kinds of questions to be asked and answered.

Once the answers to the human resource audit questions are understood, the organization is ready to begin the process of adding staff in a way that will enhance the organization's movement toward its desired state. The goal is that every hiring and retention decision is made in the context of an overall plan for where the organization is headed. All staff should be involved in the human resource audit process as well as in developing plans for bridging any identified gaps.

EXHIBIT 22.1. SAMPLE HUMAN RESOURCE AUDIT CHECKLIST

ORGANIZATION AND JOB STRUCTURE

How accurate is the organization chart? Does it reflect both formal and informal reporting relationships? Is it current? Do staff at different levels agree that it is accurate?

How up-to-date are job descriptions and statements of knowledge, skills, and abilities (KSAs)? Do hiring, performance appraisal, and promotion

---

standards support applicant matching and staff skill development for these jobs and KSAs?

Do the existing organization structure and distribution of work responsibilities match future operational plans? Which aspects of the structure seem appropriate for the next three to five years, and which will need modification?

Human Resource Planning

What skills are required for current projects? Do existing staff have the needed skills? What training might be needed?

What skills are anticipated to be needed for future projects? Does the organization have these skills on staff at this time? If not, how will they be required?

What turnover is anticipated within the next year? Will it likely be voluntary or involuntary? What gaps will this create in the organization's ability to meet its goals? What capacity may be lost due to turnover?

How strong is the internal promotion ladder? Are internal promotions a goal for this organization? If so, for what positions? How complete is the leadership succession plan?

What future hiring plans currently exist? Are there resources in place to fund these openings? What recruitment strategies have been developed in anticipation of upcoming recruitment?

How competitive is the organization in its labor market with organizations of similar size and purpose? Are salaries and benefits offered that will attract desired applicants? How does the organization's reputation affect potential recruitment success?

Organization Culture

What characteristics were identified in the organizational fit analysis as important? How well has fit been accomplished?

What were the outcomes of the internal embeddedness analysis? Which staff are embedded, and which staff are not committed? Are the more highly desired staff the more embedded? If not, how will the organization work to achieve this?

What is the state of staff motivation? What makes working in this organization desirable for staff? What are the negative aspects of the work environment? How and why do individuals vary in their motivation?

What characterizes the existing human resource culture? Is this culture consistent with the organization's mission? What values are central to the operation? What dimensions of diversity are desired?

The Staffing Plan

Nonprofits are likely to address the issue of staff planning within the broader context of the organization's strategic plan, although all nonprofits would do well to strategically consider the staffing mix at start-up, at present, and for a future desired state. The motivating question for any staffing plan is: "What are the continuing activities that need to be performed to help the organization meets its goals (and, ultimately, its mission)?" The staffing plan involves determination of the complement of staffers (full-time or full-time equivalent, part-time, volunteer, consultant, and outsourced) that will most effectively contribute to achieving the organization's purpose. It is likely that planning such levels will involve careful review of state and federal laws around fair labor standards and the designation of employees as exempt versus nonexempt. The staffing plan will also likely designate staffing positions as belonging to central administration, general operations, or program staff.

Especially in the case of small grassroots organizations transitioning to professionally staffed entities, the staffing plan must address the shift in day-to-day operations from a founding board or executive director to a supervised staff. Funding exigencies, growth projections, community and subsector expectations, and size and scope of expected service provision will all play a role in motivating or constraining the staffing levels set by organizational leaders. Staffing levels and complements for individual program areas may be set by constituent demands and supply for those services, while staffing levels and complements for central administration are likely to vary with the coordination and planning needs of the organization as a whole.

One of the most important yet most overlooked areas in staff planning in the nonprofit sector remains succession planning. In 2003, the United Way of New York City's study of CEOs, board members, and pipeline leaders confirmed sectoral fears that almost half of all New York executive directors were planning to leave their positions within five years at the same time that only one-third of all directors stated that they had a succession plan in place (Birdsell and Muzzio, 2003). Given demographic changes and likely competition for talent from other organizations and sectors, nonprofit leaders can give their organizations a leg up by engaging in reflective succession planning as well as thoughtful leadership development and training. Staffing, succession, and training and development planning will also make staff retention a less daunting challenge.

Recruitment

The first step in recruitment is figuring out what kind of staff the organization is seeking. Typically, a search is initiated by the creation of a new staff position or by the departure of staff in an existing role. In either case, it is important to begin any search with a clear idea of the characteristics the organization is seeking in a candidate. Increasing competition, especially for candidates of color, makes recruiting qualified and appropriate candidates challenging (Salamon and Geller, 2007).

Identifying Job Characteristics. In human resource terminology, these characteristics are called KSAs, for *knowledge, skills, and abilities. Knowledge* encompasses the content knowledge a staff person needs to know prior to being hired. Proficiency in many positions presumes a specific body of knowledge. Is an understanding of how arts management organizations are funded essential to the position? Is a knowledge of state laws related to nonprofit status required? When thinking about the term *knowledge,* it is useful to think about what facts an individual *should know.* The term *skills* refers to proficiency in doing things with objects or ideas. Is operating a computer necessary for this job? Does the applicant need to be able to calculate tax credits on a loan? When defining the term *skills,* think about what the applicant *needs to do.* Finally, *abilities* refers to the capacity to undertake certain work responsibilities. Does the individual need to be able to communicate effectively? Are supervisory abilities paramount? When defining *abilities,* think about what the individual *has the capacity to accomplish.*

KSAs are similar to, but not the same as, *competencies* (which are defined as capacities to act). KSAs have long been in use in government settings and made their way into the private sector nearly two decades ago. Although the term is somewhat less commonly used in the nonprofit sector, the KSA concept has an important legal distinction. In the event the nonprofit organization is required to demonstrate that a job requirement is related to the ability to perform the job, the organization will be asked to demonstrate what KSAs were used for hiring and how those KSAs are related to job performance. Thus, they serve as the underpinnings for any legal and fair recruitment process.

Effective managers begin by determining what KSAs are desired for the available position through a process called job analysis. This process of discovery usually includes interviewing current and former staff incumbents (if any), dialogue among those who will work with the individual about what they feel is needed for success in the position, and strategic planning about what is needed for the organization in that role. Job analysis is a process of uncovering various perspectives on what the staff position is, might, and should encompass.

Writing Job Descriptions. After the job analysis phase, most organizations write job descriptions. The job description serves three purposes: to help those who will select among applicants consider what is needed for the position, to advertise to potential staff what the job will entail, and for use in legal defense against discrimination charges. It is important that the job description be both comprehensive and flexible. No candidate will meet all desired aspects, and the position's requirements will be fluid over time as needs arise. The effective nonprofit manager strikes a balance, articulating clearly what the organization is seeking without writing an unrealistically rigid characterization.

There are commercially available products for job analysis and the writing of job descriptions, as well as technical assistance available from a variety of consulting firms who specialize in these tasks. Each organization must decide how it will undertake this responsibility. For larger organizations, crafting job descriptions in-house may be easier, as there may be numerous other similar positions. Conversely, it may be easier for outside consultants to compare positions with others in other organizations. For smaller organizations, the task is more difficult and is often best accomplished with outside advice from peer networks combined with sample job description materials found on the Internet.

Searching

Once the job description is in hand, the organization should consider how it will search for applicants. There are many sources of potential employees, grouped for the purpose of discussion here into external and internal types.

The primary consideration when drafting a recruitment strategy is determining the goal of the recruitment program. Is the organization trying to attract a large applicant pool? Is diversity of applications a major objective? Is promotion from within the desired outcome? What are implications of hiring from without versus hiring from within? Are the candidates likely to be available locally, or will a national search be required? Answers to these questions can help inform choices about recruitment strategies. There is significant evidence that recruitment practices do matter to organizations. For example, there is a broad and extensive literature on the effect of different recruitment strategies on applicant perception (Yu and Cable, 2014). Less is known directly about recruitment strategies and organizational effectiveness, but anecdotal research suggests there is good fodder for investigation.

External Approaches. Under some circumstances, searching for potential staff from outside the organization is deemed desirable. Several types of sources can be used, depending on the applicant pool targeted:

- *Print and online ads.* Running ads in newspapers or magazines is a broad recruitment approach: it will generate a large applicant pool with a wide range of general skills—all the more so given the huge audience that online versions of these periodicals attract. Advertising in newspapers is a good idea when the organization is entering a new market, needs a large number of staff, wants to broaden its contacts, and has the capacity to review a large number of applications. The cost is related to the advertising rates of the newspaper or magazine itself and the staff to review applications that are generated. The typical urban newspaper ad can generate as many as one thousand applicants, so be prepared to manage the volume. Most newspapers have a local readership, so newspapers allow a geographically targeted search (national newspapers will attract a national pool), although this is increasingly changing as the news goes online and worldwide. As such, this is a good approach for attracting a diverse applicant pool, as a wide array of individuals will be exposed to the advertising.

- *Websites and social networking.* Popular and very inexpensive, posting job listings through online databases and clearinghouses like Idealist.org enables nonprofits to reach out for applicants worldwide. Estimates have suggested that recruitment costs can be reduced by as much as 95 percent through online recruiting. Services differ, but they generally allow the nonprofit to specify the characteristics they are seeking and to screen out applicants who lack requisite qualifications. One related issue is that web recruiting acts as a stimulus for applicants to visit the hiring organization's website. There is evidence that website information is used by applicants to assess whether they fit with the organization or not, suggesting that nonprofits should make sure that their websites contain accurate information about the organization's mission and purpose. Also increasingly popular is the use of social networking tools (Facebook, LinkedIn, Plaxo, and YouTube Nonprofit Partners, and others) for recruiting staff, volunteers, and donors. To make the point about the importance of LinkedIn as a tool in recruitment, Zide, Elman, and Shahani-Denning (2014, p. 584) cited a Society of Human Resource Management Survey that revealed that "95 percent of the 541 HR professionals surveyed indicated that they used LinkedIn to recruit passive candidates who might not otherwise apply" and a *Forbes* article (Schwabel, 2011) that suggested "that many companies believe that the LinkedIn profile has replaced the traditional résumé" (2014, p. 584). Nonprofits that can identify the general user characteristics of these different online social networks can target their recruitment efforts for maximum yield.

- *Professional publications, associations, and conferences.* Releasing a job posting through a professional association or advertising in a professional journal is a good idea when the position the organization is seeking to fill is closely related to a specific profession. For example, if the organization is seeking a licensed social worker, advertising in professional social work outlets will attract a large proportion of qualified applicants. Conference listings are good when the organization can identify key conferences where applicants of interest would be in attendance.

- *College recruiting and internship programs.* Appropriate for positions requiring a college education, college recruiting is effective for reaching that market of applicants. For nonprofits, education about opportunities in the nonprofit sector needs to be part of on-campus recruitment efforts. Internships are particularly useful to test out staff before making a permanent hire and to allow students exposure to the organization.

- *Government job services offices and placement agencies.* These options are appropriate for locating entry and mid-level staff with little to some experience. Both types of agencies prescreen candidates, which can be a cost-saving measure for nonprofits with little time to cull through candidate files. Services are usually free to the organization; government-funded job services work for no fee, while placement agencies usually charge a fee to the applicant.

- *Professional search firms or executive recruiters.* Usually the most expensive of the options, professional search firms are a good source of high-level applicants with a specific skill set. Search firms usually offer expertise in identifying applicants with specific experience. They also offer the advantage of confidentiality, as they can make inquiries between the organization and potential applicants without identifying either party. Many search firms charge the hiring organization, not the applicant, and fees typically range from 10 to 25 percent of the first year's salary. Increasingly, search firms and recruiters are specializing in non-profit placements, and in some cases, these services may be both less expensive and more targeted for the nonprofit sector.

- *Nonprofit-specific career fairs, conferences, showcases.* During the first decade of the new millennium, there was an explosion of nonprofit-specific venues for nonprofit recruiting. Since 2001, Idealist.org has been hosting local nonprofit career fairs in cities across the United States. Job-seekers attend for free, while recruiting organizations pay a small fee to help cover costs. State and local associations of nonprofits (along with their national federations) also provide nonprofit career services to help match nonprofit professionals with nonprofit recruiters. The Alliance for Nonprofit Management, an organization dedicated to fostering the next generation of nonprofit leadership operating through college and university chapters across the United States, prepares future nonprofit staff and leaders through internships and coops with their nonprofit partners. Even Youtube.com has jumped into the mix, providing a special nonprofit program to allow third-sector organizations to tell their stories to a wide audience including job seekers.

Internal Approaches. In some cases, filling staff vacancies from inside the organization is the better strategy. The following are internal approaches that may be undertaken:

- *Employee referral.* As mentioned earlier, internal referral programs have advantages. Typically, employee referrals are relatively low in cost. Some nonprofits create staff incentive programs that give financial rewards to staff who recruit others who are hired and work successfully in the organization. Employee referrals lead to the identification of potential employees who know quite a bit about the organization and whose interest in the organization is therefore typically high. Employee referral programs tend to generate a geographically local applicant pool, and prospects are limited to candidates who are connected somehow to individuals already in the organization. One downside is that this can make diversifying the nonprofit more difficult.

- *Internal postings and promotion.* Making opportunities available to current staff is a critical dimension of a successful nonprofit. When hiring is consistently done from the outside for positions above the entry level, a signal is sent to staff that their opportunities are limited. Ensure that all staff are aware of upcoming openings, and give them access to ample information about the positions. Managing decisions to hire from the outside when there are qualified internal candidates can be difficult, but seriously considering insiders as applicants tends to lead to better perceptions of fairness, even if the internal candidates are not ultimately chosen.

- *Client and volunteer recruitment.* A rich source of candidates for nonprofits is the client and volunteer base of individuals who already have a relationship with the organization. These sources offer the benefits of familiarity with the organization and understanding of its basic operations. Many successful nonprofits make the boundaries between volunteers and paid staff permeable. Organizations with client bases can improve services by hiring clients as staff members. As already noted, many nonprofits and affirmative businesses, by mission and strategy, choose to hire mostly or exclusively from within client and volunteer ranks.

In general, what recruitment sources are most effective? Meta-analyses of studies of recruitment sources have found that individuals hired through internal sources are as much as 24 percent more likely to stay on the job for the first year (Yu and Cable, 2014) and tend to be more satisfied than those recruited from the outside. Among the competing explanations for this effect: applicants have a realistic preview of the job; there is better person-job and person-organization fit for inside referrals; internal candidates are of higher quality; and employees are more credible as sources of job information.

Finally, what information should be included in the recruitment process? Effective and accurate communication is always a goal; candidates not hired by the organization will nevertheless learn a lot about it and should be left with a good impression. More information and accurate information both lead to positive outcomes. Friendliness and timeliness on behalf of everyone in the recruitment process leads to perceptions of a fair and friendly organization that is interested in the applicant. Inclusion of women and people of color in the recruitment process signals an organization open to diversity.

Choosing a Candidate

Perhaps the most challenging human resource task is determining which candidate or candidates from the pool of applicants should be chosen. As briefly described earlier, it is important that any applicant be evaluated on whether or not he or she has the ability to perform the required tasks. In nonprofits, the needs for flexibility of staff are often paramount; thus structured approaches are often not practical and are arguably less desirable.

Most nonprofit organizations are also particularly interested in the notion of fit—in many cases, this is interpreted as the extent to which the applicant shares a commitment to the mission. Mission drift is sometimes seen as one result of hiring key staff who do not share the organization's view on its future direction. In all selection decisions, the premiere challenge is finding a qualified, motivated, and adaptable candidate on whom various staff can agree.

Particularly applicable in large nonprofit contexts, staff selection can include highly technical procedures. For example, there is a plethora of well-established selection instruments, including personality, cognitive ability, and honesty testing; assessment centers that evaluate leadership and team performance; and work sample tests that replicate actual portions of the job to be performed. We will review each of these approaches briefly (more extensive details on these topics can be found in Gatewood, Feild, and Barrick, 2015).

Once the recruitment pool has been identified, a critical first step is to review the demographics of the full pool of applicants to ensure that a diverse pool has been garnered. Once that diversity is determined, the next step is to select qualified candidates, Now is the time to apply what has been determined by the job analysis, examining which potential staff members hold the best promise based on the KSAs previously identified for the position. It is best to review a variety of applicant materials, including résumés, letters of interest, and application forms (see Table 22.1).

TABLE 22.1. The Candidate Selection Process

Questions	Aspects to Consider	Details Needed	Action to Be Taken
Is the candidate qualified?	What required qualifications does the candidate clearly meet?	Degrees, certifications, credentials, past job titles, dates of employment	*If yes:* Verify facts from sources after candidate has reached the finalist pool. *If no:* Send rejection letter.
Is the candidate among the best available?	What evidence of past performance looks applicable to this position in this organization? What limitations does past experience suggest?	Statements of accomplishments, key positions held, experience in related organizations	*If yes:* Investigate or probe into in the interview; administer selection tests, if used. *If no:* Send rejection letter.
Can this candidate (with job and organization) be verified?	Who are the key references for the applicant?	Extent to which listed references can evaluate various qualifications, experiences, motivation, and limitations; candidate consent to check other references not listed	*If yes:* Conduct reference checks after the candidate has reached the finalist pool. *If no:* Send rejection letter.
Should this candidate be selected?	What do various staff sources say? How does all the evidence collected so far add up? (Consider using a team selection process.)	Candidate who best fits the job and the organization at this time	*If yes:* Tender an offer. *If no:* Wait until an offer has been accepted before rejecting other candidates, politely, in writing.

Step 1: Determine Which Applicants Have the Required Qualifications.
Candidates who do not have the required qualifications should be immediately rejected from the pool. Most organizations write a polite letter to the candidate indicating that many other applicants who are more qualified for the position are being considered. It is important to thank candidates for their interest in the organization and to encourage them to apply for future openings as they become available. If possible, keep on file information about applicants who look promising but do not meet the organization's current needs.

For candidates who meet the required qualifications, the organization typically moves on to determine whether this is the best candidate for the position. Although the qualifications must eventually be verified (degrees actually awarded, employment checked, and so on), it is usually best to wait to verify these details until after the candidate has shown interest through the interview.

Step 2: Assess Which Candidates Are Among the Best for the Position. In
this stage of the selection process, it is necessary to choose a pool of candidates whom the organization will consider further. The size of the reduced pool will be determined by the number of qualified candidates available, the organization's resources for further investigation, and the timetable under which the decision must be made. Most organizations will reduce the qualified candidate pool to between three and five candidates.

If the organization has the available resources and assessment instruments are considered appropriate for the position being considered, at this stage the organization may ask the candidates to submit to these tests. Many organizations (particularly in the private sector) use psychological tests, the most common of which is called the "Big Five" personality test. The five characteristics, identified through either the Five Factor Index instrument (Goldberg, 1990) or the NEO-PI instrument (Costa and McCrae, 1997) are based on decades of psychological research that suggests that the stable elements of personality include openness to experience, conscientiousness, emotional stability, agreeableness, and extroversion. Of the five, conscientiousness has been shown to be the best predictor of performance overall, and extroversion best for external relations positions like sales or fundraising (Gatewood, Feild, and Barrick, 2015). Tests of general cognitive ability, which research has shown to be among the best predictors of job performance for complex jobs across the United States, with even stronger relationships across Europe (Salgado, Anderson, Moscoso, Bertua, and De Fruyt, 2003), are also widely used. In recent years, honesty tests have become popular. Research findings about the general efficacy of integrity tests exists, but questions remain about the appropriateness of their use, the ability of individuals to fake the results, the underlying conceptual reasons why integrity tests might work, and the cultural contexts in which they are appropriate (Berry, Sackett, and Wiemann, 2007).

Psychological testing has been shown to be a good predictor of future performance and to have high "predictive validity," as there is empirical evidence that the traits they test are indeed related to some kinds of job performance. Thus, such tests have generally been upheld in most court cases as legal, particularly where the organizations have tested the relationship between test scores and performance in their own organizations. However, personality tests often have low "face validity," that is, candidates may perceive the tests as inappropriate or invasive, and this sometimes gives rise to perceptions of inequity. Other organizations use work sample tests, and/or "realistic job previews" (RJPs) to assess requisite skills such as financial management, software proficiency, or industry expertise. One challenge in using work sample tests is to identify appropriate tests available for commercial sale or to develop one's own instruments in-house, an expensive undertaking that sometimes requires particular expertise. However, RJPs can take a wide variety of forms, from "homemade" videos providing "realistic" observations of typical work days/assignments to more in-depth trial assignments that may range from a few minutes to whole days on an assortment of tasks. Supporters of RJPs point to the two-way street aspect of evaluation they provide: organizations observe how the candidate actually handles the work expected, and candidates observe how the organization is actually managed. For organizations interested in "fit," RJPs provide an opportunity for both sides of the recruiting equation to test out values and work congruence.

Another popular selection tool, assessment centers, is very effective if the position requires leadership or team management skills, but their design and administration are expensive. In general, the advantage of work sample tests is that they assess work qualifications directly. Thus, they tend to have high face validity and are usually perceived by applicants as fair since they are directly related to the work to be performed.

Perhaps the holy grail in selection is the personal interview. Historically conducted face-to-face, some organizations are finding that resource constraints and large applicant pools make preliminary telephone, video, or web-based interviews an important first screening test. Empirical evidence about selection interviews is mixed. Research shows that interviews have low predictive validity for job performance but high face validity, as they are perceived as desirable by both interviewers and interviewees (Macan, 2009). Despite limitations, interviews are nearly universally conducted in selection.

We offer the following guidelines to help interviewers do a better job at conducting effective interviews:

- *Use a structured interview format.* A consistent finding in the selection literature is that the same questions should be asked of all candidates for the position. Thus, rather than using a free-flowing conversation to assess candidate appropriateness, determine ahead of the interview what questions will be asked of all candidates. This helps the organization keep the interview tied to the relevant KSAs being assessed, it encourages managers to consider carefully the characteristics they are seeking *before* the interview, and it ensures that each candidate is asked to address the same issues.

- *Stick with behaviors.* Successful interviewing relies on conversations that focus on the behaviors candidates have exhibited in past work settings. Interview questions should ask what the candidate *did* in past situations, as past behavior has been shown to be the best predictor of future performance.

- *Keep it legal.* As covered in detail earlier, there are many categories of protected employees. No interview questions should explore any protected category, either deliberately or inadvertently. For example, it is never appropriate to ask candidates whether they have made child care arrangements or they have spousal coverage on benefits (implying gender or parental status); instead, ask if the candidate is able to work the hours required. Never ask candidates when they graduated from high school or college or earned a professional certification (implying age); instead, ask if the degree has been obtained or if the certification is currently valid. Do not ask whether a candidate is a U.S. citizen; ask instead whether the candidate is authorized to work in the United States or can gain authorization if selected for the position.

- *Consider a team interview.* A relatively new development in selection involves team-based selection. Research suggests that conducting a team interview (with two to five members in diverse positions who are savvy about employment practices) and using a team selection process can enhance fit and improve commitment to selection decisions (Stewart, 2003). Team interviews also enhance the likelihood of a realistic job preview that outlines both the strengths and weaknesses of the position, making it more likely that the candidate will be informed about what the position will really entail, enhancing early commitment to the organization and encouraging self-selection out of the process for candidates who feel they would not be a good match. Realistic job previews also have the advantage of setting appropriate expectations for those accepting the position (Morse and Popovich, 2009).

Step 3: Verify Candidate Qualifications and Match. Once a candidate has passed the interview stage, it is time to check references. The candidate will have provided references in writing or listed names to be contacted. In either case, it is advisable to follow up with a telephone call with specific questions. These questions should be designed to probe information already obtained from other sources and to facilitate more detailed understanding of the candidate's qualifications.

The reference-checking process is fraught with difficulties. Many former employers will provide only very basic information, including dates of employment and whether the employee is eligible for rehire. This reluctance is sometimes due to personal preferences and at other times is the result of legal counsel's advice to avoid possible slander or libel suits. Yet reference checking is a step that should never be skipped: It is imperative to show "due diligence" in the hiring process. A legal concept called "negligent hiring" can be invoked by staff members who feel that adequate precautions were not taken to ensure that the candidate does not prove dangerous to the other staff (Gatewood, Feild, and Barrick, 2015).

Step 4: Make the Selection Decision and Tender the Offer. Once all information has been collected, it is time to make an offer to the leading candidate. Ideally, there is agreement among those involved in the selection process as to who the best candidate is. Often there is more than one leading candidate. It is a good idea to keep all top candidates in the pool until a final offer is accepted. The offer should be given by phone, followed up with details in writing. The offer letter should include the name of the position, annual (or hourly) salary, benefits to be included in the package, starting date, and terms of employment (full-time permanent, part-time temporary, and so on). The letter should include a deadline, usually within two weeks, by which the candidate must reply. Salary level should be discussed with the candidate before tendering the final offer.

Summary of the Selection Process

To summarize, the selection process should be designed to attract and hire qualified candidates who fit both the job and the organization. Throughout the process, attention must be paid to the overall hiring strategy and staff and succession planning of the organization. Performance standards must always be kept in mind during the selection process. A thorough job evaluation should help guide the criteria on which decisions are made. It is advisable to involve multiple staff members in the selection process to ensure an open dialogue among current and future staff. Legalities should be considered, and each step of the selection process should be valid in that it leads to the selection of a staff member who can succeed in the organization.

Retention Through Motivation

Once the organization has selected the right staff and the right complement of staff to achieve organizational goals, the next (ongoing) steps involve motivating and retaining (good) people. For-profit organizations and traditional business schools have spent the better part of a century trying to understand and enact the elusive motivation of staff that brings organizational effectiveness. The good news, as we noted at the beginning of this chapter, is that motivation of staff is one area where nonprofit organizations seem to have the inherent advantage. Indeed evidence shows that mission attachment of nonprofit workers enhances their satisfaction and increases their intention to stay, especially for younger and part-time workers (Brown and Yoshioka, 2003).

Study after study has demonstrated that nonprofit employees are more engaged, more motivated, and sometimes even more satisfied in and by their work than employees in other sectors (for example, De Cooman, De Gieter, Pepermans, and Jegers, 2009). Yet turning that motivation into productivity and guarding against burnout remain confounding issues for nonprofit leaders. Developing work-life balance policies, like flexible scheduling and family leaves, is key to retaining nonprofit staff (Pitt-Catsouphes, Swanberg, Bond, and Galinsky, 2004), especially for nonprofits with more than one hundred staff members. And retaining experienced workers when pay and benefits are not competitive can be difficult. Furthermore, assuming that all nonprofits have the motivation advantage is misleading. Small nonprofits motivate employees toward goal achievement differently from larger nonprofits, and great variability in motivational techniques and organizational cultures exist across (and within) nonprofit subsectors. Indeed, motivating employees in large urban hospital systems may take a very different organizational culture and set of tools than motivating employees in a small rural community development corporation.

There are any number of theories that purport to explain how organizational actors are motivated. These include needs theories that emphasize how organizational life can help satisfy individual desires (Maslow, 1943) and process approaches like equity (Adams, 1963) and expectancy theories (Vroom, 1964), which emphasize the cognitive analyses and choices that individuals make in deciding how much exertion of effort is worth their while. These concepts have then been differentially applied by the generic management literature to construct techniques and programs aimed at increasing employee motivation and concomitant productivity. In the for-profit world, management "flavors of the month" have included the recognition of individual differences in designing motivation programs, managing by objectives (using goal setting to spur effort), basing rewards on performance, and enhancing opportunities for participation in decision making. Many of these theories and applications start with the assumption that human resources need to be aligned with organizational goals, and motivation techniques exist to do just that. (Compensation strategies and designs are discussed in depth in Chapter Twenty-Three.)

These theories and applications are variably useful to nonprofit leaders as suggested by the review work of Schepers, De Gieter, Pepermans, Du Bois, Caers, and Jegers (2005). Indeed, these authors underscore our point that nonprofit employees might be differentially motivated from for-profit employees at the same time that nonprofit employees in different subsectors may also be uniquely motivated. Robert C. Clark (2006) of the Harvard Law School is quietly shopping around his potential answer to the riddle of nonprofit motivation—a strong moral system that sustains and enhances nonprofit participation through internalized values and norms and the threat of sanctions including social disapproval and guilt.

In the end, though, it might be most helpful to reconceptualize motivation in nonprofits as part of the larger human resource system embedded within the organization's culture, always with an eye toward the power of the mission. In nonprofit (and in particular service) organizations, human resources are not so much aligned with the organization as they *are* the organization. Further, it is often the case that nonprofits do not have to align employee goals with organizational goals because the selection process and the draw of the mission have already done that.

For nonprofits, then, activity around motivation might best be spent nourishing an organizational culture that values all constituencies, respecting each participant's contribution to fulfillment of mission. While such motivation may be complemented by compensation and benefit programs, it is also enacted by the management of organizational symbols, rites and rituals, and affirmative events and recognition. Progressive nonprofit cultures motivate employees through fair and humane compensation and benefits but also affirm people's value and commitment to the organization's mission in an ongoing fashion.

Discharge, Layoffs, and Voluntary Turnover

Although we hope, and textbooks infer, that organizations can motivate people to stay goal-focused and loyal, we know that organizational turnover is a fact of life. Getting a handle on voluntary turnover seems especially important to non-profit organizations that are, indeed, defined by their human resources. Costs of voluntary turnover, even in organizations not so dependent on labor, can be staggering, if not debilitating. Immediately, turnover means starting the recruiting, selecting, and even training processes all over and incurring their concomitant costs. There is also the disruption to the organization's processes, culture, and other constituents when old faces disappear.

Traditional advice to managers suggests a correlation between job satisfaction and voluntary turnover. However, many of the causes of turnover are varied and often not directly under the control of the organization. These include, most conspicuously, labor market conditions and alternative job (and life) opportunities. Recent literature has sought to explore how even these external factors might be addressed by organizational leaders eager to retain their most valued and valuable employees. A wave of literature in the for-profit sector cited earlier posits that "job embeddedness" is an even better predictor of staying the organizational course than job satisfaction, organizational commitment, job alternatives, and job search (see Mitchell, Holtom, Lee, Sablynski, and Erez, 2001). As noted earlier, these researchers define job embeddedness as a multifaceted construct that includes three core components: links between individuals and co-workers, perceptions of fit with both organization and community, and the sense of sacrifice if the position were to be relinquished.

This line of thinking takes organizational leaders out of the realm of the "at-work-only" context and suggests that leaders need to take a more holistic approach to employees' well-being. Encouraging employees' links to co-workers, boards, and clients might elevate employees' feelings of embeddedness, as would encouraging employees' connections to community activity. In many ways, these suggestions may be second-nature to leaders of community-based organizations, but their value to organizational human resources has not been so acutely supported in the past. We suggest that in the nonprofit context, job embeddedness often morphs into organizational embeddedness, which is often overlaid with a sense of community embeddedness. If organizational leaders ignore the reality of embeddedness within a job, an organization, or a community, they do so at their own peril. Conversely, finding organizationally sanctioned ways to encourage cross-linkages and social networks, as well as community involvement, will likely result in more embedded and then committed staffers and may go a long way toward supporting organization and community missions.

Particularly in economic downturns, some organizations inevitably find it necessary to lay off staff involuntarily. Inconsistent funding streams, failure to obtain grants or grant renewals, or a general downturn in demand can all lead to these difficult decisions that challenge the very fabric of a nonprofit's culture. Our general advice for downsizing (as it is bloodlessly called) is to avoid it when possible and, when it is unavoidable, to enact it mindfully. This includes careful performance-based identification of those to be eliminated, sufficient advance warning, adequate explanation of rationale, and assistance in outplacement. Perhaps paradoxically, handling these issues with a personal touch is important. Although an executive's instincts may be to avoid face-to-face conversations with those being terminated or to delegate this responsibility to staff, handling these issues openly, honestly, and directly is the best approach. Legal considerations are also important. Many downsizings target high-paid workers as a cost-cutting measure, resulting in class action lawsuits for discrimination based on age. Finally, managers also must not forget the remaining staff. Research suggests that those who retain their jobs are often haunted by stress, fatigue, and guilt.

Make or Buy? Outsourcing Human Resources

One contemporary trend is toward the outsourcing of human resource functions. For small nonprofits in particular, the attraction of delegating human resource functions to external experts may be strong: often there is little internal capacity to perform what are viewed as specialized tasks. Indeed, the outsourcing of recruitment, applicant screening, relocation services, payroll, and benefits is common in some subsectors.

Nonetheless, each organization must decide which human resource functions are core to its approach. For many organizations, this makes deciding to outsource payroll and benefits delivery (but not design) a clear choice: external vendors often have software and specialized expertise in delivering these services, and the cost can be advantageous. However, for human resource functions more central to the organization's mission, such as attracting and selecting staff, it often makes sense to keep these functions in-house. Although there can be economic benefits of scale when outsourcing recruitment and selection in small organizations, these reduced costs can sometimes also translate into loss of control of attraction of staff who fit the organization's culture. Outsourcing human resource functions that play critical roles in identifying and retaining staff who share the organization's mission are often best left inside.

One notable exception is the idea of collaborating across organizations to provide health care and retirement benefits. For small nonprofits in particular, purchasing power for health care packages and investment power for retirement are in short supply. Joining a benefits collaborative, or creating one, can dramatically decrease the cost of such services per individual employee.

When a decision to outsource is made, it is imperative to follow up with thorough management of the outsourced contracts as well as evaluation of the efficacy of those relationships after a short period. In addition to considering administrative costs, organizations are well advised to measure staff satisfaction with outsourced services.

One last outsourcing trend worth noting here is the growing industry of "rent an ED" (executive director) for nonprofits in transition. In the last decade a whole field has developed to supply transitioning nonprofits with interim executive leaders (IELs). Consulting and headhunting firms train displaced and aspiring EDs to become IELs to serve nonprofits that have been left leaderless. As talk of a coming crisis in nonprofit leadership (brought about by the en masse retirements of Baby Boomer EDs) has proliferated, so have firms, both for-profit and nonprofit, that specialize in outsourcing the ED function, at least temporarily.

Summary: Effective Human Resource Practice

If the more humanistic aspects of this chapter have been insufficient to jump-start a reluctant nonprofit human resource leader, consider this: research suggests that human costs (payroll, benefits, training, and so on) in labor-intensive nonprofit organizations can account for more than 75 percent of total costs, compared to under 15 percent in capital-intensive organizations (Macpherson, 2001). Obviously, inattention to the major resource of an organization is a recipe for trouble. And this chapter has recommended anything but inattention.

We began with the suggestion that human resources—which we define broadly as "the organization"—is usefully construed as a systems dynamic. Successful nonprofit leaders work with staff to define organizational goals around human resources as well as mission fulfillment. The parts are interconnected— breakdowns in human resource leadership (a disintegration of organizational culture, a spate of voluntary departures, and so on) will likely lead to disrupted service delivery, which can tarnish reputation, diminish the ability to acquire funds, and cause harm in myriad other ways. A smooth-running organization will devote executive-level attention to planning around human resources.

TABLE 22.2. Relevant Human Resource Questions as a Reflection of Organization Size and Life Cycle

Matter Under Consideration	Small or Start-Up	Large or Established
Culture	Do our mission, vision, and strategy support our culture? Should our human resource systems be professionalized? If so, how? Should human resource responsibilities be part of existing staff roles, or are separate positions warranted?	Do our mission, vision, and strategy support our culture? Is our staff culture consistent with the values of our mission? Has human resources remained an integral part of our strategic thinking, or has becoming functionalized make it separate? Does our large organization feel small?
Legal	At what staff size do state labor and employment laws apply? At what staff size do federal labor and employment laws apply? Are we above those levels? Is our subsector subject to further labor regulation?	Are we compliant with state labor and employment laws? Are we compliant with federal labor and employment laws? Are we superseding legal standards in promoting an equitable workplace? Is our subsector subject to further labor regulation?
Human resource audits	When and how should we allocate funds to human resource audits? Where can we find sample materials and benchmarks?	What are the goals of our human resource audits? Do our audits meet those goals? Are our human resource audits comprehensive? Are we using a variety of metrics?
Staffing Plan	Do we need to grow our staff to meet our mission? If so, how will we identify the resources to grow our staff?	Do we have the right complement of staff to meet our mission? Are we planning growth, transition, or downsizing?
Selection	Does our small size allow growth from inside, or is external recruitment more likely? Do religious orientation, regional culture, industry subsector, or other factors delimit our selection?	Does our culture promote growth from the inside? Have we identified appropriate channels through which to search for unique skills? Do religious orientation, regional culture, industry subsector, or other factors delimit our selection?
Retention and motivation	How much does our small size contribute to the culture we have developed? If we are growing, how is this affecting our culture?	What motivates our staff? How do we allocate resources to motivate and retain our proven staff? Which staff are leaving voluntarily, and why are they leaving?
Discharge, layoff, and turnover	Absent large size or long-term community track record, how do we embed our employees?	How do we leverage our size, standing, and reputation to help embed our proven employees?
Make or buy?	Do we "buy" to attempt to keep permanent staff size small?	Does our choice to "buy" alienate or support permanent internal staff?

We recognize that one size does not fit all; enabling dialogue around human resource goals is highly dependent on an organization's size and life cycle (not to mention cultural and industry or subsector norms). We argue that value-creating and value-diffusing nonprofits and their component parts are well advised to engage the whole of their labor force in the human resource process at all stages of the organization's growth. Executives in different contexts will necessarily face different human resource decisions and must ask context-relevant questions. To illustrate how some of these contextual elements might play out, a sampling of how size and life cycle of the organization influence what human resource questions should be asked is presented in Table 22.2. These questions might be periodically reviewed to take stock of how well the organization is doing in developing and maintaining their human resource approach.

Certainly, some subsectors (and within subsector, particular organizations) of the nonprofit universe are marred by less than stellar labor records, and so we underscore the importance of rethinking the organization from the standpoint of those who make it work. All nonprofit leaders can be guided by the basic questions raised by this chapter, and the answers, of course, will vary: What motivates employees? What embeds them in their jobs, organizations, and communities? What laws model best practices, even when size or subsector exempt an organization? What staffing plans best support an organization's human resource goals? What recruitment and selection processes are most likely to result in an augmentation of the most laudable components of the organization's unique culture? And finally, what are all of our goals for the people of the organization?

Since the process of answering the questions is likely to be as important as the actual answers, it is through the continuous re-creation of human resource goals that an effective nonprofit human resource culture is designed.

References

Adams, J. S. Toward an Understanding of Inequity. *Journal of Abnormal and Social Psychology*, 1963, 67, 422–426.

Beck, T. E., Lengnick-Hall, C. A., and Lengnick-Hall, M. L. Solutions Out of Context: Examining the Transfer of Business Concepts to Nonprofit Organizations. *Nonprofit Management and Leadership*, 2008, 19(2), 153–171.

Berry, C. C., Sackett, P. R., and Wiemann, S. A Review of Recent Developments in Integrity Test Research. *Personnel Psychology*, 2007, 60(2), 271–301.

Benko, C. , Erickson, R., Hagel, J., and Wong, J. Beyond Retention. *Deloitte University Press*, 2014.

Birdsell, D. S., and Muzzio, D. The Next Leaders: UWNYC Grantee Leadership Development and Succession Management Needs, 2003. unitedwaynyc.org/pdf/the_next_leaders.pdf.

Bond, G. R., Drake, R. E., and Becker, D. R. Generalizability of the Individual Placement and Support (IPS) Model of Supported Employment Outside the US. *World Psychiatry*, 2012, 11(1), 32–39.

Brown, W. A., and Yoshioka, C. F. Mission Attachment and Satisfaction as Factors in Employee Retention. *Nonprofit Management and Leadership*, 2003, 14(1), 5–18.

Chatman, J. A. Improving Interactional Organizational Research: A Model of Person-Organization Fit. *Academy of Management Review*, 1989, 14, 333–349.

Clark, R. C. Moral Systems in the Regulation of Nonprofits. Cambridge, MA: The Hauser Center for Nonprofit Organizations, Harvard University: Working Paper 33.6, 2006.

Cohen, R. Unions and the Nonprofit Workforce: A Few Considerations. *Nonprofit Quarterly Online*, 2013, August 7. Retrieved February 24, 2016, from http://nonprofitquarterly .org/2013/08/08/unions-and-the-nonprofit-workforce-a-few-considerations/.

Costa, P. T., and McCrae, R. R. Stability and Change in Personality Assessment: The Revised NEO Personality Inventory in the Year 2000. *Journal of Personality Assessment*, 1997, 68, 86–95.

Council for Disability Rights. Frequently Asked Questions, 2009. www.disabilityrights.org/ adafaq.htm#general.

De Cooman, R., De Gieter, S., Pepermans, R., and Jegers M. A Cross-Sector Comparison of Motivation-Related Concepts in For-Profit and Not-for-Profit Service Organizations. *Nonprofit and Voluntary Sector Quarterly*, 2009, 1–22.

Equal Employment Opportunity Commission. Fact Sheet on the EEOC's Final Regulations Implementing the ADAAA, 2016. www.eeoc.gov/policy/docs/902cm.html.

Equal Employment Opportunity Commission. Facts About Sexual Harassment, 2016. www .eeoc.gov/eeoc/publications/fs-sex.html.

Equal Employment Opportunity Commission. Filing a Charge of Discrimination, 2016. www.eeoc.gov/employees/charge.cfm.

Fick, B. J. *The American Bar Association Guide to Workplace Law: Everything You Need to Know About Your Rights as an Employee or Employer* (2nd ed.). New York: Times Books/Random House, 2006.

Gatewood, R. D., Feild, H. S., and Barrick, M. *Human Resource Selection* (8th ed.) Fort Worth, TX: Harcourt, 2015.

Gillett, R. What It Will Take to Get a Nonprofit Job in 2020. *Fast Company*, April 7, 2015.

Goldberg, L. R. An Alternative Description of Personality: The Big Five Factor Structure. *Journal of Personality and Social Psychology*, 1990, 59, 1216–1230.

Gregory, A. G., and Howard, D. The Nonprofit Starvation Cycle. *Stanford Social Innovation Review*, 2009, 7(4), 49–54.

Guerin, L., and DelPo, A. *Essential Guide to Federal Employment Laws* (4th ed.). Berkeley, CA: NOLO, 2013.

Halpern, R. P. *Workforce Issues in the Nonprofit Sector: Generational Leadership Change and Diversity.* Kansas City, MO: American Humanics, 2006.

Hill, C. Unionizing Nonprofits. *East Bay Express*, August 7, 2013. Retrieved February 23, 2016, from www.eastbayexpress.com/oakland/unionizing-nonprofits/Content? oid=3675593.

Hoffman, B. J., Bynum, B. H., Piccolo, R. F., & Sutton, A. W. Person–Organization Value Congruence: How Transformational Leaders Influence Work Group Effectiveness. *Academy of Management Journal*, 2011, 54, 779–796.

Holtom, B., Mitchell, T., and Lee, T. Increasing Human Capital by Applying Job Embeddedness Theory. *Organization Dynamics*, 2006, 35(4), 316–331.

Hrywna, M. 2015 NPT Best Places to Work: Mission Trumps Pay, Although Compensation Does Matter. *The Nonprofit Times*, 2012, April 1, 1–2.

Johnson, J. M., and Ng, E. S. Money Talks or Millennials Walk: The Effect of Compensation on Nonprofit Millennial Workers Sector-Switching Intentions. *Review of Public Personnel Administration*, 2015.

Koch, B. J., Galaskiewicz, J., and Pierson, A. The Effects of Networks on Organizational Missions. *Nonprofit and Voluntary Sector Quarterly*, 2015, 44(3), 510–538.

Kristof-Brown, A., Jansen, K. J., and Colbert, A. E. A Policy-Capturing Study of the Simultaneous Effects of Fit with Jobs, Groups, and Organizations. *Journal of Applied Psychology*, 2002, 87, 985–993.

Kunreuther, F. The Changing of the Guard: What Generational Differences Tell Us About Social-Change Organizations. *Nonprofit and Voluntary Sector Quarterly*, 2003, 32(3), 450–457.

Lee, T. W., Mitchell, T. R., Holtom, B. C., McDaniel, L., and Hill, J. W. The Unfolding Model of Voluntary Turnover: A Replication and Extension. *Academy of Management Journal*, 1999, 42, 450–462.

Lee, Y-J., and Sabharwai, M. Education-Job Match, Salary, and Job Satisfaction Across Public, Non-Profit and For-Profit Sectors: Survey of Recent College Graduates. *Public Management Review*, 2016, 18(1), 40–64.

Lewin, K. *Field Theory in Social Science*. New York: HarperCollins, 1951.

Light, P. C. *Sustaining Nonprofit Performance: The Case for Capacity Building and the Evidence to Support It*. Washington, DC: Brookings Institution, 2004.

Macan, T. The Employment Interview: A Review of Current Studies and Directions for Future Research. *Human Resource Management Review*, 2009, 19(3), 209–213.

Macpherson, M. Performance Measurement in Not-for-Profit and Public-Sector Organizations. *Measuring Business Excellence*, 2001, 5(2), 13–17.

Maier, F., Meyer, M., and Steinbereithner, M. Nonprofit Organizations Becoming Business-Like. *Nonprofit and Voluntary Sector Quarterly*, 2016, 45(1), 64–86.

Maslow, A. H. A Theory of Human Motivation. *Psychological Review*, 1943, 50, 370–396.

McGinnis, J. The Young and Restless: Generation Y in the Nonprofit Workforce. *Public Administration Quarterly*, 2011, 35(3) 342–362.

Mitchell, T. R., Holtom, B. C., Lee, T. W., Sablynski, C. J., and Erez, M. Why People Stay: Using Job Embeddedness to Predict Voluntary Turnover. *Academy of Management Journal*, 2001, 44, 1102–1121.

Morse, B. J., and Popovich, B. M. Realistic Recruitment Practices in Organizations. *Human Resource Management Review*, 2009, 19(1), 1–8.

National Council on Disability. *Empowerment for Americans with Disabilities: Breaking Barriers to Careers and Full Employment*. Washington, DC: National Council on Disability, October 2007.

O'Reilly, C. A., Chatman, J., and Caldwell, D. F. People and Organizational Culture: A Profile Comparison Approach to Assessing Person-Organization Fit. *Academy of Management Journal*, 1991, 34, 487–516.

Park, S. M., and Word, J. Driven to Service: Intrinsic and Extrinsic Motivation for Public and Nonprofit Managers. *Public Personnel Management*, 2012, 41(4), 705–734.

Pitt-Catsouphes, M., Swanberg, J. E., Bond, J. T., and Galinsky, E. Work Life Policies and Programs: Comparing Responsiveness of Nonprofit and For-Profit Organizations. *Nonprofit Management and Leadership*, 2004, 14(3), 291–312.

Resnick, C. J., Baltes, B. B., and Shantz, C. W. Person Organization Fit and Work-Related Attitudes and Decisions. *Journal of Applied Psychology*, 2007, 92(5), 1446–1455.

Ridder, H-G., and McCandless, A. Influences on the Architecture of Human Resources Management in Nonprofit Organizations. *Nonprofit and Voluntary Sector Quarterly*, 2010, 39(1), 124–141.

Salgado, J. F., Anderson, N., Moscoso, S. C., Bertua, C., and De Fruyt, F. International Validity Generalization and Cognitive Abilities: A European Community Meta-Analysis. *Personnel Psychology*, 2003, 56, 573–605.

Salamon, L. M., and Geller, S. L. The Nonprofit Workforce Crisis: Real or Imagined? *The Listening Post Project*, 2007, Communique #8, Johns Hopkins University.

Schepers, C., De Gieter, S., Pepermans, R., Du Bois, C., Caers, R., and Jegers, M. How Are Employees of the Nonprofit Sector Motivated? A Research Need. *Nonprofit Management & Leadership*, 2005, 16(2), 191–208.

Schwabel, D. 5 Reasons Why Your Online Presence Will Replace Your Resume in 10 Years. *Forbes Magazine*, February 21, 2011, p. 1, available at www.forbes.com/sites/danschawbel/2011/02/21/5-reasons-why-your-online-presence-will-replace-your-resume-in-10-years/.

Signorile, M. ENDA: The Nightmare Scenario in Which GOPers Push a Bad Bill That Gay Groups Dropped. *The Huffington Post, Queer Voices*. August 7, 2014. Retrieved February 24, 2016, from www.huffingtonpost.com/michelangelo-signorile/enda-the-nightmare-scenario_b_5587459.html.

Stewart, G. L. Toward an Understanding of the Multilevel Role of Personality in Teams. In M. R. Barrick and A. M. Ryan (eds.), *Personality and Work*. San Francisco: Jossey-Bass, 2003.

Swider, B. W., Zimmerman, R. D., and Barrick, M. Searching for the Right Fit: Development of Applicant Person-Organization Fit Perceptions During the Recruitment Process. *Journal of Applied Psychology*, 2015, 100(3), 880–893.

Toh, S. M., Morgeson, F. P., and Campion, M. A. Human Resource Configurations: Investigating Fit with the Organizational Context. *Journal of Applied Psychology*, 2008, 93(4), 864–882.

Vroom, V. *Work and Motivation*. New York: Wiley, 1964.

Warner, R., and Mandiberg, J. An Update on Affirmative Businesses or Social Firms for People with Mental Illness. *Psychiatric Services*, 2006, 57(10), 1488–1492.

Yu, K.Y.T., and Cable, D. M. (eds.). *The Oxford Handbook of Recruitment*. Cambridge, UK: Oxford University Press, 2014.

Zide, J., Elman, B., and Shahani-Denning, C. LinkedIn and Recruitment: How Profiles Differ Across Occupations. *Employee Relations*, 2014, 36(5), 583–604.

CHAPTER TWENTY-THREE

COMPENSATION

Total Rewards Programs in Nonprofit Organizations

Nancy E. Day

Some profit and nonprofit organizations, particularly those that are smaller and less sophisticated, consider employee compensation as an onerous and expensive obligation on which as little time as possible should be spent. Salaries and benefits may be set haphazardly, based on "gut feelings" about how much certain jobs bring on the general market or on the difficulty of attracting qualified people to key positions. These organizations view compensation as extraneous to their organization's overall mission or strategy. This is unfortunate and unwise, given that labor costs make up over 50 percent of total costs for many U.S. employers (Milkovich, Newman, and Gerhart, 2011).

It is essential that the compensation system attracts and rewards the best quality workforce it can afford, since the organization's human resources are indeed its most important resources. Without them, the organization's goals cannot be achieved and its values cannot be enacted. As Louis Mayer, of Metro Goldwyn Mayer, said, "The inventory goes home at night" (Choate, 1990). This is especially true for nonprofits.

Total Rewards: Integral to Organizational Strategy

The contemporary view of pay and benefits has become an integrative one that is more appropriately conceptualized as "total rewards" (Christofferson and King, 2006). Whereas compensation includes anything of monetary value that the organization provides its employees in exchange for their services (pay and benefits, including perquisites), "total rewards" includes all those things that will motivate workers to be attracted to the firm, join it, perform well in it, and remain with it. This definition includes not only the "basics" such as base salary, incentive pay and benefits, but also those work environment characteristics that create a "workplace of choice": good supervision, safe and attractive facilities, access to training and development, and other elements that attract potential employees and enhance their experiences once they are members of the organization. This definition is sweeping and inclusive, suggesting that the job of those managing compensation is broader and more diverse than building sound pay programs and providing adequate benefits, and includes an entire constellation of programs and practices designed to support the organization's strategic goals.

For the purposes of this chapter, space necessitates we focus most of our discussion on the more basic forms of compensation: salary, incentives, and benefits. Incentives are becoming more common in nonprofit organizations. Indeed, a survey of nonprofits conducted jointly by WorldatWork and Vivient Consulting found that 82 percent of participating organizations offered short-term incentives and 19 percent offered long-term incentives. However, it should be noted that the majority of the organizations surveyed were large (budgets between $100 million to $5 billion) and thus had resources to design and allocate more sophisticated rewards systems (WorldatWork and Vivient Consulting, 2014). But for all such nonprofits, particularly at nonexecutive levels, there is a trend to include incentives as part of the nonprofit pay package. Incentive pay is an avenue by which individual pay can be directly related to the "bottom line" results or mission of the organization, reducing fixed costs and encouraging top performance because it puts a percentage of an employee's pay "at risk." In times of tight budgets (as most are for nonprofits), pay programs that decrease fixed costs while increasing both individual and organizational performance are receiving more than passing attention from managers of nonprofit organizations.

Compensation Strategy and Organizational Mission

All organizations base their actions on goals that are either explicit or implicit. Strategic planning is done in well-managed organizations to ensure that current resources, financial, material and human, are used in the manner most effective to the organization's raison d'être. Organizations with effective performance appraisal programs will require individual employees to set performance objectives based on department goals, which in turn are driven by division and organizational goals. This "cascading" effect allows successful organizations to link broad, often ambitious, goals and values with the activities of their individual workers. Thus, ultimately the individual employee is responsible for carrying out the fundamental mission of the organization. Because of this, it is imperative that the rewards system be part of the nonprofit's strategy and plan and be consistent with the organization's goals, culture, and environmental pressures. Organizations need to decide where they want to go and how they will get there. Compensation is one of the many important cogs in the total organizational machine that must be carefully tended, frequently lubricated and repaired, and upgraded or replaced if it no longer functions adequately.

For example, an organization that is changing its organizational structure must ensure that its pay strategy fits these changes. The most effective pay for self-directed work teams is probably not a traditional salary program; careful analysis of the goals of the work teams and their structures, the reasons why teams are being implemented, and the pay strategy of the organization all must be considered to determine the best approach.

It is imperative that workers are paid for what the organization wants to reward. This obvious yet critical fact is illustrated by Steven Kerr's well-known article, "On the Folly of Rewarding A, While Hoping for B" which cannot be quoted too often:

> Whether dealing with monkeys, rats, or human beings, it is hardly controversial to state that most organisms seek information concerning what activities are rewarded, and then seek to do (or at least pretend to do) those things, often to the virtual exclusion of activities not rewarded. The extent to which this occurs of course will depend on the perceived attractiveness of the rewards offered, but neither operant nor expectancy theorists would quarrel with the essence of this notion.
>
> Nevertheless, numerous examples exist of reward systems that are fouled up in that behaviors which are rewarded are those which the rewarder is trying to *discourage*, while the behavior he desires is not being rewarded at all. (Kerr, 1975, p. 769)

A familiar example of this type of mistake occurred frequently in the early 1980s when employees were given regular, annual cost-of-living increases. Although high inflation demanded some salary escalation to keep workers even with living costs, organizations were in effect paying their employees to merely show up, whether or not they were performing in the best interests of the organization. A better way to use pay to accomplish organizational goals is to direct the largest increases at those workers who contribute the most, not equally to all employees regardless of their performance. Another more distasteful example was a situation at Green Giant, in which employees who were rewarded for finding insect pieces in the vegetables began importing "home-grown" bug parts in order to increase their incentives (as reported in Milkovich, Newman, and Gerhart, 2011).

The Need for a Rewards Policy

Environmental and market demands have significant impacts on reward systems. Organizations that have jobs requiring extremely high levels of technical skill and expertise, such as medical doctors or engineers, must design systems that reward these key positions adequately. Management needs to ensure that qualified people are attracted and retained, while at the same time carefully balancing pay relationships across jobs within the company to avoid inequity.

Edward Lawler (1990, p. 11) recommends that managers should develop an effective strategy "with an analysis of the outcomes or results they need from their pay system and then develop a core set of compensation principles and practices to support these directions." Aligning the reward system, including compensation, benefits, and work environment factors, to the organization's mission and strategic plan as well as its management style is critical. Thus, before a reward program is seriously considered, the executives and professionals responsible for designing it need to evaluate carefully the organization's goals, values, culture, and strategy to ensure that rewards plays a key role in accomplishing organizational goals. The key point here is that the nonprofit's top management should carefully and strategically assess "*What knowledge, skills, abilities, and outcomes does our organization need to reward?*" This simple yet meaningful question should become the compensation manager's motto, continually guiding him or her in making decisions about the content and process of the organization's total rewards strategy.

One way that many organizations define their total reward strategy is through the development, communication, and maintenance of a *reward policy*. This is generally a simple, relatively short statement that communicates how the organization plans to reward people, including pay, benefits, and work environment characteristics, how the system will be designed and maintained, and the philosophy of what rewards are supposed to accomplish. Also included should be a statement expressing the organization's intention to treat everyone fairly and equitably, regardless of race, sex, religion, age, disability, color, national origin, and other protected classes relevant to local laws or organizational values or policies. Notably, 89 percent of Fortune 500 organizations, as well as some jurisdictions, include LGBT (lesbian, gay, bisexual, and transgender) as a group protected by their antidiscrimination policies (Human Rights Campaign, 2015) and, indeed, there are important business reasons to do so (Day and Greene, 2008). Although the organization's rewards policy should be brief, much care and deliberation needs to go into its development, since top management must make a commitment to staunchly adhere to its precepts to maximize employee trust. The reward policy should then be communicated to employees, along with other key policies.

Using Consultants

Before embarking on any major new salary or benefits program, the nonprofit organization should consider the value and cost-effectiveness of contracting with a compensation consultant. Organizations on tight budgets, particularly nonprofits, often fall into the trap of trying to save money by developing major programs in-house. If current human resources (HR) staff have the needed expertise, this may be the appropriate avenue to take. However, even if current staff are equipped with necessary skills, the following points should be considered.

First, consultants generally have a wide range of experience across a number of organizations and therefore may know what will work best for any unique organization. Compensation programs, especially benefits, are sophisticated and complex systems, and even HR professionals with basic compensation knowledge may not have the breadth and depth of knowledge to develop and install programs that are truly a "good fit." Consultants are able to introduce innovative ideas gleaned from their work, and if they are strategically focused, will recommend the ones most suited to the organization rather than any current HR fad.

Second, consultants usually have access to a vast amount of salary and benefits survey data or have easily accessible sources and will be able to assess external competitiveness better than an organization can alone.

Third, because consultants have experience with other types of organizations, both in different sectors as well as multiple products or services, they often bring innovative and creative ideas that even the brightest HR manager within the organization wouldn't consider. They are paid for creating inventive, state-of-the-art solutions, so they may be able to generate cost-effective, unique ideas that will contribute to the organization's effectiveness or distinctiveness in the labor market.

Fourth, consultants are outsiders, and this gives them an extremely valuable commodity: objectivity. Since the consultant's salary will not be part of the new program, unlike the in-house executive's or HR professional's, he or she will be in a better position to tell top managers or the board of directors about unpopular or expensive issues (for example, critical positions that are dramatically underpaid relative to the market). Objectivity also is a great asset in explaining to employees why some jobs have been downgraded and that their topped-out employees (who are at the maximum of their grade and thus ineligible for salary increases) will not be receiving raises for the next year or so. Additionally, if the consultant is hired to conduct a specially designed salary or benefits survey, competitors may be more likely to participate and share their information, since the consultant provides a greater guarantee of confidentiality than a rival organization.

The major disadvantage of using consultants is of course cost. But keep in mind the observation cited earlier that wages often constitute over half of total organization expenses. Sometimes several thousand dollars in consulting fees is money well spent if it is able to provide the organization with a system that maximizes the value of the salary/benefit dollar.

To assist in-house compensation program development, HR professionals can gain useful technical knowledge through the certification programs of WorldatWork (formerly known as the American Compensation Association). These certifications cover everything from base pay to benefits to work-life rewards. Earning the "Certified Compensation Professional," for example, consists of completing ten seminars and exams. Those serious about establishing, installing, and maintaining a state-of-the-art rewards program should investigate these.

Let us now turn to the components of developing a sound salary and benefits program. We will begin with base compensation, usually known simply as salary or wages. Executive pay and incentive programs in nonprofit organizations will be discussed before moving on to development of benefits packages.

Traditional Base Compensation Principles

Over the last fifteen years, there has been much discussion regarding the "end of the job" (Bridges, 1994). "Jobs" are tightly defined, predetermined, and controlled, and thus said to sometimes limit organizations in responding adequately to fast-changing competitive pressures. Rather, voices of reform recommend that work should be considered "roles" that are broader and more flexible. Given the competitive nature of labor markets as well as the need for organizations to maximize the value they receive from each individual, this makes some sense. Moving away from the attitude of "it's not in my job description" allows employers to use workers' KSAs (knowledge, skills, and abilities) to their utmost in accomplishing organizational and unit goals, while at the same time providing employment that may be more rewarding, challenging and interesting than a traditional, narrowly defined job.

"To Job or Not to Job": Job- or Person-Based Systems

However, jobs provide a number of practical advantages. They also do not seem to be disappearing into the mists of time, since most organizations continue to use them (Giancola, 2007). The "job" concept often is superior to "non-job" models because of its ease in recruiting, conducting market analyses of competitors' pay levels, and training design. But it is generally true that many jobs have increased in flexibility and, in order to achieve their missions, small organizations usually require workers who are willing to wear a number of hats.

The point is that the way management views how work will be accomplished, as either carefully prescribed "jobs" or as more loose and flexible "roles," will make a difference in the type of pay systems and procedures that should be developed. Thus, nonprofits should carefully analyze their organizations' characteristics, the type of work that needs to be done, and the type of people most likely to have these skills and decide to what extent work should be conceived of as jobs or roles. One way to conceptualize this question is to ask whether the organization wants to pay for a *job* to be done, in which the work requires a defined set of tasks and duties that are relatively stable—and for which a reasonable number of candidates in the labor market could be found to fill them—or if the work requires a *person's unique set of abilities and skills* for a variety of changing organizational needs. Generally speaking, this needs to be determined organization-wide, not job-by-job or person-by-person, so that the entire pay structure is coherent and consistent. Very small organizations, such as start-ups, often by necessity use roles because the work to be done is so variable and must be responsive to quickly changing environmental demands.

Since evidence suggests that organizations, for-profit and nonprofit, have not abandoned the convenience of the job, but rather have merely broadened its content and flexibility, the emphasis of this chapter is focused on more traditional job-centered compensation systems. For readers who believe a non-job system would be more workable for their organizations, most recent compensation textbooks contain descriptions of specific non-job techniques (examples include Bergman and Scarpello, 2001; Milkovich, Newman, and Gerhart, 2011).

Job or Work Analysis

As is true for many personnel practices (recruitment, staffing, performance management, training and development, and others), the foundation of salary systems is current, accurate, and thorough analysis of the work to be done. "Job analysis" consists of a variety of techniques used to observe, examine, record, and summarize the main components of jobs. Given the interest in person-based (role or "non-job") approaches, techniques are now being developed to analyze the work accomplished in organizations outside of a traditional job context. For example, tasks within an entire department, system, process, or skill set may be investigated as the unit of analysis, where multiple people may do many interchangeable tasks (Milkovich, Newman, and Gerhart, 2011).

However, as noted above, most organizations have retained the basic "job" concept, and job analysis is still a useful term. Through job analysis, data on the content of jobs are gathered, evaluated, quality-controlled, compiled, and summarized (usually in the form of job descriptions) so that jobs are thoroughly and accurately understood. This somewhat time-consuming process is absolutely necessary for at least two reasons. First, accurate job knowledge is critical in establishing *external competitiveness* so jobs can be compared across organizations by their *content* (what the people actually do), not merely by a job title that may not truly describe it. Second, only by understanding jobs can the level of *internal equity* in the organization be assessed and, if necessary, adjusted. Internal equity involves comparing the organization's jobs, so it requires accurate and current job information be available in a useable format.

Job analysis can be conducted with a number of techniques, depending on its final use (job analysis is also used in designing programs for training, recruitment, and job design, among others). These techniques include interviews of incumbents and/or supervisors (either individually or in groups), observations of workers, highly structured questionnaires or checklists completed by the job incumbent (such as the well-known Position Analysis Questionnaire®), or open-ended questionnaires completed by the incumbent, supervisor, or both. The questionnaire approach is most frequently used by small to medium organizations, since it allows data to be gathered easily and relatively cheaply. Open-ended questionnaires are typically designed by the organization so that the data gathered fit the values and goals of the organization—in other words, they should collect data on *what the organization wants to reward*. As will be discussed later often the *compensable factors* that will be used in the job evaluation process are assessed through this questionnaire.

Organizations that do not have the resources to engage consultants or lack the in-house expertise to perform job analysis may find useful open-ended questionnaires on public-domain Internet sites. However, it is critical to keep in mind two important points. First, job analysis, as mentioned earlier, should measure jobs (or work) in relation to what the organization wants to reward. Therefore, "off-the-shelf" techniques or questionnaires that don't really measure work in ways meaningful to the design of an effective pay system may turn into a terrific waste of time. Second, job (or work) analysis can become a highly charged emotional and political activity in any organization, particularly if the results are to be used for pay determination. When employees know that job analysis results may play a role in how their jobs are valued, they have a vested interest in consciously or unconsciously making their work sound as important and complex as possible. If they believe that the process was unfair, incomplete, or contaminated, serious intra-organizational problems could arise. Thus, it is strongly recommended that compensation experts be involved in this process as early as possible.

External Competitiveness

Since the mid-1990s, external competitiveness, or the need for organizations to identify their competitors for labor and set pay levels in response to them, has increased in importance. Several changes in the national (and global) economy have shifted the weight of pay system development from internal to external considerations. A primary change is that American organizations now recognize that they exist in a highly competitive labor environment. Indeed, even in times of economic downturn, the "war" for talent continues for many technical and highly educated workers. Given projections that KSAs in the American workforce will not meet organizational needs over the next few decades (Heneman and Judge, 2009), external competitiveness has moved to the front of the line in pay system design. Further, this increase in competition for highly skilled labor has discouraged workers from limiting themselves to one sector or another. Indeed, public-sector and nonprofit organizations may find themselves in competition with for-profits for the same people who previously saw themselves as nonprofit workers. Thus, the ability to understand the entire labor market, both for-profit and nonprofit, enables the nonprofit compensation manager to make informed decisions regarding total reward strategies. Finally, rapidly increasing technology requires hiring and retaining people with skills that are "market-driven." As nonprofit organizations rely more heavily on automated information, Internet fundraising, and other functions, the need for the salary system to respond quickly and effectively to labor market forces is critical. Without adaptive systems to gauge and react to market changes, retention of highly skilled workers will be extremely difficult. To build a responsive, externally competitive system, we need to define our *relevant labor market*, identify the data we need, and decide how to use it.

With Whom Do We Compete for Employees? After ensuring that job information is complete and up-to-date, the first question that must be answered is "What are the salary markets for the jobs in this organization?" In nearly every organization, several salary markets, or *"relevant labor markets,"* will exist. The key is to determine where the needed KSAs are in the labor market. While it is true that many nonprofits will be unable to match the pay of large, private-sector companies, it is still critical to have information about the pay level of the entire relevant market. For example, clerical jobs are nearly always recruited locally, probably from both for-profit and nonprofit organizations, because that's where people with clerical KSAs can be found. Therefore, the relevant labor market for clerical jobs is usually a wide local market. Some professional jobs that are technically or specialty oriented will most likely be recruited regionally, nationally, or even internationally, often from other nonprofits with similar missions and goals, but sometimes from broader sources. If key executive positions require knowledge and skills specialized to particular nonprofit organizational needs, then their appropriate labor market will be national (or international) nonprofits in similar sectors. However, some executive roles may benefit from skills found outside the nonprofit arena. As in all positions, the relevant labor market for the nonprofit's executives must also be carefully considered and chosen, based on the organization's goals and strategies.

What Data? After identifying the relevant markets, *benchmark jobs* should be identified. These are jobs upon which the salary system will be built, so they should be well-defined and clearly understood within the organization. Every organization has its own unique jobs that do not exist in the rest of the world and for which no market data are available. However, benchmark jobs should be (1) easily found in other organizations within the relevant labor markets, (2) relatively unchanging, (3) as a group, represent nearly all levels within the organization, (4) vary in levels of compensable factors (which will be discussed later), (5) have multiple incumbents, and (6) those for which the organization is experiencing particular difficulty recruiting (Kovac, 2008; Wallace and Fay, 1988). Typically, it is desirable to choose a group of benchmarks representing 25 to 30 percent of all jobs in the organization—and many more if the organization intends its reward system to be market-driven.

A critical point is that job *contents*, not job *titles*, are determinants of benchmark jobs. Job descriptions created from the job analysis should be used to ensure valid market matches. To avoid confusion, titles should accurately reflect the contents of the job and should not be manipulated to reward employees or increase the prestige of the supervisor, as often happens in poorly designed and maintained salary systems.

Salary data are generally collected from two broad sources: published salary surveys or surveys conducted by the organization or its consultants. Published surveys are undoubtedly the easiest to obtain but have drawbacks (Exhibit 23.1 lists a variety of published surveys). First, some are extremely

---

EXHIBIT 23.1. SELECTED SALARY SURVEY SOURCES

U.S. Department of Labor, Bureau of Labor Statistics
National Compensation Survey: http://www.bls.gov/ncs/ocs/home.htm

- Data for all fifty states and metropolitan areas are available at no charge; includes benefits data.

Professional Nonprofit Associations
Center for Association Leadership (ASAE; https://www.asaecenter.org)

- The Association Compensation Interactive: An interactive web tool that allows for customized searches
- The Association Executive Compensation & Benefits Study
- The Greater Washington Area Compensation & Benefits Study

Nonprofit Industry Surveys
ERI Salary Surveys (http://salary-surveys.erieri.com/)

- Nonprofits Salary Survey
- Benefits in Nonprofit Organizations

National Consulting Groups Publishing Surveys for Various Industries and Professions
Executive Alliance (http://www.executivealliance.com/)
Korn Ferry / Hay Group (http://www.haygroup.com)
AON Hewitt: Total Compensation Center (https://www.totalcompensation center.com/TCC/home/select_site.jsp)
Mercer Human Resources Consulting (https://www.imercer.com/content/ mercer-consulting-services.aspx)
Towers Watson (http://www.towerswatson.com)

expensive. Those published by national consulting firms can cost from $100 to a few thousand dollars and more. Such cost issues may be counteracted by the payroll dollars saved in an effective salary administration program, and several organizations may form a consortium to purchase them jointly. These surveys are generally of very high quality, with the data cut in many useful ways (for example, by region, by type of industry, by budget size, number of employees, and others). However, because these surveys often are geared to the for-profit business sector, they may only have relevant data for a few jobs in a nonprofit organization. But for some high-level technical or specialized jobs, the data found in them may be essential. Luckily, there are many less expensive published sources of salary data available, such as those published by other nonprofits, including professional associations and government entities.

Finding salary data for highly paid professional jobs that exist only in other similar nonprofits may require a custom survey. An advantage of custom surveys is the organization has control over the data retrieved. The main disadvantage is that, because surveying is another fairly sophisticated and technical activity, an organization must either have the internal staff with sufficient time and expertise or hire qualified consultants. Thus, custom surveys may be as or more expensive than purchased surveys.

Determining where salary data will be found will obviously be driven by the judgment of the relevant salary markets. For local clerical markets, several sources are available. First, local human resources groups often publish salary surveys keyed to a general market. The Society for Human Resource Management (SHRM), for example, has many local chapters across the country that provide such data. Second, the Bureau of Labor Statistics has a rich variety of data available on its website (www.bls.gov/home.htm) at no charge. Third, some municipalities (often through Chambers of Commerce) and states conduct surveys of local markets, which may be available for small fees. Nonprofit managers should be particularly aware of organizations such as ERI Salary Surveys and the Center for Association Leadership that publish data specifically for nonprofit markets (as listed in Exhibit 23.1). Consultants are often helpful in identifying more obscure sources for published surveys that include unusual jobs, and associations representing specific occupations may produce surveys that are available at a reasonable cost. A word of caution regarding these, however: Be sure that these surveys have been conducted using accepted and reputable survey methodologies. Such associations sometimes overvalue their members' worth in order to improve the profession's public image, so their data should be compared with other, more objective sources to ensure their validity.

Simple Internet search engines may be able to locate hard-to-find salary sources but, as any wise web surfer knows, data from the Internet must be viewed with a degree of skepticism. This is especially true for salary data. Many managers who have had conversations about competitive salaries with employees know there is a seemingly infinite amount of Internet salary data available, and employees frequently use this information to argue for pay increases. It is therefore critical that the nonprofit manager be able to understand the basics of good salary survey methodology, discussed later, and be able to communicate the importance of using only verifiably valid and reliable data in making pay decisions.

Using the Data. Good salary surveys report several statistics for each job, usually including the average salary, weighted average, minimum, maximum, median (50th percentile) and perhaps other percentiles. Generally, the most important statistic in the salary survey is the weighted average, since it represents the average salary across all the surveyed job incumbents (not just across organizations), and thus better estimates labor market rates. Several points should be reviewed before using data from a salary source:

- How many organizations participate? Make sure the data represent a sufficiently large sample.
- Are the firms representative of the organization's relevant labor market(s)?
- How does the weighted average compare to the average salary? If they are dramatically different, it may mean that one very large organization's data are skewing the results, since weighted averages are weighted by the number of employees within each organization.
- How do the average and weighted average salaries compare with the 50th percentile (median)? Again, a large discrepancy could indicate a skewed distribution that may mean it is a nonrepresentative sample.

At least three different salary data sources should be collected for each benchmark job, more when possible. This helps to ensure that final market data averages are valid. Since survey data are collected at different points in time (high-quality surveys will cite the effective date of the data), data must be "aged" by a reasonable inflation factor so that all data are comparable. This factor should be based on the general increase in salaries and salary structures currently occurring in the market (sources for these statistics will be discussed later). Next, the individual data points for each job need to be checked to ensure they are within a reasonable range of each other; outliers, those significantly higher or lower than others, should be removed. Then data for each job should be averaged, after which the jobs can be arrayed in order of market value.

A useful means of evaluating the organization's current standing in the market is through regression analyses. Using job evaluation points (to be discussed later) as the independent variable (on the "x" axis), one regression line should be calculated with market average salaries as the dependent variable (on the "y" axis). This regression line should be plotted and compared with the regression line for which current salary is the dependent variable. By looking at the disparities between these two lines, the degree to which the organization conforms to the market can be ascertained. For example, such a comparison may show that the organization is paying competitively for lower level jobs, while upper levels jobs are being paid under their market rates (such as in Figure 23.1). Using these graphs to illustrate discrepancies helps explain compensation needs to decision makers, including boards of directors, who must consider economic impact. Especially when justifying radical departures from the organization's status quo, such as dramatic increases to formerly underpaid jobs, directors and other top decision makers are often understandably skeptical. Ensuring them

FIGURE 23.1. Regression Analysis Illustrating the Relationship of Current Salaries to Market Data

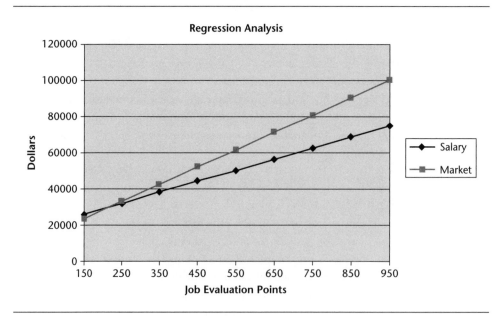

of the veracity and legitimacy of the data may be imperative to getting the new program implemented.

The convenience of adopting a job-based pay program is clearly seen when trying to gather market data for a non-job-based pay program. Simply speaking, it is quite difficult to use market surveys to price "non-jobs," because such surveys are not designed for this purpose. Flexible, unique, and highly adaptable "roles" defy collecting competitive salary data. Efforts have been made involving extrapolating key skills from job-based salary data, but this strategy, while theoretically workable, is time-consuming and difficult.

Internal Equity

Internal equity refers to the perception of fairness in pay for various jobs throughout the organization. In other words, in an internally equitable system, jobs that are of similar levels on key *compensable factors*, such as skill or knowledge required, supervisory responsibilities, accountability for budget and resources, complexity of the job, or working conditions, will be paid at the same general level. For example, a job of accounting clerk may require some post-high-school education or experience, knowledge of basic accounting principles, no supervisory responsibilities, and little accountability for financial resources. If this job is compared to a beginning employee benefits claim clerk, a job also requiring some post-high-school education or experience, basic technical knowledge, no supervisory responsibilities, and little accountability for financial resources, we would conclude that the jobs are essentially worth about the same to the organization. However, a custodian, as compared to those jobs, would probably not be valued as highly, since custodial work usually requires less education, technical knowledge, and experience. In an equitable system, these differences in internal job value would be appropriately reflected in the pay structure; in a system that is not equitable, the custodian may be paid the same or more than the accounting clerk or benefits claims clerk, or the benefits claims clerk may make significantly more or less than the accounting clerk. An important caveat here is that job evaluation addresses differences between job *content*, not employees' *performance* levels. We are interested in what the job requires, and not in what any particular individual might be able to do or how well he or she does it.

Internal equity is established using some form of *job evaluation*. This broad term describes a number of methods by which jobs are valued within the organization. Two of the most prevalent in small- to medium-sized organizations will be discussed here: slotting and point factor job evaluation.

Slotting. Slotting is appropriate for organizations wanting to emphasize external competitiveness over internal equity, that have a small number of jobs, for which a great deal of market data are available, or with highly flexible or quickly changing jobs. The slotting process begins with gathering as much market data as possible. After these data are tabulated and quality controlled using the criteria presented earlier, the jobs are listed in order of market value. Jobs for which no market data are available (usually those unique to the organization) are then *slotted* into this hierarchy. Slotting is done by comparing the job to those in the hierarchy and determining where it fits relative to other jobs based on its overall value to the organization. Slotting done in this manner is often referred to as a kind of "whole job" evaluation system, meaning that compensable factors (skill, education, working conditions, and others) are not systematically determined and compared, but that the job is looked at as a whole. Of course, in practice, the cognitive decision processes humans naturally use tend to fall back on informally derived compensable factors. However, they are not formally defined or systematically applied.

In addition to allowing market responsiveness, the major advantage of the slotting method is savings of time, effort, and cost, as compared to a more elaborate job evaluation system. Additionally, the technical skill needed to develop and install other types of systems is fairly high, and the cost of consultants in establishing internal equity can be avoided when slotting is used.

However, slotting has disadvantages. The most obvious is that some organizations have many jobs not found in the market, and thus market data may not be available for a large percentage of jobs. Second, because of the whole job technique, the system is generally lower in reliability (when two people independently slot jobs, they are likely to come up with different solutions) than in a point-factor system, and thus may be more likely to face challenges from employees.

Point-Factor Job Evaluation. Of the more complex job evaluation systems, the most common is point-factor evaluation. The well-known Hay system is a complex hybrid of the point-factor method. The basic steps in establishing and implementing a point-factor system involve:

- Identifying and weighting a set of compensable factors that uniquely describe those job characteristics for which the organization wants to pay
- Establishing levels within each factor and assigning points to each level
- Carefully comparing each job description to the factors and assigning points appropriate to each factor level

The end result is a hierarchy that ranks the jobs from highest to lowest in their value to the organization.

Organizations have used a variety of compensable factors in their job evaluation systems, including the following:

- Accountability
- Complexity of job
- Consequence of errors
- Customer service responsibility
- Decision making
- Education and training
- Experience
- Independent judgment
- Interpersonal contacts
- Interpersonal skills
- Physical exertion
- Planning responsibility
- Problem solving
- Sales responsibility
- Scope of job
- Supervision
- Technical knowledge
- Working conditions

However, empirical research using factor analysis (a statistical procedure that defines basic underlying components) has found that these numerous factors generally reduce to four basic concepts: skill, effort, responsibility, and working conditions.

Compensable factors appropriate for the organization are determined by a number of methods, ranging from sophisticated computer programs to hand-picking the factors that "sound right." However, top management must be involved in their selection, for several reasons. First, top management is closest to the mission, goals, and strategy of the organization and can translate what the organization wants to pay for into the compensable factors. Second, top management has a broad view of the organization's functions and thus should understand the scope and content of the jobs. Third, as in any management process, it is imperative that top management buys into the system. Nonprofit organizations should also consider the advisability of gaining board of directors' approval, if not including its members in the actual factor determination.

One of simplest and most straightforward methods used to guide top managers in factor choice involves five steps:

1. The manager or HR professional in charge of developing the program identifies a universe of appropriate compensable factors by reviewing a set of factors, such as those listed earlier, and eliminating those not relevant to the organization. For example, sales responsibility or physical exertion are often not relevant to nonprofits and may be removed.
2. After identifying this appropriate universe, the manager or professional carefully explains the overall point-factor evaluation concept as well as the meaning of each factor to the top managers.
3. Top managers then *individually* rank the factors.
4. The manager or HR professional compiles those rankings and uses them to select a set of factors, taking care to consider the factors that may improve the system's credibility and acceptability to employees and management. While the number of factors needed to produce a workable job hierarchy can be as few as three or four, the key is to include enough to capture the major components for which the organization wants to pay. Several years ago, it was not uncommon for job evaluation systems to include up to ten compensable factors. Currently, given the increased emphasis on market data and consideration of the cost of complex systems, point-factor systems generally include between four and seven factors.
5. The manager or HR professional presents this set to top management for discussion, asking them to ensure the set completely yet concisely describes the job characteristics for which the organization is willing to pay.

After the final compensable factors are chosen, they should then be weighted according to the relative importance of the factors to each other, in light of the organization's mission and strategy. For example, an association of physicians is probably driven by jobs that are highly dependent on education and technical training, so those factors would be heavily weighted. "Consequence of errors" may be less important, so would be weighted accordingly. An easy method to accomplish this is to ask the top managers individually to allocate or divide 100 points among all items in the set of factors. The manager or HR professional can then compile the responses into one set of weightings, which top management as a group again will review and revise or approve.

After weighting the factors, they must be divided into *levels*. An easy example is education and training. Typical levels in this factor include:

1. High school diploma or equivalent; basic reading skills required
2. High school diploma or equivalent, plus ability to operate simple equipment such as word processors; basic office or technical skills
3. Some advanced training, typically found in two-year college or certification program, or equivalent experience; ability to operate moderately complex equipment (such as for word processing); intermediate analytical skills
4. Theoretical understanding of a body of knowledge similar to that acquired in an academic field of study. May include a bachelor's degree, extensive technical training, or equivalent experience
5. Comprehensive understanding of one or several fields, normally gained through extensive study in an academic environment or business. May include a master's degree or equivalent experience
6. Knowledge of a subject to a level that the incumbent is an authority in the field; may include doctoral degree or equivalent experience

Parenthetically, we should note that the phrase "or equivalent" should be used for the education factor for two important reasons. First, it allows flexibility in staffing. Practically every organization will have individuals who may have education making them over- or under-qualified for their jobs but who are performing adequately or better. Second, it provides some protection from legal liability. Because protected classes may be adversely impacted by educational requirements, these should not be hard-and-fast requirements; they should be a general gauge of the level of education that incumbents typically have.

If no outside consultant is assisting in the project, it would be helpful at this point for the manager or HR professional to consult a compensation consultant or comprehensive textbook listing typical compensable factors. Defining appropriately sensitive factor levels requires a degree of expertise that generally comes only from previous experience. Points must also be assigned to each level within each factor, guided by the factor weightings. Table 23.1 illustrates a typical example of the assignment of these values.

The product of these efforts at this point is essentially a device by which all of the organization's jobs can be measured. The next major phase of the point-factor job evaluation process involves using this point-factor yardstick to evaluate jobs, starting with the benchmarks. Building the salary system is easier if the benchmark jobs for which market data were collected are used as markers in the job evaluation process.

The individuals responsible for evaluating the jobs must be carefully chosen. In the best of all possible worlds, a *job evaluation committee* made up of top

TABLE 23.1. Example: Assigning Points to Factor Levels

Factors	Weight	Points	1	2	3	4	5	6
Education & Training	25%	250	50	75	100	150	200	250
Accountability	20%	200	35	75	100	135	175	200
Independent Judgment	20%	150	25	50	75	100	125	150
Supervision	15%	100	15	30	45	60	80	100
Complexity of Job	10%	100	15	30	45	60	80	100
Consequence of Errors	10%	100	15	30	45	60	80	100
Total	100%	900						

managers is used. Under the guidance of a HR professional or compensation consultant, this group of five to eight executives should spend several uninterrupted hours or even days carefully discussing each benchmark job, debating its rating on each factor, and finally reaching consensus on a final rating. After the job evaluation committee has evaluated the benchmark jobs, a subcommittee, often an HR professional or consultant (or both) plus one top manager, evaluates the rest of the jobs.

Again, executives are ideal as first evaluators because they have a broad organizational perspective, are closest to the strategic goals and values of the organization, and their participation makes them more likely to buy into the system. The initial use of the new system on the benchmark jobs helps to more precisely define the meaning of the factors in the particular organizational context. Top managers then better understand and appreciate its relevance. However, the disadvantage is clear: the time and energy of executives is at a premium, particularly in these days of scaled-down management structures. Each nonprofit organization should carefully consider how much of its executives' time should be used. A cheaper but less effective strategy is to use a middle-management committee to evaluate the benchmark jobs. (Committees made up of workers below middle management are generally not recommended, since they become susceptible to political pressures from co-workers to overrate or underrate certain jobs.)

Even using time-saving tactics, the committee process can be extremely expensive in terms of executive time and productivity. An alternative but less effective process is for an HR professional, working in conjunction with a consultant or other HR staff, to evaluate all jobs, and then secure top management approval for the job hierarchy.

Regardless of the evaluation process, the same principles should be followed:

• Evaluators must understand all the factors and levels. Time should be allocated for discussion of the system and how it relates to the organization and its goals and strategies.

- Evaluators must thoroughly understand each job. This is where current and accurate job descriptions are essential. If necessary, the job's supervisor should be consulted during the discussion to ensure that essential job functions are understood.
- A critical issue for evaluators to remember is that they are evaluating *jobs* and not people. It is essential that discussions center on the requirements of the job and not on an unusually high (or low) performing job incumbent.
- Each job should be discussed in terms of how it rates on each factor and what specific job tasks or responsibilities relate to the factor.
- If possible, a consensus on the job's rating on each factor should be reached. Majority vote should be used only as a last option.

After all jobs have been evaluated, the point values should be entered into a spreadsheet (an abbreviated example is presented in Table 23.2). This enables the evaluators to "quality control" their results, ensuring face-valid and sensible relationships between the jobs are maintained.

A final step in job evaluation is to review the hierarchy with each departmental manager. The hierarchical list of jobs within the department, listed *without* point values, should be presented to the department manager. (Point values of jobs should be known only by the job evaluation committee and relevant HR staff in order to avoid misunderstandings among those who do not understand the scope or application of the system). The manager should check to see whether the hierarchy makes sense in the accepted understanding of the jobs' functions, values, and relationships. Some minimal fine-tuning may be needed. After all departments' managers have reviewed these hierarchies, a spreadsheet illustrating all jobs within departments across the organization can be produced and

TABLE 23.2. Example: Job Evaluation Spreadsheet

Job	Education & Training	Account-ability	Independent Judgment	Supervision	Complexity of Job	Consequence of Errors	Total
Receptionist	50	35	25	15	15	10	150
Accounting Clerk	75	100	75	30	45	30	355
Administrative Assistant	150	135	125	45	60	40	555
Development Director	200	175	125	60	80	80	720
Program Director	200	175	150	80	80	50	735

then reviewed by the top managers. This last step is to ensure job relationships are equitable, not only within departments, but across the organization.

Choosing and Maintaining the Right System. Regardless of the type of job evaluation method used, a system of regular review should be established so that jobs are analyzed and reevaluated about every three years, more often if they change frequently. Obviously, organizational needs as well as jobs change over time, so a regular system is necessary to maintain internal equity. Often, HR departments will systematically review one-third of the jobs each year to avoid having to face a major project every three years. Additionally, there should be a mechanism by which supervisors can appeal job evaluations at times other than this regular cycle of review, when they have a legitimate need to do so (for example, when a job significantly changes).

With innovative pay systems such as team-based pay, incentive systems, and skill-based pay increasing due to less traditional organizational structures, budget constraints, and the importance of market forces, the usefulness of extensive job evaluation programs has been questioned. All organizations, especially nonprofits, in which time and money are in extreme demand, need to determine the right balance to strike between internal and external pressures and design an internal evaluation system that is the least administratively complex. In terms of complexity, the point-factor system is definitely not for everyone.

Indeed, the hassles of creating an internally equitable salary structure are hard to exaggerate. They nearly always pay off in the long run, however. Most managers believe that inequities with the external market will foster more pay dissatisfaction than inequities in internal relationships, yet experiences in the for-profit sector with two-tiered pay systems provide a valuable lesson of the impact of internal inequity. These two-tiered systems were designed to reduce costs for financially troubled employers by paying new hires dramatically less for the same jobs than previously hired incumbents—sometimes as little as one-half of the incumbents' pay. Research and experience have shown that not only do these new employees show high levels of pay dissatisfaction, but longer-tenured, higher-paid employees are also very uncomfortable with the internal inequities. Additionally, internal inequities will be experienced by the employee on a daily, even hourly basis, as he or she continually interacts with co-workers. External market inequities, on the other hand, may only be experienced as one surfs the Internet or compares wages with a friend. Thus, every organization should be cognizant of the consequences of internal inequity and install, implement, and maintain a sound job evaluation program, no matter how simple or complex.

External Competitiveness and Internal Equity: What Roles Should They Play?

The competitive pressures of the external labor market, plus the importance of creating organizations in which employees believe they are paid equitably, require nonprofit managers to carefully weigh the relative importance of internal and external equity. It is possible for organizations that do not have the need to attract the most highly skilled, specialized, or in-demand workers to find their needs better served by first ensuring an equitable internal hierarchy of jobs and then making sure that it generally matches the relevant market. Alternatively, organizations dependent on the attraction and retention of highly skilled workers will probably need to first focus on developing a system in which jobs are paid competitively and then work to ensure internal considerations are taken care of. As always, the mantra of "What is it that the organization wants to reward?" should inform and guide this strategic decision. It is upon this decision that the amount of market data needed and the complexity of the job evaluation procedure should rest.

Building the Externally and Internally Equitable Salary Structure

A salary structure creates a means by which pay is set and administered. It serves to integrate the organization's policies relative to external competitiveness and internal equity in a manageable system that sets minimum and maximum pay levels for jobs, thereby serving to ensure pay is within the range that supports the organization's rewards strategy.

Reconciling Contradictions Between the Data. It is likely that the job hierarchies generated from market analysis and job evaluation will not match exactly. In other words, the market will probably value some jobs higher or lower than does the organization. This requires the organization to have a strategy regarding the relative importance of each. Some jobs, such as those with valuable or rare skill sets, may need to be "market-driven," meaning that their values should be based primarily if not solely on current and accurate market data. An organization with jobs particularly focused on the organization's mission and strategy may choose to pay them above their market rates. An example from a for-profit organization may be helpful. In the banking industry, one of the most notoriously low-paid jobs is teller. However, a bank that has formulated a strategy of preeminent customer service might choose to pay its tellers above the market because it wants to attract, motivate, and retain the very best candidates. Similarly, nonprofit managers must carefully consider their strategy relative to internal and external equity and whether it should differ for any particular jobs.

Pay Level Policy. As part of the rewards policy formulation, top managers must decide where they want their organization to stand relative to their job markets. This decision then directly informs how the organization prices its jobs, which is a fundamental part of building the salary structure.

Most organizations in the private sector attempt to maintain their pay levels at the median of their relevant markets. This does not mean every employee will be paid exactly the going market rate but that, overall, the salary ranges and grades reflect the current market (more will be said about this later). Some organizations make policy decisions to pay at the 60th percentile or higher, believing premium salaries will ensure they attract and retain the top performers. Some organizations may pay significantly under the market median. This strategy may be driven by the need for only low-skilled, easily hired employees performing quickly acquired duties. Obviously, the pay-level decision is critical to the organization's strategic planning, its long-range goals, and its current environmental challenges.

Structuring the Structure. The HR professional, manager, or compensation consultant must make several decisions regarding the salary structure, which is merely the set of grades and their accompanying ranges. A salary grade involves several simple but key concepts: minimum, maximum, midpoint (or control point), and range spread. The minimum is the organization's policy of the minimum value a job is worth. Generally, newly hired workers with little or no relevant job experience will be paid the minimum rate. The maximum reflects the most value the organization expects to receive from the job. Even if an incumbent performs the job superbly and has done so for the last fifty years, the job is simply worth no more than the maximum. In most cases, jobs of similar value will be grouped together in a single grade; systems using only one job per grade are usually unwieldy and inefficient.

The midpoint, or control point, is a critical concept in base salary administration. It is the point in the salary range keyed to the organization's response to the market. For example, if the market rate for accountants is $4,000 per month and the organization's policy is to pay at 110 percent of the market, the midpoint for the grade in which accountants are found will be $4,400. New hires with little or no experience will be paid at the minimum of the range, and some longer-tenured accountants may be paid more, but generally the job of accountant, when performed by a fully-performing incumbent, is worth $4,400 to that organization.

The term "control point" is preferable to "midpoint" for a couple of reasons, even though midpoint is more statistically descriptive. First, as we will explain later, all employees should not expect to advance to the maximum of their job grade, unless their performance over time is exemplary. In an effective salary structure, an employee who meets expectations for the job should receive the value the job is worth on the market (or the organization's reaction to the market as determined by its pay level policy). Using the term midpoint is often interpreted by employees to mean that they have another 50 percent of the salary structure in which to move. Only top performers, however, should be paid in the top half of the grade. Second, "control point" is descriptive of the midpoint's use in salary administration. It allows the organization to control costs around its policy toward the salary market.

Range Spread: Traditional or Broadbanding? The range spread is the difference between the maximum and the minimum amounts paid for a job and is expressed as a percentage of the minimum. In older, more traditional salary systems, range spreads typically run from 35 to 50 percent, with the smaller ranges usually used for lower-level jobs. The rationale is that incumbents in lower-level jobs will stay in the range for less time than incumbents in higher-level jobs, since the lower jobs are less complex, easier to learn, and incumbents will tend to be promoted quickly to higher levels. However, in the last couple of decades, a useful concept called "broadbanding" has been adopted by organizations seeking to make their pay systems more flexible. Broadbanding collapses what would have been several grades into a broad "band," creating a more flexible system in which the pay for jobs can be adjusted without reclassifying a position from one grade to another. Figure 23.2 illustrates this concept. Broadbanding also allows more managerial discretion, in that a manager has a wider range within which to pay people. Since a broadbanded system has fewer bands than there are grades in a traditional salary structure, it is easier to administer and maintain. While broadbanding may not formally assign a control point to the band, in practice there may be "zones" or "shadow ranges" within the band that are keyed to market rates (Klaas, 2002). In more traditional systems, salary grades group jobs together that are of the same value to the organization. In broadbanding, a certain amount of precision is lost, and jobs in the same band will differ more with regard to their organizational value than they would in a traditional system.

Broadbanding systems are useful when flexibility and nontraditional career paths (often referred to as "career networks" or "career lattices" to denote that "up" is not the only direction to build a career) are the preferred strategy of the organization. However, because there are fewer ranges and fewer minimum and maximum pay rates with which to control salaries, there is the risk of paying jobs under or over market rates. Further, the increased managerial discretion opens

FIGURE 23.2. Broadbanding Superimposed on a Traditional Salary Structure

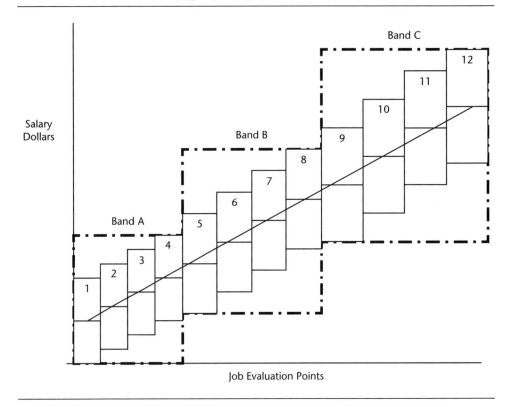

the door wider to potential for bias. As in all reward system decisions, the mission, organizational strategy, and rewards strategy need to be carefully considered in determining whether broad bands or more traditional ranges should be used.

Constructing Grades or Bands. *Control point* (or *midpoint*) *progression,* or the difference between the control points of two adjacent grades as expressed as a percentage of the lower grade's control point, should be considered in constructing grades or bands. A key consideration here is the role of promotions to the organization: If the organization wants to encourage employees to higher levels of achievement via promotion, then making control points farther apart provides more financial motivation for advancement. Also, if supervision is considered an important competency within the organization, larger progressions will more heavily reward supervisory positions. Sometimes organizations will split their structures into two: *exempt* (for professional, supervisory, and managerial workers) and *non-exempt,* divided according to the overtime provisions of the U.S. Fair Labor Standards Act. Usually, a larger control point progression is adopted for the exempt structure. An important issue is ensuring job families have sufficient differentials between them to support the value of the jobs in the marketplace and within the organization.

Salary structures are built beginning with the control points that are determined after the reconciliation of job evaluation points and market data for benchmark jobs. Minimums and maximums of each band or grade are then calculated. The widths should depend on strategic considerations: How long incumbents are expected to remain in their positions (longer time calls for wider grades or bands) and the degree to which promotional opportunities should be rewarded (greater emphasis on promotions calls for narrower grades or bands). It should be noted that creating a salary structure is art as well as science: The discrepancies in market and internal values must be managed, while at the same time creating a smooth progression up the grades that maintains appropriate relationships between the jobs within them. It is very helpful to have experience in building salary structures.

Maintaining the Structure. In order to maintain the salary structure, the market must be checked annually to ensure the organization's grades or bands remain competitive. This is done through another kind of survey, a prototype of which is WorldatWork's annual *Salary Budget Survey* (available for a reasonable fee to nonmembers). This survey presents data regionally, by industry, and by job level for present and anticipated structure increases. Organizations use the reported midpoint percentage increases to adjust their own midpoints and structures in order to keep their pay systems competitive. However, changes in the structure usually do not trigger increases to wages unless an employee's salary does not conform to the new range within which it is placed (after the change is made).

Common Issues in Installing a New System. Upon installing a new salary system, it is likely that some employees' current salaries will be over the new maximums ("red circle" employees) or under the new minimums ("green circle" employees). Theoretically, red circle employees are being paid substantially over the market rate (or midpoint or control point) for the job. Therefore, it does not make sense to continue to increase their base pay and typically it is "frozen" until the time that the structure's maximum catches up or exceeds it in the course of normal salary structure adjustment as described earlier. To maintain their level of motivation, however, many organizations will provide these individuals with lump-sum bonuses based on performance. This strategy gives the employees additional income but does not add to the fixed costs of base salaries. Green circle employees' salaries are substantially below the market rates for their jobs and, consequently, should be moved at least to the new minimum as quickly as possible. For organizations with limited resources, that may mean giving small periodic increases to gradually boost the salary. Additionally, some long-term employees may be faced with severe inequity if their salaries are at the minimum and new workers are hired to work alongside them at the same pay level. In these cases, the person managing the HR process must recommend the best approach to balance equity with financial resources. Often this will be through an "equity adjustment" of the employee's compensation. Typically, an organization will develop a simple formula that combines years of service and performance to determine where to move longer-term employees to a more equitable position in the grade or band.

Other Salary Administration Policies. Salary administration policies and procedures must be written to ensure they align with the goals and plans of the organization. There should be policies covering the salary impact of transfers, promotions, demotions, reclassifications (that is, when a job is reevaluated and placed in a different grade due to changes in its duties), and new hiring. It is essential that these be carefully thought out so that the intentions of the compensation plan are not subverted due to haphazard (and often demotivating) administrative procedures.

Pay satisfaction is popularly regarded as satisfaction with a worker's level of pay. However, research shows pay satisfaction also depends on the pay structure, administration of the program, its raises, and benefits (for example, Carraher, 1991; Heneman and Judge, 2000; Heneman and Schwab, 1985). The wise manager or HR professional will ensure these processes, as well as salary levels, are sound and equitable.

Increasing Individuals' Base Pay. In the past, many nonprofit organizations, government entities, and school districts based salary increases on seniority rather than performance. In most cases, however, seniority-based pay has come to be seen as strategically out of alignment with the leaner, more competitive operating environment of today and thus has been discontinued in favor of a merit system (merit pay generally refers to an annual salary increase based on the employee's performance appraisal; Deckop and Cirka, 2000). Accordingly, well-managed nonprofits now generally use some sort of merit-based method to increase base pay. The merit amount is determined competitively, typically using a survey such as the aforementioned WorldatWork's *Survey Budget Survey*, which reports percentage increases to actual pay across sectors, regions, and organizational types and sizes.

A Word About Performance Appraisals. An important caveat is that the success of a merit pay system depends on a performance appraisal process that is both *reliable* and *valid*. Reliability means the performance assessment must be consistent across raters (that is, if David's performance is reviewed by both Susie and Arif, assuming Susie and Arif have the same information about David's performance, they should agree within reasonable bounds on David's rating). Validity means the measure needs to be designed carefully so it is neither *contaminated* nor *deficient*. Contamination occurs when dimensions or behaviors irrelevant to good performance are measured (for example, rating a bus driver on financial acumen). Deficiency means important performance dimensions or behaviors are omitted (for example, ignoring customer service when reviewing the performance of a receptionist).

A second caveat is that valid and reliable performance measures are remarkably difficult to both design and implement. Although a deep discussion of this issue is beyond the scope of this chapter, reasons for the poor reputation of performance appraisals are lack of managerial courage, poorly articulated and communicated performance standards, insufficient training of raters, deficient allocation of time and resources, and more. In fact, bad experiences and dreadful organizational results associated with bumbling performance management systems have given rise to new processes that eliminate them in favor of technologically driven just-in-time feedback systems. There are reasons this kind of alternative might be an improvement. However, given the focus of this chapter, the main point is that careful strategy, design, and alignment of any performance management system must be in place as a new rewards strategy is considered. In nearly all cases, the two are inextricably linked.

As noted earlier, there is a trend across the nonprofit sector to move toward incentives—and sometimes even pay-at-risk plans. These more innovative pay systems do not eliminate the need for sound base compensation programs, however. Individuals must still receive a base wage, which will continue to represent a substantial expense to the organization and must be managed carefully. Therefore, the nonprofit manager or HR professional in charge of compensation must decide the best method with which to move employees through their grades or bands. In addition to merit and seniority-based systems, across-the-board or cost-of-living increases can also be used. However, like seniority-based pay, these alternatives increase the fixed costs of salaries in a manner that has no relationship to the employee's level of performance, generally unpopular in our current highly competitive economy, but occasionally necessary if an entire pay system is under the market and all salaries need to be increased quickly to ensure retention. As with all rewards decisions, these designs must be clearly linked to organizational strategy.

Communicating Salary Plans

How much to communicate, to whom, and when, are important strategic decisions that need to be carefully considered. Recently, a small number of organizations have been in the news for dropping the traditional secrecy around pay and making information about the entire system, including individual salaries and bonuses, available to anyone in the organization. This is a radical step, and it should never be undertaken without a careful assessment showing the strategy makes sense given the pay system's internal equity, external competitiveness, and administrative soundness and the culture of the organization. Unless all of these are properly aligned, a completely open pay system risks disaster. While innovative management strategies focused on egalitarian information sharing might seem optimally aligned with openness about pay, the method of communicating salary plans must be carefully aligned with the strategy and culture of the organization.

An easier case can be made for making information about the entire salary *structure* (pay grades' minimum, midpoint, and maximum values) available to all employees. Theoretically, organizations build reward strategies because they will be motivational, and if employees don't know what the structure is, the motivational benefit may be lost. Knowledge of the earning potentials of prospective jobs to which individuals aspire may motivate them to acquire the necessary skills and experiences to secure those jobs. However, if such career options do not exist and the organization's culture does not support such disclosure, it should not be done.

Organizations have to make strategic decisions regarding how much information about the plan should be available to employees. Some public organizations, like federal, state, and local governments, are legally mandated to make data regarding all salary grades and ranges available to employees as well as taxpayers, and individual salaries levels can be easily discovered by an Internet search. Other organizations are more private, and some make discussion of individual salaries among employees a disciplinary offense (however, the legality of this approach has recently been questioned). Generally speaking, most organizations make information about the minimum, midpoint, and maximum of a salary range available to the individuals whose jobs fall within it. In this way, employees are aware of the earning power of their present jobs.

A conservative and common approach is to communicate the following basic information to all employees (Rubino, 1997):

- The employee's job description and how it was obtained (job analysis)
- The general methods by which jobs are evaluated
- The organization's strategy about how market data are collected and analyzed
- The organization's approach to relating performance to pay
- How performance is measured and appraised
- Administrative policies and procedures
- Benefit plans

Going into depth and specific detail about any of these elements should be discouraged, since reward plans are often complex and may be beyond the capacity and interest of most "lay" employees to understand. Introducing more information than is needed should be avoided, so employees are neither confused nor suspicious about how their rewards are determined.

Incentive Pay in Nonprofits

Since the early 2000s, American business has had to become more competitive in many of its human resource practices. In many for-profit organizations, bonuses are now common at all levels. Many nonprofit organizations believe they are so financially constrained that incentives seem an impossible luxury, yet it is useful for the nonprofit executives and HR professionals to be aware of them since some incentives may have direct applicability to nonprofits with productivity or motivational issues.

Indeed, the use of incentive plans has increased rapidly in nonprofit organizations (Deckop and Cirka, 2000; WorldatWork and Vivient Consulting, 2014), and they can be effective in nonprofits if the following criteria are met (Wein, 1989).

- The top decision makers, including the board of directors, embrace a philosophy of pay-for-performance.
- Incentives are used only if they are based on improvements to the organization's financial condition, either through generation of revenue or enhanced cost savings. A particularly apt candidate for incentives is the development

officer, whose performance has a direct and immediate impact on organizational revenue.

- The performance upon which the incentive is based is measurable and achievable, and includes nonfinancial measures critical to the organization's mission and strategy (such as quality of service delivery).
- Employees find financial rewards motivating.
- The amount of the incentive is large enough to make a difference motivationally.
- Incentives are awarded only to employees whose performance is above average, perhaps substantially above average.
- The incentive plan is communicated effectively and employees trust that their efforts will be appropriately rewarded.

These points underscore the case that has been made throughout this chapter: Any type of rewards practice must be carefully considered and closely aligned with the organization's mission, strategy, and other HR policies and practices.

Types of Incentives

Simple short-term bonuses are probably the most widely understood incentive. These bonuses are based on a measure of performance over which the employee has some level of control and can be awarded for individually based performance, or to groups, departments, or units, depending on the desired behavior. "Spot awards," in which a supervisor allocates a small bonus to employees (usually $50 to $100, often given as a gift card) for excellent performance in isolated events, also can be powerful if carefully used.

Gainsharing programs require significant up-front design time, but may be more acceptable to board and public stakeholders because, in the nonprofit context, they focus on cost savings generated by employee performance. This type of program may be particularly appropriate for nonprofits that are experiencing unnecessarily high operating costs. While these plans vary widely in design, they nearly always include some employee-participation mechanism whereby employees' ideas and initiatives determine methods to save costs and encourage buy-in to the program. Usually, the organization will split the cost savings on an equal basis with the employees, and thus the plan benefits both the individuals and the organization. The major downside to this type of program is that it involves developing what can be a fairly complicated formula by which productivity gains will be measured, and this often requires hiring knowledgeable consultants to assist in the design and installation.

Nonprofit organizations considering incentive plans should ensure that they are in compliance with IRS regulations. While specific guidance is beyond the scope of this chapter, it should be noted that the IRS allows incentive plans as long as they do not violate rules that prohibit inappropriate private benefit or inurement by executives, managers, employees, or other insiders (Klein, McMillan, and Keating, 2002; also, see Chapter Two of this *Handbook* for general legal guidance on matters of private benefit). There are also Fair Labor Standards Act implications for U.S. nonprofits, since bonuses add to earnings and thus must be included in overtime calculations for nonexempt employees.

Nonfinancial Incentives. Nonprofit organizations are generally not cash-rich. Board members and some constituents and stakeholders also may be resistant to providing cash incentives to employees who "are just doing their jobs" and prefer those funds be directed at funding the organization's core mission. When such attitudes exist, it is encouraging to note that other types of incentives may be powerful yet less expensive motivators. For example, a popular nonfinancial incentive used by nonprofits is flextime (see, for example, "Innovative Compensation: What Should You Try? What Should You Avoid?", 1996). "Employee of the month" recognition or awards of clothing with organizational insignia can often reap motivational returns with benefit far exceeding its cost. "Recognition programs" that provide small rewards for length of service or retirement or give peers the opportunity to recognize others and reward above-and-beyond performance or specific behaviors, are widespread across organizations (WorldatWork and ITA Group, 2015). Wise managers will consider adding these options to their rewards strategies.

Executive Pay in Nonprofits

For-profit business organizations are frequently under heavy fire from the media and labor groups for their top management compensation practices, yet such was not the case for top management of nonprofit organizations until the early 1990s, when nonprofit salaries reported in the media were repudiated out-of-hand without considering the market forces that some argued made them necessary. It is imperative that top nonprofit decision makers, including board members and major funders, understand that superior performance in top management positions is critical to nonprofit success and that the best performers are often in very high demand. However, even reasonable levels of pay for their services may seem unconscionable to the uneducated, and those involved in determining executive pay should be extremely thorough in their market analyses and decision making and meticulous in communicating market pressures for top jobs to these influential leaders. Indeed, nonprofit excesses (notably Richard Grasso's executive pay package for leading the New York Stock Exchange, which is a nonprofit although not a charity) have resulted in increased disclosure requirements for nonprofit executive compensation by the U.S. Congress and Internal Revenue Service (Reilly and Cumpston, 2007).

The pay of the nonprofit executive group should be determined in a similar manner to that for other employees described earlier, using market data analyses, job evaluation, sound policies and procedures, and carefully designed incentive pay. External competitiveness issues are usually weighted much more heavily for top managers, for a couple of reasons. First, the location of these positions in the organization means internal equity considerations are more relevant for lower-level jobs. Second, these key jobs are quite visible to organizations competing for talent. Since the overall performance of the nonprofit is more clearly dependent on top management than on lower-level employees, an incentive program leveraged on achievement of the organization's mission, strategy, and goals should be seriously considered.

In response to the need for more market-based salaries, as well as external pressures for nonprofit executive pay to be correlated with organizational performance, nonprofits are increasingly turning to *variable executive pay*. In fact, a recent study of large U.S. nonprofit organizations found that 90 percent of its respondents reported having executive bonus programs in place (WorldatWork and Vivien, 2014). For-profits are usually criticized not for their base salaries, which tend to be relatively modest ("relatively" is a key word here), but for their incentive compensation, often taking the form of annual bonuses, stock options, or both. However, nonprofit organizations have less to worry about in this regard, since those nonprofit CEOs who are eligible for bonuses on average receive only about 15 percent of their base pay in incentives (Gaeta, 2003). In addition, many nonprofits are severely constrained by limited financial resources, making the magnitude of nonprofit executive pay in comparison to their for-profit counterparts seem quite modest. However, wise nonprofit decision makers will monitor the level and composition of executive compensation packages to ensure they are not only appropriate given market forces and IRS constraints, but also acceptable to key stakeholders.

The most frequent nonprofit strategy for determining executive incentive pay is a relatively subjective board judgment. A better strategy is to create performance measures clearly delineating the criteria upon which a bonus will be paid. An obvious tactic is to link executive bonuses with operational cost savings, which also serves to fund the incentives. Another financial criterion is "program ratio," or the ratio of the amount spent on delivery of mission-related services to total expenses. However, in addition to financial components, measures should be considered that reflect accomplishment of the organization's mission, such as number of clients served, as well as other practices found in balanced scorecard approaches, including investments in human capital, business processes, or innovation (Greene, 2007; Zimmerman, 2009; see Chapters Six and Ten of this book for thoughtful discussions on executive leadership, organizational effectiveness, and alternative ways of judging executive and organizational performance). David Bjork offers useful guidance on nonprofit executive compensation in his 2010 WorldatWork journal article, "Rethinking Executive Pay in Community-Based Organizations."

It is often desirable to contract with outside consultants to work with the governing board to design a salary plan for top management jobs. Not only do they have access to more data, but they generally have the objectivity needed to make recommendations to the board for compensating these critical jobs.

Benefits

Careful design and implementation of benefits programs are essential in attracting and retaining a qualified workforce. It is the rare job seeker who is willing to join an organization that does not offer a reasonable benefits package. The amount of money spent on benefits in the United States and many other nations is staggering and continues to grow. In the United States, benefits typically constitute nearly 40 percent of the average employer's total payroll (Milkovich, Newman, and Gerhart, 2011). In 2013, U.S. businesses spent $8.8 trillion on total compensation, $1.7 trillion of it on benefits (U.S. Chamber of Commerce, 2014). Thus, it is a good idea to make sure benefits are effective in attracting and retaining good employees.

The breadth and depth of guidance on the topic of benefits could easily fill several volumes, so the scope of discussion presented in this chapter necessarily must be limited. The field has become highly technical and specialized, requiring most HR professionals to solicit help in order to ensure their organizations' benefits programs are competitive and appropriate. Many consultants are available to assist in this quest—some of whom are brokers selling products and some who merely analyze organizational needs and make recommendations. Either kind can be of great assistance, although it is wise to be well-informed as to how each receives compensation for his or her work, since it can have a bearing on the nature of the recommendations.

In the United States, certain benefits are legally required (common are workers' compensation, unemployment compensation, unpaid leave for family issues per the Family and Medical Leave Act, and Social Security). Needless to say, nonprofit executives and HR professionals should take care to understand their responsibilities for compliance.

The same concepts of external competitiveness and internal equity that we discussed with regard to salary compensation are relevant in designing and implementing benefits programs. Organizations desiring to compete successfully for job candidates must design their benefits using current and reliable market data. Benefits surveys are included as adjuncts to some salary surveys, and surveys specific to benefits are also available. Because of the divergence and variety of different packages, it can be extremely difficult, frustrating, and cumbersome for an individual organization to conduct a benefits survey from scratch. Thus, if reliable and relevant data are available from a published source, it is nearly always preferable to use that data, as opposed to a survey conducted in-house.

Just as salary programs need to be developed with internal equity in mind, benefits programs should consider factors internal to the organization. The program should meet key employee needs as well as satisfy the employer in terms of financial and other policy obligations.

To meet employee needs, the organization's manager or HR professional should carefully consider the types and levels of benefits that employees want. Demographics of employee groups have an impact on benefits attractiveness. Middle-aged or older employees may be more concerned with retirement and retiree health insurance than younger employees, whose interests may revolve around beginning families and covering maternity expenses, family leave, and life insurance. However, it is a mistake to design benefits programs totally on demographics, since demographics are not always accurately predictive of the benefits employees want. Employee surveys, focus groups, or other systematic means of collecting data on the wants and needs of the organization's employees are essential.

One way organizations can satisfy diverse employee groups is through the use of flexible benefits or "cafeteria plans." These plans can be structured in many ways and include many options. In the United States the IRS allows employees to deduct pre-tax earnings from their paychecks for a limited and specific set of purposes (such as child care or medical, vision, or dental costs). This pre-tax option saves the employees taxes while allowing them to choose the benefits that are particularly attractive to them.

Benefits in the Rewards Policy

As discussed above, it is important for an organization to formulate a total rewards policy that explains what it is the organization wants its rewards system to achieve. Just as with pay and work environment considerations, the role of benefits in the overall total rewards system needs to be clearly articulated. Among the information that organizations should consider for inclusion in this policy are the following (McCaffery, 1983):

- The organization's desire to provide employees with meaningful welfare and security benefits
- The organization's intention to design benefits to fit employee needs
- The frequency and philosophy by which the program will be audited and evaluated in relation to costs, salary increases, and external factors
- The organization's desire to use benefits as a means to motivate and achieve desired levels of productivity
- How the organization plans to fund the benefits (most organizations offering benefits require employees to pay at least part of the cost)
- The organization's intention to communicate effectively, including to explain changes to benefits programs to employees
- The provision of individualized annual statements that explain to each employee the value and cost of their benefits, including the organization's contributions and the cost to employees
- The market with which benefits will be compared
- Any requirements for trustees and carriers to regularly (such as annually) submit detailed reports management and others
- The commitment that benefits plans will be evaluated regularly (annually or some other term) to ensure they meet the changing needs of the demographics of the employee group

Health Care

No U.S. reader of this book is unaware of the critical issues in health care that the United States has confronted during the past several decades. These continue to escalate and, at the time of this writing, the Patient Protection and Affordable

Care Act that was enacted by the U.S. Congress in 2010 continues to be challenged, even though most of its provisions were substantially implemented by 2014. Given the structural and political complexities of the Act (often referred to as "the ACA"), and the fact that it is based on an employer-based health care system, it is beyond the scope of this chapter to discuss employer-based health care in any depth. The ACA was enacted as an attempt to resolve the two most difficult challenges confronting the United States: controlling health care costs and ensuring access to health care to all Americans, yet it is unclear whether the ACA will resolve these challenges to the degree intended. Regardless of one's position on this specific legislation, the process of developing solutions to these complicated problems has been and will probably continue to be painful.

Nonprofit organizations in the United States are challenged by both cost and access. They are challenged directly by the rising cost of providing health insurance and, indirectly, by the need to make the difficult decision of whether to provide health insurance or have employees shop for it via the federal or state health care marketplaces developed in many locations per the requirements of the ACA. When it comes to the question of whether to provide the insurance itself, an organization that has fifty or more full-time employees must pay a penalty for each employee it does not insure (National Council of Nonprofits, 2015). Further, it is important to know the details of this act and how its provisions are enforced, since the employment of multiple part-time employees can count as full-time and cause an organization to become subject to the law's provisions. The bottom line is that many nonprofits, like many small for-profits, simply cannot afford the expense of offering health benefits to part-time (or even full-time) employees. Notably, the ACA provides individual employees an opportunity to purchase insurance within one of these "marketplaces," with the expectation that the cost would be lower than they would have paid before its enactment.

In the 1980s, one initial response to rising health insurance cost issues was the implementation of "managed care" programs by many organizations offering health benefits, both profit and nonprofit. This is a broad term for a variety of program types, ranging from Health Maintenance Organizations (HMO) to Point of Service Plans (POS) to Preferred Provider Organizations (PPO). In general, all of these types of programs require significant monitoring and management of individual health care occurrences, including ensuring that individual care selections are prudently chosen and that the costs associated with each occurrence are reasonable. Although there are many variations, generally speaking, HMOs require employees to choose physicians and other health care providers who belong to a network; POSs and PPOs reward employees who choose within their networks, but usually allow some coverage outside. In this way, employers can achieve reduced rates for medical services by either paying en masse for services or receiving discounts on certain procedures. However, most benefits professionals agree that managed care hasn't been the miracle cure for cost control that was hoped for (Employee Benefit Research Institute, 2009a).

Currently, many organizations employ more innovative measures to control costs, such as the use of "consumer driven" or "defined contribution" health care benefits. These are designed to push more decision-making responsibility about health care expenditures onto employees, through a variety of methods, from presenting multiple health care insurance choices to providing employees a certain amount of cash and letting them purchase their insurance privately. Most common among these methods, however, are those that utilize some sort of health savings account (HSAs) or health reimbursement arrangements (HRAs). HSAs are funded through a mix of employee and employer contributions and must be combined with high-deductible insurance plans. HRAs are funded solely by the employer and may or may not be paired with high-deductible insurance although, in practice, they usually are (Employee Benefit Research Institute, 2009b).

The basic advantages to organizations in all these plans are that employers' costs become more fixed and administrative costs are reduced. For employees, out-of-pocket costs may be higher, and they are required to better understand complex medical benefit plans and make more independent health care decisions.

Retirement Plans

In the past, organizations with retirement plans aimed to provide retirees with retirement income that was between 50 and 70 percent of their pre-retirement income. This was considered sufficient because, in retirement, work-related expenses are no longer accrued, employment deductions are no longer made, tax breaks give retirees a new advantage, and money is no longer being put away for retirement. However, recent experience suggests that most retirees now have little desire to scale back their lifestyles and, perhaps, even look forward to doing things they didn't have time to do earlier in life. Many financial consultants now recommend that future retirees plan to ensure a larger income, perhaps 80 to 100 percent of pre-retirement pay. Additionally, many retirees are living longer and need more funds for significant expenses (including, of course, medical expenses), for these longer retirements.

Retirement income in the United States usually is achieved through the coordination of payments from the Social Security system with income from retirement plans. However, Social Security's long-term future appears uncertain, given its projected underfunding in the coming couple of decades. This has been the focus of much political debate, yet little progress or change has occurred. Recently, a push from the political left has even demanded expanded benefits, while the efforts from the political right have been to rein them in. Proposals to make the program solvent in the future include decreasing scheduled benefit increases, changing the amount of contribution in relation to salary, and increasing the retirement age (Employee Benefit Research Institute, 2009c). It's likely a combination of these solutions will be implemented, and Americans need to be aware these changes will affect the amount and timing of retirement benefits they receive from Social Security.

All of these conditions and developments have significant implications for nonprofit organizations that wish to include retirement benefits as a part of their total rewards strategies and plans. Two general types of retirement plans exist: *defined benefit plans* and *defined contribution plans.* In the past, defined benefit plans were the norm for organizations that provided retirement plans. These plans define the income (the "benefit") the employee would receive upon retirement, based on a formula that usually included the average compensation over all or a number of the employee's years of employment. These plans require extensive actuarial guidance, incorporating assumptions regarding employees' future earning potential, number of years until retirement, and other pertinent factors. The contribution the employer makes is determined through actuarial assessments and, often, these contributions would be supplemented by the employee. Because of the expense of these programs and the requirement of a fairly large employee base to ensure their affordability, they are becoming relatively rare in all but the largest nonprofit organizations, and their numbers are in fast decline in all sectors.

Defined contribution plans, on the other hand, define the amount (the "contribution") that is put into some kind of investment vehicle for retirement. Therefore, the actual retirement income the employee will receive depends on the amount of the contribution and the success of the investment and is thus unknown, but the amount contributed to the plan by the employer is defined and limited. Often, the investment is contributed primarily by the employee with an employer match. These are commonly implemented in nonprofit organizations in the form of tax sheltered annuity programs (or TSAs) or so-called 403(b) plans.

Similar to 401(k) plans for for-profit employees, 403(b) plans and TSAs allow employees to reduce taxable income by contributing a percentage of their salaries on a pre-tax basis to one or more qualifying annuities and mutual funds.

In 2016, individuals may contribute up to $18,000 a year, with a "catch-up" provision allowing employees aged fifty or over to contribute an additional $6,000 per year.

Currently, defined contribution plans are the preferred choice of most nonprofit employers. It is important that employees be aware of the financial risks of such plans and educated about their responsibility to participate. Estimates of actual U.S. participation rates in defined contribution plans vary based on who is doing the estimation but, regardless of the source, significantly less than 100 percent of eligible employees participate. The obvious resulting problem is that a number of Americans may be extremely underfunded for their future retirement. Some employers now offer automatic enrollment in which employees must "opt out" rather than "opt in," which may increase participation. Also, many organizations offering defined contribution plans provide retirement or financial planning seminars to their employees many years before their normal retirement date to help them plan for retirement. This type of education, which generally is provided at no or low cost by providers, can assist employees in understanding the importance of investing, help them feel comfortable about their retirement prospects, and aid employers by increasing employees' sense of commitment to the organization.

Retirement plans for nonprofits in the United States, like those of for-profit organizations, are subject to extensive regulation by the IRS, the Department of Labor, and other regulatory regimes (especially the Employees' Retirement Income Security Act, or ERISA). The design and operation of such programs are well beyond the scope of this chapter. However, nonprofit executives and HR professionals who design or sponsor such retirement programs should understand that these types of programs are heavily regulated with active governmental oversight, and it is essential that they be prepared to comply with these complicated regulations.

A number of other unique and specialized benefits may deserve the attention of a nonprofit HR manager, particularly those of very large employer organizations, but space prohibits coverage of most. The Internet resource site for this *Handbook* provides a number of links to organizations and resources that have useful information. However, given their strategic importance, we will address two additional benefits that are common in the nonprofit employer world: programs that provide for paid time off, such as vacation and holidays, and programs that provide for the tuition reimbursements. These are covered in the closing section of this chapter.

Paid Time Off

Often nonprofit organizations can more easily offer paid time off than cash to reward performance. In today's business environment, employees view vacations, holidays, and sick leave as an employment right, and thus paid time off has become a standard part of the total compensation package. Determining the best mix of paid time off requires application of the same principles used to determine other reward components: internal equity and external competition considerations. The demographics of the employee base may affect the particular kind of paid time off employees prefer. Younger workers may prefer sick leave, personal time off, or family leave provisions in order to raise children. As employees age, there also may be more demand for family leave programs that allow middle-aged employees to care for elderly parents. However, as in all benefits matters, caution is advised about making unfounded assumptions based only on demographics. The best way to determine employees' preferences is to ask them, using surveys or other methods. Questions regarding preferences regarding paid time off should be included in any employee surveys or focus groups the organization uses.

Competitive market pressures also must be taken into consideration. For example, one nonprofit organization gives its employees all working days between Christmas and New Year's Day as paid holidays because a major for-profit employer a few blocks away does so. This example reflects the necessity for nonprofits to be aware of the time-off policies of organizations with which they compete for labor. All organizations should carefully evaluate what their particular labor market implications are offering before setting their own policies.

Most American employees in medium and large organizations receive an average of nine paid holidays per year, ten days of vacation at one year of service, increasing to nineteen days at twenty-five years of service (Society for Human Resource Management, 2014). Some organizations also offer floating holidays, or days that change depending on the calendar and the needs of the organization. For example, if Independence Day falls on a Thursday, Friday may be given as a "floating holiday" to create a four-day weekend that many employees will value.

Many organizations now offer what is frequently referred to as "paid time off" (PTO) or "personal days," often in lieu of separate hours for specific categories such as sick leave, holidays, and vacation (Cyboran, 2008). Policies regarding amounts vary substantially, but PTO offers a specific number of days that the employee may choose to take off for any personal reason, from sickness to birthdays to "mental health days." However, when PTO days are used up, additional time off for illness or any other reason must be taken without pay. The theory behind PTO is to encourage workers to take responsibility for their time off and to manage it in a way that fits their needs, whether it is to care for sick children, take the dog to the vet, go to the dentist, or perform any other necessary personal business. Such programs can be effective in improving or maintaining trust in and commitment to the organization, but must be carefully designed reflecting employee preferences and historical absence data so the program is as effective as possible.

There are other paid time off decisions to be determined by the organization as well, including policies regarding jury duty, military leave, and bereavement leave. Additionally, plans must be carefully formulated to ensure that policies deal fairly and appropriately with overtime pay, shift differentials, incentive pay, status of paid time off provisions during probationary periods, accrual of time off not used, and other relevant issues. Of course, in the United States, paid time off policies need to be coordinated with Family and Medical Leave Act (FMLA) requirements as well as the Uniformed Services Employment and Reemployment Rights Act (USERRA). In Europe and many other parts of the world, similar types of governmental policies and requirements exist and must be taken into account as paid time off policies are developed and implemented.

Tuition Reimbursement

About 80 percent of all U.S. companies provide tuition reimbursement (Ziehlke, 2004). Many of these organizations provide tuition reimbursement only for their employees who are pursuing degrees. Most require the student employee to receive satisfactory grades as well as to be working on a degree that is somehow related to his or her current employment or reasonably imminent promotional opportunity. Just as all compensation components need to be integrally linked to the organization's mission and strategic plan, tuition reimbursement programs should be carefully geared to some kind of career development philosophy that helps accomplish the organization's human resource strategy. In other words, nonprofits with limited resources need to understand what they are purchasing when they financially assist their student employees. It could be simply employee goodwill, recruiting a generally younger group of workers, or a more strategic goal of educating workers to fill needed professional roles or become more proficient in the use of new technologies, as identified in the human resource planning process. As with any expenditure, management should direct its tuition funds deliberately.

Communication of Benefits

Although effective communication is essential in nearly all aspects of human resources, there may be no other area so critically dependent upon communication as the benefit program. Although ERISA requires employees receive an annual summary plan description covering retirement benefits, this is not sufficient. Not only do employees need to know what their benefits are in order to effectively utilize them, but ensuring that they understand them is the only way for organizations to truly gain the "bang" for their benefit bucks. After all, both profit and nonprofit organizations spend an enormous amount of money on benefits. To obtain the optimum level of motivation and commitment from employees requires communicating the value of what they are receiving. Indeed, implementing a good benefits communication program has been shown to increase employee satisfaction by 40 percent (Kislievitz, Debgupta, and Metz, 2006). Havely and Levin-Scherz (2015) offer the following five principles for an effective benefits communication program:

1. Employ a total rewards focus in benefits communications. Help employees understand how benefits fit into their full rewards package.
2. Be consistent in overarching messages. Stress the overall purpose and strategy of the behaviors and motivations the benefits and total rewards strategy seek to encourage.
3. Target communication to unique segments of the workforce and retirees. Benefits communication is more impactful if employees see how it affects them personally.
4. Reach the audience through a variety of media, but be mindful of the message. Make sure electronic communication reaches all audiences, and make the communication mode interesting, but make sure the information communicated is on target with the strategy.
5. Measure and modify. Make sure the benefits communication is doing what it's designed to do. Goals and timetables for any communications strategies should be measureable so the program can be evaluated and improved.

Other useful recommendations are to seek input from employees and guide communication strategies around what they want to know; consider "events-centered" communication points, such as hiring, promotion, anniversaries, and so forth; test communication materials to ensure they are understandable by all employee groups; enhance employee trust by using effective and credible communicators, such as nonsupervisory benefits professionals; and ensure the communication budget is adequate (McCaffery, 1992).

Justifying Reward Costs to Directors

Some enhancements to total compensation programs may entail minimal cost increases but reap significant rewards in terms of increased employee satisfaction and retention or more successful recruitment. Often, however, improvements in salary and benefit programs result in potentially large financial outlays. In nonprofit organizations, as in many for-profit organizations, justifying such increases to boards of directors can be a formidable task. Faced with severe financial constraints and sometimes with constituent pressures, many directors are loath to approve policies that may have long-lasting and sizeable financial impact. Therefore, the managerial and HR professionals in charge of formulating and proposing the program should follow some basic guidelines.

First, decision makers will be more likely to accept a program if they are allowed some kind of input into it. Thus, no one should begin developing any part of the total compensation program without the knowledge and blessing of the CEO and board. He or she should carefully explain the need for the new program, and the means by which it will be developed and the method of installation. Graphs of turnover statistics, current salaries as compared to market data, and other preliminary information justifying the need for a new program should be presented concisely.

Second, directors should be kept informed throughout the process. Developing and installing a salary program can take anywhere from six weeks to one year, depending on the size of the employee base, the number of jobs, and the culture of the organization. As the project progresses, the board should be given regular updates.

Third, the board of directors should be involved in critical aspects of the project. It is essential, for example, that they approve the final relevant labor market determination before salary data are gathered. Unless the directors feel comfortable with the specific data sources to which jobs are being compared, any market data, no matter now painstakingly collected, will be virtually useless. Also, if an executive job evaluation committee is used, make sure at least some members of the board, preferably those of longer tenure and greater respect, are included. Ensure the board knows it will approve all final job hierarchies and salary structures. Include directors, where possible, in focus groups assessing employee needs and desires.

When nonprofit operational needs are pressing, allocating money for salaries and benefits can be an imposing challenge. However, clear, concise, and thorough justification and explanation of the needs, development process, and final recommendations to directors will allow them to make reasonable and sensible decisions regarding this critical financial issue.

Also critical is to ensure that corporate and foundation funders, as well as other major donors, understand the necessity and process by which the compensation decisions are made. Although their communication and participation should be less involved, it is important they believe the systems and processes by which these crucial decisions are made have been conducted knowledgeably, professionally, and conscientiously.

Conclusion

Organizations, both for-profit and nonprofit, are being challenged to compete effectively. In order to do this, they must have qualified employees who are motivated to accomplish the strategic goals of the organization. Attraction, motivation, and retention of high-caliber employees require a total rewards system that is carefully and thoughtfully designed and implemented. There are six key elements to accomplishing this.

First, pay strategies must fit the organization's culture and goals, and thorough consideration must be given to identifying the behaviors the organization desires and designing reward strategies to ensure they occur. To do this, effective organizations must have up-to-date salary and benefits policies and communicate them to their employees.

Second, organizations need to design and build effective base compensation programs, designed with care for how external competitiveness and internal equity will be balanced. While job evaluation programs can be effective in communicating management's intentions to pay equitably, it is important that these time-consuming and expensive systems not be overused.

Third, management must decide how it plans to encourage the key behaviors needed to accomplish strategic goals. This may be done through group or individual incentive programs, merit pay programs, or other plans. Each system has advantages and disadvantages that need to be weighed and evaluated in light of each organization's unique culture and characteristics.

Fourth, it is critical that the organization conscientiously evaluate necessary benefits levels and develop an appropriate program. It is imperative that organizations understand and balance competitive pressures, employee desires, and resource requirements.

Fifth, nonprofit organizations need to design and effectively implement administrative policies and procedures that ensure that their salary and benefits programs are consistently, equitably, and effectively delivered to employees.

And finally, it is essential that the organization effectively communicate with all employees about all facets of its total rewards approach, including compensation, benefits, recognition, training and development, and more.

Nonprofit organizations that embrace a total rewards approach to attracting, motivating, retaining, and encouraging their employees greatly increase their potential for effectively mobilizing their most precious of resources—their people—and accomplishing the goals and strategies that result in higher performance, greater impact, and long-term effectiveness in meeting the needs of the communities they exist to serve.

References

Bergman, T. J., and Scarpello, V. G. *Compensation Decision Making.* Chicago: Dryden Press. 2001.

Bjork, D. A. Rethinking Executive Pay in Community-Based Organizations. *WorldatWork Journal*, 2010, June, 53(6), 53–58.

Bridges, W. The End of the Job. *Fortune*, 1994, Sept. 18, pp. 62–68.

Carraher, S. M. A Validity Study of the Pay Satisfaction Questionnaire. *Educational and Psychological Measurement*, 1991, 51(2), 491–495.

Choate, P. Today's Worker in Tomorrow's Workplace. *Journal of Business Strategy*, 1990, 11(4), 4–7.

Christofferson, J., and King, B. The "It" Factor: A New Total Rewards Model Leads the Way. *workspan*, 2006, 4(May), 2–8.

Cyboran, S. Paid Time Off: Is It Right for Your Organization? *workspan*, 2008, 4(May), 45–48.

Day, N. E., and Greene, P. A Case for Sexual Orientation Diversity Management in Small and Large Organizations. *Human Resource Management Journal*, 2008, 47(3), 637–654.

Deckop, J. R., and Cirka, C. C. The Risk and Reward of a Double-Edged Sword: Effects of a Merit Pay Program on Intrinsic Motivation. *Nonprofit and Voluntary Sector Quarterly*, 2000, 29(3), 400–418.

Employee Benefit Research Institute. Chapter 20: Health Benefits Overview. *Fundamentals of Employee Benefit Programs* (6th ed.)., Washington, DC: Author, 2009a. www.ebri.org/pdf/publications/books/fundamentals/2009/20_Hlth-Bens-Ovrvu_HEALTH_Funds-2009_EBRI.pdf.

Employee Benefit Research Institute. Chapter 29: Managing Health Care Costs. *Fundamentals of Employee Benefit Programs* (6th ed.). Washington, DC: Author, 2009b. www.ebri.org/pdf/publications/books/fundamentals/2009/29_Mng-Costs_HEALTH_Funds-2009_EBRI.pdf.

Employee Benefit Research Institute. Social Security Reform: How Different Options Might Affect Future Funding." *ebri.org*, 2009c, September, 30(9), 13–18. www.worldatwork.org/waw/adimLink?id=34890&nonav=yes.

Gaeta, E. Nonprofits at the Crossroads: A New Look at Executive Incentives. *WorldatWork Journal*, 2003, 12(3), 64–71.

Giancola, F. Dubious Rationale for a New Compensation Policy. *Employee Benefit Plan Review*, 2007, 61(3), 11–13.

Greene, R. Caution: Sharp Turns Ahead: The Influence of Private Pay Sector Practices on Nonprofit Organizations. *workspan*, 2007, 12, 45–47.

Havely, J., and Levin-Scherz, J. 5 Key Elements for Effective Ongoing Benefits Communication. January 2015. New York: Towers Watson. Retrieved December 22, 2015, from 8nhjme4.gtrf.

Heneman, H. G., and Judge, T. A. Compensation Attitudes. In S. L. Rynes and B. Gerhart (eds.), *Compensation in Organizations: Current Research and Practice,* San Francisco: Jossey-Bass, 2000, pp. 61–103.

Heneman, H. G., and Judge, T. A. *Staffing Organizations* (6th ed.). New York: McGraw-Hill Irwin, 2009.

Heneman, H. G., and Schwab, D. P. Pay Satisfaction: Its Multidimensional Nature and Measurement. *International Journal of Psychology*, 1985, 20(2), 129–141.

Human Rights Campaign. LGBT Equality at the Fortune 500. Retrieved December 24, 2015, from www.hrc.org/resources/lgbt-equality-at-the-fortune-500.

Innovative Compensation: What Should You Try? What Should You Avoid? *Nonprofit World*, 1996, Jan/Feb, p. 54.

Kerr, S. On the Folly of Rewarding A, While Hoping for B. *Academy of Management Journal*, 1975, 18(4), 769–783.

Kislievitz, M., Debgupta, S., and Metz, D. Improving Employee Benefits Behavior Through Effective Communication. *WorldatWork Journal*, 2006, January, 52–60.

Klaas, B. S. Compensation in the Jobless Organization. *Human Resource Management Review*, 2002, 12(1), 43–61.

Klein, A., McMillan, A., and Keating, K. M. Long-Term Incentives in Not-for-Profits–An Emerging Trend. *WorldatWork Journal*, 2002, 11(3), 63–71.

Kovac, J. C, Benchmark Jobs. *workspan*, 2008, April, 50(4), 83.

Lawler, E. E., III, *Strategic Pay: Aligning Organizational Strategies and Pay Systems*. San Francisco: Jossey-Bass, 1990.

McCaffery, R. M. *Managing the Employee Benefits Program*. Boston.: PWS-Kent Publishing Company, 1983.

McCaffery, R. M. *Employee Programs: A Total Compensation Perspective*. Boston: PWS-Kent Publishing Company, 1992.

Milkovich, G. T., Newman, J. M., and Gerhart, B. *Compensation* (10th ed.). New York: McGraw-Hill Irwin, 2011.

National Council of Nonprofits. Frequently Asked Questions by Nonprofits About the Affordable Care Act. Retrieved December 21, 2015, from https://www .councilofnonprofits.org/tools-resources/frequently-asked-questions-nonprofits-about-the-affordable-care-act#small.

Reilly, M., and Cumpston, D. Executive Compensation Issues for Nonprofit Boards. *workspan*, 2007, 5, 41–46.

Rubino, J. A. *Communicating Compensation Programs*. Scottsdale, AZ: American Compensation Association, 1997.

Society for Human Resource Management. SHRM Survey Looks at 2015 Paid Holidays. November 10, 2014. Retrieved December 22, 2015, from http://shrm.org/ publications/hrnews/pages/2015-holiday-schedule-survey.aspx.

U.S. Chamber of Commerce. Thank You, American Workers! Here Is How American Employers Support Their Employees. August 2014. Retrieved December 24, 2015, from https://www.uschamber.com/above-the-fold/thank-you-american-workers-here-how-american-employers-support-their-employees.

U.S. Department of Labor, Bureau of Labor Statistics. National Compensation Survey: Employee Benefits in Private Industry in the United States, March 2006. Washington, DC: Author www.bls.gov/ncs/ebs/sp/ebsm0004.pdf. August 2006.

Wallace, M. J., and Fay, C. H. *Compensation Theory and Practice*. Boston: PWS-Kent Publishing Company, 1988.

Wein, J. R. Financial Incentives for Non-Profits. *Fund Raising Management*, 1989, 20(7), 28–35.

WorldatWork and ITA Group. Trends in Employee Recognition, 2014. Retrieved December 21, 2015, from www.worldatwork.org/adimLink?id=78679.

WorldatWork and Vivient Consulting. Incentive Pay Practices Survey: Non-Profit/Government Organizations. 2014. Retrieved December 1, 2015, from www.worldatwork.org/waw/adimLink?id=74764.

Ziehlke, E. Sharing the Costs. *Smart Business Columbus,* January 2004. www.sbnonline.com/National/Article.aspx?CID=5600.

Zimmerman, J. Using a Balanced Scorecard in a Nonprofit Organization. *Nonprofit World,* 2009, 27(3), 10–12.

CHAPTER TWENTY-FOUR

DESIGNING AND MANAGING VOLUNTEER PROGRAMS

Jeffrey L. Brudney

One of the most distinctive features of the nonprofit sector is its ability to harness the productive labor of literally millions of citizens in service to organizational goals, without benefit of remuneration. Government organizations at the federal, state, and local levels also rely on substantial volunteer labor to pursue their public purposes. This remarkable achievement does not just happen spontaneously as a consequence of compelling agency missions, although, certainly, the desire to help people through donating time to a worthwhile cause is a powerful motivation for most volunteers. The credit belongs, instead, to the volunteer program, which allows citizens to realize the helping impulse as well as a variety of other motives through work activities designed by the organization with the volunteer in mind to meet its needs and objectives. The volunteer program may be part of an organization that also has paid staff, or it may consist of a group or organization staffed entirely by volunteers.

An organized volunteer program provides a structure for meeting certain requisites: volunteers must be recruited; they must be screened and given orientation to the agency; they must be assigned to positions and afforded necessary training; they must be supervised, motivated, and accorded appropriate recognition; and they should be evaluated to assess the efficacy of their placement for themselves, as well as for the organization. This inventory focuses too narrowly on the volunteer, however, and overlooks the groundwork the organization must first lay for an effective program. The agency must determine its reasons for enlisting voluntary assistance and how it plans to involve and integrate citizen participants. Based on that philosophy, it must develop job descriptions for volunteer positions and arrange for orientation and training for employees expected to work with nonpaid staff. The agency should make clear the importance of collaborating with volunteers and hold these employees accountable for doing so. Given the infrastructure that must be created to have an effective volunteer program, an agency must exhibit or reach a certain state of preparation or readiness (Brudney, 2012).

The volunteer program is a vehicle for facilitating and coordinating the work efforts of volunteers and paid staff toward the attainment of organizational goals. The core program functions that make this achievement possible can be grouped as follows:

- Establishing the rationale for volunteer involvement
- Involving paid staff in volunteer program design
- Integrating the volunteer program into the organization
- Creating positions of program leadership
- Preparing job descriptions for volunteer positions
- Meeting the needs of volunteers
- Recruiting and retaining volunteers
- Managing volunteers
- Evaluating and recognizing volunteer effort

This chapter elaborates the essential components of the volunteer program and offers suggestions for increasing their effectiveness. Two caveats with respect to coverage are in order. First, one might reasonably add risk management for volunteers and volunteer programs to the listing above, since it has become a concern to many host organizations (Herman and Jackson, 2001). Resources on this topic are provided in the Internet resource web site for this *Handbook* and will not be covered here (for a treatment of risk management and legal holdings in relation to volunteers in the United States, see Groble and Brudney, 2015).

Second, this chapter concentrates on "service" volunteers, individuals who donate their time to help other people directly, rather than on "policy" volunteers (citizens who assume the equally vital role of sitting on boards of directors or advisory boards of nonprofit organizations). The aspects of volunteer service that are unique to boards are discussed in Chapter Five of this volume. Although the demands of managing the performance and incorporating the benefits into the agency of these two types of volunteer activity are quite distinct, some overlap does exist. Service volunteers can bring a wealth of practical experience and knowledge that might prove a great asset to a governing or advisory board. Similarly, experience in direct service might usefully shape or sharpen the observations and insights of board members. Yet service volunteers may not always possess the breadth of perspective and background important to effective policymaking, or an interest in this pursuit, whereas board members may lack the immediate skills or motivation to perform well in a service capacity. As a result of such trade-offs, a great variety of practices governs the relationship between service and policy volunteering across the nonprofit sector. Some organizations encourage service volunteers to become board members, others permit the interchange, and still others prohibit it. The term "volunteer program" conventionally refers to the organization and management of service volunteers for best results. This topic forms the core of this chapter.

Establishing the Rationale for Volunteer Involvement

No matter how overburdened an agency, constrained its human and financial resources, eager for fresh input and innovation, and enthusiastic about the potential contribution of citizens, organizational efforts to incorporate volunteers should not begin with recruitment. Unfortunately, well-intentioned but premature calls for (undifferentiated) "help" can breed apprehension among paid staff and frustration among volunteers, and exacerbate the very problems volunteerism was intended to solve. Because this scenario would reinforce negative stereotypes about volunteers and undermine their credibility as a vital service resource, it must be avoided. In fact, Susan J. Ellis (1994) begins *The Volunteer Recruitment Book* with the admonition (and chapter) "Recruitment Is the Third Step." The first step, treated in this section, is to determine why the organization wants volunteers; the second, discussed in a section below, is to design valuable work assignments for them (Ellis, 1994, pp. 5–6). The agency must resist the temptation to "call in the volunteers" until the groundwork for their sustained involvement has been put in place. "Throwing people at a problem" (rather than money) is no way to solve it. The foundation for an effective volunteer program rests, instead, on a serious consideration by the agency of the rationale for citizen involvement and the development of a philosophy or policy to guide this effort. The initial step in planning the program should be to determine the purposes for introducing the new participants into the organization. For what reasons are volunteers sought?

Especially in times of fiscal exigency, top organizational officials will often express "cost-savings" as the primary reason for enlisting volunteers. Yet the claim is misleading (Brudney, 2016). In the first place, although the labor of volunteers may be "free" or donated, a volunteer program requires expenditures, for example, for orientation, training, reimbursement, promotion, materials, and so forth. In the second, for volunteers to finance cost-savings (rather than extend agency resources), cutbacks must be exacted somewhere in the agency budget. If cutbacks are to be visited on paid staff, officials risk the kind of resentments and antagonisms that have scuttled many a volunteer program.

A more accurate description of the economic benefits that volunteers can bring to an agency is "cost-effectiveness." When a volunteer program has been designed to supplement or complement the work of paid staff with that of citizens, volunteers can help an agency to hold costs down in achieving a given level of service or to increase services for a fixed level of expenditure (Brudney, 1990, 2016; Karn, 1982–1983, 1983; Moore, 1978). From the perspective of organizational efficiency, what volunteers offer is the capacity to make more productive application of existing funds and person-power. With a relatively small investment of resources, volunteers have the potential to increase the level and quality of services that an agency can deliver to the public. Although costs are not spared in this situation, to the degree that volunteers improve the return on expenditures, they extend the resources available to an agency to meet pressing needs for assistance and services.

Additional or different purposes may drive a volunteer program. The leadership of a nonprofit organization may decide to enlist volunteers to interject a more vibrant dimension of commitment and caring into its relationships with clients. Or the goal may be to learn more about the community, nurture closer ties to citizens, and strengthen public awareness and support. Volunteers may be needed to reach clients inaccessible through normal organizational channels, that is, to engage in "outreach" activities (for example, Dorwaldt, Solomon, and Worden, 1988; May, McLaughlin, and Penner, 1991; Young, Goughler, and Larson, 1986). They may be called upon to provide professional skills not readily available to an agency, such as computer programming, legal counsel, or accounting expertise. The purpose may be to staff an experimental or pilot program otherwise doomed to fiscal austerity. Enhancing responsiveness to client groups or establishing a community perspective internally offer still other rationales for volunteer involvement.

Volunteers also make excellent fundraisers. Because the public tends to perceive them as neutral participants who will not directly benefit from monetary donations to an agency, organizations very frequently enlist citizens for this task.

In fact, in a 1989 national survey nearly half (48 percent) of the volunteers reported assignments in fundraising (Hodgkinson, Weitzman, Toppe, and Noga, 1992, p. 46). More recent survey research on volunteers shows that fundraising ranked first by frequency of mention as a volunteer assignment in surveys conducted in 1996 and 1994 (tied in 1994 with assisting the elderly, handicapped, social service recipients, or homeless not as part of an organization or group), although the percentages are much more modest (7.3 percent and 4.8 percent, respectively), probably due to differences in question wording (Hodgkinson and Weitzman, 1996, p. 34).

That the list of possible purposes for establishing a volunteer program is lengthy attests to the vitality of the approach. Before seeking volunteers, agency leaders should agree on the results to be achieved for their organization. An explicit statement of goals advances several important facets of program design and functioning. First, it begins to define the types of volunteer positions that will be needed and the number of individuals required to fill these roles. McCurley (2005) strongly cautions against over-recruitment. Such information is at the core of eventual recruitment and training of volunteers. Second, it aids in delineating concrete objectives against which the program might be evaluated once in operation. Just as in any organized effort, evaluation results are instrumental to strengthening and improving the program.

Finally, a statement of the philosophy underlying volunteer involvement and the specific ends sought through this form of participation can help alleviate possible apprehensions of paid staff that the new participants may intrude on professional prerogatives or threaten job security. Clarifying the goals for voluntary assistance can dampen idle, typically negative speculation and begin to build a sense of program ownership on the part of employees—especially if they are included in planning for the volunteer program (see next section).

It should be acknowledged that simply stating the mission or goals for volunteer involvement (or for other organizational endeavors) is insufficient. Without follow-through or commitment, even the most laudable purposes can fall easy victim to failure and frustration. Worse, rhetorical support (alone) can breed cynicism and lack of trust that can be particularly difficult to overcome. In the wake of the tragic events of September 11, 2001, for example, President Bush seemed to have the moment and the oratory to galvanize the citizenry toward greater volunteerism, self-sacrifice, and responsibility for common purposes. Approximately one year later, editorialists began to question whether the social, moral, and political capital that grew out of that terrible day had already evaporated. "Mr. Bush continues to extol the virtues of voluntary service, and this is admirable. But it is hardly enough to resist the erosion in the level of public engagement as people return to everyday routines" (*New York Times*, 2002).

Involving Paid Staff in Volunteer Program Design

The support of top-level organizational officials is crucial to the establishment and vitality of a volunteer program (for example, Ellis, 1996; Farr, 1983; Scheier, 1981; Valente, 1985). Yet they are not the only ones who should be involved in defining the mission, philosophy, and procedures of the program. Paid staff, and if they are already known to the agency or can be identified, volunteers, should also be included in relevant meetings and discussions.

A precept in the field of organizational development is to include groups to be affected by a new policy or program in its design and implementation. Involvement adds to the knowledge base for crafting policy and inculcates a sense of ownership and commitment that can prove very beneficial in gaining acceptance for innovation. Because the incorporation of volunteers into an agency can impose dramatic changes in work life, the participation of paid staff is especially important (Graff, 1984, p. 17). The sharing of needs, perspectives, and information among agency leadership, employees, and prospective volunteers that ensues plays a pivotal role in determining how the volunteer program might be most effectively designed, organized, and managed to further attainment of agency goals. At the same time, the process helps to alleviate concerns of paid staff regarding volunteer involvement and its implications for the workplace.

A primary purpose of the planning meetings and discussions is to develop policies and procedures governing volunteer involvement endorsed by all parties. Agency guidelines need not be lengthy, but they should address all major aspects of volunteer participation (see McCurley and Lynch, 1996, pp. 24, 195–202). Important aspects include

- Definition of volunteer
- Screening procedures
- Orientation and training
- Probationary period
- Assignment of volunteers
- Performance evaluation
- Benefits of service
- Length or term of service
- Grievance procedures

- Reimbursement policies
- Use of agency equipment and facilities
- Confidentiality requirements
- Disciplinary procedures
- Record-keeping requirements

In all areas these policies should be as comparable as possible to pertinent guidelines for paid staff.

Although some may lament the formality of conduct codes for volunteers as somehow inimical to the spirit of help freely given, this device is associated with positive results. Explicit policies for volunteers demonstrate that the agency takes their participation seriously and values their contribution to goal attainment. By setting standards as high for volunteers as for paid staff, an agency builds trust and credibility, increased respect and requests for volunteers from employees, a healthy work environment, and, perhaps most important, high-quality services (Deitch and Thompson, 1985; Goetter, 1987; McCurley and Lynch, 1989, 1996; Wilson, 1984). A seasoned volunteer administrator advises, "One should not have different qualifications for staff than one has for volunteers doing the same work" (Thornburg, 1992, p. 18). These guidelines and expectations greatly facilitate organizing the volunteer program, handling problem situations, protecting rights, and managing for consistent results.

Some authorities go further to argue that "Non-profits should treat volunteers as if they were paid employees" (Stoolmacher, 1991). They contend that the standard elements of volunteer administration in the United States, which have counterparts in paid employment—for example, interview, screening, placement, job description, orientation, supervision, ongoing training, performance review, maintenance of records, recognition, and fair and professional treatment—reduce the possibility for confusion and frustration on the part of volunteers that can result in an unsuccessful experience for both them and the organization. The "volunteers as unpaid staff" model is not without detractors (for example, Ilsley, 1990), and the approach should be amply leavened to take into account the needs, perspectives, and circumstances of volunteers so that volunteers are matched to missions and jobs for which they have interest, ability, skills, and input (Meijs and Brudney, 2007). Other scholars maintain that this "programme" [program] model of volunteer management may work well in certain circumstances (for example, in a larger volunteer program or in a program operated by a government agency or large nonprofit), but not in all, such as in a membership-based organization or a small cooperative (Meijs and Hoogstad, 2001).

Explicit policies for the volunteer program help solidify the "psychological contract" linking volunteers to the agency and, thus, may reduce withdrawal and turnover. In one study Jone L. Pearce (1978, pp. 276–277) found that those organizations most successful in clarifying the volunteer-agency relationship suffered the lowest rates of turnover. These agencies distributed notebooks with all written policies, formal job descriptions, and training manuals to citizen participants. By contrast, the organization with the highest turnover in Pearce's sample provided none of this information to volunteers.

In another study Steven M. Farmer and Donald B. Fedor (1999) investigated the effects of the psychological contract in a survey of 451 executive committee volunteers working in the chapters of a large, national, nonprofit fundraising health advocacy organization. Similar to the results of Pearce's study, Farmer and Fedor found that fulfillment (or violation) of the psychological contract affected the level of volunteer participation. Volunteers who reported that the organization had met their expectations participated more in the organization and perceived greater levels of organizational support for their involvement. In turn, perceived organizational support not only increased levels of participation but also reduced volunteers' turnover intentions. In another study, Matthew Liao-Troth (2001) found the attitudes of paid workers and volunteers holding similar jobs in a single hospital setting to be quite similar, including the psychological contract (with the exception of psychological contracts regarding benefits). Liao-Troth (2001, p. 437) concludes: "Volunteers may believe that they have made certain agreements with the organization as to what they will provide the organization and what the organization will provide them. If a manager is not aware of her or his volunteers' psychological contracts, then he or she may unintentionally violate the volunteers' psychological contracts, which can have negative consequences in terms of job performance."

Although volunteers may not be involved in initial discussions concerning volunteer program planning and design (at this stage they may not be known to the agency), once this effort is launched and in operation, they need to have input into major decisions affecting the program. Just as for paid employees, citizens are more likely to invest in and commit to organizational policies, and provide useful information for this purpose, if they enjoy ready access to the decision-making process. Participation in decision making is a key element of "empowerment" in volunteer administration, which is thought to result in increased ownership of the volunteer program by participants and, hence, greater commitment and effectiveness (for a full discussion, see Naylor, 1985; Scheier, 1988a, 1988b, 1988–1989). Formerly, this term seemed to center on citizen volunteers and expressed the idea that they should enjoy greater say in these programs, as well as greater recognition for the time, skills, and value they contributed. More recently, the term seems to have shifted to a focus on the administrators of these programs and expresses the conviction that they should have positions (and prerequisites), influence, authority, and status in host organizations commensurate with performing a very difficult but highly productive managerial task (Ellis, 1996; McCurley and Ellis, 2003).

Integrating the Volunteer Program into the Organization

As these comments suggest, the volunteer program must be organized to respond to the motivations and requirements of volunteers and employees. With respect to volunteers, the program should have mechanisms for determining the types of work opportunities sought and meeting those preferences, and for engendering an organizational climate in which volunteers can pursue their goals, with the acceptance if not always the avid endorsement of paid personnel. From the perspective of staff, the program must have structures and procedures in place to assume the task of volunteer administration and to generate a pool of capable citizens matched to the tasks of participating offices and departments.

To accomplish these goals, the volunteer program must be linked to the structure of the nonprofit or government host organization. A small nonprofit may accommodate volunteers with a minimum of structural adaptation, but larger agencies need to consider alternative structural configurations for integrating volunteers into their operations (Brudney, 2012; Valente and Manchester, 1984, pp. 56–57). In order of increasing comprehensiveness, these arrangements consist of ad-hoc volunteer efforts, volunteer recruitment by an outside organization with the agency otherwise responsible for management, decentralization of the program to operating departments, and a centralized approach. Each option presents a distinctive menu of advantages and disadvantages.

Volunteer efforts may arise spontaneously in an ad hoc fashion to meet exigencies confronting an organization, especially on a short-term basis. Normally, citizens motivated to share their background, training, skills, and interests with organizations that could profit by them are the catalyst. Fiscal stress, leaving an agency with few options, may quicken the helping impulse. The Service Corps of Retired Executives (SCORE), an association of primarily retired businesspersons who donate their time and skills to assist clients of the U.S. Small Business Administration, began in this way in the early 1960s; retired business executives approached the SBA to offer assistance with its huge constituency (Brudney,

1986, 1990). The responsiveness and alacrity with which an ad hoc effort can be launched and operating are inspiring. Within six months of its inception, SCORE supplied two thousand volunteers to the SBA. Crisis and emergency situations can provoke an even more spectacular response, mobilizing huge numbers of volunteers in a remarkably short time.

Spontaneous help from citizens can infuse vitality (and labor) into an agency and alert officials to the possibilities of volunteerism. Offsetting these benefits, however, is the fact that only selected parts or members of the organization may be aware of an ad hoc citizen effort and, thus, be able to take advantage of it. In addition, because energy levels and zeal wane as emergencies are tamed or fade from the limelight of publicity or attention, the ad hoc model of volunteer involvement is very vulnerable to the passage of time. A volunteer program requires not only a different type of ongoing rather than sporadic commitment from citizens, but also an organizational structure to sustain their contributions and make them accessible to all employees. Unless the agency takes steps to institutionalize participation, it risks squandering the long-term benefits of the approach.

The history of the U.S. Small Business Administration and its volunteer SCORE program offers an example of an organization-volunteer partnership that understood and surmounted this hurdle to sustainability. Almost from the start the SBA and the SCORE volunteers worked to develop an appropriate structure (Brudney, 1990). In 1989 they celebrated the twenty-fifth anniversary of a partnership that has brought a continuous stream of volunteers to the agency (thirteen thousand volunteers in 1989 alone) and assistance to an estimated 2.5 million small businesspersons (National SCORE Office, 1989). In 2014, through 348 chapters located in urban, suburban, and rural communities, SCORE (2016) volunteers donated more than 1.2 million hours of their time to help start 56,079 businesses, create 47,187 jobs, mentor and train 148,800 small business owners and entrepreneurs, and increase revenue for 107,201 clients. Working on behalf of the U.S. Small Business Administration (2016), since its inception in 1964 SCORE volunteers have assisted nearly ten million Americans.

A second option sometimes open to nonprofit agencies is to rely on the expertise and reputation of an established organization, such as the United Way and its affiliates, or a volunteer center or clearinghouse, to assist in the recruitment of volunteers, but to retain all other managerial responsibilities internally. Since recruitment is the most fundamental program function and, arguably, the most problematic, regular, professional assistance with this task can be highly beneficial, particularly for an agency just starting a volunteer program. Some private business firms seeking to develop volunteer programs for their employees have extended this model: They find it advantageous to contract with local volunteer centers not only for help with recruitment but also other primary program functions, such as volunteer placement and evaluation (Haran, Kenney, and Vermilion, 1993). A large national network of volunteer centers and affiliates of the Points of Light Institute–HandsOn Network offers these services to nonprofit organizations and government agencies (Brudney and Kim, 2003).

When this model is used, quality control presents a necessary caution, just as it does in the delegation of any organizational function. Recruiters must be familiar with the needs of the nonprofit agency seeking voluntary assistance, lest volunteers be referred who do not meet the desired profile of backgrounds, skills, and interests. A recruiter may also deal with multiple client organizations so that the priority attached to the requests of any one of them is unclear. More important, trusting recruitment to outsiders is a deterrent to developing the necessary capacity in-house, which is an essential aspect of a successful volunteer program. By all means, organizations should nurture positive relationships with agencies in the community to attract volunteers and for other purposes. But they must avoid total dependence on external sources and endeavor to implement recruitment mechanisms of their own.

The volunteer program can also be decentralized in individual departments within a larger nonprofit organization. The primary advantage offered by this approach is the flexibility to tailor programs to the needs of specific organizational units and to introduce volunteers where support for them is greatest. Yet duplication of effort across several departments, difficulties in locating sufficient expertise in volunteer management to afford multiple programs, and problems in coordination—particularly, restrictions on the ability to shift volunteers to more suitable positions or to offer them opportunities for job enrichment across the organization—are significant liabilities.

In the public sector the selective approach can unwittingly generate disincentives for managers to introduce volunteers (Brudney, 1989, p. 117). Top agency officials may mistakenly equate nonpaid work with "unimportant" activities to the detriment of a department's (and a manager's) standing in the organization, or they may seize upon the willingness to enlist volunteers as an excuse to deny a unit essential increases in budget and paid personnel. Such misunderstandings must be ameliorated prior to the introduction of volunteers.

Despite the limitations, the decentralized approach may serve an agency quite well in starting a pilot or experimental program, the results of which might guide the organization in moving toward more extensive volunteer involvement. Alternatively, a lack of tasks appropriate for volunteers in some parts of the agency or, perhaps, strong opposition from various quarters may confine voluntary assistance to selected departments. Among larger organizations that enlist volunteer assistance, the decentralized approach is likely most common.

The final structural arrangement is a centralized volunteer program serving the entire agency. With this approach a single office or department is responsible for management and coordination of the volunteer program. The volunteers may serve exclusively in this unit, or they may be deployed and supervised in line departments throughout the organization. The office provides guidelines, technical assistance, screening, training, and all other administration for volunteer activity throughout the agency. The advantages of centralization for averting duplication of effort, assigning volunteers so as to meet their needs as well as those of the organization, and producing efficient and effective voluntary services are considerable. However, the program demands broad support across the organization, especially at the top, to overcome issues that may be raised by departmental staff and any limitation in resources. When such backing is not forthcoming, the other structural arrangements may serve the nonprofit agency quite well. Although it may be tempting to conceive of the various structural arrangements as a progression from less to more "organized" volunteer involvement, they should instead be seen as corresponding to differences among agencies in acceptance and uses of volunteers.

Creating Positions of Program Leadership

Regardless of the structural arrangement by which the volunteer program is integrated into agency operations, the program requires a visible, recognized leader. All program functions, including those discussed earlier (developing a rationale, involving paid staff in program planning and design, housing the volunteer program), benefit from the establishment and staffing of a position bearing overall responsibility for management and representation of the volunteers. Such positions go by a variety of names (for example, "volunteer coordinator"); in this chapter, we label it the "director of volunteer services" (DVS) to signify the importance of the role.

James C. Fisher and Kathleen M. Cole (1993, pp. 15–18) elaborate two approaches that organizations typically take in designing the volunteer management function: personnel management and program management. The personnel management approach is most common in organizations in which volunteers are deployed in several or many units or departments and have numerous responsibilities throughout the organization. In this configuration the volunteer program manager works with the line departments in all facets of volunteer administration and supports the line departments. However, the principal accountability of the volunteer is to the paid staff (or other) supervisor in the unit where the volunteer is housed. The volunteer administrator does not directly supervise the volunteer or provide training or evaluation.

By contrast, in the program management approach the volunteer administrator normally supervises the volunteers, who are housed in a single unit under her or his leadership. As Fisher and Cole (1993, p. 18) explain, "In the program management approach, the volunteer administrator is a program developer as well as the leader of volunteer efforts integral to the organization's program delivery. In the personnel management approach, the volunteer administrator recruits, selects, and places volunteers and trains paid staff to work with them. In both approaches, the responsibilities of the volunteer administrator usually include job design, recruitment, interviewing, orientation, and recognition."

The manner by which the office of the director of volunteer services is staffed sends a forceful message to employees regarding the significance of the volunteer program to the agency and its leadership. Organizations have experimented with an assortment of staffing options for the post, including volunteers, personnel with existing duties, and employee committees. None so manifestly demonstrates a sense of organizational commitment and priorities as does a paid DVS position. Establishing the office as close to the apex of the agency's formal hierarchy as feasible conveys a similar message of resolve and purposefulness. Unfortunately, the evidence suggests that agencies do not always attend to supports for such positions (for a review, see Brudney, 1992, pp. 272–273).

Based on a nationally representative sample of charities, the Urban Institute (2004) found that only about three out of five charities (62 percent) report that they have a paid staff person whose work responsibilities include management of volunteers. The presence of a paid staff coordinator does not mean that this official spends much time on volunteer administration, or that she or he has training in the field. Consistent with other research (Brudney, 1990, 2016), the paid staff coordinators of volunteers in the Urban Institute study devote about one-third of their time on the job to the volunteer function; the median paid staff volunteer coordinator in charities spends 30 percent of her or his time on this task. Full-time managers of volunteers are especially rare. In the sample of 1,753 charities, among those charities with a paid staff volunteer coordinator, only one in eight has a staff member who devotes 100 percent of her or his time to volunteer management. Across the sample of 541 religious congregations in the Urban Institute study, only one congregation said that it has a full-time volunteer coordinator for its social service outreach activities.

Support for training of administrators of volunteers was somewhat better. About two-thirds of the paid staff coordinators in the charities (66 percent) reported receipt of a minimum level of training, defined as any formal training in volunteer administration such as coursework, workshops, or attendance at conferences that focus on volunteer management. Support for the volunteer administrator increased with organizational size or resources. Based on these findings the Urban Institute (2004, p. 9) reported that the use of staff to manage volunteers by charities lags behind their parallel need and use of staff for fundraising, and concluded:

> Taken together, the findings regarding paid staff support for management of volunteers point to low professionalization and capitalization of volunteer administration in the United States. The fact that many coordinators are getting some training suggests that many are interested in learning about how to manage volunteers. However, the small amount of time spent on volunteer administration suggests that charities and congregations do not have the resources to allocate to volunteer management or that they devote their organizational resources primarily to other efforts.

These findings point to the ongoing need to press for greater organizational support for the director of volunteer services (DVS) positions. For example, the DVS should enjoy prerogatives and responsibilities commensurate with positions at the same level in the agency hierarchy, including participation in relevant decision making and policymaking and access to superiors. In this manner the incumbent can represent the volunteers before the relevant department(s) or the organization as a whole, promote their interests, and help prevent officials from taking their contributions for granted. A part-time or full-time (as necessary) paid position lodges accountability for the program squarely with the DVS, presents a focal point for contact with the volunteer operation for those inside as well as outside the organization, implements a core structure for program administration, and rewards the office-holder in relation to the success of the volunteers.

In addition to these roles, the DVS has important duties that further substantiate the need for a dedicated position (Ellis, 1996, pp. 45–49). The DVS is responsible for volunteer recruitment and publicity, a critical function requiring active outreach in the community and highly flexible working hours. The incumbent must communicate with department and organizational officials to ascertain workloads and requirements for voluntary assistance. Assessing agency needs for volunteers, enlarging areas for their involvement, and educating staff to the approach (see earlier) should be seen not as a one-time exercise but as an ongoing responsibility of the DVS. The DVS interviews and screens all applicants for volunteer positions, maintains appropriate records, places volunteers in job assignments, provides liaison supervision, and monitors performance. The office must coordinate the bewildering variety of schedules and backgrounds brought by volunteers to the agency. The DVS also bears overall responsibility for orientation and training, as well as evaluation and recognition, of volunteers. Since employees may be unfamiliar with the approach, training may be appropriate for them as well; the DVS is the in-house source of expertise on all facets of volunteer involvement and management. Finally, as the chief advocate of the program, the DVS endeavors not only to express the volunteer perspective but to allay the apprehensions of paid staff and facilitate collaboration.

Positions of leadership for the volunteer program require extensive interaction with new and continuing volunteers. Thus, as volunteer programs increase in size, the DVS will likely need to share leadership duties with designated volunteers and/or paid staff. Given the scope of the job tasks, clerical and other support for the leadership positions is highly advisable.

Preparing Job Descriptions for Volunteer Positions

The essential building block of a successful volunteer program is the job description. Paradoxically, no intrinsic basis exists to create (or classify) a position as "paid" or "volunteer." Even among agencies that have the same purpose or mission, or that work in the same substantive or policy domain, a given position can be classified differently (for example, business counselor, computer programmer, day-care provider, receptionist, ombudsperson). Within an agency, moreover, job definitions are dynamic so that volunteers can give way to paid service professionals in some areas (Becker, 1964; Ellis and Campbell, 2005; Park, 1983; Schwartz, 1977) and gain responsibility from them in others (Brudney, 1986).

Handy, Mook, and Quarter (2008) present an analysis documenting the interchangeability of some jobs performed by paid staff and volunteers in nonprofit organizations. Based on two national surveys of nonprofit organizations and case studies of two hospitals in Canada, they find evidence that volunteers were replacing paid staff, and that paid staff were replacing volunteers, sometimes in the same organization. About two-thirds of the organizations in their study agreed that interchangeability of tasks between paid staff and volunteers occurred, although their data indicate that it was limited to about 12 percent of tasks.

Without an intrinsic basis to designate a task or position as "volunteer" or "paid," the *process* by which work responsibilities are allocated assumes paramount importance. As explained above, the most enduring basis for an effective volunteer program is for top agency officials and employees (and if possible, volunteers) to work out in advance of program implementation explicit understandings regarding the rationale for the involvement of volunteers, the nature of the jobs they are to perform, and the boundaries of their work (Brown, 1981; Ellis, 1996; Graff, 1984; Wilson, 1976). This agreement should designate (or provide the foundation for distinguishing) the jobs assigned to volunteers and those held by paid staff.

The second critical step in the job design process consists of a survey of employees, or perhaps personal interviews with them, to ascertain key factors about their jobs, and to make them aware of the potential contributions of volunteers. At a minimum, a survey should seek to identify those aspects of the job that employees most enjoy performing, those that they dislike, and those for which they lack sufficient time or expertise. The survey should also ascertain any activities or projects that employees would like to do but cannot find time to perform. Since employees may lack information regarding the assistance that volunteers might lend to them and to the agency, the survey or interview (or alternatively, in-service training) should provide resource materials regarding volunteers, such as a listing of the jobs or functions that unpaid staff are already performing in their agency or in similar organizations, new initiatives undertaken by volunteers beyond the time or expertise of paid staff, and skills and descriptions of available volunteers (compare McCurley and Lynch, 1996, pp. 25–26; McCurley and Lynch, 1989, pp. 27–28).

Popular stereotypes to the contrary, not all volunteer positions need be in supportive roles to employee endeavors. In some Maryland counties, for instance, paid staff have facilitated and supported the activities of volunteers in delivering recreation services, rather than the reverse (Marando, 1986). In certain Court Appointed Special Advocates (CASA) and Big Brothers and Big Sisters programs, paid staff also facilitate and support the core work performed by volunteers. Many organizations rely on donated labor for highly technical, professional tasks, such as accounting, economic development, and computer applications, not provided by employees and which they otherwise could not afford or obtain. For example, organized into 364 chapters across the United States, the 12,400 volunteers of SCORE (2016) provide business advice and counseling to the clients of the Small Business Administration well beyond the means and paid personnel of the SBA. Most important is that the delegation of tasks takes into account the unique capabilities that paid staff and volunteers might bring toward meeting organization needs.

To allocate work responsibilities among employees and volunteers, Ellis (1996) suggests that an agency reassess the job descriptions of the entire staff, paid and unpaid. Prime candidates for delegation to volunteers are tasks with the following characteristics:

- Those that might be performed periodically, such as once a week, rather than on a daily or inflexible basis
- Those that do not require the specialized training or expertise of paid personnel
- Those that might be done more effectively by someone with specialized training in that skill
- Those for which the position occupant feels uncomfortable or unprepared
- Those for which the agency possesses no in-house expertise
- Those which might be performed "episodically," that is, on an occasional basis using very short time intervals
- Those which might be performed "virtually" or through computer technology such as the Internet, e-mail, or online applications

The culmination of the task analysis should be a new set of job descriptions for employees and a second set for volunteers who are sensitive to prevailing organization conditions. Paid staff are primarily assigned to the most important daily functions, whereas volunteers handle work that can be done on a periodic basis or that makes use of the special talents for which the volunteers have been recruited (Ellis, 1996). The intent is to achieve the most effective deployment of both paid and nonpaid personnel. The respective tasks should be codified in formal job descriptions not only for paid but also nonpaid workers, with the stipulation that neither group will occupy the positions reserved for the other.

A pioneer in the field, Harriet H. Naylor insisted, "Most of the universally recognized principles of administration for employed personnel are even more valid for volunteer workers, who *give* their talents and time" (1973, p. 173, emphasis in original). Her insight into the parallels between the administration of paid staff and volunteers is especially pertinent with respect to job specifications, placement, and orientation. Studies undertaken by the International City/County Management Association on volunteer programs in local governments indicate that "Volunteer job descriptions are really no different than job descriptions for paid personnel. A volunteer will need the same information a paid employee would need to determine whether the position is of interest" (Manchester and Bogart, 1988, p. 59). Specifications for volunteer positions should include (McCurley and Lynch, 1996, p. 30)

- Job title and purpose
- Benefits to the occupant
- Qualifications for the position
- Time requirement (for example, hours per week)
- Proposed starting date (and ending date, if applicable)
- Job responsibilities and activities
- Authority invested in the position
- Reporting relationships and supervision
- Evaluation
- Probationary period (if necessary)

The parallels to paid administration noted by Naylor (1973) and others continue beyond the job description to other key functions of the volunteer program. Applicants for volunteer positions should be *screened* for relevant competencies and interests, as well as pertinent background and qualifications. Especially for positions that call for contact with vulnerable populations such as youth and the infirm, reference or background checks should be conducted for volunteers (in many states, such checks are required by law and agencies are responsible for compliance). Volunteers should be *interviewed* by officials from the volunteer program, the agency, or both to ensure a suitable fit of citizen and organizational needs. These new members will require an *orientation* to the agency and its volunteer component. Among the topics that orientation activities should address are the overall mission and specific objectives of the organization, its traditions and philosophy, its operating rules and procedures, the rationale and policies of the volunteer program, and the roles and interface of paid and nonpaid staff members. Finally, as needed, *training* should be provided to volunteers to assume the organizational tasks assigned to them.

New Forms of Volunteer Involvement: Virtual Volunteering and Episodic Volunteering

As mentioned briefly earlier in the listing of organizational tasks that might be accomplished through the participation of volunteers, involving volunteers virtually or online through electronic means, and episodically in short-term or nonrecurring arrangements, are new forms. Virtual volunteering refers to volunteering "at a distance" (Murray and Harrison, 2002a, 2002b, 2005) through advanced information technology such as the Internet, e-mail, or online applications. In the 1999 edition of the Independent Sector survey of *Giving and Volunteering in the United States,* just 1 percent of respondents had learned about volunteering via the Internet, a finding that prompted the authors to conclude, "Few charities are maximizing the possibilities of the Internet to stimulate giving and volunteering" (Kirsch, Hume, and Jalandoni, 2000, p. 16). By the time of the 2001 *Giving and Volunteering* survey, however, 3.3 percent of a national sample of U.S. volunteers reported that they had learned about a volunteering opportunity via an Internet posting or responded to a solicitation over the Internet (Toppe, Kirsch, and Michel, 2002, p. 41). Also in the 2001 survey, among volunteers with Internet access, about 13 percent reported that they had used the Internet to search for or learn about volunteer opportunities. About 4 percent of volunteers with Internet access reported that they had volunteered over the Internet over the past year, performing such activities as mentoring, tutoring, or website development (Toppe, Kirsch, and Michel, 2002, p. 41).

A study of virtual volunteering in Canada conducted by Vic Murray and Yvonne Harrison (2002a, 2002b) in 2001–2002 yields similar findings. Murray and Harrison found that only about 4 percent of a sample of 1,747 potential volunteers who had used the online "Volunteer Opportunities Exchange" said that they had done any virtual volunteering in the past year. Of the 494 managers of volunteer resources surveyed across Canada as part of the study, only one-third reported having any openings for virtual volunteering, and over 70 percent of them reported making fewer than five such placements in the previous year. The study showed that the top three types of virtual volunteer assignments reported by mangers of volunteer resources were desktop publishing, website development and maintenance, and research. Despite the limited use of virtual volunteering found in their study, Murray and Harrison (2002a, p. 9) concluded, "Even though the demand for virtual volunteers may not be large at present, it is likely to grow in the future."

Murray and Harrison (2002a, 2005) attribute the relatively low incidence of virtual volunteering in Canada in 2001–2002 not to a lack of potential volunteers or "supply" but to a lack of organizational readiness or "demand." They speculated that the lack of demand could emanate from several sources, including a lack of organizational capacity (funds, skills) for developing virtual volunteering positions and recruitment and management systems, negative or uninformed attitudes toward electronic technology, a genuine shortage of volunteer work that lends itself to virtual volunteering, and even fear that the electronic technology may put charitable and nonprofit organizations at risk as consequence of anti-terrorism legislation (Murray and Harrison, 2005, p. 45). They observe that this form of volunteering may require a review of all current volunteer (and possibly paid staff) positions to determine whether organizational work could be reengineered to become virtual rather than on-site (advice parallel to the discussion above regarding the possible reallocation of job tasks among paid staff and volunteers to achieve an efficient result). In addition, other major organizational changes that are likely to prove necessary could occasion reluctance, if not outright resistance, to the accommodation of virtual volunteers. Once virtual volunteer jobs have been identified, defined, and posted, for example, training, supervision, recognition, and communication systems will probably need to be redesigned to support this new type of volunteer involvement.

More contemporary data and commentary suggest that the forecasts made in the early 2000s have materialized in tremendous growth in virtual volunteering. The largest and best-known source of volunteer opportunities and placements online (the number 1 result for "volunteer" on Google and Yahoo!) is the nonprofit, virtual volunteer service VolunteerMatch (2016). VolunteerMatch claims to have 850,000 visitors monthly, and to have assisted more than 73,500 participating nonprofit organizations (and 112 corporate clients) and to have made 4.5 million volunteer referrals since 1998 (www.volunteermatch.org). Its national partnerships include such well-known nonprofits as the American Red Cross, National Multiple Sclerosis (MS) Society, National Court Appointed Special Advocates (CASA), Easter Seals, Girl Scouts USA, American Cancer Society, and Ronald McDonald House Charities. VolunteerMatch also partners with government agencies, such as the Corporation for National and Community Service program Senior Corps (2016), which links more than 270,000 Americans fifty-five years and older to service opportunities.

Jayne Cravens and Susan J. Ellis (2014) are emphatic in summarizing this trend and its implications in the provocative title of their book, *The **Last** Virtual Volunteering Guidebook* (emphasis in the title). They write, "The title we eventually chose . . . highlights the biggest and best change in the last decade: the notion of volunteering online is no longer new and has, in fact, been adopted in one way or another by a majority of organizations" (p. xiii). Although Cravens and Ellis (2014) do not substantiate their conclusion with specific statistics or studies, they propose that virtual volunteering has become so common that the need or rationale no longer exists for separate treatment of this subject, and that it should be integrated into volunteer management books and training sessions as a matter of course. "Virtual volunteering," they write, "is part of all volunteering" (p. xvi): "Some people will volunteer solely online; others will incorporate a virtual component into an online placement, and others may do their service totally hands-on. But even for this last group, increasingly we can expect some Internet contact, whether in recruitment, training, recordkeeping, or simply to communicate information" (p. xvii).

Like virtual volunteering, episodic volunteering has emerged as a central aspect of many volunteer programs (for an integrated theoretical approach to episodic volunteering, see Hyde, Dunn, Bax, and Chambers, 2016). Yet, understanding—and management—of episodic volunteering has been complicated because no universally accepted definition of this type of volunteering exists. Nancy Macduff (1995) characterizes episodic volunteers as those who give service that is short in duration (temporary) or at regular intervals for short periods of time (occasional). "A rule of thumb is that the episodic volunteer is never around longer than six months" (Macduff, 1995, p. 188). Michele A. Weber (2002, pp. 1–2) defines episodic volunteers as those who contribute their time sporadically, only during special times of the year, or consider it a one-time event. These volunteers give time without an ongoing commitment, often in the form of self-contained and time-specific projects. Weber (2002, p. 2) contrasts these volunteers with "periodic" volunteers, who give time at scheduled, recurring intervals, such as daily, weekly, or monthly. Macduff (1995, pp. 55–57) relates the growth in episodic engagement to the advent of "reflexive volunteering," in which citizens decide for themselves where, when, and how much to volunteer in creating their own "life biography." Formerly, "collective" forms of volunteering dominated, which were mediated much more strongly by organizational needs, demands, and mores.

The trend data made available by Independent Sector in its biennial national surveys illustrate the scope of episodic volunteering in the United States (Kirsch, Hume, and Jalandoni, 2000, p. 21). Over the period 1987 through 1998, reported rates of volunteering among the American public generally increased, with some perturbations. Yet the total number of hours contributed annually remained fairly constant (within the range of 19.5 to 20.5 billion) so that the average number of hours donated on a weekly basis per volunteer steadily diminished over the decade. The decline is substantial—a 25 percent decrease from an average of 4.7 hours contributed per week and 244.4 hours per year in 1987 to 3.5 hours weekly and 182.0 hours annually in 1998. Points of Light Institute CEO Michele Nunn (2000, p. 117) speculates, "This could be the result of broader participation levels of individuals who did not regularly volunteer," that is, episodic volunteers.

Given the vagaries of definition, estimates of the extent of episodic volunteering are not precise although, as suggested by the comparative data, unquestionably substantial. According to the 1999 Independent Sector survey, which assessed giving and volunteering behavior for 1998, 39 percent of volunteers preferred to volunteer at a regularly scheduled time, weekly, bi-weekly, or monthly (Kirsch, Hume, and Jalandoni, 2000, p. 5). By contrast, "For 41 percent of volunteers, serving is a sporadic, one-time activity;" another 9 percent reported volunteering only at special times of the year such as holidays or festivals. If Weber's (2002) distinction between periodic and episodic volunteering is accepted, 69 percent of volunteers could be classified as "periodic" in 2001, meaning that they volunteered at scheduled times recurring at regular intervals (for example, daily, weekly, monthly). The other 31 percent were "episodic volunteers" (Toppe, Kirsch, and Michel, 2002). With regard to the preference among potential volunteers for shorter-term, episodic engagements, McCurley and Ellis (2003, p. 1) insist, "You can find similar data in Canada, Australia, the United Kingdom, and practically every other country that's done even a casual survey of volunteer attitudes."

Host organizations that wish to attract episodic volunteers must overcome several barriers. These include potentially antagonistic attitudes of long-term volunteers and paid staff regarding the value of episodic volunteering, agency preferences for continuous service, general resistance to change, and legal liabilities (Macduff, 1995, pp. 189–191). To start or accommodate an episodic volunteer program, volunteer jobs will need to be shorter in duration; have a clearer, more limited focus; avoid those areas in which legal liability could be an issue (for example, direct contact with vulnerable populations); and have less intensive administrative procedures such as the extent of screening, interviewing, and training required for the job. An organization need not choose between having an episodic volunteer program and a more traditional one based on long-term volunteer involvement; the programs can exist side-by-side. In fact, Macduff (2005, p. 201) believes that "Supervision of short-term volunteers can be done quite effectively by long-term volunteers," a factor that could carry benefits for both parties as well as for the organization as a whole. I discuss the benefits of having such "career ladders" for volunteers in the section that follows.

McCurley and Ellis (2003) argue that, given the rising trend in short-term, episodic volunteering, the field is in danger of "using the wrong model" to design volunteer jobs, manage and supervise volunteer involvement, and integrate these vital human resources into host organizations. In light of changing volunteer attitudes, preferences, demographics, and availability, the traditional "volunteer as unpaid staff" model that conceived volunteers as holding long-term, continuous jobs albeit for many fewer hours than paid staff may well be in need of refinement for large numbers of potential volunteers (Brudney and

Meijs, 2009). Brudney and Meijs (2014) go further: They contrast "universalistic volunteer management" with "conditional volunteer management" to suggest that directors of volunteer resources must adapt their management approaches to the organizational circumstances and contingencies confronting them. As Sibylle Studer and Georg von Schnurbein (2013) show in their systematic review of the literature, the contingency factors that may affect volunteer coordination are numerous and complex (cf. Hager and Brudney, 2015). Brudney and Meijs (2014, p. 302) elaborate, "Although researchers have focused on a variety of conditions that may affect volunteer management, the most frequent contingency factors in the conditional volunteer management literature are either volunteer-focused or program/organization-focused." Volunteer characteristics include such factors as the motivations and skills of the volunteers, and program/organizational factors include the worldview and culture of the organization toward promoting radical change versus acceptance of the status quo, and more flexible versus more stable operational arrangements. Brudney and Sink (in press) present an application of the conditional approach in a chapter entitled "Volunteer Management: It All Depends."

Virtual volunteering and episodic volunteering increase the demands on agencies and their directors of volunteer services to design positions strategically to integrate new forms of productive labor and to make attendant changes in the workplace—as well as to overcome the organizational and personal hurdles and obstacles likely to result. In a volunteer world in which traditional sources of recruitment are lagging, competition for recruits is keen, new forms of participation are gaining popularity, and agency workloads are expanding, organizational investment in these emerging forms of volunteering may well be worth the effort. In light of such trends, Brudney and Meijs (2009) conceive of volunteer energy as a natural resource that must be sustained through creative involvement by host organizations.

Meeting the Needs of Volunteers

To this point, my analysis has focused primarily on the demands of nonprofit and public organizations for attracting, structuring, and managing volunteer labor. Agency needs constitute only half of the equation for a successful volunteer program, however. The other half consists of meeting the needs of volunteers. An effective volunteer program marries organizational demands for productive labor with the disparate motivations that volunteers bring for contributing their time.

The theme of voluntary action gives to the study of nonprofit institutions much of its characteristic identity. Most nonprofit organizations are vitally dependent on volunteers to carry out missions and reach objectives. Accordingly, voluminous research has been concerned, directly or indirectly, with the motivations that spur volunteers. A basic conclusion emanating from this research is that these motivations are complex and multifaceted, and that they may serve a variety of functions for the individual volunteer, including values, understanding, career, social, esteem, and protective dimensions (Clary, Snyder, and Ridge, 1992; Clary, Snyder, and Stukas, 1996). As Clary and his colleagues point out, an understanding of volunteer motivations and the functions that they perform for individuals will assist nonprofit and government organizations in recruiting and retaining volunteers—as well as lead to more satisfying experiences for these citizen participants (Clary, Snyder, and Stukas, 1996, pp. 502–503).

Although the reasons for volunteering are rich and diverse, several large, national surveys extending over more than a quarter of a century reveal a markedly consistent pattern of professed motivations. Table 24.1 displays the reasons for involvement in volunteer work as expressed most often by representative samples of Americans over time in seven surveys (the earliest taken in 1965 and the latest in 1991). Other, more recent surveys of volunteers' professed motivations have been conducted; however, they are based on different items. The survey results summarized in Table 24.1 offer the most comprehensive and consistent set of items available regarding volunteer motivation. The length of the series reinforces the reliability of the responses.

As presented in Table 24.1, the most common stimulus for volunteering is to "do something useful to help others" (or to "help people"), manifested by nearly a majority and often substantially more of the respondents in each survey. In addition, approximately one in four people mention "religious concerns." About 10 percent of volunteers, rising to 17 percent in 1991, state as a motivation that they had previously benefited from the activity; perhaps their volunteer work is motivated by a desire to "give something back" for the services or attention they had earlier received. Even allowing for the possibility of some socially desirable responses, the attention that such altruistic motivations seem to command is impressive. Although such altruistic motivations appear to drive a great amount of volunteering, more instrumental motivations are common as well. For example, in the survey findings summarized in Table 24.1, approximately 30 to 40 percent of the volunteers gave as reasons that they "enjoy doing volunteer work" or that they "had an interest in the activity or work." A substantial number of volunteers (22 to 29 percent) also said that they have a friend or relative either involved in the activity in which they volunteer or who would benefit from it.

TABLE 24.1. Motivation for Involvement in Volunteer Work by Year, 1965–1991 (in Percentages)

Motivation	1965[a]	1974	1981	1985	1987	1989	1991
Help people	38	53	45	52	–	–	70
Do something useful	–	–	–	–	56	62	61
Enjoy doing volunteer work	31	36	29	32	35	34	39
Interest in activity or work	–	–	35	36	–	–	–
Sense of duty	33	32	–	–	–	–	–
Religious concerns	–	–	21	27	22	26	31
Could not refuse request	7	15	–	–	–	–	–
Friend or relative received service[b]	–	22	23	26	27	29	29
Volunteer received service	–	–	–	–	10	9	17
Learning experience[c]	–	3	11	10	9	8	16
Nothing else to do, free time	–	4	6	10	9	10	8
Thought work would keep taxes down	–	–	5	3	–	–	–

Note: The percentages do not sum to 100 because respondents were permitted multiple responses. A dash indicates that this option was not presented to respondents (not that 0.0 percent gave this response). In the 1965 and 1974 surveys, volunteers were asked about the reason for doing their first "nonreligious" volunteer work. In the 1981, 1985, 1987, 1989, and 1991 surveys, the motivations also pertain to "informal" volunteer work, that is, work that does not involve a private-sector association or formal organization.

[a]In the 1965 survey, the question of motivations for volunteering was presented to respondents as open-ended. The responses were coded into the categories shown in the table. In the other surveys, the respondents were presented with a listing of possible motivations for volunteering and were asked which were motivations for them (see Department of Labor, 1969, p. 9).

[b]In 1974, this category referred exclusively to respondents' children; in 1989, this category stated that a family member or friend would benefit.

[c]In the 1974 survey, this category referred to the idea that volunteer work can lead to a paid job.

Sources: The data are adapted from U.S. Department of Labor (1969); ACTION (1974); Gallup Organization (1981); and Hodgkinson and Weitzman (1986, 1988, 1990, 1992).

In the surveys conducted in the 1980s, another 8 to 11 percent of respondents identified volunteering as a "learning experience" (16 percent in the 1991 survey). The educational or training benefits afforded by this opportunity are especially important to individuals who seek entry or reentry into the job market but lack requisite competencies or experience. According to one volunteer coordinator and consultant, "*Any* marketable skills can be strengthened and brought up to date in a well-structured volunteer setting" (O'Donald, 1989, p. 22; emphasis in original).

The data in Table 24.1 suggest that many people seem to hold both other-directed and self-directed motivations for volunteering simultaneously. In order to capture some of the richness of these motivations, the national surveys allowed multiple responses and, indeed, in each survey the cumulative percentages surpass 100 percent. Volunteering, thus, appears to spring from a mixture of altruistic and instrumental motivations. Volunteers can—and most likely do—pursue both types of rewards simultaneously. One can certainly help others, derive strong interest and satisfaction in the work, learn and grow from the experience, and enjoy the company of friends and co-workers in the process. These rewards emanate from the quality and meaning of the volunteer experience. As Jon Van Til (1988, pp. 1–9) observes, volunteering is helping behavior deemed beneficial by participants, even though this action "may contribute to individual goals of career exploration and development, sociability, and other forms of personal enhancement." Thus, volunteering is "pro-social" rather than self-sacrificial—that is, activity intended to benefit others but not restricting possible benefits to the volunteers as well.

It is also worth noting from Table 24.1 what the volunteering impulse is not: very few citizens apparently engage in this activity with the motivation to spare organizational funds or the conviction that their "work would keep taxes down." Only 3 to 5 percent of volunteers profess these motivations. Although, organizational pleas to "save money" with volunteers may be compelling to agency leaders, they apparently resonate with few volunteers.

How might these motivations evolve as individuals join organizations and engage in volunteer work? Strong altruistic or service motivations could reasonably lead individuals to seek productive outlets for donating their time. As might be expected, however, once they have begun to assist an organization, the immediate rewards of the work experience—such as the social aspects of volunteering and the characteristics of the job they are asked to perform—tend to rise in salience.

For example, based on a study of diverse work settings, Pearce (1983) discovered that volunteers stated that they joined the organization for predominantly service reasons, but that friendships and social interaction became more influential in their decision to remain with it. Although the long-range rewards of helping others, supporting organizational goals, and making a contribution decreased in importance to them (albeit the scores remained at high levels), the rewards of meeting people and enjoying the company of friends and co-workers increased. Similarly, in a study of volunteers to local government, the importance attached by participants to doing something useful or benefiting a family member or friend diminished over time, but interest in or enjoyment of the work grew as a motivation (Sundeen, 1989).

Pearce concludes (1983, p. 148): "The rewards individuals expected from volunteering are often not the rewards most salient to them once they have become volunteers." If not anticipated and addressed, this shift in the expected rewards from the experience can result in rapid and ruinous turnover of volunteers. The volunteer program must be designed to counteract this possibility; fortunately, many options are open.

To reinforce volunteers' initial emphasis on service motivations, they might be placed in positions in which they can contribute directly to organizational goals, for example, through contact with clients or participation in policy activities. Additionally, agencies should offer entry-level advisement and careful placement to assist volunteers in reaching their personal goals and attempt to foster a work environment conducive to their efforts. Training programs and orientation sessions should present an accurate picture of the rewards of volunteering, so that citizens—and the organizations they serve—do not fall prey to unrealistic expectations of the experience.

Agencies also need to respond to changes in the motivations of volunteers over time. While an organization may have a standard set of activities designed to recruit volunteers, retaining them is a dynamic process of reviewing performance, growth, and aspirations with the volunteer and modifying work assignments accordingly (McCurley and Lynch, 2005). In addition to the methods discussed above, to motivate the continued involvement of volunteers, organizations may offer a variety of inducements depending on individual circumstances. These include a series of steps toward greater responsibilities (volunteer career ladders), participation in problem solving and decision making, opportunities for ongoing training, supportive feedback and evaluation, and letters of recommendation documenting work performed and competencies gained. I discuss volunteer recruitment and retention in more depth in the following section.

Recruiting and Retaining Volunteers

McCurley (2005, pp. 595–596) distinguishes three types of volunteer recruitment approaches used by nonprofit and public organizations: concentric circles recruitment, warm body recruitment, and targeted recruitment. Concentric circles recruitment is the most subtle and the most endemic, by some estimates practiced by as many as 94 percent of agencies. It is intended to provide host organizations with a small but steady flow of volunteers; "turning up the heat" can yield more.

Underlying concentric circles recruitment is stakeholder interaction with the organization. An agency maintains daily contact with a variety of constituent populations or stakeholders, such as clients and their families, volunteers and their friends, staff members, people in the surrounding community, suppliers, vendors, and others. The stakeholders are aware of the existence of the agency, and many have experience with it either directly or indirectly (for example, through a relative or co-worker). Their familiarity makes them more receptive to the agency than those who do not know the organization and its work, thus facilitating volunteer recruitment. In addition, this form of recruitment "makes use of the personal appeal factor by having individuals who already know the potential volunteer convey the recruitment message, thus piggybacking on their individual credibility" (p. 596). Volunteer recruitment proceeds in concentric circles, with the agency reaching out first to its stakeholders, who then carry the recruitment message to their networks, and so forth.

The other forms of volunteer recruitment identified by McCurley (2005) are more overt. "The warm-body recruitment campaign is used when the agency needs a relatively large supply of volunteers for tasks that can be easily taught to most people in a short period of time" (p. 595). Jobs of this nature might include staffing an event, such as a clean-up campaign, a fundraising gathering, or an awards luncheon or dinner; various "thons" (bike-a-thons, walk-a-thons, and so on) also use this technique to recruit volunteers. Although detailed job descriptions are not generally necessary for warm-body recruitment, screening, orientation, and training as necessary should be provided.

The final method of attracting volunteers is targeted recruitment, which "operates in exactly the opposite fashion as the warm-body campaign" (McCurley, 2005, p. 595). Whereas warm-body recruitment seeks large numbers of volunteers with undifferentiated talents and expertise, targeted recruitment is designed to attract fewer, select volunteers for jobs that require particular skills or interests or are appropriate for specific age or cultural groups (p. 596). According to McCurley, three questions guide the targeted recruitment campaign:

1. What skills or aptitudes are needed to perform the job? This aspect considers the characteristics of the persons sought for the job.
2. Where and how can the organization find people with the requisite skills and interests? This aspect considers connections to these people, including work settings, educational attainment, leisure organizations and activities, relevant publications, and areas of the community.
3. What motivations might appeal to the persons sought? This aspect considers the psychological and other needs to be met through the job.

The intent of shaping and limiting the recruitment message and information dissemination process is to generate a small but sufficient number of suitable volunteer applicants.

Brudney (2016, pp. 121–122) has elaborated the various strategies organizations can use to attract volunteers. The first set of strategies pertains to the motivations of volunteers. Job design strategies concentrate on meeting the needs and motivations of volunteers for interesting and meaningful work, including opportunities for advancement. Closely related, human capital strategies enable participants to raise their market value for paid employment through acquiring contacts, training, and references in the volunteer environment. Ceremonial strategies allow volunteers to join groups and organizations that are important to them, work with like-minded individuals, meet policymakers and other dignitaries, and receive public recognition for service. Similarly, policy strategies, such as service on boards of directors, organizational commissions, task forces, and panels, afford volunteers the opportunity to participate actively in organizational governance.

The second set of strategies focuses on making the volunteer job and setting more attractive to volunteers. Organizational change and development strategies center on building an agency culture receptive to volunteers. This relationship begins at the outset of volunteer contact with the agency. Research suggests that many host organizations do not routinely attend to welcoming or even informing volunteers very well (Hobson and Malec, 1999). Facilitation strategies aim to make volunteer opportunities more readily available through such means as extending hours to volunteer beyond traditional (agency) work hours, reimbursing volunteers' out of pocket expenses, and providing child care as needed. Similarly, flexibility strategies broaden the nature of volunteer work to make it more convenient, and often enjoyable, to the volunteer. Examples include jobs that can be performed outside the agency (for example, at home or in an automobile), or by groups of people the volunteer knows and values (for example, the family, religious congregation, work unit, or organization), or by electronic means, such as the Internet. Finally, outreach strategies encompass publicizing the agency volunteer program both more widely and strategically to stakeholders (see earlier), to other groups and organizations (workplace, school, religious institutions, neighborhood groups, civic and other associations), and to electronic media.

The strategies to attract volunteers are, fortunately, rich and varied. However, the competition among nonprofit, government, and even for-profit organizations for them is intense (Brudney, 2016), and the rate of volunteering in the

United States has not increased. It has remained relatively stable at between 25 and 28 percent since annual surveys of volunteering by the Current Population Survey of the Bureau of Labor Statistics (2016) began in 2002. Moreover, Eisner, Grimm, Maynard, and Washburn (2009) report: "Of the 61.2 million people who volunteered in 2006, 21.7 million—more than one-third—did not donate any time to a charitable cause the following year. Because these volunteers gave about 1.9 billion hours in 2006, and the value of their donated time was about $20 per hour—that calculates to about $38 billion in lost volunteer time in one year."

Hager and Brudney (2013) understand these statistics a bit differently. Because the percentage of volunteers in the United States remained nearly constant between 2006 (26.7 percent) and 2007 (26.2 percent), the trend suggests replacement of volunteers rather than absolute loss. Since historically the annual rate of volunteering has been steady, organizations seem to be replenishing the stock of volunteers who leave over time. Hager and Brudney (2013, p. 264) observe, "Some change and churn is natural and to be expected," and nonprofit organizations in the aggregate seem to have adjusted to these societal forces by bringing in new volunteers. Thus, evidence suggests that organizations are succeeding in the volunteer "recruitment wars."

Retaining volunteers, though, is another matter. Confronted with the attrition in volunteering reported in the U.S. study, former Corporation for National and Community Service Chief Executive Officer David Eisner warned: "This report is a wakeup call for any group that uses volunteers. If you want to keep them, you need to give them serious and meaningful work that affects change in your community, and you have to remember to train, manage, and thank them the way you would any valued colleague" (Corporation for National and Community Service, 2007, p. 1). Far less is known—and published—about retaining volunteers than recruiting them (Brudney and Meijs, 2009).

Based on a nationally representative sample of charities, Hager and Brudney (2008) found that retaining volunteers is positively associated with organizations adopting recommended practices for managing volunteers, especially offering recognition activities and training and professional development opportunities for them, and using effective screening procedures to identify suitable volunteers and to match them with appropriate jobs or tasks in the agency. "These volunteer management practices all center on making the experience worthwhile for the volunteer" (Hager and Brudney, 2008, p. 20). Adoption of the volunteer management practices was not widespread among the charities, however: fewer than half of them reported that they had eight of nine recommended volunteer management practices in place "to a large degree" (cf. Urban Institute, 2004). Hager and Brudney (2008) report other steps that charities can take to increase volunteer retention and their "volunteer management capacity," including creating a culture that is welcoming to volunteers, allocating sufficient resources to support them, providing a worthwhile and productive volunteer experience that citizens will want to repeat and share, and enlisting volunteers in recruiting other volunteers.

In *Keeping Volunteers*, Steve McCurley and Rick Lynch (2005) corroborate these findings. They also provide many more guidelines for retaining volunteers. They recommend, for example, seeing to the motivational needs of volunteers (see earlier), letting volunteers do the work they want to do consistent with organizational needs, thanking volunteers, making sure that volunteers feel connected to the organization and are invested in its mission, setting high standards for volunteers, listening carefully to volunteers and providing feedback especially concerning accomplishments and goal achievement, instilling organizational values, detecting and ameliorating volunteer burnout, encouraging incremental commitment for short-term volunteers, and developing career ladders for volunteers to offer them new and expanded opportunities.

Given the mismatch between the recruitment strategies most commonly employed by host organizations and what volunteers want and need once they join an organization, it is little wonder then that host organizations encounter difficulties in retaining volunteers.

Managing Volunteers

Managing volunteers is different from managing employees. Volunteers are much less dependent on the organization to which they donate their time than are paid staff members, who must earn their livelihood from it. Volunteers can usually leave the organization and find comparable opportunities for their labor with far less effort and inconvenience than can employees. As a result, nonprofit managers and supervisors do not have as much control over volunteer workers.

These differences in control help explain some oft-noted characteristics of volunteers in the workplace. Volunteers can afford to be more selective in accepting assignments. They may insist on substantial flexibility in work hours. They may not be as faithful in observance of agency rules and regulations, particularly those they regard as burdensome or "red tape." Part of the reason may stem from the fact that nearly all who volunteer do so on a part-time basis and, thus, may have less information about organizational policies and procedures. Further, many consider these aspects of the job and agency as inimical to the spirit and practice of help freely given, and choose to evade or even ignore them. Social interaction is part of the fun and spark of volunteering, and participants may place high value on this feature of the experience (as noted earlier).

Given the relative autonomy of volunteers, a heavy-handed approach to supervision can be expected to elicit antagonism and turnover rather than productivity and compliance. Standard organizational inducements for paid employees, such as pay, promotion, and perquisites, are not operative for volunteers. Conventional organizational sanctions are likely to prove unsuccessful. For example, referring a problem to hierarchical superiors for resolution or disciplinary action (or threatening to do so) is far less apt to sway volunteers than employees.

These considerations may leave the impression that volunteers cannot be "managed," but that conclusion is unfounded. In reviewing certain "myths" (as he calls them) that people sometimes have about volunteers, Brudney (2016, pp. 122–123) debunks this notion, as well as the equally popular view that volunteers cannot be terminated or "fired." There is a reasonable course for the manager to take should a serious problem arise and persist with a volunteer: ascertain the facts of the situation, be firm in explaining both the problem and the consequences of further violation, and follow through according to agency policy if the problem continues. Eminent management authority Peter F. Drucker (1990, p. 183) agrees that in cases of egregious misconduct, volunteers "must be asked to leave." Countenancing the transgression sends the wrong message to employees, other volunteers, and agency clients that staff (nonpaid or paid) are free from organizational direction and oversight.

The message for management is decidedly more positive: the foundation for effective management of volunteers rests on applying different techniques and incentives than commonly used for paid employees to motivate and direct volunteers' work behaviors toward agency goals. Managerial investment in building trust, cooperation, teamwork, challenge, growth, achievement, values, excitement, and commitment are much more effectual strategies. In their highly influential study *In Search of Excellence,* Thomas J. Peters and Richard H. Waterman (1982) maintain that "America's best-run companies" use the same approach for paid employees—with enviable results. Although a common admonition in the volunteer management literature is to manage volunteers as if they were employees (for example, Stoolmacher, 1991), other research suggests that it is equally persuasive to recommend "managing employees as if they were volunteers" (Smith and Green, 1993).

Based on a careful examination of a volunteer program servicing a large, urban public library system, Virginia Walter (1987, p. 31) found that administrators who embraced this style of "management-by-partnership" enjoyed greater success in dealing with volunteers and meeting objectives than did those officials intent on control. In a major study of the volunteer SCORE program operated by the U.S. Small Business Administration (SBA), Brudney arrives at a similar conclusion (1990, pp. 112–114). The volunteer business counselors who assisted the SBA sometimes fit the stereotypes attributed to volunteer workers. For example, they displayed low tolerance for necessary government paperwork and "bureaucracy," uneven knowledge of SBA rules and procedures, and keen interest in deciding what cases they would accept (or reject) for counseling. Yet SBA staff rated the performance of the volunteers as comparable to their own on signal dimensions, including quality and timeliness of services to clients and dependability in work commitments. Brudney, like Walter (1987), attributes these beneficial results to the partnership approach to managing the volunteer program practiced by the SBA and SCORE.

A successful volunteer program must do more than advance changes in managerial style. It must also institute a framework or infrastructure to facilitate successful volunteer integration and involvement in the organization. To channel volunteer talents and energies productively, agencies must elucidate the behaviors expected from them. Probably no factor aids more in supervising volunteers (and paid staff) than placing them in positions where they can put their strongest motivations and best skills to work. The procedures discussed earlier in this chapter offer a viable means to elaborate and promote mutual understanding of the volunteer-agency relationship. Developing a coherent philosophy for volunteer involvement, preparing guidelines for the volunteer program, creating formal positions for volunteers, preparing the relevant job descriptions, interviewing and screening applicants and placing them in mutually satisfactory work assignments, and presenting orientation and training are potent means to define what volunteer service means to the agency and to citizens, and to coordinate the needs and motives of both parties. Jean Baldwin Grossman and Kathryn Furano (2002, p. 15) focus on three elements as "vitally important to the success of any volunteer program": screening potential volunteers to ensure appropriate entry and placement in the organization; orientation and training to provide volunteers with the skills and outlook needed; and management and ongoing support of volunteers by paid staff to ensure that volunteer time is not wasted but used as productively as possible.

Thus, effective management of volunteers calls for more than changes in managerial style, although such adjustments are certainly important. The volunteer program must also provide an infrastructure to impart a shared conception of volunteer service. Absent such a framework, managerial adaptations in themselves are likely to prove insufficient. As Grossman and Furano (2002, p. 15) aptly summarize, "No matter how well intentioned volunteers are, unless there is an infrastructure in place to support and direct their efforts, they will remain ineffective at best or, worse, become disenchanted and withdraw, potentially damaging recipients of services in the process."

Evaluating and Recognizing Volunteer Effort

Researchers contend that the evaluation function is carried out less often and less well than the other central elements of a volunteer program (Allen, 1987; Utterback and Heyman, 1984). Survey research on volunteer programs in government bears this out. In a study of 534 cities that enlisted volunteers in the delivery of services, Sydney Duncombe (1985, p. 363) found that just a handful (sixty-two, or 11.6 percent) had made an evaluation study. A study of 189 state agencies reported a comparable rate (13.6 percent) (Brudney and Kellough, 2000, p. 123). Understandably, organizations that rely on the assistance of volunteers may be reluctant to appear to question through evaluation the worth or impact of well-intentioned helping efforts. In addition, officials may be apprehensive about the effects of an evaluation policy on volunteer recruitment and retention—and on public relations. Nevertheless, for individual volunteers and the paid staff who work with them, as well as for the volunteer operation as a whole, evaluation and recognition activities are essential program functions.

Evaluation of Volunteers and Employees

The fears of organizational leadership notwithstanding, volunteers have cogent reasons to view personnel assessment in a favorable light. A powerful motivation for volunteering is to achieve worthwhile and visible results, and evaluation of performance can guide volunteers toward improvement on this dimension. No citizen contributes his or her time to have the labor wasted in misdirected activity, or to repeat easily remedied mistakes and misjudgments. That an organization might take one's work so lightly as to allow inappropriate behavior to continue is an insult to the volunteer and an affront to standards of professional conduct underlying effectiveness on the job. Clients and host organizations suffer the brunt of these lapses. Evaluation of performance, moreover, is actually a form of compliment to the volunteer (Ellis, 1996, pp. 81–82). A sincere effort at appraisal indicates that the work merits review, and that the individual has the capability and will to do a better job. For many who contribute their time, volunteering offers an opportunity to acquire or hone desirable job skills, build an attractive résumé for purposes of paid employment, or both. To deny constructive feedback to those who give their time for organizational purposes, and who could benefit from this knowledge and hope to do so, is a disservice to the volunteer.

An assortment of procedures for carrying out evaluation of volunteer performance is available to nonprofit organizations. Often the employee to whom the volunteer reports will prepare the appraisal. Or the responsibility may rest with the director of volunteer services or with the personnel department in larger organizations. A combination of these officials might also handle the task. To complement this agency-based perspective, volunteers might evaluate their own accomplishment and experience in the agency, as some suggest (for example, Manchester and Bogart, 1988; McHenry, 1988). The assessment should tap volunteer satisfaction with important facets of the work assignment, including job duties, schedule, support, training, opportunities for personal growth, and so on. The self-assessment is also a valuable tool to obtain feedback on the management and supervision of volunteers; employees should learn from the process as well. Regardless of the type of evaluation, the goal ought to be to ascertain the degree to which the needs and expectations of the volunteer and the agency are met so that job assignments can be continued, amended, or redefined as necessary.

Agency officials might recognize and show their appreciation to volunteers through a great variety of activities: award or social events (luncheons, banquets, ceremonies), media attention (newsletters, newspapers), certificates (for tenure or special achievement), expansion of opportunities (for learning, training, management), and, especially, personal expressions of gratitude from employees or clients. A heartfelt "thank you" is all the acknowledgment many volunteers want or need. Others require more formal recognition. The director of volunteer services should make letters of recommendation available to all volunteers who request them. Recognition is a highly variable activity that, optimally, should be tailored to the wants and needs of individual volunteers.

Some agencies choose to recognize volunteers who evince especially strong potential, and who seek paid employment with the agency, by considering them for such positions when available (for example, police auxiliaries). One volunteer administrator refers to this process as a "try before you buy" opportunity for paid staff (Thornburg, 1992, p. 20). The advantages offered by this procedure notwithstanding, volunteering should not be treated as a necessary credential or requirement for paid employment with a nonprofit or government organization.

In general, volunteer-based services require the participation of both volunteers and paid staff. If organizational officials are committed to having employees and volunteers work as partners, program functions of evaluation and recognition should apply to both members of the team. Although frequently neglected in job analysis, employees expected to work with volunteers should have these responsibilities written into their formal job descriptions. Equally important, performance appraisal for those who manage volunteers must assess performance in volunteer management. Just as demonstrated performance in this domain should be encouraged and rewarded, an employee's resistance to volunteers or poor work record with them should not go overlooked and, implicitly, condoned in the review. As necessary, the organization should support training activities for paid staff to develop competencies in volunteer management.

Similarly, recognition activities for volunteer programs normally focus on citizen participants rather than on both members of the team. However, employees value recognition as well, especially when awards ceremonies, social events, media coverage, agency publications, and the like bring their efforts and accomplishments with volunteers to the attention of organizational leadership. In addition, feedback on employee achievement from volunteers and the director of volunteer services belongs in agency personnel files. By taking seriously the evaluation and recognition of paid staff with regard to their collaboration with volunteers, officials provide incentives for an effective partnership.

Evaluation of the Volunteer Program

The overriding goal of a volunteer program ought to be to exert a positive effect on the external environment, better the life circumstances of agency clients, or both. Periodically, agencies that mobilize volunteers for such purposes should engage in evaluation of the impact or progress they have achieved in addressing the conditions or problems identified in their mission statements. Too often, what passes for "evaluation" of the volunteer program is a compilation of the number of volunteers who have assisted the organization, the hours they have contributed, and the number of client contacts or visits they have made.

A highly recommended but more complicated evaluation procedure is for agencies to calculate the total "equivalent dollar value" of all the jobs or services performed by volunteers, based on the market price for the labor the organization would otherwise have to pay to employed personnel to accomplish the same tasks (Ellis, 1996; Karn, 1982–1983, 1983). Anderson and Zimmerer (2003) report that the dollar value of volunteer work may be estimated in a variety of ways. At least five methods are available: calculation of value based on the average wage, or the average nonagricultural wage rate (as released annually by the U.S. Bureau of Labor Statistics and used by the Independent Sector), or a "living wage" (based on dollars required for cost of living aligned with the federal poverty level), or comparable worth (equivalent dollar valuation), or minimum wage.

Fringe benefits ranging from 10 to 12 percent may also be appropriate to include in the calculation.

Impressive and significant though these data may be—since they normally document tremendous levels of contributed effort and monetary value—they focus on the inputs or resources of a volunteer program rather than its results or accomplishments. Some researchers also complain that this approach slights the monetary costs associated with the volunteer program (for example, costs of paid staff supervision, reimbursement for expenses, training of volunteers, and use of organizational resources and facilities) (Mook, Quarter, and Richmond, 2007, p. 46; Utterback and Heyman, 1984, p. 229). To address this problem, when he conducted his analysis of the SBA's SCORE volunteer program, Brudney applied a cost-effectiveness model in which both the equivalent dollar value of volunteer services as well as the costs or expenses associated with the volunteer program are taken into account, thus resulting in a cost-effectiveness ratio (1990, pp. 40–51). Brudney's study documented that for every dollar the SBA invested in support of the SCORE program, the agency garnered volunteer services worth from $1.11 to $1.86 (pp. 40–51).

Katharine Gaskin (1999a, 1999b, 2003) similarly proposes a "Volunteer Investment and Value Audit" (VIVA) in which a cost-benefit analysis is performed based on the ratio of the comparative market value of the functions performed by volunteers to the organization's expenditures on volunteers. In her cross-national evaluation of volunteer programs, Gaskin reports very high cost-benefit ratios or returns on the investment in volunteers, ranging from 1:1.3 to 1:13.5, a finding that indicates that for every British pound invested in volunteers the "return" varied from 1.3 to 13.5 pounds (2003, p. 46).

Nonprofit organizations should consider additional forms of evaluation of the volunteer program. Much as they might be expected to do for any other operational unit, agency officials should at regular intervals assess the outcomes of the volunteer program against its stated goals or mission. Volunteer activity is other-directed; it should do more than gratify citizen participants and accommodate employees. Officials need to review the aggregate performance of the volunteers in assisting clients, addressing community problems, expediting agency operations, and meeting further objectives. Not only does the assessment yield information that can improve functioning of the program, but also it reinforces for all concerned—citizens, paid staff, and agency clients alike—the importance attached by the organization to the volunteer component.

Smith and Ellis (2003) propose, conceptually, an ambitious evaluation of volunteer programs to incorporate their contribution to economic capital, physical capital, human capital, social capital, and cultural capital. Although such a methodology has not yet been developed, they point out that a concentration on the economic impacts of volunteering to the exclusion of impacts in these other areas not only gives "a very partial picture of the total value of volunteering" but also is potentially damaging in that it serves to "reinforce the notion that volunteering is all about saving money" (p. 52). Similarly, economist Eleanor Brown (1999) recommends that we consider the value of the time and service donated to the volunteer as well as to the organization. She points out that standard accounting of volunteer time also overlooks the less tangible benefits of volunteering (such as training or career development) and the benefits that may accrue to third parties such as fellow citizens from the time devoted to people and valued causes.

Another type of evaluation, also recommended, assesses the processes of a volunteer program. Using this approach, officials would determine whether procedures to address the essential program functions discussed in this chapter (for example, volunteer screening, placement) are in place and whether they are operating effectively. Additionally, the evaluation should attempt to gauge the satisfaction of volunteers and paid staff members with the program, as well as their perceptions concerning its impact on clients and the external environment. Continuing struggles with, for example, recruitment of suitable volunteers, overly high rates of volunteer burnout and turnover, relief of staff antagonisms, and achieving mutually agreeable placements, point to flaws in program design that must be addressed. By diagnosing such difficulties, a process evaluation can enhance progress toward achievement of program objectives.

Laurie Mook, Jack Quarter, and Betty Jane Richmond (2007) have extended the concept of evaluation of volunteer programs—as well as the evaluation of the activities of nonprofit organizations and cooperatives—by placing them in the broader context of "social accounting." They focus on valuing the contributions of volunteers to the organization and its clients and the larger social impacts of these organizations (for example, their effects on clients, the community, the environment, and on the volunteers themselves). As these authors note, conventional accounting practices overlook these aspects, even though they are among the most important effects of nonprofit organizations: "Even though volunteers in the United States and Canada contribute the equivalent full-time work of almost ten million people per year (Hall, McKeown, and Roberts, 2001; Independent Sector, 2002), the value of this work, estimated to be over $250 billion, is not recognized in conventional accounting" (Mook, Quarter, and Richmond, 2007, p. 133). Mook and colleagues have introduced new types of accounting statements intended to assess the social impacts of nonprofit organizations and volunteers, including the Socioeconomic Impact Statement, the Socioeconomic Resource Statement, the Expanded Value Added Statement, and the Community Social Return on Investment Model (Mook et al., 2007).

Summary and Conclusion

According to the *2001 Survey of Giving and Volunteering in the United States*, one of the most in-depth studies of giving and volunteering ever conducted in the United States (conducted for Independent Sector by Toppe, Kirsch, and Michel in 2002), 44 percent of adults over the age of twenty-one volunteered with a formal organization in the year 2000. On average, they had volunteered fifteen hours in the preceding month. Of these formal volunteers, 69 percent reported they volunteered on a regular basis, monthly or more often. In all, an estimated 83.9 million adults formally volunteered in 2000, donating approximately 15.5 billion hours. This formal volunteer workforce represented the equivalent of over nine million full-time employees, with an estimated dollar value of $239 billion. More recently, we know from the Bureau of Labor Statistics/Current Population Survey, 62.6 million people volunteered through or for an organization at least once between September 2014 and September 2015, which is a volunteer rate of just one-quarter of the U.S. population (24.9 percent). Americans volunteered nearly 7.9 billion hours, at an attributed value for this volunteer service of nearly $184 billion (based on the estimated value of a volunteer hour provided by Independent Sector [Corporation for National and Community Service, 2016]). The level and impact of volunteering in America is amazing!

The key to integrating this staggering volume of talent and energy into nonprofit and government organizations is the volunteer program. Using the information presented in this chapter, a nonprofit leader will be able to develop and implement the central elements that are essential to a successful organizationally based volunteer program. These key elements are

- The program should begin with the establishment of a rationale or policy to guide volunteer involvement.
- Paid staff must have a central role in designing the volunteer program and creating guidelines governing its operation.
- The volunteer program must be integrated structurally into the nonprofit organization.
- The program must have formally designated leadership positions to provide direction and accountability.

- The organization must prepare job descriptions for the positions to be held by volunteers, and effectively implement the functions of screening, orientation, placement, and training.
- The volunteer program must attend to the motivations that inspire volunteers and attempt to address to them, with the goal of meeting both their needs and the needs of the organization.
- Volunteers must be attracted and recruited to the organization and retained for service.
- The organization must adapt traditional hierarchical approaches to managing volunteers, including use of teamwork and collaboration, to obtain the best results.
- All components of the volunteer effort—citizens, employees, and the program itself—will benefit from the use of appropriate evaluation and recognition activities.

This list is ambitious, yet well within the reach of most nonprofit and government organizations. So, too, are the advantages to be derived from delivering an effective volunteer program.

References

ACTION. *Americans Volunteer, 1974.* Washington, DC: ACTION, 1974.

Allen, N. J. The Role of Social and Organizational Factors in the Evaluation of Volunteer Programs. *Evaluation and Program Planning*, 1987, 10(3), 257–262.

Anderson, P. M., and Zimmerer, M. E. Dollar Value of Volunteer Time: A Review of Five Estimation Methods. *Journal of Volunteer Administration*, 2003, 21(2), 39–44.

Becker, D. G. Exit Lady Bountiful: The Volunteer and the Professional Social Worker. *Social Service Review*, 1964, 38(1), 57–72.

Brown, E. Assessing the Value of Volunteer Activity. *Nonprofit and Voluntary Sector Quarterly*, 1999, 28(1), 3–17.

Brown, K. What Goes Wrong and What Can We Do About It? *Voluntary Action Leadership*, 1981, Spring, 22–23.

Brudney, J. L. The SBA and SCORE: Coproducing Management Assistance Services. *Public Productivity Review*, 1986, 40, Winter, 57–67.

Brudney, J. L. The Use of Volunteers by Local Governments as an Approach to Fiscal Stress. In T. N. Clark, W. Lyons, and M. R. Fitzgerald (eds.), *Research in Urban Policy, Volume 3*. Greenwich, CT: JAI Press, 1989.

Brudney, J. L. *Fostering Volunteer Programs in the Public Sector: Planning, Initiating, and Managing Voluntary Activities.* San Francisco: Jossey-Bass, 1990.

Brudney, J. L. Administrators of Volunteer Services: Their Needs for Training and Research." *Nonprofit Management and Leadership*, 1992, 2, Spring, 271–282.

Brudney, J. L. Preparing the Organization for Volunteers. In T. D. Connors (ed.), *The Volunteer Management Handbook: Leadership Strategies for Success* (2nd ed.). Hoboken, NJ: John Wiley & Sons, 2012, 55–80.

Brudney, J. L. Supplanting Common Myths with Uncommon Management: The Effective Involvement of Volunteers in Delivering Public Services. In R. C. Kearney and J. D. Coggburn (eds.), *Public Human Resource Management: Problems and Prospects* (6th ed.). Thousand Oaks, CA: CQ Press, 2016, 118–131.

Brudney, J. L., and Kellough, J. E. Volunteers in State Government: Involvement, Management, and Benefits. *Nonprofit and Voluntary Sector Quarterly*, 2000, 29, March, 111–130.

Brudney, J. L., and Meijs, L.C.P.M. It Ain't Natural: Toward a New (Natural) Resource Conceptualization for Volunteer Management. *Nonprofit and Voluntary Sector Quarterly*, 2009, 38, August, 564–581.

Brudney, J. L., and Meijs, L.C.P.M. Models of Volunteer Management: Professional Volunteer Program Management in Social Work. *Human Service Organizations: Management, Leadership, and Governance*, 2014, 38(3), 297–309.

Brudney, J. L., and Sink, H. K. Volunteer Management: It All Depends. In J.K.A. Word and J. E. Sowa (eds.), *The Nonprofit Resource Handbook: From Theory to Practice*. New York: Taylor and Francis, in press.

Brudney, J. L., with Kim, D. *The 2001 Volunteer Center Survey: A Report on Findings And Implications*. Washington, DC: Points of Light Foundation, 2003.

Bureau of Labor Statistics. Volunteering in the United States, 2015. Available at www.bls .gov/news.release/volun.nr0.htm. Retrieved March 9, 2016.

Clary, E. G., Snyder, M., and Ridge, R. Volunteers' Motivations: A Functional Strategy for the Recruitment, Placement, and Retention of Volunteers. *Nonprofit Management and Leadership*, 1992, 2(4), 333–350.

Clary, E. G., Snyder, M., and Stukas, A. A. Volunteers' Motivations: Findings from a National Survey. *Nonprofit and Voluntary Sector Quarterly*, 1996, 25(4), 485–505.

Cravens, J., and Ellis, S. J. *The **Last** Virtual Volunteering Guidebook: Fully Integrating Online Service into Volunteer Involvement*. Philadelphia, PA: Energize, 2014.

Corporation for National and Community Service. New Federal Report Shows Volunteering Strong in America, but 1 in 3 Volunteers Dropped Out in 2006., 2007. Available at www.prnewswire.com/news-releases/new-federal-report-shows-volunteering-strong-in-america-but-1-in-3-volunteers-dropped-out-in-2006-58355842 .html. Retrieved January 29, 2016.

Corporation for National and Community Service. Volunteering in America. Available at www.nationalservice.gov/impact-our-nation/research-and-reports/volunteering-in-america. Retrieved February 10, 2016.

Corporation for National and Community Service. *The State of Volunteering in America, 2015*. Available at www.volunteeringinamerican.gov/infographic.cfm. Retrieved March 9, 2016.

Deitch, L. I., and Thompson, L. N. The Reserve Police Officer: One Alternative to the Need for Manpower. *Police Chief*, 1985, 52(5), 59–61.

Dorwaldt, A. L., Solomon, L. J., and Worden, J. K. Why Volunteers Helped to Promote a Community Breast Self-Exam Program. *Journal of Volunteer Administration*, 1988, 6(4), 23–30.

Drucker, P. F. *Managing the Non-Profit Organization: Practices and Principles*. New York: HarperCollins, 1990.

Duncombe, S. Volunteers in City Government: Advantages, Disadvantages and Uses. *National Civic Review*, 1985, 74(9), 356–364.

Eisner, D., Grimm, R. T., Maynard, S., and Washburn, S. The New Volunteer Workforce. *Stanford Social Innovation Review*, 2009, Winter. Available at http://ssir.org/articles/ entry/the_new_volunteer_workforce. Retrieved February 9, 2016.

Ellis, S. J. *The Volunteer Recruitment Book*. Philadelphia, PA: Energize, 1994.

Ellis, S. J. *From the Top Down: The Executive Role in Volunteer Program Success* (rev. ed.). Philadelphia, PA: Energize, 1996.

Ellis, S. J., and Campbell, K. H. *By the People: A History of Americans as Volunteers. New Century Edition*. Philadelphia, PA: Energize, 2005.

Farr, C. A. *Volunteers: Managing Volunteer Personnel in Local Government*. Washington, DC: International City Management Association, 1983.

Farmer, S. M., and Fedor, D. B. Volunteer Participation and Withdrawal: A Psychological Contract Perspective on the Role of Expectations and Organizational Support. *Nonprofit Management and Leadership*, 1999, 9(4), 349–367.

Fisher, J. C., and Cole, K. M. *Leadership and Management of Volunteer Programs: A Guide for Volunteer Administrators*. San Francisco: Jossey-Bass, 1993.

Gallup, Inc. *Americans Volunteer, 1981*. Princeton, NJ: Gallup Organization, 1981.

Gaskin, K. Valuing Volunteers in Europe: A Comparative Study of the Volunteer Investment and Value Audit. *Voluntary Action*, 1999a, 2(1), 35–49.

Gaskin, K. *VIVA in Europe: A Comparative Study of the Volunteer Investment and Value Audit*. London, UK: Institute for Volunteering Research, 1999b.

Gaskin, K. VIVA in Europe: A Comparative Study of the Volunteer Investment and Value Audit. *Journal of Volunteer Administration*, 2003, 21(2), 45–48.

Goetter, W.G.J. When You Create Ideal Conditions, Your Fledgling Volunteer Program Will Fly. *American School Board Journal*, 1987, 194(6), 34–37.

Graff, L. L. Considering the Many Facets of Volunteer/Union Relations. *Voluntary Action Leadership*, 1984, Summer, 16–20.

Groble, P., and Brudney, J. L. When Good Intentions Go Wrong: Immunity Under the Volunteer Protection Act. *Nonprofit Policy Forum*, 2015, 6(1), 3–24.

Grossman, J. B., and Furano, K. Making the Most of Volunteers. 2002. Available at Public/Private Ventures, http://ppv.issuelab.org/resource/making_the_most_of_volunteers. Retrieved February 2, 2016.

Hager, M. A., and Brudney, J. L. Management Capacity and Retention of Volunteers. In M. Liao-Troth (ed.), *Challenges in Volunteer Management*. Charlotte, NC: Information Age Publishing, 2008, 9–28.

Hager, M. A., and Brudney, J. L. Sustaining Volunteer Involvement. In K. Seel (ed.), *Volunteer Administration: Professional Practice* (2nd ed.). Markham, Ontario, Canada: LexisNexis Canada, 2013, 243–279.

Hager, M. A., and Brudney, J. L. In Search of Strategy: Universalistic, Contingent, and Configurational Adoption of Volunteer Management Practices. *Nonprofit Management and Leadership*, 2015, 25(3), 235–254.

Hall, M. H., McKeown, L., and Roberts, K. *Caring Canadians, Involved Canadians: Highlights from the 2000 National Survey of Giving, Volunteering and Participating*. Ottawa, Canada: Minister of Industry, 2001.

Handy, F., Mook, L., and Quarter, J. The Interchangeability of Paid Staff and Volunteers in Nonprofit Organizations. *Nonprofit and Voluntary Sector Quarterly*, 2008, 37, March, 76–92.

Haran, L., Kenney, S., and Vermilion, M. Contract Volunteer Services: A Model for Successful Partnership. *Leadership*, 1993, January–March, 28–30.

Herman, M. L., and Jackson, P. M. *No Surprises: Harmonizing Risk and Reward in Volunteer Management*. Washington, DC: Nonprofit Risk Management Center, 2001.

Hobson, C., and Malec, K. Initial Telephone Contact of Prospective Volunteers and Non-profits: An Operational Definition of Quality and Norms for 500 Agencies. *Journal of Volunteer Administration*, 1999, 17(4), 21–27.

Hodgkinson, V. A., and Weitzman, M. S. *The Charitable Behavior of Americans: A National Survey*. Washington, DC: Independent Sector, 1986.

Hodgkinson, V. A., and Weitzman, M. S. *Giving and Volunteering in the United States: Findings from a National Survey*. Washington, DC: Independent Sector, 1988.

Hodgkinson, V. A., and Weitzman, M. S. *Giving and Volunteering in the United States: Findings from a National Survey*. Washington, DC: Independent Sector, 1990.

Hodgkinson, V. A., and Weitzman, M. S. *Giving and Volunteering in the United States: Findings from a National Survey*. Washington, DC: Independent Sector, 1992.

Hodgkinson, V. A., and Weitzman, M. S. *Giving and Volunteering in the United States: Findings from a National Survey*. Washington, DC: Independent Sector, 1996.

Hodgkinson, V. A., Weitzman, M. S., Toppe, C. M., Noga, S. M. *Nonprofit Almanac, 1992–1993: Dimensions of the Independent Sector*. San Francisco: Jossey-Bass, 1992.

Hyde, M. K., Dunn, J., Bax, C., and Chambers, S. K. Episodic Volunteering and Retention: An Integrated Theoretical Approach. *Nonprofit and Voluntary Sector Quarterly*, 2016, 45, February, 45–63.

Ilsley, P. *Enhancing the Volunteer Experience*. San Francisco: Jossey-Bass, 1990.

Independent Sector. *Giving and Volunteering in the United States 2001: Findings from a National Survey*. Washington, DC: Independent Sector, 2002.

Karn, G. N. Money Talks: A Guide to Establishing the True Dollar Value of Volunteer Time, Part I. *Journal of Volunteer Administration*, 1982–1983, 1, Winter, 1–17.

Karn, G. N. Money Talks: A Guide to Establishing the True Dollar Value of Volunteer Time, Part II. *Journal of Volunteer Administration*, 1983, 1, Spring, 1–19.

Kirsch, A. D., Hume, K. M., and Jalandoni, N. T. *Giving and Volunteering in the United States: Findings from a National Survey 1999 Edition*. Washington, DC: Independent Sector, 2000.

Liao-Troth, M. A. Attitude Differences Between Paid Workers and Volunteers. *Nonprofit Management and Leadership*, 2001, 11(4), 423–442.

Macduff, N. Episodic Volunteering. In T. D. Connors (ed.), *The Volunteer Management Handbook*. Hoboken, NJ: John Wiley & Sons, 1995, 9–28.

Macduff, N. Principles of Training for Volunteers and Employees. In R. D. Herman (ed.), *The Jossey-Bass Handbook of Nonprofit Leadership and Management* (2nd ed.). San Francisco: Jossey-Bass, 2005, 703-730.

Manchester, L. D., and Bogart, G. S. *Contracting and Volunteerism in Local Government: A Self-Help Guide*. Washington, DC: International City Management Association, 1988.

Marando, V. L. Local Service Delivery: Volunteers and Recreation Councils. *Journal of Volunteer Administration*, 1986, 4(4), 16–24.

May, K. M., McLaughlin, R., and Penner, M. Preventing Low Birth Weight: Marketing and Volunteer Outreach. *Public Health Nursing*, 1991, 8(2), 97–104.

McHenry, C. A. Library Volunteers: Recruiting, Motivating, Keeping Them. *School Library Journal*, 1988, 35(8), 44–47.

McCurley, S. Keeping the Community Involved: Recruiting and Retaining Volunteers. In R. D. Herman (ed.), *The Jossey-Bass Handbook of Nonprofit Leadership and Management* (2nd ed.). San Francisco: Jossey-Bass, 2005, 587–622.

McCurley, S., and Ellis, S. J. Thinking the Unthinkable: Are We Using the Wrong Model for Volunteer Work?" *e-Volunteerism*, 2003, 3(1). Available at https://www.e-volunteerism.com/node/662. Retrieved February 3, 2016.

McCurley, S., and Lynch, R. *Essential Volunteer Management.* Downers Grove, IL: VM Systems and Heritage Arts Publishing, 1989.

McCurley, S., and Lynch, R. *Keeping Volunteers.* Olympia, WA: Fat Cat Publications, 2005.

McCurley, S., and Lynch, R. *Volunteer Management: Mobilizing All the Resources in the Community.* Downers Grove, IL: Heritage Arts Publishing, 1996.

McHenry, C. A. 'Library Volunteers: Recruiting, Motivating, Keeping Them. *School Library Journal,* 1988, 35(8), 44–47.

Meijs, L.C.P.M., and Brudney, J. L. Winning Volunteer Scenarios: The Soul of a New Machine. *International Journal of Volunteer Administration,* 2007, 24, Oct., 68–79.

Meijs, L.C.P.M., and Hoogstad, E. New Ways of Managing Volunteers: Combining Membership Management And Programme Management. *Voluntary Action,* 2001, 3(3), 41–61.

Mook, L.; Quarter, J.; and Richmond, B. J. *What Counts: Social Accounting for Nonprofits and Cooperatives* (2nd ed.). London: Siegel Press, 2007.

Moore, N. A. The Application of Cost-Benefit Analysis to Volunteer Programs. *Volunteer Administration,* 1978, 11(1), 13–22.

Murray, V., and Harrison, Y. Virtual Volunteering: Current Status and Future Prospects. 2002a. Available at the Canadian Centre for Philanthropy, https://www.onlinevolunteering.org/resources/documents/murray_sr2_english_web.pdf. Retrieved February 3, 2016.

Murray, V., and Harrison, Y. Virtual Volunteering in Canada. 2002b. Available at http://sectorsource.ca/sites/default/files/resources/files/Murray_FS_English.pdf. Retrieved February 3, 2016.

Murray, V., and Harrison, Y. Virtual Volunteering. In J. Brudney (ed.), *Emerging Areas of Volunteering* (2nd ed.). Indianapolis, IN: Association for Research on Nonprofit Organizations and Voluntary Action, 2005, 33–50.

National SCORE Office. *This Is SCORE.* Washington, DC: National SCORE Office, 1989 (NSO-86002 [4/89]).

Naylor, H. H. *Volunteers Today—Finding, Training and Working with Them.* Dryden, NY: Dryden Associates, 1973.

Naylor, H. H. Beyond Managing Volunteers. *Journal of Voluntary Action Research,* 1985, 14(2, 3), 25–30.

New York Times. An Uncertain Trumpet. Editorial. Sept. 8, 2002.

Nunn, M. Building the Bridge from Episodic Volunteerism to Social Capital. *Fletcher Forum of World Affairs,* 2000, 24(2), 115–127

O'Donald, E. Re-Entry Through Volunteering: The Best Jobs that Money Can't Buy. *Voluntary Action Leadership,* 1989, Fall, 22–27.

Park, J. M. *Meaning Well Is not Enough: Perspectives on Volunteering.* South Plainfield, NJ: Groupwork Today, 1983.

Pearce, J. L. Something for Nothing: An Empirical Examination of the Structures and Norms of Volunteer Organizations. Doctoral dissertation, New Haven, CT: Yale University, 1978.

Pearce, J. L. Participation in Voluntary Associations: How Membership in a Formal Organization Changes the Rewards of Participation. In D. H. Smith and J. Van Til (eds.), *International Perspectives on Voluntary Action Research.* Washington, DC: University Press of America, 1983.

Peters, T. J., and Waterman, R. H. Jr., *In Search of Excellence: Lessons from America's Best-Run Companies.* New York: Warner Books, 1982.

Scheier, I. H. Positive Staff Attitude Can Ease Volunteer Recruiting Pinch. *Hospitals*, 1981, 55(3), 61–63.

Scheier, I. H. Empowering a Profession: What's in Our Name? *Journal of Volunteer Administration*, 1988a, 6(4), 31–36.

Scheier, I. H. Empowering a Profession: Seeing Ourselves as More than Subsidiary. *Journal of Volunteer Administration*, 1988b, 7(1), 29–34.

Scheier, I. H. Empowering a Profession: Leverage Points and Process. *Journal of Volunteer Administration*, 1988–1989, 7(2), 50–57.

Schwartz, F. S. The Professional Staff and the Direct Service Volunteer: Issues and Problems. *Journal of Jewish Communal Service*, 1977, (2), 147–154.

Senior Corps. #IAmSeniorCorps. Available at www.nationalservice.gov/programs/senior-corps. Retrieved February 5, 2016.

SCORE. Our Impact. Available at https://www.score.org/our-impact. Retrieved January 29, 2016.

Small Business Administration. More About SCORE. Available at https://www.sba.gov/offices/headquarters/oed/resources/148091. Retrieved January 29, 2016.

Smith, A. C., and Green F. B. Managing Employees as If They Were Volunteers. *SAM Advanced Management Journal*, 1993, 58 3), 42–46.

Smith, J. D., and Ellis, A. Valuing Volunteering. *Journal of Volunteer Administration*, 2003, 21(2), 49–52.

Stoolmacher, I. S. Non-Profits Should Treat Volunteers as If They Were Paid Employees. *Chronicle of Philanthropy*, 1991, July 16, 3(19), 34–35.

Studer, S., and von Schnurbein, G. Organizational Factors Affecting Volunteers: A Literature Review on Volunteer Coordination. *Voluntas*, 2013, 24(2), 403–440.

Sundeen, R. A. Citizens Serving Government: Volunteer Participation in Local Public Agencies. In *Working Papers for the Spring Research Forum*. Washington, DC: Independent Sector, 1989.

Thornburg, L. What Makes an Effective Volunteer Administrator? Viewpoints from Several Practitioners. *Voluntary Action Leadership*, 1992, Summer, 18–21.

Toppe, C. M., Kirsch, A. D., and Michel, J. *Giving and Volunteering in the United States 2001: Findings from a National Survey*. Washington, DC: Independent Sector, 2002.

Urban Institute. *Volunteer Management Capacity in America's Charities and Congregations: A Briefing Report*. Washington, DC: Author, 2004. Available at www.urban.org/sites/default/files/alfresco/publication-pdfs/410963-Volunteer-Management-Capacity-in-America-s-Charities-and-Congregations.pdf. Retrieved February 3, 2016.

U.S. Department of Labor. *Americans Volunteer*. Washington, DC: Department of Labor, Manpower Administration, 1969.

Utterback, J., and Heyman, S. R. An Examination of Methods in the Evaluation of Volunteer Programs. *Evaluation and Program Planning*, 1984, 7(3), 229–235.

Valente, M. G. Volunteers Help Stretch Local Budgets. *Rural Development Perspectives*, 1985, 2(1), 30–34.

Valente, C. F., and Manchester, L. D. Rethinking Local Services: Examining Alternative Delivery Approaches. Washington, DC: International City Management Association *Information Service Special Report* (12), 1984.

Van Til, J. *Mapping the Third Sector: Voluntarism in a Changing Social Economy*. New York: Foundation Center, 1988.

VolunteerMatch. At-a-Glance VOLUNTEERMATCH. Available at http://cdn.volunteer match.org/www/about/volunteermatch_fact_sheet.pdf. Retrieved February 5, 2016.

Walter, V. Volunteers and Bureaucrats: Clarifying Roles and Creating Meaning. *Journal of Voluntary Action Research*, 1987, 16(3), 22–32.

Weber, M. A. What Can Be Learned About Episodic Volunteers from a National Survey of Giving and Volunteering? Paper presented at the Annual Meeting of the Association for Research on Nonprofit Organizations and Voluntary Action. Montreal, Quebec, Canada, November 14–16, 2002.

Wilson, M. *The Effective Management of Volunteer Programs*. Boulder, CO: Johnson Publishing, 1976.

Wilson, M. The New Frontier: Volunteer Management Training. *Training and Development Journal*, 1984, 38(7), 50–52.

Young, C. L., Goughler, D. H., and Larson, P. J. Organizational Volunteers for the Rural Frail Elderly: Outreach, Casefinding, and Service Delivery. *Gerontologist*, 1986, 26(4), 342–344.

CONCLUSION

The Future of Nonprofit Leadership and Management

David O. Renz

This fourth edition of the *Jossey-Bass Handbook of Nonprofit Leadership and Management*, which comes two decades after the publication of the first edition, describes a nonprofit sector that is very different from that of the inaugural edition. The field has grown and developed in important and amazing ways, some very positive and some less so, and the nature and content of the work of the typical nonprofit leader and manager is quite different from those earlier days. True, the purpose and functional content of nonprofit management remains substantially the same: it is the process of planning, organizing, and leading the work of the organization, including establishing goals, developing organizational strategies, securing and allocating resources, organizing the work, recruiting and mobilizing the workforce to do it, supervising the implementation of the work, evaluating the degree to which the organization is accomplishing its goals, and then refining plans and strategies to sustain and enhance the organization's performance and impact.

And yet, as Lester Salamon explains, the context of nonprofit leadership and management has changed so much in the past twenty-five years that it is not at all the same work (2010, 2012). Some things have become easier, yet much has become dramatically more complex and challenging. In his chronicle of the changes that have led to today's demanding operating environment, Salamon identifies four key types of challenges:

- The challenges of *finance,* from federal retrenchment to the changing nature of public support to a decline in the share of private giving relative to non-profit need
- The challenges of more and different kinds of *competition,* ranging from intra-sector competition among nonprofits for time, talent, and treasure to intersector competition as nonprofits and for-profits compete for attention, credibility, and business as they jockey for the opportunity to provide services in an increasingly ambivalent marketplace
- The challenge of *effectiveness* that comes of the increased demands for non-profits to demonstrate and prove performance, results, and accountability
- The challenge of *technology,* as new and increasingly sophisticated digital tech-nologies and social media become available to both the sector and to a good share of its constituents, leading to heightened expectations for new levels of communication, engagement, and responsiveness—and to new definitions of effectiveness.

Today is indeed a new day for the leader and manager of a typical non-profit! And, Salamon suggests, tomorrow promises more—more of the same, plus more that will be different (2010, 2012). Among the emerging opportunities he describes are the following:

- Major social and demographic shifts, fueling exceptional changes in the com-position and character of every society on the planet, including exceptional growth in the size of an aged population, more women in the workforce, exceptional growth in the number of children living in single-parent house-holds, and major changes in the balance among the many racial and ethnic groups that comprise civil societies across the globe
- New forms of philanthropy, some employing new strategies and vehicles and enabled or energized by new technologies, some fueled by the increasingly large intergenerational transfer of wealth
- Greater visibility and policy salience as the value and potential for impact of nonprofit and other civil society organizations are recognized and embraced by political and institutional leaders
- Resumption of governmental spending on social welfare and other civil society programming

A number of recent reports also weigh in on the changing nature of the nonprofit environment to offer their own observations about the nature of this time of fundamental change (for example, Alliance for Children and Families,

2011; Bernholz, 2014; 2015; Gowdy, Hildebrand, LaPiana, and Campos, 2009). Gowdy and colleagues (2009) assert that the nonprofit sector is at a unique point in time, "an inflection point" that will fundamentally reshape the sector, and that successful nonprofit leaders and managers will build their capacity to be attuned to rapid and continual shifts as they manage strategically in the fundamentally new operating environment. Among the key trends they suggest are converging to fuel changes are

- Shifts in demographics that lead to redefined expectations for participation, engagement, and equity
- Advances in technology, including the rise of social media, that enable (or demand?) "new ways of communicating, demanding greater openness and transparency" (p. 10)
- Development of networks (technological *and* social) that enable dialogue, work, and even decision making to be organized in multiple new and relatively more fluid ways
- Growth in interest in civic engagement, including greater expectations for new levels and multiple forms of engagement and nonprofit responsiveness
- Blurring of sectoral boundaries between nonprofits, for-profits, and governmental agencies, resulting in both competition and collaboration that enhance and sometimes confuse opportunities for the creation of both private wealth and social capital

A more recent assessment of the human services environment, prepared for the Alliance for Children and Families (2011), identifies the following as disruptive forces causing change, adaptation, and innovation: purposeful experimentation, information liberation, integration of science, an uncompromising demand for impact, branding for causes rather than organizations, and the need to attract investors rather than donors.

As challenging as these dynamics are, they are not necessarily negative. We observe effective nonprofit leaders and managers being both innovative and strategic as they explore ways to navigate and exploit the opportunities inherent in these changes. For example:

- The realization that it is impossible to operate as they have in the past has led many nonprofit organizations and their leaders to fundamentally rethink what they do and how they do it. At best, nonprofits achieve greater focus as they clarify that which is core to their mission and then seek innovative ways to address it.
- Many nonprofit organizations, as they experience the problems posed by their traditional revenue strategies, are rethinking their business and revenue

models. The exceptional growth in attention to nonprofit social entrepreneurship reflects a new level of creativity as many nonprofits employ different and more diverse ways to fund and finance their work.

- New forms of organizing are being developed and tested, particularly via the expanded use of creative forms of alliances and networks.
- There is growing use of hybrid forms of organization that extend across and blur traditional sector boundaries. Such organizations blend the practices of business, government, and nonprofit to achieve results and deliver social value that often cannot be achieved in any single sector.
- New and richer ways of understanding and ensuring accountability are being developed at both the organizational and system levels to complement those that operate within programs. Systems are being developed in ways that more effectively gather and employ data to document and enhance performance and effectiveness at both the organization and program levels of operation.
- Smaller nonprofits are investing in increasingly sophisticated yet lower cost software that makes it feasible to become more effective and data-driven in strategy and planning, decision making, constituent relations, and financial and performance management.
- Nonprofits are taking marketing more seriously and employing marketing and branding practices in more sophisticated ways (it's no longer just a euphemism for fundraising and selling). This includes adapting and employing social media and other emerging approaches and technologies to enhance constituent relations, communications, alliance and relationship building, and transparency and accountability, all at relatively low cost.
- Savvy nonprofits also are taking care to proactively address the human resources facets of nonprofit leadership and management, from developing new leadership talent to succession planning to changing the ways they engage younger generations in their work. This includes tapping the strong interest of many Millennials to engage in community-building activities. These agencies are creating new ways for young adults from all types of backgrounds to become more actively engaged in service in the sector.
- Increasing numbers are taking advantage of the phenomenal growth in the number and scope of nonprofit leadership and management programs—both formal degree programs at bachelor's and master's degree levels, and in various certificate and other non-degree programs—to build the capacity of both current and aspiring leaders.
- New forms of leadership and governance are being explored and developed as nonprofit organizations and their leaders work to capitalize on all of these trends and dynamics.

The Successful Nonprofit Leader and Manager of the Future

What does all of this mean for the future of nonprofit leadership and management? It certainly suggests that the work of leaders and managers will become even more complex and demanding. It also suggests that, while passion and commitment are essential to success, effective leaders and managers need more to succeed. The knowledge, skills, and abilities explained in this *Handbook* are central to the future success of the typical nonprofit leader and manager.

Some worry, as we continue to professionalize the management of the sector, that the distinctive character of nonprofits in civil society will be lost. But there is no reason to believe that this must be the case. Indeed, drawing on a key marketing concept, we can and must remember to regularly and clearly articulate the key differentiators that distinguish nonprofit organizations from all others. If professionalization and education are well grounded and implemented appropriately, the sector will not lose its way because, at core, effective nonprofit management must be defined in and by mission accomplishment. So the challenge, in difficult times, is to never forget why we do what we do. I am optimistic that we are unlikely to forget our mission—our volunteers and donors and community leaders will not let this happen. Although the sector's public trust ratings today are lower than I'd like, it remains true that the average citizen values the nonprofit sector and considers it an essential part of a viable society. We know this, in part, because year after year we continue to see people across the world taking the time to create thousands of new nonprofits (and a good share of them are all-volunteer organizations) to address the needs and interests of their communities and fellow citizens.

From the perspective of nonprofit management and leadership, how do we ensure the sector does not lose its distinctiveness and viability? My answer is that we lead and manage effectively! Every one of the chapters of this *Handbook* explains a unique facet of how we ensure that our sector and its organizations remain vital, viable, and distinctive. At core, this has four dimensions.

Govern, Lead, and Manage with Strategic Focus

Fundamentally, strategic leadership and management constitute the process of making choices about the best and most effective ways to achieve the intended purpose of the organization (that is, the mission). As Robert Herman argues in the second edition of this volume (2005), it is imperative that every nonprofit is "managing toward the morality of the mission." It is when a nonprofit's leaders and managers forget to or fail to keep the mission, vision, and values of the organization as the foundation for all the decisions and choices they make that we have the greatest potential for losing our way. Essentially all of the trust and accountability problems of the sector derive from our key stakeholders' fears that we are not in fact doing this and doing it well—they are warning us to take the fundamentals seriously.

Do Not Fall Prey to the "Run It Like a Business" Clichés

The oft-uttered admonition to "run it like a business" is a half-truth, valid except when it's not! Many of the most spectacular failures of nonprofit leadership and management exemplify the cultural contradictions of our sector, when nonprofit leaders think they can operate as a conventional business would operate—only to find that they had violated important conventions and rules (some written and some not) about what is acceptable for a nonprofit. All organizations today operate in an environment of increasingly complex competing and conflicting values and expectations. But businesses ultimately have the option of ignoring or shortchanging some values and expectations in favor of others (indeed, in the United States, they are legally obligated to maximize financial results for the limited group of people who are their owners—that is, their shareholders). Nonprofit leaders and managers, however, must recognize *and accommodate* a much larger array of stakeholders' competing values and perspectives as they determine what their organizations should do, how they should do it, and how to judge effectiveness and success.

Among the key distinctions: at its core, a business serves a market niche as long as it is profitable; when it's no longer profitable the well-managed business will leave the niche to pursue something that has greater promise for profit. A business is obligated, as a matter of responsible use of the owners' assets, to leave a niche or market when it cannot achieve an appropriate return on those assets (at whatever level of return is deemed acceptable by those owners). Alternatively, by definition and mandate associated with charity status, the typical nonprofit operates in a market where profitability is less viable (that is, the economist's concept of market failure). Indeed, in recent years, some nonprofits have been threatened with or even lost their nonprofit status because there was no clear distinction between their enterprise and a for-profit business. The nonprofit is mission-bound to stay in its specific (tax-exempt) business if at all possible, so key decisions turn on whether it is feasible to remain in the market (with some form of subsidization, including but not limited to tax exemption) to continue to serve its clients.

Market and Communicate Effectively

Nonprofit leaders must become more effective at explaining the true characteristics of the nonprofit world. We have failed to help many of our key constituents—including many who govern, manage, staff, and volunteer for our own organizations—understand the nature of the sector and its organizations. Lester Salamon observes:

> Thanks to the pressures they are under, and the agility they have shown in response to them, American nonprofit organizations have moved well beyond the quaint Norman Rockwell stereotype of selfless volunteers ministering to the needy and supported largely by charitable gifts. Yet popular and press images remain wedded to this older image and far too little attention has been given to bringing popular perceptions into better alignment with the realities that now exist, and to justifying these realities to a skeptical citizenry and press. (2010, p. 96)

Several of the chapters of this book examine the processes by which we engage, inform, and educate our key constituencies through marketing, strategic communication, and advocacy. We must be effective in using the guidance and insights of these fields to inform our work as leaders and managers.

Perform Well and Deliver Social Value

Ultimately, people everywhere value the nonprofit sector and civil society for the social value they add. If nonprofits cannot deliver on their missions, communities legitimately ask why they should allow them and subsidize them. The ultimate judgment in the test of whether we are effectively "managing toward the morality of the mission" comes directly from our performance and from our ability to demonstrate that progress is being made. Our constituents and stakeholders want us to succeed, and the reason they will maintain or even enhance their support is because they see the value in what we seek to accomplish. There is no question that the nature of the problems and needs addressed by the nonprofit sector is such that progress can be slow, difficult, and hard to demonstrate. For that reason, the work of marketing and communication is integral to this element. But, as Greg Dees explains in Chapter Eleven, there is only one bottom line in the nonprofit world—it is the creation of social value. Without social value that derives from the effective practice of nonprofit leadership and management, the legitimacy of the field disappears and we run the danger of becoming "just another business out to make a buck."

Does Nonprofit Management Differ from For-Profit Management?

Some question whether there is any substantive difference between "nonprofit management" and management in other types of organizations. After all, every one of the nonprofit management functions that has been explained in this *Handbook* is important to the effective management of every organization regardless of profit orientation. All the tasks of management described herein are essential to the management of profit-making organizations. So is there a difference? At core, in both nonprofit or for-profit organizations, the central purpose of management is the same—to enable the organization to function well to accomplish its mission and goals. And the fundamental difference flows directly from that point: it is the purpose to be achieved by the management system that is different. Among the distinctive dimensions of *nonprofit* management that are important to recognize because they have a distinct impact on the success of those who do this work are those discussed as follows.

The Unique Legal Context

To state the obvious, the nonprofit sector in the United States and most other nations of the world is legally distinct from the other sectors. It is neither for-profit business nor government, even as it carries certain characteristics of each, and this difference in legal context is significant to the practice of management (most notably, it limits the range of strategic options available to the leadership team). In most nations the organizations that are qualified as "nonprofit" organizations receive this distinction because they have agreed to limit the nature and scope of their work. They have been granted special privileges, such as tax-exempt status, but the price of these privileges is that these nonprofit (and nongovernmental) organizations must constrain their activities to those that address broader social or charitable purposes. Such distinctiveness applies to much of the nonprofit sector across the globe, although it is essential to recognize that there is great variation in the laws of different nations with regard to permissible and impermissible nonprofit activity. Thus, it is essential that a nonprofit manager manage with respect to the legal context of each nation in which his or her organization operates.

The Unique Ownership Structure

One of the legal differences that becomes significant to management is that of organizational ownership. In the United States and many other nations, it is generally not possible to own (that is, to have an equity stake such as stock) a nonprofit charitable organization. In practical terms, the typical U.S. charity is "owned" by the community or segment of the community that it exists to serve. Thus, its governing board and management must act as stewards of the assets of the organization on behalf of the community, even as there is no singular and clear external source of accountability or control over the affairs of the organization. Such diffusion of control and accountability creates both unique opportunities and complications for nonprofit management (for more on this, see Chapter Four, "The Many Faces of Nonprofit Accountability").

The Unique Political and Cultural Context

The aforementioned legal and ownership differences couple with the unique political context of the nonprofit sector to further complicate the work of nonprofit management. One result of the nonprofit's diffuse and unclear accountability is that the typical organization has multiple significant stakeholders, and many think they are "in charge." These stakeholders bring diverse and conflicting performance expectations to bear on the organization and, therefore, on its management team. In today's environment of heightened concern for accountability and performance, the management team cannot afford to overtly ignore most such expectations, even when they are inconsistent. Thus, one of the most challenging tasks of *nonprofit* management is to select a course of action that strikes a reasonable balance among the shifting expectations and demands of the organization's multiple stakeholders. Ebrahim also explores this issue in depth in Chapter Four. This demands that management be especially politically sophisticated and sensitive to the external environment.

Further, efficiency in the social sector cannot be assessed as it is in business. A sector that serves to address the expressive and artistic needs of a community cannot legitimately be judged by the same criteria as those that serve instrumental functions. Indeed, this is where part of the paradox of the sector arises—for many seek to turn the sector into a purely instrumental form (and in its own way, government has done more to create this dynamic than any other part of society, as Smith discusses in Chapter Twenty). Interestingly, for some nonprofits, their mere existence *is* the outcome their stakeholders seek, and we should never forget this in our press to enhance effectiveness and accountability. I am reminded of the truth of this every year as thousands (really, tens of thousands) of citizens, all over the world, invest an incredible amount of time in the founding and nurturing of new nonprofits that generate "only" good will, fellowship, camaraderie, and enhanced sense of community. In a broader sense, this, too, is a market phenomenon, yet it is not the rational-logical resource-maximizing dynamic of some economic theories—and it cannot and should not be reduced to such.

The Unique Financial and Capital Structure

Further complicating the unique work of nonprofit management is that the financial context for a typical nonprofit organization can be much more complex than it is for similarly sized for-profit businesses. The typical nonprofit's complicated mix of clients and markets, which correlates directly to complicated business models grounded in diverse and inconsistent funding and financing models, makes the work of nonprofit management distinctive. The typical for-profit business gets its financial support from a relatively uncomplicated set of sources; nonprofits increasingly must fund and finance their operations with a mix of philanthropic resources and earned income derived from a relatively diverse set of sources. This varies significantly by mission and type of work. Each source imposes its own expectations for operations, management performance, and organizational accountability. Among the most demanding are the governmental sources, since acceptance of funds from government typically intensifies the demands for procedural as well as performance accountability.

Many of these distinctions are subtle yet very real, demanding, and potentially disabling to the unprepared leader or manager. Successful business entrepreneur turned nonprofit leader and consultant, Mario Morino, described from personal experience the nature of these differences in a 2007 speech. Among the differences he articulated for his business colleagues:

- Context has an extremely significant function.... The issue itself may be crystal clear to you, but understanding the context within which the issue is framed is key (and the difference between success and failure).
- All organizations deal with external factors, but social sector organizations confront and work through more outside conditions beyond their control and that are more social and people-based in nature.
- Not all business entrepreneur traits transfer well. Some of the characteristics that were effective in the private sector may not work now.... The highly driven nature, the adrenaline kick-in, the brashness that he feels is valued in business settings, the "take it on at all costs" mentality—all have their consequences in a world where relationship, context, and social complexity play such important roles in being effective.

- Many of the factors vital to success are outside of your immediate control—the multiplicity of stakeholders, the interdependency of "supply chains," and the expectations society places on nonprofits.
- Do not make the assumption that the market forces at work in the private sector—or the systems and discipline they introduce—carry over to the social sector.
- Government funding and programs are important. There is a romantic, idealistic view that we can scale solutions without government funding. In some areas this may be true and, when possible, we should do all we can to make this a reality. But in areas where public funding approximates from 85 to 95 percent of the available funding, e.g., human services, this is simply not realistic.

Conclusion

Nonprofit organizations play increasingly significant and diverse roles in the development and maintenance of civil society and communities throughout the world. Consistent with this trend, the demand for sophistication and skill in leading and managing these organizations is growing. Leaders from across the globe are asking more and more of nonprofit organizations—more with regard to creativity and innovation, more with regard to responsiveness, and more with regard to impact and results.

A new generation of nonprofit managers is preparing to lead these important organizations—a generation that understands the increasingly complex nature of the work of nonprofit management. This new generation of nonprofit managers understands that, although passion and dedication are essential to the future of the nonprofit sector and continued development of global civil society, passion and dedication alone are inadequate. It is through the effective practice of leadership and management that the organizations of the nonprofit sector will continue to grow and develop in their capacity to successfully address the needs of a diverse and complicated world.

The practice of nonprofit leadership and management is riddled with paradox and contradiction. Indeed, it always has been. Central to public service and community leadership roles is the need to find ways to address and reconcile (to the greatest degree possible) a host of competing values and tensions. But I'd suggest that we're heading into a new era—new for the sector and new for those who aspire to lead and manage it. Nonprofits will play even more roles of pivotal significance in the shared-power global environment of tomorrow, and the successful nonprofit leaders and managers will be those who become adept at identifying, understanding, and addressing the dynamics needs and challenges of an environment characterized by greater variation and complexity, coupled with cycles of change that are deeper and faster than we traditionally have known. The pace of change and the extent of that change will demand a greater level of knowledge, sophistication, and skill from those who aspire to lead and manage these organizations.

These are exciting and challenging times for those who lead and manage nonprofit organizations, and the sector's capacity to deliver on its promises and to serve our communities and citizens well hinges directly on the effectiveness of its leaders and managers. The chapters of this fourth edition of the *Jossey-Bass Handbook of Nonprofit Leadership and Management* offer important information and guidance for both current and developing leaders and managers of the sector, preparing them with important knowledge and critical insights that will enable them to make the difference they aspire to make.

References

Alliance for Children and Families. *Disruptive Forces: Driving a Human Services Revolution.* Milwaukee, WI: Alliance for Children and Families. 2011.

Bernholz, L. *Philanthropy and Social Economy: Blueprint 2015.* Washington DC: Foundation Center, 2014.

Bernholz, L. *Philanthropy and Social Economy: Blueprint 2016.* Washington DC: Foundation Center, 2015.

Gowdy, H., Hildebrand, A., LaPiana, D., and Campos, M. M. Convergence: How Five Trends Will Reshape the Social Sector. San Francisco: The James Irvine Foundation, 2009.

Herman, R. Conclusion: The Future of Nonprofit Management. In R. Herman (ed.), *The Jossey-Bass Handbook of Nonprofit Leadership and Management.* San Francisco: Jossey-Bass, 2005, pp. 731–735.

Morino, M. Business Entrepreneurs and Philanthropy: Potential and Pitfalls. A Keynote Speech to Legacy 2007, The National Philanthropic Trust, Washington D.C., September 28, 2007.

Salamon, L. The Changing Context of Nonprofit Leadership and Management. In D. Renz (ed.), *Jossey-Bass Handbook of Nonprofit Leadership and Management* (3rd ed.). San Francisco: Jossey-Bass, 2010, pp. 77–99.

Salamon, L. M. The Resilient Sector: The Future of Nonprofit America. In L. Salamon (ed.), *The State of Nonprofit America.* Washington, DC: Brookings Institution Press, 2012.

Name Index

Subject Index

Page references followed by *fig* indicate an illustrated figure; followed by *t* indicate a table; followed by *e* indicate an exhibit.